Assessment *of* Rehabilitative *and* Quality *of* Life Issues *in* Litigation

Assessment *of* Rehabilitative *and* Quality *of* Life Issues *in* Litigation

Patricia A. Murphy, Ph.D.
John M. Williams, D.Ed.

CRC Press
Boca Raton London New York Washington, D.C.

Library of Congress Cataloging-in-Publication Data

Murphy, Patricia A., Ph.D.
Assessment of rehabilitative and quality of life issues in litigation / Patricia A. Murphy and John M. Williams
p. cm.
Includes bibliographical references and index.
ISBN 1-57444-159-0 (alk. paper)
1. Damages—United States. 2. Evidence, Expert—United States. 3. Hedonic damages—United States.
4. Lost earnings damages—United States. 5. Rehabilitation—Law and legislation—United States.
I. Williams, John M. (John Myers), 1949– II. Title.
KF8961.M87 1998
347.73′67—dc21

98-8097
CIP

International Standard Book Number 1-57444-159-0
Library of Congress Card Number 98-8097
Printed in the United States of America 1 2 3 4 5 6 7 8 9 0
Printed on acid-free paper

Preface (Times Two)

This book evolved out of collegiality between two unlikely people fostered by the American Board of Vocational Experts, an organization for rehabilitationists who provide expert witness testimony on damages in a variety of cases in civil courts. I am a Californian by experience and viewpoint, having lived all over the state while providing rehabilitation services in workers compensation systems in Los Angeles, Santa Barbara, and the California side of Lake Tahoe. My rehabilitation books have been, until now, primarily feminist in nature since it is my passionate conviction that abused women can benefit from the rehabilitation analysis in the process of recovery from traumatic abuse experiences. The 1991 Civil Rights Bill gave plaintiffs the right to seek damages for loss of enjoyment of life in sexual harassment, Americans With Disabilities Act, and other employment discrimination cases. I was riveted by this unexpected development in the federal law since the writing of *Making the Connections: Women, Work & Abuse* and *A Career & Life Planning Guide for Women Survivors: Making the Connections Workbook.* This work brought me to an understanding of how traumatic abuse was more than a matter of lost wages and psychological and/or physical injury. Sexual harassment and other forms of violence against women had an impact on every aspect of a woman's life, and the loss in her quality of life was more profound than the more traditional damages I had been trained to evaluate.

Fortunately, my relocation to New Mexico in 1992 allowed me to explore the notion of loss of enjoyment of life in more than 70 civil cases ranging from the molestation of altar boys by priests to domestic tort, sexual harassment, and a wide range of employment discrimination cases. The majority of these cases never went to trial and they were settled one after another. Then the 1994 *Daubert* decision was handed down by the Supreme Court, and everything changed. My loss of enjoyment of life cases no longer settled and I found myself in one *Daubert* hearing after another in both State and Federal Court. I was not allowed to assist the juries in evaluating this very significant damage in the lives of the injured plaintiffs I evaluated.

In the meantime, John Williams initiated a friendship with me by finding my name in the American Board of Vocational Experts (ABVE) directory. He called me to express his interest in becoming my colleague and to express his love for the Santa Fe, New Mexico area where I lived. We began a dialogue which was fostered by our meeting face to face at ABVE conferences. Our approach to the loss of enjoyment of life issue was very different. His focus came out of pain and suffering issues addressed in personal injury cases in Florida, a very different legal climate than the turbulent loss of enjoyment controversies in New Mexico. Gradually, we began to realize that together we had a holistic view of the entire issue.

And so, this book was born.

Patricia A. Murphy
February 19, 1998

I heard Dr. Murphy speak about quality of life and related issues at the semi-annual conferences of the American Board of Vocational Experts and found that we shared common interests in the well-being of persons who have experienced trauma or disability. As a result, I became keenly interested in investigating quality of life as a possible global construct to help in understanding, explaining, and possibly even predicting human behavior in response to trauma or disability. I hoped that we would find quality of life to be a multidimensional concept which would embrace human growth as well as deficit models of human behavior over the life span.

As a practicing rehabilitationist and expert in civil litigation, I have always felt that earning capacity was not only an issue of money, but also had implications for total life function. The interaction between work, enhanced self-esteem and reduced emotional turmoil is one that reaches the core of the rehabilitation process; yet, as an expert, I often felt that the therapeutic value of work, whether it be in the competitive labor market or in a sheltered setting, needed to be explained to claimants/plaintiffs, judges, and juries. Likewise, when dealing with life care planning, the rationale for offering specific care items has not been discussed in concrete, systematic terms, following a standardized model. The cost of each care item and the total dollars to be expended never made sense to me if the benefit of the care was not described. It seemed to me that enhancement of quality of life or well-being ought to be at the core of each intervention/treatment selected for inclusion in a care plan. Quality of life and cost rather than cost alone should be part of the equation in care planning. If it is possible to diminish quality of life by giving too little care, is it possible to diminish quality of life by giving too much? Such questions as this led me to believe that vocational and life care choices should be judged not only on the standard of their impact on losses or costs, but also on their impact on the person. How are we helping to make this person's life better as a result of our vocational and life care plans and interventions? As a vocational expert, one can easily look to loss of earnings as the primary issue in providing expert testimony. Yet, money does not necessarily guarantee quality of life. What does the person do when the money runs out?

Equally of concern to me as a rehabilitationist and as a student of human behavior was the notion that helping a person enhance his or her vocational, physical, psychological, financial, social, and/or intellectual functioning has never been recognized as having a concrete effect on the individual's pain and suffering. There is no question that trauma, injury, and/or disability can produce profound short-term and long-term changes in life function and one's sense of well-being. However, with care and treatment, the person can discover new aspects of life to value. The ultimate goal of the rehabilitation process is to help the person find new meaning to a life that is no longer the same. If rehabilitationists do their job well, should the person's pain and suffering actually diminish over time? Pain and suffering are not static. Life events elicit change; well-being is affected by change. Pain and suffering can be diminished through proper vocational and life care planning and care delivery. This is the dominion of the rehabilitationist who has extensive training in human behavior, disability, care planning, and related issues affecting persons who have experienced traumatic life changes.

Rehabilitation is not a simple concept or process. The rehabilitation process differs from person to person, given the individual's unique attributes, experiences and opportunities. Some people are so disabled and so limited in their capacities and resources that they have no other option than to be totally dependent on others in all aspects of life function, but most persons who have endured trauma or disability have abilities that can be tapped in order to enhance well-being. Writing this book provided a validation of my intuitive knowledge, experiential learning over 20 years of practice, academic studies as an educator and researcher, and spiritual beliefs, while putting them into a theoretical and practical paradigm that makes common sense and has empirical backing in peer-reviewed research and writings. Rehabilitation is about making people better. Quality of life provides the benchmark to define what better means in personal and global terms. I have been qualified as a rehabilitationist and not just as a vocational rehabilitation expert in a number of civil cases where I have had the opportunity to advocate for the well-being of a person, whether asked to render an opinion by the plaintiff or defense. My sincere hope is that this book demonstrates that quality of life has been and will continue to be a well-founded, scientifically sound construct upon which to judge the benefits vs. costs of rehabilitation process. Also, I believe that we have demonstrated that rehabilitation is a discipline grounded in science and that the literature on quality of life meets the standards of science stated or implied by *Daubert.* I believe that such professional credentialing groups as the American Board of Vocational Experts, the American Board of Disability Analysts, and the Commission on Rehabilitation Counselor Certification should incorporate quality of life into standards for national certification. Quality of life may be one of the best ways to demonstrate the unique knowledge and skills of the rehabilitationist who is trained in multidisciplinary, developmental approaches to the rehabilitation process.

John M. Williams
March 3, 1998

About the Authors

Patricia A. Murphy is the author of *Making the Connections: Women, Work & Abuse and A Career & Life Planning Guide for Women Survivors: Making the Connections Workbook.* She obtained her doctorate in forensic rehabilitation and women's studies, with an emphasis on traumatic abuse dynamics, in 1991 from the Union Institute. In 1991, she was awarded the NARPPS Most Innovative Rehabilitation Procedure Award in 1991 for her work on traumatic abuse and vocational impairment. Dr. Murphy provided forensic rehabilitation consultation and expert testimony in New Mexico from 1993 to 1997. She was the first recipient of the Women's Health Policy Fellowship, funded by a grant from the John D. and Catherine T. MacArthur Foundation at the Center for Research on Women and Gender at the University of Illinois at Chicago in 1994. In 1997, she was given the Founder's Award by Chicago Women Connecting, a Project of the University of Illinois Chicago Center for Research on Women and Gender for "Pioneering Research on Women Survivors of Domestic Violence." Also in 1997, Dr. Murphy relocated to Toledo, Ohio where she is now the Director of the Catharine S. Eberly Center for Women at the University of Toledo. Dr. Murphy is board certified as a vocational expert, as a rehabilitation counselor, and licensed in the state of New Mexico as a clinical mental health counselor.

John M. Williams is the co-author of *The Role of the Rehabilitation Expert in Administrative Law Proceedings* and numerous peer-reviewed journals in the field of rehabilitation. Dr. Williams earned a doctorate in counselor education with a specialization in rehabilitation counseling from the Pennsylvania State University in 1980. In 1982, he was awarded the Research Award in Counseling and Human Development by the American Educational Research Association. Dr. Williams has authored two psychometric instruments currently contained in the microfiche collection of Educational Testing Service, Princeton, NJ. Dr. Williams served as the Editor of the *NARRPS Journal & News,* published by the National Association of Rehabilitation Professionals in the Private Sector, and of the *Vocational Expert,* published by the American Board of Vocational Experts. Dr. Williams is board certified as a vocational expert, disability analyst, rehabilitation counselor, counselor, and case manager, as well as licensed as a rehabilitation provider in Florida and as a clinical mental health counselor in New Mexico. Dr. Williams was Professor of Education and Chairperson of the Department of Counseling and Human Development at Barry University, Miami Shores, FL. Dr. Williams has maintained a private practice as a rehabilitationist since 1979, and he has provided rehabilitation expert opinion in the areas of future earning capacity, life care planning, and quality of life.

Contents

Appendixes (Quality of Life Research Literature)

Introduction

In 1991, the Division of Mental Health of the World Health Organization (WHO) initiated a project involving 15 countries to develop a generic quality of life (QOL) instrument. The WHOQOL research group defines QOL as *individuals' perceptions of their position in life in the context of the culture and value systems in which they live, and in relation to their goals, expectations, standards, and concerns.* The primary objective of this project was to design an instrument broadly applicable across disease types, varying severity of illness, and diverse socioeconomic and cultural subgroups. The instrument (available in multiple languages) would be used to evaluate the effects of program interventions on QOL; compare QOL across countries; compare subgroups within countries; and measure change over time (in response to changes in life circumstances).

Bonomi and Patrick, 1997

The purpose of this book is to suggest a holistic, multidisciplinary, and reliable approach to forensic rehabilitation based upon a quality of life approach. The rise and fall of the hedonics approach in the 1980s and 1990s has served to obscure the need to have a description of what quality of life is for individuals with developmental and acquired disabilities despite the vast literature currently available in rehabilitation, health economics, clinical medicine, and the social sciences.

This book has been arranged to be user-friendly, that is, to assist the attorney and forensic rehabilitationist in having quick access to the extensive literature base in the quality of life literature. The reader may ground him- or herself in the literature in two ways. First, each chapter in the book has its own bibliography, which means that the research and theory base of each the seven domains of quality of life addressed is available. The remaining chapters, Chapter 1: Hedonic Damages and Quality of Life Approaches and Chapter 2: Rehabilitation and Quality of Life, document the current research and theory on why the hedonics approach does not meet the *Daubert* Standard and why rehabilitationists can provide the needed expertise to assist the courts in understanding quality of life issues. Second, the Appendixes provide a method by which the attorney and forensic expert can access the relevant quality of life literature by disease process, injury, disability, and population type. Since this is a rapidly developing field with research conducted worldwide, we make no claim to having a complete literature review. However, the bibliographies in this book do give the reader a good overview of what is current in the field.

A summary of the key issues or principles identified in this book regarding forensic rehabilitation and quality of life follows:

1. The consensus among researchers is that quality of life assessments must include objective and subjective data
2. The consensus among researchers is that quality of life assessments are multidisciplinary in nature and include assessments of many life domains
3. From the rehabilitationists' perspective, *satisfaction*, defined as the ability to bring aspiration and achievement together, is a more appropriate understanding of the meaning of quality of life than the vague concept of *happiness*
4. The clinical judgment of the rehabilitationist, based on the collecting of qualitative and quantitative data, will be needed by the courts in exploring quality of life issues
5. Rehabilitation can be defined as operationalizing the construct of quality of life through rehabilitation interventions which enhance life function and increase life satisfaction

6. The consensus among rehabilitation and quality of life researchers is that the ultimate goal of rehabilitation (whether programmatically or individually) is to enhance well-being or quality of life
7. Future care planning must address life satisfaction, well-being, or quality of life as well as addressing deficits if quality of life is to be restored, maintained, and enhanced
8. The international consensus (seen primarily in definitions from the World Health Organization) is that health is a state of complete mental, physical, and social well-being and not just the absence of disease or infirmity
9. The pain and suffering concept should be understood as only one aspect of the quality of life approach. Reliance on this concept diminishes a holistic and developmental understanding which focuses only on deficits in an individual's life
10. There are well-respected psychometric instruments to measure quality of life, notably the Quality of Well-Being (QWB) scale, the WHOQOL-100, the Quality of Life Index (QLI)
11. Rehabilitationists are, by training and experience, in the best position to provide a multi-dimensional perspective on the impact of impairment, disability, and/or other traumatic life events
12. The optimal credential for rehabilitationists providing testimony on quality of life issues would be a doctorate in rehabilitation, rehabilitation psychology, or a related field
13. All rehabilitationists providing such testimony need to be well-grounded in the quality of life literature
14. Quality of life is not just psychology or one's psychological well-being. Quality of life is not simply a subjective assessment of one's life, it also involves the physical, social, cognitive, vocational, leisure, and economic aspects of life
15. Researchers have found that a quality of life approach is an economically sound approach in the rehabilitation of persons with disabilities
16. The quality of life approach allows for the distinction between disability and illness, rather than the stereotypical assumption that they are one and the same. Having a disability does not preclude having a good quality of life. This has profound implications for future care planning
17. The balance between self-reliance, personal autonomy, and self-development and the need for external support and care may be found using a quality of life approach in future care planning
18. The balance between the use of assistive devices and autonomy or locus of control can be found in the quality of life approach in future care planning
19. Compliance with treatment or rehabilitation interventions by persons with injuries and/or disabilities is often based on the individual's subjective evaluation of his or her life satisfaction or well-being. This justifies the use of the quality of life approach in future care planning.
20. Global assessments of quality of life are probably more useful than disease-specific psychometric assessments. At the very least, both approaches should be used in assessing an individual's life quality
21. Every psychometric instrument assessing quality of life possesses a social domain component. The task of the rehabilitationist is to select an instrument suited to the cultural and ethnic background of the individual being assessed
22. Most psychometric tools in the quality of life field neglect the important social relationships found in people's work lives. More research is needed to understand this aspect of the social and vocational domains of quality of life
23. The search for methods for quantifying the health-related quality of life is an international pursuit found within the discipline of health economics in such concepts as *quality adjusted life years* (QALYS) and *healthy years equivalents*

24. The QALYS and HYEs approaches are consistent with rehabilitation practice and theory in that they address morbidity (dysfunction), utility (importance), and prognosis (duration of the condition) in the same way that forensic rehabilitationists are expected to address dysfunction, the importance or impact of that dysfunction on an individual's life, and the prognosis or the length of time the condition will persist within rehabilitative interventions
25. The field of health economics appears to promise solutions to the quantification of health-related quality of life and may provide economists with methods of presenting empirically based data acceptable to the courts
26. Although the concept of leisure as valuable in and of itself is suspect in our culture, leisure is an important quality of life domain in a global economy which is moving toward a decline in paid work for everyone, not just for people marginalized because of disability
27. We are now facing the possibility of having to develop a new social paradigm which is not dependent upon work as its overarching value, since the pace of technology means that the world does not need and cannot use all of the human labor available
28. The new rehabilitation speciality, therapeutic rehabilitation, may lead the way in promoting quality of life as the standard by which all rehabilitative efforts are measured because the research indicates that the development of leisure skills allows for higher levels of self-actualization, self-esteem, self-mastery, and greater life satisfaction
29. At present, work is still the overarching value and the research indicates that there is a dynamic interaction between quality of work life and quality of life in general
30. In the 1990s, career theorists noted that people now choose career paths rather than looking for careers in terms of upward mobility. In other words, careers are selected within a quality of life modality
31. Vocational choice is now better understood when using a quality of life approach
32. Work is not an isolated function in people's lives, but one aspect of their total quality of life
33. Work has a ripple effect on every other quality of life domain
34. In the rehabilitation discipline, cognitive ability is redefined in functional terms such as life skill adaptation, coping skills, and functional ability
35. In terms of quality of life issues within the cognitive domain, autonomy or loss of autonomy is the critical quality of life issue
36. Although functional ability is a critical issue in future care planning and in rehabilitation in general, no research which focused specifically on cognitive ability and quality of life could be found. Instead, the work was embedded with the quality of life literature
37. The quality of life approach or paradigm adds complexity to the discussion of damages in litigation, but it also adds accuracy.

RETHINKING FORENSIC REHABILITATION PRACTICE

To rehabilitate is to restore someone. For professionals in the field of rehabilitation who practice as rehabilitation experts in civil and administrative law proceeding, formulation of expert opinions should be based on an understanding of the injured person's total life function before and after a specific traumatic life event. We, as rehabilitationists, need to identify those specific areas of life function and the specific actions and outcomes associated with those factors which historically brought pleasure and meaning to the person's life as a baseline for determining how to restore the person to a meaningful level of function and the highest level of quality of life possible. This is not to say that a traumatic life event may not alter how one experiences life and faces its challenges. Whether positive or negative in consequences, life events and our choices in response to them shape our lives. Though we may long for our lives to remain the same so that they are predictable and, to some degree, less frightening, study of human development tells us that sameness is impossible to maintain. Avoidance of change and its consequences, whether expected or unexpected, can only result in ineffective decision-making and actions, which, in turn, result in negative life consequences and inevitably loss of quality of life. A trauma, injury, or disability is not a desired life event. One does not hope for it, plan for it, or receive it with thanks. In fact injury, impairment, and/or trauma(s) is much more likely to produce negative effects across all domains of quality of life in the short-term, while the person seeks to understand and accept the associated life changes. Rehabilitation becomes necessary for these reasons. These negative life experiences typically bring pain. The more traumatic the event and/or the more negative the consequences of behavior, the more pain (physical, psychological, cognitive, social, etc.) one experiences. The goal of rehabilitation is to return people to their pre-event levels of functioning (leading to experiencing of prior pleasure and quality of life), if their capacities and motivation allow, or when return to preevent levels of function is not possible, to maximize function across life domains while assisting people in defining new sources of pleasure and the maximum possible quality of life.

As suggested by Williams and Burlew (1995), quality of life may be the best "yardstick" by which to measure the appropriateness of available intervention options when engaging in life care planning. From a cost–benefit perspective, long-term benefits from short-term actions may provide a legitimate rationale for immediate expenditure of considerable resources (financial and human) for delivery of care designed to promote quality of life (particularly when maintenance of independence is seen as critical). Unfortunately, if care is not connected to quality of life-related outcomes, it has little hope of resulting in meaningful long-term change. Too often in the forensic rehabilitation arena, the authors of this book have seen care plans which take a "boiler plate" approach to defining care needs (giving the same type and frequency of care to all persons labeled with the same type of disability). Cost enhancement or containment (often an issue on the agenda of the attorneys in the matter) can easily take precedence over the needs of the individual (across all the domains of quality of life).

Even when dealing with the issue of future earning capacity, a common area of interest to attorneys looking to establish "hard damages" associated with civil litigation (Williams and Maze, 1994), rehabilitation experts who do not recognize that work can be extremely pleasurable and contribute greatly to quality of life may find it easier to say that the person will never work again (in order to create a greater economic loss) than to develop strategies for returning the person to the work place (even if only on the most marginal of levels). After reading Chapter 8: The Vocational Domain, if one is left unconvinced about the pervasive effects of work on other domains of life function and ultimately on one's experiencing of pleasure through productivity, then it should be easy to tell people they cannot and will not work. Even though people receive monetary compensation for work (the basis upon which a rehabilitation can compare pre and post event capacity to earn income in order to answer the question of what, if any, economic losses the person has experienced following a given event or injury), the nonmonetary benefits of work for promoting quality of life should not be missed. The field of vocational rehabilitation is based on the premise that work has the highest therapeutic value to restoring life function. Retraining for entry into a new career, for those who have a demonstrated physical and mental capacity to benefit from training and to sustain work activity thereafter, not only enhances vocational functioning, but also can provide opportunities for growth in cognitive, social, and emotional functioning as well. Ability to sustain work activity over work life expectancy may be equally dependent on growth and development in these domains of quality of life (a contention that is consistent with the "wellness" and "systemic" models of human function articulated in Chapter 2: Rehabilitation and Quality of Life). Giving expert opinion that a person is incapable of growth and development vocationally should only be offered when definitive evidence of severe impairments (typically physical and/or mental) to functioning have been identified and are well grounded in the expert's review of the subjective and objective data on impairment and functional limitations. Options such as supported or sheltered employment, both of which may have a significant associated cost, need to be explored before any persons are told they cannot work. Working part-time as opposed to full-time may preserve the therapeutic value of work for enhancing life function, although it does not lead to significant earnings.

For so many years the authors of this book have read the assessments of peers who looked at future earnings and care as mutually exclusive areas of damages in litigation. We can only think of one or two other rehabilitation experts who ever addressed the subject of quality of life in even an unsystematic, intuitive way. Forensic rehabilitation has tended to be reactive, addressing only the questions asked by attorneys from their perspective — one dominated by a concern for admissibility of opinion and simplicity of presentation to a jury or administrative officer, rather than formative. As noted throughout the chapters in this book, quality of life is not a new, experimental concept in rehabilitation. It has been seen in the developmental disabilities literature for many years (as noted in all chapters) and has been extensively used as an outcome measure in medical research more recently (as seen in Chapter 4: Physical Domain). Forensic rehabilitation experts who are not knowledgeable in human development, normalization, wellness, and related theories to quality of life and who have had minimal training in human behavior (a few courses in a master's level graduate program in rehabilitation, counseling, or a related field, most of which focused on vocational, psychological, and/or medical models of problem conceptualization and service delivery and paid little attention to human development from a wellness perspective) do not often address quality of life in their assessments. Typically, experts trained in rehabilitation and counseling at the doctoral level have had extensive exposure to theories of human growth, development, and change which emphasize strengths and capacities rather than deficits and limitations. Rehabilitationists who are sensitive to quality of life issues and who maintain a positive, growth-oriented perspective when planning care for persons who have experienced trauma or injury, provide meaningful challenges while building in sufficient supportive care to insure success. Possibilities rather than inabilities are the focal point of rehabilitation. Yet, it is too easy for the poorly informed, inexperienced, or ethically spurious rehabilitationist to co-opt the rehabilitation process by stating in or outside of the forensic arena that growth and development are not possible. Without growth people stagnate. With stagnation can easily come deterioration in quality of life. Providing people the tools to meet life's challenges (anticipated and unanticipated) successfully is a primary goal of the rehabilitation process as discussed at length in Chapter 2. It is easy for lay persons (including juries, family, friends, and well-meaning others) to only see the deficits and losses. It is the job of the rehabilitationist to identify the strengths and potential gains. As rehabilitation experts hired by the injured person's attorney, the authors of this book have routinely provided assistance in successful job finding (the result of which was mitigation of some or all of the "hard" economic damages). As defense experts, we have at times been in the position of being a stronger advocate for care for an injured person than the rehabilitation expert hired by the plaintiff's attorney. Understanding that good care produces positive results across multiple aspects of life function (impacting multiple domains of quality of life) should help an uninformed rehabilitationist to begin to see that vocational and future care issues are interdependent, since they both relate to the larger, more pervasive issue of quality of life. The pain of not becoming "all that you can be" may not be lessened in the long-term by the pleasure of acquiring money through litigation. It is a common experience for rehabilitationists to see persons focus on receipt of money as a precursor to pleasure and quality of future life during litigation and then to see the same person postlitigation without a smile, any hope, or any plan for the future. Forensic rehabilitationists are rehabilitationists first and forensic experts second. Our professional identity (our difference in training and orientation from other forensic experts in the field of human behavior such as psychiatrists and psychologists) may best be demonstrated to the courts by our unique interest in and knowledge of quality of life as an indicator of one's experiencing of life along the pleasure–pain continuum. The following discourse looks at the role of quality of life in assessing earning capacity, planning future care needs, and defining suffering in civil and/or administrative proceedings, defining the issues and methodologies appropriate for use by a rehabilitationist for forming expert opinions in these areas of forensic practice. A working model for conceptualizing how quality of life impacts earning capacity, future care planning, and human suffering is offered.

RETHINKING EARNING CAPACITY ASSESSMENT

Earning capacity in civil litigation and administrative law proceedings is one of the areas in which the rehabilitationist is typically called upon to render opinions which will impact awards, benefits, and eligibility (Williams et al., 1993). When dealing with disability, the issue of ability to work and earn a living is of primary concern when translating impairment to disability. Any unanticipated traumatic life event (injury, unemployment, loss, harm, or wrongful discharge) can necessitate significant changes in a person's life and can be disruptive to a person's lifestyle. As suggested in the models of quality of life discussed in detail in Chapter 2: Rehabilitation and Quality of Life, pursuit of a reasonable (based on both subjective and objective standards) quality of life is part of human nature. The World Health Organization, as well as medical and rehabilitation professionals, sees quality of life as a meaningful outcome upon which to judge nations as well as treatments or interventions designed to restore function across all life domains for individuals. Work, as discussed in detail in Chapter 8: Vocational Domain, is one, if not the most, influential area of life function for defining quality of life. Work produces income, but also affects one's self-esteem, social interactions, emotional well-being, leisure, and cognitive/intellectual development. This "ripple effect" makes work and income powerful sources of satisfaction with life. Therefore, how one has historically made choices about work in relationship to overall quality of life has great relevance to rehabilitationists.

Since the one finite, nonrenewable resource all humans share is time, what one does in pursuit of what one defines as an acceptable quality of life affects one's educational, social, leisure, social and vocational and economic horizons. One's real capacities in the future (following a given life event) cannot be understood unless the past decisions and behaviors are identified. One's past choices and actions relative to quality of life provide the best, objective information about quality of life in the future had the injury/event not occurred. One's work and nonwork choices and actions can limit or expand vocational and economic horizons. One person's valuing of work and/or money as a contributor(s) to quality of life can differ markedly from the valuing of another person. Any earning capacity analysis which does not look at historical choices and actions as they related to career development, earnings, and quality of life is ignoring the real person in favor of some aggregate model (commonly associated with a purely data-based approach) of earning capacity. If the courts did not historically want to know the earning capacity of an individual rather than just a class or representative sample of people (based on mean or median data), vocational experts would have never have been qualified to provide testimony on future earnings in court (a common practice seen throughout the U.S.). Williams and Reavy (1993) point out that it is the specialized knowledge in the field of vocational counseling and rehabilitation which defines the vocational and/or rehabilitation expert as the source of data about an individual's pre- and post-event earning capacity, given the individual's unique knowledge, skills, accomplishments, motivation, interests, and values. What a person believes contributes to a greater degree to quality of life is that which the person is most likely to do, whether it is to work or not to work or to perform a certain type of work vs. another type of work due to quality of life issues. The authors of this book have commonly seen persons in all age groups and with all levels of education and skill acquisition make major career changes based on a desire to change lifestyle. Persons who have experienced some traumatic life event, although required by a singular, external circumstance to change, will make choices and take steps which are consistent with their perception of their impact on quality of life, if possible. Rehabilitationists looking to restore life function must be aware of the impact of choices and strategies used to promote vocational development, checking to be sure that quality of life is restored (in its preevent or in an alternate, equally valued form). The "best fit" between work, earnings, and quality of life is one which mirrors the individual's historical quality of life or offers positive changes (as measured against objective, societal and subjective, personal criteria).

Although many examples come to mind, it is important to offer a few to illustrate the issues in merging quality of life and traditional vocational data (skills, aptitudes, academic achievement, interests). Because quality of life may differ throughout life span due to subjective and objective changes in what is considered normative, an example for a young adult (16 to 30), adult (30 to 50), older adult (50 to retirement) will be offered here. First, for a 25 year old with a sketchy work history, low historical earnings, limited (less than high school) education, and a history of unskilled to semiskilled work, current lifestyle choices associated with what is meaningful to the person in terms of quality of life may be less indicative of lifetime choices than that their historical performance was marginal, based on such objective standards as wages, grades, skills, terminations, promotions, criminal activities, or other actions/attributes which would limit occupational choices and probability of employment in the future. For persons with higher levels of demonstrated historical ability and performance, future choices may not be limited by those in the past, making it important to weigh subjective judgment about quality of life heavily in decisions about future quality of life. The less functional, more constricted (in terms of choices) person may desire a certain quality of life, but not have the realistic ability to attain it, thereby setting the person up for failure. For example, to suggest that a 25-year old with a 9th grade education and no history of task persistence in any domain of quality of life, who values money more than anything in the world, values intellectual pursuits and would have gotten an MBA from Harvard before some event/injury and cannot do so now (has lost the capacity and the associated enhancement of quality of life) is not realistically based on objective data. Likewise, it is not appropriate to say that the 25-year old who is working, going to school at night, sacrificing social life, saving money for college, and valuing accomplishment in the intellectual domain, because of limited historical financial resources or situational events of a transitory nature, does not have an earning capacity which exceeds historical earnings. A desire for quality of life (the subjective component of quality of life analysis) and demonstrated ability to learn and/or perform the tasks associated with attainment of these desires (the objective component of quality of life) creates a "goodness of fit" which leads to attainment of desired outcomes. In the case of someone with or without abilities and capacities associated with work and earning a living, if work is not valued (as noted through self-report or historical work-related behavior), then, actual pre-event earnings may be the single best representation of future earnings.

For someone 45 years of age, looking at historical vocational choices, work behavior, earnings, education, and skills development in relation to opportunities available in the labor market may have the greatest value. What one has done historically may be the best objective indicator of one's capacity to earn in the future if one has worked for an extended period of time (particularly if that work has been done in the skill areas in which a person has been most recently trained). Williams and Maze (1995) discuss the value of transferability of skills as a methodology for determining those jobs which an individual could perform (a standard in the field of forensic rehabilitation which comes out of the conceptual model for vocational expert testimony in Social Security Disability hearings developed over 20 years ago and set as a statutory standard for conceptualizing existence of jobs for a person with physical and/or mental limitations, a critical aspect of the test of disability). Skills should play heavily in any discussion of earning capacity when additional training or related learning strategy is not possible (due to the lack of internal or external resources-capacity). Education and or training options should be viewed within the context of demonstrated behavior and/or objective test results (using reliable and valid measures). Quality of life assessment adds a reference point to determine if satisfaction with work and earnings existed preevent or exists postevent. This is particularly true when quality of life instrumentation yields subtest data on leisure, recreation, and nonwork related social activities. If a person enjoyed nonwork activities more than work-related activities and identified nonwork domains as the most important areas of quality of life before an event/injury, then, nonwork issues would need to be considered in identifying future earning capacity. The person that must engage in a sporting activity or must work out nightly or sees family activities as much more important than work may take part-time or full-time jobs with certain hours or opportunities for time off as opposed to desiring the highest compensation possible. For many women and an increasing number of men, child rearing can impose constraints on vocational options. Time with family is seen as more valuable by some persons than by others. How much time someone spends in a week engaging in work and nonwork activities may be the best indicator of what that person values (back to life being a finite, nonrenewable resource). If someone is seeking academic or vocational training on personal time and with personal resources, it is quite reasonable to suggest that, if the training has been ended or interrupted, the person has experienced a loss of future earning capacity. If someone does not pursue a realistic job or educational opportunity because of a trauma/injury and the resultant physical, mental, psychological, or vocational limitations, a loss of earning capacity may ensue. Someone who has never taken a concrete step towards enhancing knowledge and skills associated with an occupation or field prior to an event/injury has not demonstrated that the outcome is valued in terms of its contribution to a desired quality of life. The concept of deferred gratification can be thought of as a short-term sacrifice of quality of life in one or more domains for a long-term gain in function in the most important, most valued domains. Instability in work history, frequent job changes, lower earnings over time, or dismissals from employment for performance or behavioral problems evidenced prior to an event/injury may speak to a low quality of life related to work and support the contention that nonwork is more important to this person. However, this could also be a person who has a clear goal and has not yet found the intervention/change strategy ideally suited to attaining the desired goal. These people recognize the role of work in promoting quality of life, but cannot implement useful methodologies to reach work goals. At times these people act as if they do not value work, but only by default (due to aversive work experiences like termination, demotion, official reprimands, loss of wage increases, discrimination). The importance of work to quality and meaning of life may hold the key to understanding why, in the same circumstances, two people with similar work, education, and wage histories act differently.

After age 50, perceptions of aging and its effects on productivity set in. It is not surprising that retraining or retooling after 50 may not produce great financial rewards. This is particularly true if retraining is necessitated by inability to perform one's past work because of some physical and/or mental impairment(s). Increased knowledge and skills (resulting from retraining) can overcome the hesitation of employers who see persons over 50 as outdate and stagnant (a stereotype which has no empirical validity, but for some has face validity). This problem is so pervasive that the Equal Opportunity Employment Commission has set the age for age discrimination as low as 40 years. Adding disability to age may only further erode one's chances of being hired. This makes it difficult for an older worker with a disability to acquire a job unless he/she has current knowledge and skills which are high demand. Physical demands must also be clearly within the older worker's functional limitations. If a worker changes a career path on his or her own, the subsequent new path can be quite informative about what the person values in life. The way someone lives and the reasons for doing so change over life span. If work provided quality of life at 30, it may not at 50.

Choices narrow as one becomes "institutionalized" in an organization. It gets harder to take risks (like seeking promotion overtly, changing jobs for a better opportunity) in the hope of increasing earnings; particularly when the benefits (total compensation when added to wages) of staying and extending one's seniority/tenure are valued for the security they provide. In the experience of the authors of this book, it is not common for someone over 50 to readily change employers, but it is even less common (the more unique skills the person possesses) to change one's major field of endeavor. When income is not growing substantially anymore, an economic fact for many persons over 50 (as articulated in Chapter 6: Economic Domain), nonwork may begin to take precedence over work in one's life. As retirement approaches, defining quality of life through nonwork activities may be a viable approach to making the transition from work to retirement. Yet, for others, being age 50 or higher may free their time for pursuing career goals (usually after re-entry into the labor market after a considerable time away). After 55, training for more than 6 to 12 months may not produce any change in work circumstances. The more training required by the job, typically the higher the skill level and the compensation. Upward mobility in the labor market in young adulthood can turn to downward mobility with aging. Disability, when added to aging, makes it even more difficult to maintain quality of life. As physical health declines and mobility and autonomy are compromised, as reviewed in detail in Chapter 4: The Physical Domain, quality of life can decline rapidly. It is not uncommon for people who found work to be important and to provide high quality of life, to the exclusion of other life domains, to have great difficulty adjusting to life with limited or no work. Retooling for a new vocation after age 50 is problematic at best. Persons over 50 should rely more on transferable skills and short-term training options to find and/or hold jobs in the labor market (as suggested in SSD regulations on transferability of skills and aging after 50). Narrowing vocational and earnings options may necessitate that persons of this age shift their attention to nonwork domains to redefine quality of life. Dramatic changes in lifestyle would not likely have occurred had the injury/trauma not occurred, making it reasonable to assume that actual earnings (when no objective evidence of preexisting, impending change has been noted) would best reflect actual future earning capacity. Likewise, dramatic preinjury/event changes in other domains of quality of life should not be considered to be likely unless concrete evidence of imminent change (not caused by a traumatic life event or injury) is provided. The underlying financial well-being of the person as well as the shifting priorities associated with lack of satisfaction with the quality of one's past lifestyle may affect vocational and financial risk-taking at this age. Security becomes a real issue after 55, when retirement is a short way off. Actual preevent/injury earnings are typically the best representation of the person's financial needs and chosen lifestyle at this age. Transferability of work skills is the best approach to dealing with postevent/injury (e.g., similar materials, products, subject matter and services as well as machines, tools, equipment, and work aides). Since this age is not good one for making career mistakes and rectifying them, reasonable goals should be set. They are defined as those which offer a high probability of resulting in employment and earning of income.

It should be noted that no matter what age, if the skills and knowledge are becoming or are obsolete, they may not be marketable. Updating existing skills (as opposed to retraining for a different occupation) may be a better option than developing all new ones; particularly when dealing with highly skilled jobs where the time required to retool is so great that it is not worth the cost (in terms of dollars or inability to pursue other nonwork activities). However, if one finds high quality of life in intellectual pursuits, the effort to participate in extensive training (committing that nonrenewable resource — time) may bring rewards other than vocational development and higher earnings. Training/education can also lead to positive changes in self-esteem, personal autonomy, social interactions, leisure, and related areas of life function. But, for most people, the loss of time and/or financial resources required to be trained must be worth the career enhancement and increased financial benefit. The quality of life approach helps define what training/educational options are best for persons, giving a "game plan" for lifestyle-related choices and actions. The more time one puts into education or work, both of which may result in changes in earning capacity, the more time one does not have for other life pursuits. At different ages and with changing life experiences, one may or may not want to devote the time required to reach an educational and/or vocational goal (even if it was once thought to be important).

RETHINKING FUTURE CARE PLANNING AND PAIN AND SUFFERING ASSESSMENT

The efficacy of any treatment or intervention strategy designed to produce change, according to the numerous authors cited in Chapter 2: Quality of Life and Rehabilitation, should be judged by its impact on quality of life. Cost–benefit analysis should include a dimension of quality of life. Quality of life offers a global measure of subjective and objective factors influencing one's life choices, actions, and outcomes. It addresses the social and leisure issues involved in life function unlike any traditional approach to life care planning (care planning being focused historically on medical and, where applicable, psychological needs almost to the exclusion of social, leisure, and purely intellectual/cognitive needs). Planning for a person's future care needs means addressing all aspects of life that give it meaning. Williams and Burlew (1995) suggest that quality of life provides a comprehensive set of criteria to judge postevent care needs. Postevent care needs should be based, in no small part, on pre-event functioning and the preexisting quality of life. Caregiving should attempt to mitigate suffering associated with the loss of function in key life areas after a traumatic/negative life event or injury. Usually, because of the investment in the medical and/or psychological model from a deficit perspective, just one or two (typically physical and/or mental) interventions or treatments are given precedence. Medication, surgery, therapy, and other care options may not be justifiable in terms of quality of life, even when on first blush, they appear to have value for restoring physiological, emotional, or mental function. Quality of life is the conceptual equivalent of holistic, wellness thinking (the whole equals more than the sum of the parts). Life care designed to promote or maintain change must address all domains of quality of life to truly understand the impact of care on one's suffering (Williams, 1995). Suffering is a relative term which has subjective and objective components. Quality of life provides the conceptual model for relieving suffering (a term preferred to pain, given that pain is a term associated with physical and mental function), because enhancement of quality of life leads to enhancement of possibilities and removal of barriers to growth and development. Loss of the capacity to grow and develop at the same or a greater level than was evidenced before a traumatic event/injury causes the person to suffer a loss of postevent/injury possibilities. Options become narrowed, behaviors become more constricted, and outcomes become less satisfying. If life care is maximally effective, possibilities may be different in the future as opposed to the past, but will be maximized. Some aspects of life may remain less satisfying than prior to the event/injury, but others can be improved in order to compensate or adjust. Without quality of life, the merging of caregivers' agendas and patients/clients' true lifestyle preferences could not occur. Quality of life provides the common conceptual ground for communicating needs, planning services, and evaluating outcomes of care on a systemic or individual level. Life care becomes care for life. Giving care across all domains which enhance quality of life is cost-effective because it restores or rehabilitates. Life may not be the same, but it is the best it can be under the circumstances. Adjustment to trauma or disability may best be defined in terms of one's ability to have an acceptable quality of life (hopefully good, no worse than it must be, and the best it can be).

THE MODEL

The desire to have a better quality of life across the domains of human function associated with quality of life is an expression of valuing, which, in turn, leads to the creation of goals (i.e., subjective expressions of desired quality of life). In the presence of capacity, goals can lead to opportunities, which, in turn, through action, can lead to accomplishment. (See the Goal–Capacity–Opportunity–Action–Accomplishment Model in Table V.). Discrepancy between one's desired and perceived quality of life in the presence of capacity, leads to realistic goal setting, a prerequisite for positive change (as opposed to unrealistic goal setting, which is likely to lead to negative change, a theoretical and empirically validated perspective found throughout the counseling and human behavior literatures). Realistic goal setting in the presence of the capacity (personal abilities/skills and external resources) to change leads to action. Action produces change (through one's interaction with one's environment), leading to growth and development. The outcome of action then alters one's perception of quality of life and the cycle renews itself.

TABLE I
GCOAA Model

Goal	Capacity	Opportunity	Action	Accomplishment
Desire	Abilities	Circumstances	Behaviors	Outcomes
Expectancy	Aptitudes	Resources	Change	Results
Standards	Learning	Community	Normalization	Acceptance
"I want"	"I can"	"It is possible."	"I am doing it."	"I did it!"

Rehabilitationists who are trained in goal setting, intervention selection, action planning and implementation, and behavioral evaluation (as articulated by such counseling and rehabilitation theorists as Rubin and Roessler, 1982; Parker, 1987; Cormier and Cormier, 1991) are uniquely trained to use this model to assess the needs, plan the care, and monitor the outcomes across all life domains. Training and experience in meeting the growth and development needs of persons who have experienced trauma and who as the result of this trauma have experienced a reduction in life function and options, rather than training in pathology, is necessary to understand quality of life. If experts and caregivers do not spend time addressing normalcy in caring for patients/clients, then quality of life will be difficult to maintain. It is certainly possible, as was cited in the cancer literature on quality of life, for a treatment or intervention to be very good at dealing with deficits, but very poor at enhancing quality of life. This is the true dilemma of traditional medical and psychological care systems, but is not so strong a concern to rehabilitationists who have been theoretically and experientially grounded in the principles of normalization and its developmental growth (rather than deficit) perspective.

The rehabilitation counselor has the unique training and perspective of a planner of care needs across all the domains of quality of life (as a case management function) and can also, because of extensive training in worker traits, vocational assessment, transferable skills, job analysis, job placement, and labor market trends, address issues related to earning capacity. Future care and earning capacity can be viewed by the rehabilitationist within the context of overall quality of life, a global measure of quality of life such as the WHOQOL being optimal for looking at the impact of changes in function after intervention on care costs and earnings capacity. Proper care and return to the highest level of earnings possible can lead to higher quality of life, and this can be seen in the empirical literature published in medical psychology, rehabilitation, counseling, and related peer reviewed journals. Rehabilitation should enhance quality of life and mitigate suffering.

The WHOQOL instrument should meet the *Daubert* standard for scientific precision and acceptance in the scientific community. It has been discussed in peer-reviewed journals and is continuing to be investigated as this book comes to press. It as already been accepted on a worldwide level by the scientific community and the United Nations. It was pilot tested, using an initial sample of 250 health care users and 50 well persons. During 1994 to 1996, 128 healthy adults were given the WHOQOL-100 (U.S. version). The ages of the three samples were as follows: childbearing women — 29.8; persons with chronic conditions — 49; and healthy adults — 41.5. Confirmatory multi-trait analysis was conducted. An alpha internal consistency reliability coefficient of 0.80 was noted across the samples; acceptable test-retest reliability coefficients (ranging from 0.83 to 0.92) were reported. Measurement of convergent and discriminant validity using the Short-Form 36-item (SF-36) and the Subjective Quality of Life Profile (SQLP) indicated that 75% of the predicted correlations were upheld for the SF-36 and 67% for the SQLP. Importance items were not validated, but are in the process of further empirical evaluation (Bonomi and Patrick, 1997). Although the instrument is designed to measure current quality of life across six domains (physical, psychological, independence, social, environmental, and spiritual), it can be administered over time to document changes in quality of life after significant life events or interventions. Its results need to be correlated clinically with self-reports about preinjury or preevent quality of life for a rehabilitation expert to assess the degree of positive or negative change in quality of life from before to after the injury or event in order to find an objective basis for measuring pain and suffering from a global, functional perspective.

The conceptual model noted above describes the impact of impairment on quality of life across life domains and offers a detailed explanation of the relationships between quality of life and the more global concept of suffering. The quality of life paradigm will not only impact earning capacity and future care costs in litigation or administrative law proceedings, but it will also provide a framework for demonstrating that care produces positive change and positive change reduces suffering. Quantification of residual suffering after expenditure of dollars on care and in light of differences in earning capacity will give a more balanced and accurate perspective on the overall cost to restore or maintain a person who has undergone a trauma or injury. The rehabilitationist is in a unique position to add insight into the impact of trauma/injury on life and the damages associated with restoration of function or compensation for loss of function.

This book attests to the scientific basis upon which quality of life is built. Its virtues and dilemmas have been articulated in peer-reviewed journals in the behavioral sciences through research which has demonstrated control of error variance in results through use of valid and reliable measures of change and accepted principles of experimental design. Quality of life adds complexity to the discussion of damages in litigation, but it also adds accuracy. Human behavior is complex and cannot be explained in simple theoretical terms. Experts in rehabilitation who understand quality of life offer the courts understanding of the impact of an injury/event on a whole person over life span. The rehabilitation expert can bring the objective and subjective aspects of a person's life function before and after a traumatic event/injury together to form a realistic and defendable picture of a person, one changed for the better and/or the worse.

It is the rehabilitation expert who can conceptualize and explain to an administrative officer, judge, or jury the net effect of the positive and negative changes in life function which occurred before and after the event/injury and will continue to occur over time. It is the experience of the authors of this book that judges will qualify rehabilitationists with demonstrated, unique knowledge in the area of quality of life as experts in quality of life. Quality of life has the empirical foundation across multiple professional disciplines that the concept of hedonics has lacked. Quality of life is based on science and global acceptance of the constructs upon which the science is built. Hedonics has not demonstrated a sound scientific base and has not enjoyed the unanimity of support in the peer-reviewed literature in rehabilitation as has quality of life across the medical, psychological, social, leisure/recreation, and rehabilitation literature. The quality of life approach provides a standard upon which to judge the cost or rehabilitation and the residual losses in earnings and pleasure of life after a traumatic event or injury. Rehabilitationists can help judges, juries, and administrative officers determine real costs of rehabilitation after losses have been mitigated to the maximum possible by care. Rehabilitationists can assist all the parties in litigation settings in using the quality of life paradigm as an approach for assessing earning capacity, future care planning, and pain and suffering.

REFERENCES

Bonomi, A. E. and Patrick, D.L. (1997). *User's Manual and Interpretation Guide for the United States Version of the World Health Organization Quality of Life (WHOQOL) Instrument.* Seattle, WA: WHOQOL Center.

Cormier, W.H. and Cormier, L.S. (1991). *Interviewing Strategies for Helpers.* Pacific Grove, CA: Brooks/Cole.

Crewe, N.C. (1997). Life stories of people with long-term spinal cord injury. *Rehabilitation Counseling Bulletin,* 41(1), 26-42.

Parker, R.M. (1987). *Rehabilitation Counseling: Basics and Beyond.* Austin, Texas: Pro-Ed.

Rubin, R.T. and Roessler, S.E. *(1982). Case Management and Rehabilitation Counseling.* Baltimore: University Park Press.

Williams, J.M. (1995). Addressing quality and pleasure of life in life care planning. *Inside Life Care Planning,* 1(2), 2.

Williams, J.M. and Burlew, L. (1995). Dealing with catastrophic injury: a developmental perspective on life care planning. *Adultspan,* 9(3), 4-8.

Williams, J.M. and Maze, M. (1994). *The Role of the Rehabilitation Expert in Civil and Administrative Law Proceedings.* Iowa City: IA: ACT.

Williams, J.M. and Maze, M. (1995). Determining future earning capacity: using computerized skills, worklife, and wage data provided in RAVE. In Mayer L. (Ed.) *Professional Issues: Assessment, Expert Testimony and Catastrophic Injury.* Topeka, KA: American Board of Vocational Experts.

Williams, J.M. and Reavy, G. (1993). Effective use of rehabilitation and economic experts in personal injury litigation: an integrated approach. In Stein, D. (Ed.) *Vocational Expert Monograph Series,* Topeka, KA: American Board of Vocational Experts.

Williams, J.M., Sawyer, H., and LaBuda, J. (1993). Forensic rehabilitation. In Thorson, R. (Ed.) *CIRS Self-Study Guide.* Rolling Meadows, IL: Certified Insurance Rehabilitation Commission.

1 Hedonic Damages and Quality of Life Approaches

THE HEDONIC DAMAGES APPROACH

> The monumental importance of the hedonic damage theory is most evident in two major premises underlying the theory, the first point being that the hedonic value of a rich person is not necessarily greater than that of a poor person. Second, a person's hedonic value is wealth. Hedonic theory fills a gap left open by additional damage remedies because it treats all human life equally.
>
> *Branch, 1992*

The origin of the notion that life itself has a value is ancient, reaching back into the Babylonian Code of Hammurabi (Smith, 1988). In modern times, the loss of this value is termed *hedonic damages*, "also referred to in different jurisdictions as damages for the *loss of enjoyment of life*, *loss of life's pleasures*, and *lost value of life*" (Airone, 1996). The word "hedonics" is derived from the Greek word "hedonikos," meaning pleasure or pleasurable. "The term *hedonic damages* was first introduced into legal parlance by the economist Stanley V. Smith in the 1985 case Sherrod v. Berry" (Airone, 1996).

Sherrod vs. Berry was a case of a young Black man shot and killed by a police officer in Joliet, IL. Mr. Sherrod's parents finally sued the officer, Mr. Berry, and the City of Joliet when they could not get their son's name cleared for a crime he did not commit. Economist Stan Smith (1992) states he

> summarized the large body of value of life literature for the jury, indicating to them the range of values. ... I further testified that, according to economic research, the value of life was considerably greater than the human capital measure. I termed this excess over the human capital measurement *hedonic damages* to distinguish it from the lost earnings measure of economic damages.

The jury awarded the Sherrod family $850,000 in hedonic damages, and although the case was eventually overturned, it was not because of the hedonic damages award. The case was never retried because the family settled with the City of Joliet (Smith, 1992).

Smith went on to publish the landmark article which outlined the Lost Pleasure of Life Scale (LPL Scale) with his co-authors Berla and Brookshire in 1990. This article described "a conceptual approach for applying estimates of the loss of the pleasure of life." "The loss of the pleasure of life, or change in quality of life, can be divided into four very broad areas, and an injured person is evaluated in these four areas. The psychologist's evaluation compares the person's postinjury lifestyle with his or her preinjury lifestyle. The four areas are:

1. **Practical functioning**. This refers to the extent a person's activity in daily living has been affected. Included in this area are any activities a person typically engages in as an integral part of daily life, such as reading, grooming, dressing, eating, sleeping, shopping, traveling, doing housework, and parenting.
2. **Emotional/psychological functioning**. This refers to a person's ability to live on a daily basis free of any debilitating emotional problems that diminish his capacity to enjoy life and compromise one's sense of self-worth, dignity, and integrity.

3. **Social functioning**. This refers to a person's capacity to derive pleasure from interacting with other people. Examples include family interactions, athletic activities, social events, hobbies, and any other interpersonal interactions.
4. **Occupational functioning**. This refers to a person's ability to engage in a career/vocation of one's choice and to derive pleasure from one's occupational identity independent of any monetary compensation.

Psychometric testing, questionnaires, and clinical interviews are used to collect data in these four areas of human function so that a determination of the severity of the hedonic loss could be made using a Lickert-like scale (0 to 17% minimal, 17 to 33% moderate, 50 to 67% severe, 67 to 83% extreme, and 83 to 100% catastrophic). Berla et al. (1990) pointed out that this rating system was quite similar to the scales used to measure degree of function and severity of stress in the *Diagnostic and Statistical Manual of Mental Disorders* (1980). It is the quantification of the loss of pleasure of life that provides a basis for an economist's assessment of the dollar value of loss of pleasure of life. If a certain percentage of loss is identified by a rehabilitationist or related professional for the relevant time periods before and after identified life event(s), then the economist has the underpinning for an analysis of the monetary loss based on a specific percentage.

According to one economist, the quantification of the value of a life can be found in "sixty-seven analyses" which "have estimated the value of a statistical life, generally from estimates of how much people pay for small changes in their survival probabilities. These analyses fall into four categories:

1. Wage-Risk Studies, which analyze compensating wage differentials associated with risky jobs,
2. Market Studies, which analyze the market for products that affect health and safety,
3. Behavioral Studies, which examine risk-avoidance behavior in inherently risky situations, and
4. Contingent Valuation Surveys, which probe how much people are willing to pay for small changes in risk. (Miller, 1992)

In a review of the studies, Miller (1992) found that the range of the value of a statistical life was between $0 to $15 million. He notes that "this wide range hinders credible use of willingness to pay in benefit-cost-analysis or court-room debate over liability damages." Miller's paper "narrows the range substantially by weeding out studies with serious flaws and adjusting out some sources of inconsistency," resulting in (after adjustment) "70% of the values of a statistical life (47 of 67) reasonably sound. The mean and median value of these studies is $2.2 million. The standard deviation is $.65 million. All the values except one survey lie within 1.96 standard deviation of the mean." He concluded that the numbers can "provide guidance to courts on the reasonable range of values for total damages."

It is not surprising that rehabilitationists would recognize that losses associated with physical or mental impairment resulting from an unanticipated life event would not be limited to what Smith (1992) refers to as the "human capital measure," or the ability to earn a living. It is the common experience of the rehabilitationists who work with industrially injured workers that psychological response to injury, loss of function, or loss of the ability to work can be equally, if not more debilitating, than the loss itself. The loss of the ability to work is not unlike the experience of loss described in the death and dying grief model of Kubler-Ross (1969). This suggests that there are emotional/psychological consequences to loss of earning capacity as well as the loss of ability to make a living. Historically, rehabilitationists are trained to help mitigate loss by restoring the person to the highest level of functioning possible, while at the same time understanding that restoration to preinjury functioning may not be possible (Williams and Fidanza, 1990). And although the rehabilitationist is ethically responsible to help people anticipate any obstacles they might encounter on the path to restoration of their highest level of functioning in and outside of the workplace, the system in which the rehabilitation effort is to take place (workers' compensation, long-term disability, state department of rehabilitation, personal injury litigation) may not recognize the need for attention to losses other than losses defined in terms of hard economic damages or earning capacity losses. And yet, quality of life issues are inherently part of the restoration or rehabilitation process. Work does not take place in a vacuum. As we will see in later chapters, the research indicates there is a dynamic interaction between quality of work life and quality of life in general (Decker and Borgen, 1993; Elizur and Shye, 1990; Loscocco and Roschelle, 1991; Shain, 1996). Losses in quality of life outside of work can dramatically affect the client's vocational behaviors, producing gains or losses in resultant lifetime earnings.

Rehabilitationists who have entered the forensic arena as experts in civil litigation or administrative law proceedings relative to disability cannot ignore the total function of the individual as it impacts the client's ability to work and earn a living. However, before the Loss of Pleasure of Life Scale (Berla et al., 1990), rehabilitationists had no theoretical model or measure to operationalize and quantify loss of pleasure of life. One of the authors of this book found the LPL Scale so attractive that she has analyzed more than 50 New Mexico state and federal cases for hedonic damages with this method. Although the trend in New Mexico is to disallow the LPL Scale analysis since *Daubert*, many such cases have been settled, and the experience in examining quality of life issues for clients in litigation has been invaluable.

Not all rehabilitationists or vocational experts adopted the LPL Scale method. Magrowski (1991a, b) published the first article on hedonics in the first monograph produced by the American Board of Vocational Experts, followed by his self-published monograph, *Introduction to Hedonics.* Magrowski examined the effects of "Work Status, Sex, Age, Severity of Injury, Regional Location, and Liability" on hedonic-type awards by using a series of six T-Tests with data from a randomly selected sample (n = 130) of 2000 Jury Verdict Research, Inc. cases. He found that "work status, severity of injury, and liability type" were shown to significantly affect award size. Regional location, age and sex were found not to affect award size." Magrowski has succeeded with his approach, as evidenced by a 1996 federal tort case where Magrowski's testimony resulted in a large hedonic award (*Wyatt vs. U.S.A.* U.S. District Court Eastern District of Missouri).

In 1992, Sackman and Ingham published an article in the *NARRPS Journal and News* which coined the term, *hedonic autopsy.* Their article presented an alternative to the Berla et al. (1990) Lost Pleasure of Life Scale. They wrote:

> The hedonic autopsy does not estimate how much a life is worth. It does estimate how much life's pleasure is worth to the person who chose to experience them. Furthermore, the hedonic autopsy does measure the value of a general concept of life's pleasures, but the value of specific kinds of life's pleasures that the victim pursued. And those specific life pleasures are valued in terms of what they cost in the competitive marketplace.

Their approach to valuation was based on the money spent in the past by the plaintiff in the pursuit of pleasure (cost of vacations, movies, baseball games, and hobbies), which was then projected over the plaintiff's expected life span. Sackman and Ingham recommend that "the hedonic autopsy and hedonic loss valuation are probably best achieved in a team effort that would include a psychologist, economist, and a vocational consultant." The role of the vocational consultant would be "to conduct the hedonic autopsy interviews and documenting the time and/or market value of each pleasure activity."

Metcalf's commentary on hedonics was also published in 1992. His approach was more cautious than that of Magrowski et al. He wrote:

> Valuation of loss of enjoyment due to injury is a complicated process involving expertise within a variety of areas, including medical, rehabilitation, vocational, psychological, ergonomic, and economic. The

> body of knowledge about the valuation of loss of enjoyment is relatively small and the field very young. There appears to be no consensus about the validity, reliability, or choice of methodology in determining hedonic loss.

Metcalf's caution was warranted. The *Daubert v. Merrell Dow Pharmaceuticals, Inc.*, 113 S.Ct. 1786 (1993) decision overturned the nearly 75-year-old *Frye* test, the *Frye v. United States* decision, which "reigned as the standard governing admissibility of scientific testimony in this country." In other words, under *Frye,* "the foundation for admissible scientific evidence had to include a showing that the underlying theory or technique enjoys general acceptance within the specialty field. (Imwinkelried, 1996)." The U.S. Supreme Court, in its *Daubert* decision, ruled that the Federal Rules of Evidence overturned Frye and "announced a new standard for determining the admissibility of scientific testimony....

> The majority stated that the pivotal question is whether the witness has empirically validated the hypothesis by appropriate scientific methodology. The majority noted that the scientific method consists of formulating a hypothesis and then engaging in experimentation and observation to falsify or verify it." (Imwinkelried, 1996)

Despite the fact that a recent survey found that claims for hedonic damages had become pervasive in 49 states (Keil and Moehring, 1995), this decision has had the effect of challenging all hedonic damages expert testimony tendered since *Daubert.*

DAUBERT AND HEDONIC DAMAGES

In a recent New Mexico case, the judge did not allow testimony by the economist and the rehabilitationist on hedonic damages:

> Prior to *Daubert*, a trend seemed to be developing to allow expert testimony on hedonic damages, those intended to compensate for the loss of pleasure and satisfaction of life.... More recent decisions, however, seem to reject hedonic damages as a proper subject for expert testimony, and indeed a *Daubert* analysis of the present record suggests the reason for the reversal of the earlier acceptance of such testimony (Black, 1996).

Judge Black (1996) referred to the Federal Rules of Evidence in writing his order.
Rule 702 reads as follows:

> If scientific, technical or other specialized knowledge will assist the trier of fact to understand the evidence or to determine a fact in issue, a witness qualified as an expert by knowledge, skill, experience, training or education may testify thereto in the form of an opinion or otherwise.

The courts should consider such matters as: (1) Whether the theory or technique can be and has been tested; (2) whether it has been subjected to peer review and publication; (3) its known rate or potential rate of error; and (4) its general acceptance in the scientific community.

Some post-*Daubert* cases where the courts rejected a number of approaches to the valuation of the loss of enjoyment of life include:

1. *Anderson v. Nebraska Department of Social Services,* 248 Neb. 651, 538 N. W. 2d 732 (1995): Stanley V. Smith's testimony on the average value per statistical life saved based on willingness-to-pay model was considered flawed and inadmissible due to the wide range of values it generates.
2. *Ayers v. Robinson,* 887 F. Supp. 1049 (ND Ill. 1995): Although the parties stipulated that the economist's testimony on loss of enjoyment of life was scientific in nature, the

Court in a comprehensive opinion undermines each basic premise behind the willingness-to-pay model.
3. *Hein v. Merck and Co., Inc*, 868 F. Supp. 230 (M.D. Tenn. 1994): Expert testimony estimating the amount of hedonic damages is not admissible under *Daubert* because it is not helpful to the jury, is unreliable, and not valid.
4. *Kurnez v. Honda North America, Inc.*, 166 FRD 386, 388 (WD Mich. 1996): "The willingness to pay model is a troubled science in the courtroom, with the vast majority of published opinions rejecting the evidence." The willingness-to-pay model was not shown to be reliable or helpful.
5. *Livingston v. United States*, 817 F. Supp. 601 (ED NC 1993): The Chestnut and Violette (1992) risk avoidance studies were rejected as a foundation for willingness to pay theory as neither reliable nor of assistance to the jury.
6. *Sullivan v. U.S. Gypsum Co.*, 862 F. Supp. 317 (D. Kan. 1994): Testimony as to hedonic damages precluded.
7. *Wilt v. Buracker*, 443 S.E.2d 196 (W. Va. 1993): Testimony by economist Michael Brookshire and a psychologist using the LPL Scale was rejected by the court, and this court held that loss of enjoyment of life is a subjective jury evaluation issue rather than an objective calculable item.

The major difficulties seen in these cases appear to rest largely with the testimony by economists and include:

1. The disagreement among scientists regarding benchmark figures for calculating the value of a statistical life
2. The problems adjusting the statistical life to the individual plaintiff (an area where the rehabilitationist's input should be found)
3. The problems with the underlying assumption of the willingness-to-pay model
4. The problems with the assumption that people accurately perceive risk and the degree of harm from the risk in choosing a job (wage-risk studies)
5. The problems with the predictions or assumptions economists make in the valuation of a statistical life or hedonic damages
6. Peer review has not led to general acceptance among economists
7. There is no accepted or established rate of error despite Miller's (1992) attempt to establish a rate of error
8. The problem of the excessive costs of hedonic damage awards (Havrilesky, 1992)

Court rulings on testimony by rehabilitationists and psychologists have not yet come down in any great number, but those mental health professionals who use the Berla et al. (1992) LPL Scale will find themselves sinking along with the economists. Magrowski (personal communication, December 30, 1996) indicated that he did not face a *Daubert* challenge in the 1996 federal tort case noted above. The judge used the State of Missouri Rules of Evidence to determine if his testimony on hedonics was admissible, and Magrowski does not use the LPL Scale method, but a method of his own devising based on physical functional capacity.

When the LPL Scale was first published in 1990 in the *Journal of Forensic Economics*, it was embraced by plaintiff attorneys (Branch, 1992; Paolicelli, 1993). It gathered critics just as quickly (Cargonne, 1993; Jones, 1994). Cargonne (1993) criticized the LPL Scale for lacking psychometric integrity, for basing it on the Axis IV, the Severity of Psychosocial Stressors Scale in the *Diagnostic and Statistical Manual of Mental Disorders — III-R*, which possesses reliability levels "being so low (.25–.44) as to be worthless," for not providing standardized guidelines from which the loss of pleasure of life can be determined, and for making "a presumption of loss having already been *a priori* … or the presence of a loss having previously assumed to have occurred."

Jones (1994) describes the use of the LPL Scale as "arbitrary," and states "the problem of linearity within and across functional groups is inherent in the BBS (LPL Scale) and all hedonic loss techniques." In other words, is the loss of pleasure of life in occupational functioning for a clerical worker and a surgeon (to use the Jones' example) the same?

Andrews et al. (1996) conducted two studies on the LPL Scale after the Cargonne and Jones reviews were published. They found moderate reliability in terms of inter-rater reliability among mental health professionals using the Scale and ecological validity in terms of financial awards for each case established by undergraduate students. Although the LPL Scale may in fact be "the only known standardized instrument that has been found to be psychometrically reliable and valid in rating loss of pleasure of life (Andrews et al., 1996)," the two studies conducted to date will most likely not be enough to stand up to the demands under *Daubert* or the Federal Rules of Evidence, which require general acceptance in the scientific community. Significant peer review of these studies has not yet taken place, and the rate of error has not yet been firmly established for the LPL Scale. Finally, the tying of the LPL Scale to currently discredited economic theory regarding the valuation of a statistical life further limits the usefulness of the LPL Scale in the courts.

THE QUALITY OF LIFE APPROACH

> Quality of life is becoming a major theme in the field of developmental disability. It is argued that some of the same issues arise in the field of aging and many of the problem and solutions are generic to the development of a range of services and systems. By examining the transfer of knowledge from the field of development study, some of the pitfalls encountered in allied systems may be avoided. Quality of life raises issues associated with cognition, emotion, and personal attributes of lifestyle. This paper (Aging, Disability, and Quality of Life: A Challenge for Society) argues for a re-evaluation of professional services in the context of quality of life which can lead to the client playing a much more dominant role in decision-making within a delivery service oriented to the individual's personal and familiar environment.
>
> *Brown, 1989*

Brown, an academic rehabilitationist in the Rehabilitation Studies Department at the University of Calgary, specializes in development disability, but calls for the transfer of knowledge of quality of life assessment from that field to the allied or related fields of rehabilitation, gerontology, and psychology (Brown, 1989; 1996). Brown and his co-authors for the essay, "Quality of Life: A Challenge for Rehabilitation Agencies," (Brown et al., 1988) have been involved in a longitudinal study of adolescents and adults who are mentally handicapped and who use the services of five rehabilitation agencies in four western provinces of Canada (1988). They point out that "the aim of the study was to examine the quality of life of the clients." Based on the results, Brown et al. (1988) have developed more than 100 recommendations for the development and change of rehabilitation programs in Canada using a quality of life approach.

The field of rehabilitation looks at the needs of the individual and the cost of providing services which have a reasonable probability of restoring the person to the highest level of function possible. This is a common thread in the ethical codes of rehabilitation professionals (Williams, 1991). Nowhere does any rehabilitation ethical code or clinical text known to the authors of this book say that the real purpose of rehabilitation is to define in "hard dollar" terms a person's noneconomic losses. The science of rehabilitation does not yet provide theoretical models for calculating loss of enjoyment of life in terms of a specific dollar amount, and there is no science which uniformly tells a rehabilitationist what an individual life is worth. Therefore, the rehabilitationist must defer to an economist in the hope that forensic economics can provide sufficient scientific data to support a specific dollar loss. It is not the rehabilitationist's job to defend the concept or methodology behind any specific dollar figure for loss of enjoyment of life. The rehabilitationist can add insight into the losses in quality of life in vocational and nonvocational areas because of the considerable volume of literature which supports the contention that work is a central life activity (Richardson, 1993), and only one of several interrelated areas of human growth and development which contribution to overall life function and well-being (Williams and Burlew, 1995). Moreover, we should be acutely aware that we are dealing with the behavioral sciences, where not all potential sources of contamination and/or chance variability in research are controlled, and not the natural sciences, where control of chance error can be more rigorous.

Quality of life terminology has nearly a 50-year history generally, and a 20- to 30-year history in rehabilitation. Roessler (1990) points out *"quality of life* began as a political slogan in the 1950s and was quickly adopted by the field of medicine. In the 1960s, quality of life was listed as an outcome criterion in *The Report of the President's Commission on National Goals*" (as cited in Schuessler and Fisher [1985]). In the 1970s, the Community Support Program initiatives of the National Institute of Mental Health for individuals with long-term mental illness (Lehman 1988) promoted quality of life assessment. In 1988, the National Institute on Disability and Rehabilitation Research published a *Rehab Brief* on "*Quality of Life Research in Rehabilitation*." Fabian, another rehabilitation academic, noted in 1991 that "15 years ago only a handful of articles were devoted to the subject" of quality of life and rehabilitation, but in the 1990s quality of life assessment is a common theme in the rehabilitation literature.

The resulting body of literature located under the term *quality of life* found in the *PsychLIT* and *ERIC* databases is staggering. The *PsychLIT* database for journal articles, book chapters, and books from January 1974 to December 1996 contained 3362 citations. The *ERIC* database was searched for journal articles and book chapters from 1966 to September of 1996 and 4087 citations were found. A great deal of this literature is not relevant for our purposes since it contains a large amount of the social indicators research developed in the 1960s and 1970s. Interestingly, a good part of the research conducted in quality of life is found in European journal articles. These articles were difficult, if not impossible to locate, although we have managed to find enough of them to understand that quality of life issues are an international research topic in the rehabilitation, clinical medicine, and psychological disciplines.

Under the terminology of "*quality of life*" and "*rehabilitation*" 275 citations were located within the *PsychLIT* database and 107 were found in *ERIC.* With our primary focus on rehabilitation and a secondary focus on clinical medicine and psychology, we have been able to locate and review more than 400 relevant articles and several books which have been organized into the appendixes found in the back of this book. The appendixes are organized by categories including disease, research methodology, and population studied.

By contrast, only 42 citations were found in the *ERIC* and *PsychLIT* databases under the terms "*loss of pleasure of life,*" "*loss of enjoyment of life,*" or "*hedonics.*" Thirty-nine citations popped up in the *PsychLIT* database under *hedonics.* Of the journal articles, 33 referred to the hedonics of taste and smell. This topic apparently became inexplicably popular in the early 1990s, but is of little use to forensic rehabilitationists except in those rare personal injury cases where impairment of taste and smell might be important. The remaining articles referred to the work done by Berla et al. (1990) and the psychiatrist, Staneyl Terman (1995).

The schism between hedonics and quality of life study and research leaves the field of hedonics without a foundation, cutting it off from its roots in the medical and social sciences. Brown's call for a knowledge transfer of quality of life assessment issues in rehabilitation fields needs to be heeded by forensic rehabilitation practitioners. Without the quality of life literature in rehabilitation and other related disciplines, hedonics (an aspect of quality of life) is easily discredited. In the field of forensic economics, the trend has been to dismiss hedonics as "voodoo economics" (Viscusi, 1992) or human life as something which cannot be valued, as unquantifiable.

Any time something is considered unquantifiable, a red warning flag should go up. As suggested by Baker (1996) in his introduction to the ground-breaking book, *Quality of Life in Health*

Promotion and Rehabilitation, the following three trends have contributed to the emergence of quality of life as a salient issue in rehabilitation and in our society in general:

1. Consumer movements among persons with disabilities
2. Broadening of the legal guarantees of equality to remove barriers that contribute to disadvantage,
3. The broadening of the perspective of human services professionals to account for aspirations of their clients

To put it another way, it is not an accident that hedonics should emerge into the forensic arena during the 1980s or after the rise of the great civil rights and women's movements of the 1960s and 1970s. The consumer movement or the independent living movement of people with disabilities also came up during these decades, resulting in the passage of the Americans with Disabilities Act of 1990. Fabian (1991) underscores the reasons for increased attention to the quality of life approach in rehabilitation research and practice:

> (a) the mounting emphasis on consumer evaluation of rehabilitation programs;
> (b) the general belief that unidimensional evaluation of programs and interventions are not satisfactory and;
> (c) the recognition that inherent to the development of all rehabilitation programs is the goal of improving the quality of life of consumers in these programs. (Fabian, 1991)

One thing we learned from these movements of disabled and disadvantaged people is that the business of quantifying and counting is a matter of power, political and economic power. Waring's (1988) book on feminist economics provides an easily understood example. In her discussion of the United Nations System of National Accounts (UNSNA), she notes that there is a

> cabal that ensures that the production of any of these goods (home-grown produce, hand-sewn garments, processing of primary commodities) by a housewife still counts for nothing. Reasons given by men for their failure to account for women's work are (1) conceptual problems and (2) the practical difficulties of collecting data (p. 80).

These two reasons for not counting women's work in the home also neatly summarize the current criticisms of the valuation of human life in the courts. This is not to discount the difficulties in conceptualizing the value of a human life or the difficulties in assembling the relevant data in order to do so, but to point out that to attempt to do this without the knowledge base currently available in the disciplines of rehabilitation, clinical medicine, psychology, psychiatry, and the social sciences is ludicrous.

Furthermore, we must ask ourselves who benefits when we decide that something cannot be counted. In the case of housework, the beneficiaries appear to be the men of the world whose lives are then deemed more valuable because they are seen as "productive," since their work is counted. If this seems overstated, consider the paper (Kurz and Prather, 1995) developed by the Association for Women in Development on the quality of life for the world's girls in which mortality, poor health care, and inadequate nutrition are more problematic for girls than for boys no matter what the overall poverty level is. That is, boys are given more food and better health care. Infanticide is more prevalent with girls than boys. Obviously, the quality of life for girls suffers by comparison to that of boys in developing countries.

Who benefits when we decide that we cannot quantify human life in the legal system or establish agreed-upon methods to do so? In the case of women with disabilities acquired as the result of a personal injury, the failure of the Bureau of Labor Statistics, U.S. Department of Labor to provide accurate statistics in terms of the worklife expectancies of contemporary women means that women with newly acquired disabilities which shortened or diminish their earning capacities and worklife expectancies are being penalized. That is, the damage to her future earning capacity cannot be accurately determined and so her damage award in a personal injury case may be less than fair. The beneficiary in this situation appears to be the insurance carrier or the defendant in the personal injury case. The beneficiary could also be the plaintiff awarded an inappropriate damage award due to lack of information by the jury, an award unfair to the defense.

The question of who benefits when we fail to quantify or come to agreement on the value of a human life is a highly controversial and politicized question which will not be answered here, since an entire book could be devoted to that topic alone, but the criticism by Jones (1994) about the "linearity" of the LPL Scale deserves mention. The LPL Scale adopts the assumption that each human life has equal value. Jones' comments tend toward gender and class bias when his example of the clerical worker (stereotypically a high school-educated female worker) and the surgeon (stereotypically a highly educated male worker) is scrutinized. His assumption seems to be that class and gender privilege ensures a greater quality of life. The reason the editors of the book, *Quality of Life in Health Promotion and Rehabilitation* (Renwick et al. 1996), are aware that their "book is not about judging the value of lives but, rather, about how we can enhance the quality of each person's life" is because they take the position that the value of the life of a person with a disability or disadvantage is the same as that of a person without disabilities or disadvantages.

The problem, then, is not how much a statistical life is worth (although an agreed-upon number would be useful — perhaps legislated?), but how much is it worth to an individual? Court decisions which have rejected testimony on hedonic damages because of the problems in adjusting the value of the statistical life to the individual plaintiff's life are, in our opinion, highly appropriate and reflect the lack of grounding found in the hedonics approach. One of the purposes of this book is to review how the disciplines of rehabilitation, clinical medicine, psychology, and other related health and social science professions have laid the groundwork for assessing the quality of an individual's life. It is our hope that the quality of life approach will bring a truly holistic, multidisciplinary, and reliable approach into the forensic arena.

TECHNICAL OR OTHER SPECIALIZED KNOWLEDGE

> Thus Rule 702 and *Daubert* leave open the possibility that a proponent of expert testimony can argue that the testimony is admissible as 'technical' knowledge or "specialized" knowledge even when the testimony falls short of qualifying as "scientific knowledge."
>
> *Imwinkelried, 1996*

In *State of Ohio v. Louis Trauth Dairy*, C-1-93-553, S. D. Ohio 1996 (an antitrust case), the U.S. District Court found that economists were allowed to testify as to their statistical and econometric analyses. The Court held that the **"*Daubert* analysis should be modified in the case of social science or other non-scientific expertise."** The reasoning of *Daubert* still applied, however, and the testimony had to meet tests of reliability and relevancy or as testimony helpful to the jury in resolving the case.

Similarly, quality of life expert testimony will most likely fall into the category of "technical" or "specialized" knowledge in the courts until the demands for "scientific" knowledge can be met. At present, there is no accepted instrument designed to measure quality of life which ties losses in quality of life to projected life expectancy in litigated settings. There are instruments which measure quality-adjusted life years (QALYs) or well-being years, but they were not designed for litigation purposes (Johannesson, 1994; Kaplan, 1991; Kaplan et al., 1991; Parmenter, 1996; Shulman and Cohen. 1993). These instruments, however, do address the issues of quality of life in an individual life, the changes in quality of life with health care interventions, the expected duration of a health condition or well-being year, and economic decision-making regarding health care interventions. These and other quality of life instruments will most likely meet the courts' demands for *Daubert* reasoning and the test for technical or other specialized knowledge, since there are many QOL instruments which have had extensive study and peer review leading to general acceptance, unlike the LPL Scale. Review of the QOL instruments will be detailed in the domain chapters which start with Chapter 3.

As might be expected, defining QOL is a complex business which generally evolves into discussions of QOL domains, models, and concepts. This book is no exception, and chapters 3 through 9 are devoted to seven domains of QOL selected by the authors as a result of their literature review and clinical experience as rehabilitationists in a variety of settings (workers' compensation practice, academia, hospital settings, sheltered workshop settings, state departments of rehabilitation, Social Security Disability Insurance, employment discrimination, personal injury, and civil sexual assault litigation consultation). The domains selected are: the psychological, physical, social, economic, leisure, vocational, and cognitive domains.

One of the better definitions found in the literature review was written by Lawton (1991).

> Quality of life is the multidimensional evaluation, by both intrapersonal and social-normative criteria, of the person-environment system of an individual in time past, current, and anticipated (p. 6).

Raphael (1996b) adds:

> Lawton's definition calls for both objective and subjective evaluations. The criteria against which judgments of quality of life are to be made include both personal perceptions of satisfaction and observer judgments based on normative criteria. Lawton sees the content domains of the *good life* as behavioral competence, perceived quality of life, objective environment, and psychological well-being (p. 295).

The authors agree that both objective and subjective evaluations are needed in order to most precisely judge quality of life for any individual. The literature review as summarized by domains in the following chapters reveals a consensus opinion among writers and researchers on this point across disciplines. The multidimensional aspects of QOL are also agreed upon. The authors also subscribe to the finding by Arnold (1991) that a majority of researchers agree that any definition of quality of life should consider physical, emotional, behavioral, intellectual, and social functioning and dysfunctioning. Life satisfaction, health perception, sexuality, economic status, and leisure were other elements often identified by researchers.

The authors take the position developed by Campbell et al. (1976) that the concept of satisfaction is better suited to the measurement of the global quality of life than the concept of happiness:

> Level of satisfaction can be precisely defined as the perceived discrepancy between aspiration and achievement, ranging from perception of fulfillment to that of deprivation. Satisfaction implies a judgment or cognitive experience, while happiness suggests an experience of feeling or affect (p. 8).

As rehabilitationists, our concern is always with function, and our work has put us in a unique position to observe and to assist with that gap between aspiration and achievement found in any rehabilitation effort with all types of rehabilitation clients. Our clients are rarely happy, and, as rehabilitationists, we don't expect them to be. We do expect, however, that clients will do their best to move from dream to reality or aspiration to achievement, and our job is to help them do so. This task is often stressful since the rehabilitation process itself is stressful, but the rehabilitation effort can also be very satisfying. We leave the business of happiness to the psychologists.

Appendix 12, titled "Domains in Quality of Life Literature" provides an overview of the range and types of domains selected from many disciplines. Some domains are quite specific, such as "breathing," as an aspect of quality of life for people with asthma. Others are quite broad such as "good health," as an aspect of quality of life for everyone. The four domains used in the LPL Scale (psychological, practical, social, and occupational) are common domains selected in the multidisciplinary quality of life literature. It is unfortunate that the LPL Scale was not firmly grounded in this source literature before its appearance in the forensic arena in 1990 (Berla et al. 1990, 1992).

Measurement issues in quality of life studies are complex. Raphael (1996a), in a brilliant chapter, "Defining Quality of Life: Eleven Debates Concerning Its Measurement," has created a table which succinctly summarizes the issues. We have not attempted to replicate Raphael's work, and for readers who are fascinated by research issues, we recommend the full reading of Raphael's chapter in *Quality of Life in Health Promotion and Rehabilitation*, published by Sage Publications in 1996. The eleven debates are:

Eleven Debates Concerning Measuring Quality of Life

Debate 1	Sociological vs. psychological perspectives
Debate 2	Positivist, idealist, and realist approaches
Debate 3	Naturalistic vs. positivist approaches
Debate 4	Quantitative vs. qualitative approaches
Debate 5	Values-based vs. values-free approaches
Debate 6	Social policy vs. basic research orientation
Debate 7	System vs. individual data collection
Debate 8	Objective vs. subjective measures
Debate 9	Self-reports vs. reports by others
Debate 10	Traditional vs. participatory approaches
Debate 11	Critical approaches (p. 147)

Our focus will, of course, be on quality of life instruments which meet the *Daubert* standard, even though we will address other measurement issues. In other words, we will point out work which is empirically based with quantifiable results (including an error rate) and which has been peer reviewed and accepted.

This is not to discount conceptual models of quality of life nor qualitative approaches. In fact, the appendixes summarizing the reviewed literature by categories include conceptual and qualitative work as well as empirically based studies. As Raphael (1996a) points out:

> Qualitative methods are especially useful for delineating new, complex areas of inquiry, whereas quantitative methods are most appropriate for hypothesis testing and generalizing to populations from samples. The implication for quality of life research of qualitative approaches, especially research among marginalized populations, is to let individuals tell their own stories rather than imposing a structure driven by theory or professional concerns and possibly devoid of the human perspectives (p. 155).

This has been particularly true in rehabilitation research in the 1990s. The National Institute on Disability and Rehabilitation Research (NIDRR) has recommended that qualitative approaches be used, due to the "credibility gap" perceived by people with disabilities and rehabilitation counselors as impractical or irrelevant (Graves, 1991; Bruyere, 1993). Participatory Action Research (PAR) was one of the methods recommended, and PAR is designed to include the members of the marginalized group (i.e., people with disabilities) in the research design, implementation, evaluation, and research outcome uses. In a review of the 75 years of the implementation of the first vocational rehabilitation program created by the Smith-Fess Act of 1920, the Director of the National Institute on Disability and Rehabilitation Research noted: "There must be continuing stress on increased consumer participation and involvement in all rehabilitation programs at all levels of operation" (Seelman and Sweeney, 1995).

The point is that despite the *Daubert* standard in the courts, clinical judgment on the part of rehabilitationist will still be needed and that will include the collecting of qualitative data in clinical interviews, reviews of client-produced data such as letters or journals, and careful listening to the clients' experiences of the quality of their lives before and after a physical or psychological injury. These data should be synthesized with objective data on the client's life (income, education, employment history, health history, etc.) and quantifiable data found in psychometrically sound instruments designed to measure the various domains of quality of life.

REFERENCES

Airone, T. J. (1996). 235 Hedonic damages and the admissibility of expert testimony in Connecticut after *Daubert* v. Merrell Dow Pharmaceuticals, Inc. *15 QLR 235*. New York: West Publishing.

American Psychiatric Association (1980). Diagnostic and Statistical Manual of Mental Disorders, 3rd ed. Washington, DC: American Psychiatric Association.

Andrews, P., Meyers, R. G., and Berla, E. P. (1996). Development of the Lost Pleasure of Life Scale. *Law and Human Behavior,* 20(1): 99-111.

Arnold, S. (1991). Measurement of quality of life in the frail elderly. In J. Birren, J. Lubben, J. Rowe, and D. Deutchman (Eds.), *The Concept and Measurement of Quality of Life in the Frail Elderly*, pp. 50-74. New York: Academic Press.

Baker, J. D. (1996). Introduction. In R. Renwick, I. Brown, and M. Nagler (Eds.). *Quality of Life in Health Promotion and Rehabilitation: Conceptual Approaches, Issues, and Applications*, p. xiv. Thousand Oaks, CA: Sage Publications.

Berla, E.P., Brookshire, M.L., and Smith, S. V. (1990). Hedonic damages and personal injury: a conceptual approach. *Journal of Forensic Economics,* 3(1), 1-8.

Berla, E.P., Brookshire, M. L., and Smith, S. V. (1992). Hedonic damages and personal injury: a conceptual approach. In J. O. Ward (Ed.), *A Hedonics Primer for Economists and Attorneys*, pp. 121-129. Tucson, AZ: Lawyers and Judges Publishing Company.

Black, B. D. (1996). McGuire v. City of Santa Fe, et al. *Memorandum opinion and order on plaintiff's hedonic damage experts.* Albuquerque, NM: U.S. District Court for the District of New Mexico.

Branch, T. W. (1992). The rise of hedonic damages and the fall of punitive damages. *Trial Diplomacy Journal*, 15: 95-100.

Brown, R. I. (1989). Aging, disability, and quality of life: a challenge for society. *Canadian Psychology,* 30(3): 551-559.

Brown, R. I., Bayer, M. B., and Brown, P. M. (1988). Quality of life: a challenge for rehabilitation agencies. *Australia and New Zealand Journal of Developmental Disabilities,* 14(3,4): 189-199.

Bruyere, S. M. (1993). Participatory action research: overview and implications for family members of persons with disabilities. *Journal of Vocational Rehabilitation*, 3(2): 62-68.

Campbell, A., Converse, P. E., and Rodgers, W. L. (1976). *The Quality of American Life: Perceptions, Evaluations, and Satisfactions.* New York: Russell Sage Foundation.

Cargonne, P. (1993). The use of the Berla scale in quantifying hedonic damages: a case management perspective. *Journal of Forensic Economics,* 7(1): 47-67.

Chestnut, L. G. and Violette, D. M. (1992). The relevance of willingness-to-pay estimates of the value of a statistical life in determining wrongful death awards. In J. O. Ward (Ed.), *A Hedonics Primer for Economists and Attorneys*, pp. 51-68. Tucson, AZ: Lawyers and Judges Publishing Company.

Decker, P. J. and Borgen, F. H. (1993). Dimension of work appraisal, stress, strain, coping, job satisfaction, and negative affectivity. *Journal of Counseling Psychology,* 40(4): 470-478.

Elizur, D. and Shye, S. (1990). Quality of work life and its relation to quality of life. *Applied Psychology: An International Review,* 39(3): 275-291.

Fabian, E. S. (1991). Using quality of life indicators in rehabilitation program evaluation. *Rehabilitation Counseling Bulletin,* 34(4): 345-356.

Graves, W. H. (1991). Participatory action research: a new paradigm for disability and rehabilitation research. *American Rehabilitation Counseling Association,* 19(1): 8-10.

Havrilesky, T. (1992). Valuing life in the courts: an overview. In J. O. Ward (Ed.), *A Hedonics Primer for Economists and Attorneys*, pp. 139-143. Tucson, AZ: Lawyers and Judges Publishing Company.

Imwinkelried, E. J. (1996). Admissibility of nonscientific expert testimony. *Trial,* 58-62.

Johannesson, M. (1994). QALYs, HYEs and individual preferences: a graphical illustration. *Social Science Medicine,* 39(12): 1623-1632.

Jones, D. D. (1994). Hedonic damages and the index number problem. *Journal of Forensic Economics,* 7(2): 193-196.

Kaplan, R. M. (1991). Health-related quality of life in patient decision making. *Journal of Social Issues,* 47(4): 69-90.

Kaplan, R. M., Debon, M., and Anderson, B. F. (1991). Effects of number of rating scale points upon utilities in a quality of well-being scale. *Medical Care,* 29(10): 1061-1064.

Keil, S. R. and Moehring, H. B. (1995). Use of hedonic loss claims in the United States: a Survey. *Litigation Economics Digest*, 1(1): 85-93.

Kubler-Ross, R. E. (1969). *On Death and Dying.* New York: Macmillan.

Kurz, K. M. and Prather, C. J. (1995). *Improving the Quality of Life of Girls.* New York: United Nations Children's Fund Programme Publications.

Lawton, M. P. (1991). A multidimensional view of quality of life in frail elders. In J. Birren, J. Lubben, J. Rowe and D. Deutchman (Eds.), *The Concept and Measurement of Quality of Life in the Frail Elderly,* pp. 3-27. New York: Academic Press.

Lehman, A. (1988). A quality of life interview for the chronically mentally ill. *Evaluation and Program Planning*, 18: 51-62.

Loscocco, K. A. and Roschelle, A. R. (1991). Influences on the quality of work and nonwork life: two decades in review. *Journal of Vocational Behavior,* 39: 182-225.

Magrowski, J. F. (1991a). Future vocational expert testimony on hedonics. *Monograph #1: The Vocational Expert's Testimony.* Topeka, KS: American Board of Vocational Experts.

Magrowski, J. F. (1991b). *Introduction to Hedonics.* St. Louis, MO: Hedonology Institute.

Metcalf, R. (1992). Loss of enjoyment, rehabilitation and hedonic damages: a comment. *Journal of Forensic Economics,* 5(3): 261-264.

Miller, T. R. (1992). The plausible range for the value of life: red herrings among the
mackerel. In J. O. Ward (Ed.). *A Hedonics Primer for Economists and Attorneys*, pp. 69-92.

National Institute on Disability and Rehabilitation Research, Office of Special Education and Rehabilitation Services, U.S. Department of Education. (1988). Quality of life research in rehabilitation. *Rehab Brief,* XI(9). Washington, D.C.: Author.

Paolicelli, D. (1993). Proving pain and suffering damages in employment discrimination cases. Paper presented at the National Employment Lawyers Association 1993 4th Annual Convention. Orlando, FL.

Parmenter, T. R. (1996). The use of quality of life as a construct for social and health policy development. In R. Renwick, I. Brown, and M. Nagler (Eds.), *Quality of Life in Health Promotion and Rehabilitation,* pp. 89-103. Thousand Oaks, CA: Sage Publications.

Raphael, D. (1996a). Defining quality of life: Eleven debates concerning its measurement. In R. Renwick, I. Brown, and M. Nagler (Eds.). *Quality of Life in Health Promotion and Rehabilitation,* pp. 146-170. Thousand Oaks, CA: Sage Publications.

Raphael, D. (1996b). Quality of life of older adults. In R. Renwick, I. Brown, and M. Nagler (Eds.). *Quality of Life in Health Promotion and Rehabilitation,* pp. 290-306. Thousand Oaks, CA: Sage Publications.

Renwick, R., Brown, I. and Nagler, M. (Eds.). (1996). *Quality of Life in Health Promotion and Rehabilitation: Conceptual Approaches, Issues, and Applications.* Thousand Oaks, CA: Sage Publications.

Richardson, M. S. (1993). Work in people's lives: a location for counseling psychologists. *Journal of Counseling Psychology,* 40(4): 425-433.

Roessler, R. T. (1990). A quality of life perspective on rehabilitation counseling. *Rehabilitation Counseling Bulletin,* 34(2): 82-91.

Sackman, B. S. and Ingham, M. (1992). Methods for calculating hedonic loss. *NARRPS Journal and News,* 7(1): 7-14.

Schuessler, K. and Fisher, G. (1985). Quality of life research and sociology. *Annual Review of Sociology,* 11: 129-149.

Seelman, K. and Sweeney, S. (1995). The changing universe of disability. *American Rehabilitation,* 21(3): 2-13.

Shain, M. (1996). Work, employment, and mental health: implications for quality of life. In R. Renwick, I. Brown, and M. Nagler (Eds.), *Quality of Life in Health Promotion and Rehabilitation,* pp. 327-341. Thousand Oaks, CA: Sage Publications.

Shulman, K. I. and Cohen, C. A. (1993). Quality of life and economic aspects of community support programs for caregivers of dementia patients. *American Journal of Geriatric Psychiatry,* 1(3): 211-220.

Smith, S. V. (1988). Hedonic damages in wrongful death cases. *ABA Journal,* 74: 70.

Smith, S. V. (1992). Hedonic damages in the courtroom setting: a bridge over troubled waters. In J. O. Ward (Ed.). *A Hedonics Primer for Economists and Attorneys*, pp. 111-120. Tucson, AZ: Lawyers and Judges Publishing Company.

Terman, S. A. (1995). Emotional damages due to wrongful death — What are they worth? *Behavioral Sciences and the Law, Vol. 11:* 43-59.

Viscusi, W. K. (1992). The value of life: Has voodoo economics come to the courts? In J. O. Ward (Ed.). *A Hedonics Primer for Economists and Attorneys*, pp. 21-38. Tucson, AZ: Lawyers and Judges Publishing Company.

Waring, M. (1988). *If Women Counted: a New Feminist Economics.* San Francisco: Harper and Row.

Williams, J. M. (1991). Providing quality service at a reasonable human and dollar cost: facing the dilemmas of serving multiple interests as professionals in private sector rehabilitation. Paper presented at the Annual Meeting of Pennsylvania Association of Rehabilitation Professionals in the Private Sector. Lake Harmony, PA.

Williams, J. M. and Burlew, L. (1995). Dealing with catastrophic injury: a developmental perspective on life care planning. *Adultspan*, 9(3): 4-8.

Williams, J. M. and Fidanza, N.S. (1990). Ensuring the success of industrial rehabilitation programs: the role of the rehabilitation counselor in return to work. *NARRPS Journal and News*, 5(5): 67-71.

2 Rehabilitation and Quality of Life

THE COMMON GROUND

> Rehabilitation is a restorative process that builds upon a person's previously acquired skills, capabilities, knowledge, experiences and attitudes regardless of the functional severity imposed by a subsequently imposed disability condition.
>
> *Rubin and Roessler, 1987*

Rehabilitation efforts are designed to restore a person to the level of function attained prior to the onset of disability, to the extent possible given the person's physical and/or mental impairments. Matkin (1985) recognized that work is the central theme of rehabilitation; entry into work (for the developmentally disabled) or return to work (for the injured worker) is the primary desired outcome of the rehabilitation process. Yet, as suggested by Wright (1980), rehabilitation encompasses more than just returning persons with disabilities to work. It is not possible to divide a person into individual parts — physical, mental, psychological, social, and economic. The rehabilitation process is seen as a systematic approach to assessing and addressing the total needs of a person with disabilities. Each person is seen as a unique individual with assets that can be developed. The ultimate goal of the rehabilitation process is to promote functional independence, where the individual is capable of economic self-sufficiency and integration into society. Every individual has equal value; in turn, equal rights under the law. Pursuit of life, liberty and happiness, as guaranteed by the Constitution of the U.S., is an unalienable right of persons with disabilities as well as those without. A rehabilitationist sees disability not as a criterion for denying equality of opportunity, but as an advocate, works diligently to enhance opportunities for persons with disabilities (McGowan and Porter, 1967). Disability affects all aspects of life and can have a negative affect on total life function if disabilities rather than abilities are emphasized in the rehabilitation process.

Attention to quality of life (QOL) provides the rehabilitationist with an opportunity to assess clients' subjective ratings of worth to self and society and compare these ratings with objective measures of life function in a number of areas, including work. Quality of life may, in fact, be a good criterion upon which to base the selection of specific rehabilitation service options, given the desire that the rehabilitation process should restore the people to pre-disability levels of function. Likewise, for the developmentally disabled who need habilitation (i.e., opportunities for growth and development equal to those offered to persons without a disability), quality of life may offer a reasonable benchmark upon which to judge the efficacy of any potential service options (Roessler, 1990), a valuable tool in rehabilitation planning.

If the discrepancy between aspiration and achievement defines one's life satisfaction, as suggested by Campbell et al. (1976), rehabilitation goal planning must clearly define goals (as an expression of aspiration) and select appropriate interventions (methods for promoting actions which lead to achievement), if life satisfaction is to be attained. Rehabilitation goals and interventions should not overemphasize personal factors (perceptions, aspirations, expectations, and/or past experience) or underestimate external factors (i.e., societal standards, employment practices, labor market trends, accessibility, attitudes towards disability, advances in medicine, new medications, or similar factors beyond the person's control) in promoting change. Cheng (1988) postulates that study of the rehabilitation interventions which lead to enhanced life function helps in building of theory about the relationship between life satisfaction and behavioral competency, assisting in defining operationally the construct of quality of life.

Furthermore, it is recognized that one may experience a high quality of life and not self-report high life satisfaction, when aspirations exceed opportunities, or, conversely, may experience low quality of life when opportunities exceed aspirations. Setting realistic and attainable goals is critical to enhancing quality of life. Kozleski and Sands (1992) point to normalization theory, the theoretical rationale for deinstitutionalization of developmentally disabled populations was an important social indicator of quality of life. The degree to which persons with disabilities have gained access to the same opportunities and have gained the same level of acceptance through accomplishment as enjoyed by nondisabled persons may be inherently the best indicator of quality of life. Quality of life may hinge more on the ability to enjoy the same opportunities for and rewards from accomplishment as offered to those one emulates than on attainment of some absolute standard of performance. In reality, normalcy encompasses a great variety of variations in human aspiration and achievement.

To Boone and Stevens (1991) quality of life is defined by one's attainment of socioeconomic status, ability to form and maintain relationships, independence/interdependence, accessibility to others who are willing to form and maintain relationships, opportunity for personal growth and fulfillment, the opportunity to participate in community and civic activities, and the opportunity to be productive. One could argue that one's quality of life is determined by the extent to which one's life matches that of peers in the community. Looking at the accomplishments of those identified by an individual as peers may give valuable clues to the standards one sets for oneself. When a person has an impairment, a sign or symptom of a disease or condition, and when that impairment leads to a disability, a restriction in ability to perform or participate in life activities, a handicap or limitation in ability to fulfill a role which is normal for that individual may occur (Wright, 1980; Cobble and Burks, 1990). The emphasis of the rehabilitation process is on learning to maximize one's residual capacities and to minimize impairments and disabilities. Rehabilitation attempts to heal the person as opposed to, in the medical model, heal the disease.

GOALS OF THE REHABILITATION PROCESS

> Total rehabilitation as a problem-solving process addresses the limitations and handicaps that remain after a medical condition is treated.
>
> *Wright, 1980*

The rehabilitationist is concerned not with the treatment of the condition, but with the impact of the condition on the person's physical, intellectual, social, vocational, economic, or emotional functioning. As Dunham and Dunham (1978) point out, a person who a disability is structurally (i.e., physically, mentally, psychologically) different from a person which would be considered to be normal, due to accident, disease, or developmental problems. The concept of normalcy can be helpful in rehabilitation in that it can provide some guidance in determining one's life choices in response to disability, but can also become a source of stigma and prejudice if disability or difference is seen to produce a tragic life-long limitation in ability to pursue life activities. Disability is different from illness in that illness implies dependency and the need for external attention and service to one's needs. Disability can be understood as merely one aspect of the human condition which may or may not create dependency, the need for care by others, or a reduced life quality. The rehabilitation model emphasizes ability as opposed to disability, seeing the inherent opportunity for growth and development in life's challenges. It is not the challenge, but the response to the challenge, which ultimately dictates life satisfaction (Hulnick and Hulnick, 1989).

In the medical model (particularly when dealing with acute care) the professional care giver has the responsibility for decision-making, and the individual spends much of the time in passively observing the care process. In the psychological model the person is asked to gain insight into self as a way of understanding his or her behavior. As in the medical model, great emphasis is placed on assessment of the intrapersonal factors influencing function, under the assumption that the more the person knows about self the greater will be the person's sense of self-worth. Enhanced self-worth is then assumed to lead to a higher level of overt function (Day and Jankey, 1996). Although the person takes a more active role in the treatment process through counseling, psychotherapy, or related structured, therapeutic programming, insight takes precedence over behavior in the assessment and intervention phases of the treatment process. The medical and psychological models both emphasize deficits (i.e., physical, emotional, mental and/or behavioral limitations) in the assessment and treatment. Treatment is seen as successful when illness and/or disease is eliminated or controlled and function reaches a level acceptable to the caregivers.

In the rehabilitation model, diagnosis of severity of impairments and/or limitations is important only because this information is helpful in teaching a "differently abled" person how to cope with life's challenges by taking responsibility for choices (i.e., developing autonomy), making responsible choices (based on internal and external feedback), and taking reasonable risks based on recognition of opportunities for growth and independence (Williams and Burlew, 1995). Cobble and Burks (1990) point out that the rehabilitation model, unlike the medical model, attempts not only to cure the disease, but also to enhance functional performance, modify social and vocational environments, prevent unnecessary complications, and help the individual and family cope with impairments. Enhancement of capacities is emphasized.

The rehabilitationist should actively assist a person with a disability in identifying the internal and external barriers to maximum performance in all areas of life function (not just in the vocational and financial areas). Hulnick and Hulnick (1989) suggest that empowering persons who are differently abled to make their own choices, act out on them, and accept responsibility for the consequences of their actions gives them an opportunity to grow, a precursor to well-being. Crose et al. (1992) suggest that well-being is multidimensional (including physical, emotional, intellectual, spiritual, and social dimensions). Well-being is not seen as a static state, but a dynamic process of growth and development. Emphasis is placed on development of the self-regulatory mechanisms to maintain a balance among and within these dimensions. Borrowing heavily from systems theory, this approach suggests that there is natural variability in the range of human behavior within each dimension of human function. When internal or external challenges to the "balance" between the areas of life function occur, well-being is threatened. The rehabilitationist seeks restoration of well-being (i.e., a term used synonymously with quality of life) and enhancement of growth and development over life span. Fabian (1991) may be correct in asserting the quality of life is a standard upon which to judge the efficacy of rehabilitation. The ultimate goal of the rehabilitation process may be enhancement of well-being or quality of life. Chandler et al. (1992) support the contention that achievement of a high level of well-being requires attainment of a homeostatic relationship between intellectual, occupational, physical, emotional, and social dimensions of human function. Their suggestion that spirituality may be the "glue" which brings all aspects of the person together into a meaningful whole reminds the rehabilitationist that for persons with or without disabilities may need to transcend their egocentric perspective in order to find sufficient quality in their lives. Issues relative to quality of life remind the rehabilitationist that human behavior is quite complex and cannot be explained simplistically. A rehabilitationist is more than a case manager, career counselor or job placement specialist — areas of rehabilitation activity mentioned by several authors (Matkin, 1985; Rasch, 1985) when describing the roles and responsibilities of rehabilitation professionals working in the private sector. The efficacy of the rehabilitation process and the professional credibility of the rehabilitationist should not rest solely on selected areas or domains of human function, but on a collective assessment of life function as a whole.

Quality of life provides a context upon which to judge the short and long-term effectiveness of rehabilitation. Renwick and Friefeld (1996) define rehabilitation as a multidisciplinary field which is concerned with physical, emotional, cognitive, and social aspects of functioning across the life span. This definition suggests that there is a strong developmental emphasis in rehabilitation. It further supports the contention that quality of life is not a static concept and is subject to change as a person develops. A single, "snapshot approach" to looking at quality of life does not account for changes which result from one's experiencing the challenges of living from birth to death and learning from interacting with life circumstances presented therein. One's health is not defined in terms of one's physical well-being, but on one's overall capacities to call upon one's energies, strengths, and abilities to interact with the environment for the purpose of promoting one's quality of life. Bergner (1989) points to the traditional perspective of rehabilitationists that quality of life centers around functional or health status; and suggests that several functional status questionnaires assess quality of life for persons with chronic illnesses in terms of such variables as gross mobility, personal care, home chores, hand activities, interpersonal activities, and mental capacity to handling finances. Sartorius (1995) points out that the primary goal of rehabilitation is restoration of quality of life, not solely the restoration of one's ability to work and earn a living. This perspective recognizes that one's lifestyle preferences rather than some absolute standard should be used as a guideline for assessing adaptation to change in life circumstances.

Individual differences rather than predetermined, historical perspectives should be used to identify rehabilitation goals. The individual identifies the importance given to each area of life function through self-report of current and historical patterns of function. Enhancement of quality of life is then based on the individual's preferences rather than societal standards of how one ought to function (Renwick and Friefeld, 1996). Day and Jankey (1996) suggest that measurement of quality of life provides a yardstick for measuring the goodness of fit between a person with a disability and the environment. The subjective weighting of the importance of each factor making up global quality of life and objective measurement of function in those areas should both be used to determine quality of life. The rehabilitationist is responsible for addressing issues relative to quality of life in the rehabilitation planning and services delivery processes rather than restoration on physical capacities only. When assessing rehabilitation outcomes, Kozleski and Sands (1992) point out that quality of life can be measured by the extent to which a person with a disability interacts with the environment and others and makes decisions compares to a person without a disability. The rehabilitation professional facilitates the planning and delivery of services which optimize productivity, social and community activities; and offer opportunities for personal growth and fulfillment, accessibility to others with whom relationships can be formed and maintained, and independence/interdependence, and socioeconomic status. Williams and Burlew (1995) recommended that future care planning for persons with disabilities should address developmental issues relative to quality of life over life span rather than focus primarily on physical care needs from a maintenance perspective. Deutsche and Sawyer (1988) identified the components of a life care plan and have articulated that quality of life was a consideration in determining the type, frequency, and duration of care. Yet, the focus of the care plans has been on medical procedures, medical-related equipment and supplies, structured care for meeting physical needs, and the like. The dollars identified in the life-care planning document are often heavily weighted towards meeting ongoing physical needs. The emphasis is on chronic illness and not on wellness. If one adopts enhancement of quality of life as the major goal or one of the major goals of the rehabilitation process, care planning should then reflect opportunities for productivity, intellectual and emotional growth, social interaction, financial growth, and leisure time. Witmer and Sweeney (1992) identify work, love, and friendship as key concepts in wellness. The interaction between internal, self-regulatory factors (i.e., sense of control, realistic beliefs, spontaneity/emotional responsiveness, intellectual stimulation/creativity, and physical fitness) and such environmental factors as education, family, community, business, and government determines one's well-being over life span. Well-being is determined based on how the whole being functions in relationship to the value given to each of the internal and external factors (Crose et al., 1992). Future care planning must emphasize wellness as well as address deficits if quality of life is to be restored, maintained, and enhanced.

WELLNESS AND QUALITY OF LIFE

> Wellness is an ongoing process. It is predicated on the person's active involvement in behavior and lifestyle choices which will empower them to live full, responsible and rewarding lives.
>
> *Hatfield and Hatfield, 1992*

Quality of life may best be understood as partially a global measure of life satisfaction and a measure of adaptive functioning or environmental mastery across multiple life domains (Fabian, 1991). Assessment of one's quality of life centers around such domains as emotional well-being, physiological state, productivity, material well-being, and performance of social roles (Felce and Perry, 1996). Wellness can best be understood as a state of being where the individual has found a dynamic balance between internal and external factors which impact life function across these same domains; where sustaining all aspects of the organism over the long-term takes precedence over gratification of short-term needs relative to one or more domain at the expense of function in others. One might report a high level of quality of life over a finite period of time while experiencing a given set of life experiences, but may not be following a lifestyle which would promote wellness. An example of this might be the person who risks losing emotional well-being and loving relationships for the long-term in an effort to earn material wealth in the short-term. Objective (behavioral) indicators of quality of life (i.e., earnings, work performance, social status, housing; personal possessions) might take precedence over subjective (self-reported) indicators (i.e., social relationships, family, self-esteem, positive affect, faith, self-respect, personal fulfillment). The stress of maintaining a lifestyle in which an imbalance occurs between internal and external factors promoting well-being may lead to erosion of wellness and increase in stress-related somatic complaints (Selye, 1974). Physical health is the one area of objective analysis of quality of life which is a good indicator of one's success in maintaining homeostasis between internal and external life domains. Conversely, erosion of physical health can create an imbalance between internal and external factors and negatively impact quality of life and wellness. For the rehabilitationist, developmental disabilities or traumatic injuries are viewed from thc perspective of the whole person. Subjective and objective indicators of quality of life and their implication for wellness over life span provide the foundation upon which to build a rationale for future care needs and to assess pain and suffering (from a whole person, developmental perspective as opposed to a static, physiological and/or emotional perspective only). As Roessler (1990) suggests, quality of life is a wellness concept which goes beyond the traditional disease or medical model found in the rehabilitation literature.

Several authors (Lehman, 1983; Kirchman, 1986) include such life domains as living situation, family and social relationships, leisure, work, finances, health, safety, and employment status in their measures of quality of life. Schalock (1996) points out that quality of life is associated with three major life domains — home and community living, school or work, and health and wellness. Kaplan and Anderson (1988) developed the Quality of Well Being Scale (QWB) as a measure of quality of life across four scales — symptoms, mobility, physical activity, and social activity. In their review of quality of life research in nursing and related medical fields, Padilla et al. (1992) identified three dimensions of content domain in the literature — psychological/psychosocial, physical/activities of daily living/functional capacities, and social support and adjustment. Interviews with 40 cancer patients with chronic pain added empirical support to physical, psychological, and interpersonal well-being as the major themes in quality of life. Tuchler et al. (1992) designed the Quality of Health and Quality of Life (OAHL) with specific questions about global life satisfaction and quality of life, physical issues (i.e., capacities, condition, sexuality, and medical treatment), and social issues (i.e., relationships and social contacts). Ferrans and Powers (1985, 1992) developed health/functioning, socioeconomic, psychological/spiritual and family subscales on the Quality of Life Index (QLI) out of recognition that these domains made up the larger construct of quality of life. These are the same domains which are discussed in the wellness literature (Crose et al., 1992; Witmer and Sweeney, 1992).

The World Health Organization (WHO, 1984) has defined health as a state of complete mental, physical, and social well-being rather than as merely the absence of disease or infirmity. The *Ottawa Charter for Health Promotion* (WHO, 1986) noted that to reach a state of physical, mental, and social well-being one must be able to identify and attain aspirations, to satisfy needs, and to change or cope with one's environment. Using this definition, WHO has worked to develop an instrument to measure quality of life out of recognition that the value of health care cannot be fully measured by assessment of its impact on disease. The World Health Organization Quality of Life scale (WHOQOL) represents the consensus of international experts on a working definition of quality of life. Quality of life is seen as "a person's perception of his/her position in life within the context of the culture and value systems in which he/she lives and in relation to his/her goals, expectations, standards, and concerns (WHOQOL Group, 1994)."

The domains of quality of life used in development of the WHOQOL were identified by conducting focus groups with healthy persons in 15 countries throughout the world.

Domain 1 — Physical gives the best insight into the role of physical pain and distressing sensations which interfere with daily life on quality of life. The assumption is that the easier it is to relieve pain, the less will be the fear of pain and its negative impact on quality of life. The constant threat of pain, even when one is not in pain, may also affect quality of life. Tolerance to and acceptance of pain varies from person to person and may moderate or exacerbate the impact of physical pain on quality of life. Constant pain reduces energy level and promotes fatigue. Stiffness, itching, and aching can be equally unpleasant sensations. The physiological pleasure of sexuality can be more than offset by the exacerbation of physical pain when engaging in sexual activity. Physical pain and suffering will diminish quality of life.

Domain 2 — Psychological examines how one experiences such positive emotions as happiness, joy, hopefulness, peace, contentment, and balance. Such negative feelings as anxiety, depression, sadness, and despair are addressed as well. One's feelings and view of the future are considered important. Respondents tend to regard this domain as synonymous with quality of life.

Domain 3 — Level of Independence deals with a person's ability to get from one place to another, to move around the home, workplace, and community. The ability to get where one wants to go without assistance is the focus of this domain. Quality of life is assumed to erode if a person is dependent on another person for mobility. Such equipment as a wheelchair or walking frame may be offered to enhance mobility and to increase quality of life. For someone who is blind, a seeing-eye dog may provide mobility without dependence on others.

In **Domain 4 — Social Relationships,** the extent to which the person experiences the companionship, support, and love of intimate relationships, shares happiness and distress with loved ones, gives love as well as receives it, and has fulfilling relationships with others is examined.

In **Domain 5 — Environment,** one's financial resources to meet one's need for a healthy and comfortable lifestyle are assessed. Satisfaction or dissatisfaction with things the person is able to attain within a given income provides insight into the person's feeling of having enough. Safety, security, leisure activities, transportation, and physical environment also contribute to this domain.

TABLE II
WHOQOL Domains and Facets

Physical	Psychological	Level of Independence	Social Relationships	Environment
Pain and discomfort	Positive feelings	Mobility	Personal relationships	Freedom, physical safety and security
Energy and fatigue	Thinking, learning, memory, and concentration	Activities of daily living	Practical social support	Home environment
Sexual activity	Self-esteem	Dependence on medical provider substances	Activities	Work satisfaction
		Dependence on nonmedical substances		Financial resources
		Communication capacity		Accessibility and quality of health and social care
		Work capacity		Opportunities for new information and skills
				Recreation/leisure activities
				Physical environment
				Transportation

Domain 6 — Spirituality/Religion/Personal Beliefs examines personal beliefs about quality of life and how one copes with difficulties and gives structure and meaning to life experiences. One's sense of belonging, meaning, strength, and purpose contributes to one's perception of quality of life. Global questions about quality of life and life satisfaction are asked out of recognition that a global perception of quality of life reflects the person's summative evaluation across all domains. Perceptions about quality of life in any one domain do not necessarily influence highly the global self-report. See Table I for a brief synopsis of the areas (facets) of inquiry associated with each domain.

For the rehabilitation professional who is preparing a life care plan or who is attempting to explain the impact of injury and disability on life function as an objective indicator of pain and suffering (realizing that pain and suffering across all the domains and not just the physical and/or psychological), an analysis of changes in quality of life from before to after the defining life event (i.e., injury or trauma) provides a rationale based on the literature and traditions in the field of rehabilitation for supporting one's professional opinions. Assessment of quality of life should include analysis of the physical, psychological, social, intellectual, vocational, and financial factors which contribute to life satisfaction.

The quality of life and wellness literature provides the rehabilitationist with theory and measures which support the construct and content associated with quality of life. This is important in that, as per the *Daubert* standard for expert testimony, an expert must offer testimony where scientific inquiry has resulted in building consensus about theory and in constructing measures which offer the opportunity to validate theory empirically. Quality of life is not the speculation of a few authors in the field of rehabilitation. It is a well-developed construct built on the consensus of cultures, peoples, and countries throughout the world, as evidenced by the commitment of WHO, as well as by clinical professionals in medicine, rehabilitation, and related health and social care fields to ongoing research on quality of life.

ASSESSMENT ISSUES

> Courts rely on ... test data and related expert testimony to answer important questions. A good test has clear instructions on administration, scoring, and interpretation. A good test is reliable. A good test is a valid test. A good test is one which contains adequate norms.
>
> *Cohen, Swerdik, and Phillips, 1996*

Although issues of quality of life and wellness are discussed in the forensic rehabilitation literature (Deutsche, 1990; Williams, 1995; Williams and Burlew, 1995), empirical assessment of quality of life (as a holistic, developmental indicator of pain and suffering) as part of a forensic rehabilitation analysis of the impact of impairment and disability on total life function has been lacking. In part, this may be due to a historical interest in "deficit thinking" when dealing with persons with disabilities in a forensic environment where the focus has been on associated dollar value of the loss. However, also it has been easy to dismiss quality of life as an issue deserving analysis due to unfamiliarity with instrumentation or dismissal of these instruments as lacking the sound psychometric properties (construction, reliability, validity, and norms) associated with more commonly used instruments. The former issue is dealt with through acquainting forensic rehabilitation experts with the rich literature in health and rehabilitation; the latter is done by looking at the state of the science in psychometric assessment of quality of life. The use of sound psychometric principles in quality of life instrumentation provides support to the position that rehabilitation expert opinion on an individual's quality of life is not speculative, but is based on sound, scientific principles consistent with those seen in other areas of the behavioral sciences. Control of measurement error and development of normative samples for disabled and nondisabled populations are critical factors in demonstrating the science required for admissibility of expert testimony on quality of life under the *Daubert* standard.

Although a complete review of the literature on measurement of quality of life is outside the scope of this book, Raphael (1996) suggests that the debate concerning measurement of quality of life contains certain signposts where one must chose a direction or path and understand the consequences of that choice. The sociological perspective looks for broad patterns of social interaction which influence an individual's quality of life, while the psychological perspective looks at the internal structure and content of well-being for an individual. The positivist suggests that the methods of hypothesis testing empirical observation and carrying out controlled experiments lead to empirical observation of social events and individual behavior, while the idealist sees the interaction between the individual and the society to produce individual meaning. The realist uses observations not to develop theory, but to understand the mechanisms which influence the development and perpetuation of quality of life (the concept of deviancy being one which lends itself to realistic assessment). The positivist relies on traditional methodologies based on the assumption that truth is out there somewhere waiting to be discovered, and believes that the boundaries of inquiry about quality of life have been sufficiently well-defined that important issues/factors will not be missed when using finite measures. Qualitative researchers are less sure that the boundaries have been well defined, that any empirical measures are sensitive to differences in individuals or subgroups of the population. Quantitative researchers suggest the empirical measures offer the advantage of comparison of the individual's performance to that of a representative population. A debate about the need to include such objective indicators of quality of life as health or work status as compared to reliance on self-report about quality of life, the subject of most of the quality of life research on measurement, is also of interest.

These debates are not meaningful to the forensic rehabilitation expert unless their relevance to meeting the *Daubert* standard is established. This standard relies heavily on traditional, positivist beliefs and scientific methodologies. Qualitative methods may be helpful for developing constructs and content of instrumentation, but provide less than persuasive evidence for comparing the quality of life of an individual before and after a traumatic life event to a normative standard of what is reasonable quality of life for the overall population of persons who have not experienced such trauma. Self-report concerning quality of life, even when offered through analysis of instruments which demonstrate adequate reliability and validity, may not fully meet the test of science unless objective, corroborative information is available for the expert to rely upon. Pooling of objective and subjective indicators in an analysis of quality of life, as suggested by Raphael et al. (1994), seems to be a reasonable approach to meeting the standard of science, recognizing that quality of life must be viewed by the standards of scientific rigor currently accepted in the peer-reviewed journals in the behavioral as opposed to the natural sciences. The behavioral sciences do not have the measurement technology to meet the standard of control of error or chance variability that the natural sciences enjoy. Quality of life research, like other research into human behavior, is not done in laboratory conditions where all variables are controlled. Yet, the behavioral sciences have sufficiently met the standards of the positivist community to allow reliance on findings as the best estimate of truth available. Experts in the behavioral sciences routinely rely on the results of instruments which have demonstrated adequate reliability and validity, as long as the available instruments allow the expert to draw conclusions about an individual under the standard of reasonable professional certainty. As suggested by Williams and Maze (1994), the rehabilitation expert is charged with the responsibility for finding the truth of the matter within his or her area of expertise. This is done by collection of all the available data, giving weight to data based on data collection methodologies which meet the prevailing standards of scientific inquiry, and comparing those data to data on the same or similar populations found in the empirical literature in the one's field. Three measures, the Quality of Well Being Scale (Kaplan, 1994), the Quality of Life Index (Ferrans and Powers, 1992), and the WHOQOL (WHOQOL Group, 1994), out of the 75 or so instruments measuring quality of life for different populations in different settings identified in a literature review, offer the most promise as sensitive, but global, measures of quality of life. Each has its strengths and weaknesses, but each addresses issues of reliability and validity to the extent that they can be considered to be useful measures for assessing current quality of life. Each holds promise for providing empirical data about differences in quality of life between nondisabled and disabled populations, a requisite for using an instrument to talk about the degree of difference between an individual's quality of life and that seen in the general population. This does not mean that a specialized quality of life instrument for dealing with the issues relevant to a unique population may not be useful. However, such instruments may be more subject to criticism because of smaller sample sizes, less diversity in age, gender, culture, and illness/disability type, and more emphasis on a few rather than all of the domains.

Ferrans and Powers (1992) felt that quality of life could be defined in terms of one's satisfaction or dissatisfaction with areas of life which are important. Subjective rating of importance of a given item is seen as an important factor in weighting the contribution of the item to the final score. The 64 items are divided into two parts. Part I measures satisfaction in a given domain (on a scale from 6 — very satisfied — to 1 — very dissatisfied), and Part II measures importance (on a scale of 6 — very important — to 1 — very unimportant). Concurrent validity studies demonstrated a 0.76 correlation between the QLI and a global question on life satisfaction for 88 graduate students and 0.65 for the dialysis patients. Cronbach's alphas (a measure of internal consistency reliability) were 0.93 for graduate students and 0.90 for dialysis patients. Factor analysis identified four factors — health and functioning, socioeconomic, psychological/spiritual, and family — as the domains for assessing quality of life. When the scores of participants earning less than \$10,000 per year (n = 155) were compared to those of persons earning over \$10,000 per year (n = 161), the only significant difference between the two groups was found on the social and economic subscale. Versions of the QLI have been developed for use with stroke, respiratory conditions, cancer, diabetes, arthritis, burn, spinal cord injury, cardiac conditions, liver conditions, and kidney transplant, as well as healthy persons.

Kaplan (1994) suggests a model of health status which includes mortality, morbidity (physical activity, mobility, and social activity), utility (relative importance — measured by independent judges), and duration. The Quality of Well-Being (QWB) scale was developed to estimate these components of the General Health Policy Model. This instrument classifies people according to objective level of function (on mobility, physical activity, and social activity subscales and according to the one most undesirable symptom). Once this is done, each individual is rated on a wellness scale from 0 — death to 1 — complete wellness. Regression weights are assigned to each item chosen from the three subscales and the symptom list. The quality of well-being score equals 1 minus the observed morbidity, physical activity, social activity, and symptom/problem regression weights (calculated from data collected from a random sample of the general population in San Diego, CA). A point-in-time wellness score is calculated and then multiplied by the number of years to identify wellness years (Kaplan et al. 1994). Where data on the number of well years with or without treatment and the cost of health care with or without a given treatment are available, a cost/utility ratio can be determined. The method of test administration is a structured interview; questions are asked concerning symptoms, mobility, physical activity, and social activity.

In a study of HIV patients using the QWB (Kaplan et al. 1995), significant relationships were seen between neurologist's ratings of impairment, neuropsychological ratings of impairment, CD4+ cells, and serum β_2 hemoglobin and quality of life scores for 514 AIDS patients. In a correlational study of the relationship between parents' ratings of the quality of life experienced by the children on the QWB scale and parental behavioral ratings concerning play and activity levels of these children (as measured by the PPS) the authors noted a significant correlation between the total QWB score and the PPS and each subscale and the PPS (Bradlyn et al. 1993). No significant gender or age differences were seen. In a similar study, Hays and Shapiro (1992) found that, with AIDS patients, the QWB was found to be a better measure of physical rather than mental health; it was seen as problematic in the study of diseases where mental health and cognitive function do not manifest themselves readily in physical or mobility deficits.

The QWB has demonstrated its psychometric soundness on repeated occasions. Andersen et al. (1989) reported interday reliability ranging from 0.78 to 0.99 with five groups — the San Diego sample, Indonesian refugees, burn victims, persons with chronic obstructive pulmonary disease, and diabetics. Andersen et al. (1986) calculated 0.90 to 0.99 correlations between self-administered and interviewer-administered versions of the QWB, suggesting that little chance error would occur. Validity studies noted a predictive value of 0.97, suggesting that only 3 times out of 100 would an optimally functional person be misclassified as dysfunctional when an interviewer administered the instrument. It appears that adequate reliability and validity have been demonstrated with a variety of populations in a number of investigations. The major strength of this instrument is the breadth and depth of the research conducted using it. It was normed on random samples of nondisabled persons (the results being used to develop the weights for the items on the symptom checklist). Also, it has correlated significantly with observed behaviors and physiological assessments across age groups and populations (patients with acute and chronic illnesses).

The WHOQOL-100 was developed to measure individuals' perception of their life in the context of the culture and value systems in which they live and in relation to their goals, expectations, standards and concerns (Bonomi and Patrick, 1997). Three hundred items were developed at 15 centers throughout the world; as a result of pilot testing with 4500 subjects, the 100 best items were selected. Specific language and cultural versions were developed for each center. The U.S. version also includes 30 questions on the importance of factors in the identified domains (i.e., allowing for individual differences in weighting of responses in each of the domains (i.e., physical, psychological, social relationships, level of independence, environment, and spiritual). For the 100 specific items relative to the identified domains, the rating scale ranges from 1 (not at all) to 5 (an extreme amount) (a Lickert-like scale). A 1 (not important) to 5 (extremely important) scale is used to rate the 30 importance items. The 14-item U.S. Supplement asks one to provide a global rating of one's quality of life within the last 2 weeks (the standard time frame for the 100 questions)

The obvious advantage of the WHOQOL measure is that it has been tested with various cultures and languages, with the items being selected for their cultural sensitivity and ease of translation. Culture- and language-specific norms can be developed using this instrument.

EXPERT ROLE AND CREDENTIALS

> An expert is one who is qualified, either by actual experience or by careful study, so as to enable him or her to form opinions with respect to a division of science, branch of art, or department of trade about which persons, who having no particular training or special study, are incapable of forming accurate opinions or drawing correct opinions.
>
> *Rogers, 1991*

As suggested by the definition of an expert offered above, one who professes expertise in assessing quality of life issues as a vehicle for enhancing understanding of a person's pain and suffering over life span, should have a unique knowledge of the literature on quality of life. Clearly, as reported in this discourse, quality of life has been an issue discussed and empirically validated in the medical and rehabilitation literature; to a lesser degree it has been addressed in the psychological literature. However, quality of life is a multidimensional issue requiring broad-based training in psychological, social, physical, vocational, intellectual, leisure, and financial development over the life span.

Williams and Maze (1994) point out that the rehabilitation professional who has completed a master's level (60 credits) rehabilitation counseling degree program is in the best position to provide a multidimensional perspective on the impact of impairment, disability, and/or other traumatic life event. Meyers (1992) points out that the history and traditions of the counseling profession emphasize enhancement of human development over life span as its primary mission, as reflected in the strategic planning documents of the American Counseling Association. Emphasis on wellness rather than illness is well established as part of professional identity of the counselor. Both the Council on Accreditation of Counseling and Related Educational Programs (CACREP) and the Council on Rehabilitation Education (CORE) require human development over life span to be part of the core curriculum and competencies of counselor trainees before entering the field of counseling. Experience in working with persons with developmental issues across the domains of quality of life noted here is also helpful. Yet, what sets the expert off from the practitioner is knowledge of the science demonstrated in the literature in the field. In accordance with the *Daubert* standard, the expert must demonstrate the use of a sound scientific knowledge base upon which expert opinions are based. Operationalizing this requirement in terms of expert credentials suggests that those with demonstrated contributions to the literature on rehabilitation, human growth and development over life span, and measurement as they relate to issues of quality of life may be most persuasive in demonstrating sufficient credentials to be experts in quality of life issues as they relate to pain and suffering over life span (from a multidimensional, developmental perspective). The typical master's level rehabilitationist may have excellent credentials as a practitioner, but will be hard pressed to demonstrate contribution to the scientific literature in the field or thorough understanding of the measurement science behind instrumentation. A doctorate in rehabilitation, rehabilitation psychology, or closely related field, with specific training in developmental, preventive theory and interventions, and principles of measurement and scientific rigor, is the optimal educational credential for demonstrating the depth and breadth of knowledge required to conduct meaningful quality of life assessments.

Certification as a rehabilitation counselor (CRC), a counselor (NCC), and as a vocational expert (ABVE) should be prerequisite to being considered an expert in quality of life issues. Certification as a case manager (CCM) or other related certifications or licensure as a psychologist (with specialization in rehabilitation psychology) may be somewhat persuasive, if the person can demonstrate training and knowledge across all domains of quality of life from a developmental perspective, rather than from the deficit orientation of the traditional medical and psychological models. Of course, professionals who have published in peer-reviewed professional journals on topics related to quality of life and have in the past been qualified in court to render opinions concerning quality of life may make the most persuasive argument for being qualified under the *Daubert* standard as experts on quality of life. The authors of this book have routinely provided quality of life assessments as part of comprehensive, rehabilitation evaluations in personal injury and employment discrimination litigation.

The following chapters, starting with Chapter 3, The Psychological Domain, address the domains of quality of life in more detail.

REFERENCES

Andersen, J. P., Bush, J. W., and Berry, C. C. (1986). Classifying function for health outcome and quality-of-life evaluation. *Medical Care*, 24(5), 454-469.

Andersen, J. P., Kaplan, R. M., Berry, C. C., Bush, J. W., and Rumbaut, R. G. (1989). Interday reliability of function assessment for a health status measure. *Medical Care*, 27(11), 1076-1084.

Bergner, M. (1989). Quality of life, health status, and clinical research. *Medical Care*, 27, 148-256.

Bonomi, A.E. and Patrick, D.L. (1997). *User's Manual and Interpretation Guide for the United States Version of the World Health Organization Quality of Life (WHOQOL) Instrument.* Seattle, WA: WHOQOL Center.

Boone, H.A. and Stevens, E. (1991). Towards an enhanced quality of life. In M. Krajicek and R. Tompkins (Eds.), *The Medically Fragmented Infant.* Austin, TX: Pro-Ed.

Bradlyn, A. S., Harris, C. V., Warner, J. E., Ritchley, A. K. and Zaboy, K. (1993). An investigation of the Quality of Well-Being scale with pediatric oncology patients. *Health Psychology,* 12(3), 246-250.

Campbell, A., Converse, P.E., and Rodgers, W. L. (1976). *Quality of Life in America.* New York: Sage Publications.

Cheng, S.T. (1988). Subjective quality of life in the planning and evaluation of programs. *Evaluation and Program Planning*, 11, 123-134.

Chandler, C. K., Holden, J. M., and Kolander, C.A. (1992). Counseling for spiritual wellness: theory and practice. *Journal of Counseling and Development*, 71, 168-175.

Cobble, N. and Burks, J. S. (1990). Introduction to principles of rehabilitation. *Journal of Neurological Rehabilitation*, 4(4), 181-185.

Cohen, R. J., Swerdik, M. E. and Phillips, S. M. (1996). *Psychological Testing and Assessment.* Mountain View, CA: Mayfield Publishing.

Crose, R., Nicholas, D. R., Gobble, D. C. and Frank, B. (1992). Gender and wellness: a multidimensional systems model of counseling. *Journal of Counseling and Development*, 71, 149-156.

Day, H. and Jankey, S. G. (1996). Lessons from the literature: towards a holistic model of quality of life. In R. Renwick, I. Brown, and M. Nagler (Eds.), *Quality of Life in Health Promotion and rehabilitation,* pp. 39-50. Thousand Oaks, CA: Sage Publications.

Deutsche, P. M. (1990). *A Guide to Rehabilitation Testimony: The Expert's Role as an Educator.* Orlando, FL: PMD Press.

Deutsche, P. M. and Sawyer, H. W. (1988). *A Guide to Rehabilitation.* New York: Matthew Bender.

Dunham, J. R. and Dunham, C.S. (1978). Psychosocial aspects of disability. In R. M. Goldson (Ed.), *Disability and Rehabilitation Handbook,* pp. 12-20. New York: McGraw-Hill.

Fabian, E. S. (1990). Quality of life: a review of theory and practice implications for individuals with long-term mental illness. *Rehabilitation Psychology,* 35(3), 161-170.

Fabian, E. S. (1991). Using quality-of-life indicators in rehabilitation program evaluation. *Rehabilitation Counseling Bulletin*, 34(4), 344-356.

Felce, D. and Perry, J. (1996). Exploring current concepts of quality of life: a model for people with and without disabilities. In R. Renwick, I. Brown, and M. Nagler (Eds.), *Quality of Life in Health Promotion and Rehabilitation*, pp. 51-62. Thousand Oaks, CA: Sage
Publications.

Ferrans, C. and Powers, M. (1985). Quality of Life Index: development and psychometric properties. *Advances in Nursing Science*, 8, 15-24.

Ferrans, C. and Powers, M. (1992). Psychometric assessment of the Quality of Life Index. *Research in Nursing and Health*, 15, 29-38.

Hatfield, T. and Hatfield, S R. (1992) As if life depended on it: promoting cognitive development to promote wellness. *Journal of Counseling and Development*, 71, 164-167.

Hays, R. D. and Shapiro, M. F. (1992). An overview of generic health-related quality of life measures for HIV research. *Quality of Life Research*, 1, 91-97.

Hullnick, M.R. and Hullnick, H. R. (1989). Life challenges: curse or opportunity? Counseling families of persons with disabilities. *Journal of Counseling and Development*, 68, 166-170.

Kaplan, R. M. (1994). Using quality of life information to set priorities in health policy. *Social Indicators Research*, 33, 121-163.

Kaplan, R. M. and Anderson, J.P. (1988). The Quality of Well Being Scale. Rationale for a single quality of life index. In S.R. Walker and R. Rosser (Eds.), *Quality of Life: Assessment and Application*. pp. 51-77. London: MTP Press.

Kaplan, R. M., Anderson, J. P., Patterson, T. L., McCutchen, J. A., Wienrich, J. D., Heaton, R. K., Atkinson, J. H., Thal, L., Chandler, J., Grant, I., and HNRC Group (1995). *Psychosomatic Medicine*, 57: 138-147.

Kaplan, R. M., McCutchen, J. A., Navarro, A. M., and Anderson, J. P. (1994). Quality adjusted survival analysis: a neglected application of the Quality of Well-Being Scale. *Psychology and
Health*, 9, 131-141.

Kirchman, M. (1986). Measuring the quality of life. *Occupational Therapy Journal of Research*, 6(1), 21-31.

Kozleski, E. B. and Sands, D. J. (1992). The yardstick of social validity: Evaluating quality of life as perceived by adults without disabilities. *Education and Training in Mental Retardation*, 119-131.

Lehman, A. (1983). The well-being of chronic mental patients. *Archives of General Psychiatry*, 40, 369-373.

Matkin, R.E. (1985). *Insurance Rehabilitation: Service Applications in Disability Compensation Systems*. Austin, TX: Pro-Ed.

McGowan, J. F. and Porter, T.L. (1967). *An Introduction to the Rehabilitation Process*. Washington, D.C.: U.S. Department of Health, Education, and Welfare, Vocational Rehabilitation Administration.

Meyers, J. E. (1992). Wellness, prevention, development: Cornerstones of the profession. *Journal of Counseling and Development*, 71, 136-139.

Padilla, G. V., Grant, M. M., and Ferrell, B. (1992). Nursing research in quality of life. *Quality of Life Research*, 1, 341-348.

Parker, R. M. (1987). *Rehabilitation Counseling*. Austin, TX: Pro-Ed.

Rasch, J.D. (1985). Rehabilitation of workers' compensation and other insurance claimants: Case management, forensic, and business aspects. Springfield, IL: Charles C Thomas.

Raphael, D. (1996) Defining quality of life: eleven debates concerning its measurement. In R. Renwick, I. Brown, and M. M. Nagler (Eds.), *Quality of Life in Health Promotion and Rehabilitation*. Thousand Oaks: CA: Sage Publications.

Raphael, D., Brown, I., Renwick, R., and Rootman, I. (1994). *Quality of Life and Health Promotion: Implications of the New Model of Quality of Life*. Toronto: University of Toronto, Center for Health Promotion.

Renwick, R. and Friefeld, S. (1996). Quality of life in rehabilitation. In R. Renwick, I. Brown, and M. M. Nagler (Eds.), *Quality of Life in Health Promotion and Rehabilitation*, pp. 26-39. Thousand Oaks, CA: Sage Publications.

Roessler, R. T. (1990). A quality of life perspective on rehabilitation counseling. *Rehabilitation Counseling Bulletin*, *34*(2), 82-90.

Rogers, R. (1991). Role of the expert witness. In R. A. Petersen (Ed.), *The Vocational Expert's Testimony*, Topeka: KA: American Board of Vocational Experts.

Rubin, S.E. and Roessler, R.T. (1987). *Foundations of the Vocational Rehabilitation Process*. Austin, Texas: Pro-Ed.

Sartorius, N. (1995). Rehabilitation and quality of life. *International Journal of Mental Health*, 24(1), 7-13.

Schalock, R. (1996). Quality of life and quality assurance. In R. Renwick, I. Brown, and M. Nagler (Eds.), *Quality of Life in Health Promotion and Rehabilitation*, pp. 104-118. Thousand Oaks, CA: Sage Publications.

Selye, H. (1974). *Stress without Distress*. New York: Lippincott.

Tuchler, H, Hofmann, S., Bernhart, M., Brugiatelli, M., Chrobak, L, Franke, A., Herold, M., Holowiecki, J., Ihle, R., Jaksic, B., Krc, I, Munteanu, N., Pawlicki, M., Sakalova, A. Schranz, V., Wolf, H., and Lutz, D. (1992). A short multi-lingual quality of life questionnaire — practicality, reliability and interlingual homogeneity. *Journal of Quality of Life*, 2, 107-117.

WHO. (1984). *Health Promotion: a Discussion Document on the Concepts and Principles*. Copenhagen: Author, Regional Office for Europe.

WHO. (1986). *Ottawa Charter for Health Promotion*. Ottawa, Canada: Canadian Public Health Association.

WHOQOL Group (1994). Development of the WHOQOL: rationale and the current status. *International Journal of Mental Health*, 23(3), 24-56.

Witmer, J. M. and Sweeney, T. J. (1992). A holistic model for wellness and prevention over life span. *Journal of Counseling and Development*, 71, 140-148.

Wright, G. N. (1980). *Total Rehabilitation*. Boston: Little, Brown & Company.

Williams, J. M. (1995). Addressing quality and pleasure of life in life care planning. *Inside Life Care Planning*, 1(2), 2.

Williams, J. M. and Burlew, L. (1995). Dealing with catastrophic injury: a developmental perspective on life care planning. *Adultspan*, 9, 4-8.

Williams, J M. and Maze, M. M. (1994). *The Role of the Rehabilitation Expert in Civil and Administrative Law Proceedings*. Iowa City: ACT.

3 The Psychological Domain

> *Psychological function* describes one's overall mental state insofar as it influences the quality of one's life. Anxiety, fear, and depression are concomitants of illness, cancer in particular, that profoundly influence the overall quality of life. ... They are not, however, the sole attributes of psychological function. Other attributes, including the sense of well-being or hope, as well as the more dissociative factors, such as denial and psychosis, clearly may influence one's perceptions of one's quality of life. Individual measures of quality of life may tap any of these issues.
>
> *Schipper, 1990*

INTRODUCTION

In deposition testimony, we (the authors) have been asked by attorneys, "Isn't this quality of life thing just psychology? Isn't it all psychological?" The question is usually designed to disqualify the rehabilitationist as not-a-psychologist, but it is also reflective of a lack of understanding about the meaning of the quality of life paradigm as used in treatment and clinical outcome studies. That quality of life is a multidimensional, multifaceted concept is the consensus of opinion among researchers (Bech, 1990; Blau, 1977; Frisch et al. 1992; Hyland, 1992; Verbrugge et al. 1994; WHOQOL Group, 1994).

Some studies have also separated out the differences between overall dysfunction and impairment and the status of one's quality of life or well-being. Bech (1990) notes that

> It is essential to differentiate between discomfort as a dimension of quality of life and clinical disability which is the manifestation of the underlying disease process.

Another way of thinking about this is to understand that researchers have also found over and over that the objective dimensions (e.g., education, income, health status, recreation, housing) of quality of life do not necessarily agree with the subjective evaluations (e.g., life satisfaction, happiness) of quality of life (Campbell et al. 1976; Deiner, 1984; McCauley and Bremer, 1991). For example, in a study of 416 patients with chronic pain, Tait et al. (1990) found that

> The results of this study support and extend prior research investigating relations between pain extent and psychological distress. Consistent with previous research, the current data indicate weak or non-existent associations with measures of depression and anxiety. In addition, patient self-reports of quality of life correlated only weakly with pain extent.

This confusion about the multidimensional nature of quality of life and the lack of agreement between objective and subjective parameters of quality of life have led to some wrong-headed, but pervasive beliefs. On the one hand, one belief is the idea that people with severe physical disabilities (respirator use, feeding assistance, powered wheelchair use) would prefer to die or should want to die. Gill (1992) writes: "The implication is that there something natural, reasonable, or proper about a disabled person's dying as opposed to a nondisabled person's dying." On the other hand, the "discomfort" or diminishment in the quality of life of persons with psychological injuries is discounted and the individual with these complaints is stigmatized as a "trouble maker." Goodman-Delahunty and

Foote (1995) have identified common psychological responses by individuals filing employment discrimination claims as Acute Stress Disorders, Disorder of Extreme Stress Not Otherwise Specified, Generalized Anxiety Disorder, Panic Disorders and Agoraphobia, Somatoform Disorder, Depression, and Posttraumatic Stress Disorder (American Psychiatric Association, 1994). In a qualitative review of employment discrimination cases and personal injury cases filed in New Mexico from 1992 to 1997 (more than 60 cases), the authors found that suicidal ideation as measured on the Employee Assistance Program Inventory (Anton and Reed, 1994) was much greater among the employment discrimination litigants than for the personal injury litigants.

That is, it does not follow that persons with severe physical disabilities have a poor quality of life and persons with psychological injuries or disabilities have a good, or at least adequate, quality of life. Hyland (1992) suggests that

> Quality of life is a casual sequence of psychological states where perceived symptoms cause problems and the problems and symptoms cause evaluations, and where the casual sequence is a complex interaction between morbidity and psychological factors.

Hyland refines this concept into three stages. In the first stage, "morbidity causes symptoms and anticipated symptoms." The patient reports "not the objective symptomatology but the subjective experience of those symptoms." This is described as a "trait mood" within the psychological factors. The second stage is the "coping style" within the psychological factors and comes about when the patient has identified the problems. The third state is for the "patients to evaluate their problems/absence of problems/symptoms on evaluative dimensions, such as *distress, lack of control, anxiety, or happiness*" or quality of life. (The last two stages, coping and evaluation, are also addressed in Chapter 9, The Cognitive Domain, in this book.)

In other words, the psychological domain of quality of life refers to the subjective aspect of quality of life, and as McCauley and Bremer (1991) state:

> Objective quality of life measures such as employment and functional status are relatively straightforward, but measuring subjective quality of life is a more complex task.

These researchers reviewed the subjective quality of life measures developed by Bradburn (1969) and Campbell et al. (1976). Bradburn's Positive and Negative Affect Scales "are accepted as among the best reliable measures of affective aspects of subjective QOL (McCauley and Bremer, 1991). Since this scale is not copyrighted and can be used without restriction, it is replicated here.

Bradburn's Affect Balance Scale

During the past few weeks, did you ever feel (circle YES or NO on each line below) ...

Particularly excited or interested in something?	YES	NO
So restless that you couldn't sit long in a chair?	YES	NO
Proud because someone complimented you on something you had done?	YES	NO
Very lonely or remote from other people?	YES	NO
Pleased about having accomplished something?	YES	NO
Bored?	YES	NO
On top of the world?	YES	NO
Depressed or very unhappy?	YES	NO
That things were going your way?	YES	NO
Upset because someone criticized you?	YES	NO

While Bradburn's approach examines positive and negative affect, Campbell's approach involves issues of life satisfaction. Campbell's instrument is also replicated here and may be used without restriction since it is not copyrighted. Readers may refer to page 50 of *The Quality of American Life* (Campbell et al. 1976) for instructions on calculating the Index of General Affect.

Campbell's Index of General Affect

Here are some words and phrases which we would like you to use to describe how you feel about your present life. For example, if you think your present life is very "boring," put an X in the box right next to the word "boring." If you think it is very "interesting," put an X in the box right next to the word "interesting." If you think it is somewhere in-between, put an X where you think it belongs. Put an X in one box on every line.

BORING	—	—	—	—	—	—	—	INTERESTING
ENJOYABLE	—	—	—	—	—	—	—	MISERABLE
USELESS	—	—	—	—	—	—	—	WORTHWHILE
FRIENDLY	—	—	—	—	—	—	—	LONELY
FULL	—	—	—	—	—	—	—	EMPTY
DISCOURAGING	—	—	—	—	—	—	—	HOPEFUL
DISAPPOINTING	—	—	—	—	—	—	—	REWARDING
BRINGS OUT THE BEST IN ME	—	—	—	—	—	—	—	DOESN'T GIVE ME MUCH CHANCE

Campbell's Overall Life Satisfaction Item

We have asked about various parts of your life, now we want to ask you about your life as whole. How satisfied are you with your life as a whole these days?

VERY SATISFIED	—	—	—	—	—	—	—	VERY DISSATISFIED

McCauley and Bremer (1991) conclude that

> Subjective QOL, as measured by scales introduced by Bradburn (1969) and Campbell et al. (1976), is a construct supported and explicated by a respectable body of research. It is more than a mood, because individual differences show substantial stability over days, weeks, and even months; but it is not so enduring as a personality trait or disposition, because the scales are sensitive to clinical outcome. It has a cognitive aspect–judgmental aspect that is assessed by the satisfaction scales of Campbell et al., and it has an affective aspect that is assessed by Bradburn's Positive and Negative Affect Scales. Internal homogeneity of the multi-item scales is consistently high, and convergent correlations of independent measures are substantial. Although the psychometric qualities of these scales may not be adequate for individual counseling or therapy, they are certainly more than adequate for group comparisons and research purposes.

We have expounded on Bradburn and Campbell's contributions to subjective quality of life measure because their work is the foundation of the field. Forensic rehabilitationists will need to bring their expertise to bear when assessing an individual's subjective quality of life in litigation by clearly understanding both individual and group measures of subjective quality of life, and since little research has been done on subjective quality of life for persons in personal injury and employment discrimination litigation, it is our hope that the use of Campbell et al. and Bradburn's scales could form the basis for such research by forensic rehabilitationists. At this point in time, we are forced to make group comparisons in litigation by type of physical injury or psychological disability. The litigation factor is left out since most subjective quality of life research is based on national survey data or clinical outcome studies. It would be very powerful to have the appropriate norm groups (persons in litigation by types of injuries or disabilities and types of litigation) studies to draw upon while also maintaining our knowledge of preexisting subjective quality of life research. In the interim, our task is to understand the breadth and depth of knowledge found in the available subjective or psychological quality of life literature.

LITERATURE REVIEW

As we shall see, the quality of life literature in the psychological domain ranges from studies of quality of life for persons with asthma to studies of traumatic brain injury.

Asthma

Hyland et al. (1991) developed the Asthma Questionnaire, despite the fact that there were several preexisting disease-specific instruments already in use. The Asthma Symptom Checklist was written to "to assess asthma attacks rather than the period between the attacks." It is not a quality of life scale. The Guyatt Scale "was designed to measure quality of life in patients with chronic airflow limitation." This scale "was not designed specifically for asthma sufferers and so has not been designed for maximum sensitivity in terms of the criteria of inclusivity and exclusivity." The Attitudes to Asthma Scale "has uncertain psychometric properties" and the derivation of items is from sources other than asthma patients, their physicians.

The Asthma Questionnaire was based on derived items from six qualitative focus groups of asthma sufferers. Items were selected based on "exclusivity (only items relevant to the condition) and inclusivity (all items relevant to the condition)." The Asthma Questionnaire is multidimensional with multiple domains, including 23 items which refer to negative and positive "dysphoric states and attitudes," or items which belong to the psychological domain. A sampling of such items includes the following:

> I feel angry with my body. I never feel fed up because I have asthma. I don't feel in control of my body. I feel anxious about not knowing when my next asthma attack is coming. I get emotionally upset when puffy. I feel inadequate because of my asthma. I have a good future ahead of me. I am in charge of my own life. I am embarrassed by having asthma, etc.

Acquiescence bias (the tendency to agree with items irrespective of the content) was managed by including both negative and positive items and by including more negative than positive items. The "validity of the scale was demonstrated by confirmation of expected group differences and the retest reliability was 0.948."

Bowel Disease

Kunsbeck et al. (1990) reviewed quality of life research for patients with inflammatory bowel disease. They emphasize the importance of the psychological domain by noting the inclusion of the patient's quality of life and the effects of medical treatments as a topic in nearly all medical fields. "This reflects a sensitization for the psychosocial aspects of illness and its treatment on the one hand and it shows a growing skepticism towards the so-called hard laboratory data as criteria of treatment on the other." These writers assert that both the subjective and objective aspects of quality of life must be taken into account. They define the "psychic" aspects of quality of life within both the subjective and objective domains by distinguishing between the subjective domain as including such terminology as "hope, anxiety, depression, self-esteem" and the objective domain including "psychopathology" as defined by a "diagnosis according to the *DSM-III R*." They note that "patients with inflammatory bowel disease (ulcerative colitis and Crohn's Disease) have been characterized as depressive, anxious and obsessive-compulsive." In their review of the research, Kunsbeck et al. (1990) conclude that quality of life data are valuable in the treatment of inflammatory bowel disease and that "quality of life measures in inflammatory bowel disease patients contain unique information relevant to their own domains and this information is complementary to laboratory data."

Cancer

Johnson et al. (1994) developed the Quality of Life Radiation Therapy Instrument (QOL-RTI) "to address a patient's quality of life by assessing components of functional (nine questions), emotional (seven questions), family-socioeconomic (six questions) and general quality of life (two questions)."

The "emotional/psychological" questions addressed "appearance, peace of mind, financial, happiness, hope, goals, religious belief." No other quality of life instruments which assess quality of life for cancer patients included patients receiving radiation therapy. This is a pilot study, and 19 patients completed the required forms. The QOL-RTI was to be administered to an additional 70 to 80 patients for further study. The correlation coefficient was 0.97 between the QOL-RTI and the Ferrans and Powers Quality of Life Cancer Version 6 (1985).

Schover's (1991) review of mastectomy vs. breast conservation quality of life studies reveals that there is one consistent finding: "women whose breasts are conserved have more positive feelings about their bodies, particularly their appearance." However, "in other important areas ... including general psychological distress, psychiatric disorders, marital happiness, frequency of sex, and sexual dissatisfaction, no significant differences are seen between treatment groups." Interestingly, other researchers also list "appearance" as a dimension of the psychological domain (Ferrans and Powers, 1992).

Cardiac Disease

The four studies reviewed in this category all emphasize the importance of psychological factors in the recovery from cardiac disease.

Young and Barboriak (1982) classified 45 male volunteers by using the Structured Interview for Type A Behavior and the Jenkins Activity Survey. They also administered 10 items from the Milwaukee Cardiovascular Life Quality Questionnaire to this group. Young and Barboriak's purpose was to compare Type A and Type B behavior. They found that the 10 items from the quality of life instrument resulted in a high agreement rating for Type A behavior with the other instruments. These 10 items were found to "provide a reliable and brief scale for rating Type A coronary-prone behavior."

Blumenthal and Emery (1988) reviewed "three classes of intervention studies" for patients with coronary heart disease: "(a) aerobic exercise training, (b) modification of Type A behavior, and (c) nonspecific psychological therapies." They did not address smoking cessation or nutritional modification in their article. Blumenthal and Emery found that exercise training research suggests that it "may improve quality of life," particularly psychological functioning. Type A behavior "is defined as a constellation of overt behavioral characteristics and underlying personality traits, including excessive and competitive drive, extreme desire for recognition and achievement, chronic feeling of time urgency and time pressure, and free-floating hostility." The available research on Type A behavior is problematic due to "a lack of consistency in the assessment." At least one study found that behavior therapy to reduce Type A behavior did result in "decreased sense of time pressure and greater life satisfaction." Blumenthal and Emery note that "emotional problems contribute to the increased risk of mortality as well as to psychological, social, and economic maladjustment in MI patients." The studies reviewed indicated that psychological treatment did result in enhanced well-being. Therefore, cardiac rehabilitation (exercise, reduction of Type A behavior, and general psychological therapies) did result in improvement of quality of life, but not necessarily in decreasing morbidity or mortality.

Mayou (1990), in a highly critical essay, notes that the "central defect" in most published work on quality of life for patients with cardiovascular disease is that "they ignore the significance of the individual meaning of illness." He notes that one common outcome measure, return to work, may or may not be a good outcome for some cardiac patients. He also writes:

> Another problem with most quality of life research is that concentration on overall changes within groups of patients has obscured the significance of individual variation. In contrast, psychosomatic research has consistently shown that the majority of patients show remarkable resilience in the face of physical adversity but that a minority (perhaps 20–30%) describe greater psychological distress and limitations which appear to be medically unnecessary.

Any rehabilitationist who has had a workers' compensation practice will quickly appreciate this point, and claims adjusters would like this finding to not be true since it is that 20 to 30% who use most of the workers' compensation systems' resources. Mayou calls for the use of more psychiatric and psychological expertise in quality of life research for cardiac patients. He asks for the use of a broader range of measures, such as the Sickness Impact Profile and Nottingham Health Profile. He also understands that

> Such changes in methodology will be impossible without acceptance that quality of life is not a simple, cheap and dubious extra but a subject deserving as much attention as physical outcome measures.

Conn et al. (1991) examined "the relationship between anxiety, depression, quality of life, and performance of suggested self-care behaviors among older adult myocardial infarction survivors." They conducted interviews with 94 adults 65 years and older. Instruments used included the Profile of Mood States to measure anxiety and depression, the Perceived Quality of Life Scale, and the Health Behavior Scale, to measure performance of self-care behaviors. Conn et al. also recommend mental health interventions as part of cardiac rehabilitation and quality of life studies for this population. They found that "depression scores accounted for a large percentage of the variance in quality of life." They also discovered that "depression was inversely related to each of the self-care behaviors." The same was not true for anxiety.

Diabetes

Rodin (1990) noted that "increased depressive and anxiety disorders have been reported in individuals with insulin-dependent diabetes mellitus (IDDM), particularly in association with more severe medical complications and low social support." Rodin's review of IDDM studies found the prevalence of psychiatric disorders for populations with IDDM. In one study, 70% of "individuals undergoing diabetes evaluations at a large medical center" had a "lifetime history of at least one psychiatric disorder." In another study, 75 patients with IDDM who were candidates for pancreatic transplantation revealed lifetime histories of major depression of 23% for females and 16% for males. An increased "prevalence of lifetime anxiety and affective disorders in individuals with IDDM" was identified by the National Institute of Mental Health in an epidemiological study. Rodin suggests that there are probably significant individual differences in treatment modalities and their impact on quality of life for IDDM patients. He notes that well-being is multidimensional and must be assessed accordingly.

Endocrine Disease

Sonino et al. (1990) focused on the psychosocial aspects of clinical care in endocrine disease. They found that although the psychoneuroendocrinology research had increased on the one hand, the study of psychological distress was ignored on the other. They note that "there has been an impressive body of literature on the relationship between stressful life events and disease onset." In one study, "the link between severe life events and the onset of physical illness was not direct but rather mediated by a depressive disorder" for women of 50 or younger. Major depressive disorders have also been found to be "a severe and life-threatening complication of endocrine disorders such Cushing's syndrome, Addison's disease, hyperthyroidism, hypothyroidism, and hyperprolactinemic amenorrhea." These writers call for a better response to the psychological quality of life by clinicians for these patients.

Epilepsy

Vickrey et al. (1992) developed the Epilepsy Surgery Inventory, "a 55-item measure of health-related quality of life for epilepsy patients." The emotional well-being scale contains five items.

They found that the greatest "level of dysfunction as in the domains of mental and general health." The instrument was administered to 200 adults with the finding that it was valid, reliable, and sensitive to differences in seizure status.

Hypertension

Hume (1989) distinguishes between emotional functioning (mood changes and sick role behaviors) and "patient perceptions regarding overall health status" which are "included in quality of life assessments because the measures of functional capacity do not always cover this area." She also notes:

> Measures of behavioral dysfunction are inherently negative and do not include positive well-being and life satisfaction, which are central to the concept of quality of life.

Hume indicates that the findings of the Treatment of Mild Hypertension Study should provide more data regarding the quality of life effects of different antihypertensive treatment agents. "A total of 850 patients between the ages of 45 and 69 years with hypertension will be enrolled."

Liver Disease

Kober et al. (1990) assert that the growing number of liver transplantations necessitates quality of life research for patients who are now living longer with liver transplants. They used the EORTC quality of life questionnaire which includes items under the dimensions of anxiety and depression, the STALX Anxiety Questionnaire which contains 20 items relating to situational anxiety, and standardized psychodiagnostic interviews. Patient samples from Chicago (20 women and 18 men) and from Hamburg (15 women and 14 men) were evaluated preoperatively and postoperatively at "2, 6, 12, 24, and 36 months." The patients received "continuous psychological support during the whole transplant course." The researchers note that most patients are in a "state of shock" by the time they get to the liver transplant stage. In the waiting period for a new liver, patients describe this time "as the most stressful in their lives." There is a decrease in anxiety when the transplant is finally to take place. However, during the intensive care period the researchers found that "about 60% of all patients experience" psychotic episodes with the content being "usually paranoid." Another finding was that patients were extremely labile directly after transplantation, "either unbelievably happy or sad to the point of crying all the time." The results of the study indicate that the use of the EORTC allowed the researchers to distinguish between patients with chronic liver disease and a healthy control group. In terms of the psychological parameters, chronic liver disease patients have a "significantly higher level of anxiety than do the healthy test individuals." This is true even 3 years after transplantation. Depression, however, is lowered after transplantation and can equal that of the healthy control group. Women had higher quality of lives than men in this study in that they had less depression. The beneficial use of continuous psychological support during this very stressful medical treatment was documented and overall quality of life improvement for liver transplantation patients was found.

Mental Illness

Four articles addressing program evaluation of programs for the mentally ill and four articles addressing measurement of subjective quality of life for persons with chronic mental illness are reviewed here.

Program Evaluation

Fabian's (1990) article is a review of both theory and practice issues for persons with chronic mental illness. She notes that most quality of life research can be found in two models, life satisfaction and adaptive functioning models. The life satisfaction models tend to include both subjective and objective measures of well-being. Studies of persons with disabilities do not the follow the commonsense approach one might expect when examining the objective factors of quality of life. That is, persons with quadriplegia or chronic mental illness show little difference in quality of life when compared to control groups of healthy persons. (Please refer to Chapter 5, The Social Domain and Chapter 9, The Cognitive Domain, for an explanation of the discrepancy theories of adaptation level, social comparison, and person–environment fit models of why the commonsense approach does not work.) The second quality of life measurement model is based on "defining quality of life in terms of environmental mastery or adaptive functioning." Fabian comments that "one of the central findings that generalized across all of quality of life literature with this population is that it represents a viable means of investigating the subjective well-being of individuals with chronic mental illness." Despite this optimism, Fabian also notes that the use of current quality of life measures as "program evaluation tools requires an understanding of theoretical and methodological issue that may arise." She cites how some quality of life scales may be highly vulnerable to response bias, "particularly social desirability." That is, individuals with disabilities who have had limited contact with a wide range of social groups may rank an unfit or inappropriate program as satisfactory or excellent due to their lack of sophistication and exposure to other alternatives. Even with these problems, Fabian recommends using quality of life measures in rehabilitation program evaluation.

Huxley and Warner (1992) used two scales developed in Great Britain, "the QOL Profile and the General Satisfaction Questionnaire … to examine the relationship between type of case management services and quality of life and satisfaction with treatment of 68 long-term psychiatric patients in Colorado." These researchers used a "computerized list of all patients with a psychotic diagnosis on the mental health center's rolls in August 1989" to obtain their study population. The QOL Profile is based on the work of Lehman (1983), but modified to include "religion as a ninth domain" in addition to Lehman's eight domains. They also assessed "positive and negative affect and self-esteem and the inclusion of a global quality of life measure." Case managers and a sample of patients "from a local health clinic for low-income persons" participated in the study as well as the patients with a history of psychosis. "The low-income group had the highest quality of life" in this study. The mental health group were worse off in terms of family and social relationships, but more satisfied in terms of work and education than the low-income group. In terms of case management style, "monitoring was the only variable that was positively associated with quality of life." Brokerage (referral to other agencies or resources) was negatively related. Huxley and Warner conclude that

> The key finding of this study is that people with serious mental health problems may respond differently to separate components of case management. There is further evidence that to enhance the clients' quality of life and satisfaction with services, direct help should be part of a case management approach.

O'Rear et al. (1996) described the program components of a wellness approach in a community rehabilitation treatment program to raise the "quality of life and promote healing for persons with psychiatric disabilities." They note that persons with psychiatric disabilities tend to have high rates of co-morbidity such as cardiovascular disease, diabetes, hypertension, etc. A program in Fredrick, MD, named Way Station, views

> wellness as a process that promotes physical, mental, emotional, and spiritual balance. Wellness is a state of being that is internally perceived and has observable, physiological correlates. It is a movement toward the absence of diseases.

Such program components as massage, nutritional counseling and food preparation training, exercise programs, and facilities with natural light are described. The results are that both members and staff at Way Station report an "increase in their sense of well-being."

Moller and Murphy (1997) conducted an epidemiological controlled case design study of 88 patients diagnosed with either schizophrenia or a mood disorder "to evaluate if enrollment in a 12-session course designed to simultaneously treat patients, families, and providers would result in a decrease in inpatient days." The treatment program is the Three R's Program: Relapse, Recovery, Rehabilitation." This program is "an interdisciplinary multiphasic comprehensive treatment program focusing on a wellness approach to the management of chronic neurobiological disorders such as schizophrenia, major depression, and the bipolar spectrum illnesses." Levels of wellness are identified in the Three R's Program as "unstable, stable, and actualized." Participants use the authors' Moller-Murphy Symptom Management Assessment Tool and the workbook, *My Symptom Management Workbook*, in the 12-session course, Symptom Management: A Wellness Expedition. Results of the study indicated that "2173.6 inpatient days were saved for the study cohort over a 2-year-time period." The savings cost was estimated at $1,086,800. Patients and families reported increased satisfaction with services, and case manager turnover was reduced since case managers who participated in the program were also more satisfied with their work.

Measurement Issues

Malm et al. (1981) developed the Quality of Life Checklist (QOLC), designed for "recording judgments of the patient's situation in a systematic way, to make sure that important areas are not overlooked." The checklist can also be completed by patients as a self-rating measure. A pilot study with 40 schizophrenia patients found that the QOLC was useful. Within the various domains covered by the QOLC, the domain most relevant in our discussion of the psychological domain of quality of life was the "inner experience" domain defined as:

> Spiritual and religious experience; inner harmony; pleasure from life; self-fulfillment; stimulation; interest; emotional contact; sense of purpose; sense of identity; peace of mind.

The authors make no claims for the psychometric properties of the checklist, indicating only that it appears to be a useful tool in the treatment of schizophrenic patients.

Endicott et al. (1993) developed the Quality of Life Enjoyment and Satisfaction Questionnaire (Q-LES-Q), "a self-report measure designed to enable investigators to easily obtain sensitive measures of the degree of enjoyment of satisfaction experienced by subjects in various areas of daily functioning." Contrary to other researchers, Endicott et al. assert that "patients with mental disorders frequently experience little enjoyment or satisfaction in many aspects of their lives. This is particularly true for patients with mood disorders." The authors' intent in developing the Q-LES-Q was to "use a format and content applicable for assessment of subject with a wide variety of mental and medical disorders." The Q-LES-Q has 93 items. There are five summary scales, and Subjective Feelings, which contains 14 items, is one of those scales. The researchers administered the instrument to patients who sought treatment for depressive symptoms and all subjects met the *DSM-III-R* criteria for major depressive disorder. They tested the assumption made by some researchers that "the ability to enjoy activities or to be satisfied with aspects of daily living represent simply an absence of depression." What they found was that the "Q-LES-Q scores are not simply reflecting the absence of depression and are therefore not totally redundant with measures of depression." The instrument was found to be valid and reliable.

Corrigan and Buican (1995) found similar results in their study of the subjective quality of life of the mentally ill. That is, they found that "quality of life is not redundant with the adhedonia common to depression." Forty-nine patients in the University of Chicago Partial Hospitalization Program participated in the study. All subjects had a history of severe mental illness with such diagnoses as schizophrenia, schizoaffective disorder, mood disorders, organic mental disorders, and substance abuse. Of these, 88% received antipsychotic medications. They had spent an average 60 or so days of the preceding 180 days receiving care on an inpatient ward. Lehman's (1983) Quality of Life Interview was used to measure quality of life for this population. The Brief Psychiatric Rating Scale was used to assess psychiatric symptoms, and the Profile of Adaptive Living (PAL) was used to assess social functioning. The Social Support Questionnaire was also administered. Of all of the quality of life studies reviewed in this book, Corrigan and Buican are the only researchers who used measures of verbal intelligence and performance intelligence, Wechsler Adult Intelligence Scale-Revised. What they found was that "an overall index of subjective quality of life was found to correlate significantly with measures of psychiatric symptoms, social functioning, social support, and verbal intelligence." Those with higher verbal intelligence reported a lower quality of life, and perhaps, understand their limitations better than those with lower intelligence. There is a significant association between subjective quality of life and depression found in this study as noted above.

Gater et al. (1995) conducted an exploratory study of 138 medical patients who scored "over the screening threshold for probable psychiatric illness" by using the Health Measurement Questionnaire (HMQ), the Psychiatric Assessment Schedule (PAS), the Nottingham Health Profile (NHP), the Rosser Index, and the Visual Analogue Scales (VAS) ("used to derive a Rosser distress (HMQ rating.") The Rosser Index is a method of rating disability and distress "by direct observation and specific questioning of patients and their nearest relatives." The remaining measures are self-report measures. When comparing the measures, the researchers found that when using VAS results

> pain, sad/depressed, and dependence on others emerged as the most significant factors in the analysis, pain explaining 31% or overall distress, sad/depressed explaining 13%, and dependence on others 6%. These three factors alone accounted for 50% of patients' distress.

Interestingly, "the clinical rater appears to be more sensitive to mild levels of distress, and to have a higher threshold for rating severe distress."

Mental Retardation

Rosen et al. (1995) developed a subjective quality of life measure, Perceived Stress, Affect, Loneliness and Satisfaction (PALS), which was "normed with 100 individuals with mental retardation residing at a large facility." The instrument focuses "exclusively upon subjective psychological dimensions that are regarded as the most relevant criteria." The instrument is administered in an interview format "with interviewers free to question in detail any response requiring further elaboration." The limitations of the PALS are described as not being suitable for persons with a level of mental retardation which does not allows them to understand or respond to questions, the small number of the sample in the study, possible acquiescence bias, and the inability to act upon the results by turning them into effective interventions. The authors call for the incorporation of quality of life measures, "particularly subjective indices, into routine quality assurance strategies."

Renal Failure

Ferrans and Powers (1992) examined the psychometric properties of the Quality of Life Index (QLI) developed by them in 1985 with a sample of 349 patients "selected randomly from the adult, in-unit hemodialysis patient population of Illinois." The QLI contains four dimensions, one of which is the psychological/spiritual dimension or domain. In this dialysis version of the QLI, the psychological/spiritual dimension or factor includes:

> Satisfaction with life; Happiness in general; Satisfaction with self in general; Achievement of personal goals; Peace of mind; Personal appearance; Personal faith in God.

Construct and convergent validity and reliability were found for the QLI-Dialysis Version.

Suicide

The now media-driven issue of physician-assisted suicide is, of course, a quality of life issue with profound ramifications for persons with severe disabilities and persons with terminal illness. The two conditions are not necessarily the same, but this simple fact has often been overlooked, and so we have significant divisions surfacing between the medical community and the Disability Rights Movement on this complex quality of life issue. In the three studies reviewed below, one addresses the changes in suicide rates for adolescents and elderly white males in the U.S. and the other two examine the problematic nature of physician- and even court-assisted suicide with persons with severe physical disabilities.

McCall (1991) examined the relationship between "suicide trends and the changing status of America's dependent populations." She points out that "since World War II, as adolescent suicide rates have risen and elderly suicide rates declined, the rates have generally converged." Her hypotheses that

> (a) the rising suicide trend among the adolescent population is associated with a deteriorating state of well-being for adolescents, and (b) the generally declining suicide trend among the elderly population is associated with an improving state of well-being for elderly persons

were examined by "using the annual suicide rates for the White male populations aged 15 to 24 and 65 and over." She used White males "primarily because White males have the highest suicide rates relative to other race–sex-specific categories." She used a social factor model which indexed well-being for adolescents as "impoverishment, family dissolution, and government expenditure." Although the review of this study could have fit into the Social Domain Chapter, we choose to put it within our discussion of the psychological domain, because McCall draws upon research regarding family dissolution which indicates that the psychological trauma of family dissolution is a factor in adolescent suicide. It is also a factor in the diminishment of well-being for this group. The well-being of elderly males, by contrast, was indexed by using "impoverishment, government expenditure, and health care availability." McCall concludes that "the findings suggest that family dissolution and White children living in poverty are associated with White male adolescent suicide trends and that societal affluence is associated with White male elderly suicide trends."

Suicide issues for persons with severe physical disabilities is also a socially based issue, as seen in the next two articles which address the pressures from medical and legal systems to either withhold life sustaining treatment from persons with physical disabilities or encourage and assist such persons in agreeing to the withdrawal of such treatments. The "Dr. Kevorkian/Dr. Death" media circus will not be addressed here, except to note that most of the people helped to die by Dr. Kevorkian so far were persons with severe physical disabilities and not persons with terminal illness.

Gill (1992), a prominent disability rights activist, writer and researcher, notes that "when a culture values human life conditionally, suicide intervention becomes selective. Devalued populations fail to receive rigorous protection, assessment, and treatment." High rates of suicide are seen among such devalued groups and, of course, persons with physical disabilities are a devalued group. Indicative of how little we value this population, there are few data collected on suicide rates for persons with disabilities. Individuals with severe disabilities who request suicide assistance are not recognized as experiencing a poor quality of life or as in psychological distress. Instead they are seen as "rational" and "logical." That is,

> For people with disabilities, as for anyone else, bouts of depression may lead to suicidal impulses. Depression and psychopathology of longstanding may also be expressed indirectly in somatic complaints, including complaints about disability. Research on depression indicates a tendency in troubled individuals toward global negative thinking and internalization. For people with disabilities, this suggests that when depressed for any reason, they are more likely to internalize society's rejection and devaluation of disability.

Coleman (1992), an attorney, addresses the withdrawal of life-sustaining treatment from persons with severe disabilities as a legal matter of equal protection for persons with disabilities by reviewing two important cases. She starts with the Elizabeth Bouvia case. Ms. Bouvia is a young woman with cerebral palsy who had "experienced a series of personal setbacks including a miscarriage, spousal abandonment, loss of certain financial benefits, and loss of an opportunity to pursue a master's degree." None of these quality of life factors were addressed in her care and resulted in her public request for assistance in dying. Ms. Bouvia had no psychological services during her suicidal crisis and by the time she had withdrawn her request, "her limbs had contracted from disuse, preventing her from using the motorized wheelchair she had used to get through college, and she became dependent upon morphine." The court decided in the Bouvia case and in the infamous Kenneth Bergstedt case that neither "had requested suicide." Instead, they were perceived as requesting a "natural death (Bouvia by self-starvation and Bergstedt by turning off his ventilator)." Kenneth Bergstedt was a young man who had used a ventilator since the age of 10, had quadriplegia, and had lived with his parents all of his life. His mother had recently died and his father was terminally ill. "The court never communicated with Mr. Bergstedt" and granted "his" petition to turn off the ventilator. Bergstedt was also not able to ever communicate with members of the disability rights community who tried to reach out to him and who had arranged assisted living for him in California. His father informed them that "he could not talk on the phone." He died without ever having been aware of his life options or the possible change and improvement in the quality of his life. Coleman calls for the overturning of these "prejudicial assessments of disability" by the courts.

Traumatic Abuse

The consequences of traumatic abuse reach into every quality of life domain. The impact on the psychological domain may be the most severe, however, because the battering of children and adult women, child sexual abuse, rape, and sexual harassment are all assaults on what Renwick and Brown (1996) describe as:

> Psychological being embodies individuals' feelings, cognitions, and evaluations concerning themselves. It focuses on self-confidence, self-control, coping with anxiety, and the initiation of possible behaviors.

Quality of life research regarding the impact of traumatic abuse is still in its infancy. However, the studies reviewed below cover a diverse range of populations in a variety of settings. Two articles specifically address the impact of traumatic abuse and well-being on persons with disabilities (Nagler, 1996; Nosek et al., 1994), and one empirical study examines well-being and sexual coercion in young adults (Zweig et al. 1997). Murphy's work (1993, 1994, 1996, 1997) is primarily focused on the vocational impairment of women which may result as a consequence of traumatic abuse, but she also recognizes that quality of life diminishment may be an even greater damage than any past or future lost wages. The report, *Sexual Harassment: Research and Resources*, prepared for the National Council for Research on Women by Siegel (1995), documents severe negative psychological outcomes resulting from sexual harassment.

Nosek and her colleagues (1994) present the results of the first phase of a National Institute of Health funded study on wellness and sexuality for women with physical disabilities. This phase of the study was qualitative and they used semistructured interviews with 31 women with various physical disabilities and diverse racial backgrounds and socioeconomic levels. "From a wellness perspective, the areas of sexuality identified in the data analysis" fell into five domains. One of these domains is "managing barriers." Barriers were described as "social, environmental, emotional, physical, and sexual abuse." The researchers emphasized that in a wellness model, women with physical disabilities will "recognize psychological, physical and sexual abuse, and exploitation and take action to reduce or eliminate it, or neutralize its impact." What the researchers found was that

> Some of the women interviewed had been so poorly informed about sexuality and life in general that they did not recognize the abuse until much later. They reported considerable psychological abuse and some physical and sexual abuse by parents, grandparents, siblings, spouses, dates, medical professionals and strangers. Many were solitary incidents, but a large number were long-term, some current.

The second phase of the study will involve a national study to determine if "the incidence and prevalence of such experiences is higher in women with disabilities than in the population as a whole."

Nagler (1996) notes that "some victims of sexual abuse are able to put the experience behind them and live normal lives. Many others, however, find it very difficult to adjust. In terms of physical and emotional health and social well-being, these individuals continue to experience psychological pain, compromised self-esteem, and stigma." In Nagler's study, 39 individuals with various disabilities from 11 different ethnic groups and 4 racial groups, and ranging in age from 18 to 73 years provided data. In addition to the usual perpetrators identified in the interpersonal violence field (family members, neighbors, dating partners, strangers), persons with disabilities are vulnerable to abuse by caretakers in institutional settings and in professional medical environments such as hospitals and clinics. Nagler cites one of the survivors: "Having been sexually abused is like having terminal cancer. It always affects you and it will affect you until the end."

The Zweig et al. (1997) study of college-enrolled and noncollege women (872) and men (527), ages 19 through 22 years, "examined the associations between sexual coercion and well-being (anger, coping, depressed mood, self-esteem, social anxiety, and social isolation)." One of the questions asked in this study was: "Did individuals who reported sexual coercion also report lower levels of well-being than those who did not report sexual coercion?" The researchers created questions to measure sexual coercion and well-being. The well-being questions included 5 items on self-esteem, 8 items on depressed mood, 5 items on anger, and 5 items on coping skills. (Social well-being items were also included but are not addressed here.) The results indicated that more women than men reported sexual coercion with 13% of the women and 1% of the men reporting rape, 18% of the women and 2% of the men experiencing sexual assault, 22% of the women and 13% of the men having intercourse in response to pressure, and 15% of the women and 2% of the men reporting sexual abuse. In terms of well-being, "men reported higher average anger than women and higher levels of coping as well." In contrast, "women reported higher levels of depressed mood than men." Overall, "compared to those who did not experience sexual coercion, individuals who experienced sexual coercion reported more anger, more depressed mood, more social isolation and lower self-esteem."

Murphy (1993, 1994, 1996, 1997) has recognized the diminishment of enjoyment or quality of life in most of her writing on traumatic abuse. When the prevalence of abuse is understood, the impact on quality of life for the survivors in particular and society in general is overwhelming by numbers alone. For example, a random national survey conducted in 1989 and 1990 indicated that about 12 million women in the U.S. have had posttraumatic stress disorder (PTSD) (Bower, 1991), and studies have clearly linked battering, rape, sexual harassment, and childhood sexual abuse to posttraumatic stress disorder symptoms in the survivors (Herman, 1992; Figley, 1985; Koss et al., 1994). The PTSD symptom of a "sense of a foreshortened future (e.g., does not expect to have a career, marriage, children, or a normal life span) (APA, 1994)" is particularly important when thinking about the quality of life of PTSD survivors, because many survivors run their lives based on this belief (*I'm going to die any time, so why bother planning ahead?*). This belief may or may not be conscious on the part of the survivor, but the result is the same: not being able to forgive themselves for not being able to finish anything or failing to keep appointments, and an inability to understand their own how behaviors damage their lives. Lowered self-esteem and depression are the outcome of this downward spiraling pattern. Simple survival becomes more important than a quality life.

Researchers have found that women suffering from posttraumatic stress disorder and depression were more likely to have been sexually harassed than those who had never experienced these problems (Gutek and Koss, 1993; Koss et al., 1994; Schneider and Swan, 1994). Although no specific quality of life research on this issue was uncovered, the current data reveal quality of life diminishment in the psychological, health-related, and work domains (Siegel, 1995).

Traumatic Brain and Spinal Cord Injury

Two studies, conducted 9 years apart, indicate that psychological or subjective quality of life issues are very important for survivors of neurotrauma or traumatic brain or spinal cord injury.

Walker et al. (1987) examined the quality of life status of 25 closed-head-injured adults. They used the MMPI, Adaptive Behavior Scale (ABS), and the Quality of Life Rating Scale (QLRS). Survivors were identified as "recovered" if they had returned to work, school, or some sort of work program. "Non-recovered" survivors were identified as those who had not met the "recovered" criteria.

> The non-recovered group was significantly higher on the Pd (Psychopathic deviate) scale. No differences were found between groups on the Sc (Schizophrenia) or K (Validity) scales. The recovered group was significantly higher on the ABS Economic Activity domain and significantly lower in the Violent and Destruction, Antisocial, Rebelliousness, Untrustworthiness, Stereotyped Behavior and Odd Mannerisms, and Psychological Disturbance behavior domains.

The QLRS indicated high levels of denial by the survivors when their elevated ratings were compared to the ratings given by relatives and significant others. As predicted, the recovered group denied their disability less than the nonrecovered group. It should be noted that no psychometric validity for the QLRS was claimed by the researchers.

The 1996 study on life satisfaction with persons with neurotrauma (traumatic brain injury (TBI) and spinal cord injury (SCI)) by Warren et al. found that "three psychosocial variables significantly increased life satisfaction for persons with SCI: closeness to family, the level of family activities, and blaming oneself for the injury." This was also true for TBI survivors, but "being employed, being married, and having memory and bowel independence" also significantly increased life satisfaction. Self-blame for the injury was found to be a significant element in life satisfaction for both groups. The study sample included 175 persons with TBI and 38 persons with SCI.

THE FORENSIC REHABILITATIONIST'S ROLE IN ASSESSING PSYCHOLOGICAL WELL-BEING

> The CHP conceptual framework makes a significant contribution to the theoretical knowledge about quality of life. It offers a broadly grounded perspective that integrates important elements of earlier conceptualizations in an innovative way as well as emphasizing new aspects of quality of life. Such theoretical work is important because there is a remarkable dearth of the comprehensive detailed conceptualizations in the literature on quality of life, particularly in the areas of health promotion and rehabilitation.
>
> *Renwick and Brown, 1996*

The Centre for Health Promotion (CHP) at the University of Toronto's Quality of Life Research Unit approach arose out of the rehabilitative disciplines, particularly the rehabilitation of persons with development disabilities in a three phase research-project. The CHP team realized early in their research that the quality of life research they were conducting had a broader relevance and that any quality of life research approach also needs to be based on the quality of life of the general population and not just a subgroup such as persons with developmental disabilities.

It is important to note that the conceptual framework of CHP was developed by a multidisciplinary research team, and this approach is a good model for the forensic rehabilitationist who must also adapt a multidisciplinary approach when examining quality of life issues in litigation. That is, the rehabilitationist must become a member of the team which addresses the rehabilitative, psychological, medical, and legal needs of the litigant. The process to be used by the rehabilitationist in a individual personal injury or employment discrimination case is not different from the process used by the CHP team.

> One process consisted of a critical evaluation of the existing literature on quality of life of persons with and without disabilities. Literature in the areas of health, rehabilitation, medicine, disability, psychology, sociology, and philosophy was reviewed.

The forensic rehabilitationist must be well-grounded in the quality of life literature of a particular injury or disability, psychological or physical, in order to meet the *Daubert* standard now demanded in the courts. Attorneys may in deposition or in cross examination in trial demand that the rehabilitationist draw upon only the literature found in rehabilitation journals. This is particularly true when the issue of the psychological domain of quality of life is involved. However, this demand represents a serious misunderstanding of the nature of the consensus of opinion by researchers world-wide. Quality of life inquiry is a multidisciplinary inquiry. The psychological domain is only one aspect of the inquiry. The demand that the rehabilitationist confine her or his opinions to literature found only in rehabilitation journals ignores publishing realities as well. That is, rehabilitation academics and researchers often publish in psychological journals, and psychologists can be found writing for rehabilitation journals. This is never more true than when examining quality of life literature as a whole. It will be the job of the forensic rehabilitationist to educate judges, juries, and attorneys as to the interdisciplinary character of the quality of life literature and research. If we fail to perform this educational process, we predict that psychologists and psychiatrists will become the "experts" in quality of life testimony and opinion in the legal system.

The second aspect of the CHP approach is "detailed consultation with prominent researchers and theorists on issues related to quality of life, health, and disability." The forensic rehabilitationist should be consulting with the psychologist, the psychiatrist, the physicians, the occupational therapist, and other health providers who may have worked with or are currently providing services to the litigant in a personal injury or employment discrimination case. Quality of life questions should be asked of these health providers, along with the usual questions regarding type and duration of treatment and the expected outcomes. Rehabilitationists may also contact prominent experts in a particular field to discuss elements of a plaintiff's case. Sometimes, the rehabilitationist will be called upon to make recommendations to attorneys regarding the use of such experts in litigation.

The third aspect of the CHP approach is the "collection of detailed information from persons with disabilities, their families ..." This can involve "personal interviews and case studies that combined interview and observational methods." These methods are the very foundation of the rehabilitation process and are known as the "initial interview" or "counseling sessions." Involvement of the family in the rehabilitative process is a perpetual drumbeat in rehabilitation literature. The forensic rehabilitationist, of course, makes extensive use of the interview process.

The CHP approach defines "psychological being" as follows. It "embodies individuals' feelings, cognitions, and evaluations concerning themselves. It focuses on self confidence, self-control, coping with anxiety, and the initiation of positive behaviors." Rehabilitation counseling engages this definition of psychological being, no matter what the counseling or evaluation setting might be: workers' compensation, psychosocial rehabilitation centers, state departments of rehabilitation, veterans' services centers, or in litigation. In fact, graduate programs in rehabilitation counseling in every state provide training to assess and empower psychological well-being for persons with physical and psychological disabilities.

The point is, the psychological domain of quality of life is not the exclusive domain of psychologists and psychiatrists. The determining factor of who is allowed to provide expert testimony in quality of life issues should not be based on training in a particular discipline, but on the training and experience of an expert in assessing quality of life issues using an interdisciplinary approach. Since the rehabilitation discipline is interdisciplinary in both theory and practice, we are in a good position to provide appropriate testimony in quality of life issues.

REFERENCES

American Psychiatric Association. (1994). *Diagnostic and Statistical Manual IV.* Washington, D.C.: Author.

Anton, W. D. and Reed, J. R. (1994). *EAPI: Professional Manual.* Odessa, FL: Psychological Assessment Resources, Inc.

Bech, P. (1990). Measurement of psychological distress and well-being. *Psychotherapy and Psychosomatics*, 54: 77-89.

Blau, T. H. (1977). Quality of life, social indicators, and criteria of change. *Professional Psychology*, 8(4): 464-473.

Blumenthal, J. A. and Emery, C. F. (1988). Rehabilitation of patients following myocardial infarction. *Journal of Consulting and Clinical Psychology*, 56(3): 374-381.

Bower, B. (1991). Women's trail of tears, (p. 141). *Science News.*

Bradburn, N.M. (1969). *The Structure of Psychological Well-being.* Chicago: Aldine.

Campbell, A., Converse, P., and Rodgers, W. (1976). *The Quality of American Life.* New York: Russell Sage.

Coleman, D. (1992). Withdrawing life-sustaining treatment from people with severe disabilities who request it: equal protection considerations. *Issues in Law and Medicine*, 8(1): 55-79.

Conn, V. S., Taylor, S. G., and Wiman, P. (1991). Anxiety, depression, quality of life, and self-care among survivors of myocardial infarction. *Issues in Mental Health Nursing*, 12: 321-331.

Corrigan, P. W. and Buican, B. (1995). The construct validity of subjective quality of life for the severely mentally ill. *Journal of Nervous and Mental Disease*, 183(5): 281-285.

Deiner, E. (1984). Subjective well-being. *Psychological Bulletin*, 95: 542-575.

Endicott, J., Nee, J., Harrison, W., and Blumenthal, R. (1993). Quality of life enjoyment and satisfaction questionnaire: a new measure. *Psychopharmacology Bulletin*, 29(2): 321-326.

Fabian, E. S. (1990). Quality of life: a review of theory and practice implications for individuals with long-term mental illness. *Rehabilitation Psychology*, 35(3): 161-170.

Ferrans, C. E. and Powers, M. J. (1992). Psychometric assessment of the quality of life index. *Research in Nursing and Health*, 15:29-38.

Ferrans, C. E. and Powers, M. J. (1985). Quality of Life Index: development and psychometric properties. *Advanced Nursing Science*, 8: 15-24.

Figley, C. R. (Ed.). (1985). *Trauma and Its Wake: The Study and Treatment of Posttraumatic Stress Disorder.* New York: Brunner/Mazel.

Frisch, M. B., Cornell, J., Villanueva, M., and Retzlaff, P. J. (1992). Clinical validation of the Quality of Life Inventory: a measure of life satisfaction for use in treatment planning and outcome assessment. *Psychological Assessment*, 4(1): 92-101.

Gater, R. A., Kind, P., and Gudex, C. (1995). Quality of life in liaison psychiatry: a comparison of patient and clinician assessment. *British Journal of Psychiatry*, 166: 515-520.

Gill, C. J. (1992). Suicide intervention for people with disabilities. *Issues in Law and Medicine*, 8(1): 37-53.

Goodman-Delahunty, J. and Foote, W. E. (1995). Compensation for pain, suffering, and other psychological injuries: the impact of *Daubert* on employment discrimination claims. *Behavioral Sciences and the Law*, 13: 183-206.

Gutek, B. and Koss, M. (1993). Changed women and changed organizations: consequences of coping with sexual harassment. *Journal of Vocational Behavior*, 42: 28-48.

Herman, J. L. (1992). *Trauma and Recovery: The Aftermath of Violence —from Domestic Abuse to Political Terror.* New York: Basic Books.

Hume, A. L. (1989). Applying quality of life data in practice: considerations for antihypertensive therapy. *Journal of Family Practice*, 29(4): 403-411.

Huxley, P. and Warner, M.B. (1992). Case management, quality of life, and satisfaction with services of long-term psychiatric patients. *Hospital and Community Psychiatry*, 43(8): 799-802.

Hyer, L., Matteson, M.A., and Siegler, I.C. (1982). Locus of control and long-term care. *Journal of Applied Gerontology*, 1: 147-160.

Hyland, M.E. (1992). A reformulation of quality of life for medical science. *Quality of Life Research*, 1: 267-272.

Hyland, M. E., Finnis, S., and Irvine, S. H. (1991). A scale for assessing quality of life in adult asthma sufferers. *Journal of Psychosomatic Research*, 15(1): 99-110.

Johnson, D. J., Casey, L., and Noriega, B. (1994). A pilot study of patient quality of life during radiation therapy treatment. *Quality of Life Research*, 3: 267-272.

Kober, B., Kuchler, Th., Broelsch, Ch., Kremer, B., and Henne-Bruns, D. (1990). A psychological support concept and quality of life research in a liver transplantation program: an interdisciplinary multicenter study. *Psychotherapy and Psychosomatics*, 54: 117-131.

Koss, M. P., Goodman, L. A., Browne, A., Fitzgerald, L. A., Keita, G. P., and Russo, N. (1994). *No Safe Haven: Male Violence Against Women at Home, at Work, and in the Community.* Washington, D.C.: American Psychological Association.

Kunsbeck, H. W., Korber, J., and Freyberger, H. (1990). Quality of life in patients with inflammatory bowel disease. *Psychotherapy and Psychosomatics*, 54: 110-116.

Lehman, A. F. (1983). The well-being of chronic mental patients: assessing their quality of life. *Archives of General Psychiatry*, 40: 369-373.

Malm, U., May, P. R. A., and Dencker, S. J. (1981). Evaluation of the quality of life of the schizophrenic outpatient: a checklist. *Schizophrenia Bulletin*, 7(3): 477-487.

Mayou, R. (1990). Quality of life in cardiovascular disease. *Psychotherapy and Psychosomatics*, 54: 99-109.

McCall, P. L. (1991). Adolescent and elderly white male suicide trends: Evidence of changing well-being? *Journal of Gerontology*, 46(1): 543-551.

McCauley, C. and Bremer, B. A. (1991). Subjective quality of life measures for evaluating medical intervention. *Evaluation and the Health Professions*, 14(4): 371-387.

Moller, M. D. Murphy, M. F. (1997). The three R's rehabilitation program: a prevention approach for the management of relapse symptoms associated with psychiatric diagnosis. *Psychiatric Rehabilitation Journal*, 20(3): 42-48.

Murphy, P. A. (1993) *Making the connections: Women, Work and Abuse.* Orlando, FL: PMD Press, Inc.

Murphy, P. A. (1994) T*he Edge of a Large Hole: Writings on the Request for Reasonable Accommodation under the American's with Disabilities Act of 1990.* Chicago: University of Illinois Center for Research on Women and Gender.

Murphy, P. A. (1996). *A Career and Life Planning Guide for Women Survivors: The Making the Connections Workbook.* Delray Beach, FL: St. Lucie Press.

Murphy, P.A. (1997). Recovering from the effects of domestic violence: Implications for welfare reform policy. *Journal of Law and Policy*, 19(2): 169-182.

Nagler, M. (1996). Quality of life of people with disabilities who have experienced sexual abuse. In R. Renwick, I. Brown, and M. Nagler (Eds.), *Quality of Life in Health Promotion and Rehabilitation*, pp. 190-203. Thousand Oaks, CA: Sage

Nosek, M. A., Howland, C. A., Young, M. E., Georgiou, D., Rintala, D. H., Foley, C. C., Bennett, J. L., and Smith, Q. (1994). Wellness models and sexuality among women with physical disabilities. *Journal of Applied Rehabilitation Counseling*, 25(1): 50-57.

O'Rear, G., Bark, L., and Hutchinson, D. S. (1996). The promotion of wellness among people with psychiatric disabilities in community rehabilitation and treatment. *Psychiatric Rehabilitation Journal*, 20(2): 82-84.

Renwick, R. and Brown, I. (1996). The Centre for Health Promotion's conceptual approach to quality of life: being, belonging, and becoming. In R. Renwick, I. Brown, and M. Nagler (Eds.). *Quality of Life in Health Promotion and Rehabilitation*, pp. 75-88. Thousand Oaks, CA: Sage Publications.

Rodin, G. (1990). Quality of life in adults with insulin-dependent diabetes mellitus. *Psychotherapy and Psychosomatics*, 54: 132-139.

Rosen, M., Simon, E. W., and McKinsey, L. (1995). Subjective measure of quality of life. *Mental Retardation*, 33(1): 31-34.

Rosenfeld, S. (1992). Factors contributing to the subjective quality of life of the seriously mentally ill. *Health and Social Behavior*, 33: 299-315.

Sartorius, N. (1995). Rehabilitation and quality of life. *International Journal of Mental Health*, 24(1): 7-13.

Schipper, H. (1990). Quality of life: principles of the clinical paradigm. *Journal of Psychosocial Oncology*, 8(2/3): 171-185.

Schneider, K. T. and Swan, S. (1994). Job-related, psychological, and health-related outcomes of sexual harassment. Presentation at Symposium on Sexual Harassment at the 9th Annual Conference of the Society of Industrial and Organizational Psychology. Nashville, TN.

Schover, L. R. (1991). The impact of breast cancer on sexuality, body image, and intimate relationships. *Ca-A Cancer Journal for Clinicians*, 41: 112-120.

Siegel, D. L. (1995). *Sexual Harassment Research and Resources.* New York: National Council for Research on Women.

Sonino, N., Fava, G. A., Fallo, F., and Boscaro, M. (1990). Psychological distress and quality of life in endocrine disease. *Psychotherapy and Psychosomatics,* 54: 140-144.

Tait, R. C., Chibnall, J. T., and Margolis, R. B. (1990). Pain extent: relations with psychological state, pain severity, pain history, and disability. *Pain*, 41: 295-301.

Verbrugge, L. M., Reoma, J. M., and Gruber-Baldini, A. L. (1994). Short-term dynamics of disability and well-being. *Journal of Health and Social Behavior*, 35: 97-117.

Vickrey, B. G., Hays, R. D., Graber, J., Rausch, R., Engel, J., and Brook, R. H. (1992). A health-related quality of life instrument for patients evaluated for epilepsy surgery. *Medical Care*, 30(4): 299-319.

Walker, D. E., Blankeship, V., Ditty, J. A., and Lynch, K. P. (1987). Prediction of recovery for closed-head-injured adults: an evaluation of the MMPI, the Adaptive Behavior Scale, and a Quality of Life Rating Scale. *Journal of Clinical Psychology*, 43(6): 699-707.

Warren, L., Wrigley, M., Yoels, W. C., and Fine, P. R. (1996). Factors associated with life satisfaction among a sample of persons with neurotrauma. *Journal of Rehabilitation Research and Development*, 33(4): 404-408.

WHOQOL Group. (1994). Development of the WHOQOL: rationale and current status. *International Journal of Mental Health*, 23(3): 24-56.

Young, L. D. and Barboriak, J. J. (1982). Reliability of a brief scale for assessment of coronary-prone behavior and standard measures of type A behavior. *Perceptual and Motor Skills*, 55: 1039-1042.

Zweig, J. M., Barber, B. L., and Eccles, J. S. (1997). Sexual coercion and well-being in young adulthood: comparisons by gender and college status. *Journal of Interpersonal Violence*, 12(2): 291-308.

4 The Physical Domain

CHRONIC ILLNESS, DISABILITY, AND QUALITY OF LIFE

> The goal of a rehabilitation team is to help the patient climb a series of steps to what we call *quality of life*.
>
> *Stover, 1995*

Quality of life has been frequently related to functional health status, natural disease processes and medical interventions (Parkerson et al., 1993) as per the definition of quality of life offered by the World Health Organization (WHO, 1959). The physical dimension of the WHO definition of health, along with such other health-related dimensions as impairments, health perception, and duration of life has been related to general life satisfaction. In his elaboration on the *International Classification of Impairments, Disabilities and Handicaps* (ICIDH), Bradley (1987) suggests that disability can be defined as the inability to perform a given physical, anatomical, and/or mental function within the standard for such function considered normal for human beings. Handicap, the inability to assume and fulfill one or more life roles, may result from a disability, but may not occur if sufficient resources (social, economic, and vocational options and opportunities), a proper physical environment (mobility and physical independence), and positive attitudes (expectancy for personal growth, goal attainment, and personal autonomy) are present. Although the relationship between impairment, disability, and handicap is complex, McDonough et al. (1995) suggest that mobility, the ability to move around effectively in one's surroundings, when limited by one's physical impairments, may be a very critical factor in determining whether disability becomes handicap. It is not surprising that age increases the likelihood that a physical impairment will occur, resulting in disability and impacting quality of life. Blake (1984) points out that 85% of adults over the age of 65 have at least one chronic health problem, and 25% will spend time in a nursing home due to physical impairment and disability. Brown (1989) points out that independence and quality of life are the primary needs of persons with disabilities and reiterates that with aging many people will face these issues. Verbrugge et al. (1994), in a study of 199 persons over age 55 who were hospitalized for fractured hip, cerebrovascular accident, diabetes, arthritis, chronic obstructive pulmonary disease, or congestive heart failure, suggested that function (i.e., the ability to engage in activities of daily living, the ability to perform discrete motions with the upper and lower extremities, and self-rated level of activity) correlated significantly with general rating of well-being (a component of quality of life). Sands and Kozleski (1994), in a survey of disabled vs. nondisabled individuals ($n = 217$), found that persons with predominantly physical disabilities were significantly less independent in choices and less satisfied with their social and leisure activities than nondisabled adults. Physical impairments and associated limitations in mobility were associated with narrowing of social and leisure/recreational options, directly affecting quality of life. Osberg et al. (1987) conducted a path analysis that revealed a close relationship between quality of life and independence in activities of daily living (ADLs). Physical functioning again appeared to be an important contributor to overall quality of life. Maintenance of quality of life appears to be an issue that most persons will need to address as part of the aging process. Aging and disability have much in common; quality of life is a relevant issue in understanding the needs and appropriate services relative to both.

Review of the literature on physical impairments, disability, and quality of life by these authors has led to organizing the literature on physical disability and quality of life into the following categories of disease/illness: (1) cancer/immune deficiency diseases; (2) spinal cord injury; (3) diabetes; (4) epilepsy, (5) cardiovascular disease, and (6) other diseases. The intent of this review is to briefly cover the essence of the existing literature on physical disabilities/illnesses on quality of life, thus establishing the legitimacy of quality of life as an indicator of the impact of impairment and disability on life function. Although discussion of seizure disorders may relate to head injury, head injury is discussed in the chapter on the cognitive domain.

Research into acquired disabilities brought about by industrial injuries, automobiles accidents, and other personal injuries has yet to reach the stage of the literature addressing disability created by disease processes. Nevertheless, the current literature provide a fertile ground for such new research to proceed.

ILLNESS, INTERVENTION, AND QUALITY OF LIFE: THE CHALLENGE FOR CARE PLANNERS

> Rehabilitation centers have tended to predominantly emphasize those tasks related to physical functioning. During the rehabilitation process much energy and time are devoted to the achievement of basic physiological and safety needs.
>
> *Coyle, Lesnik-Emas, and Kinney, 1994*

Haig et al. (1995) suggested that lack of mobility affects a disabled person's ability to obtain appropriate health care at a time when his/her needs are complex medically and psychologically. With the advent of managed care, it may be even more difficult for medical problems to be addressed by specialists until the medical problems become too complex for the primary care physician to handle. Without aggressive, appropriate treatment, one's ability to perform such important activities of daily living as dressing, bathing, ambulating, cooking, shopping, cleaning, doing laundry, interacting with others, and using public or other means of transportation may be unduly compromised, resulting in a reduction in overall quality of life and life satisfaction. Persons with such illnesses as multiple sclerosis, arthritis, stroke, head injury, Parkinson's disease, diabetes, neuropathy, orthopedic injuries, amputation, chronic pain, quadriplegia, and spondylitic myelopathy were included in a sample of 40 persons with disabilities. Results of the study indicated that recommendations for a delivery of such services as physical therapy, counseling, equipment changes, medication changes, patient instruction, diagnostic evaluations, hospitalizations, physician consultations, and social activities resulted in a significant increase in life satisfaction ($p = 0.003$), quality of life ($p = 0.01$), and self-rating of health ($p = 0.01$), all of which were significantly related to self-rating treatment effectiveness ($p = 0.0001$). Quality of life was seen as a major outcome and yardstick used in assessing the efficacy of rehabilitation interventions.

Bech (1993) points out that the medical model addresses the ability to engage in self-care and related activities of daily living; the stress model looks at how the person copes with the life circumstances associated with diminished function; and the demoralization model looks at the degree of discrepancy between the person's current situation (with all its challenges associated with illness) and his or her wishes regarding a future lifestyle. The question of who should be the decision maker about what interventions/treatments promote quality of life was equally interesting, with only a 0.50 correlation between the person's rating of quality of life and a relative's rating or between the person's rating and that of the treating physician were noted in the literature cited. This conceptualization of quality of life in relation to chronic illness reminds rehabilitation professionals that it is not just pathology and physical function which determines quality of life. Coping style and aspirations also play a role. It is ultimately what one accomplishes as a result of change in health status resulting from interventions which impacts overall quality of life.

Schipper (1990) notes that quality of life is seen as a common endpoint of medical intervention, but suggests that there are potential dilemmas in its use as a measure of the efficacy of treatments. He suggests that the best use of quality of life indicators is as a compliment to the traditional biological indicators of change (such diagnostic tools as an MRI, EEG, and EKG being indexes of biological response and not necessarily quality of life). Likewise, interventions which promote quality of life (particularly in the short-term) may not produce the desired long-term physiological effects, resulting in significant compromise of health and quality of life. Use of both biological/physiological and quality of life measures of efficacy may offer the best opportunity for judging the true merit of interventions. It is clear, however, that interventions which relieve pain (physical, functional, and emotional discomfort) result in enhanced quality of life. Conversely, quality of life may be a better indicator of global pain and suffering than simply any one or cluster of physiological measures. Therefore, interventions designed to relieve global pain and suffering inevitably must promote both physiological well-being and overall quality of life.

The medical model, where the physician acts as the singular care planner, is not likely to spontaneously result in enhanced quality of life. The opportunity for care to be so invasive to quality of life as to be suspended or terminated by the patient despite its physiological value is a realistic issue in delivery of life care for persons with disabilities. Whether done over the short-term or over life span, care planning should focus on providing all the medical and related interventions required for maintenance or enhancement of physical function, but not at the expense of quality of life. Rehabilitationists, by the nature of their multidisciplinary (i.e., medical, psychological, social, cognitive, and vocational theory and practice) training are in a unique position to understand all the issues which contribute to quality of life and seek the balance between all the forces influencing the course of the individual's life. However, historically, the physician has had the real power in planning and delivery of care, particularly when the individual in question is involved in administrative law or civil proceedings where the causation, nature, severity, functional consequences, vocational/economic results, and future care of injuries resulting from trauma are in question. The authors of this missive have seen little or no attention given in care planning to issues relative to quality of life. No dialogue about enough care vs. too much care, one type of care versus another type of care has been offered in the life care planning literature. The psychosocial impact of care options on the patient and significant others has received little attention. The life stressors created or resolved by care choices, and the congruence of care choices with the individual's desired lifestyle need to be addressed in order that overall quality of life can be maintained or enhanced. However, the focus of traditional care planning has been to identify all possible care options, the frequency and duration of their delivery, and the associated costs, with an eye to maximizing the care and providing enough monies to fund all of these possibilities over life span. The issue of providing too much care and the resulting potential to promote dependency rather than autonomy, to erode self-esteem rather than build self-confidence and identity, to reward acquiescence to the needs identified by others rather than to promote autonomy and self-reliance should be given attention. Interventions should not, as an incidental outcome, erode quality of life. Care planning built on a multidisciplinary approach to enhancing quality of life may, in fact, be more costly in the beginning, but less so in the future, as the person in question functions more effectively and autonomously. The balance between self-reliance, personal autonomy, and self-development and the need for external support and care may best be struck when quality of life is given sufficient weight in the care planning process. As suggested by Nosek and Fuhrer (1992), persons with disabilities need to exercise self-control and to self-select their own goals without undue focus on specific missing physical capacities and with appropriate focus on other (i.e., cognitive, psychological, and social) abilities and environmental factors (i.e., family support, geography, economic situation, cultural values, educational opportunities, etc.). Recognizing that persons with disabilities have frequently found themselves in a position where services have not been available due to limited personal or public funding, the authors are concerned that sufficient care be provided, but warn against providing lavish care with no real identified outcome out of a misguided belief that more is better. More can be worse, particularly when more diagnostic and treatment services are offered, not because they promote function, but because they document dysfunction. Ability rather than disability should be the focus of care planning, but often is not in a litigious environment. The rehabilitation expert may be in the unique position as the multidisciplinary planner of care to recognize that money alone will not solve problems, remove barriers, and promote life function, but if available in sufficient quantity to provide appropriate care, money can promote human growth and development, achievement of realistic life goals, and attainment of quality of life (Williams and Burlew, 1995).

REVIEW OF THE LITERATURE ON SPECIFIC PHYSICAL ILLNESSES FROM A QUALITY OF LIFE PERSPECTIVE

> There is more to life than not dying. One of the achievements of the consumer movement in health care has been a move away from the physician-dominated pre-occupation with biomedical outcomes to a patient-centered sensitivity to psychosocial aspects of health care.
>
> *Taylor, 1989*

CANCER/IMMUNE DEFICIENCY DISEASES

Because cancer and immune deficiency diseases (the most common of which is HIV) are life-threatening, the issue of quality of life should first be addressed with these populations. Traditional inpatient and outpatient HIV, oncology, and hospice agencies have espoused goals of maintenance of a high quality of life out of recognition of the physical challenges ahead and their impact on life function over the very limited amount of time a patient might remain live. Wu and Rubin (1992) make the very interesting point that quality of life may be a better indicator of the efficacy of a given pharmacological approach to treating AIDS when the desired medical outcome is palliative (stabilizing; not improving) rather than restorative. They also note that the U.S. National Institute of Health is now including a quality of life measures in the HIV clinical trials where prophylactic regimens as well as selected other interventions are offered. Schags et al. (1992) indicate that the shift in medical management of AIDS away from providing only the care required to maintain the person until death to management of chronic illness has led to greater dialogue about quality of life. Dealing with a sample of 312 participants (predominantly males [96%] incomes between $0 and $30,000; and high school to college graduates) they found that difficulty ambulating, difficulty communicating with friends and relatives, and difficulty working were among the most salient contributors to overall rating of quality of life on a self-report instrument designed for the study, the HOPES. Difficulty walking was the highest loaded item on the physical factor. It is of equal interest that as health status declined so did quality of life scores, suggesting that decline in physical function for persons with life-threatening illnesses may have greater effect on global assessment of quality of life than declines in other domains. Nichols (1997) adds that uncontrolled pain, if left untreated, could decrease the quality of life not only of the patient, but also of family members and loved ones, supporting a need to address quality of life issues in chronic illness where extreme pain is likely to occur.

Baker et al. (1992) developed the Satisfaction with Life Domains Scale for Cancer (SLDS-C), a self-report, paper-and-pencil instrument which includes items on general health, physical strength, comfort (as opposed to pain), ability to attain sexual satisfaction, ability to eat, ability to go about one's daily activities, concern regarding one's appearance, and concern regarding one's body (9 out of 18 items being related to one's physical health status), for use as a measure of quality of life with cancer patients out of recognition that quality of life is an important criterion upon which to judge the efficacy of cancer treatment. On two testing occasions (during initial treatment — $N =$ 109; 2 years after the initial survey — $N = 64$) survivors of bone marrow transplants were asked to complete the SLDS-C. A Cronbach alpha of 0.93 was obtained, indicating a relatively high reliability for the instrument; validation against Bradburn's Positive Affect and Negative Affect Scales revealed statistically significant correlations. Findings suggested that counseling relative to sexual satisfaction, intimate relations with partners, body image, and personal control, as well as pharmacological and irradiation protocols which maintained physical strength and appearance, might improve the overall effectiveness of the bone marrow transplant program.

Schag et al. (1994) used the Cancer Rehabilitation Evaluation System (CARES) and global rating of quality of life as outcome measures for judging the efficacy of treatments for lung, prostate, and colon cancer in 278 disease-free survivors of these diseases (colon — $n = 117$; lung — $n = 57$; prostate — $n = 104$). Most participants were white, high school to college graduates, not working, middle to lower income (making less than \$40,000 per year), and married. The vast majority of patients had curative long-term treatment goals, and the majority had at least one operation for cancer. Quality of life was rated on the Linear Analogue Self-Assessment, a 10-cm visual analogue scale in which the bipolar dimensions were very low and very high, with a value from 0 to 10 spaced approximately 1 cm in proximity to each other. Lung and colon cancer treatment produced significant increases in quality of life over time, but treatment for prostate cancer produced a quality of life decrease. The higher the person's functional (physical) status, the higher was the quality of life score. It appears that quality of life at least in this study was linked more to functional capacity (the degree to which a cancer survivor can carry on normal activities without limitations) than to such co-morbidity factors as medical or psychiatric history, gender, work status, time since diagnosis, or type of hospital. Difficulty with ambulation (particularly in the area of energy) and recreational activities, psychological distress, pain, and cognitive problems (primarily with memory) were noted across all groups. Sexual dysfunction was uniformly high in concern and, unlike the other variables, did not improve over time across the three types of cancer.

Johnson et al. (1994) used the Quality of Life-Radiation Therapy Instrument (QOL-RTI) to address the functional (9 questions on appetite, nausea, pain, energy/fatigue, pain/fatigue, sex life, and self-care), emotional (7 questions on appearance, peace of mind, financial status, happiness, hope, goals, and religious beliefs), and familial/social (6 questions on family, job, independence, life satisfaction, family/friends, and staff support) domains of quality of life as well as global quality of life (2 questions, 1 on general health and 1 on personal control). The QOL-RTI was found to have a Cronbach alpha coefficient of 0.87 across the 19 participants in the study, suggesting little measurement error. Concurrent validation against the Ferrans and Powers QLI revealed a corrclation of 0.47 (not a strong relationship and not surprising, given the narrow focus of the QOL-RTI). Quality of life was seen as a meaningful outcome measure for radiation therapy programs along with overall survival and disease-free survival. With this quality of life instrument, clinicians can pinpoint individual and group changes in health and allow physicians to modify the treatment protocol to minimize or prevent problems. Survival without a reasonable quality of life was not seen as a desirable outcome of treatment. Nayfield et al. (1992) point out that quality of life issues could even impact longevity for cancer patients; particularly as regards the types of treatment (a process variable in quality of life assessment) and ultimate treatment effects (an outcome variable in quality of life assessment). Quality of life is seen as a factor in judging the overall effectiveness of treatment strategies. Physical, emotional, and social function somatic/physiological complaints, and global self-perception of wellness were seen as critical elements of quality of life assessment. Till et al. (1992) go as far as to suggest that evaluation of the efficacy of treatment methodologies should not just be based on the results of randomized controlled trials designed to assess physiological changes. Evaluation of the clinical acceptability of any treatment protocol for use with cancer patients needs to consider the relative contribution of each methodology to quality of life. More specifically, these authors felt that in breast cancer research there was no reason to deny women the right to autonomy over their bodies when choosing a treatment protocol. Schover (1991) further postulates that a woman's overall well-being (a term often used synonymously with quality of life) affects postsurgical sexual satisfaction more than the extent of the damage to the breast.

These findings support the contention that quality of life issues can either detract from or enhance the efficacy of any given treatment protocol. Selection of a treatment should be based on quality of life as well as its projected physiological result and/or costs.

Since major differences in survival rates in number of years (quantity) are not being noted, quality of life during survival is becoming more and more of a factor in choosing treatments for cancer (Muthny et al. 1990). The results of such functional rating scales as the Karnofsky Index, WHO (Zubrod) Scale, and the Spitzer Index were compared with the Life Satisfaction Inventory. Those patients who were given the worst prognosis (functioning at lower levels) appeared to be more life satisfied than those who were identified as healthy. This creates a paradox which can only be resolved by recognizing that in cases where injuries or illnesses are severe and potentially life-threatening, persons cope with this knowledge by setting their internal standards for life satisfaction lower than those who perceive themselves as healthy. This also raises the question of whether self-reported high levels of quality of life after a traumatic injury or identification of a disease entity with potentially life-threatening consequences, even if equal to preinjury or event self-report of quality of life in score value, truly represent the same quantitative level of quality of life. Internal standards for measuring quality of life may change over time as a coping mechanism.

The same issues of treatment choice and efficacy found in dealing with adult cancer patients can be applied to dealing with children, although assessment of quality of life in children should rely more on checklists and observational measures completed by family members and health professionals than self-report of the child in light of developmental limitations of age. The Pediatric Oncology Quality of Life Scale (POQLS) was developed by Goodwin et al. (1994) as an appropriate measure of quality of life for use with children and acceptable reliability (0.68 to 0.87) and validity (0.71 to 0.985 correlation with child behavior, depression, and functional abilities scales) were reported. Using the Play Performance Scale for Children (PPSC) as a measure of quality of life in a pediatric oncology setting, Mulhern et al. (1990) reported high reliability between parents and physicians in rating behavior and significant correlations between quality of life and adaptive behavior, play performance, or physical symptoms. One difficulty in measuring the quality of life of children is that the same attention to global instrument development as seen with adults is not found in the literature reviewed by the authors. This is an area where significant additional research is needed.

Spinal Cord Injury

Flanagan (1978), in a survey of 1000 men and women 30 years of age, 600 men and women 40 years of age, and 600 men and women 50 years of age ($n = 2{,}200$) found one factor to be the most salient as an indicator of quality of life, one's physical well-being (95 to 98% of men and 96 to 98% of women rating health and personal safety as important or very important on a survey, and 84 to 86% of the men and 80 to 86% of the women rating their needs as being met in this area.). It is not surprising, then, that any physical illness or disease which drastically alters health and personal safety will have more potential effect on quality of life than illnesses or diseases with lesser effects on physical function and associated ability to avoid bodily harm. Work and close relationships were identified as having considerable, but lesser importance. Essentially, health and safety (consistent with Maslow's needs hierarchy) are given top priority and have the greatest impact on quality of life. Therefore, it is not surprising that the impact of spinal cord injury on quality of life would be discussed in the rehabilitation literature. Using the Quality of Life Scale (QOLS) developed by Flanagan (Cronbach's Alpha reliability coefficients ranging from 0.82 to 0.92 being reported), Burckhardt et al. (1989) surveyed 204 men and women over the age of 60 who had such chronic diseases as osteoarthritis, rheumatoid arthritis, ostomy, and diabetes found the major issues affecting quality of life to be independence and autonomy. The extreme physical limitations associated with spinal cord injury and need for intense, pervasive professional care makes maintenance of quality of life a particular challenge for persons with such injuries/disabilities.

In a 15 year study (1974 to 1989) of the adjustment of 135 patients with spinal cord injuries (SCI), Krause (1992) administered the Life Situation Questionnaire, a form of a quality of life measure (having the same domains of physical health — sitting tolerance, employment satisfaction, and financial satisfaction — as found in theoretical models of quality of life), and found that sitting tolerance, activity level, and satisfaction with general health significantly improved over time with medical care. Coyle et al. (1994), in a study of 91 SCI patients, found that health satisfaction as well as self-esteem and leisure satisfaction were major predictors of life satisfaction. Both studies support the contention that marked changes in physical function and safety impact life satisfaction (a term used in some contexts synonymously with quality of life, although a one-to-one relationship between the two variables is a subject of some debate in the literature).

Gerhart et al. (1993) shed considerable light on the relationship between physical domain and quality of life in their study of 279 individuals with long-term spinal cord injuries (having received initial and follow-up, postoperative care at a spinal cord treatment center from 20 to 47 years — 65% with lumbar, sacral, or thoracic injuries, and the remainder with cervical injuries). Significant declines over time in transfers and mobility were noted (not in dressing, toileting, homemaking/feeding, positioning/reaching/writing or in all areas combined). Almost one fourth listed fatigue/weakness as the cause of increased dependence, 18% blamed pain and stiffness, 14% blamed other injuries or age, and 5% blamed weight gain as the primary cause of decline in function. Pain in the shoulder joints was the problem noted by 45% of those who needed more medical and related care (shoulder function being critical to use of wheelchairs and other ambulation devices). For those who did not need additional assistance, quality of life increased over time, and for those whose function declined (necessitating an average of 2 hours per day of attendant care), quality of life declined. Fewer of the persons needing help rated their quality of life as excellent after 20 years (41% 20 years ago vs. 13% now). The need for and use of assistive devices (using hoists or lifts) and attendant care appears to impact perceived quality of life negatively. These findings do not suggest that care and assistive devices are not useful because the quality of life of those who received care and assistive devices was not compared to that of others who did not receive the same level of care or who did not have access to the same assistive devices. Also, general aging produces physical decline and can impact quality of life negatively. It is unclear what affect aging alone had on quality of life over 20 years, exclusive of spinal cord injury. However, it does appear that those interventions and devices which maintain or enhance mobility and transfers (attendant care, wheelchairs, hoists, etc.) have the additional effect of maintaining or increasing quality of life. However, dependence on others was seen to have the opposite effect. Therefore, it is incumbent on a rehabilitationist to request needed equipment and services in the appropriate areas and not to request the type and/or frequency of use of equipment or services which are not needed, resulting in dependence and development of a disability identity. Quality of life is maintained or enhanced when the type, frequency, and duration of such care is sufficient to meet identified functional needs. As noted by Fuhrer et al. (1992) in their study of 140 patients (100 men; 40 women) with spinal cord injuries, life satisfaction, as measured by the Life Satisfaction Index-A (a quality of life measure containing 18 items sampling such life domains as family, spiritual life, daily activities, housing, transportation, emotional well-being, general health, social life, recreational activities, money matters, sex life, and employment), was found to correlate most strongly with perceived control. Those who felt that their lives were under their control felt more satisfied than those who did not. Perceived control correlated significantly with functional independence and mobility. Therefore, an important consideration for rehabilitationists is providing sufficient equipment and assistive care to facilitate mobility and transfers, but not to provide too much care or equipment, reducing the person's sense of perceived control. Level of care should match level of need and individual preferences for retaining self-control and autonomy. These findings suggest that too much care, like too little, could result in a diminution of quality of life. For life care planners the desire to maximize or minimize life care needs in order to please referral sources should be avoided due to the potential for harm to the patient's quality of life. Quality of life should be an overriding consideration used as a rationale for specifying the type, frequency, and duration of care needs.

Steins et al. (1997) note that a sequenced, staged adjustment to injury and disability includes: (1) denial; (2) depression with internalized hostility; (3) depression with externalized hostility; (4) reaction against dependency, and (5) reconstruction of pretraumatic personality. Rehabilitation goals should reflect intervention strategies and outcomes designed to promote adjustment to injury and disability. The person should be allowed to negotiate solutions to barriers encountered in the environment. Adaptation and appropriate self-directed behavior should be encouraged. The person should be allowed to negotiate solutions to barriers encountered in the environment and to assume reasonable risks of living. It is not surprising that persons who are attempting to adjust to injury and disability may experience anger and depression. Distress is part of learning. Learning leads to adaptation. Fostering dependence by too much care can slow or impede the rehabilitation process, just like provision of too little care. Both the individual's perception of quality of life and that of caregivers and planners should be considered when care planning, but the implication of the adaptation process is that decisions are made more often by a multidisciplinary care team (including professionals, family, and significant others) in the beginning of the rehabilitation process and autonomy and self-directedness is returned to the individual as learning, and adaptation occur. Those with greater problem-solving ability, higher education, employment, more developed social skills, assertiveness, financial security, younger age, and greater internal control may adapt more readily to impairment. The more a person does for himself or herself, the greater becomes the opportunity for adaptation. Women were seen to be more adaptive than men for reasons unstated.

Use of assistive devices by persons with spinal cord injuries seems obvious; yet, little attention has been given to how they impact quality of life. Obviously, the focus of the discussion about their use has been about their impact on functional capacities. Scherer (1990) conducted a comparative case study with persons with spinal cord injury and others with cerebral palsy and found that users of assistive devices were more motivated for independent function, expressed more willingness to deal with a challenge, focused more on opportunity than on limitations, and were less withdrawn than those who did not use assistive devices (i.e., wheel chairs, vans, computers; etc.). Users functioned at a higher level educationally and vocationally than nonusers. Matching the assistive device to the person's quality of life and life satisfaction in the short-term as well as, but not solely on, potential for enhanced function and independence appears, based on the results of this study, to have value. Assistive devices do appear to impact self-reported motor functioning, overall capacities, and quality of life of persons with spinal cord injuries or cerebral palsy, but individual attitudes and temperaments should be taken into account before recommending use of an assistive device. Use of the wrong device may lead to failure, producing unanticipated negative self-perceptions and attitudes which could slow or hinder the rehabilitation process.

Similarly, satisfaction with one's residence is a salient issue related to the life satisfaction of persons with spinal cord injuries. Boschen (1996) relates barrier-free living arrangements to productivity, health, security, emotional stability, positive perceptions of disability, and social relations. The lack of accessible housing in the community has forced young persons with spinal cord injuries to live with parents beyond developmentally age-appropriate times, with the only other options being living in a structured community-based or institutional setting (a more common option with older persons with disabilities and limited or lacking family support system). The spinal cord injured person lacks autonomy because he or she lacks choice options. Self-esteem may deteriorate as well as perceived autonomy in structured, constraining living arrangements. It was postulated that higher residential choice satisfaction would be related to higher life satisfaction. Participants in the study were SCI patients averaging 28 years old, with an annual income under $10,000. Of the participants, 70% lived in private housing, 19% in apartment projects with shared attendant services, and 5% in institutions. Over one half of the participants had been forced to move to a new residence after being injured. Residential choice, residential satisfaction, health status, locus of control, and self-concept highly correlated with life satisfaction (a term used here synonymously with quality of life). The perception of choice and the freedom to relocate may be more important than the actual choice made in promoting life satisfaction. Barriers or restraints which appear to be insurmountable can alter self-esteem and have a ripple effect across all domains of life function. A barrier-free and safe home may offer the security which allows the self-esteem and productivity of the person to blossom. On the other hand, persons with long histories of low self-esteem, little productivity, low socioeconomic, and/or mental or physical health issues prior to a traumatic event which results in spinal cord injury may not experience the same incremental increase in quality of life when offered housing substantially above or below their pretraumatic standard of living or lifestyle. Steere et al. (1995) propose a model of lifestyle planning which focuses on the needs and desires of the person with a disability where the person with a disability identifies future goals, makes choices based on information. Such desired outcomes as security and safety, issues influenced by choice regarding residence, are articulated by rehabilitationists and their impact on overall quality of life over life span are discussed. Rehabilitationists should help identify services/resources designed to facilitate attainment of desire for housing as well as other rehabilitation goals which relate to quality of life domains. For persons with spinal cord injuries the challenges of finding a suitable long-term residence are likely to be greater than for other disabilities where accessibility issues are not as complex and as potentially costly.

Recognizing that such objective indicators of health status may not best represent the quality of life of persons with disabilities, Clayton and Chuban (1994) point out that such objective indicators as employment and earnings do not necessarily demonstrate higher quality of life. Using the Life Satisfaction Survey (LSS), a Lickert-type scale with 20 items rated on a continuum ranging from "agree very strongly" to "disagree very strongly," 100 individuals with spinal cord injury (80% male; mean age of 33.7; 60% Caucasian; 39% Afro-American) were surveyed via the LSS (with reported reliability of 0.87). Results of this study suggest that persons with spinal cord injuries report less quality of life than nondisabled students, cardiac patients, and persons with rheumatoid arthritis. Also, the severity of the spinal cord injury (identified through observation of physical functioning) correlated highly with quality of life (quadriplegics evidencing significantly lower scores than paraplegics). Interestingly, employment did not correlate significantly with quality of life (supporting the contention that such objective measures as employment or level of educational attainment may not demonstrate one's perception of the quality of one's life; that quality of life has an intensely subjective aspect). At least in this one study with this unique population physical capacities were a more powerful predictor of quality of life than employment and, for that matter, even income. However, social support was seen as a very powerful influence on quality of life for persons with spinal cord injury. One of the true measurement dilemmas in quality of life research is that quality of life is an intensely personal experience. Subjective measures may always be a better reflection of one's perception of quality of life, despite their appearance of being less precise and more subject to measurement error.

Diabetes

Rodin (1990) investigated the quality of life of insulin-dependent diabetics with particular interest in the effect of severity of such medical complications as nephropathy and renal failure, blindness, peripheral and autonomic neuropathy, and blindness. Of the 158 insulin-dependent adults studied, 22 had end-stage renal disease and were undergoing dialysis treatment. On the Sickness Impact Profile, as multidimensional measure of illness-related functional impairment (three categories on the physical dimension — ambulation, mobility, and body care/movement; psychosocial dimension — social interaction, communication, emotional behavior, and alertness, and five individually scored categories — eating, work, sleep, home management, and recreation/pastimes), those with more severe disease and the more intensive treatment associated therewith (less severe disease requiring less obtrusive interventions) were seen to experience short-term decline in quality of life. However, when more intensive treatment results in less long-term complications of diabetes, long-term quality of life may be enhanced. Parkerson et al. (1993) used two global measures of health-related quality of life (General Health Perception Questionnaire and the Duke Health Profile) as well as a disease-specific instrument (Diabetes Quality of Life) with 170 white, insulin-dependent diabetics ranging in age from 17 to 59, and found that on the two generic quality of life scales (not the disease-specific scale) the complications variable was a significant predictor of quality of life. Participants with complications were found to have poor health perception and significant health worry. Gender did not appear to have any predictive value. These findings suggest that severity of disability and associated complications affect quality of life; that generic measures of quality of life are preferable to disease specific measures for assessing quality of life (making research simpler to conduct and results from study to study easier to compare). Hanestad (1989) suggests that quality of life, as a construct which addresses zest for life, self-esteem, quality of interpersonal relations, and rich aesthetic experience, goes beyond the mere physiological effects of treatment for diabetes and looks at the whole human being.

Epilepsy

Helmstaedter and Elger (1994) found that for 58 adult epileptic patients their highest self-perceived area of impairment was in emotions/mood, followed by problem-solving/coping, activity/capability, and independence. Seizure frequency and financial dependency were seen as the most potent predictors of quality of life. Smith et al. (1995) postulate that severity and frequency of seizures and side effects of antiepileptic drugs can affect quality of life. The Epileptic Surgery Inventory (ESI), developed as a disease-specific measure of quality of life across 11 domains (health perceptions, energy/fatigue, overall quality of life, social function, emotional well-being, cognitive function, physical function, pain, role limitations due to physical, emotional and memory problems, and change in health status), was administered to 81 seizure patients who participated in a double-blind study of an antiseizure medication. Those who experienced reduced frequency and severity of seizures reported significantly greater happiness and control/mastery than those in the placebo condition. Similarly, significantly less anxiety, self-esteem, and mastery were reported by participants who continued to use the medication than those who stopped (the risk of toxicity being weighed against better seizure control and its effect on quality of life). Very frequent seizures were found to impact quality of life negatively, but even in patients in remission through use of medication, worry about the stigma of epilepsy was present. Frequency, severity, and social context of seizure activity appear to be the three variables which most affect quality of life for epileptic patients. Vickrey et al. (1992) administered the ESI to 200 adults (18 years or older as of 1990) who evidenced ineffective management of seizures despite anticonvulsants following surgery, a WAIS FSIQ over 70, and no progressive neurological disease, chronic psychotic condition, or medical contraindication to surgery. Reliability estimates for this health-related quality of life measure ranged from 0.68 to 0.88. Concurrent validity coefficients for the mood profile and emotional well-being, energy/fatigue, and physical function scales of the ESI ranged from 0.06 to 0.68. Significant differences in quality of life were seen between the seizure-free, aura, and seizure groups (seizure classification being based on the last 12 months of seizure activity) on health perceptions, energy/fatigue, overall quality of life, social function, emotional well-being, role limitations due to memory, emotional, or physical problems, cognitive function, physical function, and pain. Only the pain scale scores across groups did not differ significantly when adjusted for age, sex, and use of anticonvulsants (not a surprising finding, due to the less strong relationship between pain and seizure occurrence). It should be remembered that for persons with traumatic head injury, seizures may be accompanied by neuropsychological deficits which affect cognitive function, increasing the impact of head injury on health-related and overall quality of life. Seizures only compound the negative effects of brain injury on life function and related quality of life.

Cardiovascular Disease

Mayou (1990) suggests that quality of life for any cardiac disorder should be defined in terms of what is important to the patient and family, must look at specific expectations that have or have not been fulfilled, and must be sensitive to individual differences. Since the significance of psychological problems and difficulties with return to work have been cited on numerous occasions in discussions of the results of cardiac rehabilitation programs, they have not drawn attention in outcome studies focused primarily on physiology. It may be true that a treatment modality may not produce much physical benefit when added to a cardiac rehabilitation program, but it might lead to greater patient satisfaction. The example given was that of an exercise classes. Such classes have been shown to be of little benefit physiologically, but lead to greater satisfaction, longer working time, and greater frequency of sex 18 months later. The psychological benefit of such classes led to higher quality of life. Antihypertensive medications also were seen to affect quality of life. Blumenthal and Emery (1988) had previously found that exercise produced, at best, an equivocal physiological result, but clearly contributed to quality of life through enhancing morale and reducing stress. Yet, surgical and pharmacological interventions for postmyocardial patients remain the standard. Cardiac rehabilitation interventions which are grounded in a quality of life perspective inevitably are more multidisciplinary, addressing all the salient issues and needs of the individual across all life domains. The goal of treatment post myocardial infarction is not just to reduce mortality or prevent overt heart failure, but also to improve the patient's quality of life (Gorkin et al., 1994). In a study of 184 heart patients, these authors assessed the efficacy of a cardiac treatment protocol not only on physiological measures but on such quality of life variables as emotional well-being, health, social and sexual status, and cognitive function. They found that quality of life assessment played a valuable role in evaluating the efficacy of treatment protocols.

In the CAST double-blind study of antiarrythmias in patients with acute myocardial infarction, Wiklund et al. (1992) assessed quality of life through a series of questions on physical functioning, social functioning, symptoms, work status, life events, mental health, social support, social integration, and overall life satisfaction (reporting internal consistency reliability ranging from 0.10 to 0.85). Across all of these areas of quality of life, patients who experienced no dyspnea, angina, and were in a higher functional class demonstrated higher scores, suggesting that a strong relationship exists between physiological function and overall quality of life. Patients with prior congestive heart failure or myocardial infarction reported significantly less mental health, social functioning, physical functioning, and overall life satisfaction than those without such history. These findings support the contention that medical interventions produce ripple effects on other aspects of life function; and that these effects need to be understood in order to judge the true efficacy of treatment.

Other Illnesses

Although examination of the relationship between disability and quality of life has been associated most frequently in the peer-reviewed literature with the illnesses noted above, research into quality of life involving persons with the following illnesses/disabilities exists in lesser numbers: (1) pain (Tait et al., 1990); (2) renal failure (Lynch and Gallagher-Lepak, 1996); (3) back problems (Chubon, 1985); (4) inflammatory bowel disease (Kunsbeck et al., 1990); (5) neuromuscular disease (Schwartz et al., 1991); (6) Alzheimer's disease (Howard and Rockwood, 1995), and (7) hypothyroidism (Jaeschke et al., 1994). It is not surprising that most of the research on quality of life and disabilities has focused on life-threatening and/or catastrophic illnesses. However, broadening interest in quality of life only supports the contention that quality of life is an essential consideration in choosing and monitoring the efficacy of interventions designed to improve functioning of persons experiencing chronic illness and/or disability. Quality of life appears to be an important issue in planning and delivery of care across a broad range of health conditions.

CONCLUSIONS

Taylor (1989) may have said it best when he pointed out that evaluation of health status is moving from a preoccupation with death or survival as the single, dichotomous outcome upon which to judge the efficacy of any health-related intervention to an emphasis on many aspects of life and survival. Hume (1989) puts it simply when stating that the impact of any pharmacological intervention should be judged against the standard of its positive or negative effects on quality of life. Issues of well-being need to be given equal weight in selection of treatment alternatives to the physiological effects of given interventions. Fuhrer (1994) points out that persons with physical disabilities experience less subjective well-being than the general population (citing research that suggests that 90% of persons without disabilities as opposed to 68% with disabilities rate their lives as satisfying). The mechanisms by which persons with disabilities restructure their lives in order to enhance subjective well-being has received little attention. It seems reasonable to suggest that those who experience diminished subjective well-being may devalue their lives and not adhere to health maintenance practices learned through rehabilitation (potentially increasing the need for future care and associated costs). One's subjective rating of quality of life does impact one's treatment and other life choices. Quality of life is a deeply personal and inherently subjective issue.

Yet, one of the most pervasive measurement dilemmas with quality of life instrumentation is that it requires self-report of quality of life at a time (postinjury) when quality of life has diminished, creating a positive bias in which quality of life is likely to be overestimated preinjury/event because internal standards have been altered postinjury/event and there is potentially a negative bias in current (postinjury) self-report. Put simply, yesterday may look a lot better now than it did then because today is so much worse than yesterday. Today may look much worse than it might retrospectively when viewed from the future. Conversely, if yesterday offered very little quality of life, one might perceive quality of life today as improved, due to attention received from care givers after a traumatic injury/event. However, it should be noted that Anderson et al. (1986) pointed to the tendency of respondents to interview or questionnaires to underreport dysfunction when self-reporting health status, suggesting that postinjury/event subjective self-report might not be influenced by desire to "fake bad" due to attentional or economic incentives (components of secondary gain).

What instrument an expert chooses to measure quality of life should not impact the quality and accuracy of the data received (removing sources of potential error variance). Hays et al. (1993) suggest that good measures of quality of life must not only be valid and reliable, but also responsive to small, meaningful changes (making it easier to measure small changes in quality of life associated with short-term intervention). Although there has been some discussion of the relative measurement sensitivity of shorter, disease-specific and longer, general health status instruments, empirical evidence of any differences in measured outcomes using the shorter vs. longer instruments was not found by Katz et al. (1992). The number of instruments of both types reporting acceptable reliability and validity suggests that measures of health status have sufficient psychometric soundness to control for chance variability and compare successfully to more well-known measures of intelligence, personality, achievements, and related constructs seen in social science research.

The authors recognize, as a standard of practice in forensic rehabilitation, that any testing (particularly on self-report, subjective measures) needs to be based on sound psychometric principles and clinically correlated with other objective indicators. Interviewing and review of records regarding historical (preinjury/event) physical function and associated limitations in performance of life tasks should be clinically correlated with self-report data to determine consistencies and discrepancies, allowing the forensic rehabilitation expert to resolve any discrepancies through sound scientific inquiry (basing opinions about pre- and postinjury/event quality of life on all the available information from multiple sources and making judgments based on data as well as clinical judgment predicated on the expert's experience, training, and knowledge of the literature in the field of rehabilitation). Kaplan's (1994) Quality of Well Being Scale, because it asks more questions about discrete, observable physical functions, will not be as subject to variability in results due to differences in subjective standards when compared to the Ferrans and Powers' (1992) Quality of Life Index (both discussed in some detail in Chapter 2). However, the latter scale is more sensitive to the multiple domains of human function encompassing quality of life (not relying so heavily on physical functioning alone). Measurement of quality of life geared towards patients with certain illnesses, like cancer, may not have the sensitivity to all the factors affecting global, pre- and postevent quality of life; yet may control chance variability associated with responsiveness and bias. Instruments on quality of life, whether focused on physical complaints/limitations or a broader range of issues/factors or narrowed to specific issues/factors regarding one disease entity have value as an aid to rehabilitation expert decision-making. As found by Gibar (1991) in a study of 90 cancer patients who refused chemotherapy, not only was health status affected by a treatment choice, but adjustments in the family, at work, and in one's social environment were equally impacted. Rehabilitationists must be aware of all the areas of quality of life affected by treatment choices and resultant health status. Ultimately, the expert must weigh the test data along with the other evidence reviewed and give it the weight it merits. Through citation of the objective and subjective data relied in formulating opinions and the weight given to each piece of data, the rehabilitation expert can articulate opinion. Measures of health status may appear to have high validity because of their narrow focus and reliance on content related to observable, physical functions. More global measures which include items relative to subjective, psychosocial function may not appear to offer the same precision. Yet, standardized, quantitative questionnaires which measure global quality of life report reliability and validity coefficients which are comparable to those cited in the health status measures. However, incorporation of questionnaires regarding multiple domains of quality of life increases the length and complexity of the instruments. Time, cost, and related considerations make illness-specific measures more attractive to group research, but global, longer measures may have more clinical value due to sensitivity to function in multiple life domains. If global measures produce results that equal illness-specific measures, then the time should be taken to administer the global measure with or without the more narrowly focused instrument. The theoretical constructs, measures, and outcomes regarding the impact of physical challenges and limitations associated with illness and disability on quality of life are sound. Ongoing scientific inquiry will certainly improve precision and expand knowledge, but this is not a literature in its early infancy. Data exists, a multidisciplinary perspective has been developed, and use of quality of life in decision-making about care options is being made by patients and care givers. To the extent that any behavioral science research can meet the rigorous scientific standards implied by the *Daubert* standard, this literature does. Yes, it has subjective, psychosocial components to it. So do measures of depression, personality, and related psychological constructs. However, health status quality of life can be referenced to observable, discrete physical functions, unlike other measures commonly used in courts to measure abstract, less directly observable constructs related to emotional and/or cognitive function. Quality of life is a key element upon which judgment of future care needs should be built. Rehabilitationists may be distinguished from vocational rehabilitation counselors by their understanding that people function on multiple levels, interacting in complex ways with the world around them, making return to work no more inherently valuable against the standard of total life function and happiness than other domains of quality of life. Likewise, improvement in physical well-being does not necessarily result in global increases in one's quality of life or happiness. Rehabilitationists know this and develop care plans to deal with the issues and needs of a unique individual. Boilerplate life care plans where every person gets the same services with the same frequency and duration ignore issues of quality of life and do not address issues of global pain and suffering. Individualized care plans which are sensitive to quality of life issues can actually enhance quality of life where possible, where mitigating the loss to the extent possible from trauma and/or injury. For too long, care plans have been influenced by the limited knowledge and training of those writing them. Care planning for a person should be designed to do one thing, restore quality of life. Hyland (1992) suggests that medical science needs to reformulate its thinking to allow quality of life to be as pervasive a concern as physical status in decision-making about care. Life care planners in the forensic arena should do the same.

A cautionary note for rehabilitation practitioners moving from workers' compensation rehabilitation practice into forensic practice, and attorneys using the services of such rehabilitationists, is the reliance on so-called objective data provided primarily by physicians in workers' compensation systems. Such a reliance is a bias and may not be useful in quality of life assessment. That is, in some workers' compensation systems, rehabilitationists were punished for documenting psychological distress resulting from physical injury by having cases withdrawn from them or by losing a case referral source such as an insurance carrier. Competent rehabilitationists quickly learned to use their counseling skills and knowledge of psychological principles with injured workers covertly and with no documentation of psychological problems in any written reports (however ethically questionable). While this slight of hand may have been useful in a workers' compensation practice, it can be fatal in a quality of life assessment and a great disservice to the injured party. Attorneys whose focus has been on workers' compensation practice may also suffer a similar bias toward physical injury as the "real" injury and therefore not be prepared to deal with the complexity of quality of life assessment. Rehabilitationists are advised to upgrade their skills and knowledge base through continuing education in psychosocial rehabilitation courses which will allow them to offer well-grounded opinions on the relationships between physical injury and psychosocial responses to such injuries. They should also be prepared to educate attorneys and other parties in the legal system who are using a workers' compensation mind set when looking at personal injury quality of life issues.

REFERENCES

Anderson, J.P., Bush, J.W., and Berry, C.C. (1986). Classifying function for health outcome and quality-of-life evaluation. *Medical Care*, 24(5), 454-469.

Baker, F., Curbow, B., and Wingard, J. R. (1992). Development of the Satisfaction with Life Domains Scale for Cancer. *Journal of Psychosocial Oncology*, 10(3), 75-90.

Bech, P. (1993). Quality of life Measurements in chronic disorders. *Psychotherapy and Psychosomatics*, 59(1), 1-10.

Blake, R. (1984). What disables the American elderly? *Generations*, 8, 19-27.

Blumenthal, J.A. and Emery, C. F. (1988). Rehabilitation of patients following myocardial infarction. *Journal of Consulting and Clinical Psychology*, 56(3), 374-381.

Boschen, K. A. (1996). Correlates of life satisfaction, residential satisfaction, and locus of control among adults with spinal cord injuries. *Rehabilitation Counseling Bulletin*, 39(4), 230-242.

Bradley, E.M. (1987). The ICIDH: Format, application in different settings, and distinction between disability and handicap. *International Disabilities Studies*, 9, 122-125.

Burckhardt, C.S., Woods, S.L., Schultz, A.A., and Ziebarth, D.M. (1989). *Research in Nursing and Health*, 12(6), 347-354.

Chubon, R.A. (1985) Quality of life measurement of persons with back problems: some preliminary findings. *Journal of Applied Rehabilitation Counseling*, 16(2), 31-34.

Clayton, K.S. and Chuban, R.A. (1994). Factors associated with quality of life of long-term spinal cord injured persons. *Archives of Physical Medicine and Rehabilitation*, 75(June), 633-638.

Coyle, C.P., Lesnik-Emas, S., and Kinney, W.B. (1994). Predicting life satisfaction among adults with spinal cord injuries. *Rehabilitation Psychology*, 39(2), 95-112.

Ferrans, C. and Powers, M. (1992). Psychometric assessment of the Quality of Life Index. *Research in Nursing and Health*, 15, 29-38.

Flanagan, J.C. (1978). A research approach to improving our quality of life. *American Psychologist*, 33(2), 138-147.

Fuhrer, R.J. (1994). Subjective well-being: implications for medical rehabilitation outcomes and models of disablement. *American Journal of Physical Medicine and Rehabilitation*, 73(5), 358-364.

Fuhrer, R.J., Rintala, D.H., Hart, K.A., Clearman, R., and Young, M.E. (1992). Relationship of life satisfaction to impairment, disability, and handicap among persons with spinal cord injury living in the community. *Archives of Physical Medicine and Rehabilitation*, 73(June), 552-557.

Gerhart, K.A., Bergstrom, E., Charlifue, S.W., Menter, R.R., and Whiteneck, G.G. (1993). Long-term spinal cord injury: functional changes over time. *Archives of Physical Medicine and Rehabilitation*, 74, 1030-1034.

Gibar, O. (1991). The quality of life of cancer patients who refuse chemotherapy. *Social Science and Medicine*, 32(12), 1337-1340.

Goodwin, D.A.J., Boggs, S.R., and Graham-Pole, J. (1994). Development and validation of the Pediatric Oncology Quality of Life Scale. *Psychological Assessment*, 6(4), 321-328.

Gorkin, L, Follick, R.J., Geltman, E., Hamm, P., Sollano, J., Sylvia, S., Jacobson, K., Jacobson, R.J., Cochran, B.S., Sussex, B., Klein, M., Gaudette, G., Goldman, S., Carol, D., Holcombe, R., and Abern, D.K. (1994). Quality of life among patients post-myocardial infarction at baseline in the Survival and Ventricular Enlargement (SAVE) trial. *Quality of Life Research*, 3(2), 111-119.

Haig, A. J., Nagy, A., LeBreck, D., and Stein, G.L. (1995). Outpatient planning for persons with physical disabilities: a randomized prospective trial of physiatrist alone vs. a multidisciplinary team. *Archives of Physical Medicine and Rehabilitation*, 76, 341-348.

Hanestad, B.R. (1989). Insulin-dependent diabetes mellitus and quality of life. *Scandinavian Journal of Caring Sciences*, 3(3), 123-128.

Hays, R.D., Anderson, R., and Revicki, D. (1993). Psychometric considerations in evaluating health-related quality of life measures. *Quality of Life Research*, 2(6), 441-449.

Helmstaedter, C. and Elger, C.E. (1994). Cognitive-behavioral aspects of quality of life in presurgical patients with epilepsy. *Journal of Epilepsy*, 7(3), 220-231.

Howard, K. and Rockwood, K. (1995). Quality of life in Alzheimer's disease. *Dementia*, 6, 113-116.

Hume, A.L. (1989). Applying quality of life data in practice. *Journal of Family Practice*, 28(4), 403-411.

Hyland, M.E. (1992). A reformulation of quality of life for medical science. *Quality of Life Research*, 1(4), 267-272.

Jaeschke, R., Guyatt, G., Cook, D., Harper, S., and Gerstein, H.C. (1994). Spectrum of quality of life impairment in hypothyroidism. *Quality of Life Research*, 3(5), 323-327.

Johnson, D. J., Casey, L., and Noriega, B. (1994), A pilot study of patient quality of life during radiation therapy treatment. *Quality of Life Research*, 3, 267-272.

Kaplan, R.R. (1994). Using quality of life information to set priorities in health policy. *Social Indicators Research*, 33, 121-163.

Katz, J.N., Larson, M.G., Phillips, C.B., Fossel, A.H., and Liang, M.H. (1992). Comparative measurement sensitivity of short and longer health status instruments. *Medical Care*, 30(10), 917-925.

Krause, J.S. (1992). Longitudinal changes in adjustment after spinal cord injury: a 15-year study. *Archives of Physical Medicine and Rehabilitation*, 73, 564-568.

Kunsbeck, H.W., Korber, J., and Freyberger, H. (1990). Quality of life in patients with inflammatory bowel disease. *Psychotherapy and Psychosomatics*, 54, 110-116.

Lynch, R.T. and Gallagher-Lepak, S. (1996). *Journal of Applied Rehabilitation Counseling*, 27(1), 7-12.

Mayou, R. (1990). Quality of life in cardiovascular disease. *Psychotherapy and Psychosomatics*, 54 (2-3), 99-109.

McDonough, P.A., Bradley, E. M., and Tennant, A. (1995). Disability, resources, role demands and mobility handicap. *Disability and Rehabilitation*, 17(3/4), 159-168.

Mulhern, R. K., Fairclough, D. L., Freidman, A.G., and Leigh, L.D. (1990). Play Performance Scale as an index of quality of life of children with cancer. *Psychological Assessment*, 2(2), 149-155.

Muthny, F.A., Koch, U., and Stump, S. (1990). Quality of life in oncology patients. *Psychotherapy and Psychosomatics*, 54(2-3), 145-160.

Nayfield, S. G., Ganz, P. A., Cella, D. F., and Hailey, B.J. (1992). Report from the National Cancer Institute (U.S.A.) workshop on quality of life assessment in cancer clinical trials. *Quality of Life Research*, 1(3), 203-210.

Nichols, R. (1997). Managing cancer pain in managed care. *Case Management*, March/April, 49-53.

Nosek, M. A. and Fuhrer, M. J. (1992). Independence among people with disabilities: I. A heuristic model. *Rehabilitation Counseling Bulletin*, 36(1), 6-20.

Osberg, J. S., McGinnis, G. E., DeJong, G., and Seward, M. L. (1987). Life satisfaction and quality of life among disabled elderly adults. *Journal of Gerontology*, 42(2), 228-230.

Parkerson, G. R., Connis, R. T., Broadhead, W. E., Patrick, D. L., Taylor, T. R., and Tsu, C.-K. J. (1993). Disease specific vs. generic measurement of health-related quality of life in insulin dependent diabetic patients. *Medical Care*, 31(7), 629-639.

Rodin, G. (1990). Quality of life in adults with insulin-dependent diabetes mellitus. *Psychotherapy and Psychosomatics*, 31(7), 629-639.

Sands, D. J. and Kozleski, E. B. (1994) Quality of life differences between adults with and without disabilities. *Education and Training in Mental Retardation and Developmental Disabilities*, June, 90-101.

Schag, C.A.C., Ganz, P. A., Kahn, B., and Petersen, L. (1992). Assessing the needs and quality of life of patients with HIV infection: development of the HIV Overview of Problems-Evaluation System (HOPES). *Quality of Life Research*, 1(6), 397-413.

Schag, C.A., C., Ganz, P. A., Wing, D.S., Sim, M.S., and Lee, J.J. (1994). Quality of life in adult survivors of lung, colon and prostate cancer. *Quality of Life Research*, 3(2), 127-141.

Scherer, R.J. (1990). Assistive device utilization and quality of life in adults with spinal cord injuries or cerebral palsy two years later. *Journal of Applied Rehabilitation Counseling*, 21(4), 36-44.

Schipper, H. (1990). Quality of Life: principles of the clinical paradigm. *Journal of Psychosocial Oncology*, 8(2/3), 171-185.

Schover, L.R. (1991). The impact of breast cancer on sexuality, body image, and intimate relationships. *Cancer Journal for Clinicians*, 41, 112-120.

Schwartz, L.B., Devine, P.A., Schecter, C.B., and Bender, A.N. (1991). Psychosocial aspects of neuromuscular disorders. *Loss, Grief and Care*, 4(3-4), 3-21.

Smith, D., Baker, G.A., Jacoby, A., and Chadwick, D.W. (1995). The contribution of the measurement of seizure severity to quality of life research. *Quality of Life Research*, 4(2), 143-158.

Steere, D.E., Gregory, S.P., Heiny, R.W., and Butterworth, J. (1995). Lifestyle planning: Considerations for use with people with disabilities. *Rehabilitation Counseling Bulletin*, 38(3), 207-223.

Steins, S.A., Bergman, S.B., and Formal, C.S. (1997). Spinal cord injury rehabilitation. 4. Individual experience, personal adaptation, and social perspectives. *Archives of Physical Medicine and Rehabilitation*, 78, S-65-S-72.

Stover, S. (1995). Review of forty years of rehabilitation issues in spinal cord injury. *Journal of Spinal Cord Medicine*, 18(3), 175-182.

Tait, R. C., Chibnail, J.T., and Margolis, R.B. (1990). Pain extent: relations with psychological state, pain severity, pain history, and disability. *Pain*, 41, 295-301.

Taylor, T. R. (1989). Commentary. *Journal of Family Practice*, 28(4), 407.

Till, J.E., Sutherland, H.J., and Meslin, E.M. (1992). Is there role for preference assessments in research on quality of life in oncology? *Quality of Life Research*, 1(1), 31-40.

Verbrugge, L. M., Reoma, J. M., and Gruber-Baldini, A. L. (1994). Short-term dynamics of disability and well-being. *Journal of Health and Social Behavior*, 35, 97-117.

Vickrey, B.G., Hays, R. D., Graber, J., Rausch, R., Engel, J., and Brook, R.H. (1992). A health-related quality of life instrument for patients evaluated for epilepsy surgery. *Medical Care*, 30(4), 299-319.

WHO (1959). *The First Ten Years of the World Health Organization.* Geneva: World Health Organization.

Wiklund, I., Gorkin, L., Pawitan, Y., Schron, E., Schoenberger, J., Jared, L.L., and Shumaker, S. (1992). Methods for assessing quality of life in the Cardiac Arrhythmia Suppression Trial (CAST). *Quality of Life Research*, 1, 187-201.

Williams, J.M. and Burlew, L. (1995). Dealing with catastrophic injury: a developmental perspective on rehabilitation care planning. *Adultspan*, 9(3), 4-8.

Wu, A. W. and Rubin, H. R. (1992). Measuring health status and the quality of life in HIV and AIDS. *Psychology and Health*, 6(4), 251-264.

5 The Social Domain

> The recognition of quality of life as greater than simply the individualistic indicators inherent in the deficit model of disability and in equal treatment frameworks of equality places an accountability on the social, political, and economic structure to be organized in a manner that enables individuals to make appropriate life choices. Quality of life is not only a state for the individual to achieve but is inseparable from the underlying social and economic conditions without which individual and collective states of well-being cannot be achieved.
>
> *Rioux, 1996*

INTRODUCTION

Although social well-being is frequently listed as a domain of quality of life by researchers and writers in the field, the complexity of the concept cannot be underestimated. As we shall see in Chapter 7, The Leisure Domain, it is not uncommon for researchers to merge the social and leisure domains and confusingly blend them together in an unsorted mush of concepts which tend to leave out elements of the social domain such as extended family, family of origin, marital relationships, children, neighbors, and social role performance.

Siegrist and Junge (1990) conclude that the research on subjective well-being has focused on physical symptoms and psychological or emotional well-being, but research on "the social dimension in measures of subjective health measures remained undeveloped." They identified two sociological concepts used again and again by sociologists: *social support* and *social adjustment.* In the literature review below, these concepts are also present and are expanded into themes of interdependence, social roles, social being, belonging, dependently independent, interactions with others; and the impairment to social well-being (social isolation, social inactivity, environmental barriers, burden to others, and lack of independence or total dependence on others). Siegrist and Junge (1990) put this all together more elegantly:

> In keeping with our definition of treatment-related subjective health we suggest to conceptualize social health in terms of role performance, social skills, and the following components of social well-being: sense of belonging, intimacy and trust, social approval, and meaningful contribution.

A broader, meta-analysis of the social domain is addressed by Bach and Rioux (1996). They identified equality, self-determination, and democratization as the three elements of social well-being to be used as a "comprehensive standard for determining quality of life." In a review of other approaches, such as the client satisfaction, the functionalist, and the ecological approaches, they rejected the use of the client satisfaction approach since, by itself, it is not sufficient when examining the extent to which rehabilitation promotes health or how much control a person gains over his/her own life as a result of the rehabilitation process. The stigmatizing effects of disability, which lead to the exclusion of persons with disabilities from society, are also not addressed in this approach. The functionalist approach compares the individual to some standard of "normal" or "typical" as though there is some universally accepted "objective set of standards that can be constructed by the research community to guide research." The problem with this approach is that only some people have the power of definition over what people need to have a good quality of life. The ecological approach is also rejected by Bach and Rioux, even though it attempts to address the problem of focusing exclusively on either subjective measures of well-being or objective measures of quality of life. The ecological approach attempts to address the issue of "fit" between the person and his or her environment. The difficulty here is the underlying assumption that there is some way to measure the "fit" between the person and the environment.

One of the persistent underlying themes in all of quality of life literature, regardless of the domain studied, is autonomy or self-determination. In Chapter 9, The Cognitive Domain, autonomy is revealed as a critical factor in cognitive capacity or cognitive impairment. In Chapter 7, The Leisure Domain, autonomy or self-determination is found to be integral to the very definition of leisure. Similarly, self-determination is an aspect of the social domain simply because it is not possible to achieve a quality of life by one's self, and, at the same, time the integrity of the self must be maintained in relation to others. Bach and Rioux (1996) define self-determination as meaning "that choices are made autonomously and without coercion and that people consent in an informed way to their rule by others or by government." Democratization is described as a process which enables "the democratic participation of individuals and diverse groups in a wide scope of decision-making processes that directly affect their lives and their well-being" (Bach and Rioux, 1996). In this definition, interdependence is recognized as a reality of social life and is valued.

Equality is a more problematic concept, since in the traditional Northern American culture, equality has been defined by European-American men in formal legal and governmental systems. Therefore, it does not take into account difference and diversity of gender, race, ethnicity, disability, age, or sexual preference. The last half of the 20th century has seen an agonizing struggle in the attempt to incorporate difference into the concept of equality and its applications in legal and social policy processes. Bach and Rioux (1996) write:

> The principle of equality does not necessarily imply similar treatment: It may require treating people differently. In this view, differences (e.g., arising from nationality, gender, race, ethnicity, religious belief, or disability) are not a reason to deny people the supports they need to exercise their self-determination.

We will examine a wide range of quality of life literature including work from the social indicators movement; gender, age, and multicultural studies; physical and mental disability and disease dynamics; familial support and interaction patterns; and the impact of chronic pain and illness experiences on social well-being. Despite the diversity of the literature, the themes identified by Siegrist and Junge and Back and Rioux will emerge repeatedly.

LITERATURE REVIEW

> Since individuals are inevitably social and live in groups, each human being's quality of life will depend a great deal upon interactions with others in a social environment. How one is treated by others in the immediate environment affects an individual's quality of life. This is especially true of individuals who are dependent upon others because they are immature, impaired, ill, feeble, or emotionally dysfunctional.
>
> *Callahan, 1992*

In an ongoing study conducted by the National Center for Medical Rehabilitation Research on mortality after spinal cord injury, Krause (1996) reported that persons with spinal cord injuries "who were more active socially and vocationally and who had a higher overall level of subjective well-being were more likely to have survived their injuries until 1996." That is, they lived longer than their counterparts who were not as socially and vocationally active. This study underscore the critical aspects of the social domain in quality of life. Social well-being is not only about quality of life, but about being alive at all. This point is best seen in the quality of life literature, which has as its focus discrimination and stigma. The most notorious example is, of course, the Nazi justification of the murder of people with disabilities based on an ideology of "life not worthy of life" (Callahan, 1992). The Nazis used persons with disabilities to perfect their gas chambers, later used to exterminate millions of Jews, Gypsies, homosexuals, and others they deemed "deviant."

Discrimination and Stigma

On a more subtle, but still pernicious level, Rioux (1996) addresses the discrimination faced by persons with disabilities, while pointing out that her analysis could be done on other disenfranchised groups as well. She writes about the commonalities between two disenfranchised groups:

> The social and legal construction of inequality, although having some elements particularized to nation-states, also has some elements that are common across nations. ... It is clear that in nearly every nation of the world, women hold a status that is less valued than that of men. That lesser status varies from nations where women cannot vote, cannot drive a car, and cannot go out in public without their husbands to nations where they are accorded full social and legal rights but their employment opportunities and child care responsibilities result in an overall lower socioeconomic status. Likewise, in virtually every nation in the world, people with disabilities hold a lesser status than other people.

Although the inequality is then seen to be a defect of persons in the disenfranchised group, it lies, in fact, in the civic inequality imposed upon them. Rioux notes that "the indicator of quality of life from this perspective is the degree to which there has been a reduction of civic inequalities — the degree to which social and economic disadvantage has been addressed." In the U.S., the passage of the Civil Rights Bill of 1964 and the Americans with Disabilities Act of 1990 is part of the effort which move toward the reduction of civic inequality for minority groups, women, and people with disabilities.

The issue of socioeconomic status is a common thread in social well-being studies. In a study of African-American mothers on welfare (with welfare understood as a core measure of social class), Ensminger (1995) found that "welfare recipients reported less well-being on all the measures except self-esteem." In addition, almost 19% of the African-American women on welfare had chronic illness as compared to 7% of those never on welfare, and African-American women who had received welfare benefits did have problems with self-esteem and psychological distress in their later lives. The relationship between vulnerability to chronic disease and disability and welfare receipt for this group is a fascinating question when the work by Hanna and Rogovsky (1992) is considered. These authors noted that an astounding 42% of African-American women between the ages of 40 to 49 have at least "some physical disability" as contrasted to European-American and African-American men at 25%. They present a working hypothesis that "African-American women with disabilities are especially disadvantaged, and that this disadvantage is linked to their gender, race, and disability. Furthermore, the three stigmatized statuses may be interactive rather than, as usually assumed, additive. One plus one may equal four or more. The disadvantages, causes, consequences, of the interactions should be explored.

Another group whose quality of life is often overlooked or ignored is that of homeless persons. Brown's (1996) essay on the quality of life for homeless people turns out to be a discourse on self-determination by this marginal population. He identifies four "conceptual-practical problems ... in an attempt to try to understand some of the very basics of quality as it pertains to marginal people." These concepts are: "The approach to quality of life. Personal meaning of *quality* in life. Personal choice. Acceptance of marginality." That is, homeless people may not hold the same values or desires to have a home as perhaps the middle class rehabilitation professional may have. What *quality* is may have different meanings for people of different cultures and subcultures and individuals within these groups. Choices are made based on the values of each individual. The choices may not always make sense in another context. This problem speaks to the criticism of the functionalist approach by Bach and Rioux (1996), who point out that in this approach only some people have the power of definition over what people need to have a good quality of life (e.g., the rehabilitationist, the social worker rather than the homeless person). And finally, Brown (1996) recommends a movement toward inclusion which "tolerates difference, but ... goes beyond that. It tolerates difference within some general criteria that are used for all people within the society and, because these are general, they are based naturally on the common needs of human beings in most cultures." That is, they are based on accessibility to food, clothing, and shelter as well as psychological, physical, and social well-being.

The Social Indicators Movement and Related Research

Much of quality of life research arises out of the Social Indicators Movement of the 1960s and the 1970s. (Please refer to Chapter 7, The Leisure Domain, for more detail regarding this trend in social science research.)

Flanagan's 1978 report on the American Institutes for Research study of quality of life in the U.S. is a frequently cited article in the quality of life literature and in this book because the work is based on an empirically based, national sample resulting in the collection of thousands of "critical incidents" from 3000 people of "various ages, races, and backgrounds representing all regions of the country." The social domain is well described in two broad categories, relations with other people and social, community, and civic activities. Relations with other people include: "relations with spouse (girlfriend or boyfriend), having and raising children, relations with parents, siblings or other relatives, relations with friends." Social, community, and civic activities include: "activities related to helping or encouraging other people and activities related to local and national government." Recreation or leisure, unlike many essays in the quality of life literature, is described in rich detail as separate from the social domain. "Socializing" is listed under recreation, but only in the sense of entertaining or being entertained by others or participating in clubs. The study population was asked to rank the importance of the factors or domains of quality of life. Although differences in importance ranking were found by age and gender, most people found that having and raising children and close relationship with a spouse (both within the social domain) were very important and one of the areas where there was agreement that the quality of life could be improved was "participation in local and national government," another aspect of the social domain.

Rhoads and Raymond (1981) conducted a household survey with 547 adults in Phoenix, AZ with a representative population of Anglos, Blacks, and Mexican-Americans. Some interviews were conducted in Spanish. They used the Bradburn Affect–Balance Scale and Flanagan's (1978) question: "At this time in your life, would you say you are very satisfied with your life as whole, fairly satisfied, neutral, dissatisfied, or very dissatisfied?" Their study produced results consistent with other studies listed in their article which suggest that "studies which include a range of income levels in their samples consistently demonstrate a direct relationship between socioeconomic status and several different measures of well-being." Rhoads and Raymond conducted a factor analysis of the results of their work based on income level. They found that "the community factor accounted for the majority of the variance at the lowest income level while the social factor emerged as most prominent for the other two income levels."

The community factor was defined as having "opportunities for participation in activities which are traditionally provided by the community." These opportunities could include "the opportunity to obtain an education, learn a job skill, and put that education and job skill to use in earning an adequate income." The social factor was defined as "including activities which maintain contact and feedback from other persons." Rhoads and Raymond recognize the role of community, as part of the individual's social network and suggest that the unique character and needs of each community must be taken into account when designing policies to improve the quality of life of that community.

Espousing a model of community psychology which is similar to the goodness-of-fit approach noted above, Murrell and Norris (1983) postulate that "resource decisions should be dictated by the needs of the population, not those of elected officials or professional administrators." They describe a conceptual model of quality of life which should be "responsive, comprehensive, and directly usable to resource decisions." Their focus is on subjective evaluations of quality of life. In a Kentucky study of 1800 adults, "five life domains made significant contributions to QOL. In order of strongest contributions, these life domains were: Mental Health, Financial, Social Activity, Employment, and Health." Murrell and Norris propose that a quality of life approach be used as the criterion for need assessment and community psychology in order to determine the needs of a community, to identify its stresses and resources, and then to monitor the results of any interventions.

In a 1991 study, using a convenience sample of 116 people, Hadorn and Hays examined six aspects of health-related quality of life. Social relationships was one of the six aspects and was defined as:

> This area deals with the extent to which one is able to have satisfying relationships and interactions with friends and/or family including telephone calls, personal visits, and going places together. In determining the extent to which problems with Social Relationships may reduce quality of life, the following factors should be considered. How often one is alone and feeling lonely. How much enjoyment is obtained from existing social relationships.

Hadorn and Hays assert that there are only two empirically based instruments available for measuring health-related quality of life (Quality of Well-Being Scale and Sickness Impact Profile), and the purpose of their study was to "evaluate the construct validity of the survey" or a shorter method of evaluation. The construct validity was supported. They used a multitrait-multimethod (MTMM) which included both highs and lows on a quality of life scale (best possible quality of life to worst possible quality of life) and an importance scale for each aspect of quality of life (most important to least important). The social domain played an prominent role in quality of life instrument construction, suggesting that social interaction in and outside of the family play an important part in overall quality of life.

Mental Illness

Five studies underscore the importance of the social domain for people with mental illness. Bigelow et al. (1991) proposed that quality of life theory was useful for "conceptualizing and evaluating mental health services." They developed a 263-item questionnaire (Quality of Life Questionnaire — QLQ) and they generated 1154 pretests, 758 posttests, and 190 interviews with randomly selected community residents at 24 community mental health program sites. The 16 scales on the QLQ included 4 factors relevant to the social domain:

Independence — living in the community
Interpersonal interaction — satisfaction in affiliating with others
Spouse role — opportunity for affiliation, esteem, and other need satisfactions
Social support — critical to health and adjustment, having people to share good times and bad

The predictive validity of their instrument (QLQ), for the economically depressed county sample was lower, as compared to other regional groupings, in independence, interpersonal, spouse role, social support well-being, and other factors. They also found that aftercare clients were lower on interpersonal and social support factors as compared to drug, alcohol, and general psychiatric patients.

Baker et al. (1992) examined "two aspects of social support, availability and adequacy" for 729 mentally ill adults enrolled in seven state-supported community support services programs.

They used the Bradburn Positive and Negative Affect Scales and the Satisfaction with Life Domains Scales in their interview process. The researchers also added the Availability of Social Support Scale, which asked seven questions of "whether the client had:

1. friends;
2. contact with his/her immediate family;
3. a relationship with other professional staff besides the client's case manager;
4. a person that the client feel close to and has an ongoing relationship with;
5. a group of people to which he belongs and among whom he has an assured place;
6. a relationship which includes sexual activity; and
7. any people who rely on the client's advice, support or assistance."

In the Adequacy of Social Support Scale, "seven parallel questions were asked." These included: "how the client felt about the number of friends he/she had; the client's satisfaction the amount of contact that he/she had with immediate family members; the client's feelings about the level of support of his/her sexual activity, etc." The results revealed gender differences in that the "more men had a low availability of social support." Age was also a factor, with the youngest clients having the most social support and the oldest the least. Despite this, the youngest clients judged their social support as inadequate. "Schizophrenics and substance abusers were likely to have less social support ... than were clients with a primary diagnosis of affective disorders." The researchers also reported that "about half the clients remained dissatisfied with the amount of social contact they had with their families and most wanted more." Opportunities for intimate social relationships including sexual contact were also more limited than for other types of social relationships in the study.

A 1994 article by Corten and others presents a subjective quality of life clinical assessment model to be use in psychiatric rehabilitation. The researchers used semistructured interviews based on the Satisfaction with Life Domains Scale, Helps in Daily Life Scale, and Interdependencies Scale. The Interdependencies Scale consists of ten items concerning activities where most people need another person's assistance. "Each subject was asked if he could count on someone, then if someone could count on him to carry through each of these activities." There were 148 Belgian psychiatric outpatients and 40 normal controls who took part in the study. The outpatients were schizophrenics, alcoholics, anxiety disorder patients, major depressives, and heroin addicts. In terms of fulfillment of social roles, only 19.6% of the patients were married (control group 54.5%) ... and only 4.1% of them had one or more children in their care (control group 50.0%). Corten et al. conclude that a comprehensive model of how one experiences subjective quality of life includes three axes: hedonism, achievement, and conformity. The second axis, quality of life through achievement, is considered to the most important for rehabilitation professionals since, clinically, this is a frequently noted goal of development skills training programs. The abilities and social role cluster did not position itself along the same axis as the satisfaction cluster, raising the question for rehabilitationists as to whether quality of life programming designed to foster life satisfaction through self-achievement may differ from one designed to promote improvement in life satisfaction through interdependence.

Brown et al. (1997) use what Bach and Rioux (1996) have described as the ecological and functionalist approaches — that is, using both objective and subjective analyses to determine the "goodness of fit" between the person and their environment. Data were obtained from 19 severely mentally ill consumers using psychiatric rehabilitation services and their case managers. "The purpose of this study was to compare the perceptions of consumers and case managers regarding barriers interfering with life satisfaction." The case managers identified more person barriers (51%) and fewer environmental barriers (49%) as contrasted to the consumers who identified more environmental barriers (73%) and fewer person barriers (27%). Person barriers referred to "family relationships, friendships, physical health, and additional wants." Environmental barriers referred to "health care, community services, housing, neighborhood, finances, daily activities, work, and transportation." In terms of the social domain, both case managers and consumers identified "unsupportive family" as a barrier. The researchers manage to avoid the pitfall of the functionalist approach (e.g., the problem with this approach is that only some people have the power of definition over what people need to have a good quality of life) by making no claim to whose perceptions were "right." This tends to support Bach and Rioux's (1996) conclusion that self-determination is an essential aspect of social well-being. This is well supported by the authors' conclusion that "conflicting perception between professionals and consumers may compromise interventions." They suggest that the professional and the consumer need to come to consensus as to what the barriers are to life satisfaction before proceeding with an intervention. This would fall into the democratization approach also suggested by Bach and Rioux (1996) in which informed full participation in decision making is ensured by those who are governed (consumers) by others (psychiatric rehabilitation practitioners).

Whelton et al. (1997) conducted a study with families of the Hamilton Program for Schizophrenia (HPS). This is a community-based psychosocial rehabilitation and treatment program "offering long-term case management services to young adults with schizophrenia. Families of clients are included whenever possible in the rehabilitation team, and support and educational services are provided for families." The researchers sent questionnaires to 105 families representing 92 different clients. Of these, 85 were returned, with most of the respondents being mothers of the clients. The families reported:

> Illness management (medications, symptom control) as the most important service provided for their relative, followed by assistance with finding productive activities and helping to manage social relationships. The services for their relatives that they were least satisfied with were crisis management outside of office hours, and helping to provide productive activities.

The more involved family members were in the rehabilitation process, the higher level of satisfaction with HPS's services they were. This study effectively demonstrates the importance of family involvement in the psychosocial rehabilitation process and the importance of family within the social domain of quality of life research. Also, this study suggests that the quality of life of family members needs to be considered in service planning and delivery. Finding productive activities and managing social relations of persons with disabilities (mental, physical, or a combination) appear to have positive effects on the quality of life of both the person with a disability and the family. Helping the family to deal with crisis as well as chronic problems is also a valuable approach for enhancing quality of life for all concerned.

Mental Retardation/Learning Disabilities

Three studies in the fields of learning disability and mental retardation list social activity, place in society, and social and community integration and social interactions as quality of life domains. Scuccimarra and Speece (1990) examined a random sample of mildly handicapped students who exited high school in 1984. "Post-school social adjustment data included marital status, place of residence, types and frequency of social activities, friendship patterns, and satisfaction with social life." Using a 59-item instrument adapted from the Vermont Follow-Up Structured Survey Instrument, they found that 96.9% of the subjects were single and had no children (86.2%). The majority resided with their parents (76.6%), even though they would prefer to live independently (71.4%). Social activities included church attendance, movie attendance, television viewing, hobbies, sports, recreation center visits, and "hanging out" (as in a shopping mall). It should be noted that these authors do not make distinctions between the social and the leisure domains. For example, it is problematic to describe television viewing as "social" when it can be engaged in as a passive leisure activity by one's self. Because of this squashing together of the leisure and social domains, it may be difficult to use this study as a basis for comparison to other studies of social well-being for persons with learning disabilities. At any rate, this study found that 66.1% of the participants ranked themselves as "very satisfied or satisfied, and 29.2% were dissatisfied or very dissatisfied with their social life." The remainder were neutral. When examining the "employment and social data together, respondents who were working were more active socially and more often expressed satisfaction with their social lives than respondents with their social lives who were not working."

The Comprehensive Quality of Life Scale–Intellectual Disability (ComQol Scale) was developed by Cummins (1991) in an attempt to overcome the exclusively objective or subjective approaches to quality of life assessment in his instrument by pairing objective and subjective components in seven broad domains of quality of life. The Place in Society domain includes "social class, education, job status, community integration, community involvement" within the objective component and "feeling a part of the general community, being involved with people outside the home" in the subjective component. Intimacy was defined as another social domain. The objective component of intimacy includes "family, friends" and the subjective component, "having family or friends." The author invites others to collaborate with him on this instrument since it is "currently under trial." This scale recognized that satisfaction with the social domain of quality of life involved issues of intimacy, belongingness, and interaction with others.

In 1995 Perry and Felce published their article on their study "of 14 objective measures of service quality in 15 staffed houses in four counties in South Wales for people with learning disabilities." These measures were grouped under six headings which included "social and community integration and social interactions." They used the Index of Community Involvement — Form 2 and the Community Oriented Programmes Environment Scale (COPES) and the "social distance items" of the Group Home Management Schedule (GHMS) and the interactions rating within the Programme Analysis of Service Systems (PASS-3), and directly observed social activity patterns. The purpose was to compare measures and not to expound on the social domain. This article supports the contention that the social domain is a critically important part of quality of life assessment and notes that technical measurement issues associated with assessment of quality of life need to be considered.

CANCER

The two studies selected on quality of life and cancer are both studies of cultures other than the dominant European–American culture populations. The first study reviewed addresses the use of a quality of life instrument for Hispanic American cancer patients. Canales et al. (1995) conducted a study to determine if the Cancer Rehabilitation Evaluation System (CARES) could be translated for use by Spanish-speaking and bilingual patients with cancer. They offered the following commentary on the multicultural issues they encountered:

> However, in performing this study we encountered a number of methodological problems that had not been previously described in the literature, including the need for idiomatic translations, lack of familiarity with questionnaires, low acculturation and low literacy rates among Hispanic cancer patients in the southwestern USA.

They also translated the Demographic and Social Information Questionnaire which has been used in prior research with the CARES and added an Acculturation Scale and the Medical Information Form. They used a more idiomatic Spanish (Mexican–American) rather than a Castillian version of the CARES form developed in Spain. Of the 6 Hispanic male and 24 female participants (with a mean age of 46 years and an educational level of 7.7 years), 77% preferred Spanish for the interview process. The methodological difficulties in this study prevented the obtaining of reliable results. The researchers noted that the low acculturation and literacy scores meant that this population of mostly immigrants could not effectively complete the self-administered CARES, even with help from the researchers. The authors noted that the diversity among Hispanic populations in the U.S. needs to be acknowledged, and that their Spanish language version of the CARES may not be suitable for Puerto Rican, Cuban, and other Hispanic groups. This study was included in this Social Domain Chapter to point out the importance of conducting quality of life research which is designed for the ethnic or cultural group of the respondents. For assessing life satisfaction in the social domain, whether dealing with an individual or members of the individual's social network, issues of culture and language are critically important. It is possible that these differences may profoundly affect the reliability and validity of any research results generated from inadequate instruments. Yet, specific instruments for special populations have not received much attention in the research literature (not unlike the measurement dilemmas associated with other types of psychometric instruments commonly used in forensic rehabilitation, psychiatric, and psychological practice.)

Chaturvedi (1991) studied 50 randomly selected cancer patients in Bangalore, India. A list of ten items based on interviews with patients, doctors, and a review of quality of life literature was developed: "Happiness with family/relatives — happiness with relationship with family members, relatives, spouse, children, sibs, cousins, etc. (Are there any problems, discords, quarrels, disputes or distancing.?)" This was identified as the social domain in his study. He also identified four key dimensions and the social domain dimensions included

> *Marital functioning*: Performance of marital role or duties. Relationship with spouse, sexual relationship, looking after the family, bringing up children. *Marital life satisfaction*: Degree of satisfaction with the above marital role. *Social functioning:* Attending social functions, e.g., marriages, meeting friends, relatives, hosting them. Interaction with others. Social roles, participating in social gatherings. *Social satisfaction:* Degree of satisfaction with the performance of social roles.

All participants were of the Hindu religion and they ranked "peace of mind (66%), spiritual satisfaction (62%), satisfaction with religious tasks (60%), and happiness with family, relations, and social network (60%)." The author is of the opinion that sociocultural factors may have had a marked influence on the results: "Family ties, social support and spiritual as well as religious activities are considered of immense importance in a Hindu family, especially at times of disease and death." Chaturvedi suggests that the quality of life literature may be overemphasizing physical functioning as the most important element in quality of life assessment. He also notes the difficulty of measuring spiritual and religious well-being. Indeed, do religious activities belong within the social domain? Is spiritual well-being a psychological domain dimension? The researcher suggests that cultural and national cross-comparison studies on these questions would be valuable.

Deaf and Hard-of-Hearing

Mowry (1988) collected data "as a part of a follow-up study of deaf and hard-of-hearing former VR (vocational rehabilitation) clients." A total of 81 former clients were interviewed in the preferred communication mode of the study participant. Of these, 38 clients were deaf and 43 hard-of-hearing. "The self-reports on quality of life were collected using a format similar to that of Campbell et al. (1976): that is, respondents were asked to rate their satisfaction with selected aspects of their lives." Relationships with family and friends were two of the eight domains respondents were asked to rank. "When asked to rate overall satisfaction with their family lives, a large majority (92.1%) of the deaf respondents indicated that they were satisfied or very satisfied." The hard-of-hearing persons (93.1%) were also satisfied or very satisfied with family life. The majority were also satisfied with the friendships they had in their lives. Interestingly, if only the objective factors of quality of life are considered, then quality of life for this population appears limited due to financial status and poverty brought about by low earnings or receiving public assistance. The lack of agreement between objective indicators of quality of life and subjective measures is not unusual (Mowry, 1988) and has been found in other studies (Campbell et al., 1976).

Diabetes

Hanestad (1989) asserts that insulin-dependent diabetes mellitus (IDDM) "affects the overall life situation of the individual." She notes in an overview of research with people with IDDM that they may experience "impaired social interaction." Although her article is primarily a plea for quality of life study and research for people with IDDM, it is reviewed here for the descriptions of what social well-being should be. More specifically, she states that a person who has a good life quality should be able to achieve:

> Good interpersonal relations; has close, warm, and reciprocal relationship to at least one other human being; has contact, friendship, loyalty; has a feeling of identity with and belonging to a group (e.g., friends, neighbors, work mates, political group).

Hanestad also notes that the rehabilitation care planning process should address the concept of being "being dependently independent," suggesting that independence in social function for persons with disabilities is dependent upon the care of other people. This appears to be an issue of social planning which transcends ideographic needs of persons with IDDM.

Cox and Gonder-Frederick (1992) found that there have been great strides in behavioral diabetes research in the past decade and that the challenge in the "next decade is to translate these findings into interventions that improve quality of life and physical well-being for individuals with diabetes." In this detailed review of the research of the last decade, the authors list social and familial factors as providing opportunities for relationships and interactions that "can either enhance or interfere with diabetes management. Specifically, they found that "family conflict and dysfunction is predictive of adherence difficulty, whereas increased family support, cohesion, and organization are associated with better adherence and metabolic control" of diabetes. This article is one of the few articles in the quality of life literature which addresses a very important, "but empirically neglected social influence is the patient–physician relationship." This is particularly important for persons with diabetes since patients "who discontinue follow-up or infrequently attend clinics tend to be in poorer health and worse glycemic control than patients with regular follow-up." Like Hanestad (1989), Cox and Gonder-Frederick (1992) call for more quality of life research for people with diabetes. They recommend that "researchers should move away from simple correlational studies to more experimental manipulations, from assessment to treatment outcome studies, and from use of singular biological dependent variables (e.g., HbA) to incorporate broader educational, behavioral, psychosocial, and economic factors, such as knowledge, compliance, quality of life and cost effectiveness." They also note that little research has been focused on minorities and the elderly. For rehabilitation professionals, the findings abut the physician-patient relationship has implications for care planning and service delivery. Satisfaction with care givers appears to be an important variable in overall social satisfaction and in the social domain of quality of life.

Epilepsy

Helmstaedter and Elger (1994) developed their own quality of life questionnaire for patients with epilepsy. The 6-question instrument was administered to 58 German adult patients with pharmacoresistant focal epilepsies who were candidates for epilepsy surgery. Two questions directly related to the social domain are: "Due to your illness, how much of a burden do you feel you are to your family and friends? How does your partner/spouse or significant relative react when he/she is present during a seizure or thinks you are about to have one? "Respondents may choose between "Never" and "Always" or "None" and "A great deal" on a 7-point scale to answer these questions. After administering the questionnaire, Helmstaedter and Elger conducted a factor analysis which led to the development of six scales. These scales included such social domain dimensions as "relations to family and other persons" and "reduced independence" and "reduced control over life." The social domain results in this study are somewhat disturbing in that the researchers found:

"Although social reactions to the patients' disease were mostly positive and supportive, 20% of the patients experience a high degree of misunderstanding, disappointment, or anger." It is not surprising that social withdrawal by epilepsy patients is not unusual. Helmstaedter and Elger recommend that "increasing social activities, increasing the patient's responsibility for his situation, a reduction in the relatives' punishing or reinforcing behavior ..." would go a long way toward improving the person with epilepsy's social well-being.

Narcolepsy

Ferrans et al. (1992) conducted a quality of life study with a sample of 539 persons with narcolepsy. They used the Quality of Life Index — Narcolepsy Version. There are four subscales on this instrument, one of which was the social and economic domain. In this domain, 33% of the study participants

> "reported that narcolepsy had contributed moderately or a great deal to social isolation. Narcolepsy also was reported to contribute to the difficulty making or keeping friends (18.7%), difficulty with teachers in school (16.0%), and difficulty with classmates or co-workers (14.9%)."

There was also a "family domain" assessed, and the most distressing symptoms of narcolepsy "were sleep attacks and daytime drowsiness." Problems with family members (24.2%) and living partners (24.5%), and "contribute to marital problems" (13.9%) and finding a partner (14.9%) were significant, even though this was the highest quality of life domain found in the study.

Pain

Chibnall and Tait (1990) examined the impact of chronic pain on a patient's quality of life. They developed a self-report measure, the Quality of Life Scale (QOLS) on a sample of 393 chronic pain patients. In addition to the QOLS, Chibnall and Tait also administered the Beck Depression Inventory, Speilberger Trait Anxiety Inventory, Pain Disability Index, McGill Pain Questionnaire (a picture drawing which was a measure of painful body surface), Psychosomatic Symptom Checklist, and an activity level questionnaire. The QOLS variables included "social life" and "family life." Patients rated family life as giving them the most satisfaction and "hobbies/recreational activities and the experiences of daily activities (e.g., work)" the least satisfaction. The distinction between social and family life and hobbies/recreational bears noting here because of these results. That is, if social life and leisure or recreation had been put in with social life, this finding would not have surfaced. The researchers assert that the QOLS is a reliable measurement instrument which "is a measure of *satisfaction* with functioning, not level of functioning." So although the QOLS correlated moderately with the Pain Disability Index, the two instruments "do in fact measure different aspects of the chronic pain experience." That is, one is measuring the impact of pain on function (PDI) and the other life satisfaction with level of functioning (QOLS). The QOLS appears to offer promise for the forensic rehabilitationist faced with having to measure chronic pain and quality of life in civil litigation because it discretely measures quality of life and is not influenced (from a psychometric perspective) by temporal variations in levels of pain.

A 1991 article by Ferrell et al. presented a conceptual model for quality of life and the experience of pain based on a previously developed instrument, the QOL Survey. The instrument has been used extensively with groups of cancer patients and found to be "highly sensitive in documenting the impact of pain on overall QOL." The conceptual model developed is based on three earlier quantitative studies. They found that

> The importance of patient experience cannot be overstressed. The patient's expertise about his or her QOL is analogous to the importance of the patient's expertise about his or her pain.

Their model includes social well-being as a dimension of quality of life impacted by pain. This dimension includes: "caregiver burden, roles and relationships, affection/sexual function, and appearance." The researchers emphasize the significance of pain as a quality of life factor by noting that "in studies of QOL involving noncancer patients or patients without pain, pain is not mentioned as a predominant factor in overall QOL. When an individual has pain, however, it emerges as a major influence."

Spinal Cord Injury

Rintala et al. (1996) assert that persons with disabilities tend to have higher stress levels than persons without disabilities. As part of a Life Status Study, 100 men and 40 women with spinal cord injuries (SCI) were extensively interviewed and examined. A battery of instruments were administered to them including: Demographic and Injury-Related Measures, Perceived Stress Scale, the Center for Epidemiological Studies Depression Scale, Life Satisfaction Index-A, the Craig Handicap Assessment and Reporting Technique (CHART), social support questions, self-assessed health status questions, self-reported morbidity index, urinary tract infection tests and cultures, pressure ulcer skin inspection, American Spinal Injury Association Total Motor Index Score, Functional Independence Measure, and questions regarding personal assistance. In the second phase of the study, the Hassles Scale, the Life Events Scale, the Personal Independence Profile, the Personal Assistance Satisfaction Index, and the Interpersonal Support Evaluation List were administered.

The researchers found that in terms of social integration women and men reported similar scores of a mean of 84 for the women 80 for the men. Since a score of 100 is listed for the normal or nondisabled population, a lack of social integration for both women and men can be seen. High levels of satisfaction were evidenced for men and women in terms of social support; however, overall, women with SCI "have more perceived stress than men with SCI and more than women in the general population." They had more "depressive symptomatology than men." The men had more income, more education, and greater mobility than the women. Men who had more social support were found to perceive less stress or more well-being in their lives. This was not true for women. The authors concluded that stress for women with SCI is different than that of men with SCI; "it is very important to identify the causes of the stress" for women in future research. This study suggests that social well-being may not have the same meanings or effects for women and men with spinal cord injuries.

Clayton and Chubon (1994), in a study of 100 volunteer participants with SCI (80% male; 20% female; mean age of 33.7), administered the Life Situation Survey (LSS), a measure of perceived quality of life, and the Social Health Battery (SHB), a measure of social participation, in order to determine the correlation between quality of life and social participation. A significant correlation was noted between LSS scores and SHB items on frequency of interaction with friends and relatives ($r = 0.40$), number of in-home visits with friends ($r = 0.34$), number of voluntary memberships in social organizations ($r = 0.49$), and activity level in social organizations ($r = 0.45$). Of further interest was that the LSS scores for paraplegics were significantly higher than those for quadriplegics. A 0.30 correlation between LSS scores and income (more than one half the sample reporting incomes of less than $15,000 per year) and a 0.41 correlation between LSS scores and education (mean educational level being 12.6 years) were also noted. The SHB, as a measure of frequency of participation in social events, produced different scores than the LSS, a measure of qualitative social functioning. This study is particularly important for its empirical linkage of subjective social factors related to quality of life with objective criteria relative to frequency of behavior. It suggests that for catastrophically injured persons the social domain is an important area for intervention when planning care. Fuhrer et al. (1992) finding that on the Life Satisfaction Index-A (LSIA-A) SCI patients ($n = 140$) ranked social relationships as the highest area of life satisfaction (as opposed to money, sex, and employment — the lowest rated areas of life satisfaction) supports the contention that for SCI patients who have little or no involvement in work and have little or no opportunity to earn an income, social integration strategies are critically important to maintenance of quality of life. As suggested by the 15-year-follow-up study conducted by Krause (1992), significant declines in social satisfaction over time are not atypical for SCI patients. Therefore, social support interventions should be a central theme to care planning and delivery for persons with SCI if quality of life is to be maintained. The question that still remains to be investigated is what social support strategies are particularly effective in enhancing quality of life. One of the most obvious issues is whether or not an attendant would be a sufficient social stimulus to promote quality of life or what her social programming would need to be expanded to include interaction with others in the larger community. Although the latter position intuitively appears to be advantageous for promoting quality of life when compared to provision of attendant care alone (for reasons of social support), research needs to be conducted to answer such questions. The effects of aging on social functioning of SCI and other disabled persons as compared to nondisabled persons need to be investigated. This is particularly important in forensic rehabilitation where the common needs of aging must be separated from the specific needs associated with impairment or disability in order to properly judge the cost of care associated with injuries.

Traumatic Brain Injury

Kaplan (1993) studied "a group of 25 individuals (72% men) with severe brain injury, and their significant others, all of whom were interviewed" 1, 3, and 5 years after injury. "Results showed a trend of improvement in psychological and social functioning between one and five years." However, psychosocial deficits continued for some study participants, even after 5 years. Kaplan used the Portland Adaptability Inventory (PAI) for data-gathering. This instrument has three major subscales, one of which is Activities and Social Behavior. "Results also showed that Social Behavior and Activities were improved between 1 and 5 years, but not between 1 and 3 years or between 3 and 5 years." Of the participants, 48% "experienced mild problems with disrupted social relationships, and most were also rated as having fewer social contacts, less leisure activity, and continuing, albeit subtle, difficulties with social interactions." Kaplan's study was consistent with other studies which indicated that physical restoration tended to outstrip psychosocial gains. He suggests that "social functioning may not be fully remediable" for persons with traumatic brain injury. Although Kaplan does not directly address quality of life issues in general or social well-being in particular in his study, it defines the need to address the social domain of human function when addressing the needs of traumatically brain-injured persons (TBI). TBI patients find themselves not only coping with a newly acquired disability, but also, because so many brain injuries occur as the result of motor vehicle accidents, with the stress of litigation.

Granger et al. (1995) studied the overall life satisfaction of 22 TBI patients and found a significant inverse correlation between general life satisfaction and depression ($r = -0.66$). Level of life satisfaction went up as level of supervision declined, suggesting that excessive supervision (attendant care or structured day programming being the most commonly seen forms of supervision) may actually produce a negative effect on life satisfaction and supporting use of treatment strategies which promote independence where possible. Of equal interest was that ability to toilet transfer was found to be inversely related to minutes of help needed per day, while other cognitive and emotional variables were not seen as significant. It appeared from the results of this study that self-report of greater physical and psychological illness as well as fatigue and depression resulted in a reduction in overall community integration. This, in turn, suggests that social interaction with others is influenced by one's physical and psychological status, reinforcing the perception that for persons with TBI as with other persons with disabilities, socialization does not occur independent of other factors that affect life satisfaction.

THE FORENSIC REHABILITATIONIST'S ROLE IN ASSESSING SOCIAL WELL-BEING

If there is any doubt about the relationship between rehabilitation and social functioning as a paramount issue in rehabilitation practice, readers are referred to Kelley and Lambert's (1992) review of family support research in rehabilitation. They found 13,000 publications on this topic from 1980 through 1990. However, fewer than 40 of these were data-based studies. They selected 17 studies to review in depth, and the samples within these studies "were composed of persons with severe disabilities including blindness, cardiac impairments and strokes, spinal cord injuries, end-stage renal disease, sickle cell anemia, and chronic pain." The benefits of familial support were improved psychological and physical well-being, and "even mortality" as noted above in the beginning of the literature review in this Chapter. The studies were heterogeneous in their "definitions of family and social support." Three of seven studies examined "the quality of client-family interaction as the source of support; four others considered a single function of support," and "four of seven studies reported more positive outcomes in supportive interpersonal contexts." Although methodological issues and a need for more empirical studies were noted, Kelley and Lambert's 1992 review emphasizes the longstanding nature of the importance of family and social support within the purview of the rehabilitation profession.

For forensic rehabilitation consultants, it may be comforting to know that almost every quality of life instrument identified in this book has a social domain component. The task then is selecting the proper instrument which should be suited to the ethnic and cultural background of the client being evaluated. If a life care plan is proposed, particularly a life care plan without a vocational plan, then rehabilitationists are cautioned to select instruments which do not crush leisure/recreation into the social domain. If such instruments are used, then the meaningful leisure needs of the client may not be identified and regarding the overall quality of life improvements needed will not be available for considerations by the parties involved in litigation.

An interesting tendency in the quality of life literature which addresses the social domain is to put work within the social domain or to identify the work role as a social role. Indeed, in Chapter 8, The Vocational Domain, we will find that there is a dynamic interaction between quality of work life and quality of family life in more than one study. However, since the conceptual entry point for most rehabilitationists into quality of life issues is through work or work impairment, and because work has such a profound effect on most people's lives, we have separated work from the social domain. As we shall see in both the vocational domain and the social domain, there is often a curious neglect of the important social relationships which are derived from the experience of working: relationships with co-workers, supervisors, clients, customers, and colleagues. And yet, the loss of these relationships and/or the resulting destruction of these relationships because of a workers' compensation, employment discrimination, or sexual harassment lawsuit brought about by an injured person is seen over and over by forensic rehabilitationists. Work provides opportunity for social interaction; no work deprives persons with disabilities of these opportunities for social contact.

Rehabilitation care planning needs to address the impact of all interventions on the social domain of human function. Where changes in frequency and quality of social interactions has or will result from impairment or disability, rehabilitationists need to plan effectively for dealing with the social needs of the individual. Interventions designed to deal with physical, cognitive, emotional, vocational, or economic needs may have anticipated or unanticipated social consequences which need to be understood.

Readers who are interested in examining the concept of social skills as it relates to social well-being are directed to Chapter 9, The Cognitive Domain, since the authors choose to put skill, adjustment, and adaptation issues within the cognitive domain of quality of life no matter what other life quality domain may overlap. The ability to relate well to others is considered a skill, and if this is so, then it can be learned or acquired and therefore falls into the cognitive sphere.

REFERENCES

Bach, M. and Rioux, M. H. (1996). Social well-being: a framework for quality of life research. In R. Renwick, I. Brown, and M. Nagler (Eds.), *Quality of Life in Health Promotion and Rehabilitation*, pp. 63-74. Thousand Oaks, CA: Sage Publications.

Baker, F., Jodrey, D., and Intagliata, J. (1992). Social support and quality of life of community support clients. *Community Mental Health Journal*, 28(5): 397-411.

Bigelow, D. A., McFarland, B. H., and Olson, M. M. (1991). Quality of life of community mental health program clients: validating a measure. *Community Mental Health Journal*, 27(1): 43-55.

Brown, C., Cosgrove, N., and DeSelm, T. (1997). Barriers interfering with life satisfaction for individuals with severe mental illness. *Psychiatric Rehabilitation Journal*, 20(3): 67-71.

Brown, I. (1996). The quality of life of marginal citizens: homelessness. In R. Renwick, I. Brown, and M. Nagler (Eds.), *Quality of Life in Health Promotion and Rehabilitation*, pp. 204-218. Thousand Oaks, CA: Sage Publications.

Callahan, S. (1992). Quality of life. *Alzheimer Disease and Associated Disorders,* 6(3): 138-144.

Campbell, A., Converse, P. E., and Rodgers, W. L. (1976). *The Quality of American Life: Perceptions, Evaluations, and Satisfactions.* New York: Russell Sage Foundation.

Canales, S., Ganz, P. A., and Coscarelli, C.A. (1995). Translation and validation of a quality of life instrument for Hispanic American cancer patients: methodological considerations. *Quality of Life Research,* (4): 3-11.

Chaturvedi, S. K. (1991). What's important for quality of life to Indians — In relation to cancer. *Social Science Medicine*, 33(1): 91-94.

Chibnall, J. T. and Tait, R. C. (1990). The Quality of Life Scale: a preliminary study with chronic pain patients. *Psychology and Health*, 4: 283-292.

Clayton, K.S. and Chubon, R. A. (1994). Factors associated with the quality of life of long-term spinal cord injured persons. *Archives of Physical Medicine and Rehabilitation*, 75, 633-638.

Corten, P., Mercier, C. and Pele, I. (1994). Subjective quality of life: clinical model for assessment of rehabilitation treatment in psychiatry. *Social Psychiatry and Psychiatric Epidemiology*, 29(4): 178-183.

Cox, D. J. and Gonder-Frederick, L. (1992). Major developments in behavioral diabetes research. *Journal of Consulting and Clinical Psychology*, 60(4): 628-638.

Cummins, R. A. (1991). The Comprehensive Quality of Life Scale — Intellectual Disability: an instrument under development. *Australia and New Zealand Journal of Development Disabilities*, 17(2): 259-264.

Ensminger, M. E. (1995). Welfare and psychological distress: a longitudinal study of African American urban mothers. *Journal of Health and Social Behavior*, 36: 346-359.

Ferrell, B., Grant, M., Padilla, G., Vemuri, S., and Rhiner, M. (1991). The experience of pain and perceptions of quality of life: Validation of a conceptual model. *The Hospice Journal*, 7(3): 9-24.

Ferrans, C. E., Cohen, F. L., and Smith, K. M. (1992). The quality of life of persons with narcolepsy. *Loss, Grief and Care*, 5(3-4): 23-32.

Flanagan, J. C. (1978). A research approach to improving our quality of life. *American Psychologist*, 33(2): 138-147.

Fuhrer, R.J., Rintala, D.H., Hart, K.A., Clearman, R., and Young, M.E. (1992). Relationship of life satisfaction to impairment, disability, and handicap among persons with spinal cord injury living in the community. *Archives of Physical Medicine and Rehabilitation*, 73, 552-557.

Granger, C. V., Divan, N., and Fiedler, R.C. (1995). Functional assessment scales: a study of persons after traumatic brain injury. *American Journal of Physical Medicine and Rehabilitation*, 74(2), 107-113.

Hadorn, D. C. and Hays, R. D. (1991). Multitrait-multimethod analysis of health-related quality-of-life measures. *Medical Care*, 29(9): 829-840.

Hanestad, B. R. (1989). Insulin dependent diabetes mellitus and quality of life: a theoretical analysis. *Scandinavian Journal of Caring Sciences*, 3(3): 123-128.

Hanna, W. J. and Rogovsky, E. (1992). On the situation of African-American women with physical disabilities. *Journal of Applied Rehabilitation Counseling*, 23(4): 39-45.

Hays, R. D., Kallich, J. D., Mapes, D. L., Coons, S. J., and Carter, W. B. (1994). Development of the Kidney Disease Quality of Life Instrument. *Quality of Life Research*, 3: 329-338.

Helmstaedter, C. and Elger, C. E. (1994). Cognitive-behavioral aspects of quality of life in presurgical patients with epilepsy. *Journal of Epilepsy*, 7(3): 220-231.

Kaplan, S. P. (1993). Five-year tracking of psychosocial changes in people with severe traumatic brain injury. *Rehabilitation Counseling Bulletin*, 36(3): 151-159.

Kelley, S. D. M. and Lambert, S. S. (1992). Family support in rehabilitation: a review of the research, 1980-1990. *Rehabilitation Counseling Bulletin*, 36(2): 98-119.

Krause, J. S. (1996). Prediction of mortality after spinal cord injury: a 20-year prospective study. *Rehabilitation R and D Progress Reports*, 34: 298-299.

Mowry, R. L. (1988). Quality of life indicators for deaf and hard-of-hearing former VR clients. *Journal of Rehabilitation of the Deaf*, 21(3): 1-7.

Murrell, S. A. and Norris, F. H. (1983). Quality of life as the criterion for need assessment and community psychology. *Journal of Consulting Psychology*, 11(2): 88-97.

Perry, J. and Felce, D. (1995). Objective assessments of quality of life: how much do they agree with each other? *Journal of Community and Applied Social Psychology*, 5: 1-19.

Rhoads, D. L. and Raymond, J. S. (1981). Quality of life and the competent community. *American Journal of Community Psychology*, 9(3): 293-301.

Rintala, D. H., Hart, K. A., and Fuhrer, M. J. (1996). Perceived stress in individuals with spinal cord injury. In D. M. Krotoski, M. A. Nosek, and M. A. Turk (Eds.), *Women with Physical Disabilities: Achieving and Maintaining Health*, pp. 223-242. Baltimore: Paul H. Brookes Publishing.

Rioux, M. H. (1996). Overcoming the social construction of inequality as a prerequisite to quality of life. In R. Renwick, I. Brown, and M. Nagler (Eds.). *Quality of Life in Health Promotion and Rehabilitation*, pp. 119-133. Thousand Oaks, CA: Sage Publications.

Scuccimarra, D. J. and Speece, D. L. (1990). Employment outcomes and social integration of students with mild handicaps: the quality of life two years after high school. *Journal of Learning Disabilities*, 23(4): 213-219.

Sullivan, G., Wells, K. B., and Leake, B. (1992). Clinical factors associated with better quality of life in a seriously mentally ill population. *Hospital and Community Psychiatry*, 43(8): 794-798.

Siegrist, J. and Junge, A. (1990). Measuring the social dimension of subjective health in chronic illness. *Psychotherapy and Psychosomatics*, 54(2-3): 90-98.

Whelton, C., Pawlick, and Cardamone, J. (1997). Involving families in psychosocial rehabilitation. *Psychiatric Rehabilitation Journal*, 20(3): 57-60.

6 The Economic Domain

> Increasingly, the quality of life of patients is being transformed from an elusive topic for bioethicists and clinicians into a quantitative variable at home in clinical trials and economic models. Underlying this surge in quantitative representation of medical reality is the fundamental belief that the quantification of medical problems will yield meaningful solutions and thus contribute to medical progress.
>
> *Faden and LePlege, 1992*

As we discussed in the first chapter of this book, quality of life quantification has been explored in the legal system under the rubric of hedonics. Unfortunately, hedonics has not stood up to the *Daubert* challenge in the courts. This is because there is no accepted economic theory which adequately describes the value of a human life. The current forensic economic theories are presently cut off from the field of health economics as well, leaving forensic economists without a foundation in describing quality of life losses for persons with physical and psychological injuries.

As we shall see, economics plays an important role in health-related quality of life in at least three ways: discussions of quantifying quality of life and the development of the quality-adjusted life years (QALYS) or the well-being years approach, quality of life and income studies, and income and financial security as a quality of life domain in the health-related quality of life research literature.

THE QUANTIFICATION OF QUALITY OF LIFE LITERATURE REVIEW

> Quality of life scales can be used by resource allocators to aid economic planning for different groups of patients. Given finite resources, health managers look for a way for assessing the benefit of a unit cost of treatment to the quality of life of patients. This economic objective is associated particularly with the concept of Quality Adjusted Life Years (QALYS) and scales designed to measure QALYS.
>
> *Hyland, Finnis, and Irvine, 1991*

The 11 articles reviewed have been published in Great Britain, Canada, the U.S., and Sweden. The first article reviewed was published in 1973 and the last in 1996. The efforts to quantify quality of life are an international pursuit. The articles begin with the social indicators approach in 1973 and conclude with a 1996 analysis of Oregon's attempt to prioritize medical services for Medicaid recipients on a cost-effectiveness basis.

Gitter and Mostofsky (1973) address the use of social indicators to create a model for indexing quality of life. Their article is dominated by lists of questions which lay the groundwork for the problems inherent in assessing and quantifying quality of life. In some ways, all the subsequent articles attempt to address Gitter and Mostofsky's questions posed in 1973. Some of the questions are:

> How are the various aspects of a person's life related to each other? Should a social indicator be based on objective or subjective data? What is the relative importance of the respective components which constitute the entries for a single estimate of quality of life (as perceived by respondents)?

> How does the perceived quality of life affect a person's rating of the quality of his own life? How do the ratings of the level of quality and importance vary from one group to another? How are a person's ratings of the level of quality and importance of the various aspects of his life related to his personality and demographic characteristics?

Gitter and Mostofsky use the 1969 definition of quality of life domains by the U.S. Department of Health, Education and Welfare (HEW) as the HEW aspects: "health and illness, social mobility, physical environment, income and poverty, public order and safety, learning, science, and art, participation and alienation." They distinguish between objective and subjective indicators, with objective indicators being "factual information" and subjective indicators as "people's evaluations." Gitter and Mostofsky recommend the use of both sets of indicators in any quality of life assessment. They address the importance of this method by pointing out that

> although objective indicators are distinct and different from subjective ones in terms of both the nature of the data which is utilized and the information which is provided, they are related to each other. The similarity to economics is striking, insofar as people's evaluation of the economy affects their decision to buy (or sell), and thus influences, if only indirectly, the amount of goods actually produced. So too it would be reasonable to expect that a change in a subjective indicator, such as health, might influence the policy-makers to change government policy toward health, and thus change the level of health in the country.

Gitter and Mostofsky also bring up the problem of "importance" or the "weighting" of the various aspects of quality of life. This proved to be one of the important critiques of the Lost Pleasure of Life Scale (Berla et al., 1990) which uses four categories of enjoyment of life, with the weighting or assignment of weights requiring rather arbitrary judgments on the part of the investigator, which in turn might have involved purely personal values. Gitter and Mostofsky suggest that there is a way around this problem. They recommend the use of "a sample of respondents to various aspects on an Important vs. Unimportant scale .... The ratings can then be used as *empirically* derived weights for both HEW and non-HEW aspects of life." As we shall see, some researchers, notably Kaplan et al. (1991), have done just that. The purpose of this approach would be to aggregate several domains or indicators into a single index of quality of life as a whole. Gitter and Mostofsky recommend the use of such an indicator for the setting of priorities in quality of life policy and planning. They do not address the overall problem of what numerical value there is to a human life in the forensic arena, however.

The 1975 article by House et al. also identifies methodological problems similar to those identified by Gitter and Mostofsky such as "factor list generation, factor weighing and the influence of specific decisions on those weights." Both the 1973 and the 1975 articles offer models for solving the various problems listed.

Wilkins and Adams' 1983 article, published in a U.S. journal, examined health expectancy in Canada in the late 1970s. Their approach appears to be a forerunner of the QALYS concept, which they name as "quality-adjusted life expectancy." They calculated an index of health expectancy based on "estimates of activity restriction from the Canadian Health Survey, institutional data on long-term care, and survival data from vital statistics." Their Table, reprinted below (see Table II), examines health-expectancy by gender, age, region, and community size. Income levels proved to be a significant factor in "rates of activity restriction," which "were strikingly highest in the low income group, and lowest in the highest income group." Age and regional considerations were also important, and "while women outlived men by 7.5 years, that difference was reduced by half if only years free of any health-related activity restriction were considered." Wilkins and Adams also compared Canadians to U.S. citizens and found that Canadians had a "significant advantage over their American counterparts" in terms of short- or long-term disability, at both severe and moderate degrees of impairment."

TABLE III
Distribution of Health Expectancy of Each Sex, by Age, Region, Community Size, and Income Level, Canada, Late 1970s (in years)

	Life Expectancy			Disability-Free Life			Quality-Adjusted Life		
	M	F	T	M	F	T	M	F	T
Age									
At birth	70.8	78.3	74.6	59.2	62.8	61.0	65.8	71.7	68.7
15 years	57.2	64.5	60.9	46.2	49.4	47.8	52.4	58.1	55.2
25 years	48.1	54.8	51.5	37.6	40.4	39.0	43.5	48.7	46.1
45 years	29.6	35.7	32.7	20.6	23.6	22.1	25.6	30.5	28.1
65 years	14.4	18.7	16.7	8.2	9.9	9.1	11.5	14.7	13.3
75 years	8.9	11.7	10.6	4.6	5.2	5.0	6.9	8.6	7.9
Region									
Atlantic	70.5	78.3	74.4	56.7	61.8	59.2	64.4	71.2	67.8
Quebec	69.7	77.6	73.6	60.4	63.1	61.8	65.5	71.5	68.5
Ontario	71.2	78.4	74.8	59.5	63.7	61.6	66.1	72.1	69.1
Prairies	71.5	75.2	78.9	59.4	63.0	61.2	66.3	72.1	69.2
British Columbia	71.5	75.2	78.9	57.4	59.8	58.6	66.5	70.9	68.2
Community Size									
Less than 1000 and rural	69.1	76.0	72.5	56.6	63.6	60.1	63.8	71.0	67.4
1,000 — 9,999	69.9	78.1	74.0	56.7	62.2	59.4	64.3	71.6	68.0
10,000 — 99,999	69.8	77.8	73.8	58.4	64.1	61.2	64.9	72.2	68.6
100,000 — 999,999	70.1	77.7	73.9	59.1	62.1	60.0 6	65.5	71.3	68.4
1,000,000 and over	71.8	78.8	75.3	62.8	65.1	64.0	67.9	73.3	70.6
All size groups	70.2	77.5	73.8	59.3	63.2	61.3	65.6	71.7	68.6
Income Level									
Lowest	67.1	76.6	71.9	50.0	59.9	54.9	59.4	69.7	64.6
Second	70.1	77.6	73.8	57.9	61.8	59.9	64.8	71.1	68.0
Third	70.9	78.5	74.7	61.1	64.3	62.7	66.8	72.7	69.8
Fourth	72.0	79.0	75.5	62.6	63.5	63.1	68.1	72.8	70.5
Highest	73.4	79.4	76.4	64.3	67.5	65.9	69.7	74.8	72.3

From Wilkins, R. and Adams, O.B., *Am. J. Public Health,* 73(9), 1073–1080, 1983. With permission.

The researchers note the limitations inherent in their analysis. They point out the difficulty of valuing quantity and quality. That is, is it better to live a longer life in British Columbia but be less healthy than if one lived in Quebec and were male? They also addressed the disparities found in objective and subjective valuations of life in terms of "the practical difficulties of matching self-reported activity restrictions from household surveys to physician-reported causes of death from vital statistics."

The work of Wilkins and Adams was designed to be used for health planning, policy decisions and resource allocation. Consequently, this type of analysis is probably useful for examining the health of the population as a whole, but not for examining the life of an individual as forensic rehabilitationists and economists are expected to do. Such studies are important in the forensic arena, if only to establish a general pattern against which an individual can be contrasted.

Murrell and Norris' 1983 article also addresses resource allocation. They assert that "resource decisions should be dictated by the needs of the population, not those of elected officials or professional administrators." This assertion is consistent with the recommendations made by Gitter and Mostofsky in 1973. That is, the Murrell and Norris QOL–Contribution Model is based on a sophisticated needs assessment approach which is founded in the particular community under investigation. This what Gitter and Mostofsky would call the "evaluations" or the subjective indicators by the community of what is needed to improve that community's quality of life. Murrell and Norris also grapple with the weighting of life domains and offer a mathematical model to summarize their approach. They write:

> In this model, subjective QOL would be established first, perhaps by surveying a sample of the human unit. Then, with QOL known, the task is to solve for the weights for unmet need in the different life domains and types of program targets.

In other words, they also recommend getting a respondent sample in order to determine the importance or weight given to particular factors or domains.

A team of researchers at the University of California Medical Center in San Diego has developed a quality of life assessment tool based on random sampling of the San Diego population in order to determine the importance or weights of a variety of health-related symptoms in assessing quality of life. This random sampling was also completed in Oregon, with only minor differences between the two populations (Kaplan et al., 1991). The QWB-7 or Function Status Profile Classification and Quality of Well-Being Scale is "intended to be a standardized measure, meant to be used to cover all types of people in all types of situations. It is part of a resource allocation model and its purpose is to measure variations in the well-being of populations (Anderson, 1994)." The model referred to is Kaplan's (1991) General Health Policy Model (GHPM) which measures mortality (death); morbidity (dysfunction in mobility, physical, and social activity); utility (relative importance); and prognosis (duration of the illness), and translates this into QALYs or well-years by using The QWB 7. Kaplan et al. (1991) write:

> The quality of life component of the model considers behavioral scales of mobility, physical activity, social activity, and symptoms. The model also allows for the aggregation of profiles onto a single utility scale that ranges from 0 (for death) to 1.0 (optimum health), and this is a very important component of the model. These weights are derived from community surveys that assess the social preference or utility for observable states of function. A score of 0.60, for example, suggests that an individual is in observed state of functioning for which utility is about 60% of the distance between optimum functioning and death. The person remaining in this state for one year would have lost 0.40 (1.0–0.60) well-years of life.

A bibliography of 100 selected publications from the University of California San Diego group on this model and the evolution of the QWB 7 are available in the user's manual (Anderson, 1994). This is a reliable and valid instrument which has been in research and development processes since 1975. The four scales on this instrument are:

1. CPA or Symptom/Problem Complexes (CPA) with calculating measures or weights as determined in random community surveys. Examples of weighted symptoms include:
   a. Symptom #4: Itching from a rash in the genital region (0.349)
   b. Symptom #7: Pain in his feet (0.299)
   c. Symptom #8: Rash (0.292)
   d. Symptom #12: Depression (0.257)
   e. Symptom #14: Rash and Itching (0.240)
   f. Symptom #16: Need new glasses (0.230)
2. MOB or the Mobility Scale (driving, using public transportation, walking)
3. PAC or the Physical Activity Scale (performing daily activities)
4. SAC or the Social Activity Scale (includes questions about work and social roles).

When Kaplan et al. (1991) used the QWB 7 to examine quality of life issues by gender, their results looked very much like the findings of the Canadian researchers, Wilkins and Adams (1983), in that while women live longer than men, when quality of life is assessed, the female advantage is halved with only 3 additional years of health expectancy or QALYS as contrasted to the 7 to 7H years of life when quality of life is not taken into account. The advantage of using the QWB 7 is that one does not have to manipulate all the data the Canadian (or U.S. equivalent) researchers used (the Canadian Health Survey, institutional data on long-term care, and survival data from vital statistics) to get similar results. The QWB 7 assesses individual quality of life based on empirical data. For this reason, it is probably the best tool currently available for forensic rehabilitationists at this time. Research is needed to explore use of the QWB 7 with litigants filing personal injury and employment discrimination cases. Such studies would add to the luster of this well-respected approach by establishing it as a useful tool in the forensic arena. Despite this optimism, it should be understood that the New Mexico District Court did not allow testimony on the on the QWB 7 in a personal injury case. This was largely due to the remaining problem not yet solved by economists. What is the value of human life? The QWB 7 has been used primarily to ascertain whether or not health interventions are cost effective in terms of quality of life.

Jenkins' 1992 paper, published in Great Britain, is noted here, if only for its delineation for 11 conceptual and methodological issues in the assessment of health intervention outcomes or health-related quality of life. It is interesting that such papers are being published nearly 20 years after Gitter and Mostofsky's article of 1973 in which many of the same issues are raised. Jenkins cautions us all to understand that "health policy decisions will increasingly be based on outcome studies of health-related quality of life." The difference between 1973 and 1992 seems to be the use of the QALYs approach, which Jenkins describes as "futures" in his three-pronged definition of quality of life as "feelings, functions," and "futures." "Futures" is explained as follows:

> The prognosis for future continuation of adequate feelings and functions. Hypertension or cellular changes prodromal to malignancy do not involve either discomfort or dysfunction. They do lower QOL, however, because they confer a poor prognosis. The "Futures" component emphasizes that there is a time-dimension integral to all QOL determination and that duration of life must be balanced against its quality as in the concept of Quality Adjusted Life Year (QALYs).

Of course, duration of a condition is an essential element in any rehabilitative analysis and is particularly important in the forensic analysis, since duration will determine how long a plaintiff might be out of work or adjust to a disability, or have to be alive, or experience a change in his or her quality of life. Jenkins calls for moving from "judging outcomes to assessing them by a psychometrically acceptable procedure."

In addition to the use of quality of life assessment in allocating health resources, Jenkins notes that such assessment can also address questions of "individual diagnoses of the adequacy of a patient's recovery" and "as a basis for referrals for specialized rehabilitation services."

Another paper published in Great Britain by Wilkinson et al. (1992) explored the use of the QALYs approach in mental health by using the Charing Cross Health Indicator (CH-X). "The CH-X is based on assessments of (i) distress and (ii) disability." They found that their "results suggest that with respect to quality of life in mental health settings measurements of distress may be of greater importance than disability." They also found that the CH-X may "primarily reflect physical disability as opposed to social disability." The bias toward physical disability was noted in an example:

> a person with a mental disorder can score above 5 on the disability dimension only by being unconscious, confined to bed or to a wheelchair.... In the overall QALY result this would present a bias towards many medical programmes.

Jenkins notes that the CH-X is not the only health-related quality of life instrument which demonstrates such a bias. He suggests that "it should be recognized that social disability can, in some circumstances, infringe upon one's ability to pursue normal activities just as much as physical disability." He critiques the QALYs approach, which relies upon the extension of life for a health intervention, something mental health programs rarely claim. His solution for this problem is the use of program-specific quality of life assessment tools which are multidimensional in nature.

Another use of the QALY approach in a health setting was explored by Shulman and Cohen in their 1993 paper. They conducted an "economic analysis of community programs for caregivers of dementia patients" by reviewing the clinical data on caregiver stress and the effectiveness of a variety of interventions. Shulman and Cohen assert that the "traditional cost-benefit analysis may not be appropriate" for evaluating effectiveness of community support programs for caregivers. Therefore, they recommend use of the cost–utility ratio or QALYs approach.

Johannesson (1994), Swedish health economist, offers a highly technical analysis of the use of QALYs and an emerging health economic concept of Healthy-Years Equivalents (HYEs). HYEs "is the number of years in full health that is considered equivalent to the lifetime health profile." The "health expectancy" table (reprinted above) developed by the Canadian researchers, Wilkins and Adams, in 1983 appears to be a forerunner of the HYEs model. While browsing the Internet under the topic of "QALYs," we found an abstract written by Walter Ried titled, "QALYs vs. HYEs — What is Right and What is Wrong." Ried notes that the QALYs approach is now about 20 years old and was developed for the purpose of "assessing changes in mortality and morbidity in terms of individual preferences. Recently, it has been challenged by the healthy-year equivalent (HYE) approach which, according to its proponents, is theoretically superior." Readers fascinated by the technical aspects of economic theory are referred to both Johannesson's paper (1994) and Ried's abstract (1997). The May 1995 issue of the *Journal of Health Economics* may also be worth exploring, since it is devoted to the QALYs vs. HYEs debate.

Tengs (1996), a health economist at Duke University, reviews the various attempts by the state of Oregon to prioritize health care to Medicaid recipients. She notes that "Oregon, like all states, has always rationed medical care." Oregon created the Oregon Health Services Commission to prioritize medical services. In their original effort to come up with a cost-effectiveness formula, the Commission included a quality of life approach. "Quality of life was defined as the sum of the products of 1) the probability of being in a particular health state in five years, and 2) the quality of life associated with the state." They obtained data from panels of health practitioners, and a telephone survey of Oregonians was conducted using a quality of life measure. Cost-effectiveness was then defined as "quality-adjusted duration" or the number of years over which the treatment benefited the patient. Because of methodological problems, the 1990 list "was widely criticized because it included a number of obviously faulty rankings. Treatment for thumb-sucking and acute headaches, for example, received higher ranking than treatment for AIDS or cystic fibrosis." This list was quickly withdrawn and "they also completely abandoned their efforts to order the list by cost-effectiveness." As a result, quality of life considerations were also lost at that time. Tengs concludes that

> Ranking by cost-effectiveness, rigorously defined and measured, is the only algorithm that has any hope of achieving efficiency. Because Oregon did not ration care based on cost-effectiveness, their basic benefits package fails to maximize health outcomes to Medicaid recipients.

Additional browsing on the Internet under the term "QALYs" yielded a home page for the Centre for Health Economics which has six major areas of research:

> outcome measurement (quality of life measurement and the estimation of quality adjusted life years (QALYs), economic evaluation of alternative technologies (technology assessment), primary care, community care, and the determinants of health (other than health care).

The Centre for Health Economics can be found at (http://www.york.ac.uk/inst/che/che.htm).

The QALYs concept has been further developed in the Q-Twist Method (Quality-adjusted Time Without Symptoms of Disease and Toxicity of Treatment) (Gelber et al., 1995). Siegel and Brent (1997) report using this method to explore the development of a quality-adjusted-time measure in which the evaluation of time will be adjusted to reflect various "states" for schizophrenic patients, such as in-hospital, in-community without symptoms, in-community with symptoms.

The point of this part of the literature review is to emphasize that the very lively field of health economics may finally evolve to the stage where its findings and models can be extended to forensic economics, thereby providing economists with the needed tools to provide dollar valuations based on psychometrically sound assessments of quality of life conducted by rehabilitationists on the behalf of litigants filing personal injury and employment discrimination lawsuits. Such a development would mean that we would finally have a methodology based in the scientific literature using empirical methods. Regular browsing of the Internet on health economics is strongly recommended for readers who wish to keep up with this rapidly developing field.

Income and Overall Quality of Life Studies

> Financial resources: This facet explores the person's view of how his/her financial resources (and other exchangeable resources) meet his/her needs for a healthy and comfortable lifestyle. The focus is on what the person can afford or cannot afford that might affect his/her quality of life.
>
> *WHOQOL Group, 1994*

There are surprisingly few studies with an explicit focus on level of income and quality of life and none of the studies reviewed here are found in the rehabilitation literature. This is an inexplicable lack when the experience of rehabilitation providers in various rehabilitation systems (workers' compensation, Social Security Disability, state departments of rehabilitation, and litigation pertaining to vocational impairment) is considered. That is, the change in financial status and attempts to regain the previous financial status (workers' compensation, welfare-to-work programs, and litigation settings) or achieve a minimally acceptable level of income (minimum wage job, settlement, or some form of public assistance) are the very reason for the existence of the rehabilitation discipline. Rehabilitation practitioners in workers' compensation systems have directly observed the very real pain and distress experienced by injured workers who may end up losing their homes, their cars, and their credit ratings as they struggle with the greatly reduced income they receive from workers' compensation systems. Practitioners are also often called upon to exercise all of their counseling skills in assisting workers in confronting the reduced wages most face when moving from one occupation to another because of their newly acquired disability. Perhaps the obvious nature of financial status and its relationship to quality of life places it beyond the need for direct inquiry and research. That is, we just assume that financial status will influence the quality of life for all persons.

This was the finding of a 1981 article published by Rhoads and Raymond who conducted a study of 547 adults living in Phoenix, AZ. They used the Bradburn Affect–Balance Scale and a self-report regarding mental well-being in their interviews conducted in the home. They found that

> lower income was significantly related to poor self-rated mental health ..., low scores on the Bradburn Scale ..., and low levels of satisfaction with overall life quality.... In addition, low income was significantly related to low levels of satisfaction on 12 of the 15 quality of life components. The three components which were *not* related to income level were measures of satisfaction with helping others, government participation, and creative expression.

The other 12 quality of life components in this study were: health and safety, material comforts, relationship with spouse, satisfying work, learning, passive and active recreation, socializing, understanding self, close friends, community, and personal functioning.

The Select Committee on Aging, House of Representatives, conducted hearings on the quality of life of older women in the U.S. in 1988. In their summary report, when listing the factors which affect the quality of life for older women, income was on the top of the list of factors which also included health and housing. The Committee reported

> Poverty affects women disproportionately throughout their lives, but particularly in their later years. Two out of every five mid-life and older women are poor or near-poor. Women are the primary victims of poverty among the aged: 72% of all poor over 65 are women. Ethnic and racial minority women are considerably poorer than other older women.

The Committee lists some of the interrelated reasons for women's poverty as "limited or intermittent stays in the paid labor force," caretaking roles of family members (necessitating leaving paid work or reducing paid work), reduction in Social Security benefits as a result of intermittent work, and an inability to contribute to other types of pension plans. Discrimination based on gender and age are also factors. Only data relating to women's poverty levels, health status, and housing trends are addressed in this report. Other than the title of the summary report, "The Quality of Life for Older Women: Older Women Living Alone," no explicit discussion of quality of life issues was included in the report.

Mugenda et al.'s (1990) study assessed the "casual relationship among communication, money management practices, satisfaction with financial status, and quality of life. They found that "satisfaction with Quality of Life is predicted by Income (economic factors) and Satisfaction with Financial Status (subjective variable).

Morris and Lewis (1991) investigated the "relationship between entrepreneurship and societal quality of life." One of their seven components of societal quality of life is the economic dimension defined as:

> the general state of the economy as reflected by economic vitality; economic stability; the position of the economy within the world economy; and the availability of goods and services.

The "effects of entrepreneurship" on a functional basis were found to be: "Greater economic vitality via increases in GNP and the creation of jobs. Increased societal wealth and higher standards of living." On a dysfunctional basis, the effects of entrepreneurship were: "Creation of individual wealth vs. societal wealth. Higher risk use of resources. More pronounced cyclical swings in the economy. Loss in the competitive position of large, established firms."

Rettig et al. (1991) examined family life quality using a resource exchange theory. Two variables in their study were "goods resource class" and "money resource class." The goods resource class included "material goods enjoyed, things you have that are your own possessions, the space available for your privacy, adequacy of household equipment for your needs, the gifts you receive from your family at special times, the things you have access to for your hobbies." The money resource class included "money available for your own clothing, amount of money available for personal use, prospects you have for a financially secure future, family income and how it enables you to live, the cooperation you receive in working toward financial goals, amount of money the family has saved for emergencies, amount of health insurance protection you have, and amount of disability insurance protection you have." The researchers found that "the measures of the goods and money resource classes are not yet as effective as the measures of love, status, and services" in family quality of life.

In a study of African-American mothers on welfare, Ensminger (1995) found that "welfare recipients reported less well-being on all the measures except self-esteem." In addition, almost 19% of the African-American women on welfare had chronic illness as compared to 7% of those never on welfare, and African-American women who had received welfare benefits did have problems with self-esteem and psychological distress in their later lives. The relationship between vulnerability to chronic disease and disability and welfare receipt for this group is a timely issue considering the new findings on the levels of ongoing and histories of domestic violence among welfare recipients (Raphael, 1996). That is, in a national telephone survey of welfare-to-work programs, Raphael found that 50 to 80% of the recipients were either experiencing ongoing domestic violence or had histories of domestic violence. As noted in Chapter 3, The Psychological Domain, study of the impact of traumatic abuse on quality of life is in its infancy. However, the combination of trauma and the low income only available over a very short period of time in a welfare mother's life will most likely have devastating effects on her quality of life and that of her children. To date, the Welfare Reform Movement has paid scant attention to quality of life issues for the recipients and their children.

Short and Shea (1995) examined quality of life for those whose family income was below the poverty line and those who participated in Aid to Families with Dependent Children (AFDC). The data were collected from the Survey of Income and Program Participation from September to December of 1992 — that is, prior to the current enactment of the welfare reform provisions now in place. Short and Shea report that "on all the measures reported here, the poor are significantly worse off than the nonpoor." In terms of the measures of durable goods, crime and neighborhood, basic needs, and health and nutrition, the poor fell short. That is, the poor "were less likely to own or have access to a telephone." "Twenty-eight percent of the nonpoor families reported having access to a personal computer at home, while only 7 percent of persons in poor families and 4 percent of those in AFDC families had access to a personal computer." Poor families were also less likely to live in safe neighborhoods. In terms of basic needs, "twenty-six percent of the poor and 29 percent of those on AFDC lived in families that were unable to pay the full rent or mortgage at some point in the last year." Eviction rates were higher as well. Poor families were often not able to go to a doctor or dentist when they needed to and they were more likely to go without food or not have enough money to buy food. The researchers developed a "deprivation index" in order to determine the cumulative effect of various types of deprivations (e.g., having electricity turned off or phone disconnected, not having enough food). Deprivation levels among the poor were much higher than for the nonpoor.

The consensus among these studies appears to be that income near or at the poverty level has the effect of reducing life satisfaction and well-being.

INCOME AS A DOMAIN OF HEALTH-RELATED QUALITY OF LIFE

> The most common barriers (to life satisfaction) identified by consumers included inadequate finances ...
>
> *Brown, Cosgrove, and DeSelm 1997*

The World Health Organization's (WHO) Quality of Life Group (WHOQOL Group) (1994) is in the process of developing an international instrument for quality of life assessment. Financial resources are listed under the domain of Environment on the WHOQOL Group quality of life instrument. The questions are listed under two categories, perceived objective and self-report subjective as follows:

> Perceived Objective: Have you enough money to meet your needs? Do you get enough money to meet your needs? How well are you able to meet your needs with the money you have? How well can you manage on your money? Do you have financial difficulties?
>
> Self-Report Subjective: How satisfied are you with the way the money you have takes care of your needs? How satisfied are you with the amount of money you have? How satisfied are you with your financial situation? How much do you worry about money?

Response scales with cultural sensitivity have been developed for this instrument, and involve a five-point scale ranging from "Very Satisfied" to "Very Dissatisfied."

This pattern in the WHOQOL studies, examining objective and subjective quality of life issues in the economic domain, can also be found in a smattering of health-related quality of life literature which ranges from quality of life for deaf and hard-of-hearing clients to persons with spinal cord injuries.

Deaf and Hard-of-Hearing

Mowry (1988) examined the quality of life indicators for deaf and hard-of-hearing vocational rehabilitation clients 3H years after case closure. He used both objective and subjective data in his study, which engaged 81 former clients. Mowry used a quality of life format similar to that of Campbell et al. (1976), in which "respondents were asked to rate their satisfaction with selected aspects of their lives." Three of the eight dimensions were economic: financial security, savings, and standard of living. Objective data were also collected, including income levels. The results revealed that "three and a half years after closure, 63.2% (*n = 24) of the deaf and 53.5% (n = 23) of the hard-of-hearing respondents were employed in the competitive labor market." Mowry also noted that these employed workers "had weekly earnings that were considerably lower than other workers in the state of Arkansas. The deaf respondents' average earnings were $224.08 per week; the hard-of-hearing workers had average weekly earnings of $198.35."* These low earnings did not lower overall satisfaction with jobs. That is, "the majority (86.9%) of both samples said they were satisfied or very satisfied with their job." Unemployed persons included "spouses earnings, Social Security Disability Insurance, Supplemental Security Income, welfare payments, and other types of income." This income did not represent financial security for the recipients. Dissatisfaction with the economic domain in this study was found in the area of lack of savings with 66.7% of the hard-of-hearing dissatisfied or very dissatisfied and 47.4% of the deaf also expressing dissatisfaction with this element. On the other hand, 81.8% of the deaf and 67.5% of the hard-of-hearing respondents "reported being satisfied or very satisfied" with their standard of living. What is interesting about this study is that the economic domain was refined into three different elements or facets, with differing results in life satisfaction or subjective quality of life.

Mental Illness

Gerber et al.'s 1994 study of the quality of life of persons with psychiatric disabilities after discharge from hospitalization involved interviewing "43 clients 1 and 3 years following discharge from a psychiatric programme" in Ontario, Canada. These researchers utilized the Clients' Quality of Life Interview and the Uniform Client Data Instrument. Nine domains of quality of life were selected and two of the domains were economic: "amount of money received per month" and "disposable income." The data collected were primarily objective. There was no change in economic domains scores between their first year and 3 years' postdischarge interviews and data collection. On an objective level, "all clients were living below the poverty line for single individuals living in Canadian cities. The major sources of income in 1990 were disability pensions and family benefits." Although the researchers report no change from the 1988 study to the 1990 study in subjective evaluations of the respondents, they failed to report what the subjective evaluations of the psychiatrically disabled respondents were (regarding having to live at below poverty level income).

Fabian (1992) investigated the quality of life for 110 individuals with severe mental illness. She compared supported employment and nonsupported employment groups using the Quality of Life Interview which contains eight domains of quality of life. One of those domains is "finances." She also assessed global life satisfaction using a 7-point Likert scale ranging from 1 = terrible to 7 = delighted. A higher quality of life was found with the supported employment group within the domain of finances. Fabian also notes that differences between subjective and objective quality of life need to be taken into account. However, she did not address this issue in terms of the financial or economic domain.

Mental Retardation

Inge et al. (1988) reported on the quality of life for individuals placed into competitive employment vs. individuals remaining in sheltered workshop settings. Twenty individuals with mental retardation were working in competitive jobs. Twenty individuals with mental retardation in shelter workshop settings were identified as the control group. Several instruments were used, but "the Parent/Guardian Survey was developed to assess individual performance" in several life skill areas including "financial activity." The Fiscal Responsibility Subscale on this Survey "indicates gradual decline in the control group but dramatic improvement in the experimental group." The researchers caution that their study is "severely hindered by a number of procedural problems encountered throughout the study," making "clear interpretation of the results difficult." For example, the Fiscal Responsibility Subscale appears to be focused on objective data and skill acquisition. The researchers ask the following in their paper: "However, does skill acquisition translate into improvement of quality of life?" Unfortunately, they do not answer the question for us.

Sinnott-Oswald et al. (1991) also examined supported and sheltered employment for adults with mental retardation. They studied three groups: supported employment (SE), sheltered workshop employment (SW), and a control group without disabilities. Each group was assigned ten individuals. A Quality of Life Questionnaire was developed by the researchers and they also conducted a Quality of Life Survey. The Survey contained the question: "Have you noticed any change (within the past year) in income?" "Significant relationships were also found between group type and job skills ... and group type and income." The SE group had higher income. The measure of income was a perceived "change in income." The SW group did not notice a difference in income. Apparently, the economic data is subjective in nature since it is based on the participants' perceptions. No mention of objective data regarding finances was noted in this paper.

Halpern (1994) examined quality of life for students in special education making the transition from school to adulthood. Halpern identifies "physical and material well-being" as fundamental to other quality of life outcomes. Within the category of physical and material well-being, "financial security" is included as an aspect. In his review of 41 studies, Halpern found that the content area, financial security, was used 31 times with a 76% rate of use. Only career and employment, at 100%, exceeded the financial security content level in these 41 studies. Halpern does not report on a specific study but provides an overview of past studies and a model for outcome or quality of life research in school to work transition programs. The point is that financial security is considered an important quality of life domain by a majority of researchers in this field.

Older Consumers

Sherman and Schiffman (1991) reflect on

> the evolving QOL status of older consumers" by using "a two-category QOL framework consisting of *objective* components (e.g., socioeconomic indicators, health and longevity, housing, and family living arrangements, and gender differences) and *subjective* components (e.g., life satisfaction and cognitive age) to explore the QOL of older consumers.

In terms of the economic domain, the change in the objective economic status of the older consumer is noted. "Within the past twenty years, the financial situation of the elderly population has dramatically improved in comparison to younger age cohorts." The authors do note that "deep poverty subsegments" continue to exist. They include the chronically ill and frail old–elderly women. The chronic low income of older women is reported as compared to men. This statistic has tended to remain stable over time. In terms of subjective quality of life, older consumers were the least satisfied with their income. Only 59% expressed such satisfaction. Sherman and Schiffman also reported that "older respondents' economic situation (an objective index of QOL) is psychologically very important to them, and thus strongly impacts on their perceived or subjective well-being."

Renal Disease

Koch and Muthny (1990) examined the changes in life satisfaction through the kidney transplant process with 761 kidney patients in Germany. Improvement in life satisfaction in most quality of life domains were found after transplant. "No improvements were found in vocational and financial situations." Life satisfaction data were based on subjective findings.

Spinal Cord Injury

Boschen (1996) collected 92 questionnaires, Living with a Spinal Cord Injury, from 82 Canadian "urban-dwelling individuals with spinal cord injury." This study examined life satisfaction in terms of the objective data collected on income. The "average annual income was under $10,000 (Canadian), and in almost half of the cases, under $5,000 (Canadian)." They also looked at life satisfaction or subjective perceptions and "life satisfaction was found to be highly correlated with self-concept … and was also correlated with health status, income level, residential satisfaction, locus of control, residential choice, and congruence." Quality of life or life satisfaction was not correlated with disability severity or duration.

THE ROLE OF THE FORENSIC REHABILITATIONIST IN ASSESSMENT OF THE ECONOMIC DOMAIN

> There is not an easy relationship between the quantitative approaches to estimating quality of life (i.e., via Cost Utility Analysis (CUA) and Quality Adjusted Life Years (QALYs)) and qualitative measures that emphasize client–patient satisfaction and are more amenable for program planning or as process measures.
>
> *Parmenter, 1996*

The need for quality of life assessment in rehabilitation practice is not going to go away despite the current controversies about how quality of life is to be quantified. A new journal, *Journal of Rehabilitation Outcomes Research,* advertised in various professional journals in summer of 1997, is just one example of the increasing demand for quality of life assessment procedures by rehabilitationists. This is because outcomes research is quality of life research, whether or not it is taking place on a program evaluation level or on an individual level with rehabilitation consumers. The new demand for outcomes research also reflects the demand in the new managed health care era that health interventions, including rehabilitation interventions, demonstrate a cost–utility benefit or improvement in quality of life over a designated period of time. The independent living and disability rights movement of persons with disabilities also creates a demand that rehabilitation intervention be assessed in terms of their quality of life enhancement or diminishment. All of these pressures will come to bear on the forensic rehabilitationist sooner or later, depending on the legal environment where the rehabilitationist is located.

At present, we find ourselves in the very awkward position of dealing with quality of life issues for litigants on both objective and subjective levels. That is, rehabilitationists have always collected data regarding the client's objective financial status, while at the same time collecting subjective data which might impact upon the litigant's earning capacity after a physical or psychological injury. The potential earning capacity of a litigant is based on both subjective factors (e.g., vocational interest, work values, psychological health) and objective factors (e.g., disability status, educational attainment level). These data are then synthesized into what was called the "counseling hypothesis" in graduate rehabilitation counseling programs. In other words, what is the counselor's idea about the problem presented and what are the needed rehabilitative interventions? One the hypothesis was established, the counselor or evaluator would use her or his clinic judgment in order to proceed. At present, because of the current application or misapplication of the *Daubert* standard, all subjective data are suspect because they are not "objective" and all clinical judgment has now somehow become "subjective" for the forensic evaluator no matter his or her training, background, or experience. At the same time, the consensus of opinion among quality of life researchers from many disciplines is that both subjective and objective data must be gathered to get an accurate quality of life assessment. The methodology for assessing quality of life is not different from the methodology used by rehabilitation practitioners in evaluating and developing rehabilitative plans.

Feldbaum (1997) calls for the development of a "hybrid admissibility standard under *Daubert*" which would include "science, technology, and diverse areas of special knowledge." Presently, vocational and rehabilitative expert testimony has been greeted with "an inconsistent and unstandardized manner" in the admissibility of such testimony in the courts. This has proved to be absolutely true when the quantification of quality of life for an individual litigant is presented. As we have stated over and over in this book, the problem here is with the discipline of economics, which has not yet developed an acceptable methodology to value human life or quality of life. It is our opinion that such a methodology is being developed by health economists in an international effort found in the QALYs and related approaches. The problem remains, however, of the starting number. It is our opinion that such a number will have to be legislated or come to in such way as to reflect the values of the overall community much in the same way that we have legislated caps on damages in employment discrimination cases at $300,000.00. Once this has been accomplished, then the QALYs approach could be used. Without a hybrid admissibility standard under *Daubert,* however, it is not known if the QALYs approach then would be accepted.

The authors predict, however, that the development of accepted economic techniques for valuing human life will come from the health economics discipline and not from economists working on theories of hedonics. This is because health economics is grounded in outcomes research which examines the effectiveness of medical intervention with disease process and disabling conditions. Such outcomes research is now demanded in all health care disciplines, including the rehabilitation discipline, and the emerging subspecialty of life care planning or care planning within forensic rehabilitation practice is based on the concept of outcome evaluations.

REFERENCES

Anderson, J. P. (1994, May). *Interviewer Manual: Quality of Well-Being Scale Instrument QWB 7.* La Jolla, CA: University of California San Diego.

Berla, E. P., Brookshire, M. L. and Smith, S. V. (1990). Hedonic damages and personal injury: a conceptual approach. *Journal of Forensic Economics,* 3(1): 1-8.

Boschen, K. A. (1996). Correlates of life satisfaction, residential satisfaction, and locus of control among adults with spinal cord injuries. *Rehabilitation Counseling Bulletin,* 39(4): 230-243.

Brown, C., Cosgrove, N., and DeSelm, T. (1997, Winter). Barriers interfering with life satisfaction for individuals with severe mental illness. *Psychiatric Rehabilitation Journal,* 20(3): 67-71.

Campbell, A., Converse, P., and Rodgers, W. (1976). *The Quality of American Life.* New York: Russell Sage.

Ensminger, M. E. (1995). Welfare and psychological distress: a longitudinal study of African American urban mothers. *Journal of Health and Social Behavior,* 36: 346-359.

Fabian, E. S. (1992). Supported employment and the quality of life: does a job make a difference? *Rehabilitation Counseling Bulletin,* 36(2): 84-97.

Faden, R. and Leplege, A. (1992). Assessing quality of life: moral implications for clinical practice. *Medical Care*, 30(5): 166-175.

Feldbaum, C. L. (1997). The *Daubert* decision and its interaction with the federal rules. *Journal of Forensic Vocational Assessment*, 1(1): 49-73.

Gelber, R.D., Cole, B.F., Gelber, S., and Goldhirsch, A. (1995). Comparing treatments using quality-adjusted survival: the Q-TWIST method. *American Statistics,* 49: 161-169.

Gerber, G. J., Coleman, G. E., Johnston, L., and Lafave, H. G. (1994). Quality of life of people with psychiatric disabilities 1 and 3 years after discharge from hospital. *Quality of Life Research*, 3: 379-383.

Gitter, A. G. and Mostofsky, D. I. (1973). The social indicator: an index of quality of life. *Social Biology,* 20(3): 289-297.

Halpern, A. S. (1994). Quality of life for students with disabilities in transition from school to adulthood. *Social Indicators Research*, 33: 193-236.

House, P. W., Livingston, R. C., and Swinburn, C. D. (1975). Monitoring mankind: the search for quality. *Behavioral Science*, 20(1): 57-67.

Hyland, M. E., Finnis, S., and Irvine, S. H. (1991). A scale for assessing quality of life in adult asthma sufferers. *Journal of Psychosomatic Research*, 35(1): 99-110.

Inge, K. J., Banks, D., Wehman, P., Hill, J. W., and Shafer, M. S. (1988). Quality of life for individuals who are labeled mentally retarded: evaluating competitive employment versus sheltered workshop employment. *Education and Training in Mental Retardation*, 97-104.

Jenkins, C. D. (1992). Assessment of outcomes of health intervention. *Social Science Medicine,* 35(4): 367-375.

Johannesson, M. (1994). QALYs, HYEe and individual preferences: a graphical illustration. *Social Science Medicine*, 39(12): 1623-1632.

Kaplan, R. M. (1991). Health-related quality of life in patient decision making. *Journal of Social Issues,* 47(4): 69-90.

Kaplan, R. M., Debon, M., and Anderson, B. F. (1991, October). Effects of number of rating scale points upon utilities in a Quality of Well-Being Scale. *Medical Care*, 29(10): 1061-1064.

Kaplan, R. M., Anderson, J. P., and Wingard, D. L. (1991). Gender differences in health-related quality of life. *Health Psychology*, 10(2): 86-93.

Koch, U. and Muthny, F. A. (1990). Quality of life in patients with end-stage renal disease in relation to the method of treatment. *Psychotherapy and Psychosomatics*, 54: 161-171.

Morris, M. H. and Lewis, P. S. (1991). Entrepreneurship as a significant factor in societal quality of life. *Journal of Business Research*, 23: 21-36.

Mowry, R. L. (1988). Quality of life indicators for deaf and hard-of-hearing former VR clients. *Journal of Rehabilitation of the Deaf*, 21(3): 1-7.

Mugenda, O. M., Hira, T. K., and Fanslow, A. M., (1990). Assessing the causal relationship among communication, money management practices, satisfaction with financial status, and satisfaction with quality of life. *Lifestyles: Family and Economic Issues*, 11(4): 343-360.

Murrell, S. A. and Norris, F. H. (1983). Quality of life as the criterion for need assessment and community psychology. *Journal of Consulting Psychology*, 11(2): 88-97.

Parmenter, T. R. (1996). The use of quality of life as a construct for social and health policy development. In R. Renwick, I. Brown, and M. Nagler (Eds.), *Quality of Life in Health Promotion and Rehabilitation,* pp. 89-103. Thousand Oaks, CA: Sage Publications.

Raphael, J. 1996. Domestic violence and welfare receipt: toward a new feminist theory of welfare dependency. *Harvard Women's Law Journal* (Spring): 19, 201-227.

Rettig, K. D., Danes, S. M., and Bauer, J. W. (1991). Family life quality: theory and assessment in economically stressed farm families. *Social Indicators Research*, 24: 269-299.

Rhoads, D. L. and Raymond, J. S. (1981). Quality of life and the competent community. *American Journal of Community Psychology*, 9(3): 293-301.

Ried, W. (1997). *QALYs vs. HYEs — What is right and what is wrong.* <http://obelix.statistik.uni-mannheim.de/inst_vw/abstract/a54496.htm>.

Select Committee on Aging, House of Representatives. (1988, December). *The Quality of Life for Older Women: Older Women Living Alone.* Comm. Pub. No. 100-693.

Sherman, E. and Schiffman, L. G. (1991). Quality of life (QOL) assessment of older consumers: a retrospective review. *Journal of Business and Psychology*, 6(1): 107-119.

Short, K. and Shea, M. (1995). Beyond poverty, extended measures of well-being: 1992. *Current Population Reports: Household Economic Studies*, 1-4.

Shulman, K. I. and Cohen, C. A. (1993). Quality of life and economic aspects of community support programs for caregivers of dementia patients. *The American Journal of Geriatric Psychiatry*, 1(3): 211-220.

Siegel, C. and Brent, R. J. (1997). Quality-adjusted time project. *Center for the Study of Issues in Public Mental Health.* < http://www.rfmh.org/sciphm/qat.htm >

Sinnott-Oswald, M., Gliner, J. A., and Spencer, K. C. (1991). Supported and sheltered employment: quality of life issues among workers with disabilities. *Education and Training in Mental Retardation*, 26(4): 388-397.

Tengs, T. O. (1996). An evaluation of Oregon's medicaid rationing algorithms. *Health Economics*, 5: 171-181.

WHOQOL Group. (1994). Development of the WHOQOL: rationale and current status. *International Journal of Mental Health,* 23(3): 24-56.

Wilkins, R. and Adams, O. B. (1983). Health expectancy in Canada, late 1970s: demographic, regional, and social dimensions. *American Journal of Public Health*, 73(9): 1073-1080.

Wilkinson, G., Williams, B., Krekorian, J., McLees, S., and Falloon, I. (1992). QALYs in mental health: A case study. *Psychological Medicine*, 22: 725-731.

7 The Leisure Domain

> There is a substantive basis for believing that play, recreation and leisure can assist individuals to improve and maintain physical and psychological health and well-being, and that play, recreation and leisure are instrumental in creating environments that promote social acceptance and enhance life quality.
>
> *Shank, Coyle, Boyd, and Kinney, 1996*

INTRODUCTION

The role of leisure in promoting quality of life for persons with disabilities and others who have experienced traumatic life events has not received considerable attention in the rehabilitation literature, and little attention has been given to this quality of life domain in planning future care needs. The question of whether leisure has value suggests that leisure, in and of itself, has not been seen universally as meaningful and is therefore not uniformly valued by all persons or by all cultures. Leisure may be that domain of quality of life which is the most suspect for those who have difficulty in defining its meaning in a discussion of human growth and development over the life span. Since the literature on quality of life differentiates meaningful from nonmeaningful leisure (suggesting that meaningful leisure has a goal and/or purpose and therefore is to be valued differentially from leisure which lacks a defined purpose). For the purposes of this chapter, any leisure activity which enhances quality of life is assumed to have value and be meaningful. Leisure does not need to be made into something concrete and measurable (e.g., skill development, increased social contacts) to justify its existence. The real question in a discussion of quality of life and leisure is whether leisure is sufficiently powerful a variable to be given the same or lesser weight as the other domains of quality of life in an overall estimation of an individual's quality of life. The questions of the relevancy and weight given to leisure in promoting quality of life and the resources which should be allocated for leisure pursuits are important ones for the forensic rehabilitationist expert when working with someone experiencing physical and/or psychological pain. Questioning the value of leisure more than other domains of quality of life may be a reflection of the Puritan work ethic instilled in American culture and its concern that leisure is not productive and therefore, at best, useless and irrelevant and, at worst, selfish and destructive to others. Experiencing pleasure may be seen from a dichotomous "good–bad" perspective, allowing it to be dismissed on an emotional, cognitive, and/or spiritual level by those who devalue it and necessitating justification for those who do value it. Yet, the propensity for humans to pursue that which is pleasurable and avoid that which is aversive is well-documented in basic literature in human behavior (none of which needs to be repeated here).

House et al. (1975) may offer one of the best examples of the differing reactions engendered by a discussion of leisure in their article that summarized the results of a 1973 quality of life symposium "where a list of QOL factors was generated and weighted (by participants) in hope of providing a useful tool for the decision making process" in quantifying quality of life. For the purposes of the study, they defined "QOL as a function of the perceived conditions affecting a selected population and the subjective attitude toward those conditions held by persons in that population." Under the political/social category, participants were asked about their use of use of free time alone or in voluntary associations, e.g., church, clubs, etc., and variety of activities engaged in. Unfortunately, the authors concluded that no hard data could be derived from their experiment, but they did note that the topic itself generated "an unanticipated degree of hostility from the participants." This hostility is consistent with the hostility shown by third-party payers and attorneys in administrative law and civil proceedings, who view leisure as a waste of human time and effort as well as an unjustifiable expenditure. The authors of this book have observed this phenomenon as well, more than 20 years later.

Gender differences in valuing the meaning of quality of life have been observed by the authors. Women tend to perceive quality of life issues in very practical and personal terms (e.g., caring for an elderly, disabled parent) and, in a 1996 informal gathering which included the authors, the women were offended by what they perceived as the propensity for an abstract and cold discussion on the part of their male colleagues. House et al. did not provide a gender analysis of the apparently lively, and even angry, discussion which took place at their 1973 symposium. It would have been very interesting to know what happened when the topic of the use of leisure came up in the conversation because leisure, perhaps more than any other quality of life domain, has different and even hidden meanings for women and men.

Male and female experience of leisure is often very different. For example, a New Zealand recreation survey found that home-based recreational activities were used by "nine out of ten women as compared to five out of ten men" (Waring, 1988). Also, women were found to participate more frequently in cultural events than men; men, in turn, were found to participate in sporting activities. Men's involvement in sporting activities increased with the birth of children. Further, it was noted that "in a study of average housewives in twelve countries in 1975 (including the United States), the total free time per week for employed men was 34 hours, for employed women it was 14.5 hours per week, and for housewives it was 32. 6 hours per week" (p. 163). Waring indicates that the data on housewives is "highly suspect since the statistical conspiracy is such that, when women are invisible as workers, then they can be told they are at leisure when they are fulfilling unpaid domestic duties."

McCoy (1994) suggests that "very little research attention has been given to the role of leisure in women's lives." She continues: "leisure research ... has tended to focus on men's leisure and to assume that women's leisure matches this *norm*, or to ignore women's leisure entirely." Men and women tend to define leisure differently as well (McCoy, 1994). One example of this can be seen in the new research on the use of cyberspace by women and men. That is, men see computers as toys, and women view computers as tools. Or women see cyberspace as work, and men see cyberspace as another leisure opportunity. Spender (1995) asserts that this is because men have more economic and leisure access which allows them to purchase computers and other cyberspace equipment, and the time to play with cyberspace technology. (pp. 161 to 165) Spender has speculated that if women have access to the new technology at all, tend to view cyberspace as something they must fit in somewhere along with all their other life tasks.

The leisure domain, much like the cognitive domain explored in Chapter 9, is embedded in the quality of life literature and overlaps with other domains, particularly the social domain. (Fine, 1996; Terman, 1995) Terman, for example, puts the social and recreational aspects of life functioning together in one category or domain in his Loss of Enjoyment of Life — Severity Scale: "Social/recreational area of functioning refers to a person's ability to enjoy pleasure from interacting with family and friends, and to enjoy social events, hobbies and interests other than occupational."

Leisure is commonly defined as a separate domain of quality of life or is seen in the QOL literature frequently as items or questions designed to explore leisure skills, leisure access, and enjoyment of leisure. Unlike the almost completely embedded character of cognition in the quality of life literature, the study of leisure has emerged as a professional discipline grounded in the rehabilitative sciences (Shank et al., 1996), known as therapeutic recreation (Scott, 1996). The therapeutic recreation literature uses "implicit definitions" of quality of life when targeting increases in functional ability, mobility, socialization opportunities, and related variables often identified as rehabilitation goals. Rehabilitation goals may specifically include enhanced leisure activity, at least in part, out of recognition that increased leisure activity is an appropriate intervention for promoting quality of life (National Institute on Disability and Rehabilitation Research, 1988).

Sackman and Ingham (1992) considered the leisure domain so important, they used it exclusively as a basis for calculating hedonic loss in wrongful death cases. However, Sackman and Ingham's four case examples valued only the hedonic loss of men's leisure experiences. Women were present in the analysis only as the wives of the injured or wrongfully dead husbands. This tends to support the position in the question posed by the feminist economists, Leghorn and Parker (1981):

> If men are so keen to measure in terms of production, why don't they include in their statistics the production, by women, of leisure for men?

i.e., examine women's work as a method of producing leisure time for men, which seems to be the tendency the world over (Waring, 1988, p. 159). Yet, the opposite does not appear as an issue found in discussions on leisure and men. There appears to be significant gender difference in perception and experiencing of leisure as one aspect of quality of life.

This chapter will provide a sampling of the quality of life literature in the leisure domain as well as an overview of therapeutic recreation.

SOME DEFINITIONS OF LEISURE

> Leisure is defined as the activities one chooses to do in one's free time for purposes of pleasure, relaxation, self-fulfillment, or social value.
>
> *McCoy, 1994*

Fine (1996) states that "leisure is much more than occupying oneself in free time." He lists four benefits human beings derive from leisure as a method of describing what leisure is:

1. Meeting such human needs as "autonomy, relaxation, family activity, interaction with others, stimulation, skill development and use, challenge or competition, leadership or social power, and health." Good emotional health is especially associated with the use of leisure.
2. "Meaningful leisure can be tremendously helpful in reducing feelings of helplessness." Leisure in this sense provides opportunities for empowerment and self-efficacy.
3. "Leisure experiences are very likely to become critical dimensions of an individual's personal lifestyle." Self-identity can be enhanced by participation in leisure activities.
4. "Leisure participation offers people occasions to escape from everyday personal and interpersonal environments, to set aside issues and difficulties and to engage in activities that are enjoyable and personally satisfying," suggesting as do Osipow and Spokane (1987) that leisure is an effective coping strategy for dealing with the stresses and strains of life of everyday life, in particular, one's work life.

McCoy (1994) identifies the following three elements of leisure:

1. Leisure as discretionary time: this is the *free* time left over after one has fulfilled subsistence and existence need (e.g., job and household chores).
2. Leisure as a discretionary activity: for an act to be considered as leisure, it must be freely chosen, rather than being a necessity or obligation.
3. Leisure as a state of mind: leisure involves intrinsic motivations and satisfaction; that is, one engages in leisure because it is inherently satisfying.

For the purposes of this chapter and to add to these definitions of leisure, the term *leisure* will also include such words as *recreation, play, hobbies, fun, spare time with friends, outdoor activities, sports, vacation, artistic pursuits,* and *community or voluntary activities.*

LITERATURE REVIEW

The literature concerning the leisure domain as a quality of life issue can be found in the Social Indicators Movement, in the fields of mental retardation and developmental disabilities, in mental illness research, and in a scattering of quality of life articles centering around such medical conditions as asthma, chronic pain, cancer, inflammatory bowel disease, renal failure, epilepsy, hypothyroidism, traumatic brain injury, hip orthoplasty, neuromuscular disease, and spinal cord injury.

The review of this literature will start with the Social Indicators Movement, since it is the basis for national quality of life studies conducted with the general population of the U.S. and it preceded most of the health-related quality of life studies reviewed later in this chapter.

THE SOCIAL INDICATORS MOVEMENT

The Social Indicators Movement emerged in the 1960s and 1970s. In 1969, the U.S. Department of Health, Education, and Welfare used social indicators to set policy (Gitter and Mostofsky, 1973). In 1971, the Board of Directors of the American Institutes for Research reviewed 25 years of research and set the agenda for the next decade. They decided to direct a major research effort toward improving the quality of life of Americans (Flanagan, 1978). In 1973, the Environmental Protection Agency attempted to develop a methodology for the assessment and quantification of the term quality of life (House et al., 1975). In his 1977 article Blau noted that "interest in social indicators is increasing among social scientists." His article presents ten scales selected as indicators of and providing normative indexes of quality of life by persons in psychotherapy. Andrews, in his 1991 article, notes that "as the Social Indicators Movement matures, it becomes possible to explore issues of stability and change in measures of perceived life quality." This paper presents the results of administering similar measures of subjective well-being to the general adult American population 16 years apart, in 1972 and again in 1988. The leisure domain has been addressed in these studies.

Gitter and Mostofsky (1973) recommended a social indicator approach to the measurement of quality of life which "begins with the assumption that a person's life is composed of phenomena which are the elements of his everyday existence at a given point in time." Leisure and recreation were identified as key elements of quality of life. Leisure was seen as a necessary component of objective and subjective indicators of quality of life people.

Flanagan (1978) described an approach to the investigation of quality of life research developed by the American Institutes for Research (AIR). "More than 6,500 critical incidents were collected from nearly 3,000 people of various ages, races, and backgrounds representing all regions of the country." Another 2,000 additional "critical incidents were obtained from an 11-year follow-up survey." Out of this research, 15 quality of life components based on the critical incidents were identified. These 15 quality of life components were then further divided into five broad categories. Recreation was included as one of the domains of quality of life, with three subcategories of recreation being identified as follows:

1. Socializing: entertaining at home or elsewhere, attending parties or other social gatherings, meeting new people, interacting with others. It may include participation in socializing organizations and clubs.
2. Passive and observational recreational activities: participating in various kinds of passive recreation, such as watching television, listening to music, reading, going to the movies, and going to entertainment or sports events. It also involves appreciating the art and beauty in many aspects of life.

3. Active and participatory recreational activities: participating in various kinds of active recreation, such as sports, hunting, fishing, boating, camping, vacation travel, and sightseeing, etc. This may also involve playing sedentary or active games, singing, playing an instrument, dancing, acting, etc."

Once the elements of quality of life were identified, the second step in the research was to conduct a national survey of 1000 persons around the age of 15 years, another 1000 individuals at age 30 years, and a representative cohort of 1000 fifty-year-olds and another 1000 seventy-year-olds. Each interviewee was asked to report "how important each of the fifteen components defining quality of life was to them currently." Recreation was one category in which the interviewees indicated that their needs were not well met, particularly in active participatory recreation. Active recreation was one of the six areas showing the "largest correlation coefficients with overall quality of life."

In a study designed to identify normative indices of quality of life for persons undergoing psychotherapy, Blau (1977) identified leisure as one of the ten variables making up quality of life. In Blau's paradigm, the lowest anchor point for leisure is when a person has almost no time for leisure activities of choice and/or experienced stress after engaging in activities of choice. Conversely, the highest anchor point is occurs when there is a broad and frequent opportunity for a variety of unrequired activities, and the time is frequently and satisfyingly used. "Positive living" can be identified by the high anchor point (i.e., frequent and varied opportunities for leisure). According to Blau, leisure has greater relevance to the discussion of overall life function than most existing psychological tests designed only to measure emotional states. Blau notes that psychological tests of emotional states rarely emphasize quality of life and identifies "a desperate need" for valid social indicators.

Andrews (1991) reported the results of administering a subjective well-being instrument to several representative groups of American adults in 1972 and again in 1988. He noted that "the structure of the subjective well-being measures (i.e., how they relate to one another and how concern-level measures predict global-level measures) has remained remarkably constant." The leisure domain is reflected in Andrews' analysis of subjective measures suggests such common themes in questions as how much fun the person is having, how the person is spending spare time, and how much time is spent with friends. Little change was noted from 1972 to 1988 in terms of the leisure components as contrasted with gains in self-efficacy, health, and standard of living. These changes were true across the general population but differed when specific groups were examined by gender, age, race, and income level. Andrews concluded his paper by identifying one of the missions of the Social Indicators Movement as "documenting the extent, the social extensiveness, of such changes (1972 to 1988)" in a society as a whole. And although leisure was seen an important component of quality of life, change in leisure over time was not evidenced. Leisure appeared to remain constant, while other domains of quality of life experienced gains. One could argue that lack of gains points to a somewhat precarious role for leisure in a society where human growth and development is defined in terms of other variables. The authors of this book wonder whether leisure is seen as a high priority in a culture where one's functional status has more traditionally been measured by physiological assay, psychometric instruments, or accumulation of wealth. Leisure has not been given much attention in the medical and psychological models of health service delivery, possibly due to the fact that it is palliative or preventive in its orientation, not lending itself to the deficit thinking of tertiary service delivery systems. Leisure can easily be ignored and not seen as a critical area of human functioning requiring care planning when a care planner is dealing with more pressing and more debilitating physiological and/or psychological issues. Yet, if persons with disabilities are to be offered the same opportunities for quality of life as those enjoyed by the nondisabled, a moral and philosophical assumption behind normalization theory as applied for 30 years to persons with physical and mental impairments (with acquired developmentally or by some trauma), then the same opportunities for leisure must be available to disabled and nondisabled persons.

Mental Retardation, Learning Disabilities, Developmental Disabilities, Cerebral Palsy

Bratt and Johnston's (1988) review of a qualitative study of three young men and two women with profound mental handicaps and additional sensory or motor impairments revealed that the major change for these young people, when moving from hospital care to a bungalow in a busy suburban of a British city, was in the reduction of inappropriate behaviors. Such leisure activities as swimming, horse-riding sessions, and art and drama were offered as part of the therapeutic milieu along with gardening (never engaged in by the residents) and visits to the community for shopping, going to a pub, walking in a park, and having a picnic. The importance of this study lies in its linking leisure activities to interventions for reducing inappropriate behaviors. Leisure activities, as part of the rehabilitation process apparently has some therapeutic benefit and therefore need not be considered ancillary or nonessential, just because it does not fit into traditional models of rehabilitation for the developmentally disabled.

Brown et al. study (1988) suggest that choice of specific leisure activities should be based on consideration of two concepts — leisure skill development and leisure development. For example, did the bungalow residents in the previous study not use the opportunity to garden because they did not have the skills to do so? In conducting a longitudinal study with Canadians with mental disabilities who were using rehabilitation agencies, researchers found that although only 4% of the whole managed to find work over 3 years of the study, the leisure time activities of those who obtained employment was double that of those who remained in the agency, despite cognitive levels of performance being equivalent. They also found that families did not teach activities of daily living skills (e.g., changing a light bulb, using a telephone) to the clients, and so the development of leisure skills and organization also fell by the wayside. The expectation was that the rehabilitation agency would do this. This proved to be an unrealistic expectation for agencies whose funding continues to decline.

During the action research phase of the study, the researchers advocated for the clients and their requests while consulting with sponsors and parents. The leisure program options selected by the clients were based in "residential, social-education and community skills, communication, friendship, leisure, and personal development," yet, the clients perceived (and the researchers confirmed) that rehabilitation choices were based on a desire "to keep you quiet." One parent, when discussing the role of leisure in dealing with a child's behavior felt that such leisure activities as watching television, listening to a walkman with earphones, or drawing in one's bedroom were appropriate for keeping the child quiet, while activities where the individual starts learning to cook, talk on the phone, or go out into the community for leisure skills, which, for example, might bring the individual home late on occasion, producing the opposite effect, stimulating the individual to engage in a much wider range of behaviors with a potential for conflict between parents or caregivers and the individual. An adult woman may be *grounded* because she has broken her mother's rule which says you should be home at a particular time. An adult man, encouraged to be more assertive, is chastised by his residential supervisor for being difficult, rude, and unsociable because he prefers to read in his room rather than watch TV with the rest of the residents. This research raises the questions of who chooses the leisure activities.

In a 10-year followup study, Clark and Hirst (1989) examined the "attainment of adult status among a sample of 39" persons with cerebral palsy, aged 25 to 30 years. Just over half of the study participants were in paid employment. Nine participants attended day centers and four had previously done so. Although one or two reported that therapeutic day programming had enabled them to develop work skills such as typing and use of a computer, or to gain work experience of, for example, packing, assembling, or being a receptionist, in general, art and leisure activities predominated. In contrast to the Brown et al. study reviewed above, the day treatment programs activities rarely led to paid employment, and for those employed, there was no increase in leisure participation either. Services cannot, of course, guarantee successful transitions to adult life, but they can provide choice and enable those wanting to work and live independently to make decisions and take responsibility for their own lives. The study participants' use of leisure activities did not significantly differ from that of the general population. That is, they enjoyed watching television, listening to radio and tapes, reading, visiting friends, or going out for a meal, to a class or to a sporting event. The difference is as Clark and Hirst note: "People with disabilities are particularly dependent for the quality of their life on the services provided for them."

Dagan et al. (1994) administered Living in a Supervised Home: A Questionnaire on Quality of Life to 65 persons with learning disabilities who lived in 18 houses in a community in Britain. One of the factors identified on this questionnaire is leisure, an item found under the label "resident centered quality of life." Other than identification of leisure as a quality of life issue, the researchers do not address the issue any further. They did report that the quality of life instrument used had face validity, good inter-rater reliability, internal reliability, and "a factor structure that will be easily interpretable with services." Leisure was seen as one of the factors to be measured in assessing overall quality of life for persons with learning disabilities, but its singular impact on life quality was not investigated.

In a review of quality of life in applied research and in an analysis of the measures, Hughes et al. (1995) found 87 empirical studies and 1243 empirical measures. They then developed a consensual list of 15 dimensions and "corresponding components of quality of life" derived from the literature to propose a conceptual model. They focused on research that investigated: "the deinstitutionalization and community integration of adults with disabilities living in the community and the employment of individuals with disabilities working in integrated, community work settings." There were 9772 participants across the 87 studies located and almost half "had a primary diagnosis of mild or moderate mental retardation." Learning disabilities, chronic mental illness, physical disabilities, multiple handicaps, sensory impairments, behavior disorders, and autism comprised the remainder. Recreation and leisure were identified as a dimension or component of quality of life, and watching television, visiting friends, and going to a movie was mentioned 264 times across the 87 studies, with 91 different measures of this element found. This measure, the type of recreation and leisure activities, turned out to be the single component of quality of life with the greatest number and frequency of measures. By contrast, very few studies (4) assessed the "availability of leisure activities, opportunity to participate in leisure activities, and availability of a partner for leisure activities," only 4 measures included any items regarding availability and opportunity. Leisure time skills and degree of supervision needed were assessed even less often (3 times), but 6 measures were located. "Frequency of participation, active participation vs. *being kept busy*" were found in only two studies and in only two measures. The authors concluded that a consensus concerning a conceptual quality of life was in formation. They also indicated that leisure/recreation was an area needing further study.

Another study of quality of life concerns for students with disabilities in transition from school to adulthood was conducted by Halpern (1994). He points out that the three major strands in this transition were the work–study programs of the 1960s, the career education programs of the 1970s, and the transition programs of the 1980s. He surmised that the intent of all of these programs "has always been to enhance the quality of life of adolescents and young adults" with disabilities, and only the transition programs remain today. In his comprehensive discussion of quality of life outcomes research as the basis for program evaluation, Halpern notes that "the definition of quality of life for special education students in transition began in the narrowest possible way, with a focus entirely on employment." With the passage of special education legislation (P.L. 101-476), the stage is set for "a much broader interpretation of quality of life," one which recognizes three domains of life function — *physical and material well-being* (physical and mental health, food, clothing, lodging, safety from harm, financial security); *performance of adult roles* (mobility and community access, vocation, career, employment, leisure and recreation, personal relationships and social networks, educational attainment, spiritual fulfillment, citizenship, social responsibility); *personal fulfillment* (happiness, satisfaction, a sense of general well-being). Halpern considers leisure and recreation to be as significant as the other adult roles (education, work, relationships) which have received significantly more attention in the rehabilitation literature. The primary implication of this position is that leisure/recreation should be addressed as part of the process of enhancing or maintaining quality of life.

Yet in their study of quality of life benefits from competitive employment vs. sheltered workshop employment for persons "labeled mentally retarded," Inge et al. (1988) determined that the value of their study "appears to rest in its pilot nature, its preliminary findings which are encouraging, and perhaps, above all, in illuminating the methodological problems inherent in this type of research." One of the measures used in this pilot study was the Parent/Guardian Survey, which was unfortunately "found to be ineffective fairly early in the study, so several modifications had to be made to make it more practical for parental responses." This was the measure which included a leisure/recreation subscale. The other measures, the Adaptive Behavior Scale and an array of physical health measures, did not focus on the leisure domain. The encouraging results in this study were located in the cognitive domain, or increased skill development resulting from competitive employment for this population, and can be found in the literature review in Chapter 9: The Cognitive Domain. The researchers were apparently unable to replicate the positive relationship found between paid employment and leisure skill. The potency of leisure as a methodology for enhancing global quality of life within the context of multidimensional intervention programs designed primarily to achieve vocational objectives remains an area for additional research. The dilemma for care planners who have limited financial resources available for providing care or who are concerned about the cost–benefit of each potential treatment option lies in the lack of definitive data to support allocation of large proportions of available resources for leisure when significant educational, vocational, and (by implication) economic gains in function are possible.

Discussion of leisure for persons with developmental disabilities or traumatic injury must address the theory of the hypothesis that the linkage between normalization and quality of life has been forged to the extent that there is consensus that adults with developmental disabilities should have access to the activities and rhythms of life that characterize the lifestyle of typical adults, and that if access is provided, quality of life will be enhanced (Kozleski and Sands, 1992). It is in the area of developmental disabilities that exploration of this linkage is found.

Sinnott-Oswald et al. (1991) developed a quality of life survey which was administered to ten individuals with disabilities in supported community employment, ten individuals with disabilities in sheltered workshop programs, and nine persons without disabilities. They hypothesized that the quality of life for persons in supported employment would approximate the quality of life of persons without disabilities. Questions on leisure time, leisure activities, and use of leisure were included in the quality of life measure were included in the study. The researchers addressed leisure issues in some detail. They found that the supported employment group differed from the SW (sheltered workshop) group for use of leisure time and involvement in activities, with the SE (supported employment) group having significantly more time for leisure activities and being more frequently involved in activities. The authors theorize that the SE group was able to spend more time on leisure because most of them worked part-time as contrasted to the SW group who worked full-time. The other explanation was related to self-esteem, the SE group having significantly higher self-esteem than the SW group, possibly indicating that these individuals possess more confidence to become involved in more activities. Examples included an individual who had been in sheltered employment for 10 years with little participation in leisure or community activities who independently started guitar lessons after working in supported employment for one year. Another individual started karate lessons after being employed as a custodian. Active and passive recreational activities, such as eating out or shopping did not differ significantly among the three groups studied and, in other life domains such as living independently, the SE group did not differ significantly from the control group or group without disabilities.

Kozleski and Sands (1992) used the Consumer Satisfaction Survey, modified for use with adults without disabilities, to examine quality of life issues. One hundred and thirty-three surveys were returned. The overlap we have seen in other studies between the social and leisure domains is seen in this study as well as reflected in two tables. Participation in community activities included visits with close friends, relatives, or neighbors; shopping at a supermarket; eating at a restaurant; attending a church or synagogue; shopping at a mall or other retail store; going to a bar or tavern; going to the bank. Recreation and leisure activities included going to the movies, live theater, music performance, sports events, athletic clubs, community groups. Of the participants, 95% had attended movies in the past year. Over half had gone to a live theater performance and one third had seen a live music performance, and 42% had gone to a sports event. More than two thirds "reported that their current levels of activities for visiting close friends, shopping at supermarkets, eating at restaurants, attending church, shopping at malls, going to bars and banks was about right." Some respondents wanted to increase their church or synagogue attendance (33%); less than one fifth "wanted to decrease" food shopping and eating out. Most were satisfied with their leisure and wanted to increase it. Less than 10% wanted to decrease their activities. A significant relationship was not found between socioeconomic status and leisure, movie attendance, and banking. It seems that having more money "did not increase involvement in leisure activities nor did it increase access to or involvement in personal relationships." This is an important finding because "it is commonly assumed that persons in middle and upper socioeconomic strata experience a higher quality of life due to an increase in expendable income." This, in turn, leads to an assumption "that they participate in recreation and leisure activities with greater frequency." Income and leisure access and participation are only "loosely coupled" in this study. This raises serious questions about the perspective of some care planners who "throw money" at the issue of leisure pursuits. Building large sums of money for leisure may not produce any meaningful effect on quality of life. It may be necessary for care planners to engage the services of a therapeutic rehabilitation specialist in order to understand the status of leisure skill acquisition and whether or not such acquisition post injury would represents a potential for restoring quality of life.

Kozleski and Sands (1992) conclude that quality of life conceptualizations may be more complex than they had thought previously. They recommend further research which distinguishes between factors which inhibit and which enhance quality of life, and they point out that examining quality of life for people without disabilities "can assist us in achieving social validity in our services to persons with developmental disabilities." These same researchers then examined quality of life differences between adults with and without disabilities using the Consumer Satisfaction Survey mentioned above (Sands and Kozleski, 1994). One hundred and thirty-one individuals without disabilities and 86 persons with disabilities completed the survey. Of the disabled persons, 61% identified their disability as mental retardation, 13% as cerebral palsy, and 4% as head injury. Quality of life inhibitors (e.g., not having employment) and contributors (e.g., having employment) were identified as issues to be considered in the development of appropriate services for persons with disabilities. They point out that "where those inhibitors have been addressed, services can be funneled towards enhancing contributors, or those quality of life features that enhance general life satisfaction." One such support considered by Sands and Kozleski is recreation/leisure activity. They found that "persons with disabilities participated much less often in recreational activities than persons with disabilities. For every activity (see list of activities as reviewed in their earlier study above) listed, there was a significant relationship between the presence of a disability and levels of attendance." In terms of satisfaction in the six leisure activities, persons with disabilities "were more likely to want increased opportunities for attending movies and persons without disabilities were more likely to want more opportunities for attending the theater." Both groups wanted more participation in music performances, sporting events, athletic clubs, and community groups. Persons with disabilities were dissatisfied with the frequency and variety in their community, recreation, and leisure activities.

All ten of the studies in this section visited the theme of autonomy or choice as it related to leisure and recreation. Indeed, it seems that the ability to choose is intrinsic to the concept of leisure as we have seen in the definitions of leisure and in the studies found in the Social Indicators Movement. The issue of autonomy or choice will surface again in the cognitive domain as explored in Chapter 9. It may be that the freedom to choose is a quality of life domain in and of itself. We will explore that idea in our concluding chapter, Chapter 1.

MENTAL ILLNESS

Malm et al. (1981) conducted a pilot study to evaluate the usefulness of the Quality of Life Checklist with 40 patients with schizophrenia. The researchers developed a model based on their understanding of the needs of the recovering schizophrenic patient. They used this 7-dimensional model to develop a checklist on which "quick, simple assessments of the various aspects of quality of life" could be determined. One of the dimensions on this measure is described as:

> Knowledge, Education, Leisure, and Recreation: Newspapers, magazines, books; Radio, TV; Sports, games, hobbies; Movies, theater, art, music; Adult education, schools; Public information.

This section was "unsatisfactory for almost all patients," although there was variance between patients and on items in the leisure section. "Most were satisfied with their TV (35 of 40) and radio (36 of 40); 28 were satisfied with their music ... All other leisure categories contained many deficiencies." Leisure was identified as a patient-specific target area for therapeutic intervention, suggesting that very careful analysis of individual preferences, patterns of behavior, and lifestyle choices should be conducted when planning leisure activities. In the open-ended section of the checklist, patients could write in their leisure activities. These included activities such as walking, eating out, having a dog, stamp collecting, writing, and dancing. All were rated as satisfactory. The authors report that the Quality of Life Checklist can yield valuable information, since "it describes the flavor of an individual's existence in a practical way that should be readily understandable by anyone likely to be involved in caring for a schizophrenic patient."

Ciardiello and Bingham (1982) recommend that a career counseling approach be used in the vocational rehabilitation of persons with schizophrenia, because, "by definition, the career development approach is client centered," in contrast to a rehabilitative process based on a medical model, the client is empowered to set his or her own goals. This, in turn, is expected to assist the "schizophrenic client make more satisfying choices as a user of leisure time, a family member, a citizen, and worker." The authors conclude that this will lead to improvement in quality of life.

Whelton et al. (1997), in a study of young adults with schizophrenia participating in the Hamilton Program for Schizophrenia (HPS), a community-based psychosocial rehabilitation and treatment program offering long-term case management services, created a questionnaire derived from the Client Satisfaction Questionnaire. It contained categories for time or money spent by families on the behalf of their relatives with schizophrenia were created. Leisure activities were included in both the time and money categories. The researchers found that families were able to identify service needs for their relatives, but noted that these needs were incompletely addressed, including the need to be involved in meaningful and productive activities. Leisure activities were assumed to be meaningful and productive.

Fabian, a prominent researcher in quality of life and rehabilitation, has written three important articles which examine quality of life theory and practice implications for persons with long-term mental illness (1990), the use of quality of life dimensions in rehabilitation program evaluation (1991), and quality of life and supported employment for those with severe mental illness (1992). Leisure activities are identified as a quality of life dimension in all three articles, but detail is provided only in the 1992 article on supported employment and quality of life. In this article she refers to Lehman's Quality of Life Interview, a measure which uses leisure activities as one of its 8 domains, based on data from "almost 500 individuals with severe mental illness." Fabian used the Quality of Life Interview with the 110 individuals, "56 not yet placed in supported employment, and 54" in supported employment. It was noteworthy that the highest correlation (r =) was found between social relations and leisure activities. Also it was found that the subjective quality of life scores did increase for individuals with supported employment, but not for objective indicators "such as number of social or leisure activities." There was little difference between the two groups on the leisure and social domains. Fabian recommends the increased use of qualitative research to unearth the meaning of this result. These findings are significant in that they suggest relationships between leisure, work, and social domains, and by implication, the economic domain of quality of life, but suggest that the degree and direction of those relationships is variable, requiring additional research.

Slaughter et al. (1991) examined 16 quality of life studies of persons "with severe mental illness living in community residential care facilities." At least three of the studies included leisure activities as a quality of life domain. The authors offered the hypothesis that improved residential settings enhance such proximal housing outcomes as perceived comfort and satisfaction with living situation and such distal outcomes as employment status, safety, social contacts, leisure activities, and general life satisfaction. Although no further discussion of the relationship between housing and leisure was forthcoming, the question of the impact of housing on leisure as well as other domains of life quality was raised.

Huxley and Warner (1992) used the Quality of Life Profile and the General Satisfaction Questionnaire "to examine the relationship between type of case management services and quality of life and satisfaction with treatment of 68 long-term psychiatric patients in Colorado." A comparison group of 15 low-income medical patients was used. They found that the

> mental health group was significantly worse off in terms of their social and family relationships but was more satisfied in the area of work and education than the low-income group. The groups did not differ on quality of life in areas of health, religion, leisure, or finances.

Rosenfeld (1992) examined a community mental health program using a psychosocial rehabilitation model for the chronically mentally ill in Piscataway, NJ. Fourteen prevocational areas of assessment and rehabilitation are provided (e.g., clerical, transportation, cafeteria, research, and recreation). Program components included the planning of week nights, weekends, weekdays, holidays and time in recreation, leisure activities, meetings, and socializing. Although work was mentioned as the most important program component, social contacts (an aspect of leisure) was also stressed by the program participants. Another significant finding was that "the more services members (participants) receive to structure week nights and weekends, the times typically least structured for members, the greater their life satisfaction." That is, the structuring and use of leisure appears to be a necessary skill development area for this population.

Munich and Lang (1993) describe psychiatric rehabilitation as a discipline which addresses three domains of patients' lives: "clinical status, functional status, and quality of life." They indicate that rehabilitation is the discipline which addresses the functional domain, whereas the clinical domain is dealt with in the medical model and quality of life domain in a case management model. Leisure skills are considered to be within areas of overlap between clinical and functional status. The significance of this article lies in the willingness to consider leisure as a legitimate area of service planning and delivery as part of a comprehensive psychiatric rehabilitation program designed to facilitate recovery from long-term mental illness. The implication of this position is that gains in leisure functioning are appropriate target goals for rehabilitation care planning. The linkages between leisure, quality of life, and successful rehabilitation outcomes warrant additional, ongoing research.

Endicott et al. (1993) developed a self-report measure, the Quality of Life Enjoyment and Satisfaction Questionnaire (Q-LES-Q), for use with depressed patients, which included 6 items on leisure. The research was designed to determine if leisure and other domains of quality of life could be distinguished from depression. Therefore, The Hamilton Depression Scale was also administered. The researchers found that correlations between the scores more focused on activities such as leisure time and social activities do not simply not reflect the absence of depression and are therefore not totally redundant with measures of depression. This study support the contention that the domains of quality of life are separate and distinguishable from the measures of such psychological/emotional states as depression. In other words, measurement of depression is discrete from measurement of quality of life.

Gerber et al. (1994) interviewed 43 clients 1 and 3 years following discharge from a psychiatric rehabilitation program in Canada. They found that quality of life measures of "living situation, social and community living skills, and recreation improved from 1988 to 1990." They used the Clients' Quality of Life Interview and the Uniform Client Data Instrument as their measures in this study. Both measures assess recreation as a quality of life domain.

Sartorius (1995), when addressing the desired outcomes of psychiatric rehabilitation, proposed the concept of "constructive change," one in which there is some recognition that economic productivity and technological development are making projections of labor force need obsolete. This makes it at best problematic to evaluate human productivity in terms of paid work when in the near future availability of paid work may decline significantly for persons with and without disabilities. Social productivity, help and support to others, the rearing of children, creative art, and many other activities which typically receive considerably less attention and respect will need to be valued more highly. Therefore, rehabilitation goals must now include improvement of overall quality of life and not be focused on work at the expense of leisure. He calls for methods in assisting people in using their leisure time well by using it to respond to their own and other people's emotional needs. Rehabilitation needs to be thought of as "an intervention to improve the quality of people's lives." The skillful use of leisure time and activity should be a goal of psychosocial rehabilitation.

Physical Illness and Disability

Kunsbeck et al. (1990) reviewed the research on the health-related quality of life during the course of inflammatory bowel disease. Like many other researchers, they included "leisure time," along with "job satisfaction" and "money" under a component of quality of life titled, "Social." The authors do cite a study which lists "recreation" as a domain to be examined separately. Another study cited found that there was a negative change in "leisure activities" after onset of the disease for 66.7% of the patients in that study.

McGee et al. (1991) developed the Schedule for the Evaluation of Individual Quality of Life. The instrument was found to be reliable and valid in terms of measuring individual quality of life. They assessed quality of life for 42 healthy individuals, 20 persons with peptic ulcer disease, and 20 persons with irritable bowel syndrome. Recreation was a domain singled out on this measure along with family, work, religion, and health.

Baker et al. examined the quality of life of bone marrow transplant survivors (BMT) (1991) and the subjective quality of life of patients receiving aggressive cancer treatment (1992). Of these, 171 BMT survivors were administered a modified Role Checklist, the Satisfaction with Life Domains Scale, the Cantril Self-Anchoring Ladders, the Profile of Mood States, and the Positive and Negative Affect Scales. Leisure was identified as "hobbyist/amateur and participant in organizations." The main hypothesis of this study was that "role retention is significantly related to higher quality of life." The researchers found that the "decline in perceived role performance was statistically significant only for those who had retained the hobby/amateur role since before their transplants.... This is at least partly accounted for by loss of the ability to retain physically demanding hobbies such as playing various sports."

The 1992 study by Baker et al. involved the development of the Satisfaction with Life Domains Scale for Cancer (SLDS-C). Respondents were asked to rate leisure time as a domain of life satisfaction. No other commentary on the leisure domain was made.

Muthny et al. (1990), in their review of quality of life measures designed to assess the quality of life of persons with cancer, identify "leisure-time activities" as an aspect of psychosocial rehabilitation for cancer patients. The review implicitly suggests that this domain should be an aspect of any quality of life assessment for cancer patients.

Two studies of the quality of life of children with cancer were conducted by Mulhern et al. (1990) and Goodwin et al. (1994). The 1990 study "explores the reliability and validity of the Play Performance Scale for Children. Physicians and parents rated 120 children with cancer and significant inter-rater reliability was found. The 1994 study "describes the development of a 21-item, parent report measure for assessing the quality of life of children with cancer, the Pediatric Oncology Quality of Life Scale. Internal consistency reliability was high, as was interparent agreement. Both studies use the word "play" to describe the activity of children. The 1990 study provided play performance criteria ranging from "unresponsive" at zero to "fully active, normal" at 100. The 1994 study listed items such as: "My child has been able to participate in recreational activities (sports, games, etc.); My child has been able to interact/play with friends completely normally." Play as a form of leisure and as part of the developmental work of growing up appeared to have at least sufficient construct validity to be included in a discussion of the quality of life of children.

Three studies address quality of life for asthmatics. Hyland et al. (1994) administered the Living with Asthma Questionnaire and found significant improvement in the sports category (a separate category from social/leisure). Hyland et al. (1994) administered the Asthma Questionnaire to 783 patients. The scale was found to be valid and reliable. Items on the questionnaire included: "I can take part in any sports I want. I can run like other people. I never worry that going on holiday can make my asthma worse. I have difficulty doing physically demanding tasks like gardening." Christie et al. (1991) assessed asthmatic children's perceptions of their life quality, despite noting that there was a lack of a general construct of childhood functional well-being. This 3-year project focused on psychosocial factors in childhood asthma, identifying the home and social factors, peer interaction, and pets at home. This Project appears to have distinguished some leisure activities from what might be considered the "work" of a child, psychological and physical development, education, and familial relationships, suggesting that instruments designed to measure quality of life for children should contain leisure-related items which are designed to target the specific activities performed in childhood (differentiating the "work" of children from the "leisure" of children).

Chibnall and Tait (1990) examined the impact of chronic pain on patients' perceived life quality by developing and administering the Quality of Life Scale (QOLS) to 393 chronic pain patients. The preliminary results indicated that the QOLS "shared variance with measures of psychological distress, pain-related disability, and pain description." It was internally consistent, reliable, and representative of a single construct. "Hobbies/recreational" was listed as a variable on the QOLS. Other than noting a moderate correlation on this variable between the QOLS and a similar variable on the Pain Disability Index, no other discussion of leisure functioning was available.

Katz et al. (1992) administered 5 health status measures preoperatively and 3 months postoperatively to 54 patients undergoing total hip arthroplasty. The instruments were the Sickness Impact Profile, the SF-36 Functional Status Questionnaire, shortened Arthritis Impact Measurement Scales, and Modified Health Assessment Questionnaire. No measures were found to be "significantly more sensitive than the others." Four of the instruments identified "social activities" as a domain to be measured. Only one specified "recreation", the Sickness Impact Profile, as a specific domain.

Jaeschke et al. (1994) evaluated the "frequency and relative importance of health related quality of life" by surveying 200 patients with treated hypothyroidism. Endocrinologists, internists, and patients generated items for the survey. One category was "mood and emotional states." A factor in that category is described as "activities/hobbies/losing interest in going out." No separate results for this factor was reported.

Roller (1996) conducted a study of 120 polio survivors at the University of Michigan in 1991. She and her fellow researchers found that 82% "had a treatable musculoskeletal problem of some kind." They were obese, had an elevated cholesterol level, diabetes, gastrointestinal disease, and heart trouble. Sixty-two percent "had an exercise capacity below the expected and achievable levels. Based on these findings, prevention efforts that focus on improved diet and individually designed exercise plans were medically recommended." Although this book chapter was not written specifically to address quality of life issues, Roller points out that

> Polio survivors and our counterparts who have similar disabilities justly desire and deserve to maintain lifestyles that are as fully functional, diverse, and independent as possible. As we being to cope with the late effects of our disease, new questions arise: *What can I do to feel good? Could I ever feel as well as an athlete looks? ... Is it possible to have a disability, feel less pain, be more rested, and have more energy for the activities I want to participate in?*

Roller recommends the development of "satisfying leisure-time activities" as part of a health promotion strategy for women in particular and all persons with neuromuscular disabilities. In other words, Roller suggests that disability and wellness (and well-being) are not necessarily contradictory terms.

Koch and Muthny (1990) assert that chronic renal insufficiency patients are no longer faced with an early and painful death. A multidimensional quality of life concept was used to look at the subjective "strains and restrictions for patients whose lives were so dramatically changed by the permanent failure of their renal function." The study took place at the University of Freiburg in Germany in the Department of Rehabilitation Psychology. Leisure activities were identified as a factor in examining the level of psychosocial rehabilitation achieved by patients in different treatment groups. The renal transplantation group showed the most favorable outcome in leisure-time activities as compared to the hemodialysis and continuous ambulatory permanent dialysis groups.

Kaplan (1993) interviewed 25 individuals with severe brain injury and their significant others — 1, 3, and 5 years after injury. He used the Portland Adaptability Inventory (PAI) "to track and quantify the rate of change in, and interrelationships between, emotional, social, and physical aspects of recovery from TBI." Kaplan observed that at 5 years postinjury on the

> Activities and Social Behavior subscale, 48% of the participants had experienced mild problems with disrupted social relationships, and most were also rated as having fewer social contacts, less leisure activity, and continuing, albeit subtle, difficulties with appropriate social interactions.

Ferrans and Powers (1992) administered their Quality of Life Index (QLI) to "349 patients selected randomly from the adult, in-unit hemodialysis patient population of Illinois." Leisure time activities are listed under their "Factor 1: Health and Functioning" of the QLI. Ferrans and Powers suggest that the factorial complexity of the leisure category "could be broken into social, economic, and physical functioning components to reduce conceptual ambiguity" in future studies. This position is consistent with that used by several authors cited within this chapter, who constructed instruments which contained items on leisure, but did not provide a separate leisure score. Leisure may not be as discrete a domain of quality of life as the others mentioned in this book; it has clearly received the least attention in the empirical literature on quality of life and rehabilitation. However, there is evidence that changes in leisure activities are accepted as indicative of appropriate rehabilitation outcomes and that general consensus about the value of leisure for restoration of life function has been developed in the professional rehabilitation community.

REHABILITATIONIST'S ROLE IN THE LEISURE DOMAIN

> The primary purpose of this article was to place Therapeutic Recreation's body of knowledge in the context of rehabilitation sciences using a model that conceptualizes disability and disability research.
>
> *Shank, Coyle, Boyd, and Kinney (1996)*

In his 1996 address to the House Appropriations Subcommittee on Labor, Health and Human Services, Bruce Scott, Consumer Representative to the American Therapeutic Recreation Association (ATRA) asserted that

> therapeutic recreation has been demonstrated to be an effective means to assisting individuals with disabilities to achieve educational objectives and to move from school to adult life. Used as a treatment modality, recreational therapy has been found to be an effective means to assisting individuals with disabilities to increase physical and psychological functioning, and to live more independently and with greater life quality, and to maintain a level of health that prevents or delays the need for costly medical or custodial care.

Shank et al. (1996) proposed a classification scheme for therapeutic recreation research grounded in the rehabilitative sciences. The classification method is based on the model developed by the National Center for Medical Rehabilitation Research (NCMRR), created in 1992 by Congress (P.L. 101-613). The NCMRR model includes pathophysiology, impairment, functional limitation, disability, and societal limitation. The authors emphasize that

> Therapeutic recreation research fits easily into NCMRR's model, whether one chooses to emphasize recreation as a rehabilitative intervention or as an integral component of life quality, health and well-being. That is, the model's conceptualization of disability embraces both principle foci of TR services — therapy and leisure.

Perhaps, more than any speciality within the rehabilitation disciplines, therapeutic recreation will lead the way in promoting quality of life as the standard by which all rehabilitative efforts are measured. The research linking leisure and disability indicates that the development of leisure skills and use of the these skills allows persons with disabilities to achieve higher levels of self-actualization, self-esteem, self-mastery, and life satisfaction (Coyle et al., 1994; Kinney and Coyle, 1992; Weinberg, 1984). Kinney and Coyle (1992) "hypothesize that adults with disabilities go through a cognitive restructuring process that challenges the Western view of leisure as time left over after work and replaces it with a more self-actualizing conception of leisure." This is consistent with Sartorius' (1995) view of the importance of leisure as a rehabilitative issue for the 21st century in which the world population will face the decline of work, as we have known it, because of advances in technology which make workers obsolete.

In an article on planning for permanent unemployment, Macarov (1996) writes:

> The search for full employment represents a societal delusion, given that the world does not need and cannot use all of the human labor available and, as time goes on, will need less and less. The pace of technologically created unemployment is increasing, and unemployment inevitably leads to personal degradation, societal corruption, economic disaster, and global danger. A new social paradigm which does not post work as its underlying and overarching value, is needed. Among other suggestions, that for a universal basic income has attracted serious international interest.

The Canadian futurist, Frank Ogden, addressed the 27th Canadian Association of Rehabilitation Professionals in Victoria, British Columbia in 1997 (attended by an author of this book). He basically echoed Macorov's comments. The rehabilitation professionals, whose focus has been exclusively on assisting marginalized and disabled persons in entering or reentering the workforce rather than seeing enhancement of the client's overall life quality, received Ogden's commentary with fear. Indeed, unless rehabilitation reinvents itself as Sartorius (1995) has demanded, the profession will cease to exist. Rehabilitation professionals will need to be part of creating the new social paradigm will which be based on quality of life issues, and the rehabilitation speciality which offers the most promise in this regard appears to be therapeutic recreation because it offers a methodology to think about disability, illness, and quality of life in a rehabilitative framework not based on employment.

Leisure more than any other domain of quality of life, when linked to rehabilitation, may provide the greatest support for adding to the historical model of losses resulting from injury in civil and administrative law proceedings to go beyond "hard" damages associated with loss of earnings or earning capacity and with costs of future care to add the third dimension, quality of life, as the realm of human function which deals with all aspects of the person impacted by the event/injury. The concept of pain and suffering, seen as the opposite of growth and development from a quality of life analysis which addresses the other aspects of life function not covered by economic damages and medical care needs does not reflect the entire needs, costs, and outcomes of the rehabilitation process.

REFERENCES

Andrews, F. M. (1991). Stability and change in levels and structure of subjective well-being: U.S.A. 1972 and 1988. *Social Indicators Research,* 25: 1-30.

Baker, F., Curbow, B., and Wingard, J. (1991). Role retention and quality of life of bone marrow transplant survivors. *Social Science Medicine*, 32(6): 697-704.

Baker, R., Curbow, B., and Wingard, J. R. (1992). Development of the satisfaction with life domains for cancer. *Journal of Psychosocial Oncology,* 10(3): 75-90.

Blau, T. H. (1977). Quality of life, social indicators, and criteria of change. *Professional Psychology,* 8(4): 464-473.

Bratt, A. and Johnston, R. (1988). Changes in life style for young adults with profound handicaps following discharge from hospital care into a second generation housing project. *Mental Handicap Research,* 1: (1): 49-74.

Brown, R. I., Bayer, M. B., and Brown, P. M. (1988). Quality of life: a challenge for rehabilitation agencies. *Australia and New Zealand Journal of Developmental Disabilities,* 14(3,4): 189-199.

Chibnall, J. T. and Tait, R. C. (1990). The quality of life scale: a preliminary study with chronic pain patients. *Psychology and Health,* 4: 283-292.

Christie, M. J., French, D., Weatherstone, L., West, A., and the Applied Psychology Research Group. (1991). The patient's perceptions of chronic disease and its management: psychosomatics, holism and quality of life in contemporary management of childhood asthma. *Psychotherapy and Psychosomatics,* 56: 197-203.

Ciardiello, J. A. and Bingham, W. C. (1982). The career maturity of schizophrenic clients. *Rehabilitation Counseling Bulletin,* 3-9.

Clark, A. and Hirst, M. (1989). Disability in adulthood: ten-year follow-up of young people with disabilities. *Disability, Handicap and Society,* 4(3): 271-283.

Coyle, C., Lesnick,-Emas, S., and Kinney, W. (1994). Predicting life satisfaction among adults with spinal cord injuries. *Rehabilitation Psychology,* 39(2): 95-112.

Dagan, D., Jones, J., and Ruddick, L. (1994). The psychometric properties of a scale for assessing quality of life of people with learning disabilities in residential care. *The British Journal of Developmental Disabilities*, XI, Part 2(79): 98-103.

Endicott, J., Nee, J., Harrison, W., and Blumenthal, R. (1993). Quality of Life Enjoyment and Satisfaction Questionnaire: a new measure. *Psychopharmacology Bulletin,* 29(2): 321-326.

Fabian, E. S. (1990). Quality of life: a review of theory and practice implications for individuals with long-term mental illness. *Rehabilitation Psychology,* 35(3): 161-170.

Fabian, E. S. (1991). Using quality-of-life indicators in rehabilitation program evaluation. *Rehabilitation Counseling Bulletin,* 34(4): 344-356.

Fabian, E. S. (1992). Supported employment and the quality of life: does a job make a difference? *Rehabilitation Counseling Bulletin,* 36(2): 84-97.

Ferrans, C. E. and Powers, M. J. (1992). Psychometric assessment of the quality of life index. *Research in Nursing and Health,* 15: 29-38.

Fine, A. H. (1996). Leisure, living, and quality of life. In R. Renwick, I. Brown, and M. Nagler (Eds.), *Quality of Life in Health Promotion and Rehabilitation,* pp. 342-354. Thousand Oaks, CA: Sage Publications.

Flanagan, J. C. (1978). A research approach to improving our quality of life. *American Psychologist,* 33(2): 138-147.

Gerber, G. J., Coleman, G. E., Johnston, L, and Lafave, H. G. (1994). Quality of life of people with psychiatric disabilities 1 and 3 years after discharge from hospital. *Quality of Life Research*, 3: 379-383.

Gitter, A. G. and Mostofsky, D. I. (1973). The social indicator: an index of the quality of life. *Social Biology*, 20(3): 289-297.

Goodwin, D. A. J., Boggs, S. R., and Graham-Pole, J. (1994). Development and validation of the pediatric oncology quality of life scale. *Psychological Assessment*, 6(4): 321-328.

Halpern, A. S. (1994). Quality of life for students with disabilities in transition from school to adulthood. *Social Indicators Research*, 33: 193-236.

Hermann, B. P. (1995). The evolution of health-related quality of life assessment in epilepsy. *Quality of Life Research*, 4: 87-100.

House, P. W., Livingston, R. C., and Swinburn, C. D. (1975). Monitoring mankind: the search for quality. *Behavioral Science*, 20: 57-67.

Hughes, C., Hwang, B., Kim, J., Eisenman, L. T., and Killian, D. J. (1995). Quality of life in applied research: a review and analysis of empirical measures. *American Journal on Mental Retardation*, 99(6): 623-641.

Huxley, P. and Warner, R. (1992). Case management, quality of life, and satisfaction with services of long-term psychiatric patients. *Hospital and Community Psychiatry*, 43(8): 799-802.

Hyland, M. E., Finnis, S., and Irvine, S. H. (1991). A scale for assessing quality of life in adult asthma sufferers. *Journal of Psychosomatic Research*, 35(1): 99-110.

Hyland, M. E., Kenyon, C. A. P., and Jacobs, P. A. (1994). Sensitivity of quality of life domains and constructs to longitudinal change in a clinical trial comparing salmetrol with placebo in asthmatics. *Quality of Life Research*, 3: 121-126.

Inge, K. J., Banks, P. D., Wehman, P., Hill, J. W., and Shafer, M. S. (1988). Quality of life for individuals who are labeled mentally retarded: evaluating competitive employment vs. sheltered workshop employment. *Education and Training in Mental Retardation*, 97-104.

Jaeschke, R., Guyatt, G., Cook, D., Harper, S., and Gerstein, H. C. (1994). Spectrum of quality of life impairment in hypothyroidism. *Quality of Life Research*, 3: 323-327.

Kaplan, S. P. (1993). Five-year tracking of psychosocial changes in people with severe traumatic brain injury. *Rehabilitation Counseling Bulletin*, 36(3): 151-159.

Katz, J. N., Larson, M. G., Phillips, C. B., Fossel, A. H., and Liang, M. H. (1992). Comparative measurement sensitivity of short and longer health status instruments. *Medical Care*, 30(10): 917-925.

Kinney, W. and Coyle, C. (1992). Predicting satisfaction among adults with physical disabilities. *Archives of Physical Medicine and Rehabilitation*, 73(9): 863-869.

Koch, U. and Muthny, F. A. (1990). Quality of life in patients with end-stage renal disease in relation to method of treatment. *Psychotherapy and Psychosomatics*, 54:161-171.

Kozleski, E. B. and Sands, D. (1992). The yardstick of social validity: evaluating quality of life as perceived by adults without disabilities. *Education and Training in Mental Retardation*, 119-131.

Kunsbeck, H. W., Korber, J., and Freyberger, H. (1990). Quality of life in patients with inflammatory bowel disease. *Psychotherapy and Psychosomatics*, 54: 110-116.

Leghorn, L. and Parker, K. (1981). *Women's Worth: Sexual Economics and the World of Women*. Boston: Routledge and Kegan.

Macarov, D. (1996). The employment of new ends: planning for permanent unemployment. (Special issue). *The Annals of the American Academy of Political and Social Sciences*, 544: 191-202.

Malm, U., May, P. R. A., and Dencker, S. J. (1981). Evaluation of the quality of life of the schizophrenic outpatient: a checklist. *Schizophrenia Bulletin*, 7(3): 477-487.

McCoy, M. (1994). Career women's leisure: challenges and realties. In C. W. Konek and S. L. Kitch (Eds.), *Women and Careers: Issues and Challenges*, pp. 173-193. Thousand Oaks, CA: Sage Publications.

McGee, H. M., O'Boyle, A., Hickey, A., O'Malley, K., and Joyce, C. R. B. (1991). Assessing the quality of life of the individual: the SEIQoL with a health and a gastroenterology unit population. *Psychological Medicine*, 21: 749-759.

Mulhern, R. K., Fairclough, D. L., Friedman, A. G., and Leigh, L. D. (1990). Play Performance Scale as an index of quality of life of children with cancer. *Psychological Assessment*, 2(2): 149-155.

Munich, R. L. and Lang, E. (1993). The boundaries of psychiatric rehabilitation. *Hospital and Community Psychiatry*, 44(7): 661-665.

Muthny, F. A., Koch, U., and Stump, S. (1990). Quality of life in oncology patients. *Psychotherapy and Psychosomatics*, 54: 145-160.

National Institute on Disability and Rehabilitation Research. (1988). Quality-of-life research in rehabilitation. *Rehab Brief*, XI(1).

Osipow, S. H. and Spokane, A. R. (1987). *Occupational Stress Inventory Manual Research Version.* Odessa, FL: PAR Publishing.

Roller, S. (1996). Health promotion for people with chronic neuromuscular disabilities. In D. M. Krotoski, M. A. Nosek, and M. A. Turk (Eds.). *Women with Physical Disabilities: Achieving and Maintaining Health and Well-Being,* pp. 431-439. Baltimore: Paul H. Brookes.

Rosenfeld, S. (1992). Factors contributing to the subjective quality of life of the chronic mentally ill. *Journal of Health and Social Behavior,* 33: 299-315.

Sackman, B. S. and Ingham, M. (1992). Methods for calculating hedonic loss. *NARRPS Journal and News,* 7(1): 7-14.

Sands, D. J. and Kozleski (1994). Quality of life differences between adults with and without disabilities. *Education and Training in Mental Retardation and Developmental Disabilities*, 90-101.

Sartorius, N. (1995). Rehabilitation and quality of life. *International Journal of Mental Health,* 24(1): 7-13.

Scott, B. (1996). *Testimony presented by Bruce Scott, Consumer Representative on behalf of the American Therapeutic Recreation Association.* House Appropriations Subcommittee on Labor, Health and Human Services and Education. Washington, D.C.

Shank, J. W., Coyle, C. P., Boyd, R., and Kinney, W. B. (1996). A classification scheme for therapeutic recreation research grounded in the rehabilitative sciences. *Therapeutic Recreation Journal*, 179-196.

Sinnott-Oswald, M., Gliner, J. A., and Spencer, K. C. (1991). Supported and sheltered employment: Quality of life issues among workers with disabilities. *Education and Training in Mental Retardation*, 26(4): 388-397.

Slaughter, J. G., Lehman, A. F., and Meyers, C. P. (1991). Quality of life of severely mentally ill adults in residential care facilities. *Adult Residential Care Journal*, 5(2): 97-111.

Spender, D. (1995). *Nattering on the Net: Women, Power, and Cyberspace.* North Melbourne, Australia: Spinifex Press Pty Ltd.

Terman, S. A. (1995). Emotional damages due to wrongful death — What are they worth? *Behavioral Sciences and the Law,* 11: 43-59.

Waring, M. (1988). *If Women Counted: A New Feminist Economics.* San Francisco: Harper and Row.

Whelton, C., Pawlick, and Cardamone, J. (1997). Involving families in psychosocial rehabilitation. *Psychiatric Rehabilitation Journal*, 20(3): 57-60.

Weinberg, N. (1984). Physically disabled persons assess the quality of their lives. *Rehabilitation Literature,* 45: 12-15.

8 The Vocational Domain

WORK AND QUALITY OF LIFE

> Work means being a breadwinner; breadwinners can positively evaluate their contribution in providing for themselves and their families. Work also means independence or autonomy. Work also means success. Occupation has become the most important determinant of a person's position in the stratification system. Finally, work means self-respect because it establishes the mechanism through which individuals demonstrate their worth.
>
> *B. Bolton, 1982*

INTRODUCTION

Elizur and Shye (1990) suggest that one of the major issues to be faced by industrialized countries in the future will be quality of work life as a major contributor to long-term efficiency, productivity, and effectiveness of organizations and the society in general. Quality of work life has been traditionally focused on such areas as availability of jobs, training, mobility, job security, fringe benefits, and earnings. With the emergence of a societal welfare perspective in the world of work, job safety, working conditions, equitable distribution of wages, and job opportunities (Mirvis and Lawler, 1984) have been added to the list of factors influencing quality of work life. Shye (1979) believed that environmental conditions affecting general quality of life included:

1. Physical conditions-buildings, technology, materials, and physical locations
2. Economic conditions — pay, benefits and services
3. Organizational conditions-organizational structure, job design, and social conditions.

Elizur and Shye (1990), in a study of 540 employees of a large industrial corporation, found that work performance was affected by the employees' perception of their quality of life and their quality of work life. A parallelism is suggested between quality of life and quality of work life, supporting the contention that quality of work life is a powerful contributor to overall quality of life. Recognizing that as the workforce ages (51% of the workforce being between 35 and 54 by the year 2000) and becomes more diverse (dealing with greater cultural diversity, inadequate educational preparation, and the need for inclusion of persons with disabilities), a change in what people need and value from work, Jamieson and O'Mara (1991) suggested that self-development, health and wellness and lifestyle quality will be equally as important to workers as financial security, accomplishment, respect, autonomy, and involvement in the work, the more traditional approaches to enhancement of quality of work life experiences.

Pugliesi (1995) pointed out that employment status and paid work have been associated with lower depression and distress as well as greater self-esteem and life satisfaction among men and women. Happiness was found to correlate significantly with self-esteem, job satisfaction, and social support. Halpern (1994), upon examining the definitions of quality of life commonly found in the literature, suggested that assessment of quality of life should include such subjective factors as psychological well-being and life satisfaction, as well as such objective factors as economic stability, health, growth and mastery, and quality of environment. The discrepancy or convergence between one's expectations and outcomes across these factors was seen as the basis upon which ratings of quality of life are based. Quality of life would likely occur where a person needs to work and the work is available, the social milieu in which the person functions expects the person to work and the person has the ability to work, and community resources are available and they can cultivate a person's abilities. Three domains of life function were identified as being critical areas for assessment of quality of life: (1) physical and material well-being; (2) performance of adult roles, and (3) personal fulfillment. Under physical and material well-being, wages and benefits (including health benefits) associated with work can contribute to food, clothing, and lodging, safety from harm, financial security, and physical and mental health. One of the most important adult roles is that of a worker. Vocation, career, and employment as well as educational attainment (as a precursor to work) are very important adult roles. Over time, accomplishments in these areas build a sense of personal fulfillment and a durable sense of well-being. Work plays a substantive role in promoting quality of life.

Near et al. (1978), in a random survey of residents of two counties, one in New York and the other in Pennsylvania, found a significant correlation between life satisfaction and job satisfaction, health, and satisfaction over lifetime. Men were found to be healthier and more satisfied over time than women, older workers demonstrated more job and life satisfaction than younger workers (although job satisfaction was highest among managerial/professional workers), and white collar workers reported better health than blue collar workers. Job tenure was not significantly related to job or life satisfaction. Education and marital status appeared to be the most powerful demographic variable in that it correlated significantly with job satisfaction, life satisfaction, satisfaction over time, and health. The higher the level of education self-reported, the more life satisfaction, satisfaction over time, and job satisfaction and better health were evidenced. Divorced and separated people reported the lowest health and life satisfaction as compared to married and widowed persons.

Manz and Grothe (1991) noted that quality of work life is a major concern of the concern of employers facing dealing with a workforce which is now in its twenties in the 21st century. Such factors as physical work environment, job design, job clarity, personal motivation, and the meaning of the job are taking precedence over such traditional factors as desire to manage, opportunities to advance, salary, and benefits in the career decision-making of younger workers. The lack of fit between the employee and the organization was seen as a cause of deficiencies in quality of work life. Compatibility between the employee and the organization was seen to have a moderating effect on occupational stress, while maintaining or enhancing job performance. Younger workers derived significantly less quality of work life as compared to all three older groups (41 to 50, 51 to 60, and 61+) on personal motivation, personal investment, meaningfulness of the job, innovation, quality/productivity, communication of organization, policies and procedures, human resource system, management effectiveness, supervisory skills, job design, physical work environment, and career training. The contribution of work resources, policy and procedures, compensation, innovation, personal investment, and management effectiveness to quality of work life was more marked as the age group increased. Self-leadership, self-directed work design, and emphasis on education were suggested as ways to deal with changes in organizational factors influencing quality of work life. It was of interest that the sample included a disproportionately low number of persons with low income and less than a high school education. Therefore, it is difficult to generalize these results to quality of work life in the latter group.

Although employer-based quality of life issues are important, Loscocco and Spitz (1990) argued that individual work attitudes were equally as important contributors to quality of work life as structural considerations. Work values, as an indicator of affectivity, have been associated with job satisfaction (Watson and Clark, 1984). The relationship between age and work attitudes was explained by Kalleberg and Loscocco (1983) as one where people shift their expectations of work to suit the stage of career development in which they find themselves, where older workers typically have better jobs and are more satisfied, or where different cohorts of workers around the same age define the age-specific expectations from work. Several authors (Gruenberg, 1980; Lincoln and Kalleberg, 1985) have pointed out that education and the raised expectations associated therewith contribute to lack of satisfaction with job rewards.

Gender was seen as another important issue in quality of work by Loscocco and Spitz (1990) who postulated that gender and family roles were hypothesized to create differing work attitudes. Several authors (Duxbury and Higgins, 1991; Paludi, 1990) suggest that the demands of parenting have a greater effect on the career path and achievement of woman than men. Coverman (1989) noted that role overload (i.e., experiencing multiple role demands and not having enough time to fulfill them) negatively affect marital and job satisfaction in women. Feldberg and Glen (1979) and Lennon and Rosenfeld (1992) found an interaction between work and family demands. Women who had low autonomy at work were more negatively affected by competing family demands than were their more autonomous peers. Addelman (1987) noted that control over the work and income were sources of happiness for men, but found no single work characteristic which was a significant predictor of women's happiness. Lefkowitz (1994) found that occupational advancement and income level had the greatest influence on career satisfaction of men and women; and that at a given level of earnings, women were less satisfied with promotional opportunities. Gender inequities in income, status, resources, power, housework, medical and legal treatment, as well as family obligations have been addressed by authors (Travis, 1992; Green and Russo, 1993; Lefkowitz, 1994. Lerner, 1987). Women more than men need to seek a balance between their work and nonwork lives (Powell and Mainero, 1992).

Roxburgh (1996), in a study of 944 employed persons, found that highly routine work allowed women with chronic problems with children to have the time to ruminate; and thus, to experience more distress and less happiness associated with work. In contrast, men did not ruminate when performing routine tasks. Pugliesi (1995) found, in a study of 1352 full- and part-time workers that men had significantly greater control and complexity in their work and women had significantly greater social support but also greater distress. Although self-esteem and job satisfaction were both found to significantly reduce stress, self-esteem had a more powerful effect than job satisfaction. Family roles had a stronger influence on the job satisfaction of males than females, a finding that is somewhat inconsistent with historical thinking about interaction of gender, family demands, and job satisfaction.

LINKAGE BETWEEN CAREER DEVELOPMENT, FORENSIC REHABILITATION, AND QUALITY OF LIFE

> A career development approach facilitates growth of the attitudes, knowledge, behavior, and skills essential to cope adequately with the tasks of a given life stage.
>
> *Ciardiello and Bingham, 1982*

Career trends in the 1990s revolve more around selection of career paths rather than upward career development (Stoltz-Lokle, 1995). Career transitions and organizational change have become the norm, with words like *downsizing*, *relocation*, and *re-engineering* being the "buzz words" for career transitions which no longer guarantee upward mobility. Women's roles are changing in that more are working; yet, their career paths remain less continuous than those of men due to family issues, making them more vulnerable to organizational change. The role of chance in influencing career and life choices and in developing career paths has been recognized by several authors (Krumboltz, 1976; Bandura, 1982; Vondracek et al. 1983). Nicholson and West (1989) noted that orderly, step-like care development occurs only in 10% of the workforce. Goldberg (1972) found that persons with disabilities were not likely to follow the logical, sequenced stages of career development articulated by Super (1990); suggested that persons with disabilities had "spurts" of career development in response to internal changes (i.e., physical, emotional, cognitive; etc.) and external situations (i.e., life circumstances). Injuries caused by accidents are often no more anticipated than job restructuring or loss due to organizational change. One could argue that chance more than planning or reaction more than prescription are operating equally in the work lives of disabled and nondisabled persons.

Appropriate response to sudden, unanticipated career change, is not well-defined in traditional career development literature. Bejian and Salomone (1995) pointed to Super's protracted maintenance stage in the career development process as an excellent example of how chance operated in the past as opposed to the present. They suggested a sixth, "career renewal" stage to Super's five-stage model which includes self-appraisal, reorganization of personal and career priorities and reorienting to present and future planning. At this stage one re-evaluates one's life events, considers the quality of one's accomplishments, makes decisions to alter priorities, and realizes one's own mortality. Taylor et al. (1995) identified locus of control as one of the factors which influences coping style during adult career transitions, suggesting that those with internal locus of control were more likely to redefine and expand roles while those with external locus of control were more likely to respond more passively and less successfully. Cabral and Salomone (1990) felt that those individuals who had an internal locus of control were able to engage in enabling behaviors which were offered in response to chance life events. Their self-concepts were seen as more positive (i.e., thoughts of competency, strong caring; and empathetic values) than those of persons with an external locus of control. The person with the well-developed self-concept has a better filter through which to absorb the meaning of an unforeseen event and thus is more adaptive to change in life circumstances. Engels (1996) added that the person with the most internal career resilience (in response to change) and renewal has the most upward mobility (receiving greater rewards for adaptability). Adapting to unanticipated changes was seen as essential to career success.

In this time of constant change in life roles and of ongoing attempts to maintain homeostasis between the external and internal worlds, it may be more important than ever before to look to quality of life as a major indicator of career success for persons with or without disabilities. Bejian and Salomone (1995) linked career choices at times of renewal to overall life satisfaction and meaning. The efficacy of career change was to be weighed against the standard of total life function, necessitating one's consideration of quality of life for the remainder of one's life span. Brown and Crace (1996) added that life satisfaction resulted from how one's needs were satisfied when performing work and nonwork (i.e., leisure, social, marital; etc.) roles simultaneously and warned against looking at career issues outside the context of total life function. Roessler (1988) recognized the need for examining personal, social, and vocational roles when developing and implementing goals and strategies for adjustment to disability, recognizing that total life function rather than just vocational performance was a critical variable in promoting positive, long-term rehabilitation outcomes.

It appears that the interaction between internal (i.e., self-concept, values, cognitive expectancies, self-rewards; etc.) and external factors (educational options, labor market trends, financial remuneration, developmental life events, etc.) leads one to pursue a certain career path as part of an overall life path. Success in career choices and accomplishments for the disabled like the nondisabled persons appears to play a very important role in one's global assessment of quality of life. Shain (1996) points to work as a key element in one's development of mental health through encouraging development of self-worth and confidence, a feeling of belongingness, a sense of personal meaning and identity, and a desire to be involved in maintaining the social order. Mental health is seen as a prerequisite to quality of life (i.e., the experiencing of joy and happiness). When dealing with persons with or without disabilities, one could argue that vocational decision-making and career path selection should include assessment of the impact of internal as well as external issues on quality of life. Quality of life offers a conceptual framework to judge the impact of work-related decisions and resultant activities on total life function. Zunker (1990) notes that vocational self-concept, a major influence on career decision-making, develops through, in part, mental and physical growth and development. Self-concept is seen as a driving force in career development.

Such external factors as general environment, life experience with work, and identification with adult workers also impact the course of one's career path. Developmental theorists (Tiedeman and O'Hara, 1963; Ginzberg, 1984; Super, 1990) have recognized that one's ultimate life satisfaction is tied to success in making and implementing career choices. The ultimate outcome of career development is satisfaction with work. Satisfaction with work, as a central component of life function, can play a central role in total life satisfaction or quality of life.

Gender differences in well-being when confronted with work-related stressors was investigated by Roxburgh (1996). It was hypothesized that women who work had better mental health, but not necessarily better overall well-being as compared to men. Several authors (Chapman et al. 1994; Ulrich and Dunne, 1986) suggested that the need to balance home and work roles create unique stressors for women. Gutek et al. (1991) postulated that women experience higher levels of work–family conflict than men. Duxbury and Higgins (1991) found that work–family conflict was more likely to have a significantly negative impact on a woman's career than on that of a male. Pugliesi (1985) suggested that the degree of complexity of the work increases distress and well-being decreases. It was further hypothesized that women who have lesser control over their jobs were more vulnerable to stressors and experienced less well-being than those with more control over their work environment. More women than men leave the labor market or reduce their exposure to stress through part-time work. Pugliesi (1985) Findings suggested that women ($n = 524$) are exposed to a higher level of job stress through lower levels of perceived control and because of the lower complexity of their jobs than their male counterparts ($n = 542$). Women used higher co-worker support (i.e., social relationships) to buffer work stress. However, vulnerability did not correlate with gender and job complexity.

Whether one is male or female, Elizur and Shye's (1990) finding that quality of life and quality of work life affect one's performance suggests that quality of work life and quality of life in general are issues that must be addressed when looking at ways of boosting a worker's job performance.

QUALITY OF LIFE, WORK, AND FORENSIC REHABILITATION

> Satisfaction with work and life and the perceived quality of work performance are located between the QWL (quality of work life) and QOL (quality of life) regions. This indicates that employees' quality of work performance is affected by their QOL, as well as by their QWL.
>
> *Elizur and Shye, 1990*

As rehabilitationists and forensic experts, the authors of this document have seen numerous examples of failure to address quality of life issues when dealing with the vocational rehabilitation of persons with disabilities. Because injured adults need to meet their burdensome financial obligations, the desire of rehabilitationists to promote case closures, or the concern of payers to control cost of care, career decision-making can focus on return to a job, any job, without concern for the impact of job choice on total life function. Immediate financial rewards, when given greater weight than quality of life considerations in decision-making about future career paths, can appear quite attractive in the short-term and not lead to long-term life satisfaction. Quality of life, a long-term outcome of rehabilitation, may be sacrificed for the short-term "quick fix." Williams (1995) points out that enhancement of quality of life is an primary goal of the rehabilitation process; that all decisions about future interventions (i.e., vocational, medical, psychological; etc.) should be made only after a thorough understanding of their impact on quality of life in the present and future has been achieved. It is not uncommon for persons who have experienced trauma associated with unanticipated injury or harm to lack the internal or external resources to identify the appropriate career path for enhancing quality of life. Assistance from vocational rehabilitation professionals should center around strategies and interventions which restore quality of life.

Many times, for persons lacking in socioeconomic and educational resources, the primary focus of the rehabilitation professional is return to any work (Williams, 1995), without regard to educational or skill attainment, level of earnings, and the resulting socioeconomic status. Only with those persons who had a higher educational, acquired skill, earnings, and socioeconomic level before the injury or harm does quality of life become an issue, and then, only if the discussion is initiated by the injured or harmed party. Even with young adults or children, where lifestyle has not been defined and career decision-making has been tentative at best, earnings rather than total life function may be seen as the litmus test of the efficacy of identified rehabilitation strategies and outcomes. The question of whether or not an injured child or adult should be given the same opportunities to maximize their quality of life after injury or harm as they had before the event/occurrence is particularly interesting in a forensic rehabilitation setting where choices about career paths can affect overall quality of life. Maximizing income potential may or may not result in maximizing quality of life. The impact of career choices on the social, psychological, educational, leisure, and physical domains of life function as well as income needs to be explored.

As Tiedeman and Miller-Tiedeman (1984) suggest, one only has a finite amount of time to devote to all life activities. Choice of how time is allocated to the performance of work and nonwork activities determines total quality of life. Each individual must weigh the value of activities in each domain of life function against his or her personal assessment of the contribution of these activities to his or her unique perception of quality of life. One's ability to acquire goods and services across all life domains is affected by income; therefore, ability to work is a powerful factor in determination of quality of life. However, the work itself may have a greater or lesser impact on quality of life. With younger persons, time is an important asset, creating greater opportunities for choice of work which suits their perceptions of quality of life. For older adults, quality of life may need to be compromised in response to realities of available work in the labor market. As noted by Roe (1956), life circumstances within and beyond any individual's control change throughout life. Goodness of life is constantly redefined in response to changing individual and societal factors. Maintaining individual and societal stability is not a static, but rather a dynamic process. One must continuously make work-related choices, and choices influence satisfaction with work and life in general. These vocational choices affect both income and quality of life. It is important to understand that vocational choices made on the sole criterion of income may not lead to the best long-term results. One should look at one's special abilities, (aptitudes, intelligence, physical abilities and disabilities), such environmental factors as availability of educational or work options and associated costs or income, one's learning about the world of work, one's willingness to approach a task and work towards its accomplishment, one's historical learning about self from self-observation when interacting with the environment, and one's historical learning about the world from interacting with it when making vocational choices (Mitchell and Krumboltz, 1984). Vocational choice is a complex process that is looked at simplistically if only loss of earnings or earning capacity is used as the benchmark for judging the efficacy of past or future vocational decisions. Vocational choices can be better understood when looked at within the context of quality of life. Choices about future vocational behaviors, if they are to benefit total life function, should reflect the individual's historical perspective about a lifestyle which enhances quality of life. The rehabilitation expert must look at the factors which have influenced the past and will impact future vocational choices within the context of total quality of life.

Career or vocational potential is the area where loss can best be quantified and gains through appropriate rehabilitation interventions can be measured because work generates quantifiable income. Looking at vocational choices against the standard of pre- vs. post-injury differences in income has long been seen in forensic rehabilitation (Williams and Maze, 1994). However, little consideration has been given to the "ripple effects" of a vocational choice on all other areas of life function before and after an injury or event. Therefore, it is critically important to address quality of life issues in rehabilitation planning for career development over work life. It is not surprising that work and quality of life have been discussed at some length in the rehabilitation literature. It is only surprising that it has not been discussed at great length as part of vocational and/or earning capacity assessment in forensic rehabilitation. By looking at what has been done outside the forensic arena, rehabilitationists can gain insights into the interaction between career development, earning capacity, and quality of life.

DISABILITY, WORK, AND QUALITY OF LIFE: FOUNDATIONS IN THE LITERATURE

> The concept of disability has typically been associated with work. People who find pleasure in work will be more functional in work and nonwork settings, including in compliance with medical and other care regimens.
>
> *Dorto and Williams, 1997*

Disability is not just a medical or legal term. Impairment is defined by medical and/or psychological examination, testing, and expert opinion in and outside of civil or administrative law proceedings. Disability is a function of impairment (typically physical or psychosocial), limitations in function (inability to perform certain behaviors), and barriers to normal life function. As suggested by Wright (1980) and Dorto and Williams (1997), the term, "disability," as used in Social Security disability settings, workers' compensation, discrimination, and personal injury matters, requires that the impact of impairment, functional limitations, and barriers to function upon ability to work and earn income be assessed. It is possible that a person could have an impairment, functional limitations, and no disability by the nature of the physical and/or mental demands of past work, additional skills, and knowledge acquired through training that could be used to modify existing work activities or to allow entry into new types of work. Williams and Maze (1994) pointed out that even persons with limited impairments, few functional limitations, and significant skills may have difficulty being re-employed in the labor market due to employer reluctance to hire persons with impairments. Employability asks the question of whether, in light of the person's age, education, and acquired skills and physical and mental capacities, the person is able to perform the tasks associated with a given job or a number of jobs which exist in the labor market. The likelihood of placement deals with the ability of the person to acquire work in a given labor market. Therefore, assessment of disability inevitably must address the capacity to work and to secure employment. The ability to work provides an objective benchmark for determining wage losses associated with reduced function. Actual earnings associated with work can be used as a key indicator of partial or total disability. Inability to work may be the most definitive indicator of disability.

Schalock (1996) noted that work or school is one of the three major life domains in which quality of life is determined and physical and mental health or wellness is another. Since determination of disability invariably focuses on physical and mental capacities and ability to work, disability affects two of the three major domains of quality of life. The remaining domain, home and community living, also contributes to quality of life and influences work or school performance and physical and mental health and wellness. See Table III for a list of the work/school and health/wellness indicators of quality of life in this model developed by Schalock. The clarity of the relationship between work and health, as seen in this model, is best seen by days missed from work due to illness or doctor's appointments being a criterion for health. Work and health/wellness are not mutually exclusive domains. Whatever affects one may affect the other. Any discussion of disability and work is inherently addressing issues which contribute to quality of life. Quality of life may be the better global measure of disability rather than inability to earn income. However, quality of life does not translate readily to dollars. Impact of disability on work and associated changes in income can be operationalized in concrete, dollar terms. However, decisions about quality of life issues can affect vocational choices (motivating a person to change jobs, careers, relocate).

TABLE IV
Person-Centered Indicators of Quality of Life

Domain	Indicator
Work	Integrated employment
	Fair wages
	Employment benefits
	Safe work conditions
	Feedback
	Meaningful avocational activities
or	
School	Age-appropriate materials and tasks
	Functional skills training
	Integrated/"mainstreamed" classrooms
	Integrated/"mainstreamed" leisure activities
Health	Activities of daily living — eating, transfer toileting, dressing, and bathing
	Good nutrition
	Access to health care
	Mobility
	Minimum education
or	
Wellness	Number of days sick, missing work, going to doctors
	Number of hospitalizations
	Medication level
	Time out of bed
	Physical fitness — strength, agility, flexibility, and balance
	Cardiorespiratory endurance
	Activity level — number of full and partial activities

Quality of work life, although related to overall quality of life, as suggested by Elizur and Shye (1990), may or may not influence vocational choices and opportunities to a greater degree than other aspects of quality of life. The global construct of quality of life may better explain all the life choices that go into career-related decisions than just quality of work life alone. For persons with disabilities, the global construct of quality of life may be more sensitive to the interaction and interdependence of all the factors which influence career path and associated earnings than quality of work life alone. The concept of normalization, as defined by Wolfensberger (1972), has been used as a rationale for providing persons with disabilities the same access to activities and rhythms of life that have characterized the lifestyles of typical nondisabled adults out of a strongly held belief that enhanced quality of life would be the result. Work has been seen as a major contributor to mental and physical health and wellness, prerequisites to enhanced quality of life for all persons whether disabled or nondisabled (Shain, 1996); therefore, access to work as a core life activity is critical to enhancing the quality of life of persons with disabilities to the same degree that it is for persons without disabilities. Work contributes to socioeconomic status, independence/interdependence, personal development, social integration, and a sense of personal accomplishment (derived from productivity). In turn, enhanced quality of life can result in greater quality of work produced. Work is not seen as an isolated factor in overall life function. Its contribution to life function for all persons exceeds its mere ability to generate income because it does impact overall quality of life.

Differences in overall quality of life between disabled and nondisabled persons are particularly interesting to rehabilitationists who are charged with the responsibility of identifying the impact of disability on life function and for coordinating the development of care plans which articulate specific interventions which will be offered in the future. If differences in the quality of life and particularly, in quality of work life (a traditional area of interest, graduate level training, and expertise for rehabilitation professionals) between disabled and nondisabled persons can be empirically quantified, the impact of disability on quality of work life and overall quality of life can then be examined on a case-by-case basis. Development of an empirical baseline for what is normative quality of life for nondisabled populations can be used to set the standard upon which to judge the global loss of life function as the result of disability and to assess the gains from the appropriate interventions (as suggested by normalization theory). Isolating those dimensions of quality of life which are most affected by disability can be helpful in quantifying the difference in an individual's experiencing of life after a traumatic and possibly disabling life event. Wolfensberger's (1991) contention that supported employment has been the key factor in integrating persons with disabilities into the mainstream of society, a precursor to normative quality of life, points to work as a central theme in quality of life for disabled as well as nondisabled persons.

Ruchlin and Morris (1991) conducted a survey of 2682 persons between the ages of 60 and 72 and found that 85.7% of the working elderly, as opposed to 57.1% of the nonworking elderly, reported the highest quality of life rating, suggesting that work was a significant contributor to overall quality of life of older workers, many of whom had identified significant problems in the areas of health and independence. Feeling useful and valued for one's work was seen as important to overall quality of life. This finding suggested that age does not necessarily reduce the impact of work on quality of life for persons with increased health problems and reduced independence. Brown (1989) postulated that normalization theory should be applied to aging as it has been to developmental disability, supporting the contention that work and other life roles do not diminish in importance with aging as they do not with disability.

Kozleski and Sands (1992) conducted a survey of Colorado residents ($n = 133$) to determine their quality of life, as measured by a modified form of the Consumer Satisfaction Survey (Temple University, 1988). Approximately one third of the sample were men and two thirds were women. Although minorities were represented in the sample, 89.5% of the respondents were white. All of the 72 respondents who were working stated that they were either somewhat or very satisfied with their current job. At the same time, 88% reported that they were somewhat or very satisfied with life in general. When asked about their autonomy in decision-making about job choices, 77% responded positively. When asked about general level of independence, 88% responded favorably.

Sands and Kozleski (1994) surveyed 131 persons without disabilities and 86 persons with disabilities, ranging in age from 18 to 70. Although minorities were represented, 88% of the sample was white. The gender distribution in the sample was 41% male and 59% female. Of the 86 persons with disabilities responding to the survey, 61% identified their primary disability as mental retardation, 13% identified cerebral palsy, and 4% indicated head injury. The median income of persons with disabilities was $10,500 per year and of persons without disabilities was $17,500. Both the disabled and nondisabled workers saw themselves as somewhat to very satisfied with their jobs (no dissatisfaction being recorded); no significant difference in life satisfaction was seen between disabled and nondisabled participants (88% across both groups identifying themselves as being somewhat to very satisfied with life). Persons with disabilities saw themselves as more dependent than and less satisfied with the frequency and variety of their involvement in community, recreational, and leisure activities (despite their general life satisfaction) than their nondisabled counterparts. Satisfaction was not a central area of difference in life satisfaction, a finding that may reflect the efficacy of vocational services for persons with developmental disabilities, given that 74% of the disabled persons participating in the study were developmentally disabled.

In a nationwide health survey of 3251 persons from 2909 households throughout the U.S. (Lerner et al. 1994), 2474 respondents (74%) who completed the 36-item Medical Outcomes Study Short Form Health Survey (with its 8 subscales measuring physical, emotional, social, and role functioning; bodily pain; vitality, and general and mental health perceptions; with excellent internal consistency reliability [0.76–0.93] and extensive support for its validity) indicated the degree to which such work factors as job strain, job insecurity, psychological or physical demands of work, and career prospects influenced their life quality. Findings suggested that job strain had the largest impact on mental health, the high job strain group having double the odds of poor mental health. Workplace support was linked to higher odds of freedom from bodily pain as well as improved vitality. As chronic conditions (up to three or more) increased, the odds of good health decreased. Job insecurity and physically demanding work were linked in several models. Job strain could influence one's perception of quality of life and well-being directly or indirectly contribute to physical and mental disease. The significance of these findings for persons with disabilities is that any chronic condition put the person at higher risk for greater health problems when placed in a high strain work situation. Low demand and high control or high demand and high control jobs were seen as the healthiest, while high demand and low control jobs were seen as highly stressful and potentially unhealthy. The significance of these findings lies in the potential for placement of chronically ill, disabled individuals in high demand, low control unskilled (i.e., production jobs with quotas; hand assembly tasks where a conveyor belt does not stop and wait; telemarketing or other jobs with sales quotas — typical jobs offered to injured workers with limited education and little or no acquired skills) or semi-skilled jobs (i.e., feeding/offbearing jobs; clerk, typist, data entry clerk, kitchen helper) with no regard for quality of life issues. The potential for exacerbation of physical and/or mental illness as quality of life declines may partially explain why some rehabilitation clients resist placement in high demand, low control jobs. Poor adjustment of truck drivers to highly structured, controlled work settings inside and with constant pressure for production by a supervisor, as noted repeatedly by the authors of this text in their respective rehabilitation practices, may best be explained by the impact of such jobs on quality of life. Likewise, an executive, after a head injury, might not deal well with the structure, production standards, and timed productivity associated with clerical occupations, when historically as an executive, he or she would have had control over the work when dealing with high demands. Moos and Moos' (1983) finding that time urgency and pressure when coupled with restrictive structure and control in the workplace led to dissatisfaction with work and burnout may add further clarity to the reactions of some persons with disabilities to being asked to work in settings which offer the antithesis of an atmosphere that would enhance quality of life. Increased physical and/or mental illness may result from inappropriate job choices and resultant deterioration in quality of life. This study suggests that poor vocational choices (as measured against the standard of quality of life) can negatively impact quality of work life directly and indirectly impact physical and mental functioning and vitality. Thus, it appears to be safe to say that for persons with disabilities, work may play a considerable role in determining their quality of life.

The findings of Verbrugge et al. (1994) suggested that people who work may have significantly higher well-being than persons who do not work. Doing some form of work may be better than doing nothing for enhancement of quality of life among disabled and nondisabled populations. The linkage between low well-being, depression, and lack of social contact mentioned in this study lends credibility to the contention that work may be a critical factor in mitigating the negative effects of depression on well-being.

Whether dealing with persons with mental or physical disabilities or in some combination, the primary challenge for them is to secure and hold employment which can provide income to meet their financial needs. Clark and Hirst (1989), in a study of 44 (n = 100) severely physically impaired persons (between the ages 25 to 30), found that 18 persons (46%) worked in the open labor market, most in skilled, nonmanual work (9) and semiskilled manual jobs (3). Of the 19 respondents not working, almost three quarters said they would like to have a job. Scuccimarra and Speece (1990), in a study of 70 handicapped students (60 being learning disabled, 6 being mentally retarded, and the remainder being emotionally or physically impaired) 2 years after graduation from high school found that 51 (78.5%) were employed (wages: 7 at minimum wage — \$3.35; 33 at \$3.36 to \$5.00; 11 over \$5.00 per hour; skill level: 31 unskilled, 4 skilled, and 16 semiskilled). The highest percentage of workers were in the fields of clerical/sales, service, and structural occupations. Of the males 90.9% were working and of the females, 52.4% were employed.

Dikmen et al. (1994), in a study of 366 head-injured persons who completed varying types of head injury programming, found that age, educational level, severity of injury, and prior job stability were significant factors in return to work. Only 46% of those over 51 as opposed to 78% of those between 31 and 50 years of age returned to work. Only 46% of those with less than a high school education returned to work, while 87% with a bachelor's degree or higher returned to work at 24 months from the date of injury. Severity of head injury also played a significant role in return to work, with only 37% of those who had received a rating of 8 or less on the Glasgow Coma Scale as opposed to 83% of those with a score of 13 or higher returning to work. For those with stable work histories before injury, 80% returned to work, while for those with unstable work histories, 60% returned to work. In a study of 175 individuals who had been diagnosed as having severe brain injury (mean rating of 5 on the Glasgow Coma Scale) and had received intensive rehabilitation, Ponsford et al. (1995) found that 35 (33% of the 106 employed patients employed prior to their head injuries) were employed on a full-time basis, and 9 (9%) were employed on a part-time basis. Sixty-two (58%) were unemployed. Malec et al. (1993) reported that 29% of the graduates of a post-acute outpatient brain injury program were unemployed at the end of the program as compared to 52% at the time of admission; this percentage remained stable through the 1-year follow-up. Early intervention produced return-to-work outcomes superior to late intervention. Melamed et al. (1992) conducted a follow-up study on 72 traumatically brain injured patients discharged from a rehabilitation hospital and found significantly greater satisfaction with vocational activities (on the Rehabilitation Need and Status Scale, an 80-item paper-and-pencil measure of physiological, emotional-security, family, social, economic-self-esteem, economic-security, and vocational self-actualization need satisfaction) among those who worked ($n = 37$) vs. those who did not work ($n = 30$). Also, greater acceptance of disability was significantly greater for those who worked vs. those who did not. Asikainen et al. (1996) studied 496 patients who had been referred for rehabilitation and re-employment and found that for the 17 to 24-year old age group, 64% were working in the competitive labor market. It was noted that the older patients did not have as positive a vocational outcome (39% returning to competitive employment). Only 17% of the severely brain-injured patients who had a vocational/technical or college education before injury made a good recovery. It appeared that the higher one's education was prior to injury, the greater the probability of independent or subsidized work. These findings suggest that severity of brain injury and preinjury level of education affect one's probability of return to work after a head injury. Furthermore, they point to age as another important factor in return to work. Since quality of life at least in part is influenced by work, the efficacy of rehabilitation interventions for persons with head injuries should be judged on their ability to result in returning the head-injured person to work. Factors such as age, education, and severity of the injury would need to be considered when determining the feasibility of incorporating a return to work strategy into a rehabilitation plan designed to enhance quality of life. Furthermore, those rehabilitation interventions and programs which demonstrate their ability to assist head-injured patients in returning to work may be concomitantly demonstrating their ability to enhance the person's quality of life.

Similarly, any rehabilitation intervention or program that promotes return to work for any persons with disabilities may be enhancing that person's quality of life. Schmidt et al. (1995) surveyed 390 participants (41% of whom suffered from back pain, 20% from brain injury, 12% from neurological disorders, 8% from trauma, and 7% from rheumatoid arthritis) involved in a vocational rehabilitation program and found a significant positive relationship between gender and work experience and return to work. A significant inverse relationship between age and return to work was noted, a finding which was possibly influenced by the high proportion of participants who had back injuries. Persons with work experience were seen as having the highest probability of return to work; men were significantly more likely to work than women. In a study of 97 randomly selected workers with low back pain, Greenberg and Pollo (1996) found that 75 to 85%

of these previously employed workers returned to work after work hardening. Radanov et al. (1993) assessed the psychosocial stress, negative affectivity, personality traits, and attentional functioning of 97 persons with cervical sprain or strain, found that the disabled persons were significantly more anxious (demonstrating negative affectivity as assessed through use of a self-report measure on well-being) than nondisabled persons; and reported significantly greater neck pain and more back pain than the nondisabled participants. Age was also seen as a significant factor with respect to disability status. Straaton et al. (1995), in a study of 4093 recipients of vocational rehabilitation services for musculoskeletal disability, found significant relationships between successful rehabilitation outcomes and education greater or equal to 12 years, severity of disability, and employment prior to vocational rehabilitation. Osberg et al. (1987) noted that age, income, and functional capacity (both mental and physical abilities) greatly influenced life satisfaction and quality of life. It appears that the same factors affect one's probability of working and one's quality of life, suggesting a potential relationship between quality of life and working for persons with varying type and severity of musculoskeletal disabilities.

Quality of life for persons with spinal cord injuries has received some attention in the rehabilitation literature, and work has been mentioned frequently as a factor in life satisfaction for this disability group. Krause (1992) surveyed 286 former patients at an outpatient clinic (81% men; 61% quadriplegia; $n = 347$) using the Life Situation Questionnaires, a self-report measure which contains two life satisfaction subscales, one on general satisfaction (social, sex, general health, family relationships, recreational opportunities, emotional adjustment, and control over life) and the other on economic satisfaction (employment, finances). Test–retest reliability coefficients ranged from 0.71 to 0.91 over 102 days. As compared to persons who were never employed since their injuries, employed participants reported greater general and economic satisfaction and saw themselves as better adjusted, more independent, healthier, and less emotionally distressed than those who had not been employed since their spinal cord injuries. Persons who had worked saw themselves as having significantly greater life opportunities and more control over their lives than those who did not work (suggesting that independence and autonomy may result, at least in part, from work). Satisfaction with work and with finances was significantly greater among those who were working as opposed to those that were not postinjury.

Ville and Ravaud (1996) in a study of spinal cord injured persons ($n = 277$) who had been injured for at least three years and were using a wheelchair and or crutches, found that 66% (66 out of 176) men and 33.7% (34 out of 101) women were working. As education increased from primary grades to postsecondary, the percentage of spinal cord injured persons working rose from 19.2% (14 out of 73) to 65.5% (38 out of 58). Men who acquired the spinal cord injury after age 15, had completed postsecondary education, and who had a father who was an office worker or upper manager and were fathers themselves reported the highest work satisfaction. The women who were most satisfied with not working were those living as a couple, having a father who was a upper manager, having no children, and acquiring the handicap before age 15. Satisfaction with work did increase with age. Generally, across the sexes, acquiring the spinal cord injury before age 15 increased the probability that the person would work.

The traumatic abuse of women has only recently emerged in the rehabilitation literature as a vocational impairment issue for women (Murphy, 1993, 1994, 1996). Understanding posttraumatic stress disorder (PTSD) and physical disabilities caused by battering as work disabilities is still not fully appreciated in the rehabilitation profession, but has come to be a significant issue in welfare reform where welfare mothers are now expected to enter the labor market within rigid time constraints. Raphael (1997) reports that

> Four new research studies, which, although using different methods including random and nonrandom surveys of welfare caseloads and random neighborhood surveys, document high and remarkably consistent prevalence of domestic violence within welfare caseloads.

Obviously, both the quality of women's lives and their work lives are affected by the experience of traumatic abuse along with resultant disabilities for some. In a qualitative study of the request for reasonable accommodation under the Americans with Disabilities Act, Murphy (1994) noted that PTSD appeared to be a more serious barrier to obtaining and maintaining employment than the most debilitating physical disability. The research summarized above suggests that research is needed to explore quality of life and quality of work life issues for women survivors of traumatic abuse who are now facing an unprecedented demand that they enter the labor market despite their status as mothers of small children or as trauma survivors. Such research could go a long way in filling in many of the gaps in our understanding of women's lives and women's work lives.

WORK: A CRITICAL OUTCOME MEASURE FOR JUDGING THE EFFICACY OF THE REHABILITATION PROCESS FROM A QUALITY OF LIFE PERSPECTIVE

> The ultimate legal issue in determination of disability is whether or not an injured individual can return to work. Issues of adapting the home and work environment to the needs of the individual must be addressed so that wherever possible, obstacles to return to work can be overcome.
>
> *Dorto and Williams, 1997*

Specific measures of quality of work life are not plentiful in the literature on quality of life. As noted previously, Ferrans and Powers (1985) and the WHOQOL Group (1994) address work in a global fashion as part of a comprehensive assessment of quality of life. However, the authors did find one instrument which held promise as a means of assessing quality of work life. Elizur and Shye (1990) developed a 32 item questionnaire (16 items identified as the Quality of Life scale and 16 items identified as the Quality of Work Life scale) in which items on work life asked to what extent work contributed to the expression, balance, and stability of one's unique personality, physical qualities, social being, and values and beliefs. The quality of life questions asked to what extent one expresses the same factors. For the quality of work life items, a Cronbach's alpha coefficient of 0.93 and for the quality of life items of 0.85 was reported. This instrument holds promise as a discrete measure of quality of work life.

When looking to assess the impact of disability and handicap on life function, Whiteneck et al. (1992) identified five dimensions of handicap on the Craig Handicap Assessment and Reporting Technique (CHART) — physical independence, mobility, occupation, social integration, and economic self-sufficiency — that would address the impact of a handicap on one's performance of normative roles. Test–retest reliability ranged from 0.80 to 0.92 across these dimensions (subscales). A validity study comparing CHART scores with professional ratings of level of handicap showed significant relationships between the scores and ratings. The validity of each subscale was demonstrated in the same manner. This scale included occupation along with economic self-sufficiency (an outcome of work) as indicators of life satisfaction for persons with disabilities.

Halpern (1994) pointed out that employment and independent living were the major "quality of life" goals for work study and other transitional, school-to-work programs, further reinforcing the belief that work and quality of life are interrelated (for adolescents as well as adults) and recognizing that one of the most potent factors in determination of quality of life is, in fact, work. Satisfying the normative expectations of others at age-referenced points in one's vocational development was seen as a major contributor to quality of life (work being one of, if not the most, prominent indicators of adult development). People were believed to need to work and it was noted that the social milieu expects one to work. Vocational outcomes were seen as an objective indicator of quality of life. Work was considered to be an indicator of assumption of an adult roles. This position, when viewed in the context of traditional rehabilitation literature, with its focus on work as the primary outcome of services, is not surprising. The little recognized and unsaid assumption behind work as the major statutory outcome goal of state agency vocational rehabilitation is that success and satisfaction in work will permeate all aspects of life (i.e., a ripple effect). Statutory definitions of disability invariably operationalize it in terms of work. Whether the terms disability and handicap are used separately or synonymously, work is seen as a central theme and major goal of the rehabilitation process. One could argue that global quality of life in adults will be hard to enhance if rehabilitation does not result in positive vocational outcomes. Therefore, rehabilitation must result in work (where appropriate) if it is to enhance quality of life. Moller and Murphy (1997) pointed out that achieving a stable level of wellness and a wellness lifestyle in persons with mental disabilities was the goal of the rehabilitation process, suggesting that work should not be viewed as the singular factor contributing to quality of life. Relapse prevention was thought to require adopting a wellness perspective in which education, family, health and other factors as well as work were seen as contributors to quality of life. Therefore, rehabilitation interventions focused on work, although providing the opportunity for discrete measurement of success or failure for use in evaluation of rehabilitation programs and services may not be potent enough in effect to ensure long-term maintenance of change in quality of life without nonwork-specific interventions.

However, the work-related intervention which has been noted in the rehabilitation literature to enhance quality of life while achieving desired vocational outcomes is supported employment. Sinnott-Oswald et al. (1991) studied the Quality of Life of 30 persons with disabilities, 10 participants assigned at random to the sheltered employment, supported employment, or control condition, and found that supported employment significantly enhanced quality of life across such dimensions as recreation, community involvement, and personal change (mobility, job skills, and income). Similarly, Inge et al. (1988) found that mentally retarded individuals who had been placed in competitive employment had more adaptive behavior and higher quality of life than those who worked in a sheltered workshop setting. Fabian (1992) may have asked the most relevant question to the study of quality of life: Does a job make a difference? On the Quality of Life Interview, a structured interview about life experiences across eight domains: living situation, family, social relations, leisure activities, physical and mental health, safety, work and nonwork, and finances, a self-report inventory with Cronbach's alpha reliability coefficients from 0.79 (for global satisfaction) to 0.88 (for living situation), it was found that work as opposed to no work was the greatest predictor of change in quality of life before and after job placement for persons with severe mental illness.

Although supported employment and related return-to-work strategies have been shown to enhance quality of life when they result in employment of persons with disabilities, caution should be exercised to understand that rehabilitation interventions are designed to return people to work, but do not necessarily follow the person through their career path and associated job changes. Follow-up by a rehabilitation professional may enhance job prospects when life circumstances necessitate a job change. It may be reasonable that in order to maintain quality of life after the person returns to work, ongoing professional assistance with job problems/issues and acquisition over work life be offered to some persons with disabilities in order to maintain their quality of life. It seems clear that work as opposed to nonwork is a powerful influence on quality of life across disabled populations. To focus financial and human resources on return to work goals and interventions in an effort to reduce long term economic losses may also result in reduced suffering (i.e., increase in quality of life). However, as suggested by Spitz's (1983) findings with 333 patients (159 injured workers; 138 persons injured in vehicular accidents; 36 patients on long-term disability), completion of a rehabilitation process which diagnosed and treated injury-related, motivational, and other problems that interfered with return to work does not necessarily result in total success (only 54% of the subjects in this study being able to return to work; 19% not benefiting at all from rehabilitation interventions).Rehabilitation interventions focused primarily on work issues may run the risk of not dealing effectively with total lifestyle management from a quality of life perspective. Social/familial, emotional, leisure, intellectual and/or physical factors should not be ignored when developing rehabilitation strategies designed to mitigate against loss of quality of life (the developmental equivalent of pain and suffering) because nonwork factors can interfere with pleasure and/or satisfaction attained through work activity. Lifestyle analysis (which looks at the relationship between work and other life functions that promote quality of life) should be conducted. Individual differences in assignment of the importance of each area of function may necessitate giving work-related issues lower priority, when setting goals for the rehabilitation process, than the traditional emphasis on work as the primary outcome of rehabilitation might suggest. Enhanced quality and pleasure of life as opposed to increased pain and suffering (joy of accomplishment vs. the agony of dysfunction) may endure longer if return to work is viewed within the context of total life function. However, work is one of the major benchmarks of one's adjustment to adult life and attainment of "normalcy."

REFERENCES

Addelmann, P. (1987). Occupational complexity, control, and personal income: their relation to psychological well-being in men and women. *Journal of Applied Psychology*, 72: 529-537.

Asikainen, I, Kaste, M. and Sarna, S. (1996). Patients with traumatic brain injury and re-employment programme: Social and professional outcomes for 508 Finnish patients 5 or more years after injury. *Brain Injury*, 10(12): 883-899.

Bandura, A. (1982). The psychology of chance encounters and life paths. *American Psychologist*, 37: 747-755.

Bejian, D. V. and Salomone, P. R. (1995). Understanding mid-life career renewal: Implications for counselors. *Career Development Quarterly*, 44: 52-63.

Bolton, B. (1982). *Vocational Adjustment of Disabled Persons*. Baltimore, MD: University Park Press.

Brown, B. (1989). Aging, disability, and quality of life: a challenge to society. *Canadian Psychology*, 30(3): 551-558.

Brown, D. and Crace, R. K. (1996) Values in life role choices and outcomes: a conceptual model. *Career Development Quarterly*, 44(3): 211-223.

Cabral, A. C. and Salomone, P. R. (1990). Chance and careers: normative vs. contextual development. *Career Development Quarterly*, 39(1): 5-17.

Chapman, N. J., Ingersoll-Dayton, B., and Neal, M.B. (1994). Balancing the multiple roles of work and caregiving for children, adults, and elders. In G. P. Keita and J. J. Hurrell, Jr. (Eds.), *Job Stress in a Changing Workforce: Investigating Gender, Diversity, and Family Issues,* pp. 283-300. Washington, DC: American Psychological Press.

Ciardiello, J. A. and Bingham, W. C. (1982). The career maturity of schizophrenic clients. *Rehabilitation Counseling Bulletin,* 3-9.

Clark, A. and Hirst, M. (1989). Disability in adulthood: ten-year follow-up study of young people with disabilities. *Disability, Handicap and Society*, 4(3): 271-284.

Coverman, S. (1989). Role overload, role conflict, and stress: addressing the consequences of multiple role demands. *Social Forces*, 67: 965-982.

Dikmen, S.S., Temkin, N. R., Machamer, J. E., Holubkov, A. L., Fraser, R. T., and Winn, H. R. (1994). Employment following traumatic head injuries. *Archives of Neurology*, 51: 177-186.

Dorto, A. J. and Williams, J. M. (1997). Coordinating rehabilitation efforts and the disability evaluation process. *Journal of Back and Musculoskeletal Rehabilitation*, 8: 19-43.

Duxbury, L. and Higgins, C. (1991). Gender differences in work-family conflict. *Journal of Applied Psychology*, 76: 60-74.

Elizur, D. and Shye, S. (1990). Quality of work life and its relationship to quality of life. *Applied Psychology: An International Review*, 39(3): 275-291.

Engels, D. W. (1996). Common themes in midlife career transitions. *The Career Development Quarterly,* 44(1): 83-89.

Fabian, E. S. (1992). Supported employment and the quality of life: Does a job make a difference? *Rehabilitation Counseling Bulletin*, 36(2): 84-97.

Feldberg, R. L. and Glenn, E. N. (1979). Male and female: job vs. gender modules in the sociology of work. *Social Problems*, 26: 524-538.

Ferrans, C. and Powers, M. (1985). Quality of Life Index: development and psychometric properties. *Advances in Nursing Science*, 8: 15-24.

Ginzberg, E. (1984). Career development. In D. Brown and L. Brooks (Eds.), *Career Choice and Development: Applying Theories in Practice,* pp. 161-191. San Francisco: Jossey-Bass.

Goldberg, R. T. (1989). A comparative study of vocational development of able bodied and disabled persons. *International Journal of Rehabilitation Research,* 12(1): 3-15.

Green, B. L. and Russo, N. F. (1993). Work and family roles: Selected issues. In F. L. Denmark and M.A. Paludi (Eds.), *Psychology of Women: A Handbook of Issues and Theories,* pp. 685-719. Westport, CT: Greenberg Press.

Greenberg, S. N. and Pollo, R. P. (1996). The work hardening program and subsequent return to work of a client with low back pain. *JOSPT,* 24(1): 37-45.

Gruenberg, B. (1980). The happy worker: an analysis of educational and occupational differences in determinants of job satisfaction. *American Journal of Sociology,* 86: 247-271.

Gutek, B., Searle, S., and Klepa, L. (1991). Rational vs. gender role explanations for work-family conflict. *Journal of Applied Psychology,* 76: 560-568.

Halpern, A. S. (1994). Quality of life for students with disabilities in transition from school to adulthood. *Social Indicators Research,* 33: 193-236.

Inge, K. J, Banks, D. Wehman, P., Hill, J. W., and Shafer, M. S. (1988). Quality of life for individuals who are labeled mentally retarded: evaluating competitive employment vs. sheltered work employment. *Education and Training in Mental Retardation,* June, 97-104.

Jamieson, D. and O'Mara, J. (1991). *Managing Workforce 2000: Gaining the Diversity Advantage.* San Francisco: Jossey-Bass.

Kalleberg, A. L. and Loscocco, K. A. (1983). Aging, values and rewards: explaining age differences in job satisfaction, *American Psychological Review,* 48: 78-90.

Kozleski, E. B. and Sands, D. J. (1992). The yardstick of social validity: evaluating quality of life as perceived by adults without disabilities. *Education and Training in Mental Retardation,* June, 119-131.

Krause, J. S. (1992). Adjustment to life after spinal cord injury: a comparison among three participant groups based on employment status. *Rehabilitation Counseling Bulletin,* 35(4): 218-229.

Krumboltz, J. D. (1976). The Chevrolet can't float or fly. *American Psychologist,* 6: 17-19.

Krumboltz, J. D., Mitchell, A. M., and Jones G. B. (1976) A social learning theory of career selection. *Counseling Psychologist,* 6: 71-81.

Lefkowitz, J. (1984). Sex-related differences in job attitudes and dispositional variables: Now you see them, *Academy of Management Journal,* 37: 323-349.

Lennon, M. C. and Rosenfeld, S. (1992). Women and mental health: Interaction of job and family conditions. *Journal of Health and Social Behavior,* 33: 316-321.

Lerner, D. J., Levine, S. Malspeis, S., and D'Agostino, R. B. (1994). Job strain and health -related quality of life in a national sample. *American Journal of Public Health,* 84(10): 1580-1585.

Lerner, H. (1987). Work and success inhibitions in women. *Bulletin of the Menninger Clinic,* 51, 338-360.

Lincoln, J. R. and Kalleberg, A. L. (1985). Work organizations and workforce commitment: a study of plants and employees in the United States and Japan. *American Sociological Review,* 50: F38-F60.

Loscocco, K. A. and Spitz, G. (1990). Working conditions, social support, and well-being of female and male factory workers. *Journal of Health and Social Behavior,* 31: 313-327.

Malec, J. F., Smigielski, J. S., DePompolo, R. W., and Thompson, J. M. (1993). Outcome evaluation and prediction in a comprehensive, integrated post-acute outpatient brain injury rehabilitation program. *Brain Injury,* 7(1): 15-29.

Manz, C. C. and Grothe, R. (1991). Is the work force vanguard to the 21st Century a quality of life deficient-prone generation? *Journal of Business Research,* 23: 67-82.

Melamed, S., Groswasser, Z., and Stern, M. (1992). Acceptance of disability, work involvement and subjective rehabilitation status of traumatic brain-injured patients. *Brain Injury,* 6(3): 233-243.

Mirvis, P. S. and Lawler, E. E. (1984). Accountability for the quality of work life. *Journal of Occupational Behavior,* 5: 197-212.

Mitchell, L. K. and Krumboltz, J. D. (1984). Social learning approach to career decision-making: Krumboltz's theory. In D. Brown and L. Brooks (Eds.), *Career Choices and Development: Applying Theories in Practice,* pp. 235-280. San Francisco: Jossey-Bass.

Moller, M. D. and Murphy, M. F. (1997) The three R's rehabilitation program: a prevention approach for the management of relapse symptoms associated with psychiatric diagnoses. *Psychiatric Rehabilitation Journal,* 20(3): 42-48.

Moos, R. H. and Moos, B.S. (1983). Adaptation and the quality of life in work and family settings. *Journal of Community Psychology*, 11: 158-169.

Murphy, P. A. (1993) *Making the Connections: Women, work and abuse.* Orlando, FL: PMD Press.

Murphy, P. A. (1994). *The Edge of a Large Hole: Writings on the Request for Reasonable Accommodation under the Americans with Disabilities Act of 1990.* Chicago: University of Illinois Center for Research on Women and Gender.

Murphy, P. A. (1996). *A Career and Life Planning Guide for Women Survivors: The Making the Connections Workbook.* Delray Beach, FL: St. Lucie Press.

Murphy, P. A. (1997). Recovering from the effects of domestic violence: implications for welfare reform policy. *Law and Policy: Understanding Women's Poverty: a Symposium on the Relationship of Domestic Violence and Welfare Receipt,* 19(2):169-182.

Near, J. F., Rice, R. W., and Hunt, R. G. (1978). Work and extra-work correlates of life and job satisfaction. *Academy of Management Journal*, 21(2): 248-264

Nicholson, N. and West, M. (1989). Transitions, work histories and careers. In M. Arthur, D. T. Hall, and B. S. Lawrence (Eds.), *Handbook of Career Theory,* pp. 181-201, Boston, MA: Cambridge University Press.

Osberg, J. S., McGinnis, G. E., DeJong, G., and Seward, M. L. (1987). Life satisfaction and quality of life among elderly adults. *Journal of Gerontology,* 42(2): 228-230.

Paludi. M. (1990). Socio-psychological and structural factors related to women's vocational development. *Annals of the New York Academy of Science*, 602: 157-168.

Ponsford, J. L., Olver, J. H., and Curran, C. (1995). A profile of outcome: 2 years after brain injury. *Brain Injury,* 9(1): 1-10.

Powell, G. and Mainiero, L. (1992). Cross-currents in the river of time: conceptualizing the complexities of women's careers. *Journal of Management*, 18: 215-237.

Pugliesi, K. (1995). Work and well-being: gender differences in psychosocial consequences of employment. *Journal of Health and Social Behavior*, 36: 57-71.

Radanov, B. P., DiStefano, G., Schnidrig, A., and Sturzenegger, M. (1993). Psychosocial stress, cognitive performance, and disability after common whiplash. *Journal of Psychosomatic Research*, 37(1): 1-10.

Raphael, J. (1997). Welfare reform: Prescription for abuse? A report on the new research studies documenting the relationship of domestic violence and welfare. *Law and Policy: Understanding Women's Poverty: a Symposium on the Relationship of Domestic Violence and Welfare Receipt,* 19(2): 123-138.

Roe, A. (1956). *The Psychology of Occupations.* New York: Wiley.

Roessler, R. T. (1988). A conceptual framework for return to work interventions. *Rehabilitation Counseling Bulletin*, 32: 98-107.

Roxburgh, S. (1996). Gender differences in work and well-being: effects of exposure and vulnerability. *Journal of Health and Social Behavior,* 37: 265-277.

Ruchlin, H. S. and Morris, J. N. (1991). Impact of work on quality of life of community residing young elderly. *American Journal of Public Health,* 81(4): 498-500.

Sands, D. J. and Kozleski, E. B. (1994). Quality of life differences between adults with and without disabilities. *Education and Training in Mental Retardation and Developmental Disabilities*, June, 90-101.

Schalock, R. L. (1996). Quality of life nd quality assurance. In R. Renwick, I. Brown, and M. Nagler (Eds.), *Quality of Life in Health Promotion and Rehabilitation,* pp. 104-118. Thousand Oaks: CA: Sage Publications.

Schmidt, S. H., Oort-Marburger, D., and Meijman, T. F. (1995). Employment after rehabilitation for musculoskeletal impairments: the impact of vocational rehabilitation and working on a trial basis. *Archives of Physical Medicine and Rehabilitation*, 76: 950-954.

Scuccimarra, D. J. and Speece, D. L. (1990). Employment outcomes and social integration of students with mild handicaps: The quality of life two years after high school. *Journal of Learning Disabilities*, 23(4): 213-291.

Shain, M. (1996). Work, employment and mental health In R. Renwick, I. Brown, and M. Nagler (Eds.) *Quality of Life in Health Promotion and Rehabilitation,* pp. 327-341, Thousand Oaks, CA: Sage Publications.

Shye, S. (1979). *A Systematic Facet Theoretical Approach to Quality of Life*. Jerusalem: Israel Institute of Applied Social Research.

Sinnott-Oswald, M., Gliner, J. A, and Spencer, K. C. (1991). Supported employment and sheltered employment: quality of life issues among workers with disabilities, *Education and Training in Mental Retardation,* December, 388-397.

Spitz, L. K. (1983). Winning at cost containment in rehabilitation. *Risk Management*, 30: 46-48.

Stoltz-Lolke, M. (1995). Adult career transitions. *Career Development Quarterly*, 44(1): 89-92.

Straaton, K. V., Maisiak, R., Wrigley, J. M. and Fine, P. R. (1995). Musculoskeletal disability, employment, and return to work. *Journal of Rheumatology*, 22(3): 505-513.

Super, D. E. (1990). A life-span, life space approach to career development. In D. Brown and L. Brooks (Eds.), *Career Choice and Development* (2nd ed.), pp. 179-261. San Francisco, CA: Jossey-Bass.

Taylor-Carter, M. A. and Cook, K. (1995). Adaptation to retirement: role changes and psychological resources. *Career Development Quarterly*, 44: 67-82.

Temple University (1988). *A National Survey of Consumers of Services for Individuals with Developmental Disabilities. Final Survey Instrument.* Unpublished instrument. Washington, D.C.: National Developmental Disabilities Planning Council.

Tiedeman, D. V. and Miller-Tiedeman, A. (1984). Career decision-making: an individualistic perspective. In D. Brown and L. Brooks (Eds.), *Career Choice and Development: Applying Contemporary Theories in Practice,* pp. 281-310. San Francisco: Jossey-Bass.

Travis, C. (1992). *The Mismeasure of Women.* New York: Simon and Schuster.

Ulrich, D. and Dunne, Jr., H. (1986). *To Love and Work.* New York: Brunner/Mazel.

Verbrugge, L. M., Reoma, J. M., and Gruber-Baldini, A. L. (1994). Short-term dynamics of disability and well-being. *Journal of Health and Social Behavior*, 35: 97-117.

Ville, I. and Ravaud, J. F. (1996). Work, nonwork and consequent satisfaction after spinal cord injury. *International Journal of Rehabilitation Research*, 19: 241-252.

Vondracek, F. W., Lerner, R. M., and Shulenberg, J. E. (1983). The concept of development in vocational theory and intervention. *Journal of Vocational Behavior*, 23: 179-202.

Watson, D. and Clark, L. A. (1984). Negative affectivity: the disposition to experience aversive affective traits. *Psychological Bulletin*, 96: 465-490.

Whiteneck, G. G., Charlifue, S. W., Gerhart, K. A., Overholser, J. D., and Richardson, G. N. (1992). Quantifying handicap. A new measure of long-term rehabilitation outcomes. *Archives of Physical Medicine and Rehabilitation,* 73(6): 519-526.

Williams. J. M. (1995). Addressing quality and pleasure of life in life care planning. *Inside Life Care Planning*, 1(2): 2.

Williams, J. M. and Maze, M. (1994). *The Role of the Rehabilitation Expert in Civil and Administrative Law Proceedings.* Iowa City, IA: ACT.

WHOQOL Group (1994). Development of the WHOQOL: rationale and the current status. *International Journal of Mental Health*, 23(3): 24-56.

Wolfensberger, W. (1972). *Normalization: The Principle of Normalization in Human Services.* Toronto: National Institute of Mental Retardation.

Wolfensberger, W. (1991). *A Brief Introduction of Social Role Valorization as a High-Order Concept for Structuring Human Services.* Syracuse, New York: Training Institute for Human Services Planning, Leadership and Change Agency, Syracuse University.

Zunker, V. G. (1990). *Career Counseling: Applied Concepts of Life Planning.* Pacific Grove, CA: Brooks-Cole.

9 The Cognitive Domain

Growth becoming encompasses activities that promote the development of individuals' skills and knowledge, whether this involves formal or informal education and learning. These include learning new information, improving existing skills or learning new ones, and adapting to changes in their lives.

Renwick and Brown, 1996, (p. 84)

INTRODUCTION

For people with newly acquired physical and psychological disabilities as seen in personal injury and employment discrimination litigants, the demand for "growth becoming" as defined by Renwick and Brown (1996) is not only an imperative but, at the same time, highly problematic since the newly acquired disability(ies) may have damaged intellectual ability or cognition. And so while the person with an injury or disability is faced with learning new information about his/her medical and/or psychological condition, they are also faced with the need to adapt to changes in their lives. It should also be understood that like the nondisabled, even persons with chronic disabilities face life change. Disability is not a static condition (Murphy, 1994). A person who has experienced significant life changes associated with some loss of function (whether or not it is mobility, social skills, or mental stability or cognition) will need to adapt to situations and circumstances that may require acquisition of new learning, identification of the relationships between previously acquired knowledge and new learning, creative or adaptive problem-solving, and task persistence. Although change is inevitable and often results from unplanned or unforeseen events in one's life (whether one is experiencing trauma or disability), successful adaptation or coping is possible if one has the cognitive skills to do so. When cognitive abilities are diminished and awareness, understanding, and problem-solving (i.e., higher order executive functions) are compromised due to a physiological and/or an emotional trauma, inability to react to and exercise some influence over the change process is diminished or even lost. One then can lose control over one's life and experience uncontrolled downward spiral across one or more domains of quality of life. As with the other domains of quality of life, the cognitive domain presents its own issues and challenges; yet, it does not operate in isolation. As we shall see, changes in cognitive function typically lead to changes in function across the other domains.

LITERATURE REVIEW

Quality of life consists of fulfilling needs, meeting social expectations, and accessing opportunities by using abilities."

Bigelow, McFarland, and Olson, 1991

The quality of life literature on this domain or aspect of quality of life is submerged within the literature as a whole and we were not able to locate even one article which focused specifically on the singular relationship between the cognitive aspects of life and quality of life. Nevertheless, cognitive and skill development issues pervaded the literature, and are organized along the following themes: (1) Impairment and Cognitive Limitations, (2) Intellectual Level, (3) Life Skills, (4) Independence or Autonomy, and (5) Assessment Issues.

Separation of cognitive function from emotional function and/or physiological impairment is particularly challenging when discussing traumatic brain injury. Since the authors note that the singular effects of emotional, physiological, or cognitive function upon human behavior and resultant quality of life cannot be isolated in the literature on traumatic brain injury (TBI) to the satisfaction of all, the substantive issues related to TBI will be discussed under the cognitive domain in this chapter as opposed to any other chapter in this book.

Impairment or Cognitive Limitations

Impairment and/or cognitive limitations include impairment to language, long-term and short-term memory, visuospatial skills, attention cognitive function, judgment, psychomotor skills, concrete thinking, lack of problem solving ability, memory, and concentration. Recognizing the interdependence of cognitive function with other domains of quality of life, the literature review in this section is organized by a sampling of health related quality of life studies by disease, injury, or disability.

Cancer

Breevelt and Van Dam (1991) explored the puzzle of why cancer patients, when compared to other patient groups or nonpatient groups, show "no differences in most indicators of life quality, such as overall quality of life, mental functioning, fear, depression, well-being, daily activities and resumption of one's work." Adjustment to or coping with (as a cognitive decision-making paradigm resulting in implementation and evaluation of choices) traumatic life experiences was seen to occur in three phases: (1) denial (which may lead to lowered scores on depression measures); (2) crisis (a disturbance between the normal problem perception and problem-solving capacities of an individual), and (3) judgment (comparison of one's functioning to that of significant others or societal norms). Both the crisis theory and the judgment theories (adaptation and social comparison theories) are highly dependent upon cognitive functioning. More specifically, cognitive function during a crisis was described as follows:

> according to crisis theory an extremely negative situation disturbs the normal balance between problem perception and the problem solving capacity. In a later phase additional power is usually mobilized and the problem solving capacity increases or becomes more effective. Thus, a new balance may be found. The problem solving capacity proved to differ between both groups of cancer patients on the one hand and healthy persons on the other. In addition the relation between the capacity to solve problems was stronger in cancer patients who were not in crisis than in both cancer patients who were in a crisis situation and a healthy person. Thus the problem solving capacity in non-crisis patients proves to be more effective in positively influencing the quality of life.

These findings suggest that the degree of crisis may influence the impact of one's experiencing of quality of life by affecting one's choices and resultant behaviors. The greater the crisis and the more imminent its negative results, the more one's cognitive processes appear to influence the ultimate behavioral outcome and resultant quality of life. Judgment theory postulates that the cancer patient compares the factual situation surrounding the illness to some standard, typically one's earlier experience or the experiences of others in a similar situation. "A study of cancer patients found that these patients tend to make downward comparisons (looking at those who were perceived as less functional and seeing oneself in a more favorable situation)."

The relatively high scores of cancer patients on self-report measures of quality of life should, however, be viewed with caution given that a response shift in the direction of under-reporting is commonly found with such patients (such a response shift being a cognitive element in measuring quality of life in cancer patients, while being a cognitive management strategy for dealing with their negative emotional responses to the disease). Yet, as indicated by Schaafsma and Osoba (1994), in their study designed to cross-validate the Karnofsky Performance Status (KPS) scale (KPS), an observer-rated of quality of life, with the European Organization for Research and Treatment of Cancer Quality of Life Questionnaire (EORTC QLQ-C30),a self-report measure of quality of life, problems with under-reporting of quality of life by cancer patients has not been definitively demonstrated in the quality of life literature. The KPS scale, as a result of its wide use as a measure of health-related quality of life, of life in clinical oncology, and because it has been found to correlate significantly with survival in some cancers (making it a useful tool for stratification of patients in clinical trials), was weighted towards measuring physiological issues relative to quality of life, causing the authors of this article to caution that quality of life is not determined by only physical well-being. It is unclear whether under-reporting is an artifact of quality of life measures weighted heavily towards physical well-being in item content or an issue of equal concern when dealing with more balanced, global measures of quality of life. The Quality of Life Questionnaire-C30 (QLQ-C30), as a more global measure of quality of life (one which assesses symptoms, cognitive and role functioning, as well as emotional and social well-being) contains two cognitive items ("Difficulty concentrating on things" and "Had difficulty remembering things."). Out of the 139 lung cancer patients who responded to these questions, 56.8% had no problem with this, 28.1% indicated they had "a little" trouble, 10.1% noted "quite a bit," and 4.3% indicated "very much." "Not at all" was marked by 54.7% of the patients in response to the memory question, "a little" was at 32.4%, "quite a bit" was at 13.7%, and 2.9% of the patients indicated "very much." It was concluded that there is a "weak association between observer-related KPS and self-rated quality of life. These findings suggest that self-report and observer ratings may not be the same thing, a result which is not, in and of itself, surprising when one considers that cognition is not observable and must be self-reported. However, they did find that the QLQ-C30 was a valuable instrument which should be used in choices of "palliative treatment for the terminally ill." The KPS alone would not be sufficient because its focus is on physical functioning. They also found that cognitive functioning had a markedly lesser impact on quality of life than either emotional well-being or the ability to function socially. This also is not surprising, given that considerably less attention was given to cognitive elements of quality of life in instrument construction. Although the percentage of lung cancer patients reporting cognitive difficulties was not in the majority, 43.2% had some difficulty with concentration and 45.3% indicated problems with memory. This alone would indicate that lung cancer patients might need help in improving this aspect of their life quality.

Cardiovascular Disease

Romney et al. (1992) examined the components of quality of life theory by analyzing data collected from 469 patients with cardiovascular problems. They used structured interviews, self-administered questionnaires, and abstracted medical data from hospital charts on a standardized form. More than 50 items and scales were categorized and "five factors were extracted, namely, Symptoms of Illness, Neurological Dysfunctions, Interpersonal Relationships, Morale, and Socioeconomic Status (SES)." Competing hypotheses were tested using the computer program LISREL Version 6 because it provides goodness-of-fit indices. They found that

> "of two plausible competing hypotheses, the one stipulating that symptoms of illness and neurological dysfunction lead to a deterioration in SES, morale, and interpersonal relationships fitted the data very well.... The rival hypothesis that neurological dysfunction and SES lowered morale which in turn aggravated symptoms and adversely affected relationships was not confirmed."

The authors found that relationships improved slightly with cognitive impairment. They accounted for this puzzling finding by noting that it "might be explained in terms of the confused patient; eliciting sympathy and understanding from those who know him and knew what he was like before."

Romney et al. were reluctant to recommend interventions, except to note that medications could probably alleviate the patient's symptoms. They also noted that cognitive restructuring could be useful in boosting patient morale.

Dementia (in Parkinson's and Alzheimer's Disease)

Fitzsimmons and Bunting (1997) write that "individuals who develop Parkinson's Disease (PD) are confronted not only with the physical manifestations of the disorder but with the psychosocial issues that impact on the quality of life." They note "impaired verbal communication related to softening of voice" and "altered thought processes related to hallucinations and confusion." Dementia is another feature of the disease, and "it is estimated that 20% of the patients with PD will become demented." The impairments caused by dementia will involve three areas of mental activity: "language, visuospatial skills, emotionality, personality, and cognition in the presence of clear consciousness." Some patients will retain enough long-term memory and insight "to experience a clear sense of loss." In addition, the treatment for PD in the form of drug therapy may create the side effects of delirium and hallucinations, further damaging cognition. The drug therapy decisions may place patients and their families in having to make agonizing choices between motor function and mental function in terms of care since "it may be easier for a family to care for a mobile patient with PD who is cognitively impaired." The question of whose quality of life is more important arises. Is the family's quality of life an issue to be addressed in determining the quality of life of the patient and in making related treatment choices? These are interesting questions that come up in any situation where cognitive function is sufficiently diminished and assistive care is required. The authors of this book suggest that quality of life of the patient/client and the family both need to be considered when selecting care options.

Alzheimer's disease also directly alters cognitive functioning. Howard and Rockwood (1995) listed "deterioration of memory" as an important aspect of cognitive function to measure in quality of life assessment. They "reviewed and independently ranked the measurement properties of quality of life instruments currently used in anti-dementia drug trials of Alzheimer's disease." The authors noted that the most tested measure was the Progressive Deterioration Scale. This scale and the Italian Quality of Life Scale were considered to be the instruments with the most promising measurement properties. However, the authors recommend a "disease specific" quality of life measurement approach since the disease has "many manifestations, not all of which will be present in all patients." Howard and Rockwood recommend the employment of quality of life measures which will "discriminate between patterns of symptoms based on the stage of the disease." The Cognitive Rating Scale was one example. They also recommended an individualized outcome approach, challenging the use of standardized measures of quality of life generally since there is no "reversal" in Alzheimer's disease (even with treatment) the standard quality of life assessments are insensitive to clinically important changes. Howard and Rockwood concluded with the recommendation that further development in assessing the quality of life of Alzheimer's patients at various stages of the disease process is needed. It is logical to expect that an instrument which has heightened sensitivity to the impact of subtle changes in cognitive function of quality of life will inherently have more utility in measuring treatment outcomes relative to illnesses, diseases, or other life-altering events which have greater cognitive impact on a given individual than instruments designed to measure changes in physical or emotional well-being. Traditional psychometric tests, because of their preoccupation with the latter two domains of quality of life, may not be sensitive to cognitive changes which impact quality of life. Another obvious problem is that of seeking self-report data from someone with a cognitive impairment, when the impairment itself may heavily influence the ability to respond and quality of response. Asking dementia patients to self-report quality of life raises questions about validity and reliability of self-report over time; these questions deserve attention in future research.

EPILEPSY

Hays et al. (1995) investigated the impairment to cognitive function among 292 persons with epilepsy and their designated proxies or relative, friend, or significant other person in a study of quality of life reports by the patients and their proxies. The 89-term Quality of Life Inventory (QOLIE-89) was used, with the items rephrased for the proxies. The proxies "systematically reported better functioning than did patients on the three scales assessing cognitive functioning." The discriminant success across the language cognitive function was at 48%, for attention cognitive function at 64%, and for memory cognitive function, at 91%. The three cognitive function scales were among the five out of seventeen scales with mean scale scores which were significantly different between patients and proxies. The authors found that their work was consistent with previous research that indicated agreement between patients and proxies was good for observable measures of function such as physical functioning, but not as good for subjective experiences such as cognitive functioning. The authors recommended that proxy reports be used conservatively, a finding which supports the contention mentioned earlier concerning the subjective nature of cognition and its inherently subjective characteristics.

In an earlier study (Vickrey et al., 1992), a health-related quality of life measure was developed for patients evaluated for epilepsy surgery. The Epilepsy Surgery Inventory (ESI)-55 is a 55-item measure of health-related quality of life for epilepsy patients. It includes a cognitive function scale. The instrument was completed by 89% of the 224 adults who had participated in an evaluation protocol for surgery. The results of the study indicate that the ESI-55 is reliable and valid and is sensitive to differences in seizure states and their relationships to quality of life.

MENTAL ILLNESS

Bech (1990) offers a thorough analysis of the measurement issues in psychological distress and well-being. He discusses the Symptom Checklist (SCL-90), the General Health Questionnaire, the Beck Depression Inventory, the Kellner Illness Attitude Scale, the Scale of Life Events, and the Hassles Scale. He emphasizes that quality of life is multidimensional. In a review of 50 quality of life instruments used in clinical medicine research, Bech found that "cognitive, emotional, and socioeconomic" factors were important in examining what he terms "comfort" and "discomfort" rather than psychological dysfunction or mental illness. Since quality of life, pleasure of life, and life satisfaction have been used somewhat interchangeably in much of the literature reviewed for this book, all of which suggests a positive, growth-oriented perspective on human function, the importance of this article may lie in the linkage between the concept of discomfort (synonymous with the deficit thinking of the traditional medical and psychological models) and traditional measures of emotional or psychological function. Measuring discomfort through use of such traditional measures as those mentioned above may speak to issues of mental illness, but does not represent the construct of quality of life.

In a study to validate the Quality of Life Questionnaire which was developed to measure performance of mental health programs, Bigelow et al. (1991) assert that "abilities are impaired by mental illness," and that "mental health services moderate social demands, supplement opportunities, and restore abilities." The independence, adjustment, work, and leisure scales on this instrument captured the cognitive elements. The independence scale included "making everyday decision and coping with normal ambiguities, stresses, and pressures." The adjustment scale included "productivity — meeting generally sanctioned standards of effort, activity, achievement, and obtaining basic need, affiliation, esteem, autonomy, and self-actualization in this way." The work scales include ability to engage in activities of daily living, quality of work, and other performance issues. The leisure scale "consists of creative or self-improving activities." The Quality of Life Questionnaire underwent rigorous quality control and was validated in terms of sound measurement principles.

In a study of loneliness, Catana Brown (1996) noted in a convenience sample of 191 persons with severe mental illness, that

> specific social skill deficits are well documented among persons with severe mental illness. The ability for interpreting verbal and nonverbal cues, recognizing social norms, making eye contact, and initiating and sustaining conversation. A study of social competence found poor social functioning in individuals with schizophrenia on verbal, non-verbal, and role play measures of social competence.

The loneliness study found that "persons in different living situations did not experience different degrees of loneliness." This result was interpreted on the basis that "the ability to live alone may indicate a higher level of functioning and better social skills," while living with others might be very stressful for those with social deficits. This study is a good example of how cognitive functioning is embedded in the quality of life literature — in this case, in social functioning, which requires cognitive abilities.

Qualitative studies of women who have been traumatically abused (Murphy, 1993, 1994, 1996) indicate that cognitive issues identified in the posttraumatic stress disorder symptoms in the *Diagnostic and Statistical Manual* (American Psychiatric Association, 1994) had an impact on the ability of the survivors to benefit from educational and work opportunities. Inability to concentrate and impairment to memory were just two such symptoms which had the effect of diminishing the mental capacities of women trying to complete their often interrupted educational endeavors and new learning on the job. Also, the verbal abuse many victims experience is directly related to their perception of their competence (found in such abusive phrases as "You're so stupid!" or "You're so crazy!"). This has the effect of undermining the victim's sense of competence and her ability to use her mental powers for problem solving. These findings are confirmed by an ongoing study on the abuse of persons with disabilities which suggests that "quality of life among the sexually abused is an oxymoron" (Nagler, 1996). The interruption in educational attainment and inability to obtain or keep a job resulting from diminished cognitive capacity can contribute to a profound loss of life quality over the life span of abused individuals.

Sartorius (1995) underscores the important role of cognition in quality of life when he states that impairment due to mental illness often involves a reduction in the capacity to learn or memorize, which makes restoration and the acquisition of new skills quite difficult. Rehabilitation of persons with mental illness should take into account issues related to quality of life according to his model. He recommends that persons with mental illness be restored or introduced to work and to meaningful leisure as part of the rehabilitative process or to those aspects of life dependent upon improved capacity to learn and to memorize. Rehabilitation programming for the mentally ill in this model would need to include cognitive strategies designed to improve ability to learn. The obvious implication of this viewpoint is that educational and training strategies designed to enhance work or leisure function must first improve basic cognitive function before they can be successful. The interrelationships between the cognitive, work, leisure, and social domains as reflected in the multidisciplinary, multidimensional approaches to quality of life found in the literature on quality of life reported in Chapter 2 of this book are consistent with the needs of the mentally ill.

Renal Failure

Lynch and Gallagher-Lepak (1996), in their discussion of improved treatment options for persons with chronic renal failure, state that mild cognitive impairments, such as reduced ability to concentrate, may be present among persons with renal disease especially before beginning dialysis therapy and during hemodialysis treatments, particularly if the renal disease is under poor control. They encourage rehabilitation counselors to keep their knowledge updated on the improved medical treatment options for people with chronic renal failure, and to include cognitive changes in their list of functional implications for rehabilitation planning. They cite differences in the quality of life experienced by patients who have had a successful renal transplant, as contrasted to those undergoing dialysis. The list of suitable rehabilitation interventions included assessment based on a knowledge of treatment options and their side effects, counseling to enhance psychosocial outcomes (particularly maximum consumer management and control of the disease process and treatments) and advocating for the patient to move beyond the treatment regime to other options such as work. Treatment was strongly linked to cognitive goals related to acquisition of information, problem-identification, and goal selection (problem-solving). Cognitive control over treatment planning and service implementation as well as a cognitive focus on return to optimal life function was supported by this commentary.

Intellectual Level

In the quality of life literature, cognitive capacity (one's ability to think clearly and efficiently) as a concept varies widely, depending upon the population studied. For example, one of the stereotypes of the aging process is decline in cognitive capacity or intellectual level. Sherman and Schiffman's (1991) review of quality of life assessment for older persons includes the concept of *cognitive age.* They note that "age no longer can be defined in terms of chronological age," but suggest the use of *cognitive age* as a method to evaluate "an individual's age concept." Personal age dimensions such as "feel age, look age, do age, and interest age" result in many older persons perceiving themselves to be 10 or 15 years younger than their chronological age. Studies indicate that older persons who have younger cognitive ages perceive themselves "to be healthier, feel financially better off, and are less likely to want to live their lives differently." In other words, they have better quality lives.

By contrast, Brown (1989) found that when integrating the fields of aging and disability, "being old could occur at a relatively young chronological age," and that "despite, on the average, the low intellectual ability levels of the subjects, the correlations between objective measures of performance and responses of sponsors ranged (in one study) from 0.6 to 0.9. It appears that developmentally disabled persons, regardless of age, are able to recognize accurately areas of concern and need. They are aware of their own skills and deficiencies and the deficiencies of the system in which they live." Brown also points out that "so-called disabled persons were sometimes found to function in average or superior range of intellectual ability." He underscored that "in all forms of disability, individuals often show transient attention, variable memory span, and variations in fatigue, depression, self-image and motivation." For this reason, the intellectual level of developmentally disabled and older persons tends to be underestimated in terms of their ability to manage and appreciate the quality of their own lives by relatives and helping professionals.

Schalock and Lilley (1986) studied "the placement success and quality of life of 85 mentally retarded persons placed into independent housing and competitive employment 8 to 10 years before." The average full scale IQ as measured by the Wechsler Adult Intelligence Scale was 67 (range = 40 to 91, SD = 12). Data were collected on current programmatic status, current living/work placement, current financial status, family involvement, quality of life using a 30-item Quality of Life Questionnaire, behavioral skill data as obtained from the Basic Skills Screening Test, and programmatic services provided to clients. Three cognitive variables which discriminated between successful and unsuccessful living and work outcomes were sensorimotor functioning, symbolic operations, and auditory-visual processing. However, the most significant variables were family involvement, income, number of disabilities, and age. Quality of life issues for those who were unemployed or working part-time, but living independently was important since the persons in this situation were found to be "lonely and had very fragile support systems."

In a National Institutes of Health Consensus Development Conference (1990), the topic of epilepsy surgery was addressed. One of the reasons listed for considering surgical therapy was that "repeated seizures may have adverse effects on the brain, leading to progressive cerebral degeneration and more severe clinical handicaps." Coexisting disorders, including "profound developmental retardation or progressive neurodegenerative diseases," were also noted as considerations in decisions about operating. Most important, since epilepsy surgery "now may be used more often in children than in the past," the consensus was that "additional studies to determine the effects of uncontrolled seizures and antiepileptic drug therapy on the developing brain" were recommended. The assessment of cognitive or intellectual levels of the child would be included in such assessments. According to conference participants, the impact of surgery for intractable epilepsy on overall health status and quality of life "have not been yet been adequately studied." Therefore, the connections between intellectual level and quality of life for intractable seizure patients have only been identified as important issues, but no conclusions have been reached.

Other than Schalock and Lilley study referred to above, the Corrigan and Buican (1995) validity study of subjective quality of life for persons with severe mental illness is the only quality of life study found which actually measured the intellectual level of the study participants. Like Schalock and Lilley, Corrigan and Buican used the Wechsler Adult Intelligence Scale-Revised (WAIS-R). They were particularly interested in examining verbal intelligence as found on the vocabulary subtest since "it has been shown to correlate highly with verbal intelligence." They also used the WAIS-R to estimate a performance IQ. The performance IQ data yielded no significant results, but they found that verbal intelligence is independently associated with quality of life. Corrigan and Buican wrote:

> A significant inverse relationship was found between verbal intelligence and subjective quality of life. This finding supports other research which concluded that more intelligent patients are better able to understand their limitations and, therefore, experience a relatively muted quality of life.

The reader is cautioned about making the mistake described by Brown (1989) in his work on aging and disability. That is just because "those who have more insight into their illness, and therefore greater knowledge about the limitations of their life, are likely to report diminished quality of life." This does not mean that elderly persons or persons with developmental disabilities are unable to make judgments about their life quality. In fact, Corrigan and Buican assert that "subjective quality of life seems to be a complex phenomenon." This suggests that intellectual level of a person may impact the person's subjective experience of quality of life. Cognitive appreciation of the issues relative to quality of life may be required before accurate, subjective assessment of one's function in any one of the domains of quality of life is possible. One's social, occupational, and leisure functioning may be influenced greatly by one's cognitive function, implying that assessment of basic cognitive function may be helpful in determining the role of cognitive function in global and domain-specific quality of life.

Life Skills

When exploring the cognitive domain of quality of life, rehabilitationists are more likely to be interested in function, capacity, adjustment, or skills than in abstract IQ measures or constructs. Condeluci et al. (1992) illustrate this point in their review of three studies of traumatic brain injury survivors and their feelings and thoughts about the rehabilitation process outcomes. In one survey, the Profile of Personal Preferences and Skills was used to assess living arrangements, work situations, and lifestyle patterns. The life skills section of this instrument covered such domains as cognitive/executive functioning, functional communications, behavioral/emotional issues, domestic skills, community/safety issues, and vocational directions. The refinement of the life skill concept into function areas and capacity areas can be seen in Table IV.

The quality of life approach here is based on the importance rankings of outcomes by survivors, families, and payers. As can be imagined, each group ranks outcomes differently. Condeluci et al. conclude that in all three surveys of clinical or rehabilitation outcomes, "survivors value the skills leading to independence but place greater importance upon relationships and their acceptance in

TABLE V
Function and Capacity Areas

Housing	Function Areas: Vocational	Function Areas: Lifestyle	Capacity Areas: Cognitive	Capacity Areas: Physical	Capacity Areas: Behavioral
At home by self	Employed full time	Socially active	Independent	Interdependent	Appropriate
At home with parent	Employed part time	Active with minimum support	Occasional support in cueing, monitor	Occasional support with personal care	Occasional inappropriate behavior
At home with spouse	Supported employment	Active required support	Ongoing cognitive supports	Regular scheduled support	Predictable inappropriate behavior
Group home	Sheltered employment	Totally supported	Intense monitoring and support	Intense physical support	Difficult to handle
Nursing home	Unemployed	Inactive	Total support	Total support	Unmanageable
Other	Other	Other	Other	Other	Other

the community." Both payers and families ranked "independence in activities of daily living" as the most important outcome, while survivors ranked that second to the living situation.

Brown et al. (1988) also see quality of life issues as challenging issues in the delivery of rehabilitation services. These researchers from the University of Calgary have been involved since 1981 in a longitudinal study in four western provinces of Canada in terms of the "subjective performance of adolescents and adults who are mentally handicapped." They have developed more than 100 recommendations for the development and change of rehabilitation programs in Canada. The theme of underestimating the "vocational potential or functional skill from formal assessment" or standard rehabilitation procedures is repeated in this study. The authors provide the following example:

> One young woman wanted help to go from mainly peeling vegetables for six years for minimal incentive pay to working in a library. Her worker set up a half-day training program in a sympathetic little resource library, and four months later she was accepted into the university library as a part-time trainee volunteer. She is very near to independence in this work and is a lot happier. Whether she will achieve her ultimate ambition we do not know, but her general competence, confidence and self-image have improved, and she has asked meanwhile to be placed in a competitive job she could do right now.

In other words, even people with mental disabilities can get intellectually bored, potentially leading to behavioral problems which could have easily been avoided had the person been placed in a learning environment where new, valued skills could be learned. Ironically, the authors conclude that rehabilitation counselors and workers need to develop their skills so that the quality of life for persons with mental disabilities can be enhanced through appropriate support and services, those which stimulate the person's cognitive function by providing meaningful learning opportunities. Skill acquisition in any of the domains of quality of life is reliant, in part, on underlying cognitive function, and skill training programs must be sensitive to individual differences in learning capacity.

Walker et al. (1987) examined the MMPI, the Adaptive Behavior Scale (ABS), and a Quality of Life Rating Scale in predicting recovery for adult survivors of traumatic brain injury. They found that the "recovered group was significantly higher on the ABS, which defines adaptive behavior as the "effectiveness of an individual in coping with the natural and social demands of his or her environment." The ABS is scored on the ratings made by individuals in close contact with the survivors. Part One examines personal independence in the areas of economic and vocational activities and responsibility. Part Two measures maladaptive behaviors, such as violent and destructive behaviors. The Quality of Life Rating Scale (QLRS) is based on "cognitive functioning, emotional control, physical functioning, daily living skills, social functioning, educational/intellectual abilities, vocational skills, behavioral adjustment, and overall adaptation to home, work, and society." No claim for psychometric soundness was offered for this instrument. However, the researchers did predict that "subjects with successful recovery will have evidenced less denial than non-recovery subjects." Using a follow-up questionnaire administered to relatives and significant others, 15 subjects were classified as recovered and 9 as nonrecovered. "The recovery group showed a significantly higher frequency of adaptive behaviors in the economic activity domain" than the nonrecovery group. Significant differences were also found between the two groups in maladaptive behaviors, with the recovered group demonstrating fewer maladaptive behaviors. The results of the QLRS revealed that the recovery group's self-rating scores on quality of life were closer to that of ratings by relatives and others than for the nonrecovery group, whose scores were elevated. The researchers indicated that the denial process found in head-injured patients was most likely operating at a higher level in the nonrecovery group. They recommend further investigation into the denial process as it relates to function and quality of life, pointing out that denial inhibits learning of adaptive behaviors (skills) necessary for improvement in quality of life.

Schwartz et al. (1990) explored the "similarities and differences between patients with myasthenia gravis (MG), a chronic disease, and amyotrophic lateral sclerosis (ALS), a terminal disease," in terms of their impact on lifestyle. The study compared 19 ALS and 19 MG patients. Acceptable validity and reliability scores were reported on instrumentation, including a survey form. Coping styles were assessed, along with severity of illness, demographics, life satisfaction, perceived health, and social activity. Life satisfaction, perceived health, and social activity were measured using a 9-rung Cantril Ladder. The Multidimensional Health Locus of Control (MHLC) was used to measure the following: Do patients think they have control over their health? Or is their health controlled by powerful others? Or is their health a matter of luck? Psychosocial well-being was measured by adapting the Functional Living Index of Cancer (FLIC), and quality of life was measured by using the Q-L Index.

Coping methods consisted of active cognitive coping, "including attempts to manage one's appraisal of the stressfulness of the event;" active behavioral coping, "referring to overt behavioral events to deal directly with the problem and its effects;" and avoidance coping, "referring to attempts to avoid actively confronting the problem or to indirectly reduce emotional tension by eating or smoking more." Problem-focused coping included "attempts to modify or eliminate the sources of stress through one's own behavior;" and emotion-focused coping included "behavioral or cognitive responses whose primary function is to manage the emotional consequences of stressors to help maintain one's emotional equilibrium." Both MG and ALS tended to use problem-focused coping skills to manage their illness. No significant differences were found between the ALS and MG patient groups on coping styles, except for active adaptive behavioral coping.

ALS patients had a significantly higher adaptive behavior score than MG patients, a finding thought to be related to their inability to justify intellectually why they had this disease and instead the patients reverted to overt behavioral attempts to deal with the problem and its effects. MG patients had higher scores than ALS patients in life satisfaction, perceived health, social activity, and quality of life. The authors conclude that "this study provides important preliminary data showing that adjustment needs of the chronically and terminally ill differ." However, the relationship between the coping styles assessment methods and quality of life or life satisfaction parameters for these two groups was not clarified in detail. Yet, they clearly established a conceptual model of coping which includes cognitive, behavioral, and emotional components, all of which have been related at length to quality of life in this book. Acquisition and use of learned skills was clearly seen to include a cognitive component.

Scherer (1990) conducted studies on the use of assistive devices (ADs) with persons with cerebral palsy (CP) and with spinal cord injury (SCI). "The original and follow-up research was designed to provide an in-depth investigation of a small number of subject who were either assistive device users or non-users rather than a more superficial study of many subjects." Interviews and observations were used to compare users and non-users over time in "their functional capacities and temperament" and "in the perceptions of their current and future quality of life." Scherer also used the Personal Capacities Questionnaire (PCQ), "a 30-item measure of six functional areas: adaptative behavior, vocational qualifications, communication, motor functioning, physical condition, and cognitive functioning with two additional items assessing visual impairment and the need for special job requirements." The Functional Assessment Inventory (FAI) "is an item-by-item translation of the PCQ into statements completed by a rehabilitation counselor or other treatment specialist familiar with the client/subject." The Taylor-Johnson Temperament Analysis was used to examine temperament. Scherer reports:

> The findings indicate that the functional capacities and the temperament of participants with CP both tended to improve over time whereas most SCI participants seemed to become less well-adjusted in several areas. While the SCI users of ADs continued to display the best overall functioning of all participant groups, the SCI non-users reported the most functional declines over time with the gaps between them and the SCI users widening.

Scherer does not comment upon the differences in these groups in terms of quality of life (even though she uses the term "quality of life" in the title of her article) except to note that the individuals with CP seemed more content with their lives than the persons with SCI, suggesting that this may demonstrate a higher quality of life for the CP participants than for those with SCI. Functional abilities in the cognitive as well as other life domains appear to impact life satisfaction or quality of life, but more empirical study is needed with these populations in order to assess the nature and scope of this impact.

Satcher (1993) addresses quality of work life issues in terms of reasonable accommodation strategies as established by the Americans with Disabilities Act (ADA). Her focus is on the use of the reasonable accommodation provision for persons with learning disabilities, but it is likely that reasonable accommodation within the workplace would improve the quality of work life for any disability group, including the groups mentioned above (cerebral palsy, traumatic brain injury, spinal cord injury, myasthenia gravis survivors, and the mentally disabled). Satcher asserts that "the ADA provides a framework for improving quality of work life for persons with learning disabilities. These persons and their advocates, however, must assume certain responsibilities if the provisions of the ADA are to be fully realized." She makes a demand for adequate cognitive functioning by the person with a disability:

> Persons with learning disabilities must (a) understand their disabilities and resultant functional limitations and (b) be able to articulate their accommodation needs to employers.

She extends this demand to rehabilitation counselors who may assist persons with disabilities in entering the labor market by recommending that counselors assist disabled persons in feeling "comfortable in disclosing their limitations to their employers, ... to describe their limitations in functional terms and to identify accommodations to lessen the impact of these functional limitations."

Inge et al. (1988) make a compelling argument for the acquisition of skills as an aspect of the improvement of quality of life in their study of mentally retarded individuals working in competitive employment vs. sheltered workshop environments. They used the Adaptive Behavior Scale, the Parent/Guardian Survey, and an array of physical health measures. Methodological issues proved to be significant, but the study results do suggest that competitive employment has a positive effect on the quality of lives of people with mental retardation. Skill acquisition in the areas of language development, economic activity, numbers, and time (as measured on the Adaptive Behavior Scale subscales) was noted. The social/vocational and the fiscal responsibility subscales also demonstrated improvement for the competitively employed group. Inge et al. tie increased competence to acquisition of skills and, in turn, tie acquisition of identified skills to improved quality of life:

> There is no question that quality of life is very much a personal observation based on a given individual's needs, preferences, and aspirations. On the other hand, expanded competence in community participation as well as economic skill and time management is a highly valuable by-product of competitive employment. If improved quality of life translates into improved community integration and acceptance, ... then competitive employment positively affects the lives of individuals who are mentally retarded.

Skill acquisition appears to have internal and external consequences which affect quality of life (suggesting that skill acquisition associated with competitive employment positively affects the lives of persons with disabilities). When the cognitive domain is redefined in life skill, adaptation, adjustment, function, or capacity terminology, the role of the rehabilitationist emerges more clearly, reflecting the pragmatic focus of the profession. Rehabilitationists should emphasize acquisition of new knowledge and skills and not focus on the deficit model traditionally seen in the medical and psychological models. Getting people to do something new, where learning opportunities can occur, rather than simply offering such interventions as pharmacology or talk therapy, appear to impact quality of life positively.

Independence/Autonomy

Perhaps the most challenging quality of life issue within the cognitive domain lies in the area of choice, independence, and autonomy. Quality of life literature on this point is found largely in studies of quality of life and aging and developmental disability. However, the devaluation of individuals with any kind of disability can mean loss of autonomy and choice, even to the point of being put to death, as in Nazi Germany which practiced the *final solution* on persons with disabilities before they constructed the gas chambers in the death camps of Europe during World War II (Waxman, 1991).

In the late 20th century, the issue of physician-assisted suicide has emerged as the life and death issue in terms of disability, choice, independence, or autonomy. Cognitive functioning is a critical factor in the physician-assisted suicide debate. Quill et al. (1992) proposed clinical criteria for physician-assisted suicide, which include six conditions which must be met before proceeding. Three of the conditions demand clear cognition, two involve pain and suffering issues, and one centers on social functioning.

The first condition is a pain and suffering condition: "The patient must have a condition that is incurable and associated with severe, unrelenting suffering;"

The second condition is also a question of pain and suffering: "The physician must ensure that the patient's suffering and the request are not the result of inadequate comfort care;"

The third condition is a cognitive functioning condition: "The patient must clearly and repeatedly, of his or her own free will and initiative, request to die rather than continue suffering;"

The fourth condition is also a cognitive functioning condition: "The physician must be sure that the patient's judgment is not distorted;"

The fifth condition is a social functioning condition: "Physician-assisted suicide should be carried out only in the context of a meaningful doctor-patient relationship;"

And the sixth condition is another cognitive functioning condition: "Consultation with another experienced physician is required to ensure that the patient's request is voluntary and rational, the diagnosis and prognosis accurate, and the exploration of comfort-oriented alternatives thorough."

Clearly, cognitive issues associated with choice to end one's life focus on the question of autonomy. Who has the right to choose and what safeguards should be in place to protect the person's right of autonomy or choice while protecting the person from unintended self-harm? The answers to these questions have been and are being debated by medical ethicists and the courts at the present time.

The question of choice based on voluntary and rational decision-making is highly problematic for persons with disabilities. Coleman (1992), in her review of two famous right-to-die cases, comments:

> This article examines the practice and consequences of treating requests to die by persons with disabilities as rational choices and not as suicidal pleas for help and assistance in living. By selectively ignoring laws and policies for suicide prevention for persons with and those without disabilities. This double standard is based on the courts' ill-formed quality of life judgments.

In the Elizabeth Bouvia case, quality of life issues were paramount. Ms. Bouvia, a woman with cerebral palsy, had experienced a miscarriage, spousal abandonment, loss of financial benefits, and loss of educational opportunities prior to her request to die of self-starvation. By the time the court battles were done, Ms. Bouvia had given up her plan to die in that way. "Kenneth Bergstedt was a thirty-one year old man with quadriplegia who had used a ventilator since the age of ten." He lived with his parents, but had never attended school away from home, worked, or socialized. He did not have contacts with the disability community. His father was dying and his mother was deceased when "his father filed a petition in a Las Vegas court on his son's behalf," requesting that he be allowed to turn off his son's ventilator. The court never communicated with Kenneth Bergstedt and his father turned off the ventilator. The father also prevented contact between the disability community and his son.

Gill (1992) asserts that

> Lacking an informed perspective and harboring intense fears of becoming disabled, the public, including judges, ethicists, and media reporters, takes such complaints (wishing to die) at face value and looks no further for their significance. Such people readily conclude that the disabled person's wish to die is reasonable because it agrees with their own preconception that the primary problem for such individuals is the unbearable experience of a permanent disability (and/or dependence on life aids). If permanent disability is the problem, death is the solution. In this analysis, the wish to die is transformed into a desire for freedom, not suicide. If it is suicide at all, it is *rational* and, thereby, different from suicides resulting from emotional disturbance or illogical despair.

Gill then draws upon clinical descriptions of depression and notes that "one of the most dangerous aspects of despair is the development of rigid, constrictive thinking, sometimes referred to as *tunneling*." In other words, Gill has pointed out how depression can cause impairment to cognition, which is consistent with the quality of life studies reviewed earlier in this chapter under (1) Impairment and Cognitive Limitations — Mental Illness.

Most right-to-die literature is not written in terms of the quality of life paradigm, particularly for people with disabilities. This flies in the face of the disability rights movement, whose efforts could be seen as a demand for quality lives for all people with disabilities. As Nosek (1996) writes, "wellness and disability, used in the same sentence, could seriously disrupt the status quo in health care. Traditionally, disability has been equated with illness." Nosek's point is that disability is a normal part of life.

Quality of life literature in rehabilitation is keeping pace with the demand by the disability rights movement that quality of life considerations are an essential aspect of the disability experience. Sands and Kozleski (1994) surveyed adults with and without disabilities in terms of their similarities and differences on quality of life domains. The 86 persons with disabilities included 61% identifying their "primary disability as mental retardation," 13% with cerebral palsy, 4% with head injury, and the remaining with autism, deafness, and emotional disorders (6%), and with visual impairments or speech/language impairments (2%). The 131 persons without disabilities were found by random selection in a shopping area of Denver, stratified random sampling of community organization members, and a random selection of college students. Sands and Kozleski used the Consumer Satisfaction Survey which was originally designed for individuals with developmental disabilities. A modified version (minimal changes were made) was given to persons without disabilities. One of the findings was that an important difference between adults with and without disabilities is that adults with disabilities have less involvement in making choices about their lives. The authors suggest that, contrary to the rehabilitation profession's assumption that cognitive capacity limits the ability of the individual to choose, it is the lack of opportunity to participate, and "practice" choice which is more constraining than the level of cognitive ability. This has profound implications for rehabilitation service planning and delivery. One's ability to choose specific interventions and to alter those choices freely, particularly when one is experiencing chronic illness or disease which is expected to have lifelong effects on quality of life, appears to be important to the person's sense of well-being. Yet, the dilemma in working with persons with cognitive deficits (particularly in dealing with persons with moderate to severe head injury, where there is an assumption that cognition is impaired to the point that independent decision-making may not lead to useful, appropriate choices) is obvious. If a person has a mental or physical impairment which severely constricts or limits cognitive function, it becomes more difficult for the person to retain personal autonomy over choices. Also, it is not clear whether the person even retains the appreciation of the concept of autonomy. Respecting the autonomy and preserving the rights of an individual with a cognitive deficit associated with disability is at best difficult. The point at which reduced cognitive function makes appreciation of one's own autonomy and preservation of this aspect of quality of life practically meaningful has not been well-researched.

Vandergriff and Chubon (1994) conducted a multifaceted study "to assess the quality of life of persons with mental retardation residing in a variety of residential settings." They used the Program Analysis of Service Systems Implementation of Normalization Goals (PASSING), the Life Situation Survey (LSS), the Resident Choice Assessment Scale (RCAS), and, as in other studies previously reviewed, they used the Adaptive Behavior Scale (ABS). This study could have been reviewed under the category of Intellectual Level, since the findings indicated that "quality of life may be better for persons at the higher intellectual level (in a population of mentally retarded individuals)." The review is placed here since this is the only quality of life study found which measured "autonomy and freedom of choice." In this case, the freedom of choice was related to the living environment. Curiously, the Resident Choice Assessment Scale is completed by "persons familiar with the individual whose quality of life is being assessed." No discussion of the peculiarity of this arrangement is offered, even though the authors conclude that "this population was capable of making reliable and valid judgments about their condition." This conclusion appears to be based on the use of multiple assessments and agreement among assessments through self-report by clients and reports by others. Of equal interest was the finding that persons living in community residences and home settings scored higher on autonomy and choice as well as on IQ ratings than others living in more structured settings.

McGuire et al. (1991) conducted a study of elderly persons with mental disabilities living in two group homes. A lifestyle questionnaire which included questions regarding daily activities, involvement in domestic tasks, the extent of community-based activities, and the extent to which residents are responsible for, and can make decisions about, their own lives was administered in interviews with House Managers of the two groups home examined. The Social Training Achievement Record (STAR) was administered in the same way. The STAR "yields useful information about the level of competence present in a number of social skills considered necessary for successful independent living." The authors found it remarkable that "the residents studied have achieved their current level of functioning after so many depersonalizing years in large institutions." However, they also found that "even when allowed to choose things for themselves, such as what time to go to bed, many of the residents were unable to break away from the routines by which they had lived for 50 or more years." This result supports the Sands and Kozleski (1994) assertion that having the opportunity for and the ability to practice choice is important for people with mental disabilities.

Quality of life literature in the field of gerontology directly connects autonomy and choice to higher levels of competence and function for elderly persons residing in residential facilities. Hyer et al. (1982) used the Locus of Control Measure (LOC), which was designed "for the unique environment of a nursing home." Seven items measure "the expectancy of control of relevant outcomes" and seven more items measure the value or "the desirability of the outcome." Quality of life was measured using the Cantril Ladder and a life satisfaction scale, the LSI-Z, modified from the Life Satisfaction Rating. The Rosenberg Self-Esteem Scale was also included as a quality of life measure. The Behavioral Adjustment Scale, functional activities of daily living ratings, ratings by a nursing supervisor regarding pain levels, the Hamilton Depression Scale, the Bradburn Affect–Balance Scale, the Nursing Home Depression Checklist, the Short Portable Mental Status Questionnaire, the Face-Hand Test, a mental status item for short-term memory measure, the Sheltered Care Environment Scale, and four other one-item questions were all administered as part of this multifaceted approach to quality of life assessment for people in nursing homes.

Hyer, Matteson, and Seigler report that

> A major finding of this study is the locus of control adds to the understanding of the adjustment of LTC (Long Term Care) elders. Controlling for the typical background variables of age, education, sex, and the important psychiatric factors of depression and cognitive decline, the possession of an internal LOC was found to influence the various adjustment measures, particularly behavior, perception of the environment, and depression itself.

This study suggests that maintenance of locus of control for persons with organic and/or psychological deficits influence quality of life as well as overall life adjustment.

The connections among quality of life, cognitive ability or competence, and the ability to adjust are even more clear in another study of elderly persons in nursing homes. Gutheil (1991) examined "what is known about features of the physical environment of care facilities for frail older persons and their impact on quality of life." She sees the physical environment as "a tremendous resource for promoting competence and a sense of control in residents." Gutheil identifies helpful design features in residential settings and their effects. She notes that safety "is a basic building block in quality of life." Good lighting, nonslip floors, call buttons, assistive devices in bathrooms (hand rails, higher toilet seats) all increase safety, quality of life, and competence. Negotiability and orientation are also noted in design consideration. Negotiability can include easily used door handles and bannisters along walls. Orientation aids assist residents in perceiving their location in a building. This can be done with color coding, individualizing parts of the building with plants, artwork, or aquariums, distinctive wall and floor coverings, large floor numbers, and signs. The section on "Planning for Sensory Deficits" section is probably the most important when examining the cognitive domain in quality of life. Gutheil notes that "physical settings, in fact, play a role in enhancing or diminishing visual and auditory competence." Given that we have already discussed visual and auditory impairments as aspects of cognitive impairment which arise from some impairment within the individual, Gutheil's work allow us to understand that such impairments can be **imposed** upon vulnerable populations, thereby reducing their quality of life. Recommendations for solutions include adjusting lighting levels higher to meet the needs of visually impaired older adults, contrasting surfaces which need to be differentiated with texture and placement of objects as well as the creative use of color (painting doors a different color from walls and frames, selecting furniture a different color from carpets and walls), eliminating glare on surfaces, and avoiding marked differences in lighting levels. Persons with auditory impairments can be assisted by eliminating background music not related to an activity and by putting public telephones with devices to assist the hearing impaired persons in quiet spaces. Additional design factors include making privacy available to residents and allowing residents to use space to meet their needs as in being able to easily move chairs around, to control the temperature of their rooms, or to open or close curtains. Gutheil contends that "a well-planned environment supports competent behavior and individual choice" and, of course, improves quality of life. This study suggests that autonomy is affected by external, environmental factors as well as internal factors. Using assistive devices and providing a well-planned living environment can impact overall autonomy by providing choices which would not be available to a person with a disability. Cognitive function can be enhanced and quality of life can be increased by providing a physical environment which promotes choices (providing opportunities for experiencing a wide variety of life events). Providing a van, a scooter, and/or a computer to someone may be justified in terms of enhancement of cognitive function and improvement in quality of life because of the impact of each on autonomy.

Assessment Issues

The assessment of quality of life for persons with cognitive impairments is "seen as especially difficult" in a review of conceptual and methodological issues of quality of life for older people (Ory and Cox, 1994). These researchers noted that "the subjective component of quality of life measurement requires that an older person be able to express feelings, perceptions, etc. If an older person becomes cognitively impaired, other ways must be found to tap this very important aspect of the measurement."

Rosen et al. (1995) developed a subjective measure of quality of life, PALS, which contains four scales (Perceived Stress, Affect, Loneliness, and Satisfaction). They remark that "it is unfortunate that PALS is of little value for those individuals who cannot understand or respond meaningfully to the questions." They also commented on the tendency to acquiescence on the part of people with mental retardation. It was noted that inability to understand or respond and a tendency to acquiesce (issues often confronted when dealing with persons with severe cognitive deficits resulting from trauma as well as developmental issues) undermines the validity of an instrument. While noting that the dimensions of quality of life "are the same for all people," it was recommended that separate instruments are needed to "assess the quality of life of individuals functioning at different levels of mental retardation." Ouellette-Kuntz (1990) did just that. She refined the Quality of Life Interview Schedule (QUOLIS) for developmentally disabled adults "who are unable to complete a written questionnaire or a verbal interview." Interviews were conducted with parents and counselors and emphasis was placed on intra- and inter-rater agreement. Since this was a pilot study, results could not be generalized.

In addition to measurement problems focusing on the inability of individuals to provide data regarding their own assessment of their life quality, the issue of whether subjective or objective data is the most appropriate or accurate assessment technique is a constant theme in most measurement of quality of life discourse. Rosen et al. (1995) assert that their instrument, PALS, "differs from other measures of quality of life in that it is focused exclusively on subjective psychological dimensions that are regarded as the most relevant criteria." While admitting that their instrument could not be used with people "who cannot understand or respond meaningfully to the questions," they state, for such individuals, "we may be forced to rely upon objective standards, recognizing that these may represent necessary but not sufficient conditions for understanding the well-being of people."

McCauley and Bremer (1991) note that "the fit between objective conditions and the subjective experience of life is often surprisingly weak, not only for notable individuals (e.g., Mother Teresa) but also for the general population.... Frequency of sexual activity, for instance, is not the same as satisfaction with sexual activity, and employment status is not the same as satisfaction with employment." They recommend using both objective and subjective measures in order to obtain a complete assessment of quality of life. These researchers identified Bradburn's Affective Measures,

Campbell's Index of General Affect, and Campbell's Overall Life Satisfaction Items as appropriate assessment tools. They recommend using both Bradburn and Campbell since "Bradburn's measures alone will miss the cognitive-judgmental aspect" of quality of life. Objective measures "may be understood as descriptions of lifestyles, in which sociodemographic, medical, economic, and other life circumstances contribute to variations in QOL." Education, income, activity level, employment and recreation are also considered within the objective realm. McCauley and Bremer recommend using the Campbell and Bradburn measures along with these objective data. They do warn, however, that this assessment method will not be useful in meeting the needs of those who wish to understand disease-specific or disability-specific effects on quality of life. When examining quality of life within the cognitive domain, the subjective quality of life measurement is highly dependent upon the cognitive functioning of the individual being assessed. Sometimes, assessment by others (parents, helping professionals, significant others) may be the only way to obtain data. The other alternative is reliance upon objective data only.

THE FORENSIC REHABILITATIONIST'S ROLE IN THE ASSESSMENT OF COGNITIVE WELL-BEING

Rehabilitationists spend a great deal of their education, training, and professional practice time in studying and using assessment techniques to ascertain the cognitive functioning of persons with disabilities. These instruments range from the Wide Range Achievement Test, which measures spelling, reading, and arithmetic, to nonverbal intelligence testing as constructed by the RAVEN. Space does not allow for the listing of the many instruments used in rehabilitation education and practice, and this information can be easily obtained by examining any text used in graduate rehabilitation counseling measurement courses.

Therefore, it is strange that so little attention has been paid to this aspect of rehabilitation practice in terms of quality of life issues for clients being assessed in a rehabilitation process. Particularly when considering the profound effects of severe traumatic brain injury (TBI), the authors of this book would have thought much more discussion of quality of life and cognitive quality of life would have been found, particularly since there is a terminology used frequently in the TBI field, *cognitive rehabilitation.* However, Garske and Thomas (1992), in a study of 47 volunteers who were diagnosed as having severe head injuries (mean coma duration of 29.9 days, mean time since injury of 49.9 months, and mean age of 22.9 years), found a significant negative correlation ($r = -0.74$) between self-esteem measured via the Rosenberg Self-Esteem Scale (RSES — a 10-item, Lickert-type scale) and depression as measured by the Beck depression Inventory (BDI). More importantly, significant negative correlations were noted between subscales of the Human Services Scale (HHS — an 80-item measure of rehabilitation needs associated with quality of life) and the BDI (ranging from –0.31 for family to –0.78 for emotional security) and positive correlations between the RSES and the subscales of the HHS (ranging from 0.32 for economic self-esteem to 0.68 for emotional security). Only the correlation between economic self-esteem and depression was nonsignificant. Depression was seen not so much as a product of the injury, but as a reaction to experiencing of loss (in quality of life), frustration, and radical changes in lifestyle. These findings suggest that high self-esteem (one's cognitive self-reference statements) leads persons with head injuries to emphasize competencies over limitations, abilities over disabilities, and feelings of worth over feelings of hopelessness. It was noted that although mental and psychosocial factors related to functional adaptation and development of social competency were less amenable to rehabilitation efforts in the short-term, they needed to be addressed. It appears that, for persons with head injuries, what they say to themselves about their disability status influences their level of function. Cognition appears to influence rehabilitation outcomes, making it important for rehabilitation professionals to use intervention strategies which emphasize abilities and capacities rather than deficits and inabilities. Novack et al. (1992) noted that educating persons with mild head injuries about the resultant problems reduced their anxiety by making the situation more predictable. They could deal more effectively with their fears of "going crazy." Cognitive rehabilitation should focus also on developing confidence and dispelling fears, working on problem-solving, processing speed, and stamina. The Garske and Thomas' study supports the contention of the authors of this book that resumption of preinjury levels of function and lifestyle should be the goal wherever possible.

In a study of 78 TBI patients 1 to 2 years after discharge from a rehabilitation hospital, Melamed et al. (1992) administered the Rehabilitation Need and Status Scale (RNSS — an 80-item measure with 7 subscales on physiological, emotional security, family, social, economic self-esteem, economic security, and vocational self-actualization need satisfaction) as a measure of well-being/acceptance of disability (using the same constructs and content across life domains contained in the quality of life literature). Subjective rehabilitation status (SRS) improved as the functional work status of the participants in the study increased (demonstrating a positive correlation ranging from 0.41 to 0.65 between SRS and all subclasses of the RNSS except economic security. Those working in the open labor market reported the highest SRS, but it was recognized that psychosocial adjustment as well as work contributed to overall SRS rating and acceptance of disability. Warren et al. (1996) reported similarly that, with 137 TBI patients, life satisfaction, as measured on the Life Satisfaction Index-A (LSI-A), was significantly associated with increased family satisfaction, being married, increased memory, increased independence, being employed, and engaging in less self-blame for the injury.

Clearly, cognitive acceptance of disability is a critical factor in adjustment to head injury and to restoration of maximum quality of life. Forensic rehabilitationists, when developing future care plans, should encourage persons with head injuries to establish challenging goals across all life domains (in order to create positive expectancy), but to temper these goals with the realization that acceptance of limitations associated with disability is critical to acceptance of disability (not building in opportunities for failure due to having unrealistic goals that cannot be reasonably expected to be fulfilled). This balance between striving and succeeding is critical to one's perception of self. Unnecessary failures may be a source of negative expectancy; yet, low expectations (goals) may lead to little meaningful change. No literature was found in the rehabilitation journals on this point except for the literature in the speciality of mental retardation or developmental disability. Even in that literature, the tie between cognitive skills and quality of life are rarely made explicit. Since cognition is so basic to all aspects of life, perhaps we take it for granted when we think about quality of life. Because of the authors' rehabilitation backgrounds, there is an understanding of how important cognitive issues are in any rehabilitation practice, since intellectual level, as well as impairment to the use of intellectual ability such as visual and auditory damage, brain injury, or psychological damage, will often be a determining factor in the client's ability to use a rehabilitation benefit. For example, clients' intellectual levels are used to determine appropriateness for training and education in rehabilitation plans.

In rehabilitation workers' compensation practice, the authors have found that even the slightest physical injury can cast a shadow over the client's cognitive well-being. Our favorite example is that of a professional ice skater who sustained an injury to her big toe which threw her out of an occupation she had engaged in since the age of 5 years. Other quality of life issues were certainly present in her situation, but her cognitive well-being was also at risk. This is why rehabilitationists are likely to provide skills and aptitude testing in most rehabilitative situations, even though access to education and training may be the more formal or more easily understood reason. The ice skater was convinced that her competence lay only in her physical skill as a performer. She needed to know as quickly as possible that her intellectual functioning had not been damaged and she needed to know what the current level of her skills and aptitudes were. Until this issue had been cleared up, the ice skater's sense of overall well-being was diminished and she was not free to move forward in her life. It may seem odd that injured workers connect their intellectual and skill functioning to their physical integrity in this way, but in clinical practice we have observed this to be true for hundreds of injured workers. In fact, we incorporate this understanding into our counseling sessions with injured workers and justify our aptitude and skill testing to them on this basis as well as for the more formal reasons of meeting guidelines in workers' compensation systems.

Psychological injury can have a similar result. Belenky et al. (1986) found in their study of abused women that "every woman, regardless of age, social class, ethnicity, and academic achievement, needs to know she is capable of intelligent thought, and she needs to know it right away" (p. 193). This study underscores the need for aptitude and skill testing of women filing sexual harassment complaints or any civil sexual assault lawsuit, since their well-being may be immediately improved when they discover that their cognitive capacity has not abandoned them.

What the quality of life literature in rehabilitation did address was the need for rehabilitation providers to understand quality of life issues in every rehabilitation setting for every type of rehabilitation client. The cognitive domain was very present in the rehabilitation literature reviewed in this chapter and some writers have pointed out that "quality of life will probably replace deinstitutionalization, normalization, and community adjustment as the issue of the 90s" in rehabilitation (Schalock et al. 1989). The editors of *Quality of Life in Health Promotion and Rehabilitation* (Brown et al. 1996) see quality of life as a central issue in rehabilitation and health promotion. (p. 3). It remains for rehabilitation researchers to more fully address the nuances of the cognitive domain of quality of life as part of rehabilitation theory and practice.

REFERENCES

American Psychiatric Association (APA). 1994. *Diagnostic and Statistical Manual of Mental Disorders,* 4th ed. Washington, D.C.: American Psychiatric Association.

Bech, P. (1990). Measurement of psychological distress and well-being. *Psychotherapy and Psychosomatics,* 54: 77-89.

Belenky, M. F., Clinchy, B. M., Goldberger, N. R., and Tarule, J. M. (1986). *Women's Ways of Knowing: The Development of Self, Voice, and Mind.* New York: Basic Books.

Bigelow, D. A., McFarland, B. H., and Olson, M. M. (1991). Quality of life of community mental health program clients: Validating a measure. *Community Mental Health Journal,* 27(1): 43-55.

Breetvelt, I. S. and Van Dam, F. S. A. M. (1991). Underreporting by cancer patients: the case of response shift. *Social Science Medicine,* 32(9): 981-987.

Brown, C. (1996). A comparison of living situation and loneliness for people with mental illness. *Psychiatric Rehabilitation Journal,* 20(2): 59-65.

Brown, I., Renwick, R., and Nagler, M. (1996). The centrality of quality of life in health promotion and rehabilitation. In R. Renwick, I. Brown, and M. Nagler (Eds.). *Quality of Life in Health Promotion and Rehabilitation,* p. 3. Thousand Oaks, CA: Sage Publications.

Brown, R. I. (1989). Aging, disability, and quality of life: a challenge for society. *Canadian Psychology,* 30(3): 551-559.

Brown, R. I., Bayer, M. B., and Brown, P. M. (1988). Quality of life: a challenge for rehabilitation agencies. *Australia and New Zealand Journal of Developmental Disabilities,* 14(3,4): 189-199.

Coleman, D. (1992). Withdrawing life-sustaining treatment from people with severe disabilities who request it: equal protection considerations. *Issues in Law and Medicine,* 8(1): 55-79.

Condeluci, A., Ferris, L. L., and Bogdan, A. (1992). Outcome and value: the survivor perspective. *Journal of Head Trauma Rehabilitation,* 7(4): 37-45.

Corrigan, P. W. and Buican, B. (1995). The construct validity of subjective quality of life for the severely mentally ill. *The Journal of Nervous and Mental Disease,* 183(5): 281-285.

Fitzsimmons, B. and Bunting, L. K. (1997). Parkinson's disease: quality of life issues. *Http://www.cnsonline.org/www/archive/parkins/park.07.txt.*

Garske, G. G. and Thomas, K. R. (1992). Self-reported self-esteem and depression: indexes of psychosocial adjustment following severe traumatic brain injury. *Rehabilitation Counseling Bulletin,* 36(1): 44-52.

Gill, C. J. (1992). Suicide intervention for people with disabilities. *Issues in Law and Medicine,* 8(1): 37-53.

Gutheil, I. A. (1991). The physical environment and quality of life in residential facilities for frail elders. *Adult Residential Care Journal,* 52: 131-145.

Hays, R. D., Vickrey, B. G., Hermann, B. P., Perrine, K., Cramer, J., Meador, K., Spritzer, K., and Devinsky, O. (1995). Agreement between self reports and proxy reports of quality of life in epilepsy patients. *Quality of Life Research,* 4: 159-168.

Howard, K. and Rockwood, K. (1995). Quality of life in Alzheimer's disease. *Dementia,* 6: 113-116.

Hyer, L., Matteson, M.A., and Siegler, I. C. (1982). Locus of control and long-term care. *Journal of Applied Gerontology,* 1: 147-160.

Inge, K. J., Banks, P. D., Wehman, Hill, J. W., and Shafer, M. S. (1988). Quality of life for individuals who are labeled mentally retarded: evaluating competitive employment versus sheltered workshop employment. *Education and Training in Mental Retardation*, 97-104

Lynch, R. T. and Gallagher-Lepak, S. (1996). Chronic renal failure: the impact of improved medical treatment options on rehabilitation. *Journal of Applied Rehabilitation Counseling,* 27(1): 7-12.

McCauley, C. and Bremer, B. A. (1991). Subjective quality of life measures for evaluating medical intervention. *Evaluation and the Health Professions,* 14(4): 371-387.

McGuire, B. E., Choon, G., and Akuffo, E. (1991). Community living for elderly people with an intellectual disability: a pilot study. *Australia and New Zealand Journal of Developmental Disabilities,* 17(1): 25-33.

Melamed, S., Groswasser, Z., and Stern, M. J. (1992). Acceptance of disability, work involvement and subjective rehabilitation status of traumatic brain-injured (TBI) patients. *Brain Injury*, 6(3): 233-243.

Murphy, P. A. (1993). *Making the Connections: Women, Work and Abuse.* Winter Park, FL: St. Lucie Press.

Murphy, P. A. (1994). *The Edge of a Large Hole: Writings on the Request for Reasonable Accommodation under the Americans with Disabilities Act of 1990.* Chicago: Center for Research on Women and Gender University of Illinois.

Murphy, P. A. (1996). *A Career and Life Planning Guide for Women Survivors: Making the Connections Work Book.* Winter Park, FL: St. Lucie Press.

Nagler, M. (1996). Quality of life of people with disabilities who have experienced sexual abuse. In R. Renwick, I. Brown, and M. Nagler (Eds.). *Quality of Life in Health Promotion and Rehabilitation: Conceptual Approaches, Issues, and Applications,* pp. 190-203. Thousand Oaks, CA: Sage Publications.

National Institutes of Health. (1990). Surgery for Epilepsy. *NIH Consensus Statement Online,* 8(2): 1-20.

Nosek, M. A. (1996). Wellness among women with physical disabilities. In D. M. Krotoski, M. A. Nosek, and M. A. Turk (Eds.), *Women with Physical Disabilities: Achieving and Maintaining Health and Well-Being,* pp. 17-33. Baltimore: Paul H. Brookes Publishing.

Novack, D., Roth, L., and Boll, T. J. (1988). Treatment alternatives following mild head injury. *Rehabilitation Counseling Bulletin*, 31(4): 313-324.

Ory, M. O. and Cox, D. M. (1994). Forging ahead: linking health and behavior to improve quality of life in older people. *Social Indicators Research*, 33: 89-120.

Ouellette-Kuntz, H. (1990). A pilot study in the use of the quality of life interview schedule. *Social Indicators Research,* 23: 283-298.

Quill, T. E., Cassel, C. K., and Meier, D. E. (1992). Care of the hopelessly ill: proposed clinical criteria for physician-assisted suicide. *New England Journal of Medicine,* 327(19): 1380-1384.

Renwick, R. and Brown, I. (1996). The Centre for Health Promotion's conceptual approach to quality of life: Being, belonging, and becoming. In R. Renwick, I. Brown, and M. Nagler (Eds.), *Quality of Life in Health Promotion and Rehabilitation,* pp. 75-86. Thousand Oaks, CA: Sage Publications.

Romney, D. M., Jenkins, C. D., and Bynner, J. M. (1992). A structural analysis of health-related quality of life dimensions. *Human Relations,* 45(2): 165-176.

Rosen, M., Simon, E. W., and McKinsey, L. (1995). Subjective measure of quality of life. *Mental Retardation,* 33(1): 31-34.

Sands, D. J. and Kozleski, E. B. (1994). Quality of life differences between adults with and without disabilities. *Education and Training in Mental Retardation and Developmental Disabilities,* 90-101.

Sartorius, N. (1995). Rehabilitation and Quality of Life. *International Journal of Mental Health,* 24(1): 7-13.

Satcher, J. (1993). Improving the quality of work life for persons with learning disabilities: ADA rights and responsibilities. *Journal of Applied Rehabilitation Counseling*, 24(1): 16-18.

Schaafsma, J. and Osoba, D. (1994). The Karnofsky performance status scale re-examined: a cross-validation with the EORTC-C30. *Quality of Life Research,* 3: 413-424.

Schalock, R. L., Keith, K. D., Hoffman, K., and Karan, U. D. (1989). Quality of life: perspectives and issues. *Mental Retardation*, 27: 25-31.

Schalock, R. L. and Lilley, M. A. (1986). Placement from community-based mental retardation programs: how well do clients do after 8 to 10 years? *American Journal of Mental Deficiency*, 90(6): 669-676.

Scherer, M. J. (1990). Assistive device utilization and quality of life in adults with spinal cord injuries or cerebral palsy two years later. *Journal of Applied Rehabilitation Counseling*, 21(4): 36-44.

Schwartz, L. B., Devine, P. A., Schechter, C. B., and Bender, A. N. (1990). Impact of illness on lifestyle. *Loss, Grief, and Care*, 4(3-4): 3-21.

Sherman, E. and Schiffman, L. G. (1991). Quality-of-life (QOL) assessment of older consumers: a retrospective review. *Journal of Business and Psychology*, 6(1): 107-119.

Vandergriff, D. V. and Chubon, R. A. (1994). Quality of life experienced by persons with mental retardation in various residential settings. *Journal of Rehabilitation*, 30-37.

Vickrey, B. G., Hays, R. D., Graber, J., Rausch, R., Engel, J., and Brook, R. H. (1992). A health-related quality of life instrument for patients evaluated for epilepsy surgery. *Medical Care*, 30(4): 299-319.

Walker, D. E., Blankenship, V., Ditty, J. A., and Lynch, K. P. (1987). Prediction of recovery for closed-head-injured adults: an evaluation of the MMPI, the Adaptive Behavior Scale, and a Quality of Life Rating Scale. *Journal of Clinical Psychology,* 43(6): 699-707.

Warren, L., Wrigley, M., Yoels, W. C., and Fine, P. R. (1996). Factors associated with life satisfaction among a sample of persons with neurotrauma. *Journal of Rehabilitation Research and Development,* 33(4): 404-408.

Waxman, B. F. (1991). Hatred: the unacknowledged dimension in violence against disabled people. *Sexuality and Disability*, 9(3): 185-199.

Appendices (Quality of Life Research Literature)

APPENDIX 1
Alzheimer's Disease and Quality of Life (QOL) Literature

Source	Population	Measures/Method	Domains
Callahan (1992)	Alzheimer's patients	Essay	Subjective experience, social interaction, and environment
Howard and Rockwood (1995)	Examined QOL instruments measuring Alzheimer's disease and QOL	Reviewed and ranked measurement properties of QOL instruments; need for more validation of QOL instruments for Alzheimer's patients	Behavioral competence.

References

Callahan, S. (1992). Quality of life. *Alzheimer Disease and Associated Disorders,* 6(3): 138-144.

Howard, K. and Rockwood, K. (1995). Quality of life in Alzheimer's disease. *Dementia,* 6: 113-116.

APPENDIX 2
Arthritis and Quality of Life (QOL) Research Literature

Source	Population	Measures/Method	Domains
Perlman, Connell, Clark, et al. (1990)	43 Rheumatoid arthritis patients	Self-report and doctors' and history, dance-based exercise, Arthritis Impact Measurement Scales	Disease states, physical medical function, psychological function

References

Perlman, S. G., Connell, K. J., Clark, A., Robinson, M.S., Conlon, P., Gecht, M., Caldron, P., and Sinacore, J. M. (1990). Dance-based aerobic exercise of rheumatoid arthritis. *Arthritis Care and Research,* 3(1): 29-35.

APPENDIX 3
Asthma and Breathing Problems and Quality of Life (QOL) Studies

Source	Population	Measures/Method	Domains
Christie, French, Weatherstone, West, and the Applied Psychology Research Group (1991)	Children with asthma	3-Year development for developing tools to assess QOL in childhood asthma; questionnaire and open-ended discussion with children with and without asthma	Psychological, medical factors, home and social factors, and educational factors
Hyland, Bott, Singh, and Kenyon (1994)	40 Patients with breathing problems	Breathing Problems Questionnaire and review of other QOL measures	Walking, bending or reaching, washing and bathing, household chores, social interactions, effects of weather and temperature, effects of smells and fumes, effects of colds, sleeping, medicines, dysphoric states, eating, excretion urgency
Hyland, Finnis, and Irvine (1991)	783 Asthma patients	Asthma Questionnaire, a 68-item quality of life scale	Social/leisure, sport, holidays, sleep, work, colds, mobility, effects on others, medication usage, sex, dysphoric states and attitudes
Hyland, Kenyon, and Jacobs (1994)	41 Patients with asthma receiving salmeterol and 38 to placebo	Living with Asthma Questionnaire (LWAQ)	Social/leisure, sport, holidays, sleep, work, and other activities, colds, mobility, effects on others, medication usage, sex and dysphoric states and attitudes

References

Christie, M. J., French, D., Weatherstone, L., West, A., and the Applied Research Group. (1991). The patient's perceptions of chronic disease and its management: psychosomatic, holism and quality of life in contemporary management of childhood asthma. *Psychotherapy and Psychosomatics,* 56: 197-203.

Hyland, M. E., Bott, J., Singh, S., and Kenyon, C. A. P. (1994). Domains, constructs and the development of the breathing problems questionnaire. *Quality of Life Research,* 3: 245-256.

Hyland, M. E., Finnis, S., and Irvine, S. H. (1991). A scale for assessing quality of life in adult asthma sufferers. *Journal of Psychosomatic Research,* 35(2): 99-110.

Hyland, M. E., Kenyon, C. A. P., and Jacobs, P. A. (1994). Sensitivity of quality of life domains and constructs to longitudinal change in a clinical trial comparing salmeterol with placebo in asthmatics. *Quality of Life Research,* 3: 121-126.

APPENDIX 4
Cancer and Quality of Life (QOL) Literature

Source	Population	Measures/Method	Domains
Baker, Curbow, and Wingard (1992)	109 Long-term cancer survivors who have received bone marrow transplants	Development of the Satisfaction with Life Domains Scale for Cancer (SLDS-C)	18 Domains listed as questions on the SLDS-C. Include: relationships, health, appearance, leisure time, ability to eat, physical strength
Breetvelt and Van Dam (1991)	Cancer patients	Review of subjective QOL measures for cancer patients	Underreporting phenomenon of complaints in psychological domains as opposed to consistent reporting of physical health complaints
Canales, Ganz, and Coscarelli (1995)	Hispanic cancer patients — 6 males and 24 females.	Interviews, translated Cancer Rehabilitation Evaluation System (CARES) into Spanish	Marital status, gender, age, employment, education, ethnicity, religion, income, children at home, changes since diagnosis
Chaturvedi (1991)	50 Hindu adults with and without cancer	Interviews based on QOL list prepared before the interviews	Peace of mind, spiritual tasks (meditation), religion, family, basic need fulfillment, self-esteem, satisfaction with functioning, physical health, psychological health, individual functioning and marital, occupational, social, and self care
Edbril and Rieker (1989)	74 Adult male patient survivors of testicular cancer	Cancer Behavior Scale, Profile of Mood States, Brannon Masculinity Scale	Work status, career mobility and aspirations, work satisfaction and emotional state
Fava (1990)	Cardiovascular and cancer patients	Review of research on QOL issues	Physical, psychological, and social
Ferrell, Grant, Padilla, Vemuri, and Rhiner (1991)	Cancer patients	Open-ended interviews based on earlier quantitative studies to assess relationship of QOL to pain	Physical well-being, symptoms, psychological well-being, spiritual well-being
Ganz, Day, Ware, Fisher (1995)	9749 Participants in randomized trials for use of tamoxifen or placebo in 119 clinical centers in U.S. and Canada treating invasive breast cancer	Health-related QOL questionnaire which includes a depression scale, a symptom checklist for Medical Outcomes Study -37SF and MOS sexual problems questions	Age, ethnicity, Redmond, and education, employment, occupation, income, marital status, health behaviors, estrogen, hysterectomy, ovaries removed, and menstrual cycle
Ganz, Bernhard, and Hurny (1991)	Oncology patients	Survey of British and European investigators regarding QOL research on psychosocial oncology	Surveyed research on measurement techniques and validation, clinical trials and QOL, coping techniques, rehabilitation and supportive needs
Gelber, Cole, Gelber, and Goldhirsh (1995)	Patients with breast cancer and pediatric AIDS and cancer	Q-TWIST method	With symptoms, QOL when in treatment, without symptoms

APPENDIX 4 (continued)
Cancer and Quality of Life (QOL) Literature

Source	Population	Measures/Method	Domains
Gilbar (1991)	51 Cancer patients who dropped out of chemotherapy, 19 who refused treatment, and 70 who completed treatment	Psychosocial Adjustment to Physical Illness Scale, Brief Symptom Inventory, and interviews at patients' homes.	Heath care, work, home, sexual relationship, extended family, social and psychological distress. Somatization and psychological symptoms
Goodwin, Boggs, and Graham-Pole (1994)	210 parents of children with cancer	Development of a 21-item parent report measure of QOL, the Pediatric Oncology Quality of Life Scale	Physical function, role restriction, emotional distress, reaction to current medical treatment
Gottschalk and Lolas (1992)	Small group of cancer patients	Patients were asked to speak into a tape recorder for 5 min about the "quality of your life" at the present time. Used the Content Analysis of Verbal Behavior and then used the Social Alienation-Personal Disorganization Scale, the Human Relations Scale, the Hope Scale, and the Health-Sickness Scale to locate facets of QOL	Well-being, health, work, anxiety, self, hope, others, spiritual,symptoms
Johnson, Casey, and Noriega (1994)	21 Radiation therapy patients	Review of Functional Assessment Cancer Tool and development of the QOL Radiation Therapy Instrument	*Functional/Health:* appetite, nausea, pain, energy/fatigue, fatigue pain, pain, sex life, self care; *General QOL:* general health, personal control; *Emotional Psychological:* appearance, peace of mind, financial, happiness, hope, goals, religious beliefs; *Socioeconomic/Family:* family, job, independence, life satisfaction, family/friends support, staff support
Lindley, Hirsch, O'Neill, Tansau, Gilbert, and Osterhaus (1992)	Cancer patients receiving chemotherapy	Used the Functional Living Index — Cancer as model to create Functional Living Index — Emesis	Physical well-being and ability, emotional state, sociability, family situation, and nausea
Mulhern, Fairclough, Friedman, and Leigh (1990)	120 Children with cancer	Play Performance Scale for Children and Vineland Adaptive Behavior Scales with parent and physician ratings	Acute psychological problems, somatic toxicities of various treatments, and residual psychological problems

APPENDIX 4 (continued)
Cancer and Quality of Life (QOL) Literature

Source	Population	Measures/Method	Domains
Muthny, Koch, and Stump (1990)	Oncology patients	Review of QOL instruments used	Physical concerns, functional ability, family well-being, emotional well-being, spirituality, treatment satisfaction, future hopes and plans, sexuality, social and occupational functioning
Nayfield, Ganz, Moinpour, Cella, and Hailey (1992)	Cancer clinical trials research and QOL research	Workshop with 4 working groups of clinical cancer trials and QOL research experts	Group recommended that, as a minimum, QOL assessment in cancer clinical trials should include: physical, emotional, social functioning, somatic/physiological complaints (symptoms and side effects associated with treatment)
Nichols (1997)	Cancer patients	Essay on management of cancer pain	Pain affects activity, sleep, appetite, and brings about depression, anxiety, and hostility and also affects psychological and social stress, impairing life quality
Osoba (1992)	Cancer patients	Reports on work of QOL Committee in Canada regarding use of QOL measures in all cancer clinical trials	No domains listed
Schaafsma and Osoba (1994)	139 Lung cancer patients	Karnofsky Performance Status and item 30 of the QOL questionnaire developed by the European Organization for Research and Treatment of Cancer Study Group	Physical functioning, emotional functioning, breathing, social functioning, and cognition, pain, and fatigue
Schover (1991)	Women with breast cancer	Review of studies on the impact of breast cancer on sexuality, body image, and intimate relationships	Psychological health, relationship satisfaction, premorbid sexual life, choice in treatment options, and types of treatment options
Till, Sutherland, and Meslin (1992)	Cancer patients	Recommends that patient preference should be included in clinical cancer trials re QOL issues	Preferences might include: personal factors, values, and attitudes; psychosocial factors; activities of daily living; family; survival; and sexuality

References

Baker, F., Curbow, B., and Wingard, J. R. (1992). Development of the Satisfaction with Life Domains Scale for Cancer. *Journal of Psychosocial Oncology,* 10(3): 75-90.

Breetvelt, I. S. and Van Dam, F. S. A. M. (1991). Underreporting by cancer patients: The case of response shift. *Social Science Medicine,* 32(9): 981-987.

Canales, S., Ganz, P. A., and Coscarelli, C. A. (1995). Translation and validation of a quality of life instrument for Hispanic American cancer patients: Methodological considerations. *Quality of Life Research,* 4: 3-11.

Chaturvedi, S. K. (1991). What's important for quality of life to Indians — In relation to cancer. *Social Science Medicine,* 33(1): 91-94.

Edbril, S. D. and Rieker, P. P. (1989). The impact of testicular cancer on the work lives of survivors. *Journal of Psychosocial Oncology,* 7(3): 17-29.

Fava, G. A. (1990). Methodological and conceptual issues in research on quality of life. *Psychotherapy and Psychosomatics,* 54: 70-76.

Ferrel, B., Grant, M., Padilla, G., Vemuri, S., and Rhiner, M. (1991). The experience of pain and perceptions of the quality of life: validation of a conceptual model. *Hospice Journal,* 7(3): 9-22.

Ganz, P. A., Bernahrd, J., and Hurny, C. (1991). Quality of life and psychosocial oncology research in Europe: state of the art. *Journal of Psychosocial Oncology,* 9(1): 1-22.

Ganz, P. A., Day, R., Ware, J. E., Redmond, C. and Fisher, B. (1995). Base-line quality-of-life assessment in national surgical adjuvant breast and bowel project cancer. *Journal of the National Cancer Institute,* 87(18): 1372-1382.

Gelber, R.D., Cole, B.F., Gelber, S., and Goldhirsch, A. (1995). Comparing treatments using quality-adjusted survival: The Q-TWIST method. *American Statistics,* 49: 161-169.

Gilbar, O. (1991). The quality of life of cancer patients who refuse chemotherapy. *Social Science Medicine,* 32(12): 1337-1340.

Goodwin, D. A. J., Boggs, S. R., and Graham-Poole, J. (1994). Development and validation of the pediatric oncology quality of life scale. *Psychological Assessment,* 6(4): 321-328.

Gottschalk, L. A. and Lolas, F. (1992). The measurement of quality of life through the content analysis of verbal behavior. *Psychotherapy and Psychosomatics,* 58: 69-78.

Johnson, D. J., Casey, L., and Noriega, B. (1994). A pilot study of patient quality of life during radiation therapy treatment. *Quality of Life Research,* 3: 267-272.

Lindley, C. M., Hirsch, J. D., O'Neill, C. V., Tansau, M. C., Gilbert, C. S., and Osterhaus, J. T. (1992). Quality of life consequences of chemotherapy-induced emesis. *Quality of Life Research,* 1: 331-340.

Mulhern, R. K., Fairclough, D. L., Friedman, A. G., and Leigh, L. D. (1990). Play Performance Scale as an index of quality of life of children with cancer. *Psychological Assessment,* 2(2): 149-155.

Muthny, F. A., Koch, U., and Stump, S. (1990). Quality of life in oncology patients. *Psychotherapy and Psychosomatics,* 54: 145-160.

Nayfield, S. G., Ganz, P. A., Moinpour, C. M., Cella, D. F., and Hailey, B. J. (1992). Report from a National Cancer Institute (U.S.A.) workshop on quality of life assessment in cancer clinical trials. *Quality of Life Research,* 1: 203-210.

Nichols, R. (1997). Managing cancer pain in managed care. *Case Manager,* 49-53.

Osoba, D. (1992). The quality of life committee of the clinical trials groups of the National Cancer Institute of Canada: organization and functions. *Quality of Life Research,* 1: 211-218.

Schaafsma, J. and Osoba, D. (1994). The Karnofsky performance status scale re-examined: a cross-validation with the EORTC-C30. *Quality of Life Research,* 3: 413-424.

Schover, L. R. (1991). The impact of breast cancer on sexuality, body image, and intimate relationships. *Cancer Journal for Clinicians,* 41: 112-120.

Till, J. E., Sutherland, H. J., and Meslin, E. M. (1992). Is there a role for preference assessments in research on quality of life in oncology? *Quality of Life Research,* 1: 31-40.

APPENDIX 5
Children and Quality of Life (QOL) Studies

Source	Population	Measures/Method	Domains
Christie, French, Weatherstone, West, and the Applied Psychology Research Group (1991)	Children with asthma	3-Year development for developing tools to assess QOL in childhood asthma. Questionnaire and open-ended discussion with children with and without asthma	Psychological, medical factors, home and social factors, and educational factors.
Coulter (1990)	Children with disabilities	Essay on conceptualizing QOL for very young children	Independence, participation, responsibility
Gelber, Cole, Gelber, and Goldhirsh (1995)	Patients with breast cancer and pediatric AIDS and cancer	Q-TWIST method	With symptoms, QOL when in treatment, without symptoms
Goodwin, Boggs, and Graham-Pole (1994)	210 Parents of children with cancer	Development of a 21-item parent report measure of QOL, the Pediatric Oncology Quality of Life Scale	Physical function, role restriction, emotional distress, reaction to current medical treatment
Kurz and Prather (1995)	Girls — birth to 19 years in the world's developing countries	Findings of the Association of Women in Development Forum	Mortality, poor health care, inadequate nutrition, lack of education, female genital mutilation, child labor, pregnancy and sexual activity, violence, prostitution, poor self concept
McCall (1991)	Suicide rates in elderly and adolescent males	Used annual suicide rates for U.S. from *Annual Vital Health Statistics Report 1947-1987*	Impoverishment, family dissolution, and government expenditures
McLanahan and Adams (1989)	Effects of children on adult well-being	Two Americans View Their Mental Health Surveys (AVTHM) 1957 and 1976	Happiness, satisfaction, worries, psychological distress, and perceptions of parenthood
McPhail (1996)	Effects of children with disabilities on the lives of family members	Recommendations regarding improving QOL for families with members with disabilities	Growth opportunities, community membership, choice, in-home health care support, inclusion of parents in decision making, inclusive services which support the family unit, inclusion in regular schooling
Mulhern, Fairclough, Friedman, and Leigh (1990)	120 Children with cancer	Play Performance Scale for Children and Vineland Adaptive Behavior Scales with parent and physician ratings	Acute psychological problems, somatic toxicity of various treatments, and residual psychological problems
Raphael (1996)	10- to 25-year olds or adolescent health	Review of adolescent health and QOL issues	*Global:* macro environment, human rights and welfare policies; *External:* work, income, housing; *Interpersonal:* family structure and function, intimate friends, extended social; *Personal:* physical, mental, spiritual

References

Christie, M. J., French, D., Weatherstone, L., West, A., and the Applied Research Group. (1991). The patient's perceptions of chronic disease and its management: psychosomatics, holism and quality of life in contemporary management of childhood asthma. *Psychotherapy and Psychosomatics,* 56: 197-203.

Coulter, D. L. (1990). Home is the place: quality of life for young children with developmental disabilities. In R. L. Schalock (Ed.). *Quality of Life: Perspectives and Issues,* pp. 61-69. Washington, D.C.: American Association of Mental Retardation.

Gelber, R.D., Cole, B.F., Gelber, S., and Goldhirsch, A. (1995). Comparing treatments using quality-adjusted survival: the Q-TWIST method. *American Statistics,* 49: 161-169.

Goodwin, D. A. J., Boggs, S. R., and Graham-Poole, J. (1994). Development and validation of the pediatric oncology quality of life scale. *Psychological Assessment,* 6(4): 321-328.

Kurz, K. M. and Prather, C. J. (1995). *Improving the Quality of Life of Girls.* New York: United Nations Children's Fund Programme Publications.

McCall, P. L. (1991). Adolescent and elderly white male suicide trends: evidence of changing well-being? *Journal of Gerontology,* 46(1): 843-851.

McLanahan, S. and Adams, J. (1989). The effects of children on adults' psychological well-being: 1957-1976. *Social Forces,* 68(1): 124-146.

McPhail, E. R. (1996). A parent's perspective: quality of life in families with a member with disabilities. In R. Renwick, I. Brown, and M. Nagler (Eds.), *Quality of Life in Health Promotion and Rehabilitation,* pp. 279-289. Thousand Oaks, CA: Sage Publications.

Mulhern, R. K., Fairclough, D. L., Friedman, A. G., and Leigh, L. D. (1990). Play Performance Scale as an index of quality of life of children with cancer. *Psychological Assessment,* 2(2): 149-155.

Raphael, D. (1996). Quality of life and adolescent health. In R. Renwick, I. Brown, and M. Nagler (Eds.), *Quality of Life in Health Promotion and Rehabilitation,* pp. 307-326. Thousand Oaks, CA: Sage Publications.

APPENDIX 6
Chronic Pain and Illness, and Quality of Life (QOL) Studies

Source	Population	Measures/Method	Domains
Chibnall and Tait (1990)	444 Chronic Pain patients at multidisciplinary pain clinic	QOL Scale, Beck Depression Inventory, Speilberger Trait Anxiety Inventory, Pain Disability Index, McGill Pain Questionnaire, Psychosomatic Symptom Checklist	Social life, family life, recreational, education intellectual, daily activities (work), romantic experiences, expectations/hopes.
Ferrell, Grant, Padilla, Vemuri, and Rhiner (1991)	Cancer patients	Open-ended interviews based on earlier quantitative studies to assess relationship of QOL to pain	Physical well-being, symptoms, psychological well-being, spiritual well-being
Nichols (1997)	Cancer patients	Essay on management of cancer pain	Pain affects activity, sleep, appetite, and brings about depression, anxiety, and hostility and also affects psychological and social stress, impairing life quality

APPENDIX 6 (continued)
Chronic Pain and Illness, and Quality of Life (QOL) Studies

Source	Population	Measures/Method	Domains
Siegrist and Junge (1990)	Chronic illness patients	The Katz Adjustment Scale, Social Maladjustment Schedule, Social Dysfunction Rating Scale, Structured and Scaled Interview to Assess Maladjustment, Reintegration to Normal Living Index	Physical, psychological, and social dimensions of health
Tait, Chibnall, and Margolis (1990)	416 Patients with chronic pain	Beck Depression Inventory, Spielberger Anxiety Inventory, Psychosomatic Symptom Checklist, QOL Scale, and Pain Disability Index	Pain extent, psychological state, pain severity, disability, pain history, age, education

References

Chibnall, J. T. and Tait, R. C. (1990). The Quality of Life Scale: a preliminary study with chronic pain patients. *Psychology and Health,* 4: 283-292.

Ferrell, B., Grant, M., Padilla, G., Vemuri, S., and Rhiner, M. (1991). The experience of pain and perceptions of the quality of life: validation of a conceptual model. *Hospice Journal,* 7(3): 9-22.

Nichols, R. (1997). Managing cancer pain in managed care. *The Case Manager,* 49-53.

Siegrist, J. and Junge, A. (1990). Measuring the social dimension of subjective health in chronic illness. *Psychotherapy and Psychosomatics,* 54: 90-98.

Tait, R. C., Chibnall, J. T., and Margolis, R. B. (1990). Pain extent: relations with psychological state, pain severity, pain history, and disability. *Pain,* 41(3): 295-301.

APPENDIX 7
Communication Disorders and Quality of Life (QOL) Research Literature

Source	Population	Measures/Method	Domains
Maas (1991)	Persons after laryngectomy	Theoretical model for QOL after laryngectomy	Speech impairment, social, psychological, vocational
O'Keefe (1996)	Persons with communication disorders	Essay recommending that recognition be given to the QOL issues in this impairment and research be conducted	Being, belonging, and becoming

References

Maas, A. (1992). A model for quality of life after laryngectomy. *Social Science Medicine,* 33(12): 1373-1377.

O'Keefe, B. M. (1996). Communication disorders: just minor inconveniences? In R. Renwick, I. Brown, and M. Nagler (Eds.), *Quality of Life in Health Promotion and Rehabilitation,* pp. 219-236. Thousand Oaks, CA: Sage Publications.

APPENDIX 8
Deafness and Hard-of-Hearing in Quality of Life (QOL) Literature

Source	Population	Measures/Method	Domains
Mason (1996)	Deaf and hard-of-hearing people	Essay on the cultural meaning of deafness and hard-of-hearing as a QOL issue	Culturally deaf, oral deaf, hard-of-hearing, late deafened persons
Mowry (1988)	81 Former VR deaf and hard-of-hearing clients	Interviews in the preferred mode of the former VR client	Health, employment, financial security, home, savings, standard of living, relationships with family and friends

References

Mason, D. G. (1996). Quality of life for deaf and hard-of-hearing people. In R. Renwick, I. Brown, and M. Nagler (Eds.), *Quality of Life in Health Promotion and Rehabilitation,* pp. 237-252. Thousand Oaks, CA: Sage Publications.

Mowry, R. L. (1988). Quality of life indicators for deaf and hard-of-hearing former VR clients. *Journal of Rehabilitation of the Deaf,* 21(3): 1-7.

APPENDIX 9
Death and Dying Issues in Quality of Life (QOL) Research Literature

Source	Population	Measures/Method	Domains
Logue (1991)	Death and dying issues for women	Overview article on research needs on age, sex, race, social class, primary diagnosis, co-morbidities of those whose deaths are negotiated	QOL and choosing death, premature death and delayed death, women as recipients of informal and formal care systems, competency, the experts, and feminist health goals
McCall (1991)	Suicide rates in elderly and adolescent males	Use annual suicide rates for U.S. from *Annual Vital Health Statistics Report 1947-1987*	Impoverishment, family dissolution, and government expenditures
Terman (1995)	Wrongful death cases in civil lawsuits	Introduces the Loss of Enjoyment of Life-Severity Scale (LEL-SS), partially based on Global Assessment of Functioning in DSM	Physical/practical functioning, emotional/psychological functioning, social/recreational functioning, occupational/homemaking/scholastic functioning
Tigges (1993)	Hospice care patients	Review of QOL literature re hospice care	Control of pain and symptoms, personal care and comfort, support of respite to the primary caregiver/family member, pastoral care, and bereavement services for survivors. Tigges' defines a sense of excellence of character; being useful, productive, needed and valued; personal safety and security; and the ability to interact with others as the domains to be assessed

References

Logue, B. J. (1991). Taking charge: Death control as an emergent women's issue. *Women and Health,* 17(4): 97-121.

McCall, P. L. (1991). Adolescent and elderly white male suicide trends: evidence of changing well-being? *Journal of Gerontology,* 46(1): 843-851.

Terman, S. A. (1995). Emotional damages due to wrongful death — What are they worth? *Behavioral Sciences and the Law,* 11: 43-59.

Tigges, K. N. (1993). Quality of life: reality or Rhetoric? *Loss, Grief, and Care,* 7(1-2): 157-167.

APPENDIX 10
Developmental Disabilities in Quality of Life (QOL) Research Literature

Source	Population	Measures/Method	Domains
Bellamy, Newton, LeBaron, and Horner (1990)	Persons with developmental disabilities	Essay on residential services and QOL lifestyle outcomes	Independence, enhanced adaptive functioning, activities of daily living, income, choice
Borthwick-Duffy (1990)	Persons with profound mental retardation	Essay on QOL models and measures for this population	Education, employment, language delays, choices in daily living, self-report on QOL
Bratt and Johnston (1988)	5 Young adults with a mental disability leaving a hospital to live in a group home	Recorded visits to the home; trips made out of the home; activity patterns, staff opinions	Reduction in inappropriate behavior; increase in overall interactions; more outside contact; more appropriate leisure activities
Brown, Bayer, and Brown (1988)	Adolescents and adults with mental disabilities: 73 males, 75 females	Evaluate if clients' perceptions match statements by sponsors (usually parents), a longitudinal study	Emotional support, assertiveness, reading, preparing meals, housekeeping, leisure skills, budgeting, work, housing, guardianship, spiritual, filling out forms, shopping
Brown, R. I. (1996)	240 Persons with developmental disabilities between 18–63 in Canadian rehabilitation service programs	Essay on QOL issues for persons with development disabilities. Used WAIS, Adaptive Functioning Index, and Quality of Life Questionnaire	Staff in agencies, employment, living conditions, choices and perceptions, client and sponsor perceptions, emotional needs
Clark and Hirst (1989)	39 Adults with physical impairments.	Sample drawn from previous study of 89 young people with cerebral palsy; Survey questionnaire	Work, household composition, living arrangements, income, leisure and social activities, mobility, perceived needs and aspirations
Conroy and Feinstein (1990)	Persons with mental retardation	Essay on QOL measurement to include an outcome orientation	Individual happiness, family satisfaction, increasing productivity, increased integration, status, and acceptance in society
Coulter (1990)	Children with disabilities QOL for very young children	Essay on conceptualizing	Independence, participation, responsibility
Crutcher (1990)	Parent of a child with mental retardation	Essay on QOL vs. QOL judgments by others	Psychological, physical, social, and mental functioning

APPENDIX 10 (continued)
Developmental Disabilities in Quality of Life (QOL) Research Literature

Source	Population	Measures/Method	Domains
Cummins (1991)	Review of a QOL Scale for people with intellectual disabilities	Comprehensive QOLScale or ComQOL	Material well-being, physical well-being, productivity, intimacy, safety, place in society, emotional well-being
Dagan, Jones, and Ruddick (1994)	18 People with learning people disabilities	Questionnaire on Quality of Life which has good inter-rater and internal reliability and factor structure usable in services to people with learning disabilities living in residential care facilities	Factors or domains include: physical details, community access, leisure, routines, education and training, staff behavior, decision making
Edgerton (1990)	Persons with mental retardation	Longitudinal perspectives on QOL research	Self-esteem, social functioning, life satisfaction and well-being, work, physical health
Goode (1990)	Persons with disabilities and their families	Review of QOL literature from point of view of the individual	Objective variables: life events, health, mental health, and socioeconomic status, outcome behaviors, environment
Heal and Sigelman (1990)	Persons with mental retardation	Essay on methodological issues for measuring QOL	Income, housing, behavior, life satisfaction, subjective perceptions.
Houser and Chace (1993)	18 Males and 9 females with disabilities placed into jobs in a project with industry setting	Minnesota Satisfaction Questionnaire	Keeping busy, work alone, variety, status, supervision, ethics, tenure, service, leadership, working up to capacity, fair policies, advancement, exercise judgment, try out new methods, working conditions, relationships with co-workers, praise, and accomplishment
Inge, Banks, Wehman, Hill, and Shafer (1988)	20 Persons with mental retardation	Adaptive Behavior Scale, Parent/Guardian Survey, Quality of Life Matching Scale	Domestic skills, appearance, community participation, leisure/recreation, social/vocational skills and financial activity
Jacoby (1990)	A sibling of a sister with spina bifida	Essay by a brother on his sister's QOL	Physical health, finances, mobility, education, and leisure activities
Janicki (1990)	Older persons with a lifelong disability	Essay on aging with a lifelong disability and QOL issues	Physical, material, social, cognitive well-being
Keith (1990)	Persons with mental retardation	Essay on QOL issues in community integration	Health, employment, education, well-being, living situation, familial and social relations, leisure, work, learning, creative expression, safety, and finances
Kiernan and Knutson (1990)	Persons with disabilities	Essay on QOL and quality of work life (QWL)	Productivity and job satisfaction, participant management style, flexibility

APPENDIX 10 (continued)
Developmental Disabilities in Quality of Life (QOL) Research Literature

Source	Population	Measures/Method	Domains
Luckasson (1990)	Person with mental retardation	Legal perspective on QOL terminology	Normalization, integration, and worth of all human beings
Martinez (1990)	A woman with mental retardation	Her essay on her perception of QOL for herself	Family support, education, and independent living
McGuire, Choon, and Akuffo (1991)	19 Elderly people with a developmental disability	Used a lifestyle questionnaire and the Social Training Achievement Record Profile through interviews	Activities of daily life, community-based activities, domestic tasks, areas of personal responsibility
Oullette-Kuntz (1990)	Ten interviews with mentally retarded adults	Use of Quality of Life Interview Schedule with emphasis on intra- and inter-rater agreement	Health services, family-guardianship, income, education, training, and employment, housing and safety, transportation, social, recreational, religious/cultural, case management, advocacy, aesthetics, and counseling
Ouellette-Kuntz and McCreary (1996)	Persons with severe developmental disabilities	Development of the QOL Interview Schedule	Communication, disabilities, personal characteristics, and recent life events
Perry and Felce (1995)	People with learning disabilities in 15 staffed houses	Review of 14 objective measures of service quality in residential facilities	Quality of housing, social and community integration, social interactions, development, activity, and autonomy and choice
Rosen, Simon, and McKinsey (1995)	100 Individuals with mental retardation	Developed subjective QOL instrument — PALS	Perceived Stress, Affect, Loneliness, and Satisfaction
Sands and Kozleski (1994)	131 persons without disabilities and 86 persons with disabilities (cerebral palsy, mental retardation, and head injury) living in community settings	Used the Consumer Satisfaction Survey and modified version with nondisabled sample	Experience with advocacy organizations, services and satisfaction, independence interdependence, participation in community activities, and in recreation activities, and satisfaction with these activities
Schalock (1990a)	Persons with developmental disabilities	Essay on conceptualizing and measuring QOL, QOL variables in mental retardation literature	Social and psychological indicators, goodness-of-fit/social policy
Schalock (1990b)	Persons with mental retardation	Essay on QOL disability policy and service delivery systems	Living, learning, working, choice, independence, productivity, and community integration
Schalock and Lilley (1986)	85 Mentally retarded persons	Quality of Life Questionnaire	Environmental control (daily schedule, income, appointments, shopping, home decorations, pets); social interaction (neighbors, co-inhabitants, friends); community utilization (transportation, recreation, education)

APPENDIX 10 (continued)
Developmental Disabilities in Quality of Life (QOL) Research Literature

Source	Population	Measures/Method	Domains
Scuccimarra and Speece (1990)	65 Mildly handicapped students who exited high school in 1984	59-Item instrument was developed and adapted from the Vermont Follow-up Structured Survey Instrument	Employment status and social activity
Sinnott-Oswald, Gliner, and Spencer (1991)	Ten persons with disabilities in supported community employment, ten persons with disabilities in sheltered workshop employment, and nine persons without disabilities	QOL Index, Adaptive Behavior Scale, physical health measures, Parent-Guardian Survey	Leisure activities, use of leisure time, self-esteem, involvement in activities, mobility, job skill perceptions, and perceptions regarding changes in income
Stark and Goldsbury (1990)	Persons with mental retardation	Essay on QOL over the life span	General well-being, age, sex, social/cultural background, level of cognitive/adaptive functioning, education, health, living environment, family, social/emotional, work, and leisure
Taylor and Bodgan (1990)	Persons with mental retardation	Definitions and conceptions of QOL; subjective aspects of QOL	Cognitive, activities of daily living, social and family functioning, subjective experience of QOL
Vandergriff and Chubon (1994)	120 Persons withmental retardation	Program Analysis of Service System Implementation of Normalization Goals, Life Situation Survey, Resident Choice Assessment Scale, American Association on Mental Deficiency Adaptive Behavior Scale	Internal standards and evaluations of life by individuals, socionormative, and person–environment systems
Ward (1990)	A woman with mental retardation	Her essay on her reflections on QOL	Work, independent living, housing, social function, family and education
West, Kregel, and Banks (1990)	1550 individuals placed in supported employment (65% with mental retardation, 9% with long-term mental illness, and 10% with head injuries and cerebral palsy)	*Data Management System Operations Manual* for form completion by 96 provider agencies	Evaluation of QOL in worklife by looking availability of fringe benefits

APPENDIX 10 (continued)
Developmental Disabilities in Quality of Life (QOL) Research Literature

Source	Population	Measures/Method	Domains
Whitaker (1989)	Persons with profound mental handicaps (mental retardation)	Essay regarding a conceptual model	*Individual behavior:* level of skills and abilities, level of adaptive engagement, level of negative behavior; and *Factors regarding the environment:* conditions of physical environment in terms of comfort, food, health care; opportunities to mix with local community; variability and amount of varied activities available; opportunity to make choices; and treated as valued individuals in society

References

Bellamy, G. T., Newton, J. S., LeBaron, N. M., and Horner, R. H. (1990). Quality of life and lifestyle outcomes: a challenge for residential programs. In R. L. Schalock (Ed.), *Quality of Life: Perspectives and Issues,* pp. 127-137. Washington, D.C.: American Association of Mental Retardation.

Borthwick-Duffy, S. A. (1990). Quality of life of persons with severe or profound mental retardation. In R. L. Schalock (Ed.), *Quality of Life: Perspectives and Issues,* pp. 177-189. Washington, D.C.: American Association of Mental Retardation.

Bratt, A. and Johnston, R. (1988). Changes in life style for young adults with profound handicaps following discharge from hospital care into a "second generation" housing project. *Mental Handicap Research,* 1(1): 49-74.

Brown, R. I., Bayer, M. B., and Brown, P. M. (1988). Quality of life: a challenge for rehabilitation agencies. *Australia and New Zealand Journal of Developmental Disabilities,* 14(3,4): 189-199.

Brown, R. I. (1996). People with developmental disabilities: applying quality of life to assessment and intervention. In R. Renwick, I. Brown, and M. Nagler (Eds.), *Quality of Life in Health Promotion and Rehabilitation,* pp. 253-267. Thousand Oaks, CA: Sage Publications.

Clark, A. and Hirst, M. (1989). Disability in adulthood: ten-year follow-up of young people with disabilities. *Disability, Handicap and Society,* 4(3): 271-283.

Conroy, J. W. and Feinstein, C. S. (1990). Measuring quality of life: Where have we been? Where are we going? In R. L. Schalock (Ed.), *Quality of Life: Perspectives and Issues,* pp. 227-233. Washington, D.C.: American Association of Mental Retardation.

Coulter, D. L. (1990). Home is the place: quality of life for young children with developmental disabilities. In R. L. Schalock (Ed.). *Quality of Life: Perspectives and Issues,* pp. 61-69. Washington, D.C.: American Association of Mental Retardation.

Crutcher, D. M. (1990). Quality of life vs. quality of life judgments: A parent's perspective. In R. L. Schalock (Ed.). *Quality of life: Perspectives and issues,* pp. 17-22. Washington, D.C.: American Association of Mental Retardation.

Cummins, R. A. (1991). The Comprehensive Quality of Life Scale — Intellectual Disability: an instrument under development. *Australia and New Zealand Journal of Developmental Disabilities,* 17(2): 259-264.

Dagan, D., Jones, J., and Ruddick, L. (1994). The psychometric properties of a scale for assessing the quality of life of people with learning disabilities in residential care. *British Journal of Developmental Disabilities,* XL(79): 98-103.

Edgerton, R. B. (1990). Quality of life from a longitudinal research perspective. In R. L. Schalock (Ed.). *Quality of Life: Perspectives and issues,* pp. 149-160. Washington, D.C.: American Association of Mental Retardation.

Goode, D. A. (1990). Thinking about and discussing quality of life. In R. L. Schalock (Ed.), *Quality of Life: Perspectives and issues,* pp. 41-57. Washington, D.C.: American Association of Mental Retardation.

Heal, L. W. and Sigelman, C. K. (1990). Methodological issues in measuring quality of life of individuals with mental retardation. In R. L. Schalock (Ed.). *Quality of life: Perspectives and issues,* pp. 161-176. Washington, D.C.: American Association of Mental Retardation.

Houser, R. and Chace, A. (1993). Job satisfaction of people with disabilities placed through a project with industry. *Journal of Rehabilitation,* 59(1): 45-48.

Inge, K. J., Banks, P. D., Wehman, Hill, J. W., and Shafer, M. S. (1988). Quality of life for individuals who are labeled mentally retarded: evaluating competitive employment versus sheltered workshop employment. *Education and Training in Mental Retardation,* 97-104.

Jacoby, J. (1990). My sister Angie: a sibling's perspective. In R. L. Schalock (Ed.), *Quality of Life: Perspectives and Issues,* pp. 23-26. Washington, D.C.: American Association of Mental Retardation.

Janicki, M. P. (1990). Growing old with dignity: on quality of life for older persons with a lifelong disability. In R. L. Schalock (Ed.), *Quality of Life: Perspectives and Issues,* pp. 115-125. Washington, D.C.: American Association of Mental Retardation.

Keith, K. D. (1990). Quality of life: issues in community integration. In R. L. Schalock (Ed.), *Quality of Life: Perspectives and Issues,* pp. 93-100. Washington, D.C.: American Association of Mental Retardation.

Kiernan, W. E. and Knutson, K. (1990). Quality of work life. In R. L. Schalock (Ed.), *Quality of Life: Perspectives and Issues,* pp. 101-114. Washington, D.C.: American Association of Mental Retardation.

Luckasson, R. (1990). A lawyer's perspective on quality of life. In R. L. Schalock (Ed.). *Quality of Life: Perspectives and Issues,* pp. 211-214. Washington, D.C.: American Association of Mental Retardation.

Martinez, C. (1990). A dream for myself. In R. L. Schalock (Ed.), *Quality of Life: Perspectives and Issues,* pp. 3-8. Washington, D.C.: American Association of Mental Retardation.

McGuire, B. E., Choon, G., and Akuffo, E. (1991). Community living for elderly people with an intellectual disability: a pilot study. *Australia and New Zealand Journal of Developmental Disabilities,* 17(1): 25-33.

Ouellette-Kuntz, H. (1990). A pilot study in the use of the quality of life interview schedule. *Social Indicators Research,* 23: 283-298.

Ouellette-Kuntz, H. and McCreary, B. (1996). Quality of life assessment for persons with severe developmental disabilities. In R. Renwick, I. Brown, and M. Nagler (Eds.), *Quality of Life in Health Promotion and Rehabilitation,* (pp. 268-278). Thousand Oaks, CA: Sage Publications.

Perry, J. and Felce, D. (1995). Objective assessments of quality of life: how much do they agree with each other? *Journal of Community and Applied Social Psychology,* 5: 1-19.

Rosen, M., Simon, E. W., and McKinsey, L. (1995). Subjective measure of quality of life. *Mental Retardation,* 33(1): 31-34.

Sands, D. J. and Kozleski, E. B. (1994). Quality of life differences between adults with and without disabilities. *Education and Training in Mental Retardation and Developmental Disabilities,* 90-101.

Schalock, R. L. (1990a). Attempts to conceptualize and measure quality of life. In R. L. Schalock, (Ed.), *Quality of Life: Perspectives and Issues,* pp. 141-148 . Washington, D.C.: American Association of Mental Retardation.

Schalock, R. L. (1990b). Where do we go from here? In R. L. Schalock, (Ed.), *Quality of Life: Perspectives and Issues,* pp. 235-240. Washington, D.C.: American Association of Mental Retardation.

Schalock, R. L. and Lilley, M. A. (1986). Placement from community-based mental retardation programs: how well do clients do after 8 to 10 years? *American Journal of Mental Deficiency,* 90(6): 669-676.

Scuccimarra, D. J. and Speece, D. L. (1990). Employment outcomes and social integration of students with mild handicaps: The quality of life two years after high school. *Journal of Learning Disabilities,* 23(4): 213-219.

Sinnott-Oswald, M., Gliner, J. A., and Spencer, K. C. (1991). Supported and sheltered employment: quality of life issues among workers with disabilities. *Education and Training in Mental Retardation,* 388-397.

Stark, J. A. and Goldsbury, R. (1990). Quality of life from childhood to adulthood. In R. L. Schalock, (Ed.), *Quality of Life: Perspectives and Issues,* pp. 71-92 . Washington, D.C.: American Association of Mental Retardation.
Taylor, S. J. and Bogdan, R. (1990). Quality of life and the individual's perspective. In R. L. Schalock, R. L. (Ed.). *Quality of life: Perspectives and issues,* pp. 27-40. Washington, D.C.: American Association of Mental Retardation.
Vandergriff, D. V. and Chubon, R. A. (1994). Quality of life experienced by persons with mental retardation in various residential settings. *Journal of Rehabilitation,* 30-37.
Ward, N. (1990). Reflections on my quality of life: then and now. In R. L. Schalock (Ed.), *Quality of Life: Perspectives and Issues,* pp. 9-16. Washington, D.C.: American Association of Mental Retardation.
West, M., Kregel, J., and Banks, P. D. (1990). Fringe benefits available to supported employment participants. *Rehabilitation Counseling Bulletin,* 34(2): 126-138.
Whitaker, S. (1989). Quality of life and people with a very profound handicap. *British Journal of Mental Subnormality,* 35(68): 3-7.

APPENDIX 11
Diabetes and Quality of Life (QOL) Studies

Source	Population	Measures/Method	Domains
Cox and Gonder-Frederick (1992)	Diabetes and patient behavior	Literature review of quality of life and physical well-being: 1982 to 1992	Self-treatment, social and familial factors, environmental factors, psychosocial impact, psychological stress, weight loss, cognitive motor deficits, transient
Handestad (1989)	Insulin-dependent patients	Theoretical analysis of QOL and insulin-dependency	Active, interpersonal relationships, self-esteem, aesthetic experiences, finances, physical capacity, and permanent effects
Rodin (1990)	Adults with insulin-dependent diabetes mellitus (158 subjects)	Rand General Well-Being Scale, General Health Questionnaire	Physical functioning, social functioning, emotional functioning, burden of symptoms, and the sense of well-being

References

Cox, D. J. and Gonder-Frederick, L. (1992). Major developments in behavioral diabetes research. *Journal of Consulting and Clinical Psychology,* 60(4): 628-638.
Handestad, B. R. (1989). Insulin-dependent diabetes mellitus and quality of life: a theoretical analysis. *Scandinavian Journal of Caring,* 3(3): 123-128.
Rodin, G. (1990). Quality of life in adults with insulin-dependent diabetes mellitus. *Psychotherapy and Psychosomatics,* 54: 132-139.

APPENDIX 12
Domains (Overview) in Quality of Life (QOL) Literature

Source	Population	Measures/Method	Domains
American Academy of Ophthalmology and American Society of Cataract and Refractive Surgery (1997)	Patients with cataracts	Glare and contrast sensitivity testing, Activities of Daily Vision Scale, and the Visual Activities Questionnaire	Functional capacity, visual acuity, and results of treatment
Andrew (1991)	1972 Surveys based on probability samples had 2369 respondents; and 616 adult Americans were sampled in 1988	Used life quality measures: global well-being and 24 assessments of specific life concerns	Domains included: self, fun, health, income, job, leisure, community, and general environment
Andrews, Meyer, and Berla (1996)	Personal injury plaintiffs	Development of descriptors for the LPL Scale to determine inter-rater reliability and development of 15 case vignettes to test ecological validity	Practical, psychological, social, and occupational
Askins (1997)	Persons with disabilities	Description of therapeutic recreation offered	Leisure values in one's lifestyle, ADA issues, problem-solving, and assertiveness training; no QOL issues specifically identified
Bach and Rioux (1996)	Rehabilitation clients	Critique of health promotion and QOL research	Self-determination, equality, democratization, well-being
Baker, Curbow, and Wingard (1992)	109 Long-term cancer survivors who have received bone marrow transplants	Development of the Satisfaction with Life Domains Scale for Cancer (SLDS-C)	18 Domains listed as questions on the SLDS-C. Include: relationships, health, appearance, leisure time, ability to eat, physical strength, etc.
Baker, Jodrey, and Intagliata (1992)	729 Mentally ill adults in state supported programs	Repeated (9 months apart) questionnaires, QOL interviews, Bradburn Positive and Negative Affect Scales, Satisfaction with Life Domains Scale	Availability and adequacy of social support needed for quality of life
Bech (1990)	General population	Examination of objective (nomothetic) and subjective (idographic) approaches to measuring QOL	Psychological, psychosocial
Bellamy, Newton, LeBaron, and Horner (1990)	Persons with developmental disabilities	Essay on residential services and QOL lifestyle outcomes	Independence, enhanced adaptive functioning, activities of daily living, income, choice

APPENDIX 12 (continued)
Domains (Overview) in Quality of Life (QOL) Literature

Source	Population	Measures/Method	Domains
Ben-Ari and Tater (1984)	53 Male and 46 female clients in 5 governmental rehabilitation centers in Israel	Minnesota Satisfaction Questionnaire and interviews of social workers working with clients	Duration of injury and educational level were related to 3 categories of satisfaction: internal, external, and overall satisfaction
Berla, Brookshire, and Smith (1990)	Personal injury plaintiffs	LPL Scale from 0 to 100% across the domains	Practical, psychological, social, and occupational domains
Bigelow, McFarland, and Olson (1991)	Community samples, client samples from 24 mental health agencies	Interviews and QOL Questionnaire	Psychological distress and well-being, tolerance of stress, independence, interdependence, interpersonal interactions, spouse role, work at home, social support, employability, meaningful use of time, substance abuse.
Blandford and Chappell (1990)	193 Interviews with Treaty and Metis Indians in Winnipeg and 300 non-Natives in Winnipeg	UCLA Loneliness Scale and Overall Life Satisfaction Scale	Age, gender, marital status, work, income, functional disability, chronic conditions, perceived health, family
Blau (1977)	Persons in psychotherapy	Persons in psychotherapy selected QOL variables or domains	Working, leisure eating, sleeping, social contact, earning, parenting, loving, environment, self-acceptance
Blumenthal and Emery (1988)	Cardiac patients	Review of three behavioral strategies to examine the value of cardiac rehabilitation as a method for improving QOL	Cardiovascular functioning, psychological functioning, physical fitness, and psychosocial functioning
Boschen (1996)	222 Young adults with spinal cord injuries living in Toronto	Living with a Spinal Cord Injury Questionnaire, Latitude of Choice Scale, Self-Concept Semantic Differential Scale, Locus of Control Scale	Autonomy, control, and daily life choices with postinjury accommodations
Borthwick-Duffy (1990)	Persons with profound mental retardation	Essay on QOL models and measures for this population	Education, employment, language delays, choices in daily living, self-report on QOL
Bratt and Johnston (1988)	5 Young adults with a mental disability leaving a hospital to live in a group home	Recorded visits to the home; trips made out of the home; activity patterns, staff opinions	Reduction in inappropriate behavior, increase in overall interactions, more outside contact, more appropriate leisure activities
Breetvelt and Van Dam (1991)	Cancer patients	Review of subjective QOL measures for cancer patients	Underreporting phenomenon of complaints in psychological domains as opposed to consistent reporting of physical health complaints

APPENDIX 12 (continued)
Domains (Overview) in Quality of Life (QOL) Literature

Source	Population	Measures/Method	Domains
Brown, C. (1996)	105 Males and 86 females with severe mental illness	Assessed loneliness using UCLA Loneliness Scale	Loneliness as a QOL issue dependent upon living situation or social skills and social networks and the experience of the individual with severe mental illness
Brown, I. (1996)	Homeless adults	Essay on QOL issues and homelessness	Physical, psychological, social well-being, housed, homed, homeless, houseless
Brown, R. I. (1989)	240 Adults with disabilities	Quality of Life Questionnaire compared to objective measures of performance and observations of sponsors (high correlations found)	Home, social, and recreational aspects of life
Brown, R. I. (1996)	240 Persons with developmental disabilities between 18–63 in Canadian rehabilitation service programs	Essay on QOL issues for persons with development disabilities; used WAIS, Adaptive Functioning Index, and Quality of Life Questionnaire	Staff in agencies, employment, living conditions, choices and perceptions, client and sponsor perceptions, emotional needs
Brown, Bayer, and Brown (1988)	Adolescents and adults with mental disabilities: 73 males, 75 females	Evaluate if clients' perceptions match statements by sponsors (usually parents), a longitudinal study	Emotional support, assertiveness, reading, preparing meals, housekeeping, leisure skills, budgeting, work, housing, guardianship, spiritual, filling out forms, shopping
Brown, Cosgrove, and DeSelm (1997)	19 Consumers of mental health services and their case managers	Compared perceptions of consumers and case managers regarding barriers interfering with life satisfaction using a structured interview	Family, friendships, health care, community services, housing, neighborhood, finances, daily activities, work, transportation, physical health
Brown, Renwick, and Nagler (1996)	Rehabilitation clients	Essay on the centrality of QOL in health promotion and rehabilitation	Physical, social, psychological, and environmental
Brydolf, Berndtsson, Lindholm, and Berglund (1994)	36 Patients with ostomies and 12 without	Used Ostomy Adjustment Scale and a visual analog scale to measure total QOL	Physical function, psychological strain, and social interaction
Burton and Volpe (1993)	33 Persons with traumatic brain injury	Social Adjustment Scale to evaluate functioning in various categories unit	Work, social and leisure, extended family, marital, parental, family
Callahan (1992)	Alzheimer's patients	Essay	Subjective experience, social interaction, and environment
Campbell (1976)	National study of persons 18 years and older living in 48 states based on a probability sample — 2,164 women and men	Interviews with a structured questionnaire	Life cycle, urbanicity, age, race, working, family income, work of head of household, education, religion, and sex

APPENDIX 12 (continued)
Domains (Overview) in Quality of Life (QOL) Literature

Source	Population	Measures/Method	Domains
Campbell, Converse, and Rodgers (1976)	Same as Campbell above	583-Page book describing the national study	Same as Campbell above
Canales, Ganz, and Coscarelli (1995)	Hispanic cancer patients — 6 males and 24 females.	Interviews, translated Cancer Rehabilitation Evaluation System (CARES) into Spanish	Marital status, gender, age, employment, education, ethnicity, religion, income, children at home, changes since diagnosis
Carksy, Dolan, and Free (1991)	Housewives working at home-based businesses	A proposed model to examine the effects of women's at-home income generation on family life and satisfaction	*Worker/family characteristics:* role orientation, family demands, and tolerance for distraction; *Nature of Work:* degree of entrepreneurship, business/work site, absorptiveness; *Home/work environment:* time and income
Centers for Disease Control and Prevention (1995)	102,263 Respondents in all states except Wyoming	Health-Related QOL measures for U.S.	Physical, psychological, and social functioning during usual daily activities
Chaturvedi (1991)	50 Hindu adults with and without cancer	Interviews based on QOL list prepared before the interviews	Peace of mind, spiritual tasks (meditation), religion, family, basic need fulfillment, self-esteem, satisfaction with functioning, physical health, psychological health, individual functioning and marital, occupational, social, and self care
Cheng (1988)			
Chibnall and Tait (1990)	444 Chronic Pain patients at multidisciplinary pain clinic	QOL Scale, Beck Depression Inventory, Speilberger Trait Anxiety Inventory, Pain Disability Index, McGill Pain Questionnaire, Psychosomatic Symptom Checklist	Social life, family life, recreational, education/intellectual, daily activities (work), romantic experiences, expectations/hopes
Christie, French, Weatherstone, West, and the Applied Psychology Research Group (1991)	Children with asthma	3-Year development for developing tools to assess QOL in childhood asthma; questionnaire and open-ended discussion with children with and without asthma	Psychological, medicalfactors, home andsocial factors, andeducational factors
Chubon (1985)	Nondisabled graduate students and persons with chronic back problems, and prison inmates	Life Situation Survey	Pain tolerance, satisfaction of life quality

APPENDIX 12 (continued)
Domains (Overview) in Quality of Life (QOL) Literature

Source	Population	Measures/Method	Domains
Ciardiello and Bingham (1962)	Schizophrenic clients	Review of a career maturity construct and how a career development approach improves QOL	Use of leisure, family, citizenship, and work roles
Clark and Hirst (1989)	39 Adults with physical impairments.	Sample drawn from previous study of 89 young people with cerebral palsy; survey questionnaire.	Work, household composition, living arrangements, income, leisure and social activities, mobility, perceived needs and aspirations
Clayton and Chubon (1994)	100 SCI patients (89% male, 20% female)	Life Situation Survey, Social Health Battery	Educational level, employment status, income, social activities, and severity of disability
Condeluci, Ferris, and Bogdan (1992)	Persons in head injury rehabilitation	Review of three surveys from the survivors' perspective	Independence in activities of daily living, living situation, communication skills, health status, mobility, problem behaviors, need for rehabilitation and supervision, employment status, family, income, and educational status
Conn, Taylor, and Wiman (1991)	94 Older adult myocardial infarction survivors	Interviews and Profile of Mood States, Perceived QOL Scale, Health Behavior Scale	Anxiety, depression, exercise, diet, medications, stress, smoking
Conroy and Feinstein (1990)	Persons with mental retardation	Essay on QOL measurement to include an outcome orientation	Individual happiness, family satisfaction, increasing productivity, increased integration, status, and acceptance in society
Corrigan and Buican (1995)	49 Patients with severe mental illness	Interview-based measure of quality of life using a multiple regression analysis to separate depression and subjective quality of life	Psychiatric symptoms, social functioning and support, intellectual functioning
Corten, Mercier, and Pele (1994)	148 Patients with DSM diagnoses and control group of 40 randomly selected from general population	Semistructured interviews, Satisfaction with Life Domains Scale, Helps in Daily Life Scale, and Interdependencies Scale administered to all	*Satisfaction in life domains:* personal aspirations, intensity of interdependencies, good health; Achievement factor; *Conformity Factor:* social anxiety
Coulter (1990)	Children with disabilities	Essay on conceptualizing QOL for very young children	Independence, participation, responsibility
Cox and Gonder-Frederick (1992)	Diabetes and patient behavior	Literature review of quality of life and physical well-being: 1982–1992	Self-treatment, social and familial factors, environmental factors, psychosocial impact, psychological stress, weight loss, cognitive motor deficits, transient and permanent effects

APPENDIX 12 (continued)
Domains (Overview) in Quality of Life (QOL) Literature

Source	Population	Measures/Method	Domains
Crews (1991)	Older persons with blindness in rehabilitation	Model of strategic planning for fostering independent living	Independent living, consumer input, gains in function, family, services
Crutcher (1990)	Parent of a child with mental retardation	Essay on QOL vs. QOL judgments by others	Psychological, physical, social, and mental functioning
Cummins (1991)	Review of a QOL Scale for people with intellectual disabilities	Comprehensive QOL Scale or ComQOL	Material well-being, physical well-being, productivity, intimacy, safety, place in society, emotional well-being
Dagan, Jones, and Ruddick (1994)	18 People with learning disabilities	Questionnaire on Quality of Life which has good inter-rater and internal reliability and factor structure usable in services to people with learning disabilities living in residential care facilities	Factors or domains include: physical details, community access, leisure, routines, education and training, staff behavior, decision making
Day and Jankey (1996)	Rehabilitation clients	Review of QOL origins and limitations due to originating disciplines; proposes holistic model of QOL	Genetic disposition, domains, goals and achievements, values, personality, circumstances, evaluation process, experiences, comparisons, external reactions
Dellario and Anthony (1981)	Psychiatrically disabled persons	Review of research studies regarding client outcome of institutional vs. alternative placements; a model for psychiatric rehabilitation	Physical, intellectual, emotional, work, and community
Edbril and Rieker (1989)	74 Adult male patient survivors of testicular cancer	Cancer Behavior Scale, Profile of Mood States, Brannon Masculinity Scale	Work status, career mobility and aspirations, work satisfaction and emotional state
Edgerton (1990)	Persons with mental retardation	Longitudinal perspectives on QOL research	Self-esteem, social functioning, life satisfaction and well-being, work, physical health
Elizur and Shye (1990)	540 Employees of large corporation in Hungary	Given QOLand Quality of Work Life (QWL) questionnaires — 16 items each	QOL and QWL share the same domains: *Mode of functioning:* expressive, integrative, adaptive, or conservative; *Field of Functioning:* social or cultural, psychological, physical; and *Life area:* work and life in general

APPENDIX 12 (continued)
Domains (Overview) in Quality of Life (QOL) Literature

Source	Population	Measures/Method	Domains
Endicott, Nee, Harrison, and Blumenthal (1993)	Depressed patients	Quality of Life Enjoyment and Satisfaction Questionnaire	Physical health, subjective feelings, leisure time, social relationships, and general activities; household duties, work, and school
Ensminger (1995)	836 African-American mothers on welfare	Interviews based on selected measures	Psychological distress, welfare, earlier life conditions, region of U.S.A., teenage mother, chronic burdens, number of children, single parent, self perceptions of health, self-esteem, psychological and physical well-being
Evans, Dingus, and Haselkorn (1993)	Persons with disabilities	Review of QOL and disability studies, (52) articles, 1985-1989	Functional capacity, subjective QOL, and objective QOL
Fabian (1990)	Individuals with long-term mental illness	Review of two models of QOL: life satisfaction and adaptive functioning and instruments designed to measure them	Housing, leisure, work, overall life satisfaction, subjective well-being
Fabian (1991)	Individuals with disabilities	Review of QOL as life satisfaction, adaptive functioning, social indicator measure of programs and services	Housing, neighborhood, leisure, work, socialactivities, health
Fabian (1992)	110 Mentally ill persons in 2 supported employment programs	Control group study of those in community programs to those in supported employment	Living situation, family, social relations, leisure activities, physical and mental health, safety, work or nonwork, and finances
Fabian (1995)	People with disabilities	Overview of QOL in rehabilitation research	Life satisfaction, independence, adaptive functioning, self-mastery, and self-efficacy
Fava (1990)	Cardiovascular and cancer patients	Review of research on QOL issues	Physical, psychological, and social
Felce and Perry (1996)	People with and without disabilities	Development of a multidimensional model — essay	Physical well-being, material well-being, social well-being, development and activity, emotional well-being
Ferrans, Cohen, and Smith (1992)	539 Persons with narcolepsy	QOL Index — Narcolepsy	Health and functioning, social and economic aspects, psychological/spiritual aspects, and family
Ferrans and Powers (1992)	349 Adult hemodialysis patients	Quality of Life Index — Dialysis version	Life satisfaction, self-esteem, health, and functioning

APPENDIX 12 (continued)
Domains (Overview) in Quality of Life (QOL) Literature

Source	Population	Measures/Method	Domains
Ferrell, Grant, Padilla, Vemuri, and Rhiner (1991)	Cancer patients	Open-ended interviews based on earlier quantitative studies to assess relationship ofQOL to pain	Physical well-being, symptoms, psychological well-being, spiritual well-being
Fields and Thacker (1992)	293 Employees in intervention one and 119 employees in intervention two.	Used Company Commitment measure, Job Satisfaction measure, Union Commitment Scale, Quality of Work Life Scale	Loyalty, responsibility, belief in unionism, willingness, organizal commitment, job satisfaction
Fine (1996)	Persons with disabilities	Essay on leisure and QOL issues	Safety, pleasantness, friends and companions, self-esteem, fun, accomplishments, productivity, excitement, leisure
Fitzsimmons and Bunting (1997)	Persons with Parkinson's Disease (PD)	Essay on the psychosocial aspects of PD and QOL	Social roles, mental acuity, emotional states, subjective well-being, interrelationships, life satisfaction and physical health
Flanagan (1978)	3 Age groups of 30, 50, and 70 year olds	6,500 Critical incidents were collected from 3,000 people of various ages, races, and backgrounds from all over the U.S. in order to use an inductive process to locate 15 categories of QOL	Material well-being, financial security; health and personal safety; spousal relations, having children, parents, siblings, friends; helping others, local and national government activities; intellectual development and personal understanding and planning; work role; creativity and expression; socializing, passive and observational and active recreational activities
Frisch, Cronell, and Villanueva (1992)	54 VA inpatient, 51 VA recovered, 18 private inpatient, 19 offender, 272 general undergraduates, and 127 counseling center persons in psychotherapy	Used QOL Inventory and validated against the Global Severity Scale, Positive Total Symptom, Positive Symptom Distress Index, Beck Depression Inventory, Symptoms Checklist-90-R, Millon Clinical Multi-axial Inventory, Generalized Expectancy for Success Scale, etc.	Health, self-regard, philosophy of life, standard of living, work, recreation, learning, creativity, social service, civic action, love relationships, friends, relationships with children and relatives, home, neighborhood, and community

APPENDIX 12 (continued)
Domains (Overview) in Quality of Life (QOL) Literature

Source	Population	Measures/Method	Domains
Ganz, Bernhard, and Hurny (1991)	Oncology patients	Survey of British and European investigators regarding QOL research on psychosocial oncology	Surveyed research on measurement techniques and validation, clinical trials and QOL, coping techniques, rehabilitation and supportive needs
Ganz, Day, Ware, Redmond, and Fisher (1995)	9749 Participants in randomized trials for use of tamoxifen or placebo in 119 clinical centers in U.S. and Canada treating invasive breast cancer	Health-related QOL questionnaire which includes a depression scale, a symptom checklist for Medical Outcomes Study-37SF and MOS sexual problems questions	Age, ethnicity, education, employment, occupation, income, marital status, health behaviors, estrogen, hysterectomy, ovaries removed, and menstrual cycle
Gater, Kind, and Gudex (1995)	138 Medical patients scoring over the threshold for probable psychiatric illness	Health Measurement Questionnaire, (HMQ) Nottingham Health Profile, Psychiatric Assessment Scale, Rosser Index	Compared self-rating and observer-completed; a strong correlation was found between measures, HMQ and QOL, and agreement between self and observer ratings
Gelber, Cole, Gelber, and Goldhirsh (1995)	Patients with breast cancer and pediatric AIDS and cancer	Q-TWIST method	With symptoms, QOL when in treatment, without symptoms
George and Bearon (1980)	Older persons	A book reviewing QOL concepts, dimensions, and measures	*Subjective evaluations:* life satisfaction and self-esteem. *Objective measures:* general health, functional status, and socioeconomic status
Gerber, Coleman, Johnston, and Lavfave (1994)	43 clients discharged 1 and 3 years after psychiatric rehabilitation	Structured interviews, Mulern and Manderscheid Clients' Quality of Life Interview, Uniform Client Data Instrument	Found that QOL was maintained or improved post discharge on all QOL measures
Gilbar (1991)	51 Cancer patients who dropped out of chemotherapy, 19 who refused treatment, and 70 who completed treatment	Psychosocial Adjust-ment to Physical Illness Scale, Brief Symptom Inventory, and interviews at patients' homes.	Heath care, work, home, sexual relationship, extended family, social and psychological distress; somatization and psychological symptoms
Gitter and Mostofsky (1973)	General population	Goal is to construct an objective and parallel subjective indicator of quality of life	HEW aspects: health and illness; social mobility, income and poverty, public order and safety, learning, science and art, participation and alienation
Goode (1990)	Persons with disabilities and their families	Review of QOL literature from point of view of the individual	Objective variables: life events, health, mental health, and socioeconomic status, outcome behaviors, environment

APPENDIX 12 (continued)
Domains (Overview) in Quality of Life (QOL) Literature

Source	Population	Measures/Method	Domains
Goodwin, Boggs, and Graham-Pole (1994)	210 Parents of children with cancer	Development of a 21-item parent report measure of QOL, the Pediatric Oncology Quality of Life Scale	Physical function, role restriction, emotional distress, reaction to current medical treatment
Gottschalk and Lolas (1992)	Small group of cancer patients	Patients were asked to speak into a tape recorder for 5 min about "the quality of your life at the present time." Used the Content Analysis of Verbal Behavior and then used the Social Alienation-Personal Disorganization Scale, the Human Relations Scale, the Hope Scale, and the Health-Sickness Scale to locate facets of QOL	Well-being, health, work, anxiety, self, hope, others, spiritual, symptoms
Granger, Divan, and Fiedler (1995)	22 Traumatic brain injury patients	Functional assessment scales	Cognitive, social, psychological function
Gutheil (1991)	Frail elderly in residential facilities	Review of literature regarding features of physical environment of residential settings for frail older persons	Adequate space, essential furnishings, clean and orderly surroundings, self-worth, satisfaction with life, territorial needs, privacy, meaning
Guyatt (1994)	Heart failure patients	Minnesota Living with Heart Failure Questionnaire is reliable and valid	Disease specific with domains as emotional function, dyspnea (labored breathing), and fatigue with use of Digoxin
Hadorn and Hays (1991)	Convenience sample of 116 persons in elderly care homes, renal dialysis unit, low-income neighborhood health centers, meetings of clergy and social workers	Self-report on the 6 domains asking for problem levels and positive responses, and importance selection	General health, physical suffering, self-care activities, outlook on life, meaningful activities, and social relationships
Halpern (1994)	Special education students in high school in school-to-community transition to set standards	Developed Community Transition Team Model (CTTM)	Physical and material well-being, performance of adult roles, personal fulfillment
Hanestad (1989)	Insulin-dependent patients	Theoretical analysis of QOL and insulin-dependency	Active, interpersonal relationships, self-esteem, aesthetic experiences, finances, physical capacity

APPENDIX 12 (continued)
Domains (Overview) in Quality of Life (QOL) Literature

Source	Population	Measures/Method	Domains
Hanestad (1990)	Patients requiring nursing care	Structured interviews and questionnaires are reviewed as methods for collecting reliable data on QOL	Examines errors of measurement such as systematic errors found in self-assessment when people lie in a negative or positive direction; agreement bias (tend to say yes), social idealization, cultural and linguistic errors
Hardison and Vanier (1976)	130 Men and 153 women in California	Part of a research project funded by Urban Mass Transit Administration	Traffic, parking, transportation mode, pollution, physical condition, life stress, social conflict, mental illness, good old days, too many people, fast change, dominated by machines, getting ahead
Harper (1990)	Couples in couple therapy dealing with the recovery of a chemically dependent partner	Treatment model with three phases of recovery for the relationship in which their QOL is questioned	Trust, communication, intimacy, sex, and partnership
Hays, Kallich, Mapes, Coons, and Carter (1994)	165 Patients with kidney disease	Development of the Kidney Disease QOL Instrument (KDQOL)	Physical functioning, emotional functioning, social functioning, pain, energy/fatigue, and general health perceptions
Hays and Shapiro (1992)	HIV patients	Use of Quality of Well-Being Scale	Symptoms/problems complexes, mobility, physical activity, and social activity
Hays, Vickrey, Hermann, Perrine, Cramer, Meador, Spritzer, and Devinsky (1995)	292 Patients with epilepsy and their designated proxies.	Used 89-item QOL Inventory	Physical functioning, pain, health perception, role disability (due to physical or emotional health) support, emotional well-being, overall QOL, social isolation, energy/fatigue, language/memory/attention cognitive function, seizure distress, work and driving
Headey, Veenhoven, and Wearing (1991)	QOL survey of 942 persons conducted in 4 waves (1981, 1983, 1985, 1987) in Victoria, Australia	Used Life-as-a-Whole Index, Delighted–Terrible Scale, Eyesenck Personality Inventory, and socioeconomic status by gender in examining subjective well-being	Marriage, work, material standard of living, leisure, friendship, and health
Heal and Sigelman	Persons with mental retardation	Essay on (1990) methodological issues for measuring QOL	Income, housing, behavior, life satisfaction, subjective perceptions

APPENDIX 12 (continued)
Domains (Overview) in Quality of Life (QOL) Literature

Source	Population	Measures/Method	Domains
Helmstaedter and Elger (1994)	Presurgical epileptic patients	Evaluated subjective reports of psychosocial impairments with a questionnaire	Physical status, emotional status, capability, work, social life, independence and self-determination
Hennessy, Moriarty, Zack, Scherr, and Brackbill (1994)	General population	QOL public health surveillance by CDCP using Behavioral Risk Factor Surveillance System, a state-based telephone surveillance system	Self-perceived health, recent physical health, recent mental health, recent activity limitation
Herbert (1996)	Persons with disabilities	Literature review of of adventure-based counseling for persons with disabilities	QOL not a specific goal but more favorable attitude toward disability, improvement in independent living skills, positive self-concept, enhancement of self image, sense of responsibility, and cooperation with others, and greater life satisfaction result
Hermann (1995)	Epilepsy patients	Reviews phases of QOL research for epilepsy patients.	Cognitive, behavioral, psychosocial function; fear of seizures, social effects, perceived stigma, limitations and discrimination, behavior ratings, personality, psychosocial
Hickey and Stilwell (1992)	Aging and chronic illness issues	Essay on personal-conceptual model of age-related changes in health status	*Health perceptions:* aging illness beliefs; *Health status:* illness characteristics and comorbidities; *Health outlook:* assessment and treatment barriers and coping skills
House, Livingston, and Swinburn (1973)	General population	Experiment conducted at QOL symposium to develop list of QOL factors were generated and weighted; results analysis indicated the use of dissatisfaction indices may be better than trying to measure happiness	*Factor list included:* political/social; economic; and environment
Howard and Rockwood (1995)	Examined QOL instruments measuring Alzheimer's Disease and QOL	Reviewed and ranked measurement properties of QOL instruments; need for more validation of QOL instruments for Alzheimer's patients	Behavioral competence

APPENDIX 12 (continued)
Domains (Overview) in Quality of Life (QOL) Literature

Source	Population	Measures/Method	Domains
Hughes (1993)	Older adults and their caregivers	Model of comprehensive assessment processes	Personal characteristics, attitude to self, health, functioning, environment, finance and material circumstance, recreation and activities, family, community relationships, and support network
Hughes, Hwang, Kim, Eisenman, and Killian (1995)	People with disabilities	Review of 87 empirical studies analyzed and a model proposed	Social relationships, psychological well-being, employment, self-determination, recreation and leisure, personal competence, residential environment, community integration, normalization, support services, demographic indicators, personal development and fulfillment, social acceptance, physical and material well-being, civic responsibility.
Hume (1989)	Patients with hypertension	Review of the findings of the Treatment of Mild Hypertension Study as it relates to the addition of hydrochlorothiazide to other pharamacologic agents.	Functional capacity perceptions, and symptoms including mobility and independence. *Social functioning:* family, friends, community. *Cognitive functioning:* reasoning, memory, judgment and alertness. Psychological distress. Economic status
Huxley and Warner (1992)	68 Long-term psychiatric patients	Quality of Life Profile and General Satisfaction Questionnaire	Used interviews and modified the QOL Profile to include a 9th domain of religion, and used the client database to conduct study
Hyer, Matteson, and Siegler (1982)	Elderly in long-term care facilities	Use of a Locus of Control measure as a tool to facilitate quality of life	Age, education, sex, depression, and cognitive decline
Hyland (1992)	Overview article	Multifaceted approach recommended for economic decision-making in health systems	Physical status and functional ability, psychological status and well-being, social interactions, and economic status

APPENDIX 12 (continued)
Domains (Overview) in Quality of Life (QOL) Literature

Source	Population	Measures/Method	Domains
Hyland, Bott, Singh, and Kenyon (1994)	40 patients with breathing problems	Breathing Problems Questionnaire and review of other QOL measures	Walking, bending or reaching, washing and bathing, household chores, social interactions, effects of weather and temperature, effects of smells and fumes, effects of colds, sleeping, medicines, dysphoric states, eating, excretion urgency
Hyland, Finnis, and Irvine (1991)	783 asthma patients	Asthma Questionnaire, a 68-item quality of life scale	Social/leisure, sport, holidays, sleep, work, colds, mobility, effects on others, medication usage, sex, dysphoric states and attitudes
Hyland, Kenyon, and Jacobs (1994)	41 patients with asthma receiving salmeterol and 38 to placebo	Living with Asthma Questionnaire (LWAQ)	Social/leisure, sport, holidays, sleep, work, and other activities, colds, mobility, effects on others, medication usage, sex and dysphoric states and attitudes
Idler and Benyamini 1997)	Representative community samples	Review of 27 empirical community studies on self-rate health and mortality	Age and general health
Inge, Banks, Wehman, Hill, and Shafer (1988)	20 Persons with mental retardation	Adaptive Behavior Scale, Parent/Guardian Survey, Quality of Life Matching Scale	Domestic skills, appearance, community participation, leisure/recreation, social/vocational skills and financial activity
Jacoby (1990)	A sibling of a sister with spina bifida	Essay by a brother on his sister's QOL	Physical health, finances, mobility, education, and leisure activities
Jaeschke, Guyatt, Cook, Harper, and Gerstein (1994)	200 Patients with treated hypothyroidism	Took a survey of 200 patients to generate items, then distributed 70 questionnaires to family doctors and specialists, and 150 questionnaires to the Thyroid Foundation; 70 responses total received from the 2 groups	Physical problems, energy and general well-being problems, mood and emotional problems
Janicki (1990)	Older persons with a lifelong disability	Essay on aging with a lifelong disability and QOL issues	Physical, material, social, cognitive well-being
Jenkins (1992)	Assessing health issues generally	Review of methodological issues in assessing health-related QOL	Feelings, functions, and futures or biological, psychological, interpersonal–social, and economic

APPENDIX 12 (continued)
Domains (Overview) in Quality of Life (QOL) Literature

Source	Population	Measures/Method	Domains
Johnson, Casey, and Noriega (1994)	21 Radiation therapy patients	Review of Functional Assessment Cancer Tool and development of the QOL Radiation Therapy Instrument	*Functional/Health:* appetite, nausea, pain, energy/fatigue, fatigue pain, pain, sex life, self care. *General QOL:* general health, personal control. *Emotional psychological:* appearance, peace of mind, financial, happiness, hope, goals, religious beliefs. *Socioeconomic/family:* family, job, independence, life satisfaction, family/friends support, staff support
Kaplan (1991)	Patient and doctors sharing health-related decision making	Essay on General Health Policy Model (GHPM)	Mortality (death); morbidity (dysfunction in mobility, physical, and social activity); utility (relative importance); and prognosis (duration of the illness)
Kaplan, R. M.(1994)	Health problems such as diabetes, HIV, arthritis, neonatal circumcision, and tobacco tax	Quality of Well-Being Scale (QWB) is a questionnaire which classifies patients by objective levels of functioning	Levels of functioning are represented by mobility, physical activity, and social activity
Kaplan, S. P. (1993)	25 Individuals with traumatic brain injury	Portland Adaptability Inventory	Temperament and emotionality, activities and social behavior, physical capabilities
Kaplan, Anderson, and Wingard (1991)	Random sample of 1,034 men and women from San Diego	Analysis of well-years by gender using General Health Policy Model	Mobility, physical activity, social activity
Katz, Larson, Phillips, Fossel, and Liang (1992)	54 Patients undergoing total hip arthroplasty	Sickness Impact Profile, Arthritis Impact Measurement Scales, and Modified Health Assessment Questionnaire	Physical, psychological, global dimensions
Keith (1990)	Persons with mental retardation	Essay on QOL issues in community integration	Health, employment, education, well-being, living situation, familial and social relations, leisure, work, learning, creative expression, safety, and finances

APPENDIX 12 (continued)
Domains (Overview) in Quality of Life (QOL) Literature

Source	Population	Measures/Method	Domains
Kelley and Lambert(1992)	Review of 30 empirical studies on family support in rehabilitation regarding adaptation to chronic illness and disability.	Selected 4 types of studies to review: (a) observational studies — randomized and nonrandomized intervention studies; (b) surveys, (c) case studies, and (d) randomized controlled trials of interventions of support-outcome relationships	No coherent theory yet available since study of efficacy of family-centered vs. client-centered rehabilitation not been conducted. However, empirical research does clearly demonstrated that adaptation to disability (including QOL) is multidimensional in nature. Adaptation to disability and subsequent community adjustment are recognized as a biopsychosocial phenomenon
Kim (1997)	Patients with Chronic Obstructive Pulmonary Disease (COPD)	Review of methods to evaluate functional status of patients with COPD: Sickness Impact Profile (SIP), Activity of Daily Living (ADL), Quality of Well-Being (QWB), Medical Outcome Study (MOS), Nottingham Health Profile (NHP), Chronic Respiratory Disease Questionnaire (CRDQ), St. George Respiratory Questionnaire (SGRQ), Pulmonary Functional Scale (PFSS), Functional Limitation Profile (FLP)	Functional status, functional ability, quality of life, and health status
Kloseck, Crilly, Ellis, and Lammers (1996)	Geriatric rehabilitation population — 114 persons (47 male and 67 female)	Leisure Competence Measure, Life Satisfaction Index, Geriatric Depression Scale, Folstein Mini-Mental State Examination	Leisure awareness, skills, attitude, social appropriateness, group interaction skills, social context, and community participation
Kober, Kuchler, Broelsch, Kremer, and Henne-Bruns (1990)	29 Liver transplant patients from Hamburg and 38 patients from Chicago	EORTC quality of life questionnaire, the STALX Anxiety Questionnaire, psychodiagnostic interviews, routine laboratory parameters	Functional status, ability to work, general symptoms, liver symptoms, anxiety, depression, social integration, pain, treatment strain, overall physical condition and overall QOL

APPENDIX 12 (continued)
Domains (Overview) in Quality of Life (QOL) Literature

Source	Population	Measures/Method	Domains
Koch and Muthny (1990)	More than 2,000 patients with kidney disease	Questionnaire	Physical/psychosomatic complaints, emotional well-being, partnership and family, vocational rehabilitation, hobbies, leisure activities, and satisfaction with treatment.
Kozleski and Sands (1992)	133 Individuals from the general Colorado population	Consumer Satisfaction Survey	Services and satisfaction, support services and assistance needed, independence/interdependence, integration, activities, personal relationships
Krause (1996)	449 Persons with spinal cord injuries	Life Situation Questionnaire and collection of prospective data on life adjustment in 1974, 1985, 1989	Subjective well-being, social and vocational functioning, and life satisfaction
Kristiansen (1989)	58 British females and 52 British males	Rokeach's Value Survey	World peace, inner harmony, mature love, social recognition, friendship, comfortable life, health, security, wisdom, self-respect
Kunsbeck, Korber, and Freyberger (1990)	Patients with inflammatory bowel disease	Review of empirical research	Energy, leisure, work or school, mobility, body image, psychic status, enjoyment, sexuality, family, friends, and partnership
Kurz and Prather (1995)	Girls — birth to 19 years in the world's developing countries	Findings of the Association of Women in Development Forum	Mortality, poor health care, inadequate nutrition, lack of education, female genital mutilation, child labor, pregnancy and sexual activity, violence, prostitution, poor self concept
Labonte (1996)	Persons with disabilities and disadvantages	Discussion of power issues in determining QOL	Quality of life, health, and empowerment
Lance, Lautenschlager, and Sloan (1989)	150 Assistant, associate, and full professors from University of Georgia	Job Stress Scale, Depressed Mood Scale, Minnesota Satisfaction Questionnaire	Marital satisfaction, satisfaction with social activities, job satisfaction
Langfitt (1995)	71 Epilepsy patients	Epilepsy Surgery Inventory, Sickness Impact Profile, Washington Psychosocial Seizure Inventory	Symptoms, functional status, self-care, mobility, physical activity, energy and vitality, sleep and rest, social functioning, emotional status, cognition, health perceptions, general life satisfaction, work and household management

APPENDIX 12 (continued)
Domains (Overview) in Quality of Life (QOL) Literature

Source	Population	Measures/Method	Domains
Larson (1991)	International health status of nations	Health Status 1 and Health Status 2 derived from Physical Quality of Life Index	Physical, mental, and social well-being
Latten (1989)	3000 Respondents over 18 years in the Netherlands	Quality of Life Surveys	Serious physical injury or illness, death of family member, widow(er)hood, and serious tension at home, aging
Lehman, Reed, and Possidente (1982)	278 Randomly selected psychiatric patients in board and care homes in Los Angeles	Quality of Life Interview	Living situation, family, social relations, leisure time, employment, finances, personal safety, and health
Lennon (1994)	300 Employed women, 202 full-time homemakers, 302 employed men	Investigated the role of work conditions in mediating the effect of employment status on married women's psychological well-being	Autonomy, time pressure, responsibility for things outside of one's control, interruptions, physical effort, and routine
Lennox (1994)	Chronic substance abusers	Center for Epidemiological Studies Depression Scale	Somatic complaints, depressed affect, positive affect, and interpersonal relations
Lerner, Levine, Malspeis, and D'Agostino (1994)	1,319 Working adults	Job Content Questionnaire Medical Outcomes Study Short-Form Health Survey	Physical, role functioning as relates to health, vitality, social functioning, and mental health
Limacher, Dahler, Bosch, and Egli (1991)	Back pain patients	Questionnaire completed by 5 general practitioners for first 20 patients seen for consultation	Work, leisure, partnership, family, housing, stress, misfortune, care availability, and nursing
Lindley, Hirsch, O'Neill, Tansau, Gilbert, and Osterhaus (1992)	Cancer patients receiving chemotherapy	Used the Functional Living Index — Cancer as model to create Functional Living Index — Emesis	Physical well-being and ability, emotional state, sociability, family situation, and nausea
Logue (1990)	Elderly long-term American Indian, Black and White patients (over 45 years)	Data obtained from Public Use Microdata Samples for Oklahoma from 1980 decennial census and from a query on Public Transportation Disability	Social risk, aging, disability, economic status, health, race, gender, educational attainment, marital status, area of residence
Logue (1991)	Death and dying issues for women	Overview article on research needs on age, sex, race, social class, primary diagnosis, co-morbidities of those whose deaths are negotiated	QOL and choosing death, premature death and delayed death, women as recipients of informal and formal care systems, competency, the experts, and feminist health goals
Loscocco and Roschelle (1991)	Working and non-working adults	Literature review of quality of work and nonwork life: 1971–1991	Personality, education, gender, family roles, job characteristics, organizational characteristics, unions, promotions, social context

APPENDIX 12 (continued)
Domains (Overview) in Quality of Life (QOL) Literature

Source	Population	Measures/Method	Domains
Luckasson (1990)	Person with mental retardation	Legal perspective on QOL terminology	Normalization, integration, and worth of all human beings
Lynch and Gallagher-Lepak (1996)	Patients with chronic renal failure	Essay on updating rehabilitation professionals on impact of improved medical treatment	Functional outcomes: weakness/fatigue, reduced endurance, cognitive changes, and psychological distress
Lyons (1993)	Persons with disabilities	Overview article on the need for "total rehabilitation" which would include referral and training in use of leisure time for people with disabilities	Problem of free time, meaningful activity, evolution of recreation services for people with disabilities
Maas (1991)	Persons after laryngectomy	Theoretical model for QOL after laryngectomy	Speech impairment, social, psychological, vocational
Malm, May, and Dencker (1981)	Schizophrenic outpatients — 27 males and 13 females	Used Quality of Life Checklist	Medical care, social, standard of living, communication and transportation, work, safety, education, leisure, spiritual/religious
Manz and Grothe(1991)	Approximately 4000 employees in a midwestern computer manufacturing company	Quality of Work Life Survey	Personal motivation, personal investment, meaningfulness of job, innovation, quality/productivity, communication of organization mission, policies and procedures, human resource systems, management effectiveness, management understanding, commitment to employees, participation, performance evaluation, respect for the individual, supervisory skills, nonfinancial rewards, job clarity, trust and support, team productivity, team communication, job stress, work load, job design, equity, benefits, compensation, career training, physical work environment, work resources
Martinez (1990)	A woman with mental retardation	Her essay on her perception of QOL for herself	Family support, education, and independent living
Mason (1996)	Deaf and hard-of-hearing people	Essay on the cultural meaning of deafness and hard-of-hearing as a QOL issue	Culturally deaf, oral deaf, hard-of-hearing, late-deafened persons

APPENDIX 12 (continued)
Domains (Overview) in Quality of Life (QOL) Literature

Source	Population	Measures/Method	Domains
Mathias, Fifer, andPatrick (1994)	International QOL clinical trials	8-Step protocol for rapidly translating a QOL questionnaire into multiple languages	Health well-being, psychosocial well-being, health distress, depression, self-esteem, emotional functioning, and work loss
Mayou (1990)	Cardiovascular disease patients	Recommends greater use of psychosomatic research including interview-based and self-report measures as well as physical outcome measures	Symptoms, mental state, general health status, types of cardiac disorder
McCall (1991)	Success rates in elderly and adolescent males	Use annual suicide rates for U.S. from *Annual Vital Health Statistics Report 1947–1987*	Impoverishment, family dissolution, and government expenditures
McCauley and Bremer (1991)	Medical patients	Recommends use of Bradburn Affect Balance Scale and Campbell's Scale of General Affect	Sociodemographic, medical economic, income, employment, education, recreation, intrapsychic or psychological
McCoy (1994)	439 Professional women	Survey of working women's leisure time	Discretionary time, discretionary activity, leisure as a state of mind
McGee, O'Boyle, Hickey, O'Malley, and Joyce (1991)	20 Irritable bowel syndrome and 20 peptic ulcer disease patients as compared to 42 healthy individuals	Used the Schedule for Evaluation of Individual QOL	Family, work, recreation, religion, and health
McGuire, Choon, and Akuffo (1991)	19 Elderly people with a developmental disability	Used a lifestyle questionnaire and the Social Training Achievement Record Profile through interviews	Activities of daily life, community-based activities, domestic tasks, areas of personal responsibility
McLanahan and Adams (1989)	Effects of children on adult well-being	Two Americans View Their Mental Health Surveys (AVTHM) 1957 and 1976	Happiness, satisfaction, worries, psychological distress, and perceptions of parenthood
McPhail (1996)	Effects of children with disabilities on the lives of family members	Recommendations regarding improving QOL for families with members with disabilities	Growth opportunities, community membership, choice, in-home health care support, inclusion of parents in decision making, inclusive services which support the family unit, inclusion in regular schooling
Mehrabian and Ross (1979)	293 Undergraduate students	Checklists, questionnaires, and measures of personality	Life changes, physical illness and symptoms, psychosomatic symptoms, accidents, psychological symptoms

APPENDIX 12 (continued)
Domains (Overview) in Quality of Life (QOL) Literature

Source	Population	Measures/Method	Domains
Metcalf (1992)	Plaintiffs in civil law suits with disabilities	Commentary on loss of pleasure of life as testified to by rehabilitationists	Physical, emotional, spiritual, cognitive
Moller and Murphy (1997)	176 Patients with psychiatric disabilities	Clients, family members, and case managers enrolled in course, *"Symptom Management: A Wellness Expedition"*	Number of inpatient days, cost savings, and participant satisfaction
Moos and Moos(1983)	32 Staff members in residential care and 42 staff members in a community mental health center	Development of a set of social climate scales; Work Environment Scale, Family Environment Scale	Relationships, personal growth, and system growth and change
Morris and Lewis (1991)	Entrepreneurship	Framework of further theory development and hypothesis testing concerning the entrepreneurship/QOL interface	Societal QOL: economic, health, social, technological, work, institutional, ecological
Moss (1980)	69 Older clients from 2 similar rehabilitation workshops	Clients assigned to random groups to receive group counseling or social activities. Dean Alienation Scale, Havighhurst Life Satisfaction Index A, Sociometric Questionnaire	Life satisfaction, work productivity, alienation
Mowry (1988)	81 Former VR deaf and hard-of-hearing clients	Interviews in the preferred mode of the former VR client	Health, employment, financial security, home, savings, standard of living, relationships with family and friends
Mugenda, Hira, and Fanslow (1990)	123 Adults in the midwest	Obtained data re household size and net worth, marital status, employment status of money manager, and money management practices	Level of living, savings, staying out of debt, assets, paying debts, meeting emergency expenses, satisfaction with QOL
Mulhern, Fairclough, Friedman, and Leigh (1990)	120 Children with cancer	Play Performance Scale for Children and Vineland Adaptive Behavior Scales with parent and physician ratings	Acute psychological problems, somatic toxicities of various treatments, and residual psychological problems
Munich and Lang (1993)	Persons with psychiatric disabilities	Argument for rehabilitation as a central discipline which integrates clinical and functional status and QOL	Biopsychosocial issues including learning, compensation, adaptation. autonomy, least professional intervention
Murrell and Norris (1983)	1800 Adults living in Kentucky	Use of a subjective measure of QOL	Mental health, financial, social activity, employment, and health

APPENDIX 12 (continued)
Domains (Overview) in Quality of Life (QOL) Literature

Source	Population	Measures/Method	Domains
Muthny, Koch, and Stump (1990)	Oncology patients	Review of QOL instruments used	Physical concerns, functional ability, family well-being, emotional well-being, spirituality, treatment satisfaction, future hopes and plans, sexuality, social and occupational functioning
Nagler (1996)	39 Persons with disabilities who have experienced sexual abuse	Interviews and essay on QOL issues and sexual abuse	Social, emotional, sexuality, work, friends, self-esteem, marriage, education, emotional and physical well-being
Nation, Benshoff and Malkin (1996)	Adolescents in substance abuse treatment facilities	Random survey of substance abuse treatment programs using therapeutic recreation	Social skills, self-esteem, self-efficacy and improve cooperation and trust; QOL not a specific goal
National Association of Rehabilitation Facilities (NARF) (1988)	Persons with disabilities using NARF facilities	Position statement by NARF on QOL and quality of work life	Empowerment, friendship, being valued, supported employment
National Eye Institute (1997)	600 Newly diagnosed patients with glaucoma	Medicine vs. glaucoma filtering surgery	Overall patient satisfaction and quality of life based on treatment type
National Institute on Disability and Rehabilitation Research (1988)	Persons with disabilities	Essay on research in rehabilitation and QOL	Mobility, environmental control, community resources and know-how, reliance on loved ones or significant others from time to time, self-acceptance andmotivation to be productive and happy
National Institutes of Health (1990)	A consensus development conference on surgery for epilepsy with neurologists, neurosurgeons, psychologists, and other health care providers	Addressed issues of epilepsy surgery including patient selection and management	Seizure elimination or reduction, short-term surgical outcome, physical health, mental health, cognitive function and memory, social health, general health
Nayfield, Ganz, Moinpour, Cella, and Hailey (1992)	Cancer clinical trials research and QOL research	Workshop with 4 working groups of clinical cancer trials and QOL research experts	Group recommended that, as a minimum, QOL assessment in cancer clinical trials should include: physical, emotional, social functioning, somatic/physiological complaints (symptoms and side effects associated with treatment)
Near, Rice, and Hunt (1978)	1041 Probability sample of adults living in New York state	4 Subjective QOL measures	Life satisfaction, life satisfaction over time, job satisfaction, and health

APPENDIX 12 (continued)
Domains (Overview) in Quality of Life (QOL) Literature

Source	Population	Measures/Method	Domains
Newfield and Duet (1976)	The work of curriculum developers	A review of QOL Indexes for the purpose of comparing their characteristics to that of the goal of education	Public order and safety, physical environment, health, affection and sociability, income and poverty, education and skills attainment, participation and alienation, availability and utilization of leisure, self-respect, aesthetics, communication, enjoyment of art, finer things, learning, and morality
Nichols (1997)	Cancer patients	Essay on management of cancer pain	Pain affects activity, sleep, appetite, and bring about depression, anxiety, and hostility and also affect psychological and social stress, impairing life quality
Nosek, Howland, Young, Georgiou, Rintala, Foley, Bennett, and Smith (1994)	31 Women with physical disabilities	Qualitative interviews regarding disability	Positive sexual self-concept, having sexuality and sexuality information, good relationships, managing barriers, good health and physical functioning
O'Keefe (1996)	Persons with communication disorders	Essay recommending that recognition and be given to the QOL issues in this impairment and research be conducted	Being, belonging, and becoming
Oliver, Holloway, and Carson (1995)	Patients using mental health services	Review of objective, subjective, and health-related concepts of QOL	Adequate income, housing, occupation, opportunities to make social relationships
O'Rear, Bark, and Hutchinson (1996)	Persons with psychiatric disabilities	Essay on promoting wellness activities which improve QOL	Physical, mental, emotional, and spiritual wellness
Ory and Cox (1994)	Elderly people	Review of conceptual and methodological issues related to health promotion and disability for older people	Social and environmental factors, physical and mental health, health-related behaviors
Osberg, McGinnis, DeJong, and Seward (1987)	97 Elderly disabled adults	Markides and Martin's (1979) path analysis model to assess QOL, Barthel Index, self-administered questionnaire	Income, age, marital status, functional capacity, independence
Osoba (1992)	Cancer patients	Reports on work of QOL Committee in Canada regarding use of QOL measures in all cancer clinical trials	No domains listed

APPENDIX 12 (continued)
Domains (Overview) in Quality of Life (QOL) Literature

Source	Population	Measures/Method	Domains
Ouellette-Kuntz (1990)	Ten interviews with mentally retarded adults	Use of Quality of Life Interview Schedule with emphasis on intra- and inter-rater agreement	Health services, family-guardianship, income, education, training, and employment, housing and safety, transportation, social, recreational, religious/cultural, case management, advocacy, aesthetics, and counseling
Ouellette-Kuntz and McCreary (1996)	Persons with severe developmental disabilities	Development of the QOL Interview Schedule	Communication, disabilities, personal characteristics, and recent life events
Parmenter (1996)	For everyone	Discussion of the quality-adjusted life-year (QALYs) approach	A plurality of independent vectors based on an individual life
Perlman et al. (1990)	43 Rheumatoid arthritis patients	Self-report and doctors' medical history, dance-based exercise, Arthritis Impact Measurement Scales	Disease states, physical function, and pscyhological function
Perry and Felce (1995)	People with learning disabilities in 15 staffed houses	Review of 14 objective measures of service quality in residential facilities	Quality of housing, social and community integration, social interactions, development, activity, and autonomy and choice
Pugliesi (1995)	599 Women and 753 men from a national data set	Refinement of differential exposure or vulnerability models	Work characteristics, social and psychological resources, well-being, role and status variables — gender, marital status, ethnicity, and parenthood
Pumpian, Szeto, and Sax (1996)	Young adults with disabilities	Demonstration project to enhance the lives of persons with significant disabilities using customized assistive technology	Functional capacity, independent living skills, supported employment, rehabilitation services
Raeburn and Rootman (1996)	For everyone	Essay on a conceptual model of QOL	Being, belonging, and becoming
Raphael (1996a)	For everyone	11 Debates concerning measurement of QOL	Social, psychological, quantitative vs. qualitative, objective vs. subjective, self-report vs. reports by others
Raphael (1996b)	10- to 25-year olds or adolescent health	Review of adolescent health and QOL issues	*Global:* macro environment, human rights and welfare policies; *External:* work, income, housing; *Interpersonal:* family structure and function, intimate friends, extended social. *Personal:* physical, mental, spiritual

APPENDIX 12 (continued)
Domains (Overview) in Quality of Life (QOL) Literature

Source	Population	Measures/Method	Domains
Raphael (1996c)	12 Group meetings, 120 seniors in the community	Development of Quality of Life Profile: Seniors Version	Physical being, psychological being, spiritual being, physical belonging, social belonging, community belonging, practical becoming, leisure becoming, growth becoming
Recchia, et al. (1991)	Elderly patients	Recommends QOL measures for elderly patients	Daily life functions, productivity and economic status, performance of social roles, intellectual capabilities, emotional stability, assessment of satisfaction with life, signs and symptoms of illness
Reich and Zautra (1983)	70 Middle and older aged persons and a college sample of 104 students	Life Events Questionnaire, Depressive Adjective Checklist, Perceived Quality of Life Scale	Demands, desires, positive and negative components of well-being, psychiatric symptoms
Renwick and Brown (1996)	People with disabilities, service providers, and families of persons with disabilities	Focus groups, literature review, consultation with the experts for Centre for Health Promotion (CHP) in Toronto approach	*Being:* physical, psychological, spiritual. *Belonging:* physical, social, community. *Becoming:* practical, leisure, growth
Renwick, Brown, Rootman, and Nagler (1996)	For everyone	Recommendations for further research	Conceptual frameworks: person–environment interactions, empowerment of individuals, generic approaches suited to general and specific populations, personal meanings, broad range of domains, and relationships between health and QOL
Renwick and Friefeld (1996)	Rehabilitation clients	Recommendations for going beyond functional and health status measures such as the Barethel Index, Functional Status Index, Functional Activities Questionnaire, Sickness Impact Profile, Nottingham Health Profile, Arthritis Impact Measurement Scale	Physical, emotional, cognitive, social aspects of functioning in the major areas of life (e.g., mobility, communication, activities of daily living, vocational activities, social relationships, leisure and recreation)

APPENDIX 12 (continued)
Domains (Overview) in Quality of Life (QOL) Literature

Source	Population	Measures/Method	Domains
Renwick and Friedland (1996)	107 Males and 13 females with HIV	Quality of Life Questionnaire, Fanning Quality of Life Scale, Life Appraisal and Life Satisfaction Questionnaire, Interpersonal Support Evaluation List, Ways of Coping, Recent Life Changes Questionnaire	Job satisfaction, relations with others, work relations, altruistic behavior, creative–aesthetic behavior, significant other relationships, marital (partner) relations, job characteristics, political behavior, extended family relations, vacation behavior, personal growth, material well-being, sports activity, and physical well-being
Rettig, Danes, and Bauer (1991)	592 Women and men from farm families	Survey and Delighted–Terrible Scale	Love, status, services, information, goods, money resources received from family
Rhoads and Raymond (1981)	547 Adults from Phoenix area	Interviews, Bradburn Affect–Balance Scale	Age, sex, family income, personal, social, community, income
Rintala, Hart, and Fuhrer (1996)	661 Persons with spinal cord injuries	Questionnaires and Perceived Stress Scale, Center for Epidemiological Studies Depression Scale, Life Satisfaction Index, Craig Handicap Assessment and Reporting Technique, ASIA Total Motor Index, Functional Independence Measure, Hassles Scale, Life Events Scale, Personal Independence Profile, Satisfaction with Personal Assistance, Interpersonal Support Evaluation List	Depression, life satisfaction, morbidity, mobility, occupation, social integration and support, independence, pressure sores
Rioux (1996)	Persons with disabilities	Essay on disability as a social construct	Social, political, and economic structures are inseparable from individual and collective states of well-being
Rodin (1990)	Adults with insulin-dependent diabetes mellitus (158 subjects)	Rand General Well-Being Scale, General Health Questionnaire	Physical functioning, social functioning, emotional functioning, burden of symptoms, and the sense of well-being

APPENDIX 12 (continued)
Domains (Overview) in Quality of Life (QOL) Literature

Source	Population	Measures/Method	Domains
Roessler (1990)	Rehabilitation counseling clients	Recommends QOL approach in rehabilitation of persons with disabilities	Health, public safety, education, employment, earnings and income, poverty, housing, family stability, equality, well-being, happiness
Roller (1996)	People with late effects of polio	Advocates 2 health promotion models used in German and U.S. for increasing physical fitness	Alleviate, manage, and prevent secondary conditions; promote good health and wellness; introduce new health promotion tactics; facilitate long-term adoption of health-enhancing behaviors
Romney, Jenkins, and Bynner (1992)	469 Patients with cardiovascular problems	Use LISREL to test competing hypothesis	Symptoms of illness, neurological dysfunction, interpersonal relationships, morale, and socioeconomic status
Rosen, Simon, and McKinsey (1995)	100 Individuals with mental retardation	Developed subjective QOL instrument — PALS	Perceived Stress, Affect, Loneliness, and Satisfaction
Rosenfeld, S. (1992)	157 Members of a psychosocial rehabilitation program	Interviews, Delighted–Terrible Scale, Lehman's QOL, Moos' Community-Oriented Program Environment Scale	Importance of program components, vocational rehabilitation, financial services, empowerment approaches to service delivery
Roxburgh (1996)	994 Employed Canadians	Tested Job Stress Models	Differential exposure and vulnerability by gender to job stress, occupational self-direction, job demands, co-worker social support
Ruchlin and Morris (1991)	310 Young elderly between ages of 65–74.	Modified Spitzer Uniscale QL index	Marital Status, self-assessed health status, functional status, self-assessed financial status, and work status
Ruffing-Rahal (1991)	182 Community-dwelling elderly adults	The Integration Inventory, Philadelphia Geriatric Center Morale Scale, the Spiritual Well-Being Scale, and 4 measures of self-rated well-being	Well-being, absence of loneliness, positive attitude toward aging, self-rated happiness, self-rated health, self-rated life satisfaction, absence of agitation, religious well-being
Sands and Kozleski (1994)	131 Persons without disabilities and 86 persons with disabilities (cerebral palsy, mental retardation, and head injury)living in community settings	Used the Consumer Satisfaction Survey and modified version with nondisabled sample	Experience with advocacy organizations, services and satisfaction, independence interdependence, participation in community activities, and in recreation activities, and satisfaction with these activities

APPENDIX 12 (continued)
Domains (Overview) in Quality of Life (QOL) Literature

Source	Population	Measures/Method	Domains
Sartorius (1995)	Psychiatric rehabilitation clients	Review essay	Not specific, but leisure, work, family, community, aesthetic, and health are mentioned
Satcher (1993)	Persons with learning disabilities	Essay on ADA and its potential for improvement of quality of work life	Job restructuring, modified work schedule, reassignment to vacant positions, acquiring or modifying equipment or devices, modifying examinations, training materials or policies, providing qualified readers
Schaafsma and Osoba (1994)	139 Lung cancer patients	Karnofsky Performance Status and item 30 of the QOL questionnaire developed by the European Organization for Research and Treatment of Cancer Study Group	Physical functioning, emotional functioning, breathing, social functioning, and cognition, pain, and fatigue
Schalock (1990a)	Persons with developmental disabilities	Essay on conceptualizing and measuring QOL, QOL variables in mental retardation literature	Social and psychological indicators, goodness-of-fit/social policy
Schalock (1990b)	Persons with mental retardation	Essay on QOL disability policy and service delivery systems	Living, learning, working, choice, independence, productivity, and community integration
Schalock (1996)	For everyone	Proposes a quality assurance model for QOL evaluation	Home and community living, work-school, and health and wellness
Schalock and Lilley(1986)	85 Mentally retarded persons place in independent housing and competitive employment	Quality of Life Questionnaire	Environmental control (daily schedule, income, appointments, shopping, home decorations, pets); social interaction(neighbors, coinhabitants, friends); community utilization (transportation, recreation, education)
Scherer (1990)	Persons with spinal cord injury (SCI) and cerebral palsy (CP)	Compared persons with SCI and CP using assistive devices (AD), interviews and observations, Personal Capacities Questionnaire, Functional Assessment Inventory, Taylor-Johnson Temperament Analysis	Personal capacities, adaptive behavior, vocational qualifications, motor functioning

APPENDIX 12 (continued)
Domains (Overview) in Quality of Life (QOL) Literature

Source	Population	Measures/Method	Domains
Schipper (1990)	Cancer patients	Essay on QOL paradigms based on patient-outcome measures	Definition is patient centered and functional. Physical and occupational function, social intervention, somatic sensational, and psychological state
Schover (1991)	Women with breast cancer	Review of studies on the impact of breast cancer on sexuality, body image, and intimate relationships	Psychological health, relationship satisfaction, premorbid sexual life, choice in treatment options, and types of treatment options
Schwartz, Devine, Schechter, and Bender (1990)	19 Myasthenia gravis and 19 amyotrophic lateral sclerosis patients	9-Rung Cantril Ladder, Multidimensional Health Locus of Control, Functional Living Index for Cancer, Quality of Life Index	Demographics, severity of illness, coping styles, life satisfaction, perceived health and social activity, control of health, psychosocial well-being, public and body image, and QOL
Scott (1996)	Persons with disabilities in integrated community recreation programs vs. those in segregated programs	Testimony before the House Appropriations Subcommittee on Labor, Health, and Human Services and Education	Work performance, family relations, physical health, overall health status and independent functioning at home
Scuccimarra and Speece (1990)	65 Mildly handicapped students who exited high school in 1984	59-Item instrument was developed, adapted from the Vermont Follow-up Structured Survey Instrument	Employment status and social activity
Select House Committee on Aging (1989)	Older women living alone	Chairman Roybal's report on hearings on QOL of older women living alone	Income, health, safety, housing
Shank, Coyle, Boyd, and Kinney (1996)	Persons with disabilities	Therapeutic recreation according to a model used by the National Center for Medical Rehabilitation Research	Functional limitations, physical, psychological cognitive, and social functioning
Sherman and Schiffman (1991)	Older consumers	Historical reflections on past 20 to 30 years of QOL status of older consumers	Socioeconomic indicators, health and longevity, housing and family living, gender differences, life satisfaction, cognitive age, leisure, occupation, health
Short and Shea (1995)	Families below the poverty line and AFDC families	From data collected in Survey of Income and Program Participation	Access to consumer durables, living conditions, crime and neighborhood, basic needs, health and nutrition, index of deprivation
Shye (1989)	General population	Examined QOL Model vs. Residents Reports	Personality, Physical, Social, Cultural as the functioning modes of the QOL Model

APPENDIX 12 (continued)
Domains (Overview) in Quality of Life (QOL) Literature

Source	Population	Measures/Method	Domains
Siegel and Brent (1997)	Schizophrenic patients	Q-TWIST method	In-hospital, in-community without symptoms, in-community with symptoms.
Siegrist and Junge (1990)	Chronic illness patients	The Katz Adjustment Scale, Social Maladjustment Schedule, Social Dysfunction Rating Scale, Structured and Scaled Interview to Assess Maladjustment, Reintegration to Normal Living Index	Physical, psychological, and social dimensions of health
Sinnott-Oswald, Gliner, and Spencer (1991)	Ten persons with disabilities in supported community employment, ten persons with disabilities in sheltered workshop employment, and nine persons without disabilities	QOL Index, Adaptive Behavior Scale, physical health measures, Parent–Guardian Survey	Leisure activities, use of leisure time, self-esteem, involvement in activities, mobility, job skill perceptions, and perceptions regarding changes in income
Slaughter, Lehman, Myers (1991)	Severely mentally ill adults in residential care facilities	Literature review of 16 studies	Employment status, and safety, social contacts, leisure activities, and general life satisfaction
Sonino, Fava, Fallo, and Boscaro (1990)	Patients with endocrine disease	Recommends use of the psychosomatic approach in QOL with these patients	Life events preceding disease onset, psychological distress, abnormal illness behavior
Spreitzer and Snyder (1989)	Toledo adults	Life Satisfaction, Job Satisfaction, and Self-Esteem items used in a telephone interview	Self-esteem, job and life satisfaction, and leisure
Stark and Goldsbury (1990)	Persons with mental retardation	Essay on QOL over the life span	General well-being, age, sex, social/cultural background, level of cognitive/adaptive functioning, education, health, living environment, family, social/emotional, work, and leisure
Stewart and King (1991)	Older adults	Conceptual framework presented of QOL concepts for evaluating the efficacy of physical activity in older adults	Physical functioning, cognitive functioning, activities, bodily well-being, emotional well-being, self-concept, and global perceptions of health and life satisfaction
Stillson, White, and Harris (1986)	Alcoholism treatment personnel	Review of aspects of stress management techniques to improve QOL	Psychotherapy, meditation/visualization and time management

APPENDIX 12 (continued)
Domains (Overview) in Quality of Life (QOL) Literature

Source	Population	Measures/Method	Domains
Sullivan, Wells, and Leake (1992)	101 former acute care psychiatric inpatients living in Mississippi	Quality of Life Index, Drug Attitude Inventory, The Symptom Checklist	Living situation, social life, personal health, finances, global rating, depressive symptoms, psychotic symptoms, medications compliance, side effects, alcohol abuse, social skills, living skills, criticism by family
Tait, Chibnall, and Margolis (1990)	416 Patients with chronic pain	Beck Depression, Spielberger Inventory, Anxiety Inventory, Psychosomatic Symptom Checklist, QOL Scale, and Pain Disability Index	Pain extent, psychological state, pain severity, disability, pain history, age, education
Taylor (1989)	Patients with hypertension	Commentary on Hume; suggests methods of evaluation	Disease-specific, physical functioning, emotional functioning, social functioning and general health perceptions
Taylor and Bodgan (1990)	Persons with mental retardation	Definitions and conceptions of QOL; subjective aspects of QOL	Cognitive, activities of daily living, social and family functioning, subjective experience of QOL
Tengs (1996)	Medicaid recipients	Evaluation of Oregon's Medicaid rationing algorithms	Cost, duration of benefit with treatment for health problems, symptoms, adverse health outcomes including death
Terman (1995)	Wrongful death cases in civil lawsuits	Introduces the Loss of Enjoyment of Life-Severity Scale (LEL-SS) partially based on Global Assessment of Functioning in DSM	Physical/practical functioning, emotional/psychological functioning, social/recreational functioning, occupational/homemaking/scholastic functioning.
Tigges (1993)	Hospice care patients	Review of QOL literature re hospice care	Control of pain and symptoms, personal care and comfort, support of respite to the primary caregiver/family member, pastoral care, and bereavement services for survivors. Tigges' defines a sense of excellence of character; being useful, productive, needed and valued; personal safety and security; and the ability to interact with others as the domains to be assessed

APPENDIX 12 (continued)
Domains (Overview) in Quality of Life (QOL) Literature

Source	Population	Measures/Method	Domains
Till, Sutherland, Meslin (1992)	Cancer patients	Recommends that patient preference should be included in clinical cancer trials re QOL issues	Preferences might and include: personal factors, values, and attitudes; psychosocial factors; activities of daily living; family; survival; and sexuality
Tsevat, Goldman, Lamas, Pfeffer, Chapin, Connors, and Lee (1991)	80 Myocardial infarction survivors	Visual Analogue Scale, Verbal Rating Scale, Time Trade-off, Transformed Time Trade-off Mean, Karnofsky Index, Specific Anxiety Scale Class, and NY Heart Association Class	Gender, employment, exercise, pain, functional status
Tuchler, Hofmann, Bernhart, et al. (1992)	1,014 Adult patients in European countries	QOL Questionnaire	Physical condition,QOL, relationships and social contacts, health, overall life situation, medical treatment, sexuality, recovery chances, physical capacity, life satisfaction
Turk (1996)	Women with disabilities: neuromuscular diseases, late effects of polio, spinal cord pathology, multiple sclerosis, osteoporosis in disability	Essay on fitness as an optimal state of physical well-being. Call for research on fitness issues for women with physical disabilities	Flexibility, muscular strength and endurance, cardiopulmonary conditioning
Vandergriff and Chubon (1994)	120 Persons with mental retardation	Program Analysis of Service System Implementation of Normalization Goals, Life Situation Survey, Resident Choice Assessment Scale, American Association on Mental Deficiency Adaptive Behavior Scale	Internal standards and evaluations of life by individuals, socionormative, and person–environment systems
Vaughan and Hobson (1990)	179 Elderly adults using low-vision devices	Report on a project of 39 counties of rural Missouri to screen and provide low-vision devices to elderly persons in need	Increase in independent living: read mail, write checks, thread needles,and read large print,better general functioning in everyday tasks and QOL
Verbrugge, Reoma, and Gruber-Baldini (1994)	165 Persons withchronic disability	Mental Status Questionnaire, Beck Depression Inventory, Activities of Daily Living, Six Motions to determine physical functioning, and Index of Well-Being	Cognitive, emotional, social, physical, and global well-being

APPENDIX 12 (continued)
Domains (Overview) in Quality of Life (QOL) Literature

Source	Population	Measures/Method	Domains
Vickrey, Hays, Graber et al. (1992)	239 Adults with epilepsy	Epilepsy Surgery Inventory, Mood Profile, Seizure Classification	Energy/fatigue, overall QOL, social function, emotional well-being, cognitive function, physical function, pain, role limitations
Walker, Blankenship, Ditty, and Lynch (1987)	25 Closed-head-injured adults (1 female and 24 males)	MMPI, Adaptive Behavior Scale, Quality of Life Rating Scale	Vocational, educational, family participation, community service, avocational, artistic, and scholarly pursuits
Wallston, Hoover-Dempsey, and Brissie (1989)	78 Working women	Job Satisfaction Scale, Self-esteem Scale, and Life Satisfaction Scale	Gatekeeping transactions, flexibility, outcome/success, negativity, job satisfaction, self-esteem, quality of life, substance use
Ward (1990)	A woman with mental retardation	Her essay on her reflections on QOL	Work, independent living, housing, social function, family and education
Warren, Wrigley, Yoels, and Fine (1996)	137 Persons with traumatic brain injury, 38 spinal cord injury persons	Life Satisfaction Index–A, Functional Independence Measure, Family Satisfaction Scale	Family satisfaction, employment status, memory independence, bowel independence, marital status, self blame
West, Kregel, and Banks (1990)	1550 Individuals placed in supported employment (65% with mental retardation, 9% with long-term mental illness, and 10% with head injuries and cerebral palsy)	*Data Management System Operations Manual* for form completion by 96 provider agencies	Evaluation of QOL in worklife by looking availability of fringe benefits
Whelton, Pawlick, and Cardamone (1997)	105 families with 92 Family members with psychiatric disabilities	Questionnaires sent to families regarding the Hamilton Program for Schizophrenia to determine levels of satisfaction with the program	Time and money spent by family members for their relatives with disabilities and reduction of caregiving by program; quality of relationship with relative; illness management.
Whitaker (1989)	Persons with profound mental handicaps (mental retardation).	Essay regarding a conceptual model	*Individual behavior:* level of skills and abilities, level of adaptive engagement, level of negative behavior; and *Factor about the environment:* conditions of physical environment in terms of comfort, food, health care; opportunities to mix with local community; variability and amount of varied activities available; opportunity to make choices; and treated as valued individuals in society

APPENDIX 12 (continued)
Domains (Overview) in Quality of Life (QOL) Literature

Source	Population	Measures/Method	Domains
WHOQOL Group (1994)	Field centers in development of instrument in 15 countries	Development of World Health Organization Quality of Life instrument using consensus of definition of QOL by international expert review, qualitative pilot with focus groups, field tests to develop psychometric properties	Physical, psychological, level of independence, social relationships, environment, spiritual religion/personal beliefs
Wilkinson, Williams, Krekorian, McLees, and Falloon (1992)	32 Adults with functional mental disorders	Structured interview schedule, Charing Cross Health Indicator, Clinical Global Impression Scale	Adaptive functioning, social performance, patient and family distress, economic, and sociodemographic factors
Williams, Eyring, Gaynor, and Long (1991)	734 College students and adults	Life Satisfaction Index, Satisfaction with Life Scale, Spiritual Well-Being Scale	Inherent value of life, effective life management, and sense of health
Wolkenstein and Butler (1992)	96 Healthy elderly (65 years and over)	Questionnaire, opinion surveys, group interviews	Outside world and others, inner world of the self, coping with loss, interaction with treating physician
Wood and Johnson (1989)	15 Elderly rural adults selected for qualitative study and 392 elderly rural adults in quantitative study	Used a life satisfaction questionnaire and analysis of qualitative data.	Housing, health, self-esteem, friendship, and family
Wood, Matthews, and Norris (1992)	457 Women and men over 60 years in urban and rural Canada	Structured interviews and Guelph Satellite Method	Spouse, health, housing, and friendship
Woodruff and Conway (1992)	519 U.S. Navy personnel randomly selected	Questionnaires based on QOL research to examine health and fitness factors and changes in QOL	Overall QOL, health/fitness, and health behavior
Wozner (1982)	Persons in various institutions — jails, residential facilities, hospitals (internats)	Conceptual framework based on the QOL Map	Personality, physical, societal, and cultural
Young and Barboriak (1982)	45 Male volunteers classified for Type A behavior	Structured Interview, Jenkins Activity Survey, Milwaukee Cardiovascular Life Quality Questionnaire	Competition on the job, hard driving, temper, job deadlines, getting ahead, vacations, rest
Zautra (1982)	537 community residents	Life Cycle Measurements, Social Resource Measurements, Negative Life Events, Perceived Quality of Life Scale, 22-item Psychiatric Screening Inventory	Self-reliance, supportive others, social responsibility, social network blame, positive affect, negative affect, psychiatric distress, overall life quality, number of negative events

APPENDIX 12 (continued)
Domains (Overview) in Quality of Life (QOL) Literature

Source	Population	Measures/Method	Domains
Zautra and Reich (1983)	General population	Review of 15 studies measuring effects of positive and negative events on psychiatric distress	Positive life events, negative life events, psychological well-being
Zweig, Barber, and Eccles (1997)	Young adults: 872 women and 527 men	Data from MI Study of Adolescent Life used to examine sexual coercion and well-being	Psychological and social adjustment, depressed mood, self-esteem, coping

References

Parameters for selecting articles reviewed and charted by QOL domains:

1. **Had to have clearly delineated domains regarding QOL.**
2. **QOL had to be addressed within the context of QOL research literature or not just the use of QOL terminology without placing it in any context.**

American Academy of Ophthalmology and American Society of Cataract and Refractive Surgery. (1997). *White paper on cataract surgery.* http//www.eyenet.org.

Andrew, F. M. (1991). Stability and change in levels and structure of subjective well-being: USA 1972 and 1988. *Social Indicators Research,* 25: 1-30.

Andrews, P., Meyer, R. G., and Berla, E. P. (1996). Development of the Lost Pleasure of Life Scale. *Law and Human Behavior,* 20(1): 99-111.

Askins, J. (1997). Gone fishin'. *Team Rehab Report,* 35-37.

Bach, M. and Rioux, M. H. (1996). Social well-being: a framework for quality of life research. In R. Renwick, I. Brown, and M. Nagler (Eds.), *Quality of Life in Health Promotion and Rehabilitation,* pp. 63-74. Thousand Oaks, CA: Sage Publications.

Baker, F., Curbow, B., and Wingard, J. R. (1992). Development of the Satisfaction with Life Domains Scale for Cancer. *Journal of Psychosocial Oncology,* 10(3): 75-90.

Baker, F., Jodrey, D., and Intagliata, J. (1992). Social support and quality of life of community support clients. *Community Mental Health Journal,* 29(5): 397-411.

Bech, P. (1990). Measurement of psychological distress and well-being. *Psychotherapy and Psychosomatics,* 54: 77-89.

Bellamy, G. T., Newton, J. S., LeBaron, N. M., and Horner, R. H. (1990). Quality of life and lifestyle outcomes: A challenge for residential programs. In R. L. Schalock (Ed.), *Quality of Life: Perspectives and Issues,* pp. 127-137. Washington, D.C.: American Association of Mental Retardation.

Ben-Ari, A. and Taler, Y. (1984). The relationship between absenteeism rate and satisfaction among clients in vocational rehabilitation. *Journal of Applied Rehabilitation Counseling,* 15(4): 39-47.

Berla, E., Brookshire, M., and Smith, (1990). Hedonic damages and personal injury: a conceptual approach. *Journal of Forensic Economics,* 1-8.

Bigelow, D. A., McFarland, B. H., and Olson, M. M. (1991). Quality of life of community mental health program clients: validating a measure. *Community Mental Health Journal,* 27(1): 43-55.

Blandford, A. A. and Campbell, N. L. (1990). Subjective well-being among native and non-native elderly persons: do differences exist? *Canadian Journal on Aging,* 9(4): 386-399.

Blau, T. H. (1977). Quality of life, social indicators, and criteria of change. *Professional Psychology,* 464-473.

Blumenthal, J. A. and Emery, C. F. (1988). Rehabilitation of patients following myocardial infarction. *Journal of Consulting and Clinical Psychology,* 56(3): 374-381.

Boschen, K. A. (1996). Correlates of life satisfaction, residential satisfaction, and locus of control among adults with spinal cord injuries. *Rehabilitation Counseling Bulletin,* 39(4): 230-243.

Borthwick-Duffy, S. A. (1990). Quality of life of persons with severe or profound mental retardation. In R.L. Schalock (Ed.), *Quality of Life: Perspectives and Issues,* pp. 177-189. Washington, D.C.: American Association of Mental Retardation.

Bratt, A. and Johnston, R. (1988). Changes in life style for young adults with profound handicaps following discharge from hospital care into a "second generation" housing project. *Mental Handicap Research,* 1(1): 49-74.

Breetvelt, I. S. and Van Dam, F. S. A. M. (1991). Underreporting by cancer patients: the case of response shift. *Social Science Medicine,* 32(9): 981-987.

Brown, C. (1996). *A* comparison of living situation and loneliness for people with mental illness. *Psychiatric Rehabilitation Journal,* 20(2): 59-65.

Brown, I. (1996). The quality of life of marginal citizens: homelessness. In R. Renwick, I. Brown, and M. Nagler (Eds.), *Quality of Life in Health Promotion and Rehabilitation,* pp. 204-218. Thousand Oaks, CA: Sage Publications.

Brown, I., Renwick, R., and Nagler, M. (1996). The centrality of quality of life in health promotion and rehabilitation. In R. Renwick, I. Brown, and M. Nagler (Eds.), *Quality of Life in Health Promotion and Rehabilitation,* pp. 3-13. Thousand Oaks, CA: Sage Publications.

Brown, R. I. (1989). Aging, disability, and quality of life: a challenge for society. *Canadian Psychology,* 30(3): 551-559.

Brown, R. I. (1996). People with developmental disabilities: applying quality of life to assessment and intervention. In R. Renwick, I. Brown, and M. Nagler (Eds.), *Quality of Life in Health Promotion and Rehabilitation,* pp. 253-267. Thousand Oaks, CA: Sage Publications.

Brown, R. I., Bayer, M. B., and Brown, P. M. (1988). Quality of life: a challenge for rehabilitation agencies. *Australia and New Zealand Journal of Developmental Disabilities,* 14(3,4): 189-199.

Brown, C., Cosgrove, N., and De Selm, T. (1997). Barriers interfering with life satisfaction for individuals with severe mental illness. *Psychiatric Rehabilitation Journal,* 20(3): 67-71.

Brydolf, M., Berndtsson, I., Lindholm, E., and Berglund, B. (1994). Evaluation of a Swedish version of the Ostomy Adjustment Scale. *Scandinavian Journal of Caring Science,* 8: 179-183.

Burton, L. A. and Volpe, B. (1993). Social adjustment scale assessments in traumatic brain injury. *Journal of Rehabilitation,* 34-37.

Callahan, S. (1992). Quality of life. *Alzheimer Disease and Associated Disorders,* 6(3): 138-144.

Campbell, A. (1976). Subjective measures of well-being. *American Psychologist,* 117-124.

Campbell, A., Converse, P. E., and Rodgers, W. L. (1976). *The Quality of American Life: Perceptions, Evaluations, and Satisfactions.* New York: Russell Sage Foundation.

Canales, S., Ganz, P. A., and Coscarelli, C. A. (1995). Translation and validation of a quality of life instrument for Hispanic American cancer patients: methodological considerations. *Quality of Life Research,* 4: 3-11.

Carsky, M. L., Dolan, E. M., and Free, R. K. (1991). An integrated model of homebased work: Effects on family quality of life. *Journal of Business Research,* 23: 37-49.

Centers for Disease Control and Prevention. (1995). Health-related quality of life measures — United States, 1993. *Morbidity and Mortality Weekly Report,* 44(11): 195-200.

Chaturvedi, S. K. (1991). What's important for quality of life to Indians — In relation to cancer. *Social Science Medicine,* 33(1): 91-94.

Cheng, S.T. (1988). Subjective quality of life in the planning and evaluation of programs. *Evaluation and Program Planning,* 11, 123-134.

Chibnall, J. T. and Tait, R. C. (1990). The Quality of Life Scale: a preliminary study with chronic pain patients. *Psychology and Health,* 4: 283-292.

Christie, M. J., French, D., Weatherstone, L., West, A., and the Applied Research Group. (1991). The patient's perceptions of chronic disease and its management: Psychosomatics, holism and quality of life in contemporary management of childhood asthma. *Psychotherapy and Psychosomatics,* 56: 197-203.

Chubon, R. A. (1985). Quality of life measurement of persons with back problems: some preliminary findings. *Journal of Applied Rehabilitation Counseling,* 16(2): 31-34.

Ciardiello, J. A. and Bingham, W. C. (1962). The career maturity of schizophrenic clients. *Rehabilitation Counseling Bulletin,* 3-9.

Clark, A. and Hirst, M. (1989). Disability in adulthood: ten-year follow-up of young people with disabilities. *Disability, Handicap and Society,* 4(3): 271-283.

Clayton, K.S. and Chubon, R. A. (1994). Factors associated with the quality of life of long-term spinal cord injured persons. *Archives of Physical Medicine and Rehabilitation,* 75: 633-638.

Condeluci, A., Ferris, L. L., and Bogdan, A. (1992). Outcome and value: the survivor perspective. *Journal of Head Trauma Rehabilitation,* 7(4): 37-45.

Conn, V. S., Taylor, S. G., and Wiman, P. (1991). Anxiety, depression, quality of life, and self-care among survivors of myocardial infarction. *Issues in Mental Health Nursing,* 12: 321-331.

Conroy, J. W. and Feinstein, C. S. (1990). Measuring quality of life: Where have we been? Where are we going? In R. L. Schalock (Ed.), *Quality of Life: Perspectives and Issues,* pp. 227-233. Washington, D.C.: American Association of Mental Retardation.

Corrigan, P. W. and Buican, B. (1995). The construct validity of subjective quality of life for the severely mentally ill. *Journal of Nervous and Mental Disease,* 183(5): 281-285.

Corten, P., Mercier, C., and Pele, I. (1994). Subjective quality of life: clinical model for assessment of rehabilitation treatment in psychiatry. *Social Psychiatric Epidemiology,* 29: 178-183.

Coulter, D. L. (1990). Home is the place: quality of life for young children with developmental disabilities. In R. L. Schalock (Ed.), *Quality of Life: Perspectives and Issues,* pp. 61-69. Washington, D.C.: American Association of Mental Retardation.

Cox, D. J. and Gonder-Frederick, L. (1992). Major developments in behavioral diabetes research. *Journal of Consulting and Clinical Psychology,* 60(4): 628-638.

Crews, J. E. (1991). Strategic planning and independent living for elders who are blind. *Journal of Visual Impairment and Blindness,* 52-57.

Crutcher, D. M. (1990). Quality of life vs. quality of life judgments: a parent's perspective. In R. L. Schalock (Ed.), *Quality of Life: Perspectives and Issues,* pp. 17-26. Washington, D.C.: American Association of Mental Retardation.

Cummins, R. A. (1991). The Comprehensive Quality of Life Scale — Intellectual Disability: an instrument under development. *Australia and New Zealand Journal of Developmental Disabilities,* 17(2): 259-264.

Dagan, D., Jones, J., and Ruddick, L. (1994). The psychometric properties of a scale for assessing the quality of life of people with learning disabilities in residential care. *British Journal of Developmental Disabilities,* XL(79): 98-103.

Day, H. and Jankey, S. G. (1996). Lessons from the literature: toward a holistic model of quality of life. In R. Renwick, I. Brown, and M. Nagler (Eds.), *Quality of Life in Health Promotion and Rehabilitation,* pp. 39-50. Thousand Oaks, CA: Sage Publications.

Dellario, D. J. and Anthony, W. A. (1981). On the relative effectiveness of institutional and alternative placement for the psychiatrically disabled. *Journal of Social Issues,* 37(3): 21-33.

Edbril, S. D. and Rieker, P. P. (1989). The impact of testicular cancer on the work lives of survivors. *Journal of Psychosocial Oncology,* 7(3): 17-29.

Edgerton, R. B. (1990). Quality of life from a longitudinal research perspective. In R. L. Schalock (Ed.), *Quality of Life: Perspectives and Issues,* pp. 149-160. Washington, D.C.: American Association of Mental Retardation.

Elizur, D. and Shye, S. (1990). Quality of work life and its relation to quality of life. *Applied Psychology: An International Review,* 39(3): 275-291.

Endicott, J., Nee, J., Harrison, W., and Blumenthal, R. (1993). Quality of Life Enjoyment and Satisfaction Questionnaire: a new measure. *Psychopharmacology Bulletin,* 29: 321-326.

Ensminger, M. E. (1995). Welfare and psychological distress: a longitudinal study of African American urban mothers. *Journal of Health and Social Behavior,* 36: 346-359.

Evans, R. L., Dingus, C. M., and Haselkorn, J. K. (1993). Living with a disability: a synthesis and critique of the literature on quality of life, 1985–1989. *Psychological Reports,* 72: 771-777.

Fabian, E. S. (1990). Quality of life: a review of theory and practice implications for individuals with long-term mental illness. *Rehabilitation Psychology,* 35(3): 161-170.

Fabian, E. S. (1991). Using quality of life indicators in rehabilitation program evaluation. *Rehabilitation Counseling Bulletin,* 34(4): 345-356.

Fabian, E. S. (1992). Supported employment and quality of life: Does a job make a difference? *Rehabilitation Counseling Bulletin,* 36(2): 85-87.

Fabian, E. S. (1995). Quality of life. In A. E. Dell Orto and R. P. Martinelli, (Eds.), *Encylopedia of Disability and Rehabilitation*, pp. 607-609. New York: Macmillan.

Fava, G. A. (1990). Methodological and conceptual issues in research on quality of life. *Psychotherapy and Psychosomatics,* 54: 70-76.

Felce, D. and Perry, J. (1996). Exploring current concepts of quality of life. In R. Renwick, I. Brown, and M. Nagler (Eds.), *Quality of Life in Health Promotion and Rehabilitation,* pp. 51-62. Thousand Oaks, CA: Sage Publications.

Ferrans, C. E., Cohen, F. L., and Smith, K. M. (1992). The quality of life of persons with narcolepsy. Psychosocial aspects of narcolepsy, *Loss, Grief, and Care,* 5(3-4): 23-32.

Ferrans, C. and Powers, M. (1992). Psychometric assessment of the Quality of Life Index. *Research in Nursing and Health,* 15: 111-119.

Ferrel, B., Grant, M., Padilla, G., Vemuri, S., and Rhiner, M. (1991). The experience of pain and perceptions of the quality of life: validation of a conceptual model. *Hospice Journal,* 7(3): 9-22.

Fields, M. W. and Thacker, J. W. (1992). Influence of quality of work life on company and union commitment. *Academy of Management Journal,* 35(2): 439-450.

Fine, A. H. (1996). Leisure, living, and quality of life. In R. Renwick, I. Brown, and M. Nagler (Eds.), *Quality of Life in Health Promotion and Rehabilitation,* pp. 342-356. Thousand Oaks, CA: Sage Publications.

Fitzsimmons, B. and Bunting, L. K. (1997). Parkinson's Disease: quality of life issues. http://www.cnsonline.org/www/archive/parkins/park.07.txt.

Flanagan, J. C. (1978). A research approach to improving our quality of life. *American Psychologist,* (33)(2): 138-147.

Frisch, M. B., Cornell, J., and Villanueva. (1992). Clinical validation of the Quality of Life Inventory: a measure of life satisfaction for use in treatment planning and outcome assessment. *Psychological Assessment,* 4(1): 92-101.

Ganz, P. A., Bernahrd, J., and Hurny, C. (1991). Quality of life and psychosocial oncology research in Europe: state of the Art. *Journal of Psychosocial Oncology,* 9(1): 1-22.

Ganz, P. A., Day, R., Ware, J. E., Redmond, C. and Fisher, B. (1995). Base-line quality-of-life assessment in national surgical adjuvant breast and bowel project cancer. *Journal of the National Cancer Institute,* 87(18): 1372-1382.

Gater, R. A., Kind, P., and Gudex, C. (1995). Quality of life in liaison psychiatry: a comparison of patient and clinician assessment. *British Journal of Psychiatry,* 166: 515-520.

Gelber, R.D., Cole, B.F., Gelber, S., and Goldhirsch, A. (1995). Comparing treatments using quality-adjusted survival: the Q-TWIST method. *American Statistics,* 49: 161-169.

Gerber, G. J., Coleman, G. E., Johnston, L., and Lafave, H. G. (1994). Quality of life of people with psychiatric disabilities 1 and 3 years after discharge from hospital. *Quality of Life Research,* 3: 379-383.

George, L. K. and Bearon, L. B. (1980). *Quality of Life in Older Persons: Meaning and Measurement.* New York: Human Sciences Press.

Gilbar, O. (1991). The quality of life of cancer patients who refuse chemotherapy. *Social Science Medicine,* 32(12): 1337-1340.

Gitter, A. G. and Mostofsky, D. I. (1973). The social indicator: an index of the quality of life. *Social-Biology,* 20(3): 289-297.

Goode, D. A. (1990). Thinking about and discussing quality of life. In R. L. Schalock (Ed.), *Quality of Life: Perspectives and Issues,* pp. 41-57. Washington, D.C.: American Association of Mental Retardation.

Goodwin, D. A. J., Boggs, S. R., and Graham-Poole, J. (1994). Development and validation of the pediatric oncology quality of life scale. *Psychological Assessment,* 6(4): 321-328.

Gottschalk, L. A. and Lolas, F. (1992). The measurement of quality of life through the content analysis of verbal behavior. *Psychotherapy and Psychosomatics,* 58: 69-78.

Granger, C. V., Divan, N., and Fiedler, R.C. (1995). Functional assessment scales: a study of persons after traumatic brain injury. *American Journal of Physical Medicine and Rehabilitation*, 74(2), 107-113.

Gutheil, I. A. (1991). The physical environment and quality of life in residential facilities for frail elders. *Adult Residential Care Journal,* 52: 131-145.

Guyatt, G. H. (1994). Measurement of health-related quality of life in heart failure. *Irish Journal of Psychology,* 15(1): 148-163.

Hadorn, D. C. and Hays, R. D. (1991). Multitrait-multimethod analysis of health-related quality of life measures. *Medical Care,* 29(9): 829-840.

Halpern, A. S. (1994). Quality of life for students with disabilities in transition from school to adulthood. *Social Indicators Research,* 33: 193-236.

Hanestad, B. R. (1990). Errors of measurement affecting the reliability and validity of data acquired from self-assessed quality of life. *Scandinavian Journal of Caring Science,* 4(1): 29-34.

Hanestad, B. R. (1989). Insulin-dependent diabetes mellitus and quality of life: a theoretical analysis. *Scandanvian Journal of Caring,* 3(3): 123-128.

Hardison, N. M. and Vanier, D. J. (1976). Environment and quality of life: attitudinal measurement and analysis. *Psychological Reports,* 39: 959-965.

Harper, J. (1990). Recovery for the relationship: a treatment model for couples with a recovering chemically dependent partner. *Alcoholism Treatment Quarterly,* 7(2): 1-21.

Hays, R. D., Kallich, J. D., Mapes, D. L., Coons, S. J., and Carter, W. B. (1994). Development of the Kidney Disease Quality of Life (KDQOL) Instrument. *Quality of Life Research,* 3: 329-338.

Hays, R. D. and Shapiro, M. F. (1992). An overview of generic health-related quality of life measures for HIV research. *Quality of Life Research,* 1: 91-97.

Hays, R. D., Vickrey, B. G., Hermann, B. P., Perrine, K., Cramer, J., Meador, K., Spritzer, K., and Devinsky, O. (1995). Agreement between self reports and proxy reports of quality of life in epilepsy patients. *Quality of Life Research,* 4: 159-168.

Heady, B, Veenhoven, R., and Wearing, A. (1991). Top-down vs. bottom-up theories of subjective well-being. *Social Indicators Research,* 24: 81-100.

Heal, L. W. and Sigelman, C. K. (1990). Methodological issues in measuring quality of life of individuals with mental retardation. In R. L. Schalock (Ed.), *Quality of Life: Perspectives and Issues,* pp. 161-176. Washington, D.C.: American Association of Mental Retardation.

Helmstaedter, C. and Elger, C. E. (1994). Cognitive-behavioral aspects of quality of life in presurgical patients with epilepsy. *Journal of Epilepsy,* 7: 220-231.

Hennessy, C. H., Moriarty, D. G., Zack, M. M., Scherr, P. A., and Brackbill, R. (1994). Measuring health-related quality of life for public health surveillance. *Public Health Reports,* 106(5): 665-672.

Herbert, J. T. (1996). Use of of adventure-based counseling programs for persons with disabilities. *Journal of Rehabilitation,* 3-9.

Hermann, B. P. (1995). The evolution of health-related quality of life assessment in epilepsy. *Quality of Life Research,* 4: 87-100.

Hickey, T. and Stilwell, D. L. (1992). Chronic illness and aging: A personal-contextual model of age-related changes in health status. *Educational Gerontology,* 18: 1-15.

House, P. W., Livingston, R. C., and Swinburn, C. D. (1973). Monitoring mankind: the search for quality. *Behavioral Science,* 20: 57-67.

Howard, K. and Rockwood, K. (1995). Quality of life in Alzheimer's disease. *Dementia,* 6: 113-116.

Hughes, B. (1993). A model for the comprehensive assessment of older people and their carers. *British Journal of Social Work,* 23: 345-364.

Hughes, C., Hwang, B., Kim, J. H., Eisenman, L. T., and Killian, D. J. (1995). Quality of life in applied research: a review and analysis of empirical measures. *American Journal on Mental Retardation,* 99(6): 623-641.

Hume, A. L. (1989). Applying quality of life data in practice: considerations for antihypertensive therapy. *The Journal of Family Practice,* 28(4): 403-411.

Huxley, P. and Warner, R. (1992). Case management, quality of life, and satisfaction with services of long-term psychiatric patients. *Hospital and Community Psychiatry,* 43(8): 799-802.

Hyer, L. Matteson, M.A., and Siegler, I. C. (1982). Locus of control and long-term care. *Journal of Applied Gerontology,* 1: 147-160.

Hyland, M. E. (1992). A reformation of quality of life for medial science. *Quality of Life Research,* 1: 267-272.

Hyland, M. E., Bott, J., Singh, S., and Kenyon, C. A. P. (1994). Domains, constructs and the development of the breathing problems questionnaire. *Quality of Life Research,* 3: 245-256.

Hyland, M. E., Finnis, S., and Irvine, S. H. (1991). A scale for assessing quality of life in adult asthma sufferers. *Journal of Psychosomatic Research,* 35(2): 99-110.

Hyland, M. E., Kenyon, C. A. P., and Jacobs, P. A. (1994). Sensitivity of quality of life domains and constructs to longitudinal change in a clinical trial comparing salmeterol with placebo in asthmatics. *Quality of Life Research,* 3: 121-126.

Idler, E. I. and Benyamini, Y. (1997). Self-rated health and mortality: a review of twenty-seven community studies. *Journal of Health and Social Behavior*, 38: 21-37.

Inge, K. J., Banks, P. D., Wehman, Hill, J. W., and Shafer, M. S. (1988). Quality of life for individuals who are labeled mentally retarded: evaluating competitive employment versus sheltered workshop employment. *Education and Training in Mental Retardation*, 97-104.

Jacoby, J. (1990). My sister Angie: a sibling's perspective. In R. L. Schalock (Ed.), *Quality of Life: Perspectives and Issues*, pp. 23-26. Washington, D.C.: American Association of Mental Retardation.

Jaeschke, R., Guyatt, G., Cook, S., Harper, S., and Gerstein, H. C. (1994). Spectrum of quality of life impairment in hypothyroidism. *Quality of Life Research*, 3: 323-327.

Janicki, M. P. (1990). Growing old with dignity: on quality of life for older persons with a lifelong disability. In R. L. Schalock (Ed.), *Quality of Life: Perspectives and Issues*, pp. 115-125. Washington, D.C.: American Association of Mental Retardation.

Jenkins, C. D. (1992). Assessment of outcomes of health intervention. *Social Science Medicine*, 35(4): 367-375.

Johnson, D. J., Casey, L., and Noriega, B. (1994). A pilot study of patient quality of life during radiation therapy treatment. *Quality of Life Research*, 3: 267-272.

Kaplan, R. M. (1991). Health-related quality of life in patient decision making. *Journal of Social Issues*, 47(4): 69-90.

Kaplan, R. M. (1994). Using quality of life information to set priorities in health policy. *Social Indicators Research*, 33: 121-163.

Kaplan, R. M., Anderson, J. P., and Wingard, D. L. (1991). Gender differences in health-related quality of life. *Health Psychology*, 10(2): 86-93.

Kaplan, S. P. (1993). Five-year tracking of psychosocial changes in people with severe traumatic brain injury. *Rehabilitation Counseling Bulletin*, 36(3): 151-159.

Katz, J. N., Larson, M. G., Phillips, C. B., Fossel, A. H., and Liang, M. H. (1992). *Medical Care*, 30(10): 917-925.

Keith, K. D. (1990). Quality of life: issues in community integration. In R. L. Schalock (Ed.), *Quality of Life: Perspectives and Issues*, pp. 93-100. Washington, D.C.: American Association of Mental Retardation.

Kelley, D. M. S. and Lambert, S. S. (1992). Family support in rehabilitation: a review of the research, 1980–1990. *Rehabilitation Counseling Bulletin*, 36(2): 98-111.

Kim, E. (1997). Methodological Issues in the Study of Functional Performance in Patients with COPD. Unpublished manuscript. Chicago: Department of Medical-Surgical Nursing, University of Illinois.

Kloseck, M., Crilly, R. G., Ellis, G. D., and Lammers, E. (1996). Leisure Competence Measure: development and reliability testing of a scale to measure functional outcomes in therapeutic recreation. *Therapeutic Recreation Journal*, 13-26.

Kober, B., Kuchler, T., Broelsch, C., Kremer, B., and Henne-Bruns, D. (1990). A psychological support concept and quality of life research in a liver transplantation program: an interdisciplinary multicenter study. *Psychotherapy and Psychosomatics*, 54: 117-131.

Koch, U. and Muthny, F. A. (1990). Quality of life in patients with end-stage renal disease in relation to the method of treatment. *Psychotherapy and Psychosomatics*, 54: 161-171.

Kozleski, E. B. and Sands, D. J. (1992). The yardstick of social validity: evaluating quality of life as perceived by adults without disabilities. *Education and Training in Mental Retardation*, 119-131.

Krause, J. S. (1996). Prediction of mortality after spinal cord injury: a 20-year prospective study. *Rehabilitation R & D Progress Reports*, 34: 298-299.

Kristiansen, C. M. (1989). Gender differences in the meaning of "health." *Social Behavior*, 4: 185-188.

Kunsebeck, H. W., Korber, J., and Freyberger, H. (1990). Quality of life in patients with inflammatory bowel disease, *Psychotherapy and Psychosomatics*, 54: 110-116.

Kurz, K. M. and Prather, C. J. (1995). *Improving the quality of life of girls*. New York: United Nations Children's Fund Programme Publications.

Labonte, R. (1996). Measurement and practice: power issues in quality of life, health promotion, and empowerment. In R. Renwick, I. Brown, and M. Nagler (Eds.), *Quality of Life in Health Promotion and Rehabilitation*, pp. 132-145. Thousand Oaks, CA: Sage Publications.

Lance, C. E., Lautenschlager, G. J., and Sloan, C. E. (1989). A comparison between bottom-up, top-down, and bidirectional models of relationships between global and life facet satisfaction. *Journal of Personality*, 57(3): 601-624.

Langfitt, J. T. (1995). Comparison of the psychometric characteristics of three quality of life measures in intractable epilepsy. *Quality of Life Research,* 4: 101-114.

Larson, J. S. (1991). Two scales for measuring international health status. *Evaluation and the Health Professions,* 14(4): 422-437.

Latten, J. J. (1989). Life-course and satisfaction, equal for every-one? *Social Indicators Research,* 21: 599-610.

Lehman, A. F., Reed, S. K., and Possidente, S. M. (1982). Priorities for long-term care: Comments from board-and-care residents. *Psychiatric Quarterly,* 54(3): 181-189.

Lennon, M. C. (1994). Women, work, and well-being: the importance of work conditions. *Journal of Health and Social Behavior,* 35: 235-247.

Lennox, R. D. (1994). Measurement error issues in substance abuse services research: lessons from structural equation modeling and psychometric theory. *Evaluation and Program Planning,* 17(4): 399-407.

Lerner, D. J., Levin, S., Malspeis, S., and D'Agostino, R. B. (1994). Job strain and health-related quality of life in a national sample. *American Journal of Public Health,* 84(10): 1580-1585.

Limacher, B., Dahler, E., Bosch, J., and Egli, N. (1991). Color me multi-colored: a note on problems in clinical research methodology. *Family Systems Medicine,* 9(1): 65-68.

Lindley, C. M., Hirsch, J. D., O'Neill, C. V., Tansau, M. C., Gilbert, C. S., and Osterhaus, J. T. (1992). Quality of life consequences of chemotherapy-induced emesis. *Quality of Life Research,* 1: 331-340.

Logue, B. J. (1990). Race differences in long-term disability: middle-aged and older American Indians, Blacks and Whites in Oklahoma. *Social Science Journal,* 27(3): 253-272.

Logue, B. J. (1991). Taking charge: Death control as an emergent women's issue. *Women and Health,* 17(4): 97-121.

Loscocco, K. A. and Roschelle, A. R. (1991). Influences on the quality of work and nonwork life: two decades in review. *Journal of Vocational Behavior,* 39: 182-225.

Luckasson, R. (1990). A lawyer's perspective on quality of life. In R. L. Schalock (Ed.), *Quality of Life: Perspectives and Issues,* pp. 211-214. Washington, D.C.: American Association of Mental Retardation.

Lynch, R. T. and Gallagher-Lepak, S. (1996). Chronic renal failure: the impact of improved medical treatment options on rehabilitation. *Journal of Applied Rehabilitation Counseling,* 27(1): 7-12.

Lyons, R. F. (1993). Meaningful activity and disability: capitalizing upon the potential of outreach recreation networks in Canada. *Canadian Journal of Rehabilitation,* 6(4): 256-265.

Maas, A. (1992). A model for quality of life after laryngectomy. *Social Science Medicine,* 33(12): 1373-1377.

Malm, U., May, P. R. A., and Dencker, S. J. (1981). Evaluation of the quality of life of the schizophrenic outpatient: a checklist. *Schizophrenia Bulletin,* 7(3): 477-487.

Manz, C. C. and Grothe, R. (1991). Is the work force vanguard to the 21st century a quality of work life deficient-prone generation? *Journal of Business Research,* 23: 67-82.

Martinez, C. (1990). A dream for myself. In R. L. Schalock (Ed.), *Quality of Life: Perspectives and Issues,* pp. 3-8. Washington, D.C.: American Association of Mental Retardation.

Mason, D. G. (1996). Quality of life for deaf and hard-of-hearing people. In R. Renwick, I. Brown, and M. Nagler (Eds.), *Quality of Life in Health Promotion and Rehabilitation,* pp. 237-252. Thousand Oaks, CA: Sage Publications.

Mathias, S. D., Fifer, S. K., and Patrick, D. L. (1994). Rapid translation of quality of life measures for international clinical trials: avoiding errors in the minimalist approach. *Quality of Life Research,* 3: 403-412.

Mayou, R. (1990). Quality of life in cardiovascular disease. *Psychotherapy and Psychosomatics,* 54: 99-109.

McCall, P. L. (1991). Adolescent and elderly white male suicide trends: evidence of changing well-being? *Journal of Gerontology,* 46(1): 843-851.

McCauley, C. and Bremer, B. A. (1991). Subjective quality of life measures for evaluating medical intervention. *Evaluation and the Health Professions,* 14(4): 371-387.

McCoy, M. L. (1994). Career women's leisure: challenges and realities. In C. W. Konek and S. L. Kitch (Eds.), *Women and Careers: Issues and Challenges,* pp. 173-286. Thousand Oaks, CA: Sage Publications.

McGee, H. M., O'Boyle, C. A., Hickey, A., O'Malley, K., and Joyce, C. R. B. (1991). Assessing the quality of life of the individual: the SEIQoL with a healthy and a gastroenterology unit population. *Psychological Medicine,* 21: 749-759.

McGuire, B. E., Choon, G., and Akuffo, E. (1991). Community living for elderly people with an intellectual disability: a pilot study. *Australia and New Zealand Journal of Developmental Disabilities,* 17(1): 25-33.

McLanahan, S. and Adams, J. (1989). The effects of children on adults' psychological well-being: 1957–1976. *Social Forces,* 68(1): 124-146.

McPhail, E. R. (1996). A parent's perspective: quality of life in families with a member with disabilities. In R. Renwick, I. Brown, and M. Nagler (Eds.), *Quality of Life in Health Promotion and Rehabilitation,* pp. 279-289. Thousand Oaks, CA: Sage Publications.

Mehrabian, A. and Ross, M. (1979). Illness, accidents, and alcohol use as functions of the arousing quality and pleasantness of life changes. *Psychological Reports,* 45: 31-43.

Metcalf, R. (1992). Loss of enjoyment, rehabilitation and hedonic damages. *Journal of Forensic Economics,* 5(3): 261-264.

Moller, M. D. and Murphy, M. F. (1997). The Three R's Rehabilitation Program: a prevention approach for the management of relapse symptoms associated with psychiatric diagnosis. *Psychiatric Rehabilitation Journal,* 20(3): 42-48.

Moos, R. H. and Moos, B. S. (1983). Adaptation and the quality of life in work and family settings. *Journal of Consulting Psychology,* 11: 158-170.

Morris, M. H. and Lewis, P. S. (1991). Entrepreneurship as a significant factor in societal quality of life. *Journal of Business Research,* 23: 21-36.

Moss, E. (1980). Geriatric rehabilitation: Group conseling vs. Recreational programming for older workshop clients. *Journal of Applied Rehabilitation Counseling,* 11(3): 145-148.

Mowry, R. L. (1988). Quality of life indicators for deaf and hard-of-hearing former VR clients. *Journal of Rehabilitation of the Deaf,* 21(3): 1-7.

Mugenda, O. M., Hira, T. K., and Fanslow, A. M. (1990). Assessing the causal relationship among communication, money management practices, satisfaction with financial status, and satisfaction with quality of life. *Lifestyles: Family and Economic Issues,* 11(4): 343-360.

Mulhern, R. K., Fairclough, D. L., Friedman, A. G., and Leigh, L. D. (1990). Play Performance Scale as an index of quality of life of children with cancer. *Psychological Assessment,* 2(2): 149-155.

Munich, R. L. and Lang, E. (1993). The boundaries of psychiatric rehabilitation. *Hospital and Community Psychiatry,* 44(7): 661-665.

Murrell, S. A. and Norris, F. H. (1983). Quality of life as the criterion for need assessment and community psychology. *Journal of Consulting Psychology,* 11: 88-97.

Muthny, F. A., Koch, U., and Stump, S. (1990). Quality of life in oncology patients. *Psychotherapy and Psychosomatics,* 54: 145-160.

Nagler, M. (1996). Quality of life of people with disabilities who have experienced sexual abuse. In R. Renwick, I. Brown, and M. Nagler (Eds.), *Quality of Life in Health Promotion and Rehabilitation,* pp. 190-203. Thousand Oaks, CA: Sage Publications.

Nation, J. M., Benshoff, J. J., and Malkin, M. M. (1996). Therapeutic recreation programs for adolescents in substance abuse treatment facilities. *Journal of Rehabilitation,* 10-16.

National Association of Rehabilitation Facilities. (1988). Quality of life. *NARF Monograph Series.*

National Eye Institute. (1997). *The Collaborative Initial Glaucoma Treatment Study.* Ann Arbor, MI: University of Michigan, National Study Coordinator.

National Institute on Disability and Rehabilitation Research. (1988). Quality-of-life research in rehabilitation. *Rehab Brief,* XI(1).

National Institutes of Health. (1990). Surgery for Epilepsy. *NIH Consensus Statement Online,* 8(2): 1-20.

Nayfield, S. G., Ganz, P. A., Moinpour, C. M., Cella, D. F., and Hailey, B. J. (1992). Report from a National Cancer Institute (U.S.A.) workshop on quality of life assessment in cancer clinical trials. *Quality of Life Research,* 1: 203-210.

Near, J. P., Rice, R. W. and Hunt, R. G. (1978). Work and extra-work correlates of life and job satisfaction. *Academy of Management Journal,* 21(2): 248-264.

Newfield, J. W. and Duet, C. P. (1976). Implications of quality of life for goal setting tasks of the curriculum workers. *Education,* 97(2): 135.

Nichols, R. (1997). Managing cancer pain in managed care. *The Case Manager,* 49-53.

Nosek, M. A., Howland, C.A., Young, M. E., Georgiou, D., Rintala, D. H., Foley, C. C., Bennett, J. L., and Smith, Q. (1994). Wellness models and sexuality among women with physical disabilities. *Journal of Applied Rehabilitation Counseling,* 25(1): 50-57.

O'Keefe, B. M. (1996). Communication disorders: just minor inconveniences? In R. Renwick, I. Brown, and M. Nagler (Eds.), *Quality of Life in Health Promotion and Rehabilitation,* pp. 219-236. Thousand Oaks, CA: Sage Publications.

Oliver, N., Holloway, F., and Carson, J. (1995). Deconstructing quality of life. *Journal of Mental Health,* 4: 1-4.

O'Rear, G., Bark, L., and Hutchinson, D. S. (1996). The promotion of wellness among people with psychiatric disabilities in community rehabilitation and treatment. *Psychiatric Rehabilitation Journal,* 20(2): 82-84.

Ory, M. O. and Cox, D. M. (1994). Forging ahead: linking health and behavior to improve quality of life in older people. *Social Indicators Research,* 33: 89-120.

Osberg, J. S., McGinnis, G. E., DeJong, G., and Seward, M. L. (1987). Life satisfaction and quality of life among disabled elderly adults. *Journal of Gerontology,* 42(2): 228-230.

Osoba, D. (1992). The quality of life committee of the clinical trials groups of the National Cancer Institute of Canada: organization and functions. *Quality of Life Research,* 1: 211-218.

Ouellette-Kuntz, H. (1990). A pilot study in the use of the quality of life interview schedule. *Social Indicators Research,* 23: 283-298.

Ouellette-Kuntz, H. and McCreary, B. (1996). Quality of life assessment for persons with severe developmental disabilities. In R. Renwick, I. Brown, and M. Nagler (Eds.), *Quality of Life in Health Promotion and Rehabilitation,* pp. 268-278. Thousand Oaks, CA: Sage Publications.

Parmenter, T. R. (1996). The use of quality of life as a construct for social and health policy development. In R. Renwick, I. Brown, and M. Nagler (Eds.), *Quality of Life in Health Promotion and Rehabilitation,* pp. 89-103. Thousand Oaks, CA: Sage Publications.

Perlman, S. G., Connell, K. J., Clark, A., Robinson, M.S., Conlon, P., Gecht, M., Caldron, P. and Sinacore, J. M. (1990). Dance-based aerobic exercise of rheumatoid arthritis. *Arthritis Care and Research,* 3(1): 29-35.

Perry, J. and Felce, D. (1995). Objective assessments of quality of life: how much do they agree with each other? *Journal of Community and Applied Social Psychology,* 5: 1-19.

Pugliesi, K. (1995). Work and well-being: gender differences in the psychological consequences of employment. *Journal of Health and Social Behavior,* 36: 57-71.

Pumpian, I. R., Szeto, A. Y J., and Sax, C. L. (1996). Special projects and demonstration: applications of technology to enhance quality of life — A community model. *Rehabilitation R & D Progress Reports,* 34: 138-139.

Raeburn, J. M. and Rootman, I. (1996). Quality of life and health promotion. In R. Renwick, I. Brown, and M. Nagler (Eds.), *Quality of Life in Health Promotion and Rehabilitation,* pp. 14-25. Thousand Oaks, CA: Sage Publications.

Raphael, D. (1996a). Defining quality of life: eleven debates concerning its measurement. In R. Renwick, I. Brown, and M. Nagler (Eds.), *Quality of Life in Health Promotion and Rehabilitation,* pp. 146-170. Thousand Oaks, CA: Sage Publications.

Raphael, D. (1996b) . Quality of life and adolescent health. In R. Renwick, I. Brown, and M. Nagler (Eds.), *Quality of Life in Health Promotion and Rehabilitation,* pp. 307-326. Thousand Oaks, CA: Sage Publications.

Raphael, D. (1996c) . Quality of life for older adults: toward the optimization of the aging process. In R. Renwick, I. Brown, and M. Nagler (Eds.), *Quality of Life in Health Promotion and Rehabilitation,* pp. 290-306. Thousand Oaks, CA: Sage Publications.

Recchia, G., de Carli, G., Parise, G., Zerbini, O., Fostini, R., Catelloe, C., and Rizzini, P. (1991). Quality of life: a new approach to the assessment of the pharmacological treatment in the elderly patient. *Archives of Gerontology and Geriatrics; 1991 Supplement,* 2: 33-37.

Reich, J. W. and Zautra, A. J. (1983). Demands and desires in daily life: some influences on well-being. *American Journal of Community Psychology,* 11(1): 41-59.

Renwick, R. and Brown, I. (1996). The Centre for Health Promotion's conceptual approach to quality of life: being, belonging, and becoming. In R. Renwick, I. Brown, and M. Nagler (Eds.), *Quality of Life in Health Promotion and Rehabilitation,* pp. 75-86. Thousand Oaks, CA: Sage Publications.

Renwick, R., Brown, I, Rootman, I., and Nagler, M. (1996). Conceptualization, research, and application: future directions. In R. Renwick, I. Brown, and M. Nagler (Eds.), *Quality of Life in Health Promotion and Rehabilitation,* pp. 357-367. Thousand Oaks, CA: Sage Publications.

Renwick, R. and Friefeld, S. (1996). Quality of life and rehabilitation. In R. Renwick, I. Brown, and M. Nagler (Eds.), *Quality of Life in Health Promotion and Rehabilitation,* pp. 26-38. Thousand Oaks, CA: Sage Publications.

Renwick, R. and Friedland, J. (1996). Quality of life experienced by a sample of adults with HIV. In R. Renwick, I. Brown, and M. Nagler (Eds.), *Quality of Life in Health Promotion and Rehabilitation,* pp. 171-189. Thousand Oaks, CA: Sage Publications.

Rettig, K. D., Danes, S. M., and Bauer, J. W. (1991). Family life quality: theory and assessment in economically stressed farm families. *Social Indicators Research,* 24: 269-299.

Rhoads, D. L. and Raymond, J. S. (1981). Quality of life and the competent community. *American Journal of Community Psychology,* 9(3): 293-301.

Rintala, D. H., Hart, K. A., and Fuhrer, M. J. (1996). Perceived stress in individuals with spinal cord injuries. In D. M. Krotoski, M. A. Nosek, and M. A. Turk (Eds.), *Women with Physical Disabilities: Achieving and Maintaining Health and Well-Being,* pp. 223-242. Baltimore: Paul H. Brookes Publishing.

Rioux, M. H. (1996). Overcoming the social construction of inequality as a prerequisite to quality of life. In R. Renwick, I. Brown, and M. Nagler (Eds.), *Quality of Life in Health Promotion and Rehabilitation,* pp. 119-131. Thousand Oaks, CA: Sage Publications.

Rodin, G. (1990). Quality of life in adults with insulin-dependent diabetes mellitus. *Psychotherapy and Psychosomatics,* 54: 132-139.

Roessler, R. T. (1990). A quality of life perspective on rehabilitation counseling. *Rehabilitation Counseling Bulletin,* 34(2): 82-91.

Roller, S. (1996). Health promotion for people with chronic neuromuscular disabilities. In D. M. Krotoski, M. A. Nosek, and M. A. Turk (Eds.), *Women with Physical Disabilities: Achieving and Maintaining Health and Well-Being,* pp. 391-401. Baltimore: Paul H. Brookes.

Romney, D. M., Jenkins, C. D., and Bynner, J. M. (1992). A structural analysis of health-related quality of life dimensions. *Human Relations,* 45(2): 165-176.

Rosen, M., Simon, E. W., and McKinsey, L. (1995). Subjective measure of quality of life. *Mental Retardation,* 33(1): 31-34.

Rosenfeld, S. (1992). Factors contributing to the subjective quality of life of the chronic mentally ill. *Journal of Health and Social Behavior,* 33: 299-315.

Roxburgh, S. (1996). Gender differences in work and well-being: Effects of exposure and vulnerability. *Journal of Health and Social Behavior,* 37: 265-277.

Ruchlin, H. S. and Morris, J. N. (1991). Impact of work on the quality of life of community-residing young elderly. *American Journal of Public Health,* 81(4): 498-500.

Ruffing-Rahal, M. A. (1991). Initial psychometric evaluation of a qualitative evaluation well-being measure: the Integration Inventory. *Health Values,* 15(2): 10-20.

Sands, D. J. and Kozleski, E. B. (1994). Quality of life differences between adults with and without disabilities. *Education and Training in Mental Retardation and Developmental Disabilities,* 90-101.

Sartorius, N. (1995). Rehabilitation and quality of Life. *International Journal of Mental Health,* 24(1): 7-13.

Satcher, J. (1993). Improving the quality of work life for persons with learning disabilities: ADA rights and responsibilities. *Journal of Applied Rehabilitation Counseling,* 24(1): 16-18.

Schaafsma, J. and Osoba, D. (1994). The Karnofsky performance status scale re-examined: a cross-validation with the EORTC-C30. *Quality of Life Research,* 3: 413-424.

Schalock, R. L. (1996). Quality of life and quality assurance. In Renwick, I. Brown, and M. Nagler (Eds.), *Quality of Life in Health Promotion and Rehabilitation,* pp. 104-118. Thousand Oaks, CA: Sage Publications.

Schalock, R. L. (1990a). Attempts to conceptualize and measure quality of life. In R. L. Schalock, (Ed.), *Quality of Life: Perspectives and Issues,* pp. 141-148 . Washington, D.C.: American Association of Mental Retardation.

Schalock, R. L. (1990b). Where do we go from here? In R. L. Schalock, (Ed.), *Quality of Life: Perspectives and Issues,* pp. 235-240. Washington, D.C.: American Association of Mental Retardation.

Schalock, R. L. and Lilley, M. A. (1986). Placement from community-based mental retardation programs: how well do clients do after 8 to 10 years? *American Journal of Mental Deficiency,* 90(6): 669-676.

Scherer, M. J. (1990). Assistive device utilization and quality of life in adults with spinal cord injuries or cerebral palsy two years later. *Journal of Applied Rehabilitation Counseling,* 21(4): 36-44.

Schipper, H. (1990). Quality of life: principles of the clinical paradigm. *Journal of Psychosocial Oncology,* 8(2/3): 171-184.

Schover, L. R. (1991). The impact of breast cancer on sexuality, body image, and intimate relationships. *Cancer Journal for Clinicians,* 41: 112-120.

Schwartz, L. B., Devine, P. A., Schechter, C. B., and Bender, A. N. (1990). Impact of illness on lifestyle. *Loss, Grief, and Care*, 4(3-4): 3-21.

Scott, B. (1996). Testimony presented by Bruce Scott, Consumer Representative, on the behalf of the American Therapeutic Recreation Association to the House Appropriations Subcommittee on Labor, Health and Human Services, and Education.
http://cwis.unomaha.edu/%7Ebrasile/testimny.htm

Scuccimarra, D. J. and Speece, D. L. (1990). Employment outcomes and social integration of students with mild handicaps: the quality of life two years after high school. *Journal of Learning Disabilities,* 23(4): 213-219.

Select Committee on Aging, House of Representatives. (1989). *The Quality of Life for Older Women: Older Women Living Alone.* Washington, D.C.: U.S. Government Printing Office.

Shain, M. (1996). Work, employment, and mental health: Implications for quality of life. In R. Renwick, I. Brown, and M. Nagler (Eds.), *Quality of Life in Health Promotion and Rehabilitation,* pp. 327-341. Thousand Oaks, CA: Sage Publications.

Shank, J. W., Coyle, C. P., Boyd, R., and Kinney, W. B. (1996). A classification scheme for therapeutic recreation research grounded in the rehabilitative sciences. *Therapeutic Research Journal,* 178-196.

Sherman, E. and Schiffman, L. G. (1991). Quality-of-life (QOL) assessment of older consumers: a retrospective review. *Journal of Business and Psychology*, 6(1): 107-119.

Short, K. and Shea, M. (1995). Beyond poverty, extended measures of well-being: 1992. *Current Population Reports,* P70-SORV. Washington, D.C.: U.S. Dept. of Commerce, Economics and Statistics Administration.

Shye, S. (1989). Systemic life quality model. *Social Indicators Research,* 21: 343-378.

Siegel, C. and Brent, R. J. (1997). Quality-adjusted time project. *Center for the Study of Issues in Public Mental Health.*
< http://www.rfmh.org/sciphm/qat.htm >

Siegrist, J. and Junge, A. (1990). Measuring the social dimension of subjective health in chronic illness. *Psychotherapy and Psychosomatics*, 54: 90-98.

Sinnott-Oswald, M., Gliner, J. A., and Spencer, K. C. (1991). Supported and sheltered employment: quality of life issues among workers with disabilities. *Education and Training in Mental Retardation,* 388-397.

Slaughter, J. G., Lehman, A. F., and Myers, C. P. (1991). Quality of life of severely mentally ill adults in residential care facilities. *Adult Residential Care Journal*, 5(2): 97-111.

Sonino, N., Fava, G. A., Fallo, F., and Boscaro, M. (1990). Psychological distress and quality of life in endocrine disease. *Psychotherapy and Psychosomatics*, 54: 140-144.

Spreitzer, E. and Snyder, E. E. (1989). Sports involvement and quality of life dimensions. *Journal of Sport Behavior,* 12(1): 3-11.

Stark, J. A. and Goldsbury, R. (1990). Quality of life from childhood to adulthood. In R. L. Schalock, (Ed.), *Quality of Life: Perspectives and Issues,* pp. 71-92 . Washington, D.C.: American Association of Mental Retardation.

Stewart, A. L. and King, A. C. (1991). Evaluating the efficacy of physical activity for influencing quality-of-life outcomes in older adults. *Annals of Behavioral Medicine*, 13(3): 108-116.

Stillson, K., White, J., and Harris, E. F. (1986). Helping the helper: stress management for alcoholism treatment personnel. *Alcoholism Treatment Quarterly,* 3(3): 107-123.

Sullivan, G., Wells, K. B., and Leake, B. (1992). Clinical factors associated with better quality of life in a seriously mental ill population. *Hospital and Community Psychiatry,* 43(8): 794-798.

Tait, R. C., Chibnall, J. T., and Margolis, R. B. (1990). Pain extent: relations with psychological state, pain severity, pain history, and disability. *Pain,* 41: 295-301.

Taylor, S. J. and Bogdan, R. (1990). Quality of life and the individual's perspective. In R. L. Schalock (Ed.), *Quality of Life: Perspectives and Issues,* pp. 27-40. Washington, D.C.: American Association of Mental Retardation.

Taylor, T. T. (1989). Commentary. *The Journal of Family Practice,* 28(4): 407-411.

Tengs, T. O. (1996). An evaluation of Oregon's Medicaid rationing algorithms. *Health Economics*, 5: 171-181.

Terman, S. A. (1995). Emotional damages due to wrongful death — What are they worth? *Behavioral Sciences and the Law,* 11: 43-59.

Tigges, K. N. (1993). Quality of life: reality or rhetoric? *Loss, Grief, and Care,* 7(1-2): 157-167.

Till, J. E., Sutherland, H. J., and Meslin, E. M. (1992). Is there a role for preference assessments in research on quality of life in oncology? *Quality of Life Research*, 1: 31-40.

Tsevat, J., Goldman, L., Lamas, G. A., Pfeffer, M. A., Chapin, C.C., Connors, K. F., and Lee, T. H. (1991). Functional status vs. utilities in survivors of myocardial infarction. *Medical Care*, 29(11): 1153-1159.

Tuchler, H., Hofmann, S., Bernhart, M., Bruglatelli, M., Chrobak, L., Franke, A., Herold, M., Holowiechki, J., Ihle, R., Jaksic, B., Krc, I., Munteanue, N., Pawlicki, M., Sakalova, A., Schranz, V., Wolf, H., and Lutz, D. (1992). A short multilingual quality of life questionnaire — practicability, reliability, and interlingual homogeneity. *Quality of Life Research*, 1: 107-117.

Turk, M. A. (1996). The impact of disability on fitness in women: musculoskeletal issues. In D. M. Krotoski, M. A. Nosek, and M. A. Turk (Eds.). *Women with Physical Disabilities: Achieving and Maintaining Health and Well-Being,* pp. 391-401. Baltimore: Paul H. Brookes Publishing.

Vandergriff, D. V. and Chubon, R. A. (1994). Quality of life experienced by persons with mental retardation in various residential settings. *Journal of Rehabilitation*, 30-37.

Vaughan, C. E. and Hobson, S. (1990). Reducing late-life dependence resulting from declining visual acuity. *Journal of Visual Impairment and Blindness*, 370-372.

Verbrugge, L. M., Reoma, J. M., and Gruber-Baldini, A. L. (1994). Short-term dynamics of disability and well-being. *Journal of Health and Social Behavior,* 35: 97-117.

Vickrey, B. G., Hays, R. D., Graber, J., Rausch, R., Engel, J., and Brook, R. H. (1992). A health-related quality of life instrument for patients evaluated for epilepsy surgery. *Medical Care*, 30(4): 299-319.

Walker, D. E., Blankenship, V., Ditty, J. A., and Lynch, K. P. (1987). Prediction of recovery for closed-head-injured adults: an evaluation of the MMPI, the Adaptive Behavior Scale, and a Quality of Life Rating Scale. *Journal of Clinical Psychology,* 43(6): 699-707.

Wallston, B. S., Hoover-Dempsey, K. V., and Brissie, J. S. (1989). Gatekeeping transactions: Women's resource acquisition and mental health in the workplace. *Psychology of Women Quarterly*, 13: 205-222.

Ward, N. (1990). Reflections on my quality of life: then and now. In R. L. Schalock (Ed.), *Quality of Life: Perspectives and Issues,* pp. 9-16. Washington, D.C.: American Association of Mental Retardation.

Warren, L., Wrigley, M., Yoels, W. C., and Fine, P. R. (1996). Factors associated with life satisfaction among a sample of persons with neurotrauma. *Journal of Rehabilitation Research and Development,* 33(4): 404-408.

West, M., Kregel, J., and Banks, P. D. (1990). Fringe benefits available to supported employment participants. *Rehabilitation Counseling Bulletin,* 34(2): 126-138.

Whelton, C., Pawlick, J., and Cardamone, J. (1997). Involving families in psychosocial rehabilitation. *Psychiatric Rehabilitation Journal*, 20(3): 57-60.

Whitaker, S. (1989). Quality of life and people with a very profound handicap. *British Journal of Mental Subnormality,* 35(68): 3-7.

WHOQOL Group. (1994). Development of the WHOQOL: rationale and current status. *International Journal of Mental Health,* 23(3): 24-56.

Wilkinson, G., Williams, B., Krekorian, H., McLees, S., and Falloon, I. (1992). QALYs in mental health: A case study. *Psychological Medicine,* 22: 725-731.

Williams, R. L., Eyring, M., Gaynor, P., and Long, J. D. (1991). Development of Views of Life Scale. *Psychology and Health*, 5: 165-181.

Wolkenstein, A. S. and Butler, D. J. (1992). Quality of life among the elderly: self-perspectives of some healthy elderly. *Gerontology and Geriatrics Education,* 12(4): 59-68.

Wood, L. A. and Johnson, J. (1989). Life satisfaction among the rural elderly: what do the numbers mean? *Social Indicators Research,* 21: 379-408.

Wood, L. A., Matthews, A. M., and Norris, J. (1992). Gerontological research on the quality of life: the Guelph Satellite Method. *Social Indicators Research,* 27: 345-361.

Woodruff, S. I., and Conway, T. L. (1992). A longitudinal assessment of the impact of health/fitness and health behavior on perceived quality of life. *Perceptual and Motor Skills,* 75: 3-14.

Wozner, Y. (1982). Assessing the quality of internat life. *Human Relations*, 35(11): 1059-1072.

Young, L. D. and Barboriak, J. J. (1982). Reliability of a brief scale for assessment of coronary-prone behavior and standard measures of Type A behavior. *Perceptual and Motor Skills*, 55: 1039-1042.

Zautra, A. J. (1983). Social resources and the quality of life. *American Journal of Community Psychology,* 11(3): 275-289.

Zautra, A. J. and Reich, J. W. (1983). Life events and perceptions of life quality: Developments in a two-factor approach. *Journal of Community Psychology,* 11(2): 121-132.

Zweig, J. M., Barber, B. L., and Eccles, J. S. (1997). Sexual coercion and well-being in young adulthood: Comparisons by gender and college status. *Journal of Interpersonal Violence,* 12(2): 291-308.

APPENDIX 13
Elderly Persons and Quality of Life (QOL) Literature

Source	Population	Measures/Method	Domains
Crews (1991)	Older persons with blindness in rehabilitation	Model of strategic planning for fostering independent living	Independent living, consumer input, gains in function, family, services
George and Bearon (1980)	Older persons	A book reviewing QOL concepts, dimensions, and measures	*Subjective evaluations:* life satisfaction and self-esteem. *Objective measures:* general health, functional status, and socioeconomic status
Gutheil (1991)	Frail elderly in residential facilities	Review of literature regarding features of physical environment of residential settings for frail older persons	Adequate space, essential furnishings, clean and orderly surroundings, self-worth, satisfaction with life, territorial needs, privacy, meaning
Hickey and Stilwell (1992)	Aging and chronic illness issues	Essay on personal–conceptual model of age-related changes in health status	*Health perceptions:* aging illness beliefs; *Health status:* illness characteristics and comorbidities; *Health outlook:* assessment and treatment barriers and coping skills
Howard and Rockwood (1995)	Examined QOL instruments measuring Alzheimer's Disease and QOL	Reviewed and ranked measurement properties of QOL instruments; need for more validation of QOL instruments for Alzheimer's patients	Behavioral competence
Hughes (1993)	Older adults and their care-givers	Model of comprehensive assessment processes	Personal characteristics, attitude to self, health, functioning, environment, finance and material circumstance, recreation and activities, family, community relationships, and support network
Hyer, Matteson, and Siegler (1982)	Elderly in long-term care facilities	Use of a Locus of Control measure as a tool to facilitate quality of life	Age, education, sex, depression, and cognitive decline
Idler and Benyamini (1997)	Representative community samples	Review of 27 empirical community studies on self-rate health and mortality	Age and general health
Janicki (1990)	Older persons with a lifelong disability	Essay on aging with a lifelong disability and QOL issues	Physical, material, social, cognitive well-being
Kloseck, Crilly, Ellis, and Lammers (1996)	Geriatric rehabilitation population — 114 persons (47 male and 67 female)	Leisure Competence Measure, Life Satisfaction Index, Geriatric Depression Scale, Folstein Mini-Mental State Examination	Leisure awareness, skiils, attitude, social appropriateness, group interaction skills, social context, and community participation

APPENDIX 13 (continued)
Elderly Persons and Quality of Life (QOL) Literature

Source	Population	Measures/Method	Domains
Logue (1990)	Elderly long-term American Indian, Black, and White patients (over 45 years)	Data obtained from Public Use Microdata Samples for Oklahoma from 1980 decennial census and from a query on Public Transportation Disability	Social risk, aging, disability, economic status, health, race, gender, educational attainment, marital status, area of residence
McCall (1991)	Suicide rates in elderly and adolescent males	Used annual suicide rates for U.S. from *Annual Vital Health Statistics Report 1947–1987*	Impoverishment, family dissolution, and government expenditures
McGuire, Choon, and Akuffo (1991)	19 Elderly people with a developmental disability	Used a lifestyle questionnaire and the Social Training Achievement Record Profile through interviews	Activities of daily life, community-based activities, domestic tasks, areas of personal responsibility
Moss (1980)	69 Older clients from 2 similar rehabilitation workshops	Clients assigned to random groups to receive group counseling or social activities; Dean Alienation Scale, Havighhurst Life Satisfaction Index A, Sociometric Questionnaire	Life satisfaction, work productivity, alienation
Ory and Cox (1994)	Elderly people	Review of conceptual and methodological issues related to health promotion and disability for older people	Social and environmental factors, physical and mental health, health-related behaviors
Osberg, McGinnis, DeJong, and Seward (1987)	97 Elderly disabled adults	Path analysis model to assess QOL, Barthel Index, self-administered questionnaire	Income, age, marital status, functional capacity, independence
Raphael (1996)	12 Group meetings 120 seniors in the community	Development of Quality of Life Profile: Seniors Version	Physical being, psychological being, spiritual being, physical belonging, social belonging, community belonging, practical becoming, leisure becoming, growth becoming
Recchia, de Carli, Parise, Zerbini et al. (1991)	Elderly patients	Recommends QOL measures for elderly patients	Daily life functions, productivity and economic status, performance of social roles, intellectual capabilities, emotional stability, assessment of satisfaction with life, signs and symptoms of illness
Ruchlin and Morris (1991)	310 Young elderly between ages of 65–74.	Modified Spitzer Uniscale QL index	Marital Status, self-assessed health status, functional status, self-assessed financial status, and work status

APPENDIX 13 (continued)
Elderly Persons and Quality of Life (QOL) Literature

Source	Population	Measures/Method	Domains
Ruffing-Rahal (1991)	182 Community-dwelling elderly adults	The Integration Inventory, Philadelphia Geriatric Center Morale Scale, the Spiritual Well-Being Scale, and 4 measures of self-rated well being	Well-being, absence of loneliness, positive attitude toward aging, self-rated happiness, self-rated health, self-rated life satisfaction, absence of agitation, religious well-being
Select House Committee on Aging (1989)	Older women living alone	Chairman Roybal's report on hearings on QOL of older women living alone	Income, health, safety, housing
Sherman and Schiffman (1991)	Older consumers	Historical reflections on past 20 to 30 years of QOL status of older consumers	Socioeconomic indicators, health and longevity, housing and family living, gender differences, life satisfaction, cognitive age, leisure, occupation, health
Stewart and King (1991)	Older adults	Conceptual framework presented of QOL concepts for evaluating the efficacy of physical activity in older adults	Physical functioning, cognitive functioning, activities, bodily well-being, emotional well-being, self-concept, and global perceptions of health and life satisfaction
Vaughan and Hobson (1990)	179 Elderly adults using low-vision devices	Report on a project of 39 counties of rural Missouri to screen and provide low vision devices to elderly persons in need	Increase in independent living: read mail, write checks, thread needles, and read large print, better general functioning in everyday tasks and QOL
Wolkenstein and Butler (1992)	96 Healthy elderly (65 years and over)	Questionnaire, opinion surveys, group interviews	Outside world and others, inner world of the self, coping with loss, interaction with treating physician
Wood and Johnson (1989)	15 Elderly rural adults selected for qualitative study and 392 elderly rural adults in quantitative study	Used a life satisfaction questionnaire and analysis of qualitative data	Housing, health, self-esteem, friendship, and family
Wood, Matthews, and Norris (1992)	457 Women and men over 60 years in urban and rural Canada	Structured interviews and Guelph Satellite Method	Spouse, health, housing, and friendship

References

Crews, J. E. (1991). Strategic planning and independent living for elders who are blind. *Journal of Visual Impairment and Blindness*, 52-57.

George, L. K. and Bearon, L. B. (1980). *Quality of Life in Older Persons: Meaning and Measurement.* New York: Human Sciences Press.

Gutheil, I. A. (1991). The physical environment and quality of life in residential facilities for frail elders. *Adult Residential Care Journal,* 5(2): 131-145.

Hickey, T. and Stilwell, D. L. (1992). Chronic illness and aging: a personal-contextual model of age-related changes in health status. *Educational Gerontology,* 18: 1-15.

Howard, K. and Rockwood, K. (1995). Quality of life in Alzheimer's disease. *Dementia,* 6: 113-116.

Hughes, B. (1993). A model for comprehensive assessment of older people and their carers. *British Journal of Social Work,* 23: 345-365.

Hyer, L. Matteson, M.A., and Siegler, I. C. (1982). Locus of control and long-term care. *Journal of Applied Gerontology,* 1: 147-160.

Idler, E. I. and Benyamini, Y. (1997). Self-rated health and mortality: a review of twenty-seven community studies. *Journal of Health and Social Behavior,* 38: 21-37

Janicki, M. P. (1990). Growing old with dignity: on quality of life for older persons with a lifelong disability. In R. L. Schalock (Ed.), *Quality of Life: Perspectives and Issues,* pp. 115-125. Washington, D.C.: American Association of Mental Retardation.

Kloseck, M., Crilly, R. G., Ellis, G. D., and Lammers, E. (1996). Leisure Competence Measure: development and reliability testing of a scale to measure functional outcomes in therapeutic recreation. *Therapeutic Recreation Journal,* 13-26.

Logue, B. J. (1990). Race differences in long-term disability: middle-aged and older American Indians, Blacks and Whites in Oklahoma. *Social Science Journal,* 27(3): 253-272.

McCall, P. L. (1991). Adolescent and elderly white male suicide trends: evidence of changing well-being? *Journal of Gerontology,* 46(1): 843-851.

McGuire, B. E., Choon, G., and Akuffo, E. (1991). Community living for elderly people with an intellectual disability: a pilot study. *Australia and New Zealand Journal of Developmental Disabilities,* 17(1): 25-33.

Ory, M. O. and Cox, D. M. (1994). Forging ahead: linking health and behavior to improve quality of life in older people. *Social Indicators Research,* 33: 89-120.

Osberg, J. S., McGinnis, G. E., DeJong, G., and Seward, M. L. (1987). Life satisfaction and quality of life among disabled elderly adults. *Journal of Gerontology,* 42(2): 228-230.

Raphael, D. (1996). Quality of life for older adults: toward the optimization of the aging process. In R. Renwick, I. Brown, and M. Nagler (Eds.), *Quality of Life in Health Promotion and Rehabilitation,* pp. 290-306. Thousand Oaks, CA: Sage Publications.

Recchia, G., De Carli, G., Parise, G., Zerbini, O., Fostini, R., Catelloe, C., and Rizzini, P. (1991). Quality of life: a new approach to the assessment of the pharmacological treatment in the elderly patient. *Archives of Gerontology and Geriatrics; 1991 Supplement,* 2: 33-37.

Ruchlin, H. S. and Morris, J. N. (1991). Impact of work on quality of life of community-residing young elderly. *American Journal of Public Health,* 81(4): 498-500.

Ruffing-Rahal, M. A. (1991). Initial psychometric evaluation of a qualitative evaluation well-being measure: The Integration Inventory. *Health Values,* 15(2): 10-20.

Select Committee on Aging, House of Representatives. (1989). *The Quality of Life for Older Women: Older Women Living Alone.* Washington, D.C.: U.S. Government Printing Office.

Sherman, E. and Schiffman, L. G. (1991). Quality-of-life (QOL) assessment of older consumers: a retrospective review. *Journal of Business and Psychology,* 6(1): 107-119.

Stewart, A. L. and King, A. C. (1991). Evaluating the efficacy of physical activity for influencing quality-of-life outcomes in older adults. *Annals of Behavioral Medicine,* 13(3): 108-116.

Vaughan, C. E. and Hobson, S. (1990). Reducing late-life dependence resulting from declining visual acuity. *Journal of Visual Impairment and Blindness,* 370-372.

Wolkenstein, A. S. and Butler, D. J. (1992). Quality of life among the elderly: self-perspectives of some healthy elderly. *Gerontology and Geriatrics Education,* 12(4): 59-68.

Wood, L. A. and Johnson, J. (1989). Life satisfaction among the rural elderly: what do the numbers mean? *Social Indicators Research,* 21: 379-408.

Wood, L. A., Matthews, A. M., and Norris, J. (1992). Gerontological research on the quality of life: the Guelph Satellite Method. *Social Indicators Research,* 27: 345-361.

APPENDIX 14
Endocrine Disease and Quality of Life (QOL) Research Literature

Source	Population	Measures/Method	Domains
Sonino, Fava, Fallo, and Boscaro (1990)	Patients with endocrine disease	Recommends use of the psychosomatic approach in QOL issues with these patients	Life events preceding disease onset, psychological distress, abnormal illness behavior

References

Sonino, N., Fava, G. A., Fallo, F., and Boscaro, M. (1990). Psychological distress and quality of life in endocrine disease. *Psychotherapy and Psychosomatics*, 54: 140-144.

APPENDIX 15
Ethics and Quality of Life (QOL) Literature

Source	Discipline	Measurement Issues
Faden and Leplege (1992)	Clinical medicine and Research	QOL measurement in clinical care: screening, monitoring, and decision making. The subjective values of the patient must be heeded. The rush to quantification must not overlook the individual patient

References

Faden, R. and Leplege, A. (1992). Assessing quality of life: moral implications for clinical practice. *Medical Care,* 30(5): 166-175.

APPENDIX 16
Gender and Quality of Life (QOL) Studies

Source	Population	Measures/Method	Domains
Carsky, Dolan, and Free (1991)	Housewives working at home-based businesses	A proposed model to examine the effects of women's at-home income generation on family life and satisfaction	*Worker/family characteristics:* role orientation, family demands, and tolerance for distraction. *Nature of work:* degree of entrepreneurship, business/work site, absorptiveness. *Home/work environment:* time and income

APPENDIX 16 (continued)
Gender and Quality of Life (QOL) Studies

Source	Population	Measures/Method	Domains
Ensminger (1995)	836 African-American mothers on welfare	Interviews based on selected measures	Psychological distress, welfare, earlier life conditions, region of U.S., teenage mother, chronic burdens, number of children, single parent, self perceptions of health, self-esteem, psychological and physical well-being
Ganz, Day, Redmond, Ware, and Fisher (1995)	9,749 Participants in randomized trials for use of tamoxifen or placebo in 119 clinical centers in U.S. and Canada treating invasive breast cancer	Health-related QOL questionnaire which includes a depression scale, a symptom checklist for Medical Outcomes Study - 37SF and MOS sexual problems questions	Age, ethnicity, education, employment, occupation, income, marital status, health behaviors, estrogen, hysterectomy, ovaries removed, and menstrual cycle
Hardison and Vanier (1976)	130 Men and 153 women in California	Part of a research project funded by Urban Mass Transit Administration	Traffic, parking, transportation mode, pollution, physical condition, life stress, social conflict, mental illness, good old days, too many people, fast change, dominated by machines, getting ahead
Kaplan, Anderson, and Wingard (1991)	Random sample of 1,034 men and women from San Diego	Analysis of well-years by gender using General Health Policy Model	Mobility, Physical activity, social activity
Kober, Kuchler, Broelsch, Kremer, and Henne-Bruns (1990)	29 Liver transplant patients from Hamburg and 38 patients from Chicago	EORTC quality of life questionnaire, the STALX Anxiety Questionnaire, psychodiagnostic interviews, routine laboratory parameters	Functional status, ability to work, general symptoms, liver symptoms, anxiety, depression, social integration, pain, treatment strain, overall physical condition and overall QOL
Kristiansen (1989)	58 British females and 52 British males	Rokeach's Value Survey	World peace, inner harmony, mature love, social recognition, friendship, comfortable life, health, security, wisdom, self-respect
Kurz and Prather (1995)	Girls — birth to 19 years in the world's developing countries	Findings of the Association of Women in Development Forum	Mortality, poor health care, inadequate nutrition, lack of education, female genital mutilation, child labor, pregnancy and sexual activity, violence, prostitution, poor self concept

APPENDIX 16 (continued)
Gender and Quality of Life (QOL) Studies

Source	Population	Measures/Method	Domains
Lennon (1994)	300 Employed women, 202 full-time homemakers, 302 employed men	Investigated the role of work conditions in mediating the effect of employment status on married women's psychological well-being	Autonomy, time pressure, responsibility for things outside of one's control, interruptions, physical effort, and routine
Logue (1990)	Elderly long-term American Indian, Black and White patients (over 45 years)	Data obtained from Public Use Microdata Samples for Oklahoma from 1980 decennial census and from a query on Public Transportation Disability	Social risk, aging, disability, economic status, health, race, gender, educational attainment, marital status, area of residence
Logue (1991)	Death and dying issues for women	Overview article on research needs on age, sex, race, social class, primary diagnosis, co-morbidities of those whose deaths are negotiated	QOL and choosing death, premature death and delayed death, women as recipients of informal and formal care systems, competency, the experts, and feminist health goals
McCall (1991)	Suicide rates in elderly and adolescent males	Use annual suicide rates for U.S. from *Annual Vital Health Statistics Report 1947-1987*	Impoverishment, family dissolution, and government expenditures
McCoy (1994)	439 professional women	Survey of working women's leisure time	Discretionary time, discretionary activity, leisure as a state of mind
Nosek, Holland, Young, Georgiou, Rintala, Foley Bennett, and Smith (1994)	31 Women with physical disabilities	Qualitative interviews regarding disability and sexuality	Positive sexual self-concept, having sexuality information, good relationships, managing barriers, good health, and physical functioning
Pugliesi (1995)	599 Women and 753 men from a national data set	Refinement of differential exposure or vulnerability models	Work characteristics, social and psychological resources, well-being, role and status variables — gender, marital status, ethnicity, and parenthood
Roxburgh (1996)	994 Employed Canadians	Tested Job Stress Models	Differential exposure and vulnerability by gender to job stress, occupational self-direction, job demands, co-worker social support
Schover (1991)	Women with breast cancer	Review of studies on the impact of breast cancer on sexuality, body image, and intimate relationships	Psychological health, relationship satisfaction, pre-morbid sexual life, choice in treatment options, and types of treatment options

APPENDIX 16 (continued)
Gender and Quality of Life (QOL) Studies

Source	Population	Measures/Method	Domains
Select House Committee on Aging (1989)	Older women living alone	Chairman Roybal's report on hearings on QOL of older women living alone	Income, health, safety, housing
Sherman and Schiffman (1991)	Older consumers	Historical reflections on past 20 to 30 years of QOL status of older consumers	Socioeconomic indicators, health and longevity, housing and family living, gender differences, life satisfaction, cognitive age, leisure, occupation, health, gender
Turk (1996)	Women with disabilities: neuromuscular diseases, late effects of polio, spinal cord pathology, multiple sclerosis, osteoporosis in disability	Essay on fitness as an optimal state of physical well-being; call for research on fitness issues for women with physical disabilities	Flexibility, muscular strength and endurance, cardiopulmonary conditioning
Wallston, Hoover-Dempsey, and Brissie (1989)	78 Working women	Job Satisfaction, Scale Self-esteem Scale, and Life Satisfaction Scale	Gatekeeping transactions, flexibility, outcome/success, negativity, job satisfaction, self-esteem, quality of life, substance use
Young and Barboriak (1982)	45 Male volunteers classified for Type A behavior	Structured Interview, Jenkins Activity Survey, Milwaukee Cardiovascular Life Quality Questionnaire	Competition on the job, hard driving, temper, job deadlines, getting ahead, vacations, rest
Zweig, Barber, and Eccles (1997)	Young adults: 872 women and 527 men	Data from MI Study of Adolescent Life used to examine sexual coercion and well-being	Psychological and social adjustment, depressed mood, self-esteem, coping

References

Carsky, M. L., Dolan, E. M., and Free, R. K. (1991). An integrated model of homebased work: effects on family quality of life. *Journal of Business Research*, 23: 37-49.

Ensminger, M. E. (1995). Welfare and psychological distress: a longitudinal study of African American urban mothers. *Journal of Health and Social Behavior,* 36: 346-359.

Ganz, P. A., Day, R., Ware, J. E., Redmond, C., and Fisher, B. (1995). Base-line quality-of-life assessment in national surgical adjuvant breast and bowel project cancer. *Journal of the National Cancer Institute*, 87(18): 1372-1382.

Hardison, N. M. and Vanier, D. J. (1976). Environment and quality of life: attitudinal measurement and analysis. *Psychological Reports,* 39: 959-965.

Kaplan, R. M., Anderson, J. P., and Wingard, D. L. (1991). Gender differences in health-related quality of life. *Health Psychology,* 10(2): 86-93.

Kober, B., Kuchler, T., Broelsch, C., Kremer, B., and Henne-Bruns, D. (1990). A psychological support concept and quality of life research in a liver transplantation program: an interdisciplinary multicenter study. *Psychotherapy and Psychosomatics,* 54: 117-131.

Kristiansen, C. M. (1989). Gender differences in the meaning of "health." *Social Behavior,* 4: 185-188.

Kurz, K. M. and Prather, C. J. (1995). *Improving the Quality of Life of Girls.* New York: United Nations Children's Fund Programme Publications.

Lennon, M. C. (1994). Women, work, and well-being: the importance of work conditions. *Journal of Health and Social Behavior*, 35: 235-247.

Logue, B. J. (1990). Race differences in long-term disability: middle-aged and older American Indians, Blacks and Whites in Oklahoma. *Social Science Journal*, 27(3): 253-272.

Logue, B. J. (1991). Taking charge: death control as an emergent women's issue. *Women and Health*, 17(4): 97-121.

McCall, P. L. (1991). Adolescent and elderly white male suicide trends: evidence of changing well-being? *Journal of Gerontology*, 46(1): 843-851.

McCoy, M. L. (1994). Career women's leisure: challenges and realities. In C. W. Konek and S. L. Kitch (Eds.), *Women and Careers: Issues and Challenges*, pp. 173-286. Thousand Oaks, CA: Sage Publications.

Nosek, M. A., Howland, C. A., Young M. E., Georgiou, D., Rintala, D. H., Foley, C. C., Bennett, J. L., and Smith, Q. (1994). Wellness models and sexuality among women with physical disabilities. *Journal of Applied Rehabilitation Counseling*, 24(1): 50-57.

Pugliesi, K. (1995). Work and well-being: gender differences in the psychological consequences of employment. *Journal of Health and Social Behavior*, 36: 57-71.

Roxburgh, S. (1996). Gender differences in work and well-being: effects of exposure and vulnerability. *Journal of Health and Social Behavior*, 37: 265-277.

Schover, L. R. (1991). The impact of breast cancer on sexuality, body image, and intimate relationships. *Cancer Journal for Clinicians*, 41: 112-120.

Select Committee on Aging, House of Representatives. (1989). *The Quality of Life for Older Women: Older Women Living Alone*. Washington, D.C.: U.S. Government Printing Office.

Sherman, E. and Schiffman, L. G. (1991). Quality-of-life (QOL) assessment of older consumers: a retrospective review. *Journal of Business and Psychology*, 6(1): 107-119.

Turk, M. A. (1996). The impact of disability on fitness in women: musculoskeletal issues. In D. M. Krotoski, M. A. Nosek, and M. A. Turk (Eds.), *Women with Physical Disabilities: Achieving and Maintaining Health and Well-Being*, pp. 391-401. Baltimore: Paul H. Brookes.

Wallston, B. S., Hoover-Dempsey, K. V., and Brissie, J. S. (1989). Gatekeeping transactions: women's resource acquisition and mental health in the workplace. *Psychology of Women Quarterly*, 13: 205-222.

Young, L. D. and Barboriak, J. J. (1982). Reliability of a brief scale for assessment of coronary-prone behavior and standard measures of Type A behavior. *Perceptual and Motor Skills*, 55: 1039-1042.

Zweig, J. M., Barber, B. L., and Eccles, J. S. (1997). Sexual coercion and well-being in young adulthood: comparisons by gender and college status. *Journal of Interpersonal Violence*, 12(2): 291-308.

APPENDIX 17
General Population and Quality of Life Literature

Source	Population	Measures/Method	Domains
Andrew (1991)	1972 Surveys based on probability samples had 2,369 respondents; and 616 adult Americans were sampled in 1988	Used life quality measures: global well-being and 24 assessments of specific life concerns	Domains included: self, fun, health, income, job, leisure, community, and general environment
Campbell (1976)	National study of persons 18 years and older living in 48 states, based on a probability sample — 2,164 women and men	Interviews with a structured questionnaire	Life cycle, urbanicity, age, race, working, family income, work of head of household, education, religion, and sex
Campbell, Converse, and Rodgers (1976)	Same as Campbell above	583-Page book describing the national study	Same as Campbell above

APPENDIX 17 (continued)
General Population and Quality of Life Literature

Source	Population	Measures/Method	Domains
Carsky, Dolan, and Free (1991)	Housewives working at home-based businesses	A proposed model to examine the effects of women's at-home income generation on family life and satisfaction	*Worker/family characteristics:* role orientation, family demands, and tolerance for distraction. *Nature of work:* degree of entrepreneurship, business/work site, absorptiveness. *Home/work Environment:* time and income
Center for Disease Control and Prevention (1995)	102,263 respondents in all states except Wyoming	Health-Related QOL measures for U.S.	Physical, psychological, and social functioning during usual daily activities
Elizur and Shye (1990)	540 Employees of large corporation in Hungary	Given QOL and Quality of Work Life (QWL) questionnaires — 16 items each	QOL and QWL share the same domains: *Mode of functioning:* expressive, integrative, adaptive, or conservative. *Field of Functioning:* social or cultural, psychological, physical. *Life area: work and life in general*
Fields and Thacker (1992)	293 Employees in intervention one and 119 employees in intervention two	Used Company Commitment measure, Job Satisfaction measure, Union Commitment Scale, Quality of Work Life Scale	Loyalty, responsibility, belief in unionism, willingness, organizational commitment, job satisfaction
Gitter and Mostofsky (1973)	General population	Goal is to construct an objective and parallel subjective indicator of quality of life	HEW aspects: health and illness; social mobility, income and poverty, public order and safety, learning, science, and art, participation and alienation
Hardison and Vanier (1976)	130 Men and 153 women in California	Part of a research project funded by Urban Mass Transit Administration.	Traffic, parking, transportation mode, pollution, physical condition, life stress, social conflict, mental illness, good old days, too many people, fast change, dominated by machines, getting ahead
Headey, Veenhoven, and Wearing (1991)	QOL survey of 942 persons conducted in 4 waves (1981, 1983, 1985, 1987) in Victoria, Australia	Used Life-as-a-Whole Index, Delighted–Terrible Scale, Eyesenck Personality Inventory, and socioeconomic status by gender in examining subjective well-being	Marriage, work, material standard of living, leisure, friendship, and health
Hennessy, Moriarty, Zack, Scherr, and Brackbill (1994)	General population	QOL public health surveillance by CDCP using Behavioral Risk Factor Surveillance System, a state-based telephone surveillance system	Self-perceived health, recent physical health, recent mental health, recent activity limitation
House, Livingston, and Swinburn (1973)	General population	Experiment conducted at QOL symposium to develop list of QOL factors which were generated and weighted; results analysis indicated the use of dissatisfaction indices may be better than trying to measure happiness	Factor list included: political/social; economic; and environment

APPENDIX 17 (continued)
General Population and Quality of Life Literature

Source	Population	Measures/Method	Domains
Idler and Benyamini (1997)	Representative community samples	Review of 27 empirical community studies on self-rate health and mortality	Age and general health
Kozleski and Sands (1992)	133 Individuals from the general Colorado population	Consumer Satisfaction Survey	Services and satisfaction, support services and assistance needed, independence/interdependence, integration, activities, personal relationships
Kristiansen (1989)	58 British females and 52 British males	Rokeach's Value Survey	World peace, inner harmony, mature love, social recognition, friendship, comfortable life, health, security, wisdom, self-respect
Lance, Lautenschlager, and Sloan (1989)	150 assistant, associate, and full professors from University of Georgia	Job Stress Scale, Depressed Mood Scale, Minnesota Satisfaction Questionnaire	Marital satisfaction, satisfaction with social activities, job satisfaction
Larson (1991)	International health status of nations	Health Status 1 and Health Status 2 derived from Physical Quality of Life Index	Physical, mental, and social well-being
Latten (1989)	3000 Respondents over 18 years in the Netherlands	Quality of Life Surveys	Serious physical injury or illness, death of family member, widow(er)hood, and serious tension at home, aging
Lerner, Levine, Malspeis, and D'Agostino (1994)	1,319 Working adults	Job Content Questionnaire, Medical Outcomes Study, Short-Form Health Survey	Physical, role functioning as relates to health, vitality, social functioning, and mental health
Loscocco and Roschelle (1991)	Working and nonworking adults	Literature review of quality of work and nonwork life: 1971–1991	Personality, education, gender, family roles, job characteristics, organizational characteristics, unions, promotions, social context
Manz and Grothe (1991)	Approximately 4000 employees in a midwestern computer manufacturing company	Quality of Work Life Survey	Personal motivation, personal investment, meaningfulness of job, innovation, quality/productivity, communication of organization mission, policies and procedures, human resource systems, management effectiveness, management understanding, commitment to employees, participation, performance evaluation, respect for the individual, supervisory skills, nonfinancial rewards, job clarity, trust and support, team productivity, team communication, job stress, work load, job design, equity, benefits, compensation, career training, physical work environment, work resources
McCoy (1994)	439 Professional women	Survey of working women's leisure time	Discretionary time, discretionary activity, leisure as a state of mind

APPENDIX 17 (continued)
General Population and Quality of Life Literature

Source	Population	Measures/Method	Domains
McGee, O'Boyle, Hickey, O'Malley, and Joyce (1991)	20 Irritable bowel syndrome and 20 peptic ulcer disease patients as compared to 42 healthy individuals	Used the Schedule for Evaluation of Individual Quality of Life	Family, work, recreation, religion, and health
McLanahan and Adams (1989)	Effects of children on adult well-being	Two Americans View Their Mental Health Surveys (AVTHM) 1957 and 1976	Happiness, satisfaction, worries, psychological distress, and perceptions of parenthood
Mehrabian and Ross (1979)	293 Undergraduate students	Checklists, questionnaires, and measures of personality	Life changes, physical illness and symptoms, psychosomatic symptoms, accidents, psychological symptoms
Moos and Moos (1983)	32 Staff members in residential care and 42 staff members in a community mental health center	Development of a set of social climate scales; Work Environment Scale, Family Environment Scale	Relationships, personal growth, and system growth and change
Mugenda, Hira, and Fanslow (1990)	123 Adults in the midwest	Obtained data re household size and net worth, marital status, employment status of money manager, and money management practices	Level of living, savings, staying out of debt, assets, paying debts, meeting emergency expenses, satisfaction with QOL
Murrell and Norris (1983)	1800 Adults living in Kentucky	Use of a subjective measure of QOL	Mental health, financial, social activity, employment, and health
Near, Rice, and Hunt (1978)	1041 Probability sample of adults living in New York state	4 Subjective QOL measures	Life satisfaction, life satisfaction over time, job satisfaction, and health
Newfield and Duet (1976)	The work of curriculum developers	A review of QOL Indexes for the purpose of comparing their characteristics to that of the goal of education	Public order and safety, physical environment, health, affection and sociability, income and poverty, education and skills attainment, participation and alienation, availability and utilization of leisure, self-respect, aesthetics, communication, enjoyment of art, finer things, learning, and morality
Reich and Zautra (1983)	70 Middle and older aged persons and a college sample of 104 students	Life Events Questionnaire, Depressive Adjective Checklist, Perceived Quality of Life Scale	Demands, desires, positive and negative components of well-being, psychiatric symptoms
Rettig, Danes, and Bauer (1991)	592 Women and men from farm families	Survey and Delighted–Terrible Scale	Love, status, services, information, goods, money resources received from family
Rhoads and Raymond (1981)	547 Adults from Phoenix area	Interviews, Bradburn Affect–Balance-Scale	Age, sex, family income, personal, social, community, income
Ruchlin and Morris (1991)	310 Young elderly between ages of 65–74.	Modified Spitzer Uniscale QL index	Marital Status, self-assessed health status, functional status, self-assessed financial status, and work status
Schalock (1996)	For everyone	Proposes a quality assurance model for QOL evaulation	Home and community living, work-school, and health and wellness

APPENDIX 17 (continued)
General Population and Quality of Life Literature

Source	Population	Measures/Method	Domains
Shain (1996)	For everyone	Analyzes study: *Influences on Wellness in the Workplace: A Multivariate Approach*	Personal health practices, perceived stressors at home and at work, personal resources, demographic and socioeconomic factors
Sherman and Schiffman (1991)	Older consumers	Historical reflections on past 20 to 30 years of QOL status of older consumers	Socioeconomic indicators, health and longevity, housing and family living, gender differences, life satisfaction, cognitive age, leisure, occupation, health
Short and Shea (1995)	Families below the poverty line and AFDC families	From data collected in Survey of Income and Program Participation	Access to consumer durables, living conditions, crime and neighborhood, basic needs, health and nutrition, index of deprivation
Shye (1989)	General population	Examined QOL Model vs. Residents' Reports	Personality, Physical, Social, Cultural as the functioning modes of the QOL Model
Spreitzer and Snyder (1989)	Toledo adults	Life Satisfaction, Job Satisfaction, and Self-Esteem items used in a telephone interview	Self-esteem, job and life satisfaction, and leisure
Stewart and King (1991)	Older adults	Conceptual framework presented of QOL concepts for evaluating the efficacy of physical activity in older adults	Physical functioning, cognitive functioning, activities, bodily well-being, emotional well-being, self-concept, and global perceptions of health and life satisfaction
Stillson, White, and Harris (1986)	Alcoholism treatment personnel	Review of aspects of stress management techniques to improve QOL	Psychotherapy, meditation/visualization and time management
Williams, Eyring, Gaynor, and Long (1991)	734 College students and adults	Life Satisfaction Index, Satisfaction with Life Scale, Spiritual Well-Being Scale	Inherent value of life, effective life management, and sense of health
Wolkenstein and Butler (1992)	96 Healthy elderly (65 years and over)	Questionnaire, opinion surveys, group interviews	Outside world and others, inner world of the self, coping with loss, interaction with treating physician
Wood and Johnson (1989)	15 Elderly rural adults selected for qualitative study and 392 elderly rural adults in quantitative study	Used a life satisfaction questionnaire and analysis of qualitative data	Housing, health, self-esteem, friendship, and family
Wood, Matthews, and Norris (1992)	457 Women and men over 60 years in urban and rural Canada	Structured interviews and Guelph Satellite Method	Spouse, health, housing, and friendship
Woodruff and Conway (1992)	519 U.S. Navy personnel randomly selected	Questionnaires based on QOL research to examine health and fitness factors and changes in QOL	Overall QOL, health/fitness, and health behavior

APPENDIX 17 (continued)
General Population and Quality of Life Literature

Source	Population	Measures/Method	Domains
Zautra (1982)	537 Community residents	Life Cycle Measurements, Social Resource Measurements, Negative Life Events, Perceived Quality of Life Scale, 22-item Psychiatric Screening Inventory	Self-reliance, supportive others, social responsibility, social network blame, positive affect, negative affect, psychiatric distress, overall life quality, number of negative events
Zautra and Reich (1983)	General population	Review of 15 studies measuring effects of positive and negative events on psychiatric distress	Positive life events, negative life events, psychological well-being

References

Andrew, F. M. (1991). Stability and change in levels and structure of subjective well-being: USA 1972 and 1988. *Social Indicators Research,* 25: 1-30.

Campbell, A. (1976). Subjective measures of well-being. *American Psychologist,* 117-124.

Campbell, A., Converse, P. E., and Rodgers, W. L. (1976). *The Quality of American Life: Perceptions, Evaluations, and Satisfactions.* New York: Russell Sage Foundation.

Carsky, M. L., Dolan, E. M., and Free, R. K. (1991). An integrated model of homebased work: effects on family quality of life. *Journal of Business Research,* 23: 37-49.

Center for Disease Control and Prevention. (1995). Health-related quality of life measures — United States, 1993. *Morbidity and Mortality Weekly Report,* 44(11): 195-200.

Elizur, D. and Shye, S. (1990). Quality of work life and its relation to quality of life. *Applied Psychology: An International Review,* 39(3): 275-291.

Fields, M. W. and Thacker, J. W. (1992). Influence of quality of work life on company and union commitment. *Academy of Management Journal,* 35(2): 439-450.

Gitter, A. G. and Mostofsky, D. I. (1973). The social indicator: an index of the quality of life. *Social-Biology,* 20(3): 289-297.

Hardison, N. M. and Vanier, D. J. (1976). Environment and quality of life: attitudinal measurement and analysis. *Psychological Reports,* 39: 959-965.

Headey, B, Veenhoven, R., and Wearing, A. (1991). Top-down vs. bottom-up theories of subjective well-being. *Social Indicators Research,* 24: 81-100.

Hennessy, C. H., Moriarty, D. G., Zack, M. M., Scherr, P. A., and Brackbill, R. (1994). Measuring health-related quality of life for public health surveillance. *Public Health Reports,* 106(5): 665-672.

House, P. W., Livingston, R. C., and Swinburn, C. D. (1973). Monitoring mankind: the search for quality. *Behavioral Science,* 20: 57-67.

Idler, E. I. and Benyamini, Y. (1997). Self-rated health and mortality: a review of twenty-seven community studies. *Journal of Health and Social Behavior,* 38: 21-37.

Kozleski, E. B. and Sands, D. J. (1992). The yardstick of social validity: evaluating quality of life as perceived by adults without disabilities. *Education and Training in Mental Retardation,* 119-131.

Kristiansen, C. M. (1989). Gender differences in the meaning of "health." *Social Behavior,* 4: 185-188.

Lance, C. E., Lautenschlager, G. J., and Sloan, C. E. (1989). A comparison between bottom-up, top-down, and bi-directional models of relationships between global and life facet satisfaction. *Journal of Personality,* 57(3): 601-624.

Larson, J. S. (1991). Two scales for measuring international health status. *Evaluation and the Health Professions,* 14(4): 422-437.

Latten, J. J. (1989). Life-course and satisfaction, equal for every-one? *Social Indicators Research,* 21: 599-610.

Lerner, D. J., Leaven, S., Malspeis, S., and D'Agostino, R. B. (1994). Job strain and health-related quality of life in a national sample. *American Journal of Public Health,* 84(10): 1580-1585.

Loscocco, K. A. and Roschelle, A. R. (1991). Influences on the quality of work and nonwork life: two decades in review. *Journal of Vocational Behavior,* 39: 182-225.

Manz, C. C. and Grothe, R. (1991). Is the work force vanguard to the 21st century a quality of work life deficient-prone generation? *Journal of Business Research,* 23: 67-82.

McCoy, M. L. (1994). Career women's leisure: challenges and realities. In C. W. Knock and S. L. Kith (Eds.), *Women and careers: issues and challenges,* pp. 173-286. Thousand Oaks, CA: Sage Publications.

McGee, H. M., O'Boyle, C. A., Hickey, A., O'Malley, K., and Joyce, C. R. B. (1991). Assessing the quality of life of the individual: the sequel with a healthy and a gastroenterology unit population. *Psychological Medicine,* 21: 749-759.

McLanahan, S. and Adams, J. (1989). The effects of children on adults' psychological well-being: 1957–1976. *Social Forces,* 68(1): 124-146.

Mehrabian, A. and Ross, M. (1979). Illness, accidents, and alcohol use as functions of the arousing quality and pleasantness of life changes. *Psychological Reports,* 45: 31-43.

Moos, R. H. and Moos, B. S. (1983). Adaptation and the quality of life in work and family settings. *Journal of Consulting Psychology,* 11: 158-170.

Mugenda, O. M., Hira, T. K., and Fanslow, A. M. (1990). Assessing the causal relationship among communication, money management practices, satisfaction with financial status, and satisfaction with quality of life. *Lifestyles: Family and Economic Issues,* 11(4): 343-360.

Murrell, S. A. and Norris, F. H. (1983). Quality of life as the criterion for need assessment and community psychology. *Journal of Consulting Psychology,* 11: 88-97.

Near, J. P., Rice, R. W. and Hunt, R. G. (1978). Work and extra-work correlates of life and job satisfaction. *Academy of Management Journal,* 21(2): 248-264.

Newfield, J. W. and Duet, C. P. (1976). Implications of quality of life for goal setting tasks of the curriculum workers. *Education,* 97(2): 135.

Reich, J. W. and Zautra, A. J. (1983). Demands and desires in daily life: some influences on well-being. *American Journal of Community Psychology,* 11(1): 41-59.

Rettig, K. D., Danes, S. M., and Bauer, J. W. (1991). Family life quality: theory and assessment in economically stress farm families. *Social Indicators Research,* 24: 269-299.

Rhoads, D. L. and Raymond, J. S. (1981). Quality of life and the competent community. *American Journal of Community Psychology,* 9(3): 293-301.

Ruchlin, H. S. and Morris, J. N. (1991). Impact of work on quality of life of community-residing young elderly. *American Journal of Public Health,* 81(4): 498-500.

Schalock, R. L. (1996). Quality of life and quality assurance. In R. Renwick, I. Brown, and M. Nagler (Eds.), *Quality of Life in Health Promotion and Rehabilitation,* pp. 104-118. Thousand Oaks, CA: Sage Publications.

Shain, M. (1996). Work, employment, and mental health: implications for quality of life. In R. Renwick, I. Brown, and M. Nagler (Eds.), *Quality of Life in Health Promotion and Rehabilitation,* pp. 327-341. Thousand Oaks, CA: Sage Publications.

Sherman, E. and Schiffman, L. G. (1991). Quality-of-life (QOL) assessment of older consumers: a retrospective review. *Journal of Business and Psychology,* 6(1): 107-119.

Short, K. and Shea, M. (1995). Beyond poverty, extended measures of well-being: 1992. *Current Population Reports,* P70-SORV, Washington, D.C.: U.S. Dept. of Commerce, Economics, and Statistics Administration.

Shye, S. (1989). Systemic life quality model. *Social Indicators Research,* 21: 343-378.

Spreitzer, E. and Snyder, E. E. (1989). Sports involvement and quality of life dimensions. *Journal of Sport Behavior,* 12(1): 3-11.

Stewart, A. L. and King, A. C. (1991). Evaluating the efficacy of physical activity for influencing quality-of-life outcomes in older adults. *Annals of Behavioral Medicine,* 13(3): 108-116.

Stillson, K., White, J., and Harris, E. F. (1986). Helping the helper: stress management for alcoholism treatment personnel. *Alcoholism Treatment Quarterly,* 3(3): 107-123.

Williams, R. L., Eyring, M., Gaynor, P., and Long, J. D. (1991). Development of Views of Life Scale. *Psychology and Health,* 5: 165-181.

Wolkenstein, A. S. and Butler, D. J. (1992). Quality of life among the elderly: self-perspectives of some healthy elderly. *Gerontology and Geriatrics Education,* 12(4): 59-68.

Wood, L. A. and Johnson, J. (1989). Life satisfaction among the rural elderly: what do the numbers mean? *Social Indicators Research,* 21: 379-408.

Wood, L. A., Matthews, A. M., and Norris, J. (1992). Gerontological research on the quality of life: the Guelph Satellite Method. *Social Indicators Research,* 27: 345-361.

Woodruff, S. I., and Conway, T. L. (1992). A longitudinal assessment of the impact of health/fitness and health behavior on perceived quality of life. *Perceptual and Motor Skills,* 75: 3-14.

Zautra, A. J. (1983). Social resources and the quality of life. *American Journal of Community Psychology,* 11(3): 275-289.

Zautra, A. J. and Reich, J. W. (1983). Life events and perceptions of life quality: developments in a two-factor approach. *Journal of Community Psychology,* 11(2): 121-132

APPENDIX 18
Heart Disease and Quality of Life (QOL) Studies

Source	Population	Measures/Method	Domains
Blumenthal and Emery (1988)	Cardiac patients	Review of three behavioral strategies to examine the value of cardiac rehabilitation as a method for improving QOL	Cardiovascular functioning, psychological functioning, physical fitness, and psychosocial functioning
Conn, Taylor, and Wiman (1991)	94 Older adult myocardial infarction survivors	Interviews and Profile of Mood States, Perceived QOL Scale, Health Behavior Scale	Anxiety, depression, exercise, diet, medications, stress, smoking
Fava (1990)	Cardiovascular and cancer patients	Review of research on QOL issues	Physical, psychological, and social
Guyatt (1994)	Heart failure patients	Minnesota Living with Heart Failure Questionnaire is reliable and valid	Disease specific with domains as emotional function, dyspnea (labored breathing), and fatigue with use of digoxin
Mayou (1990)	Cardiovascular disease patients	Recommends greater use of psychosomatic research including interview-based and self-report measures as well as physical outcome measures	Symptoms, mental state, general health status, types of cardiac disorder
Romney, Jenkins, and Bynner (1992)	469 Patients with cardiovascular problems	Use LISREL to test competing hypothesis	Symptoms of illness, neurological dysfunction, interpersonal relationsips, morale, and socioeconomic status
Tsevat, Goldman, Lamas, Pfeffer, Chapin, Connors, and Lee (1991)	80 Myocardial infarction survivors	Visual Analogue Scale, Verbal Rating Scale, Time Trade-off, Transformed Time Trade-off Mean, Karnofsky Index, Specific Anxiety Scale Class, and NY Heart Association Class	Gender, employment, exercise, pain, functional status
Young and Barboriak (1982)	45 Male volunteers classified for Type A behavior	Structured Interview, Jenkins Activity Survey, Milwaukee Cardiovascular Life Quality Questionnaire	Competition on the job, hard driving, temper, job deadlines, getting ahead, vacations, rest

References

Blumenthal, J. A. and Emery, C. F. (1988). Rehabilitation of patients following myocardial infarction. *Journal of Consulting and Clinical Psychology,* 56(3): 374-381.

Conn, V. S., Taylor, S. G., and Wiman, P. (1991). Anxiety, depression, quality of life, and self-care among survivors of myocardial infarction. *Issues in Mental Health Nursing,* 12: 321-331.

Fava, G. A. (1990). Methodological and conceptual issues in research on quality of life. *Psychotherapy and Psychosomatics,* 54: 70-76.

Guyatt, G. H. (1994). Measurement of health-related quality of life in heart failure. *Irish Journal of Psychology,* 15(1): 148-163.

Mayou, R. (1990). Quality of life in cardiovascular disease. *Psychotherapy and Psychosomatics,* 54: 99-109.

Romney, D. M., Jenkins, C. D., and Bynner, J. M. (1992). A structural analysis of health-related quality of life dimensions. *Human Relations,* 45(2): 165-176.

Tsevat, J., Goldman, L., Lamas, G. A., Pfeffer, M. A., Chapin, C.C., Connors, K. F., and Lee, T. H. (1991). Functional status vs. utilities in survivors of myocardial infarction. *Medical Care,* 29(11): 1153-1159.

Young, L. D. and Barboriak, J. J. (1982). Reliability of a brief scale for assessment of coronary-prone behavior and standard measures of type A behavior. *Perceptual and Motor Skills,* 55: 1039-1042.

APPENDIX 19
Homelessness and Quality of Life (QOL) Research Literature

Source	Population	Measures/Method	Domains
Brown (1996)	Homeless adults	Essay on QOL issues and homelessness	Physical, psychological, social well-being, housed, homed, homeless, houseless

References

Brown, I. (1996). The quality of life of marginal citizens: homelessness. In R. Renwick, I. Brown, and M. Nagler (Eds.), *Quality of Life in Health Promotion and Rehabilitation,* pp. 204-218. Thousand Oaks, CA: Sage Publications.

APPENDIX 20
Inflammatory Bowel Disease and Quality of Life Literature

Source	Population	Measures/Method	Domains
Kunsbeck, Korber, and Freyberger (1990)	Patients with inflammatory bowel disease	Review of empirical research	Energy, leisure, work or school, mobility, body image, psychic status, enjoyment, sexuality, family, friends, and partnership

References

Kunsbeck, H. W., Korber, J., and Freyberger, H. (1990). Quality of life in patients with inflammatory bowel disease, *Psychotherapy and Psychosomatics,* 54: 110-116.

APPENDIX 21
HIV and Quality of Life (QOL) Literature

Source	Population	Measures/Method	Domains
Hays and Shapiro (1992)	HIV Patients	Use of Quality of Well-Being Scale	Symptoms/problems complexes, mobility, physical activity, and social activity
Renwick and Friedland (1996)	107 Males and 13 females with HIV	Quality of Life Questionnaire, Fanning Quality of Life Scale, Life Appraisal and Life Satisfaction Questionnaire, Interpersonal Support Evaluation List, Ways of Coping, Recent Life Changes Questionnaire	Job satisfaction, relations with others, work relations, altruistic behavior, creative–aesthetic behavior, significant other relationships, marital (partner) relations, job characteristics, political behavior, extended family relations, vacation behavior, personal growth, material well-being, sports activity, and physical well-being

References

Hays, R. D. and Shapiro, M. F. (1992). An overview of generic health-related quality of life measures for HIV research. *Quality of Life Research,* 1: 91-97.

Renwick, R. and Friedland, J. (1996). Quality of life experienced by a sample of adults with HIV. In R. Renwick, I. Brown, and M. Nagler (Eds.), *Quality of Life in Health Promotion and Rehabilitation,* pp. 171-189. Thousand Oaks, CA: Sage Publications.

APPENDIX 22
Hypertension and Quality of Life (QOL) Literature

Source	Population	Measures/Method	Domains
Hume (1989)	Patients with hypertension	Review of the findings of the Treatment of Mild Hypertension Study as it relates to the addition of hydrochlorothiazide to other pharamacologic agents	Functional capacity perceptions, and symptoms including mobility and independence. *Social functioning:* family, friends, community. *Cognitive functioning:* reasoning, memory, judgment and alertness. Psychological distress. Economic status.
Taylor (1989)	Patients with hypertension	Commentary on Hume; suggests methods of evaluation	Disease-specific, physical functioning, emotional functioning, social functioning and general health perceptions.

References

Hume, A. L. (1989). Applying quality of life data in practice: considerations for antihypertensive therapy. *Journal of Family Practice,* 28(4): 403-407.

Taylor, T. T. (1989). Commentary. *Journal of Family Practice,* 28(4): 407-411.

APPENDIX 23
Hypothyroidism and Quality of Life (QOL) Literature

Source	Population	Measures/Method	Domains
Jaeschke, Guyatt, Cook, Harper, and Gerstein (1994)	200 Patients with treated hypothyroidism	Took a survey of 200 patients to generate items; then distributed 70 questionnaires to family doctors and specialists, and 150 questionnaires to the Thyroid Foundation. 70 responses total received from the 2 groups	Physical problems, energy and general well-being problems, mood and emotional problems

References

Jaeschke, R., Guyatt, G., Cook, S., Harper, S., and Gerstein, H. C. (1994). Spectrum of quality of life impairment in hypothyroidism. *Quality of Life Research,* 3: 323-327.

APPENDIX 24
Kidney Disease and Quality of Life (QOL) Literature

Source	Population	Measures/Method	Domains
Ferrans and Powers (1992)	349 adult hemodialysis patients	Quality of Life Index — Dialysis version	Life satisfaction, self-esteem, health, and functioning
Hays, Kallich, Mapes, Coons, and Carter (1994)	165 Patients with kidney disease	Development of the Kidney Disease QOL Instrument (KDQOL)	Physical functioning, emotional functioning, social functioning, pain, energy-fatigue, and general health perceptions
Koch and Muthny (1990)	More than 2,000 patients with kidney disease	Questionnaire	Physical/psychosomatic complaints, emotional well-being, partnership and family, vocational rehabilitation, hobbies, leisure activities, and satisfaction with treatment
Lynch and Gallagher-Lepak (1996)	Patients with chronic renal failure	Essay on updating rehabilitation professionals on impact of improved medical treatment	Functional outcomes: weakness/fatigue, reduced endurance, cognitive changes, and psychological distress

References

Ferrans, C. and Powers, M. (1992). Psychometric assessment of the Quality of Life Index. *Research in Nursing and Health,* 15: 111-119.

Hays, R. D., Kallich, J. D., Mapes, D. L., Coons, S. J., and Carter, W. B. (1994). Development of the Kidney Disease Quality of Life (KDQOL) Instrument. *Quality of Life Research,* 3: 329-338.

Koch, U. and Muthny, F. A. (1990). Quality of life in patients with end-stage renal disease in relation to the method of treatment. *Psychotherapy and Psychosomatics,* 54: 161-171.

Lynch, R. T. and Gallagher-Lepak, S. (1996). Chronic renal failure: the impact of improved medical treatment options on rehabilitation. *Journal of Applied Rehabilitation Counseling,* 27(1): 7-12.

APPENDIX 25
Liver Disease and Quality of Life (QOL) Literature

Source	Population	Measures/Method	Domains
Kober, Kuchler, Broelsch, Kremer, and Henne-Bruns (1990)	29 Liver transplant patients from Hamburg and 38 patients from Chicago	EORTC quality of life questionnaire, the STALX Anxiety Questionnaire, psychodiagnostic interviews, routine laboratory parameters	Functional status, ability to work, general symptoms, liver symptoms, anxiety, depression, social integration, pain, treatment strain, overall physical condition and overall QOL

References

Kober, B., Kuchler, T., Broelsch, C., Kremer, B., and Henne-Bruns, D. (1990). A psychological support concept and quality of life research in a liver transplantation program: an interdisciplinary multicenter study. *Psychotherapy and Psychosomatics,* 54: 117-131.

APPENDIX 26
Mental Illness and Quality of Life (QOL) Literature

Source	Population	Measures/Method	Domains
Baker, Jodrey, and Intagliata (1992)	729 Mentally ill adults in state-supported programs	Repeated (9 months apart) questionnaires, QOL interviews, Bradburn Positive and Negative Affect Scales, Availability of Social Support Scale; Advocacy of Social Support Scale	Satisfaction with Life Domains Scale correlates found
Bigelow, McFarland, and Olson (1991)	Community samples, client samples from 24 mental health agencies	Interviews by trained interviewers	QOL Questionnaire developed by this method
Brown (1996)	105 Males and 86 females with severe mental illness	Assessed loneliness using UCLA Loneliness Scale	Loneliness as a QOL issue dependent upon living situation or social skills and social networks and the experience of the individual with severe mental illness
Brown, Cosgrove, and DeSelm (1997)	19 Consumers of mental health services and their case managers	Compared perceptions of consumers and case managers regarding barriers interfering with life satisfaction using a structured interview	Family, friendships, health care, community services, housing, neighborhood, finances, daily activities, work, transportation, physical health
Ciardiello and Bingham (1962)	Schizophrenic clients	Review of a career maturity construct and how a career development approach improves QOL	Use of leisure, family, citizenship, and work roles

APPENDIX 26 (continued)
Mental Illness and Quality of Life (QOL) Literature

Source	Population	Measures/Method	Domains
Corrigan and Buican (1995)	49 Patients with severe mental illness	Interview-based measures of quality of life: Brief Psychiatric Rating Scale, Profile of Adaptive Living, Social Support Questionnaire, Wechsler Adult Intelligence Scale Revised	Correlations found between QOL Interview and variables on other instruments. QOL is not redundant with adhedonia common to depression
Corten, Mercier, and Pele (1994)	148 Patients with DSM diagnoses and control group of 40 randomly selected from general population	Semistructured interviews, Satisfaction with Life Domains Scale, Helps in Daily Life Scale, and Scale Conformity	3 Significant factors found for comprehensive model for QOL: hedonist factor, achievement factor, and conformity factor
Dellario and Anthony (1981)	Psychiatrically disabled persons	Review of research studies regarding client outcomes of institutional vs. alternative placements; a model for psychiatric rehabilitation	Physical, intellectual, emotional, work, and community
Elizur and Shye (1990)	540 Employees of large corporation in Hungary	Given QOL and Quality of Work Life (QWL) questionnaires — 16 items each	QOL and QWL share the same domains
Endicott, Nee, Harrison, and Blumenthal (1993)	Depressed patients	Quality of Life Enjoyment and Satisfaction Questionnaire	Physical health, subjective feelings, leisure time, social relationships, and general activities; household duties, work, and school
Fabian (1990)	Individuals with long-term mental illness	Review of two models of QOL: life satisfaction and adaptive functioning and instruments designed to measure them	Housing, leisure, work, overall life satisfaction, subjective well-being
Fitzsimmons and Bunting (1997)	Persons with Parkinson's Disease (PD)	Essay on the psychosocial aspects of PD and QOL	Social roles, mental acuity, emotional states, subjective well-being, interrelationships, life satisfaction and physical health
Frisch, Cronell, and Villanueva (1992)	54 VA inpatient, 51 VA recovered, 18 private inpatient, 19 offender, 272 general undergraduates, and 127 counseling center persons in psychotherapy	The Global Severity Scale, Positive Symptom Total, Positive Symptom Distress Index, Beck Depression Inventory, Symptoms Checklist-90-R, Millon Clinical Multiaxial Inventory, Generalized Expectancy for Success Scale	Quality of Life Inventory correlations with variables on other instruments found

APPENDIX 26 (continued)
Mental Illness and Quality of Life (QOL) Literature

Source	Population	Measures/Method	Domains
Gater, Kind, and Gudex (1995)	138 Medical patients scoring over the threshold for probable psychiatric illness	Health Measurement Questionnaire, (HMQ) Nottingham Health Profile, Psychiatric Assessment Scale, Rosser Index	Compared self-rating and observer-completed; a strong correlation was found between measures, HMQ and QOL and agreement between self and observer ratings
Gerber, Coleman, Johnston, and Lavfave (1994)	43 Clients discharged 1 and 3 years after psychiatric rehabilitation	Structured interviews, Mulern and Manderscheid Clients' Quality of Life Interview, Uniform Client Data Instrument	Found that QOL was maintained or improved postdischarge on all QOL measures
Huxley and Warner (1992)	68 Long-term psychiatric patients	Quality of Life Profile and General Satisfaction Questionnaire	Used interviews modified the QOL Profile to include a 9th domain of religion, and used the client database to conduct study
Jablensky (1992)	Psychiatry as a medical discipline	Historical review of psychiatry as social control of the deviant, advocacy of the right to be different, and the effects of the latter on QOL issues	Cognitive models of human nature, social organization, technology available to manipulate human behavior
Lehman, Reed, and Possidente (1982)	278 Randomly selected psychiatric patients in board and care homes in Los Angeles	Quality of Life Interview	Living situation, family, social relations, leisure time, employment, finances, personal safety, and health
Lerner, Levine, Malspeis, and D'Agostino (1994)	1319 Working men and women, 18–64 years	Job Content Questionnaire, Medical Outcomes Study, Short-Form Health Survey, and a health distress scale	Job strain was associated with components of health-related QOL: physical functioning, role functioning, vitality, social functioning and mental health
Malm, May, and Dencker (1981)	Schizophrenic outpatients — 27 males and 13 females	Used Quality of Life Checklist	Medical care, social, standard of living, communication and transportation, work, safety, education, leisure, spiritual/religious
Moller and Murphy (1997)	176 Patients with psychiatric disabilities	Clients, family members, and case managers enrolled in course, *Symptom Management: A Wellness Expedition*	Number of inpatient days, cost savings, and participant satisfaction
Munich and Lang (1993)	Persons with psychiatric disabilities	Argument for rehabilitation as a central discipline which integrates clinical and functional status and QOL	Biopsychosocial issues including learning, compensation, adaptation. autonomy, least professional intervention
Oliver, Holloway, and Carson (1995)	Patients using mental health services	Review of objective, subjective, and health-related concepts of QOL	Adequate income, housing, occupation, opportunities to make social relationships

APPENDIX 26 (continued)
Mental Illness and Quality of Life (QOL) Literature

Source	Population	Measures/Method	Domains
O'Rear, Bark, and Hutchinson (1996)	Persons with psychiatric disabilities	Essay on promoting wellness activities which improve QOL	Physical, mental, emotional, and spiritual wellness
Rosenfeld, S. (1992)	157 Members of a psychosocial rehabilitation program	Interviews, Delighted–Terrible Scale, Lehman's QOL, Moos' Community-Oriented Program Environment Scale	Importance of program components, vocational rehabilitation, financial services, empowerment approaches to service delivery
Roessler (1990)	Essay on QOL as an outcome to be sought by rehabilitation counselors	Use of objective and subjective factors in examining QOL	*Objective factors include:* health and employment records, earnings and income, and use of Lehman's QOL measure. *Subjective factors include:* self-rating in specific domains of a person's life regarding perceived satisfaction
Sartorius (1995)	Psychiatric rehabilitation clients	Review essay	Not specific, but leisure, work, family, community, aesthetic, and health are mentioned
Siegel and Brent (1997)	Schizophrenic patients	Q-TWIST method	In-hospital, in-community without symptoms, in-community with symptoms
Slaughter, Lehman, and Myers (1991)	Severely mentally ill adults in residential care facilities	Literature review of 16 studies	Employment status, safety, social contacts, leisure activities, and general life satisfaction
Sonino, Fava, Fallo, and Boscaro (1990)	Patients with endocrine disease	Recommends use of the psychosomatic approach in QOL with these patients	Life events preceding disease onset, psychological distress, abnormal illness behavior
Sullivan, Wells, and Leake (1992)	101 Former acute care psychiatric inpatients living in Mississippi	Quality of Life Index, Drug Attitude Inventory, the Symptom Checklist	Living situation, social life, personal health, finances, global rating, depressive symptoms, psychotic symptoms, medications compliance, side effects, alcohol abuse, social skills, living skills, criticism by family
West, Kregel, and Banks (1990)	1550 Individuals placed in supported employment (65% with mental retardation, 9% with long-term mental illness, and 10% with head injuries and cerebral palsy)	*Data Management System Operations Manual* for form completion by 96 provider agencies	Evaluation of QOL in worklife by looking availability of fringe benefits

APPENDIX 26 (continued)
Mental Illness and Quality of Life (QOL) Literature

Source	Population	Measures/Method	Domains
Whelton, Pawlick, and Cardamone (1997)	105 Families with 92 family members with psychiatric disabilities	Questionnaires sent to families regarding the Hamilton Program for Schizophrenia to determine levels of satisfaction with the program	Time and money spent by family members for their relatives with disabilities and reduction of caregiving by program. Quality of relationship with relative illness management
Wilkinson, Williams, Krekorian, McLees, and Falloon (1992)	32 Adults with functional mental disorders	Structured Interview schedule, Charing Cross Health Indicator, Clinical Global Impression Scale	Adaptive functioning, social performance, patient and family distress, economic, and sociodemographic factors

References

Baker, F., Jodrey, D., and Intagliata, J. (1992). Social support and quality of life of community support clients. *Community Mental Health Journal,* 29(5): 397-411.

Bigelow, D. A., McFarland, B. H., and Olson, M. M. (1991). Quality of life of community mental health program clients: validating a measure. *Community Mental Health Journal,* 27(1): 43-55.

Brown, C. (1996). *A* comparison of living situation and loneliness for people with mental illness. *Psychiatric Rehabilitation Journal,* 20(2): 59-65.

Brown, C., Cosgrove, N., and De Selm, T. (1997). Barriers interfering with life satisfaction for individuals with severe mental illness. *Psychiatric Rehabilitation Journal,* 20(3): 67-71.

Ciardiello, J. A. and Bingham, W. C. (1962). The career maturity of schizophrenic clients. *Rehabilitation Counseling Bulletin,* 3-9.

Corrigan, P. W. and Buican, B. (1995). The construct validity of subjective quality of life for the severely mentally ill. *Journal of Nervous and Mental Disease,* 183(5): 281-285.

Corten, P., Mercier, C., and Pele, I. (1994). Subjective quality of life: clinical model for assessment of rehabilitation treatment in psychiatry. *Social Psychiatric Epidemiology,* 29: 178-183.

Dellario, D. J. and Anthony, W. A. (1981). On the relative effectiveness of institutional and alternative placement for the psychiatrically disabled. *Journal of Social Issues,* 37(3): 21-33.

Elizur, D. and Shye, S. (1990). Quality of work life and its relation to quality of life. *Applied Psychology: An International Review,* 39(3): 275-291.

Endicott, J., Nee, J., Harrison, W., and Blumenthal, R. (1993). Quality of life enjoyment and satisfaction questionnaire: a new measure. *Psychopharmacology Bulletin,* 29: 321-326.

Fabian, E. S. (1990). Quality of life: a review of theory and practice implications for individuals with long-term mental illness. *Rehabilitation Psychology,* 35(3): 161-170.

Fabian, E. S. (1992). Supported employment and quality of life: does a job make a difference? *Rehabilitation Counseling Bulletin,* 36(2): 85-87.

Fitzsimmons, B. and Bunting, L. K. (1997). Parkinson's Disease: Quality of life issues. http://www.cnsonline.org/www/archive/parkins/park.07.txt

Frisch, M. B., Cornell, J., and Villanueva. (1992). Clinical validation of the Quality of Life Inventory: a measure of life satisfaction for use in treatment planning and outcome assessment. *Psychological Assessment,* 4(1): 92-101.

Gater, R. A., Kind, P., and Gudex, C. (1995). Quality of life in liaison psychiatry: a comparison of patient and clinician assessment. *British Journal of Psychiatry,* 166: 515-520.

Gerber, G. J., Coleman, G. E., Johnston, L., and Lafave, H. G. (1994). Quality of life of people with psychiatric disabilities 1 and 3 years after discharge from hospital. *Quality of Life Research,* 3: 379-383.

Huxley, P. and Warner, R. (1992). Case management, quality of life, and satisfaction with services of long-term psychiatric patients. *Hospital and Community Psychiatry,* 43(8): 799-802.

Jablensky, A. (1992). Politics and mental health. *International Journal of Social Psychiatry,* 38(1): 24-29.

Lehman, A. F., Reed, S. K., and Possidente, S. M. (1982). Priorities for long-term care: comments from board-and-care residents. *Psychiatric Quarterly,* 54(3): 181-189

Lerner, D. J., Levine, S., Malspeis, and D'Agostino, R. B. (1994). Job strain and health-related quality of life in a national sample. *American Journal of Public Health,* 84(10): 1580-1585.

Malm, U., May, P. R. A., and Dencker, S. J. (1981). Evaluation of the quality of life of the schizophrenic outpatient: a checklist. *Schizophrenia Bulletin,* 7(3): 477-487.

Moller, M. D. and Murphy, M. F. (1997). The Three R's Rehabilitation Program: A prevention approach for the management of relapse symptoms associated with psychiatric diagnosis. *Psychiatric Rehabilitation Journal,* 20(3): 42-48.

Munich, R. L. and Lang, E. (1993). The boundaries of psychiatric rehabilitation. *Hospital and Community Psychiatry,* 44(7): 661-665.

Oliver, N., Holloway, F., and Carson, J. (1995). Deconstructing quality of life. *Journal of Mental Health,* 4: 1-4.

O'Rear, G., Bark, L., and Hutchinson, D. S. (1996). The promotion of wellness among people with psychiatric disabilities in community rehabilitation and treatment. *Psychiatric Rehabilitation Journal,* 20(2): 82-84.

Roessler, R. T. (1990). A quality of life perspective on rehabilitation counseling. *Rehabilitation Counseling Bulletin,* 34(2): 82-91.

Rosenfeld, S. (1992). Factors contributing to the subjective quality of life of the chronic mentally ill. *Journal of Health and Social Behavior,* 33: 299-315.

Sartorius, N. (1995). Rehabilitation and Quality of Life. *International Journal of Mental Health,* 24(1): 7-13.

Shain, M. (1996). Work, employment, and mental health: implications for quality of life. In R. Renwick, I. Brown, and M. Nagler (Eds.), *Quality of Life in Health Promotion and Rehabilitation,* pp. 327-341. Thousand Oaks, CA: Sage Publications.

Siegel, C. and Brent, R. J. (1997). Quality-adjusted time project. *Center for the Study of Issues in Public Mental Health.*
http://www.rfmh.org/sciphm/qat.htm

Slaughter, J. G., Lehman, A. F., and Myers, C. P. (1991). Quality of life of severely mentally ill adults in residential care facilities. *Adult Residential Care Journal,* 5(2): 97-111.

Sonino, N., Fava, G. A., Fallo, F., and Boscaro, M. (1990). Psychological distress and quality of life in endocrine disease. *Psychotherapy and Psychosomatics,* 54: 140-144.

Sullivan, G., Wells, K. B., and Leake, B. (1992). Clinical factors associated with better quality of life in a seriously mental ill population. *Hospital and Community Psychiatry,* 43(8): 794-798.

West, M., Kregel, J., and Banks, P. D. (1990). Fringe benefits available to supported employment participants. *Rehabilitation Counseling Bulletin,* 34(2): 126-138.

Whelton, C., Pawlick, J., and Cardamone, J. (1997). Involving families in psychosocial rehabilitation. *Psychiatric Rehabilitation Journal,* 20(3): 57-60.

Wilkinson, G., Williams, B., Krekorian, H., McLees, S., and Falloon, I. (1992). QALYs in mental health: a case study. *Psychological Medicine,* 22: 725-731.

APPENDIX 27
Multicultural Studies in Quality of Life Literature

Source	Population	Measures/Method	Domains
Blandford and Chappell (1990)	193 Interviews with Treaty and Metis Indians in Winnipeg and 300 non-Natives in Winnipeg	UCLA Loneliness Scale and Overall Life Satisfaction Scale	Age, gender, marital status, work, income, functional disability, chronic conditions, perceived health, family

APPENDIX 27 (continued)
Multicultural Studies in Quality of Life Literature

Source	Population	Measures/Method	Domains
Canales, Ganz, and Coscarelli (1995)	Hispanic cancer patients — 6 males and 24 females	Interviews, translated Cancer Rehabilitation Evaluation System (CARES) into Spanish	Marital status, gender, age, employment, education, ethnicity, religion, income, children at home, changes since diagnosis
Chaturvedi (1991)	50 Hindu adults with and without Cancer	Interviews based on QOL list prepared before the interviews	Peace of mind, spiritual tasks (meditation), religion, family, basic need fulfillment, self-esteem, satisfaction with functioning, physical health, psychological health, individual functioning and marital, occupational, social, and self care
Ensminger (1995)	836 African-American mothers on welfare	Interviews based on selected measures	Psychological distress, welfare, earlier life conditions, region of U.S., teenage mother, chronic burdens, number of children, single parent, self perceptions of health, self-esteem, psychological and physical well-being
Ganz, Bernhard, and Hurny (1991)	Oncology patients	Survey of British and European investigators regarding QOL research on psychosocial oncology	Surveyed research on measurement techniques and validation, clinical trials and QOL, coping techniques, rehabilitation and supportive needs
Gilbar (1991)	51 Cancer patients who dropped out of chemotherapy, 19 who refused treatment, and 70 who completed treatment	Psychosocial Adjustment to Physical Illness Scale, Brief Symptom Inventory, and interviews at patients' homes.	Heath care, work, home, sexual relationship, extended family, social and psychological distress. Somatization and psychological symptoms
Headey, Veenhoven, and Wearing (1991)	QOL survey of 942 persons conducted in 4 waves (1981, 1983, 1985, 1987) in Victoria, Australia	Used Life-as-a-Whole Index, Delighted–Terrible Scale, Eyesenck Personality Inventory, and socioeconomic status by gender in examining subjective well-being	Marriage, work, material standard of living, leisure, friendship, and health
Kurz and Prather (1995)	Girls — birth to 19 years in the world's developing countries	Findings of the Association of Women in Development Forum	Mortality, poor health care, inadequate nutrition, lack of education, female genital mutilation, child labor, pregnancy and sexual activity, violence, prostitution, poor self concept

APPENDIX 27 (continued)
Multicultural Studies in Quality of Life Literature

Source	Population	Measures/Method	Domains
Logue (1990)	Elderly long-term American Indian, Black, and White patients (over 45 years)	Data obtained from Public Use Microdata Samples for Oklahoma from 1980 decennial census and from a query on Public Transportation Disability	Social risk, aging, disability, economic status, health, race, gender, educational attainment, marital status, area of residence
Mathias, Fifer, and Patrick (1994)	International QOL clinical trials	8-Step protocol for rapidly translating a QOL questionnaire into multiple languages	Health well-being, psychosocial well-being, health distress, depression, self-esteem, emotional functioning, and work loss
Tuchler, Hofmann, Bernahart et al. (1992)	1014 Adult patients in European countries	QOL Questionnaire	Physical condition, QOL, relationships and social contacts, health, overall life situation, medical treatment, sexuality, recovery chances, physical capacity, life satisfaction
WHOQOL Group (1994)	Field centers in development of instrument in 15 countries	Development of World Health Organization Quality of Life instrument using consensus of definition of QOL by international expert review, qualitative pilot with focus groups, field tests to develop psychometric properties	Physical, psychological, level of independence, social relationships, environment, spiritual religion/personal beliefs

References

Blandford, A. A. and Campbell, N. L. (1990). Subjective well-being among native and non-native elderly persons: do differences exist? *Canadian Journal on Aging,* 9(4): 386-399.

Canales, S., Ganz, P. A., and Coscarelli, C. A. (1995). Translation and validation of a quality of life instrument for Hispanic American cancer patients: methodological considerations. *Quality of Life Research,* 4: 3-11.

Chaturvedi, S. K. (1991). What's important for quality of life to Indians — In relation to cancer. *Social Science Medicine,* 33(1): 91-94.

Ensminger, M. E. (1995). Welfare and psychological distress: a longitudinal study of African American urban mothers. *Journal of Health and Social Behavior,* 36: 346-359.

Ganz, P. A., Bernahrd, J., and Hurny, C. (1991). Quality of life and psychosocial oncology research in Europe: state of the art. *Journal of Psychosocial Oncology,* 9(1): 1-22.

Gilbar, O. (1991). The quality of life of cancer patients who refuse chemotherapy. *Social Science Medicine,* 32(12): 1337-1340.

Heady, B, Veenhoven, R., and Wearing, A. (1991). Top-down vs. bottom-up theories of subjective well-being. *Social Indicators Research,* 24: 81-100.

Kurz, K. M. and Prather, C. J. (1995). *Improving the Quality of Life of Girls.* New York: United Nations Children's Fund Programme Publications.

Logue, B. J. (1990). Race differences in long-term disability: middle-aged and older American Indians, Blacks and Whites in Oklahoma. *Social Science Journal,* 27(3): 253-272.

Mathias, S. D., Fifer, S. K., and Patrick, D. L. (1994). Rapid translation of quality of life measures for international clinical trials: avoiding errors in the minimalist approach. *Quality of Life Research,* 3: 403-412.

Tuchler, H., Hofmann, S., Bernahart, M., Bruglatelli, M., Chrobak, L., Franke, A., Herold, M., Holowiechki, J., Ihle, R., Jaksic, B., Krc, I., Munteanue, N., Pawlicki, M., Sakalova, A., Schranz, V., Wolf, H., and Lutz, D. (1992). A short multilingual quality of life questionnaire — practicability, reliability, and interlingual homogeneity. *Quality of Life Research*, 1: 107-117.

WHOQOL Group. (1994). Development of the WHOQOL: rationale and current status. *International Journal of Mental Health,* 23(3): 24-56.

APPENDIX 28
Neuromuscular Disorders and Quality of Life (QOL) Literature

Source	Population	Measures/Method	Domains
Fitzsimmons and Bunting (1997)	Persons with Parkinson's Disease (PD)	Essay on the psycho-social aspects of PD and QOL	Social roles, mental acuity, emotional states, subjective well-being, interrelationships, life satisfaction and physical health
Schwartz, Devine, Schechter, and Bender (1990)	19 Myasthenia gravis and 19 amyotrophic lateral sclerosis patients	9-Rung Cantril Ladder, Multidimensional Health Locus of Control, Functional Living Index for Cancer, Quality of Life Index	Demographics, severity of illness, coping styles, life satisfaction, perceived health and social activity, control of health, psychosocial well-being, public and body image, and QOL
Turk (1996)	Women with disabilities: neuromuscular diseases, late effects of polio, spinal cord pathology, multiple sclerosis, osteoporosis in disability	Essay on fitness as an optimal state of physical well-being; call for research on fitness issues for women with physical disabilities	Flexibility, muscular strength and endurance, cardiopulmonary conditioning

References

Fitzsimmons, B. and Bunting, L. K. (1997). Parkinson's Disease: quality of life issues http://www.cnsonline.org/www/archive/parkins/park.07.txt

Schwartz, L. B., Devine, P. A., Schechter, C. B., and Bender, A. N. (1990). Impact of illness on lifestyle. *Loss, Grief, and Care*, 4(3-4): 3-21.

Turk, M. A. (1996). The impact of disability on fitness in women: musculoskeletal issues. In D. M. Krotoski, M. A. Nosek, and M. A. Turk (Eds.), *Women with Physical Disabilities: Achieving and Maintaining Health and Well-Being,* pp. 391-401. Baltimore: Paul H. Brookes.

APPENDIX 29
Orthopedic Injuries and Quality of Life (QOL) Literature

Source	Population	Measures/Method	Domains
Chubon (1985)	Nondisabled graduate students and persons with chronic back problems, and prison inmates	Life Situation Survey	Pain tolerance, satisfaction with life quality

APPENDIX 29
Orthopedic Injuries and Quality of Life (QOL) Literature

Source	Population	Measures/Method	Domains
Katz, Larson, Phillips, Fossel, and Liang (1992)	54 Patients undergoing total hip arthroplasty	Sickness Impact Profile, Arthritis Impact Measurement Scales, and Modified Health Assessment Questionnaire	Physical, psychological, global dimensions
Limacher, Dahler, Bosch, and Egli (1991)	Back pain patients	Questionnaire completed by 5 general practitioners for first 20 patients seen for consultation	Work, leisure, partnership, family, housing, stress, misfortune, care availability, and nursing
Osberg, McGinnis, DeJong, and Seward (1987)	97 Elderly disabled adults (31 with hip fractures or replacements	Path analysis model to assess QOL, Barthel Index, self-administered questionnaire	Income, age, marital status, functional capacity, independence
Verbrugge, Reoma, and Gruber-Baldini (1994)	165 Persons with chronic disability	Mental Status Questionnaire, Beck Depression Inventory, Activities of Daily Living, Six Motions to determine physical functioning, and Index of Well-Being	Cognitive, emotional, social, physical, and global well-being

References

Chubon, R. A. (1985). Quality of life measurement of persons with back problems: some preliminary findings. *Journal of Applied Rehabilitation Counseling,* 16(2): 31-34.

Katz, J. N., Larson, M. G., Phillips, C. B., Fossel, A. H., and Liang, M. H. (1992). *Medical Care,* 30(10): 917-925.

Limacher, B., Dahler, E., Bosch, J., and Egli, N. (1991). Color me multi-colored: a note on problems in clinical research methodology. *Family Systems Medicine,* 9(1): 65-68.

Osberg, J. S., McGinnis, G. E., DeJong, G., and Seward, M. L. (1987). Life satisfaction and quality of life among disabled elderly adults. *Journal of Gerontology,* 42(2): 228-230.

Verbrugge, L. M., Reoma, J. M., and Gruber-Baldini, A. L. (1994). Short-term dynamics of disability and well-being. *Journal of Health and Social Behavior,* 35: 97-117.

APPENDIX 30
Ostomy Patients and Quality of Life (QOL) Literature

Source	Population	Measures/Method	Domains
Brydolf, Berndtsson, Lindholm, and Berglund (1994)	36 Patients with ostomies and 12 without	Used Ostomy Adjustment Scale and a visual analog scale to measure total QOL	Physical function, psychological strain, and social interaction
McGee, O'Boyle, Hickey, O'Malley, and Joyce (1991)	20 Irritable bowel syndrome and 20 peptic ulcer disease patients as compared to 42 healthy individuals	Used the Schedule for Evaluation of Individual Quality of Life	Family, work, recreation, religion, and health

References

Brydolf, M., Berndtsson, I., Lindholm, E., and Berglund, B. (1994). Evaluation of a Swedish version of the Ostomy Adjustment Scale. *Scandinavian Journal of Caring Science,* 8: 179-183.

McGee, H. M., O'Boyle, C. A., Hickey, A., O'Malley, K., and Joyce, C. R. B. (1991). Assessing the quality of life of the individual: the SEIQoL with a healthy and a gastroenterology unit population. *Psychological Medicine,* 21: 749-759.

APPENDIX 31
Review of Quality of Life (QOL) Instruments

Authors	Instrument	Purpose
Andrews, Meyer, and Berla (1996)	Lost Pleasure of Life Scale (LPL Scale)	Development of descriptors for the LPL Scale to determine inter-rater reliability and development of 15 case vignettes to test ecological validity
Andrews and Withey (1976) cited in Baker Jodrey, and Intagliata (1992)	Satisfaction with Life Domains (SLDS)	A measure of respondent satisfaction with 15 life domains
Baker, Curbow, and Wingard (1992)	Satisfaction with Life Domains Scale for Cancer (SLDS-C)	A self-report instrument for assessing subjective QOL of patients receiving aggressive cancer treatment
Bech (1990)	Examination of objective (nomothetic) and subjective (idographic) approaches to measuring QOL	Discusses advantages and disadvantages of both approaches in measurement
Bigelow et al. (1991) cited in Corrigan and Buican (1995)	Quality of Life Questionnaire	Designed to measure subjective QOL
Bradburn (1969) cited in Baker, Jodrey, and Intagliata (1992)	Bradburn Positive Negative Affect Scales	To assess the client's sense of psychological well-being
Brown, Bayer, and MacFarlane (1989)	Quality of Life Questionnaire	Developed for a study dealing with developmentally handicapped adults
Brydoff, Berndtsson, Lindholm, and Berglund (1994)	Ostomy Adjustment Scale, Swedish version (OAS)	To adapt the OAS for Swedish patients and their adjustment to an ostomy
Cox and Gonder–Frederick (1992)	Summary of IS Instruments	To measure well-being of insulin-dependent diabetics
Cragg and Harrison (1986)	Questionnaire	To measure the QOL of people with learning disabilities in residential care
Cunny and Perri (1991)	Short-Form General Health Survey of the Medical Outcomes Study	Single-item measure of health-related QOL when multiple-item measures of health-related QOL are not suitable.
Dagan, Jones, and Ruddick (1994)	Questionnaire	To determine psychometric properties of Cragg and Harrison's (1986) *Quality of Life Questionnaire*
Endicott et al. (1993) cited in Corrigan and Buican (1995)	Quality of Life Enjoyment and Satisfaction Questionnaire	Designed to measure subjective QOL
Endicott, Nee, Harrison, and Blumenthal (1993)	Quality of Life Enjoyment and Satisfaction Questionnaire	Designed to measure subjective QOL, based on life satisfaction and enjoyment
Evans, Dingus, and Haselkorn (1993)	Review of QOL and disability studies, (52) articles, 1985–1989	16% of the articles included data about QOL and disability requiring rehabilitation. Only 13% were randomized clinical trials.

APPENDIX 31 (continued)
Review of Quality of Life (QOL) Instruments

Authors	Instrument	Purpose
Ferrans, Cohen, and Smith (1992)	QOL Index — Narcolepsy version	Designed to measure symptoms, activity/experience, problems or satisfaction of life, self-esteem and health and functioning
Ferrans and Powers (1992)	Quality of Life Index — Dialysis version	Measures life satisfaction and importance of domains of satisfaction of life, self-esteem and health and functioning
George and Bearon (1980)	Kutner Morale Scale, Life Satisfaction Index, Cantril Ladder, Philadelphia Geriatric Morale Scale, Affect Balance Scale, Self-Esteem Scale, Self-Acceptance Scale, Tennessee Self-Concept Scale, Self-Esteem Inventory, Semantic Differential Scale, Health Index, Subjective Health Rating, Function Status Index, OARS Multidimensional Functional Assessment Questionnaire, Stockon Geriatric Rating Scale, North-Hatt Occupational Prestige Ratings, Duncan Socioeconomic Index, Hollingshead Two-Factor Index of Social Position, Measure of Income, Measure of Net Worth, U.S. Government Poverty Measure	The authors reviewed psychometric instruments designed to examine QOL for elderly persons
Goodwin, Boggs, and Graham-Pole (1994)	Development of a 21-item parent report measure of QOL, the Pediatric Oncology Quality of Life Scale	Physical function, role restriction, emotional distress, reaction to current medical treatment
Hays, Kallich, Mapes, Coons, and Carter (1994)	Development of the Kidney Disease QOL Instrument (KDQOL)	Targeted physical functioning, emotional functioning, social functioning, pain, energy-fatigue, and general health perceptions
Hays and Shapiro (1992)	Use of Quality of Well-Being Scale, HIV Overview of Problems/Evaluation System, COOP Charts for visual acuity, Medical Outcomes Study-derived measures	Ideal measures taps multiple dimensions (physical function, emotional well-being, social interaction) and allows for integration of these dimensions into an aggregate score. Reviews each instrument selected
Hays, Vickrey, Hermann, Perrine, Cramer, Meador, Spritzer, and Devinsky (1995)	Used 89-item QOL Inventory	Differences found in agreement by proxies and patients on subjective measures, but moderate agreement in directly observable functions
Heinrichs et al. (1984) cited in Corrigan and Buican (1995)	Quality of Life Scale	Designed to measure subjective QOL
Henderson et al. (1980) cited in Baker, Jodrey, and Intagliata (1992)	Availability of Social Support Scale	Examined availability of key social relationships
Hennessy, Moriarty, Zack, Scherr, and Brackbill (1994)	QOL public health using Behavioral Risk Factor Surveillance System, a state-based telephone surveillance system — Health-Related QOL	Self-perceived health, recent physical health, recent mental health, and recent activity limitations
Hermann (1995)	Reviews phases of QOL research for epilepsy patients	(1) Clinical evaluation and generic measures; (2) epilepsy-specific measures; and (3) QOL epilepsy measures such as ESI-55, QOLIE-89, and Seizure Severity Scale

APPENDIX 31 (continued)
Review of Quality of Life (QOL) Instruments

Authors	Instrument	Purpose
Howard and Rockwood (1995)	Reviewed and ranked measurement properties of QOL instruments. Need for more validation of QOL instruments for Alzheimer's patients	Progressive Deterioration Scale and Italian Quality of Life Scale had the most promising measurement properties
Hughes, Hwang, Kim, Eisenman, and Killian	Review of 87 empirical studies analyzed and a model proposed	Found 15 dimensions of QOL for people with disabilities, resulting in 1,243 different measures. A growing consensus in the research for a conceptual model of QOL that is multidimensional and interactional
Huxley and Warner (1992) cited in Corrigan and Buican (1995)	Quality of Life Profile	Designed to measure subjective QOL
Johannesson (1994)	Using quality-adjusted life years (QALYs) and healthy-years equivalents (HYEs) as outcome measures in health care	Recommends further empirical work to validate ranking risky health profiles according to individual preferences
Johnson, Casey, and Noriega (1994)	Functional Assessment Cancer Tool and development of the QOL Radiation Therapy Instrument	Review of QOL instrument designed to measure QOL for radiation therapy patients
Kaplan (1991)	General Health Policy Model (GHPM)	Measures mortality (death); morbidity (dysfunction in mobility, physical, and social activity); utility (relative importance); and prognosis (duration of the illness)
Kaplan, Debon, and Anderson (1991)	Quality of Well-Being Scale	Study of rating scale points upon utilities in the scale; designed to measure well-years
Kloseck, Crilly, Ellis, and Lammers (1996)	Leisure Competence Measure	Leisure awareness, skills, attitude, social appropriateness, group interaction skills, social context, and community participation — all seven scales found valid and reliable
Lehman (1983, 1988) cited in Corrigan and Buican (1995)	Quality of Life Interview	Designed to measure subjective QOL
Malm et al. (1981) cited in Corrigan and Buican (1995)	Quality of Life Checklist	Designed to measure subjective QOL
Malm, May, and Dencker (1981)	Quality of Life Checklist	To measure QOL in medical care, social, standard of living, communication and transportation, work, safety, education, leisure, spiritual/religious
Mathias, Fifer, and Patrick (1994)	8-Step protocol for rapidly translating into multiple languages	For international clinical trials
McCauley and Bremer (1991)	Bradburn Affect Balance Scale and Campbell's Scale of General Affect	Recommends use in addition to objective QOL factors such as health, medical records, employment
McCulloch (1991)	Rosser Matrix and Functional Limitations Profile	Not appropriate for measuring outcomes in occupational therapy
Mulhern, Fairclough, Friedman, and Leigh (1990)	Play Performance Scale for Children (PPSC) and Vineland Adaptive Behavior Scales	The PPSC will need major revisions to measure QOL in children with cancer

APPENDIX 31 (continued)
Review of Quality of Life (QOL) Instruments

Authors	Instrument	Purpose
Muthny, Koch, and Stump (1990)	Review of QOL instruments used to assess QOL for oncology patients	Visual Analog Scale, Quality of Adjusted Life Years, Time without Symptoms, Karnofsky Index, Eastern Cooperative Oncology Group, World Health Organization Scales, Ability Index, Linear Analog Self-Assessment, Functional Living Index for Cancer, QOL Index, European Organization for Research and Treatment Cancer QOL Questionnaire, Padilla QOL Index, Ontario Cancer Institute QOL Questionnaire, Sickness Impact Profile, Psychosocial Adjustment to Illness Scale, Nottingham Health Profile
Osipow and Spokane (1987) cited in Decker and Borgen (1991)	Occupational Stress Inventory (OSI)	To measure stress, strain, and coping on the job
Ouellette-Kuntz (1990)	Use of Quality of Life Interview Schedule of ten mentally retarded adults	Emphasis on intra- and inter-rater agreement
Ouellette-Kuntz and McCreary (1996)	Development of the QOL Interview Schedule	To be used for persons whose disabilities disallow them to identify QOL issues — used with two key persons, usually a family member and paid caregiver
Perry and Felce (1995)	Review of 14 objective measures of service quality in residential staffed houses	Characteristics of the Physical Environment Scale, Physical Quality Scale, Programme Analysis of Service Systems, Index of Community Involvement, Community Oriented Programmes Environment Scale, Group Home Management Schedule, Characteristics of the Treatment Environment Scale, Choice Making Scale
Pinkney et al. (1991) cited in Corrigan and Buican (1995)	Client's Quality of Life Instrument	Designed to measure subjective QOL
Raphael (1996)	Quality of Life Profile: Seniors Version QOLPSV	Designed to examine QOL for senior citizens
Rosen, Simon, and McKinsey (1995)	Developed subjective QOL instrument — PALS	Designed to measure Perceived Stress, Affect, Loneliness, and Satisfaction
Rosser and Watts (1972) cited in Wilkinson, Williams, Krekorian, McLees, and Falloon (1992)	Charing Cross Health Indicator	Measures a single value outcome for Quality Adjusted Life Years
Ruffing-Rahal (1991)	The Integration Inventory	An appraisal of the construct validity using the revised Philadelphia Geriatric Center Morale Scale, the Spiritual Well-Being Scale, and 4 measures of self-rated well being
Schaafsma and Osoba (1994)	Karnofsky Performance Status and item 30 of the QOL questionnaire developed by the European Organization for Research and Treatment of Cancer Study Group	QOL is a much broader concept than the Karnofsky, since it captures more than physical functioning

APPENDIX 31 (continued)
Review of Quality of Life (QOL) Instruments

Authors	Instrument	Purpose
Skantze et al. (1992) cited in Corrigan and Buican (1995)	Quality of Life Self-Assessment	Designed to measure subjective QOL
Spilker, Molinek, Johnston, Simpson, et al. (1990)	Comprehensive bibliography of published articles in which QOL instruments are described or printed	Three indexes: (1) papers which refer to particular QOL instruments; (2) QOL papers which discuss different therapeutic categories; and (3) QOL instruments used in specific therapeutic categories
Terman (1995)	Introduces the Loss of Enjoyment of Life-Severity Scale (LEL-SS) partially based on Global Assessment of Functioning in DSM	Purpose is to assist in settling cases more frequently without need for trial
Thapa and Rowland (1989) cited in Corrigan and Buican (1995)	Quality of Life Questionnaire	Designed to measure subjective QOL
Tuchler, Hofmann, Bernhart et al. (1992)	Quality of Life Questionnaire	Objective was to examine practicability, reliability, and interlingual homogeneity in versions in Czech, German, Hungarian, Italian, Croation, Polish, Romanian, and Slovakian
Vickrey, Hays, Graber et al. (1992)	Epilepsy Surgery Inventory-55	Development of instrument for patients facing epilepsy surgery; found to be reliable, valid, and sensitive to differences in seizure status
Walker, Blankenship, Ditty, and Lynch (1987)	MMPI, Adaptive Behavior Scale, Quality of Life Rating Scale	The "nonrecovered" group of head-injured rehabilitation clients was significantly higher on PD scale; "recovered" group significantly higher on economic activity domain and lower on psychosocial dysfunction. The self-ratings of the "nonrecovered" subjects were significantly more distinct from ratings made by their relatives or significant others than those of "recovered" subjects
WHOQOL Group (1994)	Development of World Health Organization Quality of Life instrument	Using consensus of definition of QOL by international expert review, qualitative pilot with focus groups, field tests to develop psychometric properties. Studies being done in 15 centers in the world, including Seattle
Williams, Eyring, Gaynor, and Long (1991)	Development of the Views of Life Scale	Reliability, convergent and divergent validity, and high internal consistency found

References

Andrews, P., Meyer, R. G., and Berla, E. P. (1996). Development of the Lost Pleasure of Life Scale. *Law and Human Behavior, 20*(1): 99-111.

Andrews, F. M. and Withey, S. B. (1976). *Social Indicators of Well-Being: American's Perceptions of Life Quality.* New York: Plenum.

Baker, F., Curbow, B., and Wingard, J. R. (1992). Development of the Satisfaction with Life Domains Scale for Cancer. *Journal of Psychosocial Oncology,* 10(3): 75-90.

Baker, F., Jodrey, D., and Intagliata, J. (1992). Social support and quality of life of community support clients. *Community Mental Health Journal,* 29(5): 397-411.

Bech, P. (1990). Measurement of psychological distress and well-being. *Psychotherapy and Psychosomatics,* 54: 77-89.
Bigelow, D. A., MacFarland, B. H., and Olson, M. M. (1991). Quality of life of community mental health program clients: validating a measure. *Community Mental Health Journal,* 27: 43-55.
Bradburn, N. M. (1969). *The Structure of Psychological Well-Being.* Chicago: Aldine.
Brown, R. I. (1989). Aging, disability, and quality of life: a challenge for society. *Canadian Psychology,* 30(3): 551-558.
Brown, R. I., Bayer, M.B., and MacFarlane, C. (1989). *Rehabilitation Programmes: Performance and Quality of Life of Adults with Developmental Handicaps.* Toronto: Lugus.
Brydolf, M., Berndtsson, I., Lindholm, E., and Berglund, B. (1994). Evaluation of a Swedish version of the Ostomy Adjustment Scale. *Scandinavian Journal of Caring Science,* 8: 179-183.
Corrigan, P. W. and Buican, B. (1995). The construct validity of subjective quality of life for the severely mentally ill. *Journal of Nervous and Mental Disease,* 183(5): 281-285.
Cox, D. J. and Gonder–Frederick, L. (1992). Major developments in behavioral diabetes research. *Journal of Consulting and Clinical Psychology,* 60(4): 628-638.
Cragg, R. and Harrison, J. (1986). *Living in a Supervised Home: A Questionnaire on Quality of Life.* Wolverley, Kidderminster, Worcester, U.K.: West Midlands Campaign for People with a Mental Handicap.
Cunny, K. A. and Perri, M. (1991). Single-item vs. multiple-item measures of health-related quality of life. *Psychological Reports,* 69: 127-130.
Dagan, D., Jones, J., and Ruddick, L. (1994). The psychometric properties of a scale for assessing the quality of life of people with learning disabilities in residential care. *British Journal of Developmental Disabilities,* XL(79): 98-103.
Decker, P. J. and Borgen, F. H. (1991). Dimensions of work appraisal: stress, strain, coping, job satisfaction, and negative affectivity. *Journal of Counseling Psychology,* 40(4): 470-478.
Endicott, J., Nee, J., Harrison, W., and Blumenthal, R. (1993). Quality of Life Enjoyment and Satisfaction Questionnaire: A new measure. *Psychopharmacolgy Bulletin,* 29: 321-326.
Evans, R. L., Dingus, C. M., and Haselkorn, J. K. (1993). Living with a disability: A synthesis and critique of the literature on quality of life, 1985-1989. *Psychological Reports,* 72: 771-777.
Ferrans, C. E., Cohen, F. L., and Smith, K. M. (1992). The quality of life of persons with narcolepsy. Psychosocial aspects of narcolepsy. *Loss, Grief, and Care,* 5(3-4): 23-32.
Ferrans, C. and Powers, M. (1992). Psychometric assessment of the Quality of Life Index. *Research in Nursing and Health,* 15: 111-119.
George, L. K. and Bearon, L. B. (1980). *Quality of Life in Older Persons: Meaning and Measurement.* New York: Human Sciences Press.
Goodwin, D. A. J., Boggs, S. R., and Graham-Poole, J. (1994). Development and validation of the pediatric oncology quality of life scale. *Psychological Assessment,* 6(4): 321-328.
Hays, R. D., Kallich, J. D., Mapes, D. L., Coons, S. J., and Carter, W. B. (1994). Development of the Kidney Disease Quality of Life (KDQOL) Instrument. *Quality of Life Research,* 3: 329-338.
Hays, R. D. and Shapiro, M. F. (1992). An overview of generic health-related quality of life measures for HIV research. *Quality of Life Research,* 1: 91-97.
Hays, R. D., Vickrey, B. G., Hermann, B. P., Perrine, K., Cramer, J., Meador, K., Spritzer, K., and Devinsky, O. (1995). Agreement between self reports and proxy reports of quality of life in epilepsy patients. *Quality of Life Research,* 4: 159-168.
Heinrichs, D. W., Hanlon, T. E., and Carpenter, W. T. (1984). The Quality of Life Scale: an instrument for rating the schizophrenic deficit syndrome. *Schizophrenia Bulletin,* 10: 388-398.
Henderson, S., Duncan-Jones, P., Byrne, D. G., and Scott, R. (1980). Measuring social relations: the interview schedule for social interaction. *Psychological Medicine,* 10, 723-734.
Hennessy, C. H., Moriarty, D. G., Zack, M. M., Scherr, P. A., and Brackbill, R. (1994). Measuring health-related quality of life for public health surveillance. *Public Health Reports,* 106(5): 665-672.
Hermann, B. P. (1995). The evolution of health-related quality of life assessment in epilepsy. *Quality of Life Research,* 4: 87-100.
Howard, K. and Rockwood, K. (1995). Quality of life in Alzheimer's disease. *Dementia,* 6: 113-116.
Hughes, C., Hwang, B., Kim, J. H., Eisenman, L. T., and Killian, D. J. (1995). Quality of life in applied research: a review and analysis of empirical measures. *American Journal on Mental Retardation,* 99(6): 623-641.
Huxley, P. J., and Warner, R. (1992). Case management, quality of life, and satisfaction with services of long-term psychiatric patients. *Hospital Community Psychiatry,* 43: 799-802.

Johannesson, M. (1994). QALYs, HYEs, and individual preferences: a graphical illustration. *Social Science Medicine,* 39(12): 1623-1632.

Johnson, D. J., Casey, L., and Noriega, B. (1994). A pilot study of patient quality of life during radiation therapy treatment. *Quality of Life Research,* 3: 267-272.

Kaplan, R. M. (1991). Health-related quality of life in patient decision making. *Journal of Social Issues,* 47(4): 69-90.

Kaplan, R. M., Debon, M., and Anderson, B. F. (1991). Effects of number of rating scale points upon utilities in a Quality of Well-Being Scale. *Medical Care,* 29(10): 1061-1064.

Kloseck, M., Crilly, R. G., Ellis, G. D., and Lammers, E. (1996). Leisure Competence Measure: Development and reliability testing of a scale to measure functional outcomes in therapeutic recreation. *Therapeutic Recreation Journal,* 13-26.

Lehman, A. F. (1983). The well-being of chronic mental patients. *Archives of General Psychiatry,* 40: 369-373.

Lehman, A. F. (1988). A quality of life interview for chronically mentally ill. *Evaluation Program Plan,* 11: 51-62.

Malm, U., May, P. R. A., and Dencker, S. J. (1981). Evaluation of the quality of life of the schizophrenic outpatient: a checklist. *Schizophrenia Bulletin,* 7: 477-487.

Mathias, S. D., Fifer, S. K., and Patrick, D. L. (1994). Rapid translation of quality of life measures for international clinical trials: avoiding errors in the minimalist approach. *Quality of Life Research,* 3: 403-412.

McCauley, C. and Bremer, B. A. (1991). Subjective quality of life measures for evaluating medical intervention. *Evaluation and the Health Professions,* 14(4): 371-387.

McCulloch, D. (1991). Can we measure 'output'? Quality-adjusted life years, health indices and occupational therapy. *British Journal of Occupational Therapy,* 54(6): 219-221.

Mulhern, R. K., Fairclough, D. L., Friedman, A. G., and Leigh, L. D. (1990). Play Performance Scale as an index of quality of life of children with cancer. *Psychological Assessment,* 2(2): 149-155.

Muthny, F.A., Koch, U., and Stump, S. (1990). Quality of life in oncology patients. *Psychotherapy and Psychosomatics,* 54: 145-160.

Osipow, S. H. and Spokane, A. R. (1987). *Manual for the Occupational Stress Inventory.* Odessa, FL: Psychological Assessment Resources.

Ouellette-Kuntz, H. (1990). A pilot study in the use of the quality of life interview schedule. *Social Indicators Research,* 23: 283-298.

Ouellette-Kuntz, H. and McCreary, B. (1996). Quality of life assessment for persons with severe developmental disabilities. In R. Renwick, I. Brown, and M. Nagler (Eds.), *Quality of Life in Health Promotion and Rehabilitation,* pp. 268-278. Thousand Oaks, CA: Sage Publications.

Perry, J. and Felce, D. (1995). Objective assessments of quality of life: how much do they agree with each other? *Journal of Community and Applied Social Psychology,* 5: 1-19.

Pinkney, A. A., Gerber, G. J., and Lafave, H. G. (1991). Quality of life after psychiatric rehabilitation: the client's perspective. *Acta Psychiatrica Scandanavica,* 83: 86-91.

Raphael, D. (1996). Quality of life for older adults: toward the optimization of the aging process. In R. Renwick, I. Brown, and M. Nagler (Eds.), *Quality of Life in Health Promotion and Rehabilitation,* pp. 290-306. Thousand Oaks, CA: Sage Publications.

Rosen, M., Simon, E. W., and McKinsey, L. (1995). Subjective measure of quality of life. *Mental Retardation,* 33(1): 31-34.

Rosser, R. M. and Watts, V. C. (1972). The measurement of hospital output. *International Journal of Epidemiology,* 7: 347-357.

Ruffing-Rahal, M. A. (1991). Initial psychometric evaluation of a qualitative evaluation well-being measure: the Integration Inventory. *Health Values,* 15(2): 10-20.

Schaafsma, J. and Osoba, D. (1994). The Karnofsky performance status scale re-examined: a cross-validation with the EORTC-C30. *Quality of Life Research,* 3: 413-424.

Skantze, K., Malm, U., Dencker, S. J., May P. R. A., and Corrigan, P. W. (1992). Comparisons of quality of life to standard of living in schizophrenic outpatients. *British Journal of Psychiatry,* 161: 797-801.

Spilker, B., Molinek, F. R., Johnston, K. A., Simpson, R. L. et al. (1990). Quality of life bibliography and indexes. *Medical Care,* 28(12, Suppl.): DS1-DS77.

Terman, S. A. (1995). Emotional damages due to wrongful death — What are they worth? *Behavioral Sciences and the Law,* 11: 43-59.

Thapa, K., and Rowland, L. A. (1989). Quality of life perspectives in long-term care: staff and patient perceptions. *Acta Psychiatrica Scandanavica,* 80: 267-271.

Tuchler, H., Hofmann, S., Bernhart, M., Bruglatelli, M., Chrobak, L., Franke, A., Herold, M., Holowiechki, J., Ihle, R., Jaksic, B., Krc, I., Munteanue, N., Pawlicki, M., Sakalova, A., Schranz, V., Wolf, H., and Lutz, D. (1992). A short multilingual quality of life questionnaire — practicability, reliability, and interlingual homogeneity. *Quality of Life Research*, 1: 107-117.

Vickrey, B. G., Hays, R. D., Graber, J., Rausch, R., Engel, J., and Brook, R. H. (1992). A health-related quality of life instrument for patients evaluated for epilepsy surgery. *Medical Care*, 30(4): 299-319.

Walker, D. E., Blankenship, V., Ditty, J. A., and Lynch, K. P. (1987). Prediction of recovery for closed-head-injured adults: an evaluation of the MMPI, the Adaptive Behavior Scale, and a Quality of Life Rating Scale. *Journal of Clinical Psychology,* 43(6): 699-707.

WHOQOL Group. (1994). Development of the WHOQOL: rationale and current status. *International Journal of Mental Health,* 23(3): 24-56.

Wilkinson, G., Williams, B., Krekorian, H., McLees, S., and Falloon, I. (1992). QALYs in mental health: a case study. *Psychological Medicine,* 22: 725-731.

Williams, R. L., Eyring, M., Gaynor, P., and Long, J. D. (1991). Development of Views of Life Scale. *Psychology and Health*, 5: 165-181.

APPENDIX 32
Qualitative Methods in Quality of Life (QOL) Literature

Source	Population	Measures/Method	Domains
Bach and Rioux (1996)	Rehabilitation clients	Critique of health promotion and QOL research	Self-determination, equality, democratization, well-being
Baker, Jodrey, and Intagliata (1992)	729 Mentally ill adults in state-supported programs	Repeated (9 months apart) questionnaires, QOL interviews, Bradburn Positive and Negative Affect Scales, Satisfaction with Life Domains Scale	Availability and adequacy of social support needed for quality of life
Bellamy, Newton, LeBaron, and Horner (1990)	Persons with developmental disabilities	Essay on residential services and QOL lifestyle outcomes	Independence, enhanced adaptive functioning, activities of daily living, income, choice
Berla, Brookshire, and Smith (1990)	Personal injury plaintiffs	LPL Scale from 0 to 100% across the domains	Practical, psychological, social, and occupational domains
Bigelow, McFarland, and Olson (1991)	Community samples, client samples from 24 mental health agencies	Interviews and QOL Questionnaire	Psychological distress and well-being, tolerance of stress, independence, interdependence, interpersonal interactions, spouse role, work at home, social support, employability, meaningful use of time, substance abuse
Blumenthal and Emery (1988)	Cardiac patients	Review of three behavioral strategies to examine the value of cardiac rehabilitation as a method for improving QOL	Cardiovascular functioning, psychological functioning, physical fitness, and psychosocial functioning
Borthwick-Duffy (1990)	Persons with profound mental retardation	Essay on QOL models and measures for this population	Education, employment, language delays, choices in daily living, self-report on QOL

APPENDIX 32 (continued)
Qualitative Methods in Quality of Life (QOL) Literature

Source	Population	Measures/Method	Domains
Bratt and Johnston (1988)	5 Young adults with a mental disability, leaving a hospital to live in a group home	Recorded visits to the home; trips made out of the home; activity patterns, staff opinions	Reduction in inappropriate behavior; increase in overall interactions; more outside contact, more appropriate leisure activities
Brown, I. (1996)	Homeless adults	Essay on QOL issues and homelessness	Physical, psychological, social well-being, housed, homed, homeless, houseless
Brown, R. I. (1996)	240 Persons with developmental disabilities between 18–63 in Canadian rehabilitation service programs	Essay on QOL issues for persons with development disabilities. Used WAIS, Adaptive Functioning Index, and Quality of Life Questionnaire	Staff in agencies, employment, living conditions, choices and perceptions, client and sponsor perceptions, emotional needs
Canales, Ganz, and Coscarelli (1995)	Hispanic cancer patients — 6 males and 24 females	Interviews, translated Cancer Rehabilitation Evaluation System (CARES) into Spanish	Marital status, gender, age, employment, education, ethnicity, religion, income, children at home, changes since diagnosis
Carsky, Dolan, and Free (1991)	Housewives working at home-based businesses	A proposed model to examine the effects of women's at-home income generation on family life and satisfaction	*Worker/family characteristics:* role orientation, family demands, and tolerance for distraction. *Nature of Work:* degree of entrepreneurship, business/work site, absorptiveness. *Home/work environment:* time and income
Chaturvedi (1991)	50 Hindu adults with and without cancer	Interviews based on QOL list prepared before the interviews	Peace of mind, spiritual tasks (meditation), religion, family, basic need fulfillment, self-esteem, satisfaction with functioning, physical health, psychological health, individual functioning and marital, occupational, social, and self care
Christie, French, Weatherstone, West, and the Applied Psychology Research Group (1991)	Children with asthma	3-Year development for developing tools to assess QOL in childhood asthma. Questionnaire and open-ended discussion with children with and without asthma	Psychological, medical factors, home and social factors, and educational factors
Ciardiello and Bingham (1962)	Schizophrenic clients	Review of a career maturity construct and how a career development approach improves QOL	Use of leisure, family, citizenship, and work roles

APPENDIX 32 (continued)
Qualitative Methods in Quality of Life (QOL) Literature

Source	Population	Measures/Method	Domains
Clark and Hirst (1989)	39 Adults with physical impairments.	Sample drawn from previous study of 89 young people with cerebral palsy. Survey questionnaire.	Work, household composition, living arrangements, income, leisure and social activities, mobility, perceived needs and aspirations
Condeluci, Ferris, and Bogdan (1992)	Persons in head injury rehabilitation	Review of three surveys from the survivors' perspective	Independence in activities of daily living, living situation, communication skills, health status, mobility, problem behaviors, need for rehabilitation and supervision, employment status, family, income, and educational status
Conroy and Feinstein (1990)	Persons with mental retardation	Essay on QOL measurement to include an outcome orientation	Individual happiness, family satisfaction, increasing productivity, increased integration, status, and acceptance in society
Coulter (1990)	Children with disabilities	Essay on conceptualizing QOL for very young children	Independence, participation, responsibility
Crews (1991)	Older persons with blindness in rehabilitation	Model of strategic planning for fostering independent living	Independent living, consumer input, gains in function, family, services
Day and Jankey (1996)	Rehabilitation clients	Review of QOL origins and limitations due to originating disciplines. Proposes holistic model of QOL	Genetic disposition, domains, goals and achievements, values, personality, circumstances, evaluation process, experiences, comparisons, external reactions
Dellario and Anthony (1981)	Psychiatrically disabled persons	Review of research studies regarding client outcome of institutional vs. alternative placements; a model for psychiatric rehabilitation	Physical, intellectual, emotional, work, and community
Edbril and Rieker (1989)	74 Adult male patient survivors of testicular cancer	Cancer Behavior Scale, Profile of Mood States, Brannon Masculinity Scale	Work status, career mobility and aspirations, work satisfaction and emotional state
Edgerton (1990)	Persons with mental retardation	Longitudinal perspectives on QOL research	Self-esteem, social functioning, life satisfaction and well-being, work, physical health
Engel (1990)	Essay	Promotes the ancient triad of introspection, observation, and dialogue — the basic scientific method of clinical study	QOL as experienced can itself influence health and even duration of life
Fabian (1995)	People with disabilities	Overview of QOL in rehabilitation research	Life satisfaction, independence, adaptive functioning, self-mastery, and self-efficacy

APPENDIX 32 (continued)
Qualitative Methods in Quality of Life (QOL) Literature

Source	Population	Measures/Method	Domains
Felce and Perry (1996)	People with and without disabilities	Development of a multidimensional model–essay.	Physical well-being, material well-being, social well-being, development and activity, emotional well-being
Fine (1996)	Persons with disabilities	Essay on leisure and QOL issues	Safety, pleasantness, friends and companions, self-esteem, fun, accomplishments, productivity, excitement, leisure
Fitzsimmons and Bunting (1997)	Persons with Parkinson's Disease (PD)	Essay on the psychosocial aspects of PD and QOL	Social roles, mental acuity, emotional states, subjective well-being, interrelationships, life satisfaction and physical health
Frisch, Cronell, and Villanueva (1992)	54 VA inpatient, 51 VA recovered, 18 private inpatient, 19 offender, 272 general undergraduates, and 127 counseling center persons in psychotherapy	Used QOL Inventory and validated against the Global Severity Scale, Positive Total Symptom, Positive Symptom Distress Index, Beck Depression Inventory, Symptoms Checklist-90-R, Millon Clinical Multiaxial Inventory, Generalized Expectancy for Success Scale	Health, self-regard, philosophy of life, standard of living, work, recreation, learning, creativity, social service, civic action, love relationships, friends, relationships with children and relatives, home, neighborhood, and community
Gerber, Coleman, Johnston, and Lafave (1994)	43 Clients discharged 1 and 3 years after psychiatric rehabilitation	Structured interviews, Mulern and Manderscheid Clients' Quality of Life Interview, Uniform Client Data Instrument	Found that QOL was maintained or improved postdischarge on all QOL measures
Gottschalk and Lolas (1992)	Small group of cancer patients	Patients were asked to speak into a tape recorder for 5 minutes about "the quality of your life" at the present time. Used the Content Analysis of Verbal Behavior and then used the Social Alienation-Personal Disorganization Scale, the Human Relations Scale, the Hope Scale, and the Health-Sickness Scale to locate facets of QOL	Well-being, health, work, anxiety, self, hope, others, spiritual, symptoms
Gutheil (1991)	Frail elderly in residential facilities	Review of literature regarding features of physical environment of residential settings for frail older persons	Adequate space, essential furnishings, clean and orderly surroundings, self-worth, satisfaction with life, territorial needs, privacy, meaning

APPENDIX 32 (continued)
Qualitative Methods in Quality of Life (QOL) Literature

Source	Population	Measures/Method	Domains
Hanestad (1989)	Insulin-dependent patients	Theoretical analysis of QOL and insulin-dependency	Active, interpersonal relationships, self-esteem, aesthetic experiences, finances, physical capacity
Hanestad (1990)	Patients requiring nursing care	Structured interviews and questionnaires are reviewed as methods for collecting reliable data on QOL	Examines errors of measurement such as systematic errors found in self-assessment when people lie in a negative or positive direction; agreement bias (tend to say "yes"), social idealization, cultural and linguistic errors
Harper (1990)	Couples in couple therapy dealing with the recovery of a chemically dependent partner	Treatment model with three phases of recovery for the relationship in which their QOL is questioned	Trust, communication, intimacy, sex, and partnership
Heal and Sigelman	Persons with mental retardation	Essay on (1990) methodological issues for measuring QOL	Income, housing, behavior, life satisfaction, subjective perceptions.
Hickey and Stilwell (1992)	Aging and chronic illness issues	Essay on personal-conceptual model of age-related changes in health status	*Health perceptions:* aging illness beliefs. *Health status:* illness characteristics and co-morbidities. *Health outlook:* assessment and treatment barriers and coping skills
Hughes (1993)	Older adults and their care-givers	Model of comprehensive assessment processes	Personal characteristics, attitude to self, health, functioning, environment, finance and material circumstance, recreation and activities, family, community relationships, and support network
Hume (1989)	Patients with hypertension	Review of the findings of the Treatment of Mild Hypertension Study as it relates to the addition of hydrochlorothiazide to other pharamacologic agents.	Functional capacity perceptions, and symptoms including mobility and independence. *Social functioning:* family, friends, community. *Cognitive functioning:* reasoning, memory, judgment and alertness. *Psychological distress. Economic status*
Hyland (1992)	Overview article	Multifaceted approach recommended for economic decision-making in health systems	Physical status and functional ability, psychological status and well-being, social interactions, and economic status

APPENDIX 32 (continued)
Qualitative Methods in Quality of Life (QOL) Literature

Source	Population	Measures/Method	Domains
Jablensky (1992)	Psychiatry as a medical discipline	Historical review of psychiatry as social control of the deviant, advocacy of the right to be different, and the effects of the latter on QOL issues	Cognitive models of human nature, social organization, technology available to manipulate human behavior
Janicki (1990)	Older persons with a lifelong disability	Essay on aging with a lifelong disability and QOL issues	Physical, material, social, cognitive well-being
Keith (1990)	Persons with mental retardation	Essay on QOL issues in community integration	Health, employment, education, well-being, living situation, familial and social relations, leisure, work, learning, creative expression, safety, and finances
Kiernan and Knutson (1990)	Persons with disabilities	Essay on QOL and quality of work life (QWL)	Productivity and job satisfaction, participate management style, flexibility
Labonte (1996)	Persons with disabilities and disadvantages	Discussion of power issues in determining QOL	Quality of life, health, and empowerment
Limacher, Dahler, Bosch, and Egli (1991)	Back pain patients	Questionnaire completed by 5 general practitioners for first 20 patients seen for consultation	Work, leisure, partnership, family, housing, stress, misfortune, care availability, and nursing
Logue (1991)	Death and dying issues for women	Overview article on research needs on age, sex, race, social class, primary diagnosis, co-morbidities of those whose deaths are negotiated	QOL and choosing death, premature death and delayed death, women as recipients of informal and formal care systems, competency, the experts, and feminist health goals
Loscocco and Roschelle (1991)	Working and nonworking adults	Literature review of quality of work and nonwork life: 1971–1991	Personality, education, gender, family roles, job characteristics, organizational characteristics, unions, promotions, social context
Luckasson (1990)	Person with mental retardation	Legal perspective on QOL terminology	Normalization, integration, and worth of all human beings
Lynch and Gallagher-Lepak (1996)	Patients with chronic renal failure	Essay on updating rehabilitation professionals on impact of improved medical treatment	Functional outcomes: weakness/fatigue, reduced endurance, cognitive changes, and psychological distress
Maas (1991)	Persons after laryngectomy	Theoretical model for QOL after laryngectomy	Speech impairment, social, psychological, vocational
Malm, May, and Dencker (1981)	Schizophrenic outpatients — 27 males and 13 females	Used Quality of Life Checklist	Medical care, social, standard of living, communication and transportation, work, safety, education, leisure, spiritual/religious
Mason (1996)	Deaf and hard-of-hearing people	Essay on the cultural meaning of deafness and hard-of-hearing as a QOL issue	Culturally deaf, oral deaf, hard-of-hearing, late-deafened persons

APPENDIX 32 (continued)
Qualitative Methods in Quality of Life (QOL) Literature

Source	Population	Measures/Method	Domains
Mathias, Fifer, and Patrick (1994)	International QOL clinical trials	8-Step protocol for rapidly translating a QOL questionnaire into multiple languages	Health well-being, psychosocial well-being, health distress, depression, self-esteem, emotional functioning, and work loss
Mayou (1990)	Cardiovascular disease patients	Recommends greater use of psychosomatic research, including interview-based and self-report measures as well as physical outcome measures	Symptoms, mental state, general health status, types of cardiac disorder
McPhail (1996)	Effects of children with disabilities on the lives of family members	Recommendations regarding improving QOL for families with members with disabilities	Growth opportunities, community membership, choice, in-home health care support, inclusion of parents in decision making, inclusive services which support the family unit, inclusion in regular schooling
Morris and Lewis (1991)	Entrepreneurship	Framework of further theory development and hypothesis testing concerning the entrepreneurship/QOL interface	Societal QOL: economic, health, social, technological, work, institutional, ecological
Munich and Lang (1993)	Persons with psychiatric disabilities	Argument for rehabilitation as a central discipline which integrates clinical and functional status and QOL	Biopsychosocial issues including learning, compensation, adaptation. autonomy, least professional intervention
Nagler (1996)	39 persons with disabilities who have experienced sexual abuse	Interviews and essay on QOL issues and sexual abuse	Social, emotional, sexuality, work, friends, self-esteem, marriage, education, emotional and physical well-being
National Association of Rehabilitation Facilities (NARF) (1988)	Persons with disabilities using NARF facilities	Position statement by NARF on QOL and quality of work life	Empowerment, friendship, being valued, supported employment
National Institute on Disability and Rehabilitation Research (1988)	Persons with disabilities	Essay on research in rehabilitation and QOL	Mobility, environmental control, community resources and know-how, reliance on loved ones or significant others from time to time, self-acceptance and motivation to be productive and happy

APPENDIX 32 (continued)
Qualitative Methods in Quality of Life (QOL) Literature

Source	Population	Measures/Method	Domains
Newfield and Duet (1976)	The work of curriculum developers	A review of QOL Indexes for the purpose of comparing their characteristics to that of the goal of education	Public order and safety, physical environment, health, affection and sociability, income and poverty, education and skills attainment, participation and alienation, availability and utilization of leisure, self-respect, aesthetics, communication, enjoyment of art, finer things, learning, and morality
Nosek, Holland, Young, Georgiou, Rintala, Foley, Bennett, and Smith (1994)	31 Women with physical disabilities	Qualitative interviews regarding disability and sexuality	Positive sexual concept, having good relationships, managing barriers, good health and physical functioning
O'Keefe (1996)	Persons with communication disorders	Essay recommending that recognition and be given to the QOL issues in this impairment and research be conducted	Being, belonging, and becoming
Oliver, Holloway, and Carson (1995)	Patients using mental health services	Review of objective, subjective, and health-related concepts of QOL	Adequate income, housing, occupation, opportunities to make social relationships
O'Rear, Bark, and Hutchinson (1996)	Persons with psychiatric disabilities	Essay on promoting wellness activities which improve QOL	Physical, mental, emotional, and spiritual wellness
Ory and Cox (1994)	Elderly people	Review of conceptual and methodological issues related to health promotion and disability for older people	Social and environmental factors, physical and mental health, health-related behaviors
Osoba (1992)	Cancer patients	Reports on work of QOL Committee in Canada regarding use of QOL measures in all cancer clinical trials	No domains listed
Ouellette-Kuntz and McCreary (1996)	Persons with severe developmental disabilities	Development of the QOL Interview Schedule	Communication, disabilities, personal characteristics, and recent life events
Parmenter (1996)	For everyone	Discussion of the quality-adjusted life-year (QALYs) approach	A plurality of independent vectors based on an individual life
Raeburn and Rootman (1996)	For everyone	Essay on a conceptual model of QOL	Being, belonging, and becoming

APPENDIX 32 (continued)
Qualitative Methods in Quality of Life (QOL) Literature

Source	Population	Measures/Method	Domains
Roller (1996)	People with late effects of polio	Advocates 2 health promotion models used in Germany and U.S. for increasing physical fitness	Alleviate, manage, and prevent secondary conditions; promote good health and wellness; introduce new health promotion tactics; facilitate long-term adoption of health-enhancing behaviors
Raphael (1996a)	For everyone	11 Debates concerning measurement of QOL	Social, psychological, quantitative vs. qualitative, objective vs. subjective, self-report vs. reports by others
Raphael (1996b)	10- to 25-year olds or adolescent health	Review of adolescent health and QOL issues	*Global:* macro environment, human rights and welfare policies. *External:* work, income, housing. *Interpersonal:* family structure and function, intimate friends, extended social. *Personal:* physical, mental, spiritual
Raphael (1996c)	12 Group meetings — 120 seniors in the community	Development of Quality of Life Profile: Seniors Version	Physical being, psychological being, spiritual being, physical belonging, social belonging, community belonging, practical becoming, leisure becoming, growth becoming
Renwick and Brown (1996)	People with disabilities, service providers, and families of persons with disabilities	Focus groups, literature review, consultation with the experts for Centre for Health Promotion (CHP) in Toronto approach	*Being:* physical, psychological, spiritual. *Belonging:* physical, social, community. *Becoming:* practical, leisure, growth
Renwick, Brown, Rootman, and Nagler (1996)	For everyone	Recommendations for further research	Conceptual frameworks: person–environment interactions, empowerment of individuals, generic approaches suited to general and specific populations, personal meanings, broad range of domains, and relationships between health and QOL
Renwick and Friefeld (1996)	Rehabilitation clients	Recommendations for going beyond functional and health status measures such as the Barthel Index, Functional Status Index, Functional Activities Questionnaire, Sickness Impact Profile, Nottingham Health Profile, Arthritis Impact Measurement Scale	Physical, emotional, cognitive, social aspects of functioning in the major areas of life (e.g., mobility, communication, activities of daily living, vocational activities, social relationships, leisure and recreation)

APPENDIX 32 (continued)
Qualitative Methods in Quality of Life (QOL) Literature

Source	Population	Measures/Method	Domains
Rioux (1996)	Persons with disabilities	Essay on disability as a social construct	Social, political, and economic structures are inseparable from individual and collective states of well-being
Roessler (1990)	Rehabilitation clients	Recommends QOL approach in rehabilitation of persons with disabilities	Health, public safety, education, employment, earnings and income, poverty, housing, family stability, equality, well-being, happiness
Ruffing-Rahal (1991)	182 Community-dwelling elderly adults	The Integration Inventory, Philadelphia Geriatric Center Morale Scale, the Spiritual Well-Being Scale, and 4 measures of self-rated well-being	Well-being, absence of loneliness, positive attitude toward aging, self-rated happiness, self-rated health, self-rated life satisfaction, absence of agitation, religious well-being
Sartorius (1995)	Psychiatric rehabilitation clients	Review essay	Not specific, but leisure, work, family, community, aesthetic, and health are mentioned
Satcher (1993)	Persons with learning disabilities	Essay on ADA and its potential for improvement of quality of work life	Job restructuring, modified work schedule, reassignment to vacant positions, acquiring or modifying equipment or devices, modifying examinations, training materials or policies, providing qualified readers
Schalock (1990a)	Persons with developmental disabilities	Essay on conceptualizing and measuring QOL, QOL variables in mental retardation literature	Social and psychological indicators, goodness-of-fit/social policy
Schalock (1990b)	Persons with mental retardation	Essay on QOL disability policy and service delivery systems	Living, learning, working, choice, independence, productivity, and community integration
Schalock (1996)	For everyone	Proposes a quality assurance model for QOL evaluation	Home and community living, work-school, and health and wellness
Scherer (1990)	Persons with spinal cord injury (SCI) and cerebral palsy (CP)	Compared persons with SCI and CP using assistive devices (AD), interviews and observations, Personal Capacities Questionnaire, Functional Assessment Inventory, Taylor-Johnson Temperament Analysis	Personal capacities, adaptive behavior vocational qualifications, motor functioning
Select House Committee on Aging (1989)	Older women living alone	Chairman Roybal's report on hearings on QOL of older women living alone	Income, health, safety, housing

APPENDIX 32 (continued)
Qualitative Methods in Quality of Life (QOL) Literature

Source	Population	Measures/Method	Domains
Shain (1996)	For everyone	Analyzes study: *Influences on Wellness in the Workplace: A Multivariate Approach*	Personal health practices, perceived stressors at home and at work, personal resources, demographic and socioeconomic factors
Sherman and Schiffman (1991)	Older consumers	Historical reflections on past 20 to 30 years of QOL status of older consumers	Socioeconomic indicators, health and longevity, housing and family living, gender differences, life satisfaction, cognitive age, leisure, occupation, health
Siegrist and Junge (1990)	Chronic illness patients	Katz Adjustment Scale, Social Maladjustment Schedule, Social Dysfunction Rating Scale, Structured and Scaled Interview to Assess Maladjustment, Reintegration to Normal Living Index	Physical, psychological, and social dimensions of health
Slaughter, Lehman, and Myers (1991)	Severely mentally ill adults in residential care facilities	Literature review of 16 studies	Employment status, safety, social contacts, leisure activities, and general life satisfaction
Sonino, Fava, Fallo, and Boscaro (1990)	Patients with endocrine disease	Recommends use of the psychosomatic approach in QOL issues with these patients	Life events preceding disease onset, psychological distress, abnormal illness, behavior
Stark and Goldsbury (1990)	Persons with mental retardation	Essay on QOL over the life span	General well-being, age, sex, social/cultural background, level of cognitive/adaptive functioning, education, health, living environment, family, social/emotional, work, and leisure
Stewart and King (1991)	Older adults	Conceptual framework presented of QOL concepts for evaluating the efficacy of physical activity in older adults	Physical functioning, cognitive functioning, activities, bodily well-being, emotional well-being, self-concept, and global perceptions of health and life satisfaction
Stillson, White, and Harris (1986)	Alcoholism treatment personnel	Review of aspects of stress management techniques to improve QOL	Psychotherapy, meditation/visualization and time management

APPENDIX 32 (continued)
Qualitative Methods in Quality of Life (QOL) Literature

Source	Population	Measures/Method	Domains
Tigges (1993)	Hospice care patients	Review of QOL literature re hospice care	Control of pain and symptoms, personal care and comfort, support of respite to the primary caregiver/family member, pastoral care, and bereavement services for survivors. Tigges' defines a sense of excellence of character; being useful, productive, needed and valued; personal safety and security; and the ability to interact with others as the domains to be assessed
Till, Sutherland, and Meslin (1992)	Cancer patients	Recommends that patient preference should be included in clinical cancer trials re QOL issues	Preferences might include: personal factors, values, and attitudes; psychosocial factors; activities of daily living; family; survival; and sexuality
Vaughan and Hobson (1990)	179 Elderly adults using low-vision devices	Report on a project of 39 counties of rural Missouri to screen and provide low-vision devices to elderly persons in need	Increase in independent living: read mail, write checks, thread needles, and read large print, better general functioning in everyday tasks and QOL
Whitaker (1989)	Persons with profound mental handicaps (mental retardation).	Essay regarding a conceptual model.	*Individual behavior:* level of skills and abilities, level of adaptive engagement, level of negative behavior. *Factor about the environment:* conditions of physical environment in terms of comfort, food, health care; opportunities to mix with local community; variability and amount of varied activities available; opportunity to make choices; and treated as valued individuals in society
Wolkenstein and Butler (1992)	96 Healthy elderly (65 years and over)	Questionnaire, opinion surveys, group interviews	Outside world and others, inner world of the self, coping with loss, interaction with treating physician
Wood and Johnson (1989)	15 Elderly rural adults selected for qualitative study and 392 elderly rural adults in quantitative study	Used a life satisfaction questionnaire and analysis of qualitative data	Housing, health, self-esteem, friendship, and family
Wozner (1982)	Persons in various institutions — jails, residential facilities, hospitals (internats)	Conceptual framework based on the QOL Map	Personality, physical, societal, and cultural

APPENDIX 32 (continued)
Qualitative Methods in Quality of Life (QOL) Literature

Source	Population	Measures/Method	Domains
Zautra and Reich (1983)	General population	Review of 15 studies measuring effects of positive and negative events on psychiatric distress	Positive life events, negative life events, psychological well-being

References

Bach, M. and Rioux, M. H. (1996). Social well-being: a framework for quality of life research. In R. Renwick, I. Brown, and M. Nagler (Eds.), *Quality of Life in Health Promotion and Rehabilitation,* pp. 63-74. Thousand Oaks, CA: Sage Publications.

Baker, F., Jodrey, D., and Intagliata, J. (1992). Social support and quality of life of community support clients. *Community Mental Health Journal,* 29(5): 397-411.

Bellamy, G. T., Newton, J. S., LeBaron, N. M., and Horner, R. H. (1990). Quality of life and lifestyle outcomes: a challenge for residential programs. In R. L. Schalock (Ed.), *Quality of Life: Perspectives and Issues,* pp. 127-137. Washington, D.C.: American Association of Mental Retardation.

Berla, E., Brookshire, M., and Smith, (1990). Hedonic damages and personal injury: a conceptual approach. *Journal of Forensic Economics,* 1-8.

Bigelow, D. A., McFarland, B. H., and Olson, M. M. (1991). Quality of life of community mental health program clients: validating a measure. *Community Mental Health Journal,* 27(1): 43-55.

Blumenthal, J. A. and Emery, C. F. (1988). Rehabilitation of patients following myocardial infarction. *Journal of Consulting and Clinical Psychology,* 56(3): 374-381.

Borthwick-Duffy, S. A. (1990). Quality of life of persons with severe or profound mental retardation. In R. L. Schalock (Ed.), *Quality of Life: Perspectives and Issues,* pp. 177-189. Washington, D.C.: American Association of Mental Retardation.

Bratt, A. and Johnston, R. (1988). Changes in life style for young adults with profound handicaps following discharge from hospital care into a “second generation” housing project. *Mental Handicap Research,* 1(1): 49-74.

Brown, I. (1996). The quality of life of marginal citizens: homelessness. In R. Renwick, I. Brown, and M. Nagler (Eds.), *Quality of Life in Health Promotion and Rehabilitation,* pp. 204-218. Thousand Oaks, CA: Sage Publications.

Brown, R. I. (1996). People with developmental disabilities: applying quality of life to assessment and intervention. In R. Renwick, I. Brown, and M. Nagler (Eds.), *Quality of Life in Health Promotion and Rehabilitation,* pp. 253-267. Thousand Oaks, CA: Sage Publications.

Canales, S., Ganz, P. A., and Coscarelli, C. A. (1995). Translation and validation of a quality of life instrument for Hispanic American cancer patients: methodological considerations. *Quality of Life Research,* 4: 3-11.

Carsky, M. L., Dolan, E. M., and Free, R. K. (1991). An integrated model of homebased work: effects on family quality of life. *Journal of Business Research*, 23: 37-49.

Chaturvedi, S. K. (1991). What's important for quality of life to Indians — In relation to cancer. *Social Science Medicine,* 33(1): 91-94.

Christie, M. J., French, D., Weatherstone, L., West, A., and the Applied Research Group. (1991). The patient's perceptions of chronic disease and its management: psychosomatics, holism and quality of life in contemporary management of childhood asthma. *Psychotherapy and Psychosomatics,* 56: 197-203.

Ciardiello, J. A. and Bingham, W. C. (1962). The career maturity of schizophrenic clients. *Rehabilitation Counseling Bulletin,* 3-9.

Clark, A. and Hirst, M. (1989). Disability in adulthood: ten-year follow-up of young people with disabilities. *Disability, Handicap and Society,* 4(3): 271-283.

Condeluci, A., Ferris, L. L., and Bogdan, A. (1992). Outcome and value: the survivor perspective. *Journal of Head Trauma Rehabilitation,* 7(4): 37-45.

Conroy, J. W. and Feinstein, C. S. (1990). Measuring quality of life: where have we been? Where are we going? In R. L. Schalock (Ed.), *Quality of Life: Perspectives and Issues,* pp. 227-233. Washington, D.C.: American Association of Mental Retardation.

Coulter, D. L. (1990). Home is the place: quality of life for young children with developmental disabilities. In R. L. Schalock (Ed.), *Quality of Life: Perspectives and Issues,* pp. 61-69. Washington, D.C.: American Association of Mental Retardation.

Crews, J. E. (1991). Strategic planning and independent living for elders who are blind. *Journal of Visual Impairment and Blindness,* 52-57.

Day, H. and Jankey, S. G. (1996). Lessons from the literature: toward a holistic model of quality of life. In R. Renwick, I. Brown, and M. Nagler (Eds.), *Quality of Life in Health Promotion and Rehabilitation,* pp. 39-50. Thousand Oaks, CA: Sage Publications.

Dellario, D. J. and Anthony, W. A. (1981). On the relative effectiveness of institutional and alternative placement for the psychiatrically disabled. *Journal of Social Issues,* 37(3): 21-33.

Edbril, S. D. and Rieker, P. P. (1989). The impact of testicular cancer on the work lives of survivors. *Journal of Psychosocial Oncology,* 7(3): 17-29.

Edgerton, R. B. (1990). Quality of life from a longitudinal research perspective. In R. L. Schalock (Ed.), *Quality of Life: Perspectives and Issues,* pp. 149-160. Washington, D.C.: American Association of Mental Retardation.

Engel, G. L. (1990). On looking inward and being scientific: a tribute to Arthur H. Schmale, MD. *Psychotherapy and Psychosomatics,* 54: 63-69.

Fabian, E. S. (1995). Quality of life. In Dell Orto, A.E. and Martinelli, R. P. (Eds.), *Encylopedia of Disability and Rehabilitation,* pp. 607-609. New York: Macmillan Publishing.

Felce, D. and Perry, J. (1996). Exploring current concepts of quality of life. In R. Renwick, I. Brown, and M. Nagler (Eds.), *Quality of Life in Health Promotion and Rehabilitation,* pp. 51-62. Thousand Oaks, CA: Sage Publications.

Fine, A. H. (1996). Leisure, living, and quality of life. In R. Renwick, I. Brown, and M. Nagler (Eds.), *Quality of Life in Health Promotion and Rehabilitation,* pp. 342-356. Thousand Oaks, CA: Sage Publications.

Fitzsimmons, B. and Bunting, L. K. (1997). Parkinson's Disease: quality of life issues. http://www.cnsonline.org/www/archive/parkins/park.07.txt

Frisch, M. B., Cornell, J., and Villanueva. (1992). Clinical validation of the Quality of Life Inventory: a measure of life satisfaction for use in treatment planning and outcome assessment. *Psychological Assessment,* 4(1): 92-101.

Gerber, G. J., Coleman, G. E., Johnston, L., and Lafave, H. G. (1994). Quality of life of people with psychiatric disabilities 1 and 3 years after discharge from hospital. *Quality of Life Research,* 3: 379-383.

Gottschalk, L. A. and Lolas, F. (1992). The measurement of quality of life through the content analysis of verbal behavior. *Psychotherapy and Psychosomatics,* 58: 69-78.

Gutheil, I. A. (1991). The physical environment and quality of life in residential facilities for frail elders. *Adult Residential Care Journal,* 5(2): 131-145.

Handestad, B. R. (1989). Insulin-dependent diabetes mellitus and quality of life: a theoretical analysis. *Scandanavian Journal of Caring,* 3(3): 123-128.

Hanestad, B. R. (1990). Errors of measurement affecting the reliability and validity of data acquired from self-assessed quality of life. *Scandanavian Journal of Caring,* 4(1): 29-34.

Harper, J. (1990). Recovery for the relationship: a treatment model for couples with a recovering chemically dependent partner. *Alcoholism Treatment Quarterly,* 7(2): 1-21.

Heal, L. W. and Sigelman, C. K. (1990). Methodological issues in measuring quality of life of individuals with mental retardation. In R. L. Schalock (Ed.), *Quality of Life: Perspectives and Issues,* pp. 161-176. Washington, D.C.: American Association of Mental Retardation.

Hickey, T. and Stilwell, D. L. (1992). Chronic illness and aging: a personal-contextual model of age-related changes in health status. *Educational Gerontology,* 18: 1-15.

Hughes, B. (1993). A model for the comprehensive assessment of older people and their carers. *British Journal of Social Work,* 23: 345-364.

Hume, A. L. (1989). Applying quality of life data in practice: considerations for antihypertensive therapy. *Journal of Family Practice,* 28(4): 403-407.

Hyland, M. E. (1992). A reformulation of quality of life for medial science. *Quality of Life Research,* 1: 267-272.

Jablensky, A. (1992). Politics and mental health. *International Journal of Social Psychiatry,* 38(1): 24-29.

Janicki, M. P. (1990). Growing old with dignity: on quality of life for older persons with a lifelong disability. In R. L. Schalock (Ed.), *Quality of Life: Perspectives and Issues,* pp. 115-125. Washington, D.C.: American Association of Mental Retardation.

Keith, K. D. (1990). Quality of life: issues in community integration. In R. L. Schalock (Ed.), *Quality of Life: Perspectives and Issues,* pp. 93-100. Washington, D.C.: American Association of Mental Retardation.

Kiernan, W. E. and Knutson, K. (1990). Quality of work life. In R. L. Schalock (Ed.), *Quality of Life: Perspectives and Issues,* pp. 101-114. Washington, D.C.: American Association of Mental Retardation.

Labonte, R. (1996). Measurement and practice: power issues in quality of life, health promotion, and empowerment. In R. Renwick, I. Brown, and M. Nagler (Eds.), *Quality of Life in Health Promotion and Rehabilitation,* pp. 132-145. Thousand Oaks, CA: Sage Publications.

Limacher, B., Dahler, E., Bosch, J., and Egli, N. (1991). Color me multi-colored: a note on problems in clinical research methodology. *Family Systems Medicine,* 9(1): 65-68.

Logue, B. J. (1991). Taking charge: death control as an emergent women's issue. *Women and Health,* 17(4): 97-121.

Loscocco, K. A. and Roschelle, A. R. (1991). Influences on the quality of work and nonwork life: two decades in review. *Journal of Vocational Behavior,* 39: 182-225.

Luckasson, R. (1990). A lawyer's perspective on quality of life. In R. L. Schalock (Ed.), *Quality of Life: Perspectives and Issues,* pp. 211-214. Washington, D.C.: American Association of Mental Retardation.

Lynch, R. T. and Gallagher-Lepak, S. (1996). Chronic renal failure: the impact of improved medical treatment options on rehabilitation. *Journal of Applied Rehabilitation Counseling,* 27(1): 7-12.

Maas, A. (1992). A model for quality of life after laryngectomy. *Social Science Medicine,* 33(12): 1373-1377.

Malm, U., May, P. R. A., and Dencker, S. J. (1981). Evaluation of the quality of life of the schizophrenic outpatient: a checklist. *Schizophrenia Bulletin,* 7(3): 477-487.

Mason, D. G. (1996). Quality of life for deaf and hard-of-hearing people. In R. Renwick, I. Brown, and M. Nagler (Eds.), *Quality of Life in Health Promotion and Rehabilitation,* pp. 237-252. Thousand Oaks, CA: Sage Publications.

Mathias, S. D., Fifer, S. K., and Patrick, D. L. (1994). Rapid translation of quality of life measures for international clinical trials: avoiding errors in the minimalist approach. *Quality of Life Research,* 3: 403-412.

Mayou, R. (1990). Quality of life in cardiovascular disease. *Psychotherapy and Psychosomatics*, 54: 99-109.

McPhail, E. R. (1996). A parent's perspective: quality of life in families with a member with disabilities. In R. Renwick, I. Brown, and M. Nagler (Eds.), *Quality of Life in Health Promotion and Rehabilitation,* pp. 279-289. Thousand Oaks, CA: Sage Publications.

Morris, M. H. and Lewis, P. S. (1991). Entrepreneurship as a significant factor in societal quality of life. *Journal of Business Research*, 23: 21-36.

Munich, R. L. and Lang, E. (1993). The boundaries of psychiatric rehabilitation. *Hospital and Community Psychiatry*, 44(7): 661-665.

Nagler, M. (1996). Quality of life of people with disabilities who have experienced sexual abuse. In R. Renwick, I. Brown, and M. Nagler (Eds.), *Quality of Life in Health Promotion and Rehabilitation,* pp. 190-203. Thousand Oaks, CA: Sage Publications.

National Association of Rehabilitation Facilities. (1988). Quality of life. *NARF Monograph Series.*

National Institute on Disability and Rehabilitation Research. (1988). Quality-of-life research in rehabilitation. *Rehab Brief*, XI(1).

Newfield, J. W. and Duet, C. P. (1976). Implications of quality of life for goal setting tasks of the curriculum workers. *Education,* 97(2): 135.

Nosek, M. A., Howland, C.A., Young, M. E., Georgiou, D., Rintala, D. H., Foley, C. C., Bennett, J. L., and Smith, Q. (1994). Wellness models and sexuality among women with physical disabilities. *Journal of Applied Rehabilitation Counseling*, 25(1): 50-57.

O'Keefe, B. M. (1996). Communication disorders: just minor inconveniences? In R. Renwick, I. Brown, and M. Nagler (Eds.), *Quality of Life in Health Promotion and Rehabilitation,* pp. 219-236. Thousand Oaks, CA: Sage Publications.

Oliver, N., Holloway, F., and Carson, J. (1995). Deconstructing quality of life. *Journal of Mental Health,* 4: 1-4.

O'Rear, G., Bark, L., and Hutchinson, D. S. (1996). The promotion of wellness among people with psychiatric disabilities in community rehabilitation and treatment. *Psychiatric Rehabilitation Journal*, 20(2): 82-84.

Ory, M. O. and Cox, D. M. (1994). Forging ahead: linking health and behavior to improve quality of life in older people. *Social Indicators Research,* 33: 89-120.

Osoba, D. (1992). The quality of life committee of the clinical trials groups of the National Cancer Institute of Canada: organization and functions. *Quality of Life Research,* 1: 211-218.

Ouellette-Kuntz, H. and McCreary, B. (1996). Quality of life assessment for persons with severe developmental disabilities. In R. Renwick, I. Brown, and M. Nagler (Eds.), *Quality of Life in Health Promotion and Rehabilitation,* pp. 268-278. Thousand Oaks, CA: Sage Publications.

Parmenter, T. R. (1996). The use of quality of life as a construct for social and health policy development. In R. Renwick, I. Brown, and M. Nagler (Eds.), *Quality of Life in Health Promotion and Rehabilitation,* pp. 89-103. Thousand Oaks, CA: Sage Publications.

Raeburn, J. M. and Rootman, I. (1996). Quality of life and health promotion. In R. Renwick, I. Brown, and M. Nagler (Eds.), *Quality of Life in Health Promotion and Rehabilitation,* pp. 14-25. Thousand Oaks, CA: Sage Publications.

Raphael, D. (1996a). Defining quality of life: eleven debates concerning its measurement. In R. Renwick, I. Brown, and M. Nagler (Eds.), *Quality of Life in Health Promotion and Rehabilitation,* pp. 146-170. Thousand Oaks, CA: Sage Publications.

Raphael, D. (1996b) . Quality of life and adolescent health. In R. Renwick, I. Brown, and M. Nagler (Eds.), *Quality of Life in Health Promotion and Rehabilitation,* pp. 307-326. Thousand Oaks, CA: Sage Publications.

Raphael, D. (1996c) . Quality of life for older adults: toward the optimization of the aging process. In R. Renwick, I. Brown, and M. Nagler (Eds.), *Quality of Life in Health Promotion and Rehabilitation,* pp. 290-306. Thousand Oaks, CA: Sage Publications.

Renwick, R. and Brown, I. (1996). The Centre for Health Promotion's conceptual approach to quality of life: being, belonging, and becoming. In R. Renwick, I. Brown, and M. Nagler (Eds.), *Quality of Life in Health Promotion and Rehabilitation,* pp. 75-86. Thousand Oaks, CA: Sage Publications.

Renwick, R., Brown, I, Rootman, I., and Nagler, M. (1996). Conceptualization, research, and application: future directions. In R. Renwick, I. Brown, and M. Nagler (Eds.), *Quality of Life in Health Promotion and Rehabilitation,* pp. 357-367. Thousand Oaks, CA: Sage Publications.

Renwick, R. and Friefeld, S. (1996). Quality of life and rehabilitation. In Renwick, I. Brown, and M. Nagler (Eds.), *Quality of Life in Health Promotion and Rehabilitation,* pp. 26-36. Thousand Oaks, CA: Sage Publications.

Rioux, M. H. (1996). Overcoming the social construction of inequality as a prerequisite to quality of life. In R. Renwick, I. Brown, and M. Nagler (Eds.), *Quality of Life in Health Promotion and Rehabilitation,* pp. 119-131. Thousand Oaks, CA: Sage Publications.

Roessler, R. T. (1990). A quality of life perspective on rehabilitation counseling. *Rehabilitation Counseling Bulletin,* 34(2): 82-91.

Roller, S. (1996). Health promotion for people with chronic neuromuscular disabilities. In D. M. Krotoski, M. A. Nosek, and M. A. Turk (Eds.), *Women with Physical Disabilities: Achieving and Maintaining Health and Well-Being,* pp. 431-439. Baltimore: Paul H. Brookes Publishing.

Ruffing-Rahal, M. A. (1991). Initial psychometric evaluation of a qualitative evaluation well-being measure: the Integration Inventory. *Health Values,* 15(2): 10-20.

Sartorius, N. (1995). Rehabilitation and Quality of Life. *International Journal of Mental Health,* 24(1): 7-13.

Satcher, J. (1993). Improving the quality of work life for persons with learning disabilities: ADA rights and responsibilities. *Journal of Applied Rehabilitation Counseling,* 24(1): 16-18.

Schalock, R. L. (1996). Quality of life and quality assurance. In Renwick, I. Brown, and M. Nagler (Eds.), *Quality of Life in Health Promotion and Rehabilitation,* pp. 104-118. Thousand Oaks, CA: Sage Publications.

Schalock, R. L. (1990a). Attempts to conceptualize and measure quality of life. In R. L. Schalock, (Ed.), *Quality of Life: Perspectives and Issues,* pp. 141-148 . Washington, D.C.: American Association of Mental Retardation.

Schalock, R. L. (1990b). Where do we go from here? In R. L. Schalock, (Ed.), *Quality of Life: Perspectives and Issues,* pp. 235-240. Washington, D.C.: American Association of Mental Retardation.

Scherer, M. J. (1990). Assistive device utilization and quality of life in adults with spinal cord injuries or cerebral palsy two years later. *Journal of Applied Rehabilitation Counseling,* 21(4): 36-44.

Select Committee on Aging, House of Representatives. (1989). *The Quality of Life for Older Women: Older Women Living Alone.* Washington, D.C.: U.S. Government Printing Office.

Shain, M. (1996). Work, employment, and mental health: implications for quality of life. In R. Renwick, I. Brown, and M. Nagler (Eds.), *Quality of Life in Health Promotion and Rehabilitation,* pp. 327-341. Thousand Oaks, CA: Sage Publications.

Sherman, E. and Schiffman, L. G. (1991). Quality-of-life (QOL) assessment of older consumers: A retrospective review. *Journal of Business and Psychology,* 6(1): 107-119.

Siegrist, J. and Junge, A. (1990). Measuring the social dimension of subjective health in chronic illness. *Psychotherapy and Psychosomatics,* 54: 90-98.

Slaughter, J. G., Lehman, A. F., and Myers, C. P. (1991). Quality of life of severely mentally ill adults in residential care facilities. *Adult Residential Care Journal,* 5(2): 97-111.

Sonino, N., Fava, G. A., Fallo, F., and Boscaro, M. (1990). Psychological distress and quality of life in endocrine disease. *Psychotherapy and Psychosomatics,* 54: 140-144.

Stark, J. A. and Goldsbury, R. (1990). Quality of life from childhood to adulthood. In R. L. Schalock, (Ed.), *Quality of Life: Perspectives and Issues,* pp. 71-92 . Washington, D.C.: American Association of Mental Retardation.

Stewart, A. L. and King, A. C. (1991). Evaluating the efficacy of physical activity for influencing quality-of-life outcomes in older adults. *Annals of Behavioral Medicine,* 13(3): 108-116.

Stillson, K., White, J., and Harris, E. F. (1986). Helping the helper: stress management for alcoholism treatment personnel. *Alcoholism Treatment Quarterly,* 3(3): 107-123.

Tigges, K. N. (1993). Quality of life: reality or rhetoric? *Loss, Grief, and Care,* 7(1-2): 157-167.

Till, J. E., Sutherland, H. J., and Meslin, E. M. (1992). Is there a role for preference assessments in research on quality of life in oncology? *Quality of Life Research,* 1: 31-40.

Vaughan, C. E. and Hobson, S. (1990). Reducing late-life dependence resulting from declining visual acuity. *Journal of Visual Impairment and Blindness,* 370-372.

Whitaker, S. (1989). Quality of life and people with a very profound handicap. *British Journal of Mental Subnormality,* 35(68): 3-7.

Wolkenstein, A. S. and Butler, D. J. (1992). Quality of life among the elderly: self-perspectives of some healthy elderly. *Gerontology and Geriatrics Education,* 12(4): 59-68.

Wood, L. A. and Johnson, J. (1989). Life satisfaction among the rural elderly: What do the numbers mean? *Social Indicators Research,* 21: 379-408.

Wozner, Y. (1982). Assessing the quality of internal life. *Human Relations,* 35(11): 1059-1072.

Zautra, A. J. and Reich, J. W. (1983). Life events and perceptions of life quality: developments in a two-factor approach. *Journal of Community Psychology,* 11(2): 121-132.

APPENDIX 33
Studies Using Quantitative Methods in Quality of Life (QOL) Research

Source	Population	Measures/Method	Domains
Baker, Curbow, and Wingard (1992)	109 Long-term cancer survivors who have received bone marrow transplants	Development of the Satisfaction with Life Domains Scale for Cancer (SLDS-C)	18 Domains listed as questions on the SLDS-C. Include: relationships, health, appearance, leisure time, ability to eat, physical strength
Baker, Jodrey, and Intagliata (1992)	729 Mentally ill adults in state-supported programs	Repeated (9 months apart) questionnaires, QOL interviews, Bradburn Positive and Negative Affect Scales, Satisfaction with Life Domains Scale	Availability and adequacy of social support needed for quality of life
Ben-Ari and Tater (1984)	53 Male and 46 female clients in 5 governmental rehabilitation centers In Israel	Minnesota Satisfaction Questionnaire and interviews of social workers working with clients	Duration of injury and educational level were related to 3 categories of satisfaction: internal, external, and overall satisfaction

APPENDIX 33 (continued)
Studies Using Quantitative Methods in Quality of Life (QOL) Research

Source	Population	Measures/Method	Domains
Bigelow, McFarland, and Olson (1991)	Community samples, client samples from 24 mental health agencies	Interviews and QOL Questionnaire	Psychological distress and well-being, tolerance of stress, independence, interdependence, interpersonal interactions, spouse role, work at home, social support, employability, meaningful use of time, substance abuse
Boschen (1996)	222 Young adults with spinal cord injuries living in Toronto	Living with a Spinal Cord Injury Questionnaire, Latitude of Choice Scale, Self-Concept Semantic Differential Scale, Locus of Control Scale	Autonomy, control, and daily life choices with postinjury accommodations
Brown (1996)	105 Males and 86 females with severe mental illness	Assessed loneliness using UCLA Loneliness Scale	Loneliness as a QOL issue dependent upon living situation or social skills and social networks and the experience of the individual with severe mental illness
Brown, Cosgrove, and DeSelm (1997)	19 Consumers of mental health services and their case managers	Compared perceptions of consumers and case managers regarding barriers interfering with life satisfaction using a structured interview	Family, friendships, health care, community services, housing, neighborhood, finances, daily activities, work, transportation, physical health
Campbell (1976)	National study of persons 18 years and older living in 48 states based on a probability sample — 2,164 women and men	Interviews using a structured questionnaire	Life cycle, urbanicity, age, race, working, family income, work of head of household, education, religion, and sex
Center for Disease Control and Prevention (1995)	102,263 respondents in all states except Wyoming	Health-Related QOL measures for U.S.	Physical, psychological, and social functioning during usual daily activities
Chibnall and Tait (1990)	444 Chronic pain patients at multidisciplinary pain clinic	QOL Scale, Beck Depression Inventory, Speilberger Trait Anxiety Inventory, Pain Disability Index, McGill Pain Questionnaire, Psychosomatic Symptom Checklist	Social life, family life, recreational, education/intellectual, daily activities (work), romantic experiences, expectations/hopes
Chubon (1985)	Nondisabled graduate students and persons with chronic back problems, and prison inmates	Life Situation Survey	Pain tolerance, satisfaction of life quality
Clayton and Chubon (1994)	100 SCI patients (80% male, 20% female)	Life Situation Survey Social Health Battery	Educational level, employment status, income, social activities, and severity of disability
Conn, Taylor, and Wiman (1991)	94 Older adult myocardial infarction survivors	Interviews and Profile of Mood States, Perceived QOL Scale, Health Behavior Scale	Anxiety, depression, exercise, diet, medications, stress, smoking

APPENDIX 33 (continued)
Studies Using Quantitative Methods in Quality of Life (QOL) Research

Source	Population	Measures/Method	Domains
Corrigan and Buican (1995)	49 Patients with severe mental illness	Interview-based measures of quality of life: Brief Psychiatric Rating Scale, Profile of Adaptive Living, Social Support Questionnaire, Wechsler Adult Intelligence Scale Revised	Correlations found between QOL Interview and variables on other instruments. QOL is not redundant with adhedonia common to depression
Dagan, Jones, and Ruddick (1994)	18 People with learning people disabilities	Questionnaire on Quality of Life which has good inter-rater and internal reliability and factor structure usable in services to people with learning disabilities living in residential care facilities	Factors or domains include: physical details, community access, leisure, routines, education and training, staff behavior, decision making
Decker and Borgen (1993)	249 Adults	Occupational Stress Inventory	Vocational, Psychological, Gender, Age, Education, Job Tenure, Negative Affectivity, Stress, and Coping
Elizur and Shye (1990)	540 Employees of large corporation in Hungary	Given QOL and Quality of Work Life (QWL) questionnaires — 16 items each	QOL and QWL share the same domains: *Mode of functioning:* expressive, integrative, adaptive, or conservative; *Field of Functioning:* social or cultural, psychological, physical; and *Life area:* work and life in general
Endicott, Nee, Harrison, and Blumenthal (1993)	Depressed patients	Quality of Life Enjoyment and Satisfaction Questionnaire	Physical health, subjective feelings, leisure time, social relationships, and general activities; Household duties, work, and school
Ensminger (1995)	836 African-American mothers on welfare	Interviews based on selected measures	Psychological distress, welfare, earlier life conditions, region of U.S., teenage mother, chronic burdens, number of children, single parent, self perceptions of health, self-esteem, psychological and physical well-being
Fabian (1992)	110 Mentally ill persons in 2 supported employment programs	Control group study of those in community programs to those in supported employment	Living situation, family, social relations, leisure activities, physical and mental health, safety, work or nonwork, and finances
Ferrans, Cohen, and Smith (1992)	539 Persons with narcolepsy	QOL Index — Narcolepsy	Health and functioning, social and economic aspects, psychological/spiritual aspects, and family
Ferrans and Powers (1992)	349 Adult hemodialysis patients	Quality of Life Index — Dialysis version	Life satisfaction, self-esteem, health, and functioning

APPENDIX 33 (continued)
Studies Using Quantitative Methods in Quality of Life (QOL) Research

Source	Population	Measures/Method	Domains
Fields and Thacker (1992)	293 Employees in intervention one and 119 employees in intervention two	Used Company Commitment measure, Job Satisfaction measure, Union Commitment Scale, Quality of Work Life Scale	Loyalty, responsibility, belief in unionism, willingness, organizational commitment, job satisfaction
Frisch, Cornell, and Villanueva (1992)	54 VA inpatient, 51 VA recovered, 18 private inpatient, 19 offender, 272 general undergraduates, and 127 counseling center persons in psychotherapy	Used QOL Inventory and validated against the Global Severity Scale, Positive Total Symptom, Positive Symptom Distress Index, Beck Depression Inventory, Symptoms Checklist-90-R, Millon Clinical Multiaxial Inventory, Generalized Expectancy for Success Scale	Health, self-regard, philosophy of life, standard of living, work, recreation, learning, creativity, social service, civic action, love relationships, friends, relationships with children and relatives, home, neighborhood, and community
Ganz, Day, Ware, Redmond, and Fisher (1995)	9749 Participants in randomized trials for use of tamoxifen or placebo in 119 clinical centers in U.S. and Canada treating invasive breast cancer	Health-related QOL questionnaire which includes a depression scale, a symptom checklist for Medical Outcomes Study 37SF and MOS sexual problems questions	Age, ethnicity, education, employment, occupation, income, marital status, health behaviors, estrogen, hysterectomy, ovaries removed, and menstrual cycle
Gater, Kind, and Gudex (1995)	138 Medical patients scoring over the threshold for probable psychiatric illness	Health Measurement Questionnaire, (HMQ) Nottingham Health Profile, Psychiatric Assessment Scale, Rosser Index	Compared self-rating and observer-completed; A strong correlation was found between measures, HMQ and QOL and agreement between self- and observer ratings
Gerber, Coleman, Johnston, and Lavfave (1994)	43 Clients discharged 1 and 3 years after psychiatric rehabilitation	Structured interviews, Mulern and Manderscheid Clients' Quality of Life Interview, Uniform Client Data Instrument	Found that QOL was maintained or improved post discharge on all QOL measures
Gilbar (1991)	51 Cancer patients who dropped out of chemotherapy, 19 who refused treatment, and 70 who completed treatment	Psychosocial Adjustment to Physical Illness Scale, Brief Symptom Inventory, and interviews at patients' homes	Heath care, work, home, sexual relationship, extended family, social and psychological distress; somatization and psychological symptoms
Goodwin, Boggs, and Graham-Pole (1994)	210 Parents of children with cancer	Development of a 21-item parent report measure of QOL, the Pediatric Oncology Quality of Life Scale	Physical function, role restriction, emotional distress, reaction to current medical treatment
Guyatt (1994)	Heart failure patients	Minnesota Living with Heart Failure Questionnaire is reliable and valid	Disease specific with domains as emotional function, dyspnea (labored breathing), and fatigue with use of digoxin

APPENDIX 33 (continued)
Studies Using Quantitative Methods in Quality of Life (QOL) Research

Source	Population	Measures/Method	Domains
Hadorn and Hays (1991)	Convenience sample of 116 persons in elderly care homes, renal dialysis unit, low-income neighborhood health centers, meetings of clergy and social workers	Self-report on the 6 domains asking for problem levels and positive responses, and importance selection	General health, physical suffering, self-care activities, outlook on life, meaningful activities, and social relationships
Hardison and Vanier (1976)	130 Men and 153 women in California	Part of a research project funded by Urban Mass Transit Administration	Traffic, parking, transportation mode, pollution, physical condition, life stress, social conflict, mental illness, good old days, too many people, fast change, dominated by machines, getting ahead
Hays, Kallich, Mapes, Coons, and Carter (1994)	165 Patients with kidney disease	Development of the Kidney Disease QOL Instrument (KDQOL)	Physical functioning, emotional functioning, social functioning, pain, energy–fatigue, and general health perceptions
Hays, Vickrey, Hermann, Perrine, Cramer, Meador, Spritzer, and Devinsky (1995)	292 Patients with epilepsy and their designated proxies	Used 89-item QOL Inventory	Physical functioning, pain, health perception, role disability (due to physical or emotional health) support, emotional well-being, overall QOL, social isolation, energy/fatigue, language/memory/attention cognitive function, seizure distress, work and driving
Headey, Veenhoven, and Wearing (1991)	QOL survey of 942 persons conducted in 4 waves (1981, 1983, 1985, 1987) in Victoria, Australia	Used Life-as-a-Whole Index, Delighted–Terrible Scale, Eyesenck Personality Inventory, and socioeconomic status by gender in examining subjective well-being	Marriage, work, material standard of living, leisure, friendship, and health
Helmstaedter and Elger (1994)	Presurgical epileptic patients	Evaluated subjective reports of psychosocial impairments with a questionnaire	Physical status, emotional status, capability, work, social life, independence and self-determination
Hennessy, Moriarty, Zack, Scherr, and Brackbill (1994)	General population	QOL public health surveillance by CDCP using Behavioral Risk Factor Surveillance System, a state-based telephone surveillance system	Self-perceived health, recent physical health, recent mental health, recent activity limitation
Houser and Chace (1993)	18 Males and 9 females with disabilities placed into jobs in a project with industry setting	Minnesota Satisfaction Questionnaire	Keeping busy, work alone, variety, status, supervision, ethics, tenure, service, leadership, working up to capacity, fair policies, advancement, exercise judgment, try out new methods, working conditions, relationships with co-workers, praise, and accomplishment

APPENDIX 33 (continued)
Studies Using Quantitative Methods in Quality of Life (QOL) Research

Source	Population	Measures/Method	Domains
Hughes, Hwang, Kim, Eisenman, and Killian (1995)	People with disabilities	Review of 87 empirical studies analyzed and a model proposed	Social relationships, psychological well-being, employment, self-determination, recreation and leisure, personal competence, residential environment, community integration, normalization, support services, demographic indicators, personal development and fulfillment, social acceptance, physical and material well-being, civic responsibility
Huxley and Warner (1992)	68 Long-term psychiatric patients	Quality of Life Profile and General Satisfaction Questionnaire	Used interviews modified the QOL Profile to include a 9th domain of religion, and used the client database to conduct study
Hyer, Matteson, and Siegler (1982)	Elderly in long-term care facilities	Use of a Locus of Control measure as a tool to facilitate quality of life	Age, education, sex, depression, and cognitive decline
Hyland, Bott, Singh, and Kenyon (1994)	40 Patients with breathing problems	Breathing Problems Questionnaire and review of other QOL measures	Walking, bending or reaching, washing and bathing, household chores, social interactions, effects of weather and temperature, effects of smells and fumes, effects of colds, sleeping, medicines, dysphoric states, eating, excretion urgency
Hyland, Finnis, and Irvine (1991)	783 Asthma patients	Asthma Questionnaire, a 68-item quality of life scale	Social/leisure, sport, holidays, sleep, work, colds, mobility, effects on others, medication usage, sex, dysphoric states and attitudes
Hyland, Kenyon, and Jacobs (1994)	41 Patients with asthma receiving salmeterol and 38 to placebo	Living with Asthma Questionnaire (LWAQ)	Social/leisure, sport, holidays, sleep, work, and other activities, colds, mobility, effects on others, medication usage, sex and dysphoric states and attitudes
Inge, Banks, Wehman, Hill, and Shafer (1988)	20 Persons with mental retardation	Adaptive Behavior Scale, Parent/Guardian Survey, Quality of Life Matching Scale	Domestic skills, appearance, community participation, leisure/recreation, social/vocational skills and financial activity
Jaeschke, Guyatt, Cook, Harper, and Gerstein (1994)	200 Patients with treated hypothyroidism	Took a survey of 200 patients to generate items. Then distributed 70 questionnaires to family doctors and specialists, and 150 questionnaires to the Thyroid Foundation. 70 responses total received from the 2 groups	Physical problems, energy and general well-being problems, mood and emotional problems

APPENDIX 33 (continued)
Studies Using Quantitative Methods in Quality of Life (QOL) Research

Source	Population	Measures/Method	Domains
Kaplan, R. M. (1994)	Health problems such as diabetes, HIV, arthritis, neonatal circumcision, and tobacco tax	Quality of Well-Being Scale (QWB) is a questionnaire which classifies patients by objective levels of functioning	Levels of functioning are represented by mobility, physical activity, and social activity
Kaplan, Anderson, and Wingard (1991)	Random sample of 1,034 men and women from San Diego	Analysis of well-years by gender using General Health Policy Model	Mobility, physical activity, social activity
Kaplan, S. P. (1993)	25 Individuals with traumatic brain injury	Portland Adaptability Inventory	Temperament and emotionality, activities and social behavior, physical capabilities
Katz, Larson, Phillips, Fossel, and Liang (1992)	54 Patients undergoing total hip arthroplasty	Sickness Impact Profile, Arthritis Impact Measurement Scales, and Modified Health Assessment Questionnaire	Physical, psychological, global dimensions
Kloseck, Crilly, Ellis, and Lammers (1996)	Geriatric rehabilitation population — 114 persons (47 male and 67 female)	Leisure Competence Measure, Life Satisfaction Index, Geriatric Depression Scale, Folstein Mini-Mental State Examination	Leisure awareness, skills, attitude, social appropriateness, group interaction skills, social context, and community participation
Kober, Kuchler, Broelsch, Kremer, and Henne-Bruns (1990)	29 Liver transplant patients from Hamburg and 38 patients from Chicago	EORTC quality of life questionnaire, the STALX Anxiety Questionnaire, psychodiagnostic interviews, routine laboratory parameters	Functional status, ability to work, general symptoms, liver symptoms, anxiety, depression, social integration, pain, treatment strain, overall physical condition and overall QOL
Koch and Muthny (1990)	More than 2000 patients with kidney disease	Questionnaire	Physical/psychosomatic complaints, emotional well-being, partnership and family, vocational rehabilitation, hobbies, leisure activities, and satisfaction with treatment
Kristiansen (1989)	58 British females and 52 British males	Rokeach's Value Survey	World peace, inner harmony, mature love, social recognition, friendship, comfortable life, health, security, wisdom, self-respect
Lance, Lautenschlager, and Sloan (1989)	150 Assistant, associate, and full professors from University of Georgia	Job Stress Scale, Depressed Mood Scale, Minnesota Satisfaction Questionnaire	Marital satisfaction, satisfaction with social activities, job satisfaction
Langfitt (1995)	71 Epilepsy patients	Epilepsy Surgery Inventory, Sickness Impact Profile, Washington Psychosocial Seizure Inventory	Symptoms, functional status, self-care, mobility, physical activity, energy and vitality, sleep and rest, social functioning, emotional status, cognition, health perceptions, general life satisfaction, work and household management
Larson (1991)	International health status of nations	Health Status 1 and Health Status 2 derived from Physical Quality of Life Index	Physical, mental, and social well-being

APPENDIX 33 (continued)
Studies Using Quantitative Methods in Quality of Life (QOL) Research

Source	Population	Measures/Method	Domains
Latten (1989)	3,000 Respondents over 18 years in the Netherlands	Quality of Life Surveys	Serious physical injury or illness, death of family member, widow(er)hood, and serious tension at home, aging
Lehman, Reed, and Possidente (1982)	278 Randomly selected psychiatric patients in board and care homes in Los Angeles	Quality of Life Interview	Living situation, family, social relations, leisure time, employment, finances, personal safety, and health
Lennon (1994)	300 Employed women, 202 full-time homemakers, 302 employed men	Investigated the role of work conditions in mediating the effect of employment status on married women's psychological well-being	Autonomy, time pressure, responsibility for things outside of one's control, interruptions, physical effort, and routine
Lennox (1994)	Chronic substance abusers	Center for Epidemiological Studies Depression Scale	Somatic complaints, depressed affect, positive affect, and interpersonal relations
Lerner, Levine, Malspeis, and D'Agostino (1994)	1,319 Working adults	Job Content Questionnaire Medical Outcomes Study Short-Form Health Survey	Physical, role functioning as relates to health, vitality, social functioning, and mental health
Lindley, Hirsch, O'Neill, Tansau, Gilbert, and Osterhaus (1992)	Cancer patients receiving chemotherapy	Used the Functional Living Index — Cancer as model to create Functional Living Index — Emesis	Physical well-being and ability, emotional state, sociability, family situation, and nausea
Logue (1990)	Elderly long-term American Indian, Black, and White patients (over 45 years)	Data obtained from Public Use Microdata Samples for Oklahoma from 1980 decennial census and from a query on Public Transportation Disability	Social risk, aging, disability, economic status, health, race, gender, educational attainment, marital status, area of residence
Manz and Grothe (1991)	Approximately 4,000 employees in a midwestern computer manufacturing company	Quality of Work Life Survey	Personal motivation, personal investment, meaningfulness of job, innovation, quality/productivity, communication of organization mission, policies and procedures, human resource systems, management effectiveness, management understanding, commitment to employees, participation, performance evaluation, respect for the individual, supervisory skills, nonfinancial rewards, job clarity, trust and support, team productivity, team communication, job stress, work load, job design, equity, benefits, compensation, career training, physical work environment, work resources

APPENDIX 33 (continued)
Studies Using Quantitative Methods in Quality of Life (QOL) Research

Source	Population	Measures/Method	Domains
McCall (1991)	Suicide rates in elderly and adolescent males	Used annual suicide rates for U.S. from *Annual Vital Health Statistics Report 1947–1987*	Impoverishment, family dissolution, and government expenditures
McCoy (1994)	439 Professional women	Survey of working women's leisure time	Discretionary time, discretionary activity, leisure as a state of mind
McGee, O'Boyle, Hickey, O'Malley, and Joyce (1991)	20 Irritable bowel syndrome and 20 peptic ulcer disease patients as compared to 42 healthy individuals	Used the Schedule for Evaluation of Individual Quality of Life	Family, work, recreation, religion, and health
McGuire, Choon, and Akuffo (1991)	19 Elderly people with a developmental disability	Used a lifestyle questionnaire and the Social Training Achievement Record Profile through interviews	Activities of daily life, community-based activities, domestic tasks, areas of personal responsibility
McLanahan and Adams (1989)	Effects of children on adult well-being	Two Americans View Their Mental Health Surveys (AVTHM) 1957 and 1976	Happiness, satisfaction, worries, psychological distress, and perceptions of parenthood
Mehrabian and Ross (1979)	293 Undergraduate students	Checklists, questionnaires, and measures of personality	Life changes, physical illness and symptoms, psychosomatic symptoms, accidents, psychological symptoms
Moller and Murphy (1997)	176 Patients with psychiatric disabilities	Clients, family members, and case managers enrolled in course, *Symptom Management: A Wellness Expedition*	Number of inpatient days, cost savings, and participant satisfaction
Moss (1980)	69 Older clients from 2 similar rehabilitation workshops	Clients assigned to random groups to receive group counseling or social activities; Dean Alienation Scale, Havighhurst Life Satisfaction Index A, Sociometric Questionnaire	Life satisfaction, work productivity, alienation
Mugenda, Hira, and Fanslow (1990)	123 Adults in the midwest	Obtained data re household size and net worth, marital status, employment status of money manager, and money management practices	Level of living, savings, staying out of debt, assets, paying debts, meeting emergency expenses, satisfaction with QOL
Mulhern, Fairclough, Friedman, and Leigh (1990)	120 Children with cancer	Play Performance Scale for Children and Vineland Adaptive Behavior Scales with parent and physician ratings	Acute psychological problems, somatic toxicity of various treatments, and residual psychological problems
Murrell and Norris (1983)	1,800 Adults living in Kentucky	Use of a subjective measure of QOL	Mental health, financial, social activity, employment, and health
Nation, Benshoff, and Malkin (1996)	Adolescents in substance abuse treatment facilities	Random survey of substance abuse treatment programs using therapeutic recreation	Social skills, self-esteem, self-efficacy and improve cooperation and trust; QOL not a specific goal

APPENDIX 33 (continued)
Studies Using Quantitative Methods in Quality of Life (QOL) Research

Source	Population	Measures/Method	Domains
Near, Rice, and Hunt (1978)	1041 Probability sample of adults living in New York state	4 subjective QOL measures	Life satisfaction, life satisfaction over time, job satisfaction, and health
Osberg, McGinnis, DeJong, and Seward (1987)	97 Elderly disabled adults	Markides and Martin's (1979) path analysis model to assess QOL, Barthel Index, self-administered questionnaire	Income, age, marital status, functional capacity, independence
Ouellette-Kuntz (1990)	Ten interviews with mentally retarded adults	Use of Quality of Life Interview Schedule with emphasis on intra- and inter-rater agreement	Health services, family-guardianship, income, education, training, and employment, housing and safety, transportation, social, recreational, religious/cultural, case management, advocacy, aesthetics, and counseling
Perlman, Connell, Clark et al. (1990)	43 Rheumatoid arthritis patients	Self-report and doctors' medical history, dance-based exercise, Arthritis Impact Measurement Scales	Disease states, physical function, and pscyhological function
Perry and Felce (1995)	People with learning disabilities in 15 staffed houses	Review of 14 objective measures of service quality in residential facilities	Quality of housing, social and community integration, social interactions, development, activity, and autonomy and choice
Pugliesi (1995)	599 Women and 753 men from a national data set	Refinement of differential exposure or vulnerability models	Work characteristics, social and psychological resources, well-being, role and status variables — gender, marital status, ethnicity, and parenthood
Reich and Zautra (1983)	70 Middle and older aged persons and a college sample of 104 students	Life Events Questionnaire, Depressive Adjective Checklist, Perceived Quality of Life Scale	Demands, desires, positive and negative components of well-being, psychiatric symptoms
Renwick and Friedland (1996)	107 Males and 13 females with HIV	Quality of Life Questionnaire, Fanning Quality of Life Scale, Life Appraisal and Life Satisfaction Questionnaire, Interpersonal Support Evaluation List, Ways of Coping, Recent Life Changes Questionnaire	Job satisfaction, relations with others, work relations, altruistic behavior, creative–aesthetic behavior, significant other relationships, marital (partner) relations, job characteristics, political behavior, extended family relations, vacation behavior, personal growth, material well-being, sports activity, and physical well-being
Rettig, Danes, and Bauer (1991)	592 Women and men from farm families	Survey and Delighted–Terrible Scale	Love, status, services, information, goods, money resources received from family
Rhoads and Raymond (1981)	547 Adults from Phoenix area	Interviews, Bradburn Affect–Balance-Scale	Age, sex, family income, personal, social, community, income

APPENDIX 33 (continued)
Studies Using Quantitative Methods in Quality of Life (QOL) Research

Source	Population	Measures/Method	Domains
Rintala, Hart, and Fuhrer (1996)	661 Persons with spinal cord injuries	Questionnaires and Perceived Stress Scale, Center for Epidemiological Studies Depression Scale, Life Satisfaction Index, Craig Handicap Assessment and Reporting Technique, ASIA Total Motor Index, Functional Independence Measure, Hassles Scale, Life Events Scale, Personal Independence Profile, Satisfaction with Personal Assistance, Interpersonal Support Evaluation List	Depression, life satisfaction, morbidity, mobility, occupation, social integration and support, independence, pressure sores
Rodin (1990)	Adults with insulin-dependent diabetes mellitus (158 subjects)	Rand General Well-Being Scale, General Health Questionnaire	Physical functioning, social functioning, emotional functioning, burden of symptoms, and the sense of well-being
Romney, Jenkins, and Bynner (1992)	469 Patients with cardiovascular problems	Use LISREL to test competing hypothesis	Symptoms of illness, neurological dysfunction, interpersonal relationships, morale, and socioeconomic status
Rosen, Simon, and McKinsey (1995)	100 Individuals with mental retardation	Developed subjective QOL instrument — PALS	Perceived Stress, Affect, Loneliness, and Satisfaction
Rosenfeld, S. (1992)	157 Members of a psychosocial rehabilitation program	Interviews, Delighted–Terrible Scale, Lehman's QOL, Moos' Community-Oriented Program Environment Scale	Importance of program components, vocational rehabilitation, financial services, empowerment approaches to service delivery
Roxburgh (1996)	994 Employed Canadians	Tested Job Stress Models	Differential exposure and vulnerability by gender to job stress, occupational self-direction, job demands, co-worker social support
Ruchlin and Morris (1991)	310 Young elderly between ages of 65-74.	Modified Spitzer Uniscale QL index	Marital Status, self-assessed health status, functional status, self-assessed financial status, and work status
Ruffing-Rahal (1991)	182 Community-dwelling elderly adults	Integration Inventory, Philadelphia Geriatric Center Morale Scale, the Spiritual Well-Being Scale, and 4 measures of self-rated well-being	Well-being, absence of loneliness, positive attitude toward aging, self-rated happiness, self-rated health, self-rated life satisfaction, absence of agitation, religious well-being
Sands and Kozleski (1994)	131 Persons without disabilities and 86 persons with disabilities (cerebral palsy, mental retardation, and head injury) living in community settings	Used the Consumer Satisfaction Survey and modified version with nondisabled sample	Experience with advocacy organizations, services and satisfaction, independence interdependence, participation in community activities, and in recreation activities, and satisfaction with these activities

APPENDIX 33 (continued)
Studies Using Quantitative Methods in Quality of Life (QOL) Research

Source	Population	Measures/Method	Domains
Schaafsma and Osoba (1994)	139 Lung cancer patients	Karnofsky Performance Status and item 30 of the QOL questionnaire developed by the European Organization for Research and Treatment of Cancer Study Group	Physical functioning, emotional functioning, breathing, social functioning, and cognition, pain, and fatigue
Schalock and Lilley (1986)	85 Mentally retarded persons	Quality of Life Questionnaire	Environmental control (daily schedule, income, appointments, shopping, home decorations, pets); social interaction (neighbors, co-inhabitants, friends); community utilization (transportation, recreation, education)
Scherer (1990)	Persons with spinal cord injury (SCI) and cerebral palsy (CP)	Compared persons with SCI and CP using assistive devices (AD), interviews and observations, Personal Capacities Questionnaire, Functional Assessment Inventory, Taylor-Johnson Temperament Analysis	Personal capacities, adaptive behavior, vocational qualifications, motor functioning
Schwartz, Devine, Schechter, and Bender (1990)	19 Myasthenia gravis and 19 amyotrophic lateral sclerosis patients	9-Rung Cantril Ladder, Multidimensional Health Locus of Control, Functional Living Index for Cancer, Quality of Life Index	Demographics, severity of illness, coping styles, life satisfaction, perceived health and social activity, control of health, psychosocial well-being, public and body image, and QOL
Scuccimarra and Speece (1990)	65 Mildly handicapped students who exited high school in 1984	59-Item instrument was developed adapted from the Vermont Follow-up Structured Survey Instrument	Employment status and social activity
Short and Shea (1995)	Families below the poverty line and AFDC families	From data collected in Survey of Income and Program Participation	Access to consumer durables, living conditions, crime and neighborhood, basic needs, health and nutrition, index of deprivation
Shye (1989)	General population	Examined QOL Model vs. Residents Reports	Personality, physical, social, cultural
Sinnott-Oswald, Gliner, and Spencer (1991)	Ten persons with disabilities in supported community employment, ten persons with disabilities in sheltered workshop employment, and nine persons without disabilities	QOL Index, Adaptive Behavior Scale, physical health measures, Parent–Guardian Survey	Leisure activities, use of leisure time, self-esteem, involvement in activities, mobility, job skill perceptions, and perceptions regarding changes in income

APPENDIX 33 (continued)
Studies Using Quantitative Methods in Quality of Life (QOL) Research

Source	Population	Measures/Method	Domains
Spreitzer and Snyder (1989)	Toledo adults	Life Satisfaction, Job Satisfaction, and Self-Esteem items used in telephone interviews	Self-esteem, job and life satisfaction, and leisure
Sullivan, Wells, and Leake (1992)	101 Former acute care psychiatric inpatients living in Mississippi	Quality of Life Index, Drug Attitude Inventory, the Symptom Checklist	Living situation, social life, personal health, finances, global rating, depressive symptoms, psychotic symptoms, medications compliance, side effects, alcohol abuse, social skills, living skills, criticism by family
Tait, Chibnall, and Margolis (1990)	416 Patients with chronic pain	Beck Depression Inventory, Speilberger Anxiety Inventory, Psychosomatic Symptom Checklist, QOL Scale, and Pain Disability Index	Pain extent, psychological state, pain severity, disability, pain history, age, education
Tsevat, Goldman, Lamas, Pfeffer, Chapin, Connors, and Lee (1991)	80 Myocardial infarction survivors	Visual Analogue Scale, Verbal Rating Scale, Time Trade-off, Transformed Time Trade-off Mean, Karnofsky Index, Specific Anxiety Scale Class, and NY Heart Association Class	Gender, employment, exercise, pain, functional status
Tuchler, Hofmann, Bernahart et al. (1992)	1014 Adult patients in European countries	QOL Questionnaire	Physical condition, QOL, relationships and social contacts, health, overall life situation, medical treatment, sexuality, recovery chances, physical capacity, life satisfaction
Vandergriff and Chubon (1994)	120 Persons with mental retardation	Program Analysis of Service System Implementation of Normalization Goals, Life Situation Survey, Resident Choice Assessment Scale, American Association on Mental Deficiency Adaptive Behavior Scale	Internal standards and evaluations of life by individuals, socionormative, and person–environment systems
Verbrugge, Reoma, and Gruber-Baldini (1994)	165 Persons with chronic disability	Mental Status Questionnaire, Beck Depression Inventory, Activities of Daily Living, Six Motions to determine physical functioning, and Index of Well-Being	Cognitive, emotional, social, physical, and global well-being
Vickrey, Hays, Graber et al. (1992)	239 Adults with epilepsy	Epilepsy Surgery Inventory, Mood Profile, Seizure Classification	Energy/fatigue, overall QOL, social function, emotional well-being, cognitive function, physical function, pain, role limitations

APPENDIX 33 (continued)
Studies Using Quantitative Methods in Quality of Life (QOL) Research

Source	Population	Measures/Method	Domains
Walker, Blankenship, Ditty, and Lynch (1987)	25 Closed-head-injured adults (1 female and 24 males)	MMPI, Adaptive Behavior Scale, Quality of Life Rating Scale	Vocational, educational, family participation, community service, avocational, artistic, and scholarly pursuits
Wallston, Hoover-Dempsey, and Brissie (1989)	78 Working women	Job Satisfaction, Scale Self-esteem Scale, and Life Satisfaction Scale	Gatekeeping transactions, flexibility, outcome/success, negativity, job satisfaction, self-esteem, quality of life, substance use
Warren, Wrigley, Yoels, and Fine (1996)	137 Persons with traumatic brain injury, 38 spinal cord injury persons	Life Satisfaction Index–A, Functional Independence Measure, Family Satisfaction Scale	Family satisfaction, employment status, memory independence, bowel independence, marital status, self blame
West, Kregel, and Banks (1990)	1,550 Individuals placed in supported employment (65% with mental retardation, 9% with long-term mental illness, and 10% with head injuries and cerebral palsy)	*Data Management System Operations Manual* for form completion by 96 provider agencies	Evaluation of QOL in worklife by looking availability of fringe benefits
Whelton, Pawlick, and Cardamone (1997)	105 Families with 92 family members with psychiatric disabilities	Questionnaires sent to families regarding the Hamilton Program for Schizophrenia to determine levels of satisfaction with the program	Time and money spent by family members for their relatives with disabilities and reduction of caregiving by program. Quality of relationship with relative. Illness management
Wilkinson, Williams, Krekorian, McLees, and Falloon (1992)	32 Adults with functional mental disorders	Structured Interview schedule, Charing Cross Health Indicator, Clinical Global Impression Scale	Adaptive functioning, social performance, patient and family distress, economic, and sociodemographic factors
Williams, Eyring, Gaynor, and Long (1991)	734 College students and adults	Life Satisfaction Index, Satisfaction with Life Scale, Spiritual Well-Being Scale	Inherent value of life, effective life management, and sense of health
Wood and Johnson (1989)	15 Elderly rural adults selected for qualitative study and 392 elderly rural adults in quantitative study	Used a life satisfaction questionnaire and analysis of qualitative data	Housing, health, self-esteem, friendship, and family
Woodruff and Conway (1992)	519 U.S. Navy personnel randomly selected	Questionnaires based on QOL research to examine health and fitness factors and changes in QOL	Overall QOL, health/fitness, and health behavior
Young and Barboriak (1982)	45 Male volunteers classified for Type A behavior	Structured Interview, Jenkins Activity Survey, Milwaukee Cardiovascular Life Quality Questionnaire	Competition on the job, hard driving, temper, job deadlines, getting ahead, vacations, rest

APPENDIX 33 (continued)
Studies Using Quantitative Methods in Quality of Life (QOL) Research

Source	Population	Measures/Method	Domains
Zautra (1982)	537 Community residents	Life Cycle Measurements, Social Resource Measurements, Negative Life Events, Perceived Quality of Life Scale, 22-item Psychiatric Screening Inventory	Self-reliance, supportive others, social responsibility, social network blame, positive affect, negative affect, psychiatric distress, overall life quality, number of negative events
Zweig, Barber, and Eccles (1997)	Young adults: 872 women and 527 men	Data from MI Study of Adolescent Life used to examine sexual coercion and well-being	Psychological and social adjustment, depressed mood, self-esteem, coping

References

Baker, F., Curbow, B., and Wingard, J. R. (1992). Development of the Satisfaction with Life Domains Scale for Cancer. *Journal of Psychosocial Oncology,* 10(3): 75-90.

Baker, F., Jodrey, D., and Intagliata, J. (1992). Social support and quality of life of community support clients. *Community Mental Health Journal,* 29(5): 397-411.

Ben-Ari, A. and Taler, Y. (1984). The relationship between absenteeism rate and satisfaction among clients in vocational rehabilitation centers. *Journal of Applied Rehabilitation Counseling,* 15(4): 39-47.

Bigelow, D. A., McFarland, B. H., and Olson, M. M. (1991). Quality of life of community mental health program clients: validating a measure. *Community Mental Health Journal,* 27(1): 43-55.

Boschen, K. A. (1996). Correlates of life satisfaction, residential satisfaction, and locus of control among adults with spinal cord injuries. *Rehabilitation Counseling Bulletin,* 39(4): 230-243.

Brown, C. (1996). A comparison of living situation and loneliness for people with mental illness. *Psychiatric Rehabilitation Journal,* 20(2): 59-65.

Brown, C., Cosgrove, N., and De Selm, T. (1997). Barriers interfering with life satisfaction for individuals with severe mental illness. *Psychiatric Rehabilitation Journal,* 20(3): 67-71.

Campbell, A. (1976). Subjective measures of well-being. *American Psychologist,* 117-124.

Centers for Disease Control and Prevention. (1995). Health-related quality of life measures — United States, 1993. *Morbidity and Mortality Weekly Report,* 44(11): 195-200.

Chibnall, J. T. and Tait, R. C. (1990). The Quality of Life Scale: a preliminary study with chronic pain patients. *Psychology and Health,* 4: 283-292.

Chubon, R. A. (1985). Quality of life measurement of persons with back problems: some preliminary findings. *Journal of Applied Rehabilitation Counseling,* 16(2): 31-34.

Clayton, K.S. and Chubon, R. A. (1994). Factors associated with the quality of life of long-term spinal cord injured persons. *Archives of Physical Medicine and Rehabilitation,* 75 (June), 633-638.

Conn, V. S., Taylor, S. G., and Wiman, P. (1991). Anxiety, depression, quality of life, and self-care among survivors of myocardial infarction. *Issues in Mental Health Nursing,* 12: 321-331.

Corrigan, P. W. and Buican, B. (1995). The construct validity of subjective quality of life for the severely mentally ill. *The Journal of Nervous and Mental Disease,* 183(5): 281-285.

Dagan, D., Jones, J., and Ruddick, L. (1994). The psychometric properties of a scale for assessing the quality of life of people with learning disabilities in residential care. *The British Journal of Developmental Disabilities, XL* (79): 98-103.

Decker, P. J. and Borgen, F. H. (1993). Dimension of work appraisal, stress, strain, coping, job satisfaction, and negative affectivity. *Journal of Counseling Psychology,* 40(4): 470-478.

Elizur, D. and Shye, S. (1990). Quality of work life and its relation to quality of life. *Applied Psychology: An International Review,* 39(3): 275-291.

Endicott, J., Nee, J., Harrison, W., and Blumenthal, R. (1993). Quality of Life Enjoyment and Satisfaction Questionnaire: a new measure. *Psychopharmacology Bulletin,* 29: 321-326

Ensminger, M. E. (1995). Welfare and psychological distress: a longitudinal study of African American urban mothers. *Journal of Health and Social Behavior,* 36: 346-359.

Fabian, E. S. (1992). Supported employment and quality of life: does a job make a difference? *Rehabilitation Counseling Bulletin,* 36(2): 85-87.

Ferrans, C. E., Cohen, F. L., and Smith, K. M. (1992). The quality of life of persons with narcolepsy. *Psychosocial aspects of narcolepsy.* Haworth Press.

Ferrans, C. and Powers, M. (1992). Psychometric assessment of the Quality of Life Index. *Research in Nursing and Health,* 15: 111-119.

Fields, M. W. and Thacker, J. W. (1992). Influence of quality of work life on company and union commitment. *Academy of Management Journal,* 35(2): 439-450.

Frisch, M. B., Cornell, J., and Villanueva. (1992). Clinical validation of the Quality of Life Inventory: a measure of life satisfaction for use in treatment planning and outcome assessment. *Psychological Assessment,* 4(1): 92-101.

Ganz, P. A., Day, R., Ware, J. E., Redmond, C., and Fisher, B. (1995). Base-line quality-of-life assessment in national surgical adjuvant breast and bowel project cancer. *Journal of the National Cancer Institute,* 87(18): 1372-1382.

Gater, R. A., Kind, P., and Gudex, C. (1995). Quality of life in liaison psychiatry: a comparison of patient and clinician assessment. *British Journal of Psychiatry,* 166: 515-520.

Gerber, G. J., Coleman, G. E., Johnston, L., and Lafave, H. G. (1994). Quality of life of people with psychiatric disabilities 1 and 3 years after discharge from hospital. *Quality of Life Research,* 3: 379-383.

Gilbar, O. (1991). The quality of life of cancer patients who refuse chemotherapy. *Social Science Medicine,* 32(12): 1337-1340.

Goodwin, D. A. J., Boggs, S. R., and Graham-Poole, J. (1994). Development and validation of the pediatric oncology quality of life scale. *Psychological Assessment,* 6(4): 321-328.

Guyatt, G. H. (1994). Measurement of health-related quality of life in heart failure. *Irish Journal of Psychology,* 15(1): 148-163.

Hadorn, D. C. and Hays, R. D. (1991). Multitrait-multimethod analysis of health-related quality of life measures. *Medical Care,* 29(9): 829-840.

Hardison, N. M. and Vanier, D. J. (1976). Environment and quality of life: attitudinal measurement and analysis. *Psychological Reports,* 39: 959-965.

Hays, R. D., Kallich, J. D., Mapes, D. L., Coons, S. J., and Carter, W. B. (1994). Development of the Kidney Disease Quality of Life (KDQOL) Instrument. *Quality of Life Research,* 3: 329-338.

Hays, R. D., Vickrey, B. G., Hermann, B. P., Perrine, K., Cramer, J., Meador, K., Spritzer, K., and Devinsky, O. (1995). Agreement between self reports and proxy reports of quality of life in epilepsy patients. *Quality of Life Research,* 4: 159-168.

Headey, B, Veenhoven, R., and Wearing, A. (1991). Top-down vs. bottom-up theories of subjective well-being. *Social Indicators Research,* 24: 81-100.

Helmstaedter, C. and Elger, C. E. (1994). Cognitive-behavioral aspects of quality of life in presurgical patients with epilepsy. *Journal of Epilepsy,* 7: 220-231.

Hennessy, C. H., Moriarty, D. G., Zack, M. M., Scherr, P. A., and Brackbill, R. (1994). Measuring health-related quality of life for public health surveillance. *Public Health Reports,* 106(5): 665-672.

Houser, R, and Chace, A. (1993). Job satisfaction of people with disabilities place through a project with industry. *Journal of Rehabilitation,* 45-48.

Hughes, C., Hwang, B., Kim, J. H., Eisenman, L. T., and Killian, D. J. (1995). Quality of life in applied research: a review and analysis of empirical measures. *American Journal on Mental Retardation,* 99(6): 623-641.

Huxley, P. and Warner, R. (1992). Case management, quality of life, and satisfaction with services of long-term psychiatric patients. *Hospital and Community Psychiatry,* 43(8): 799-802.

Hyer, L. Matteson, M.A., and Siegler, I. C. (1982). Locus of control and long-term care. *Journal of Applied Gerontology,* 1: 147-160.

Hyland, M. E., Bott, J., Singh, S., and Kenyon, C. A. P. (1994). Domains, constructs and the development of the breathing problems questionnaire. *Quality of Life Research,* 3: 245-256.

Hyland, M. E., Finnis, S., and Irvine, S. H. (1991). A scale for assessing quality of life in adult asthma sufferers. *Journal of Psychosomatic Research,* 35(2): 99-110.

Hyland, M. E., Kenyon, C. A. P., and Jacobs, P. A. (1994). Sensitivity of quality of life domains and constructs to longitudinal change in a clinical trial comparing salmeterol with placebo in asthmatics. *Quality of Life Research,* 3: 121-126.

Inge, K. J., Banks, P. D., Wehman, Hill, J. W., and Shafer, M. S. (1988). Quality of life for individuals who are labeled mentally retarded: evaluating competitive employment versus sheltered workshop employment. *Education and Training in Mental Retardation*, 97-104.

Jaeschke, R., Guyatt, G., Cook, S., Harper, S., and Gerstein, H. C. (1994). Spectrum of quality of life impairment in hypothyroidism. *Quality of Life Research,* 3: 323-327.

Kaplan, R. M. (1994). Using quality of life information to set priorities in health policy. *Social Indicators Research,* 33: 121-163.

Kaplan, R. M., Anderson, J. P., and Wingard, D. L. (1991). Gender differences in health-related quality of life. *Health Psychology,* 10(2): 86-93.

Kaplan, S. P. (1993). Five-year tracking of psychosocial changes in people with severe traumatic brain injury. *Rehabilitation Counseling Bulletin,* 36(3): 151-159.

Katz, J. N., Larson, M. G., Phillips, C. B., Fossel, A. H., and Liang, M. H. (1992). *Medical Care,* 30(10): 917-925.

Kloseck, M., Crilly, R. G., Ellis, G. D., and Lammers, E. (1996). Leisure Competence Measure: development and reliability testing of a scale to measure functional outcomes in therapeutic recreation. *Therapeutic Recreation Journal,* 13-26.

Kober, B., Kuchler, T., Broelsch, C., Kremer, B., and Henne-Bruns, D. (1990). A psychological support concept and quality of life research in a liver transplantation program: an interdisciplinary multicenter study. *Psychotherapy and Psychosomatics,* 54: 117-131.

Koch, U. and Muthny, F. A. (1990). Quality of life in patients with end-stage renal disease in relation to the method of treatment. *Psychotherapy and Psychosomatics,* 54: 161-171.

Kristiansen, C. M. (1989). Gender differences in the meaning of "health." *Social Behavior,* 4: 185-188.

Lance, C. E., Lautenschlager, G. J., and Sloan, C. E. (1989). A comparison between bottom-up, top-down, and bidirectional models of relationships between global and life facet satisfaction. *Journal of Personality,* 57(3): 601-624.

Langfitt, J. T. (1995). Comparison of the psychometric characteristics of three quality of life measures in intractable epilepsy. *Quality of Life Research,* 4: 101-114.

Larson, J. S. (1991). Two scales for measuring international health status. *Evaluation and the Health Professions,* 14(4): 422-437.

Latten, J. J. (1989). Life-course and satisfaction, equal for every-one? *Social Indicators Research,* 21: 599-610.

Lehman, A. F., Reed, S. K., and Possidente, S. M. (1982). Priorities for long-term care: comments from board-and-care residents. *Psychiatric Quarterly,* 54(3): 181-189.

Lennon, M. C. (1994). Women, work, and well-being: the importance of work conditions. *Journal of Health and Social Behavior,* 35: 235-247.

Lennox, R. D. (1994). Measurement error issues in substance abuse services research: lessons from structural equation modeling and psychometric theory. *Evaluation and Program Planning,* 17(4): 399-407.

Lerner, D. J., Levin, S., Malspeis, S., and D'Agostino, R. B. (1994). Job strain and health-related quality of life in a national sample. *American Journal of Public Health,* 84(10): 1580-1585.

Lindley, C. M., Hirsch, J. D., O'Neill, C. V., Tansau, M. C., Gilbert, C. S., and Osterhaus, J. T. (1992). Quality of life consequences of chemotherapy-induced emesis. *Quality of Life Research,* 1: 331-340.

Logue, B. J. (1990). Race differences in long-term disability: middle-aged and older American Indians, Blacks and Whites in Oklahoma. *Social Science Journal,* 27(3): 253-272.

Manz, C. C. and Grothe, R. (1991). Is the work force vanguard to the 21st century a quality of work life deficient-prone generation? *Journal of Business Research,* 23: 67-82.

McCall, P. L. (1991). Adolescent and elderly white male suicide trends: evidence of changing well-being? *Journal of Gerontology,* 46(1): 843-851.

McCoy, M. L. (1994). Career women's leisure: challenges and realities. In C. W. Konek and S. L. Kitch (Eds.), *Women and Careers: Issues and Challenges,* pp. 173-286. Thousand Oaks, CA: Sage Publications.

McGee, H. M., O'Boyle, C. A., Hickey, A., O'Malley, K., and Joyce, C. R. B. (1991). Assessing the quality of life of the individual: the SEIQoL with a healthy and a gastroenterology unit population. *Psychological Medicine,* 21: 749-759.

McGuire, B. E., Choon, G., and Akuffo, E. (1991). Community living for elderly people with an intellectual disability: a pilot study. *Australia and New Zealand Journal of Developmental Disabilities,* 17(1): 25-33.

McLanahan, S. and Adams, J. (1989). The effects of children on adults' psychological well-being: 1957–1976. *Social Forces,* 68(1): 124-146.

Mehrabian, A. and Ross, M. (1979). Illness, accidents, and alcohol use as functions of the arousing quality and pleasantness of life changes. *Psychological Reports,* 45: 31-43.

Moller, M. D. and Murphy, M. F. (1997). The Three R's Rehabilitation Program: a prevention approach for the management of relapse symptoms associated with psychiatric diagnosis. *Psychiatric Rehabilitation Journal,* 20(3): 42-48.

Moss, E. (1980). Geriatric rehabilitation: group conseling vs. recreational programming for older workshop clients. *Journal of Applied Rehabilitation Counseling,* 11(3): 145-148.

Mugenda, O. M., Hira, T. K., and Fanslow, A. M. (1990). Assessing the causal relationship among communication, money management practices, satisfaction with financial status, and satisfaction with quality of life. *Lifestyles: Family and Economic Issues,* 11(4): 343-360.

Mulhern, R. K., Fairclough, D. L., Friedman, A. G., and Leigh, L. D. (1990). Play Performance Scale as an index of quality of life of children with cancer. *Psychological Assessment,* 2(2): 149-155.

Murrell, S. A. and Norris, F. H. (1983). Quality of life as the criterion for need assessment and community psychology. *Journal of Consulting Psychology,* 11: 88-97.

Nation, J. M., Benshoff, J. J., and Malkin, M. M. (1996). Therapeutic recreation programs for adolescents in substance abuse treatment facilities. *Journal of Rehabilitation,* 10-16.

Near, J. P., Rice, R. W. and Hunt, R. G. (1978). Work and extra-work correlates of life and job satisfaction. *Academy of Management Journal,* 21(2): 248-264.

Osberg, J. S., McGinnis, G. E., DeJong, G., and Seward, M. L. (1987). Life satisfaction and quality of life among disabled elderly adults. *Journal of Gerontology,* 42(2): 228-230.

Ouellette-Kuntz, H. (1990). A pilot study in the use of the quality of life interview schedule. *Social Indicators Research,* 23: 283-298.

Perlman, S. G., Connell, K. J., Clark, A., Robinson, M.S., Conlon, P., Gecht, M., Caldron, P. and Sinacore, J. M. (1990). Dance-based aerobic exercise of rheumatoid arthritis. *Arthritis Care and Research,* 3(1): 29-35.

Perry, J. and Felce, D. (1995). Objective assessments of quality of life: how much do they agree with each other? *Journal of Community and Applied Social Psychology,* 5: 1-19.

Pugliesi, K. (1995). Work and well-being: gender differences in the psychological consequences of employment. *Journal of Health and Social Behavior,* 36: 57-71.

Reich, J. W. and Zautra, A. J. (1983). Demands and desires in daily life: some influences on well-being. *American Journal of Community Psychology,* 11(1): 41-59.

Renwick, R. and Friedland, J. (1996). Quality of life experienced by a sample of adults with HIV. In R. Renwick, I. Brown, and M. Nagler (Eds.), *Quality of Life in Health Promotion and Rehabilitation,* pp. 171-189. Thousand Oaks, CA: Sage Publications.

Rettig, K. D., Danes, S. M., and Bauer, J. W. (1991). Family life quality: theory and assessment in economically stress farm families. *Social Indicators Research,* 24: 269-299.

Rhoads, D. L. and Raymond, J. S. (1981). Quality of life and the competent community. *American Journal of Community Psychology,* 9(3): 293-301.

Rintala, D. H., Hart, K. A., and Fuhrer, M. J. (1996). Perceived stress in individuals with spinal cord injuries. In D. M. Krotoski, M. A. Nosek, and M. A. Turk (Eds.), *Women with Physical Disabilities: Achieving and Maintaining Health and Well-Being,* pp. 223-242. Baltimore: Paul H. Brookes Publishing.

Rodin, G. (1990). Quality of life in adults with insulin-dependent diabetes mellitus. *Psychotherapy and Psychosomatics,* 54: 132-139.

Romney, D. M., Jenkins, C. D., and Bynner, J. M. (1992). A structural analysis of health-related quality of life dimensions. *Human Relations,* 45(2): 165-176.

Rosen, M., Simon, E. W., and McKinsey, L. (1995). Subjective measure of quality of life. *Mental Retardation,* 33(1): 31-34.

Rosenfeld, S. (1992). Factors contributing to the subjective quality of life of the chronic mentally ill. *Journal of Health and Social Behavior,* 33: 299-315.

Roxburgh, S. (1996). Gender differences in work and well-being: effects of exposure and vulnerability. *Journal of Health and Social Behavior,* 37: 265-277.

Ruchlin, H. S. and Morris, J. N. (1991). Impact of work on quality of life of community-residing young elderly. *American Journal of Public Health,* 81(4): 498-500.

Ruffing-Rahal, M. A. (1991). Initial psychometric evaluation of a qualitative evaluation well-being measure: the Integration Inventory. *Health Values,* 15(2): 10-20.

Sands, D. J. and Kozleski, E. B. (1994). Quality of life differences between adults with and without disabilities. *Education and Training in Mental Retardation and Developmental Disabilities,* 90-101.

Schaafsma, J. and Osoba, D. (1994). The Karnofsky performance status scale re-examined: a cross-validation with the EORTC-C30. *Quality of Life Research,* 3: 413-424.

Schalock, R. L. and Lilley, M. A. (1986). Placement from community-based mental retardation programs: how well do clients do after 8 to 10 years? *American Journal of Mental Deficiency,* 90(6): 669-676.

Scherer, M. J. (1990). Assistive device utilization and quality of life in adults with spinal cord injuries or cerebral palsy two years later. *Journal of Applied Rehabilitation Counseling,* 21(4): 36-44.

Schwartz, L. B., Devine, P. A., Schechter, C. B., and Bender, A. N. (1990). Impact of illness on lifestyle. *Loss, Grief, and Care,* 4(3-4): 3-21.

Scuccimarra, D. J. and Speece, D. L. (1990). Employment outcomes and social integration of students with mild handicaps: the quality of life two years after high school. *Journal of Learning Disabilities,* 23(4): 213-219.

Short, K. and Shea, M. (1995). Beyond poverty, extended measures of well-being: 1992. *Current Population Reports.*

Shye, S. (1989). Systemic life quality model. *Social Indicators Research,* 21: 343-378.

Sinnott-Oswald, M., Gliner, J. A., and Spencer, K. C. (1991). Supported and sheltered employment: quality of life issues among workers with disabilities. *Education and Training in Mental Retardation,* 388-397.

Spreitzer, E. and Snyder, E. E. (1989). Sports involvement and quality of life dimensions. *Journal of Sport Behavior,* 12(1): 3-11.

Sullivan, G., Wells, K. B., and Leake, B. (1992). Clinical factors associated with better quality of life in a seriously mental ill population. *Hospital and Community Psychiatry,* 43(8): 794-798.

Tait, R. C., Chibnall, J. T., and Margolis, R. B. (1990). Pain extent: relations with psychological state, pain severity, pain history, and disability.

Tsevat, J., Goldman, L., Lamas, G. A., Pfeffer, M. A., Chapin, C.C., Connors, K. F., Lee, T. H. (1991). Functional status vs. utilities in survivors of myocardial infarction. *Medical Care,* 29(11): 1153-1159.

Tuchler, H., Hofmann, S., Bernhart, M., Bruglatelli, M., Chrobak, L., Franke, A., Herold, M., Holowiechki, J., Ihle, R., Jaksic, B., Krc, I., Munteanue, N., Pawlicki, M., Sakalova, A., Schranz, V., Wolf, H., and Lutz, D. (1992). A short multilingual quality of life questionnaire — practicability, reliability, and interlingual homogeneity. *Quality of Life Research,* 1: 107-117.

Vandergriff, D. V. and Chubon, R. A. (1994). Quality of life experienced by persons with mental retardation in various residential settings. *Journal of Rehabilitation,* 30-37.

Verbrugge, L. M., Reoma, J. M., and Gruber-Baldini, A. L. (1994). Short-term dynamics of disability and well-being. *Journal of Health and Social Behavior,* 35: 97-117.

Vickrey, B. G., Hays, R. D., Graber, J., Rausch, R., Engel, J., and Brook, R. H. (1992). A health-related quality of life instrument for patients evaluated for epilepsy surgery. *Medical Care,* 30(4): 299-319.

Walker, D. E., Blankenship, V., Ditty, J. A., and Lynch, K. P. (1987). Prediction of recovery for closed-head-injured adults: an evaluation of the MMPI, the Adaptive Behavior Scale, and a Quality of Life Rating Scale. *Journal of Clinical Psychology,* 43(6): 699-707.

Wallston, B. S., Hoover-Dempsey, K. V., and Brissie, J. S. (1989). Gatekeeping transactions: women's resource acquisition and mental health in the workplace. *Psychology of Women Quarterly,* 13: 205-222.

Warren, L., Wrigley, M., Yoels, W. C., and Fine, P. R. (1996). Factors associated with life satisfaction among a sample of persons with neurotrauma. *Journal of Rehabilitation Research and Development,* 33(4): 404-408.

West, M., Kregel, J., and Banks, P. D. (1990). Fringe benefits available to supported employment participants. *Rehabilitation Counseling Bulletin,* 34(2): 126-138.

Whelton, C., Pawlick, J., and Cardamone, J. (1997). Involving families in psychosocial rehabilitation. *Psychiatric Rehabilitation Journal*, 20(3): 57-60.
Wilkinson, G., Williams, B., Krekorian, H., McLees, S., and Falloon, I. (1992). QALYs in mental health: a case study. *Psychological Medicine,* 22: 725-731.
Williams, R. L., Eyring, M., Gaynor, P., and Long, J. D. (1991). Development of Views of Life Scale. *Psychology and Health*, 5: 165-181.
Wood, L. A. and Johnson, J. (1989). Life satisfaction among the rural elderly: what do the numbers mean? *Social Indicators Research,* 21: 379-408.
Woodruff, S. I., and Conway, T. L. (1992). A longitudinal assessment of the impact of health/fitness and health behavior on perceived quality of life. *Perceptual and Motor Skills,* 75: 3-14.
Young, L. D. and Barboriak, J. J. (1982). Reliability of a brief scale for assessment of coronary-prone behavior and standard measures of Type A behavior. *Perceptual and Motor Skills*, 55: 1039-1042.
Zautra, A. J. (1983). Social resources and the quality of life. *American Journal of Community Psychology,* 11(3): 275-289.
Zweig, J. M., Barber, B. L., and Eccles, J. S. (1997). Sexual coercion and well-being in young adulthood: comparisons by gender and college status. *Journal of Interpersonal Violence,* 12(2): 291-308.

APPENDIX 34
Rehabilitation and Quality of Life (QOL) Literature

Source	Population	Measures/Method	Domains
Bach and Rioux (1996)	Rehabilitation clients	Critique of health promotion and QOL research	Self-determination, equality, democratization, well-being
Bellamy, Newton, LeBaron, and Horner (1990)	Persons with developmental disabilities	Essay on residential services and QOL lifestyle outcomes	Independence, enhanced adaptive functioning, activities of daily living, income, choice
Ben-Ari and Tater (1984)	53 Male and 46 female clients in 5 governmental rehabilitation centers In Israel	Minnesota Satisfaction Questionnaire and interviews of social workers working with clients	Duration of injury and educational level were related to 3 categories of satisfaction: internal, external, and overall satisfaction
Blumenthal and Emcry (1988)	Cardiac patients	Review of three behavioral strategies to examine the value of cardiac rehabilitation as a method for improving QOL	Cardiovascular functioning, psychological functioning, physical fitness, and psychosocial functioning
Borthwick-Duffy (1990)	Persons with profound mental retardation	Essay on QOL models and measures for this population	Education, employment, language delays, choices in daily living, self-report on QOL
Boschen (1996)	222 Young adults with spinal cord injuries living in Toronto	Living with a Spinal Cord Injury Questionnaire, Latitude of Choice Scale, Self-Concept Semantic Differential Scale, Locus of Control Scale	Autonomy, control, and daily life choices with postinjury accommodations
Bratt and Johnston (1988)	5 Young adults with a mental disability leaving a hospital to live in a group home	Recorded visits to the home; trips made out of the home; activity patterns, staff opinions.	Reduction in inappropriate behavior, Increase in overall interactions; more outside contact, more appropriate leisure activities
Brown, C. (1996)	105 Males and 86 females with severe mental illness	Assessed loneliness using UCLA Loneliness Scale	Loneliness as a QOL issue dependent upon living situation or social skills and social networks and the experience of the individual with severe mental illness

APPENDIX 34 (continued)
Rehabilitation and Quality of Life (QOL) Literature

Source	Population	Measures/Method	Domains
Brown, I. (1996)	Homeless adults	Essay on QOL issues and homelessness	Physical, psychological, social well-being, housed, homed, homeless, houseless
Brown, R. I. (1989)	240 Adults with disabilities	Quality of Life Questionnaire compared to objective measures of performance and observations of sponsors (high correlations found)	Home, social, and recreational aspects of life
Brown, R. I. (1996)	240 Persons with developmental disabilities between 18–63 in Canadian rehabilitation service programs	Essay on QOL issues for persons with development disabilities. Used WAIS, Adaptive Functioning Index, and Quality of Life Questionnaire	Staff in agencies, employment, living conditions, choices and perceptions, client and sponsor perceptions, emotional needs
Brown, R. I. Bayer, and Brown (1988)	Adolescents and adults with mental disabilities: 73 males, 75 females	Evaluate if clients' perceptions match statements by sponsors (usually parents), a longitudinal study	Emotional support, assertiveness, reading, preparing meals, housekeeping, leisure skills, budgeting, work, housing, guardianship, spiritual, filling out forms, shopping
Brown, C. Cosgrove, and DeSelm (1997)	19 Consumers of mental health services and their case managers	Compared perceptions of consumers and case managers regarding barriers interfering with life satisfaction using a structured interview	Family, friendships, health care, community services, housing, neighborhood, finances, daily activities, work, transportation, physical health
Brown, I. Renwick, and Nagler (1996)	Rehabilitation clients	Essay on the centrality of QOL in health promotion and rehabilitation	Physical, social, psychological, and environmental
Burton and Volpe (1993)	33 Persons with traumatic brain injury	Social Adjustment Scale to evaluate functioning in various categories unit	Work, social and leisure, extended family, marital, parental, family
Chubon (1985)	Nondisabled graduate students and persons with chronic back problems, and prison inmates	Life Situation Survey	Pain tolerance, satisfaction of life quality
Ciardiello and Bingham (1962)	Schizophrenic clients	Review of a career maturity construct and how a career development approach improves QOL	Use of leisure, family, citizenship, and work roles
Clark and Hirst (1989)	39 Adults with physical impairments	Sample drawn from previous study of 89 young people with cerebral palsy; survey questionnaire	Work, household composition, living arrangements, income, leisure and social activities, mobility, perceived needs and aspirations

APPENDIX 34 (continued)
Rehabilitation and Quality of Life (QOL) Literature

Source	Population	Measures/Method	Domains
Condeluci, Ferris, and Bogdan (1992)	Persons in head Injury rehabilitation	Review of three surveys from the survivors' perspective	Independence in activities of daily living, living situation, communication skills, health status, mobility, problem behaviors, need for rehabilitation and supervision, employment status, family, income, and educational status
Conroy and Feinstein (1990)	Persons with Mental retardation	Essay on QOL measurement to include an outcome orientation	Individual happiness, family satisfaction, increasing productivity, increased integration, status, and acceptance in society
Crews (1991)	Older persons with blindness in rehabilitation	Model of strategic planning for fostering independent living	Independent living, consumer input, gains in function, family, services
Crutcher (1990)	Parent of a child with mental retardation	Essay on QOL vs. QOL judgments by others	Psychological, physical, social, and mental functioning
Cummins (1991)	Review of a QOL Scale for people with intellectual disabilities	Comprehensive QOL Scale or ComQOL	Material well-being, physical well-being, productivity, intimacy, safety, place in society, emotional well-being
Dagan, Jones, and Ruddick (1994)	18 People with learning people disabilities	Questionnaire on Quality of Life which has good inter-rater and internal reliability and factor structure usable in services to people with learning disabilities living in residential care facilities	Factors or domains include: physical details, community access, leisure, routines, education and training, staff behavior, decision making
Day and Jankey (1996)	Rehabilitation clients	Review of QOL origins and limitations due to originating disciplines. Proposes holistic model of QOL	Genetic disposition, domains, goals and achievements, values, personality, circumstances, evaluation process, experiences, comparisons, external reactions
Dellario and Anthony (1981)	Psychiatrically disabled persons	Review of research studies regarding client outcome of institutional vs. alternative placements; a model for psychiatric rehabilitation	Physical, intellectual, emotional, work, and community
Edgerton (1990)	Persons with mental retardation	Longitudinal perspectives on QOL research	Self-esteem, social functioning, life satisfaction and well-being, work, physical health
Evans, Dingus, and Haselkorn (1993)	Persons with disabilities	Review of QOL and Disability Studies, (52) articles, 1985–1989	Functional capacity, subjective QOL, and objective QOL
Fabian (1991)	Individuals with disabilities	Review of QOL as life satisfaction, adaptive functioning, social indicator measure of programs and services	Housing, neighborhood, leisure, work, social activities, health

APPENDIX 34 (continued)
Rehabilitation and Quality of Life (QOL) Literature

Source	Population	Measures/Method	Domains
Fabian (1992)	110 Mentally ill persons in 2 supported employment programs	Control group study of those in community programs to those in supported employment	Living situation, family, social relations, leisure activities, physical and mental health, safety, work or nonwork, and finances
Fabian (1995)	People with disabilities	Overview of QOL in rehabilitation research	Life satisfaction, independence, adaptive functioning, self-mastery, and self-efficacy
Felce and Perry (1996)	People with and without disabilities	Development of a multidimensional model — essay	Physical well-being, material well-being, social well-being, development and activity, emotional well-being
Fine (1996)	Persons with disabilities	Essay on leisure and QOL issues	Safety, pleasantness, friends and companions, self-esteem, fun, accomplishments, productivity, excitement, leisure
Goode (1990)	Persons with disabilities and their families	Review of QOL literature from point of view of the individual	Objective variables: life events, health, mental health, and socioeconomic status, outcome behaviors, environment
Halpern (1994)	Special education students in high school in school to community transition. to set standards	Developed Community Transition Team Model (CTTM)	Physical and material well-being, performance of adult roles, personal fulfillment
Heal and Sigelman	Persons with mental retardation	Essay on (1990) methodological issues for measuring QOL	Income, housing, behavior, life satisfaction, subjective perceptions
Herbert (1996)	Persons with disabilities	Literature review of of adventure-based counseling for persons with disabilities	QOL not a specific goal but more favorable attitude toward disability, improvement in independent living skills, positive self-concept, enhancement of self image, sense of responsibility, and cooperation with others, and greater life satisfaction result
Houser and Chace (1993)	18 Males and 9 females with disabilities placed into jobs in a project with industry setting	Minnesota Satisfaction Questionnaire	Keeping busy, work alone, variety, status, supervision, ethics, tenure, service, leadership, working up to capacity, fair policies, advancement, exercise judgment, try out new methods, working conditions, relationships with co-workers, praise, and accomplishment

APPENDIX 34 (continued)
Rehabilitation and Quality of Life (QOL) Literature

Source	Population	Measures/Method	Domains
Hughes, Hwang, Kim, Eisenman, and Killian (1995)	People with disabilities	Review of 87 empirical studies analyzed and a model proposed	Social relationships, psychological well-being, employment, self-determination, recreation and leisure, personal competence, residential environment, community integration, normalization, support services, demographic indicators, personal development and fulfillment, social acceptance, physical and material well-being, civic responsibility
Inge, Banks, Wehman, Hill, and Shafer (1988)	20 Persons with mental retardation	Adaptive Behavior Scale, Parent/Guardian Survey, Quality of Life Matching Scale	Domestic skills, appearance, community participation, leisure/recreation, social/vocational skills and financial activity
Jacoby (1990)	A sibling of a sister with spina bifida	Essay by a brother on his sister's QOL	Physical health, finances, mobility, education, and leisure activities
Janicki (1990)	Older persons with a lifelong disability	Essay on aging with a lifelong disability and QOL issues	Physical, material, social, cognitive well-being
Kaplan, (1993)	25 Individuals with traumatic brain injury	Portland Adaptability Inventory	Temperament and emotionality, activities and social behavior, physical capabilities
Keith (1990)	Persons with mental retardation	Essay on QOL issues in community integration	Health, employment, education, well-being, living situation, familial and social relations, leisure, work, learning, creative expression, safety, and finances
Kelley and Lambert (1992)	Review of 30 empirical studies on family support in rehabilitation regarding adaptation to chronic illness and disability	Selected 4 types of studies to review: (a) observational studies — randomized and nonrandomized intervention studies; (b) surveys, (c) case studies, and (d) randomized controlled trials of interventions of support-outcome relationships	No coherent theory yet available since study of efficacy of family-centered vs. client-centered rehabilitation not been conducted. However, empirical research does clearly demonstrated that adaptation to disability (including QOL) is multidimensional in nature. Adaptation to disability and subsequent community adjustment are recognized as a biopsychosocial phenomenon
Kiernan and Knutson (1990)	Persons with disabilities	Essay on QOL and quality of work life (QWL)	Productivity and job satisfaction, participate management style, flexibility
Kloseck, Crilly, Ellis, and Lammers (1996)	Geriatric rehabilitation population — 114 persons (47 male and 67 female)	Leisure Competence Measure, Life Satisfaction Index, Geriatric Depression Scale, Folstein Mini-Mental State Examination	Leisure awareness, skills, attitude, social appropriateness, group interaction skills, social context, and community participation

APPENDIX 34 (continued)
Rehabilitation and Quality of Life (QOL) Literature

Source	Population	Measures/Method	Domains
Kozleski and Sands (1992)	133 Individuals from the general Colorado population	Consumer Satisfaction Survey	Services and satisfaction, support services and assistance needed, independence/interdependence, integration, activities, personal relationships
Krause (1996)	449 Persons with spinal cord injuries	Life Situation Questionnaire and collection of prospective data on life adjustment in 1974, 1985, 1989	Subjective well-being, social and vocational functioning, and life satisfaction
Labonte (1996)	Persons with disabilities and disadvantages	Discussion of power issues in determining QOL	Quality of life, health, and empowerment
Luckasson (1990)	Person with mental retardation	Legal perspective on QOL terminology	Normalization, integration, and worth of all human beings
Lynch and Gallagher-Lepak (1996)	Patients with chronic renal failure	Essay on updating rehabilitation professionals on impact of improved medical treatment	Functional outcomes: weakness/fatigue, reduced endurance, cognitive changes, and psychological distress
Lyons (1993)	Persons with disabilities	Overview article on the need for "total rehabilitation" which would include referral and training in use of leisure time for people with disabilities	Problem of free time, meaningful activity, evolution of recreation services for people with disabilities
Maas (1991)	Persons after laryngectomy	Theoretical model for QOL after laryngectomy	Speech impairment, social, psychological, vocational
Martinez (1990)	A woman with mental retardation	Her essay on her perception of QOL for herself	Family support, education, and independent living
Mason (1996)	Deaf and hard-of-hearing people	Essay on the cultural meaning of deafness and hard-of-hearing as a QOL issue	Culturally deaf, oral deaf, hard-of-hearing, late-deafened persons
McGuire, Choon, and Akuffo (1991)	19 Elderly people with a developmental disability	Used a lifestyle questionnaire and the Social Training Achievement Record Profile through interviews	Activities of daily life, community-based activities, domestic tasks, areas of personal responsibility
McPhail (1996)	Effects of children with disabilities on the lives of family members	Recommendations regarding improving QOL for families with members with disabilities	Growth opportunities, community membership, choice, in-home health care support, inclusion of parents in decision making, inclusive services which support the family unit, inclusion in regular schooling
Metcalf (1992)	Plaintiffs in civil law suits with disabilities	Commentary on loss of pleasure of life as testified to by rehabilitationists	Physical, emotional, spiritual, cognitive
Moller and Murphy (1997)	176 Patients with psychiatric disabilities	Clients, family members, and case managers enrolled in course, *Symptom Management: A Wellness Expedition*	Number of inpatient days, cost savings, and participant satisfaction

APPENDIX 34 (continued)
Rehabilitation and Quality of Life (QOL) Literature

Source	Population	Measures/Method	Domains
Moss (1980)	69 Older clients from 2 similar rehabilitation workshops	Clients assigned to random groups to receive group counseling or social activities. Dean Alienation Scale, Havighhurst Life Satisfaction Index A, Sociometric Questionnaire	Life satisfaction, work productivity, alienation
Mowry (1988)	81 Deaf and hard-of-hearing former vocational rehabilitation clients	Self-reports of QOL	Health, employment, financial security, home, savings, standard of living, family and friends relationships
Munich and Lang (1993)	Persons with psychiatric disabilities	Argument for rehabilitation as a central discipline which integrates clinical and functional status and QOL	Biopsychosocial issues including learning, compensation, adaptation autonomy, least professional intervention
Nagler (1996)	39 Persons with disabilities who have experienced sexual abuse	Interviews and essay on QOL issues and sexual abuse	Social, emotional, sexuality, work, friends, self-esteem, marriage, education, emotional and physical well-being
Nation, Benshoff and Malkin (1996)	Adolescents in substance abuse treatment facilities	Random survey of substance abuse treatment programs using therapeutic recreation	Social skills, self-esteem, self-efficacy and improve cooperation and trust. QOL not a specific goal
National Institute on Disability and Research (1988)	Persons with disabilities	Essay on research in rehabilitation and QOL	Mobility, environmental control, community Rehabilitation resources and know-how, reliance on loved ones or significant others from time to time, self-acceptance and motivation to be productive and happy
National Association of Rehabilitation Facilities (NARF) (1988)	Persons with disabilities using NARF facilities	Position statement by NARF on QOL and quality of work life	Empowerment, friendship, being valued, supported employment
Nosek, Holland, Young, Georgiou, Rintala, Foley, Bennett, and Smith (1994)	31 Women with physical disabilities	Qualitative interviews regarding disability and sexuality	Positive sexual self-concept, having sexuality information, good relationships, managing barriers, good health and physical functioning
O'Keefe (1996)	Persons with communication disorders	Essay recommending that recognition and be given to the QOL issues in this impairment and research be conducted	Being, belonging, and becoming
O'Rear, Bark, and Hutchinson (1996)	Persons with psychiatric disabilities	Essay on promoting wellness activities which improve QOL	Physical, mental, emotional, and spiritual wellness
Osberg, McGinnis, DeJong, and Seward (1987)	97 Elderly disabled adults	Markides and Martin's (1979) path analysis model to assess QOL, Barthel Index, self-administered questionnaire	Income, age, marital status, functional capacity, independence

APPENDIX 34 (continued)
Rehabilitation and Quality of Life (QOL) Literature

Source	Population	Measures/Method	Domains
Ouellette-Kuntz (1990)	Ten interviews with mentally retarded adults	Use of Quality of Life Interview Schedule with emphasis on intra- and inter-rater agreement	Health services, family-guardianship, income, education, training, and employment, housing and safety, transportation, social, recreational, religious/cultural, case management, advocacy, aesthetics, and counseling
Ouellette-Kuntz and McCreary (1996)	Persons with severe developmental disabilities	Development of the QOL Interview Schedule	Communication, disabilities, personal characteristics, and recent life events
Parmenter (1996)	For everyone	Discussion of the quality-adjusted life-year (QALYs) approach	A plurality of independent vectors based on an individual life
Perry and Felce (1995)	People with learning disabilities in 15 staffed houses	Review of 14 objective measures of service quality in residential facilities	Quality of housing, social and community integration, social interactions, development, activity, and autonomy and choice
Pumpian, Szeto, and Sax (1996)	Young adults with disabilities	Demonstration project to enhance the lives of persons with significant disabilities using customized assistive technology	Functional capacity, independent living skills, supported employment, rehabilitation services
Raeburn and Rootman (1996)	For everyone	Essay on a conceptual model of QOL	Being, belonging, and becoming
Raphael (1996a)	For everyone	11 Debates concerning measurement of QOL	Social, psychological, quantitative vs. qualitative, objective vs. subjective, self-report vs. reports by others
Raphael (1996b)	10- to 25-year olds or adolescent health	Review of adolescent health and QOL issues	*Global:* macro environment, human rights and welfare policies; *External:* work, income, housing; *Interpersonal:* family structure and function, intimate friends, extended social; *Personal:* physical, mental, spiritual
Raphael (1996c)	12 Group meetings; 120 seniors in the community	Development of Quality of Life Profile: Seniors Version	Physical being, psychological being, spiritual being, physical belonging, social belonging, community belonging, practical becoming, leisure becoming, growth becoming
Renwick and Brown (1996)	People with disabilities, service providers, and families of persons with disabilities	Focus groups, literature review, consultation with the experts for Centre for Health Promotion (CHP) in Toronto approach	*Being:* physical, psychological, spiritual. *Belonging:* physical, social, community. *Becoming:* practical, leisure, growth

APPENDIX 34 (continued)
Rehabilitation and Quality of Life (QOL) Literature

Source	Population	Measures/Method	Domains
Renwick, Brown, Rootman, and Nagler (1996)	For everyone	Recommendations for further research	Conceptual frameworks: person-environment interactions, empowerment of individuals, generic approaches suited to general and specific populations, personal meanings, broad range of domains, and relationships between health and QOL
Renwick and Friefeld (1996)	Rehabilitation clients	Recommendations for going beyond functional and health status measures such as the Barthel Index, Functional Status Index, Functional Activities Questionnaire, Sickness Impact Profile, Nottingham Health Profile, Arthritis Impact Measurement Scale	Physical, emotional, cognitive, social aspects of functioning in the major areas of life (e.g., mobility, communication, activities of daily living, vocational activities, social relationships, leisure and recreation)
Renwick and Friedland (1996)	107 Males and 13 females with HIV	Quality of Life Questionnaire, Fanning Quality of Life Scale, Life Appraisal and Life Satisfaction Questionnaire, Interpersonal Support Evaluation List, Ways of Coping, Recent Life Changes Questionnaire	Job satisfaction, relations with others, work relations, altruistic behavior, creative–aesthetic behavior, significant other relationships, marital (partner) relations, job characteristics, political behavior, extended family relations, vacation behavior, personal growth, material well-being, sports activity, and physical well-being
Rintala, Hart, and Fuhrer (1996)	661 Persons with spinal cord injuries	Questionnaires and Perceived Stress Scale, Center for Epidemiological Studies Depression Scale, Life Satisfaction Index, Craig Handicap Assessment and Reporting Technique, ASIA Total Motor Index, Functional Independence Measure, Hassles Scale, Life Events Scale, Personal Independence Profile, Satisfaction with Personal Assistance, Interpersonal Support Evaluation List	Depression, life satisfaction, morbidity, mobility, occupation, social integration and support, independence, pressure sores
Rioux (1996)	Persons with disabilities	Essay on disability as a social construct	Social, political, and economic structures are inseparable from individual and collective states of well-being
Roessler (1990)	Rehabilitation counseling clients	Recommends QOL approach in rehabilitation of persons with disabilities	Health, public safety, education, employment, earnings and income, poverty, housing, family stability, equality, well-being, happiness

APPENDIX 34 (continued)
Rehabilitation and Quality of Life (QOL) Literature

Source	Population	Measures/Method	Domains
Roller (1996)	People with late effects of polio	Advocates 2 health promotion models used in German and U.S. for increasing physical fitness	Alleviate, manage, and prevent secondary conditions; promote good health and wellness; introduce new health promotion tactics; facilitate long-term adoption of health-enhancing behaviors
Rosen, Simon, and McKinsey (1995)	100 Individuals with mental retardation	Developed subjective QOL instrument — PALS	Perceived Stress, Affect, Loneliness, and Satisfaction
Rosenfeld (1992)	157 Members of a psychosocial rehabilitation program	Interviews, Delighted–Terrible Scale, Lehman's QOL, Moos' Community-Oriented Program Environment Scale	Importance of program components, vocational rehabilitation, financial services, empowerment approaches to service delivery
Sackman and Ingham (1992)	Methods for calculating loss of enjoyment of life	Examples of using value of leisure time as equal to earnings as a measure of loss	Varies by case — mostly wrongful death cases
Sands and Kozleski (1994)	131 Persons without disabilities and 86 persons with disabilities (cerebral palsy, mental retardation, and head injury)	Used the Consumer Satisfaction Survey and modified version with nondisabled sample	Experience with advocacy organizations, services and satisfaction, independent living interdependence, participation in community activities and in recreation activities, and satisfaction with these activities
Sartorius (1995)	Psychiatric rehabilitation clients	Review essay	Not specific, but leisure, work, family, community, aesthetic, and health are mentioned
Satcher (1993)	Persons with learning disabilities	Essay on ADA and its potential for improvement of quality of work life	Job restructuring, modified work schedule, reassignment to vacant positions, acquiring or modifying equipment or devices, modifying examinations, training materials or policies, providing qualified readers
Schalock (1990a)	Persons with developmental disabilities	Essay on conceptualizing and measuring QOL, QOL variables in mental retardation literature	Social and psychological indicators, goodness-of-fit/social policy
Schalock (1990b)	Persons with mental retardation	Essay on QOL disability policy and service delivery systems	Living, learning, working, choice, independence, productivity, and community integration
Schalock (1996)	For everyone	Proposes a quality assurance model for QOL evaluation	Home and community living, work-school, and health and wellness
Schalock and Lilley (1986)	85 Mentally retarded persons	Quality of Life Questionnaire	Environmental control (daily schedule, income, appointments, shopping, home decorations, pets); social interaction (neighbors, co-inhabitants, friends); community utilization (transportation, recreation, education)

APPENDIX 34 (continued)
Rehabilitation and Quality of Life (QOL) Literature

Source	Population	Measures/Method	Domains
Scherer (1990)	Persons with spinal cord injury (SCI) and cerebral palsy (CP)	Compared persons with SCI and CP using assistive devices (AD), interviews and observations, Personal Capacities Questionnaire, Functional Assessment Inventory, Taylor-Johnson Temperament Analysis	Personal capacities, adaptive behavior, vocational qualifications, motor functioning
Scott (1996)	Persons with disabilities in integrated community recreation programs vs. those in segregated programs	Testimony before the House Appropriations Subcommittee on Labor, Health, and Human Services and Education	Work performance, family relations, physical health, overall health status and independent functioning at home
Scuccimarra and Speece (1990)	65 Mildly handicapped students who exited high school in 1984	59-Item instrument was developed, adapted from the Vermont Follow-up Structured Survey Instrument	Employment status and social activity
Shain (1996)	For everyone	Analyzes study: *Influences on Wellness in the Workplace: A Multivariate Approach*	Personal health practices, perceived stressors at home and at work, personal resources, demographic and socioeconomic factors
Shank, Coyle, Boyd, and Kinney (1996)	Persons with disabilities	Therapeutic recreation according to a model used by the National Center for Medical Rehabilitation Research	Functional limitations, physical, psychological cognitive, and social functioning
Sinnott-Oswald, Gliner, and Spencer (1991)	Ten persons with disabilities in supported community employment, ten persons with disabilities in sheltered workshop employment, and nine persons without disabilities	QOL Index, Adaptive Behavior Scale, physical health measures, Parent-Guardian Survey	Leisure activities, use of leisure time, self-esteem, involvement in activities, mobility, job skill perceptions, and perceptions regarding changes in income
Stark and Goldsbury (1990)	Persons with mental retardation	Essay on QOL over the life span	General well-being, age, sex, social/cultural background, level of cognitive/adaptive functioning, education, health, living environment, family, social/emotional, work, and leisure
Taylor and Bodgan (1990)	Persons with mental retardation	Definitions and conceptions of QOL; subjective aspects of QOL	Cognitive, activities of daily living, social and family functioning, subjective experience of QOL

APPENDIX 34 (continued)
Rehabilitation and Quality of Life (QOL) Literature

Source	Population	Measures/Method	Domains
Turk (1996)	Women with disabilities: neuromuscular diseases, late effects of polio, spinal cord pathology, multiple sclerosis, osteoporosis in disability	Essay on fitness as an optimal state of physical well-being; call for research on fitness issues for women with physical disabilities	Flexibility, muscular strength and endurance, cardiopulmonary conditioning
Vandergriff and Chubon (1994)	120 Persons with mental retardation	Program Analysis of Service System Implementation of Normalization Goals, Life Situation Survey, Resident Choice Assessment Scale, American Association on Mental Deficiency Adaptive Behavior Scale	Internal standards and evaluations of life by individuals, socio-normative, and person-environment systems
Vaughan and Hobson (1990)	179 Elderly adults using low-vision devices	Report on a project of 39 counties of rural Missouri to screen and provide low-vision devices to elderly persons in need	Increase in independent living: read mail, write checks, thread needles, and read large print, better general functioning in everyday tasks and QOL
Verbrugge, Reoma, and Gruber-Baldini (1994)	165 Persons with chronic disability	Mental Status Questionnaire, Beck Depression Inventory, Activities of Daily Living, Six Motions to determine physical functioning, and Index of Well-Being	Cognitive, emotional, social, physical, and global well-being
Walker, Blankenship, Ditty, and Lynch (1987)	25 Closed-head-injured adults (1 female and 24 males)	MMPI, Adaptive Behavior Scale, Quality of Life Rating Scale	Vocational, educational, family participation, community service, avocational, artistic, and scholarly pursuits
Ward (1990)	A woman with mental retardation	Her essay on her reflections on QOL	Work, independent living, housing, social function, family and education
Warren, Wrigley, Yoels, and Fine (1996)	137 Persons with traumatic brain injury	Life Satisfaction Index–A, Functional Independence Measure, Family Satisfaction Scale	Family satisfaction, employment status, memory independence, bowel independence, marital status, self blame
West, Kregel, and Banks (1990)	1,550 Individuals placed in supported employment (65% with mental retardation, 9% with long-term mental illness, and 10% with head injuries and cerebral palsy)	*Data Management System Operations Manual* for form completion by 96 provider agencies	Evaluation of QOL in worklife by looking availability of fringe benefits

APPENDIX 34 (continued)
Rehabilitation and Quality of Life (QOL) Literature

Source	Population	Measures/Method	Domains
Whelton, Pawlick, and Cardamone (1997)	105 Families with 92 family members with psychiatric disabilities	Questionnaires sent to families regarding the Hamilton Program for Schizophrenia to determine levels of satisfaction with the program	Time and money spent by family members for their relatives with disabilities and reduction of caregiving by program. Quality of relationship with relative. Illness management.
Whitaker (1989)	Persons with profound mental handicaps (mental retardation)	Essay regarding a conceptual model	*Individual behavior:* level of skills and abilities, level of adaptive engagement, level of negative behavior; and *Factor about the environment:* conditions of physical environment in terms of comfort, food, health care; opportunities to mix with local community; variability and amount of varied activities available; opportunity to make choices; and treated as valued individuals in society

References

Bach, M. and Rioux, M. H. (1996). Social well-being: a framework for quality of life research. In R. Renwick, I. Brown, and M. Nagler (Eds.), *Quality of Life in Health Promotion and Rehabilitation,* pp. 63-74. Thousand Oaks, CA: Sage Publications.

Bellamy, G. T., Newton, J. S., LeBaron, N. M., and Horner, R. H. (1990). Quality of life and lifestyle outcomes: a challenge for residential programs. In R. L. Schalock (Ed.), *Quality of Life: Perspectives and Issues,* pp. 127-137. Washington, D.C.: American Association of Mental Retardation.

Ben-Ari, A. and Taler, Y. (1984). The relationship between absenteeism rate and satisfaction among clients in vocational rehabilitation centers. *Journal of Applied Rehabilitation Counseling,* 15(4): 39-47.

Blumenthal, J. A. and Emery, C. F. (1988). Rehabilitation of patients following myocardial infarction. *Journal of Consulting and Clinical Psychology,* 56(3): 374-381.

Boschen, K. A. (1996). Correlates of life satisfaction, residential satisfaction, and locus of control among adults with spinal cord injuries. *Rehabilitation Counseling Bulletin,* 39(4): 230-243.

Borthwick-Duffy, S. A. (1990). Quality of life of persons with severe or profound mental retardation. In R. L. Schalock (Ed.), *Quality of Life: Perspectives and Issues,* pp. 177-189. Washington, D.C.: American Association of Mental Retardation.

Bratt, A. and Johnston, R. (1988). Changes in life style for young adults with profound handicaps following discharge from hospital care into a "second generation" housing project. *Mental Handicap Research,* 1(1): 49-74.

Brown, C. (1996). A comparison of living situation and loneliness for people with mental illness. *Psychiatric Rehabilitation Journal*, 20(2): 59-65.

Brown, C., Cosgrove, N., and De Selm, T. (1997). Barriers interfering with life satisfaction for individuals with severe mental illness. *Psychiatric Rehabilitation Journal*, 20(3): 67-71.

Brown, I. (1996). The quality of life of marginal citizens: homelessness. In R. Renwick, I. Brown, and M. Nagler (Eds.), *Quality of Life in Health Promotion and Rehabilitation,* pp. 204-218. Thousand Oaks, CA: Sage Publications.

Brown, I., Renwick, R., and Nagler, M. (1996). The centrality of quality of life in health promotion and rehabilitation. In R. Renwick, I. Brown, and M. Nagler (Eds.), *Quality of Life in Health Promotion and Rehabilitation,* pp. 3-13. Thousand Oaks, CA: Sage Publications.

Brown, R. I. (1989). Aging, disability, and quality of life: a challenge for society. *Canadian Psychology,* 30(3): 551-559.

Brown, R. I. (1996). People with developmental disabilities: applying quality of life to assessment and intervention. In R. Renwick, I. Brown, and M. Nagler (Eds.), *Quality of Life in Health Promotion and Rehabilitation,* pp. 253-267. Thousand Oaks, CA: Sage Publications.

Brown, R. I., Bayer, M. B., and Brown, P. M. (1988). Quality of life: a challenge for rehabilitation agencies. *Australia and New Zealand Journal of Developmental Disabilities,* 14(3,4): 189-199.

Burton, L. A. and Volpe, B. (1993). Social adjustment scale assessments in traumatic brain injury. *Journal of Rehabilitation,* 34-37.

Chubon, R. A. (1985). Quality of life measurement of persons with back problems: some preliminary findings. *Journal of Applied Rehabilitation Counseling,* 16(2): 31-34.

Ciardiello, J. A. and Bingham, W. C. (1962). The career maturity of schizophrenic clients. *Rehabilitation Counseling Bulletin,* 3-9.

Clark, A. and Hirst, M. (1989). Disability in adulthood: ten-year follow-up of young people with disabilities. *Disability, Handicap and Society,* 4(3): 271-283.

Cobble, N. and Burks, J. S. (1990). Introduction to principles of rehabilitation. *Journal of Neurological Rehabilitation,* 4(4): 1818-185.

Condeluci, A., Ferris, L. L., and Bogdan, A. (1992). Outcome and value: the survivor perspective. *Journal of Head Trauma Rehabilitation,* 7(4): 37-45.

Conroy, J. W. and Feinstein, C. S. (1990). Measuring quality of life: where have we been? Where are we going? In R. L. Schalock (Ed.), *Quality of Life: Perspectives and Issues,* pp. 227-233. Washington, D.C.: American Association of Mental Retardation.

Crews, J. E. (1991). Strategic planning and independent living for elders who are blind. *Journal of Visual Impairment and Blindness,* 52-57.

Crutcher, D. M. (1990). Quality of life vs. quality of life judgments: a parent's perspective. In R. L. Schalock (Ed.), *Quality of Life: Perspectives and Issues,* pp. 17-22. Washington, D.C.: American Association of Mental Retardation.

Cummins, R. A. (1991). The Comprehensive Quality of Life Scale — Intellectual Disability: an instrument under development. *Australia and New Zealand Journal of Developmental Disabilities,* 17(2): 259-264.

Dagan, D., Jones, J., and Ruddick, L. (1994). The psychometric properties of a scale for assessing the quality of life of people with learning disabilities in residential care. *The British Journal of Developmental Disabilities,* XL(79): 98-103.

Day, H. and Jankey, S. G. (1996). Lessons from the literature: toward a holistic model of quality of life. In R. Renwick, I. Brown, and M. Nagler (Eds.), *Quality of Life in Health Promotion and Rehabilitation,* pp. 39-50. Thousand Oaks, CA: Sage Publications.

Dellario, D. J. and Anthony, W. A. (1981). On the relative effectiveness of institutional and alternative placement for the psychiatrically disabled. *Journal of Social Issues,* 37(3): 21-33.

Edgerton, R. B. (1990). Quality of life from a longitudinal research perspective. In R. L. Schalock (Ed.), *Quality of Life: Perspectives and Issues,* pp. 149-160. Washington, D.C.: American Association of Mental Retardation.

Evans, R. L., Dingus, C. M., and Haselkorn, J. K. (1993). Living with a disability: a synthesis and critique of the literature on quality of life, 1985–1989. *Psychological Reports,* 72: 771-777.

Fabian, E. S. (1991). Using quality of life indicators in rehabilitation program evaluation. *Rehabilitation Counseling Bulletin,* 34(4): 345-356.

Fabian, E. S. (1992). Supported employment and quality of life: does a job make a difference? *Rehabilitation Counseling Bulletin,* 36(2): 85-87.

Fabian, E. S. (1995). Quality of life. In Dell Orto, A.E. and Martinelli, R. P. (Eds.), *Encylopedia of Disability and Rehabilitation,* pp. 607-609. New York: Macmillan Publishing.

Felce, D. and Perry, J. (1996). Exploring current concepts of quality of life. In R. Renwick, I. Brown, and M. Nagler (Eds.), *Quality of Life in Health Promotion and Rehabilitation,* pp. 51-62. Thousand Oaks, CA: Sage Publications.

Fine, A. H. (1996). Leisure, living, and quality of life. In R. Renwick, I. Brown, and M. Nagler (Eds.), *Quality of Life in Health Promotion and Rehabilitation,* pp. 342-356. Thousand Oaks, CA: Sage Publications.

Goode, D. A. (1990). Thinking about and discussing quality of life. In R. L. Schalock (Ed.), *Quality of Life: Perspectives and Issues,* pp. 41-57. Washington, D.C.: American Association of Mental Retardation.

Halpern, A. S. (1994). Quality of life for students with disabilities in transition from school to adulthood. *Social Indicators Research,* 33: 193-236.

Heal, L. W. and Sigelman, C. K. (1990). Methodological issues in measuring quality of life of individuals with mental retardation. In R. L. Schalock (Ed.), *Quality of Life: Perspectives and Issues,* pp. 161-176. Washington, D.C.: American Association of Mental Retardation.

Herbert, J. T. (1996). Use of of adventure-based counseling programs for persons with disabilities. *Journal of Rehabilitation,* 3-9.

Houser, R. and Chace, A. (1993). Job satisfaction of people with disabilities placed through a project with industry. *Journal of Rehabilitation,* 59(1): 45-48.

Hughes, C., Hwang, B., Kim, J. H., Eisenman, L. T., and Killian, D. J. (1995). Quality of life in applied research: a review and analysis of empirical measures. *American Journal on Mental Retardation,* 99(6): 623-641.

Inge, K. J., Banks, P. D., Wehman, Hill, J. W., and Shafer, M. S. (1988). Quality of life for individuals who are labeled mentally retarded: evaluating competitive employment versus sheltered workshop employment. *Education and Training in Mental Retardation,* 97-104.

Jacoby, J. (1990). My sister Angie: a sibling's perspective. In R. L. Schalock (Ed.), *Quality of Life: Perspectives and Issues,* pp. 23-26. Washington, D.C.: American Association of Mental Retardation.

Janicki, M. P. (1990). Growing old with dignity: on quality of life for older persons with a lifelong disability. In R. L. Schalock (Ed.), *Quality of Life: Perspectives and Issues,* pp. 115-125. Washington, D.C.: American Association of Mental Retardation.

Kaplan, S. P. (1993). Five-year tracking of psychosocial changes in people with severe traumatic brain injury. *Rehabilitation Counseling Bulletin,* 36(3): 151-159.

Keith, K. D. (1990). Quality of life: issues in community integration. In R. L. Schalock (Ed.), *Quality of Life: Perspectives and Issues,* pp. 93-100. Washington, D.C.: American Association of Mental Retardation.

Kelley, D. M. S. and Lambert, S. S. (1992). Family support in rehabilitation: a review of the research, 1980–1990. *Rehabilitation Counseling Bulletin,* 36(2): 98-111.

Kiernan, W. E. and Knutson, K. (1990). Quality of work life. In R. L. Schalock (Ed.), *Quality of Life: Perspectives and Issues,* pp. 101-114. Washington, D.C.: American Association of Mental Retardation.

Kloseck, M., Crilly, R. G., Ellis, G. D., and Lammers, E. (1996). Leisure Competence Measure: development and reliability testing of a scale to measure functional outcomes in therapeutic recreation. *Therapeutic Recreation Journal,* 13-26.

Kozleski, E. B. and Sands, D. J. (1992). The yardstick of social validity: evaluating the quality of life as perceived by adults without disabilities. *Education and Training in Mental Retardation,* 119-131.

Krause, J. S. (1996). Prediction of mortality after spinal cord injury: a 20-year prospective study. *Rehabilitation R & D Progress Reports,* 34: 298-299.

Labonte, R. (1996). Measurement and practice: power issues in quality of life, health promotion, and empowerment. In R. Renwick, I. Brown, and M. Nagler (Eds.), *Quality of Life in Health Promotion and Rehabilitation,* pp. 132-145. Thousand Oaks, CA: Sage Publications.

Luckasson, R. (1990). A lawyer's perspective on quality of life. In R. L. Schalock (Ed.), *Quality of Life: Perspectives and Issues,* pp. 211-214. Washington, D.C.: American Association of Mental Retardation.

Lynch, R. T. and Gallagher-Lepak, S. (1996). Chronic renal failure: the impact of improved medical treatment options on rehabilitation. *Journal of Applied Rehabilitation Counseling,*27(1): 7-12.

Lyons, R. F. (1993). Meaningful activity and disability: capitalizing upon the potential of outreach recreation networks in Canada. *Canadian Journal of Rehabilitation,* (6)4: 256-265.

Maas, A. (1992). A model for quality of life after laryngectomy. *Social Science Medicine,* 33(12): 1373-1377.

Martinez, C. (1990). A dream for myself. In R. L. Schalock (Ed.), *Quality of Life: Perspectives and Issues,* pp. 3-8. Washington, D.C.: American Association of Mental Retardation.

Mason, D. G. (1996). Quality of life for deaf and hard-of-hearing people. In R. Renwick, I. Brown, and M. Nagler (Eds.), *Quality of Life in Health Promotion and Rehabilitation,* pp. 237-252. Thousand Oaks, CA: Sage Publications.

McGuire, B. E., Choon, G., and Akuffo, E. (1991). Community living for elderly people with an intellectual disability: a pilot study. *Australia and New Zealand Journal of Developmental Disabilities,* 17(1): 25-33.

McPhail, E. R. (1996). A parent's perspective: quality of life in families with a member with disabilities. In R. Renwick, I. Brown, and M. Nagler (Eds.), *Quality of Life in Health Promotion and Rehabilitation,* pp. 279-289. Thousand Oaks, CA: Sage Publications.

Metcalf, R. (1992). Loss of enjoyment, rehabilitation and hedonic damages: a comment. *Journal of Forensic Economics,* 5(3): 261-264.

Moller, M. D. and Murphy, M. F. (1997). The Three R's Rehabilitation Program: a prevention approach for the management of relapse symptoms associated with psychiatric diagnosis. *Psychiatric Rehabilitation Journal,* 20(3): 42-48.

Moss, E. (1980). Geriatric rehabilitation: group counseling vs. recreational programming for older workshop clients. *Journal of Applied Rehabilitation Counseling,* 11(3): 145-148.

Mowry, R. L. (1988). Quality of life indicators for deaf and hard-of-hearing former VR clients. *Journal of Rehabilitation of the Deaf,* 21(3): 1-7.

Munich, R. L. and Lang, E. (1993). The boundaries of psychiatric rehabilitation. *Hospital and Community Psychiatry,* 44(7): 661-665.

Nagler, M. (1996). Quality of life of people with disabilities who have experienced sexual abuse. In R. Renwick, I. Brown, and M. Nagler (Eds.), *Quality of Life in Health Promotion and Rehabilitation,* pp. 190-203. Thousand Oaks, CA: Sage Publications.

Nation, J. M., Benshoff, J. J., and Malkin, M. M. (1996). Therapeutic recreation programs for adolescents in substance abuse treatment facilities. *Journal of Rehabilitation,* 10-16.

National Association of Rehabilitation Facilities. (1988). Quality of life. *NARF Monograph Series.* Washington, D.C.

National Institute on Disability and Rehabilitation Research. (1988). Quality-of-life research in rehabilitation. *Rehab Brief,* XI(1).

Nosek, M. A., Howland, C. A., Young M. E., Georgiou, D., Rintala, D. H., Foley, C. C., Bennett, J. L., and Smith, Q. (1994). Wellness models and sexuality among women with physical disabilities. *Journal of Applied Rehabilitation Counseling,* 24(1): 50-57.

O'Keefe, B. M. (1996). Communication disorders: just minor inconveniences? In R. Renwick, I. Brown, and M. Nagler (Eds.), *Quality of Life in Health Promotion and Rehabilitation,* pp. 219-237. Thousand Oaks, CA: Sage Publications.

O'Rear, G., Bark, L., and Hutchinson, D. S. (1996). The promotion of wellness among people with psychiatric disabilities in community rehabilitation and treatment. *Psychiatric Rehabilitation Journal,* 20(2): 82-84.

Osberg, J. S., McGinnis, G. E., DeJong, G., and Seward, M. L. (1987). Life satisfaction and quality of life among disabled elderly adults. *Journal of Gerontology,* 42(2): 228-230.

Ouellette-Kuntz, H. (1990). A pilot study in the use of the quality of life interview schedule. *Social Indicators Research,* 23: 283-298.

Ouellette-Kuntz, H. and McCreary, B. (1996). Quality of life assessment for persons with severe developmental disabilities. In R. Renwick, I. Brown, and M. Nagler (Eds.), *Quality of Life in Health Promotion and Rehabilitation,* pp. 268-278. Thousand Oaks, CA: Sage Publications.

Parmenter, T. R. (1996). The use of quality of life as a construct for social and health policy development, In R. Renwick, I. Brown, and M. Nagler (Eds.), *Quality of Life in Health Promotion and Rehabilitation,* pp. 89-103. Thousand Oaks, CA: Sage Publications.

Perry, J. and Felce, D. (1995). Objective assessments of quality of life: how much do they agree with each other? *Journal of Community and Applied Social Psychology,* 5: 1-19.

Pumpian, I. R., Szeto, A. Y J., and Sax, C. L. (1996). Special projects and demonstration: applications of technology to enhance quality of life — A community model. *Rehabilitation R & D Progress Reports,* 34: 138-139.

Raeburn, J. M. and Rootman, I. (1996). Quality of life and health promotion. In R. Renwick, I. Brown, and M. Nagler (Eds.), *Quality of Life in Health Promotion and Rehabilitation,* pp. 14-25. Thousand Oaks, CA: Sage Publications.

Raphael, D. (1996a). Defining quality of life: eleven debates concerning its measurement. In R. Renwick, I. Brown, and M. Nagler (Eds.), *Quality of Life in Health Promotion and Rehabilitation,* pp. 146-170. Thousand Oaks, CA: Sage Publications.

Raphael, D. (1996b) . Quality of life and adolescent health. In R. Renwick, I. Brown, and M. Nagler (Eds.), *Quality of Life in Health Promotion and Rehabilitation,* pp. 307-326. Thousand Oaks, CA: Sage Publications.

Raphael, D. (1996c) . Quality of life for older adults: toward the optimization of the aging process. In R. Renwick, I. Brown, and M. Nagler (Eds.), *Quality of Life in Health Promotion and Rehabilitation,* pp. 290-306. Thousand Oaks, CA: Sage Publications.

Renwick, R. and Brown, I. (1996). The Centre for Health Promotion's conceptual approach to quality of life: being, belonging, and becoming. In R. Renwick, I. Brown, and M. Nagler (Eds.), *Quality of Life in Health Promotion and Rehabilitation,* pp. 64-75. Thousand Oaks, CA: Sage Publications.

Renwick, R., Brown, I, Rootman, I., and Nagler, M. (1996). conceptualization, research, and application: future directions. In R. Renwick, I. Brown, and M. Nagler (Eds.), *Quality of Life in Health Promotion and Rehabilitation,* pp. 357-367. Thousand Oaks, CA: Sage Publications.

Renwick, R. and Friefeld, S. (1996). Quality of life and rehabilitation. In R. Renwick, I. Brown, and M. Nagler (Eds.), *Quality of Life in Health Promotion and Rehabilitation,* pp. 26-36. Thousand Oaks, CA: Sage Publications.

Renwick, R. and Friedland, J. (1996). Quality of life experienced by a sample of adults with HIV. In R. Renwick, I. Brown, and M. Nagler (Eds.), *Quality of Life in Health Promotion and Rehabilitation,* pp. 171-189. Thousand Oaks, CA: Sage Publications.

Rintala, D. H., Hart, K. A., and Fuhrer, M. J. (1996). Perceived stress in individuals with spinal cord injuries. In D. M. Krotoski, M. A. Nosek, and M. A. Turk (Eds.), *Women with Physical Disabilities: Achieving and Maintaining Health and Well-Being,* pp. 223-242. Baltimore: Paul H. Brookes Publishing.

Rioux, M. H. (1996). Overcoming the social construction of inequality as a prerequisite to quality of life. In R. Renwick, I. Brown, and M. Nagler (Eds.), *Quality of Life in Health Promotion and Rehabilitation,* pp. 119-131. Thousand Oaks, CA: Sage Publications.

Roessler, R. T. (1990). A quality of life perspective on rehabilitation counseling. *Rehabilitation Counseling Bulletin,* 34(2): 82-91.

Roller, S. (1996). Health promotion for people with chronic neuromuscular disabilities. In D. M. Krotoski, M. A. Nosek, and M. A. Turk (Eds.), *Women with Physical Disabilities: Achieving and Maintaining Health and Well-Being,* pp. 391-401. Baltimore: Paul H. Brookes.

Rosen, M., Simon, E. W., and McKinsey, L. (1995). Subjective measure of quality of life. *Mental Retardation,* 33(1): 31-34.

Rosenfeld, S. (1992). Factors contributing to the subjective quality of life of the chronic mentally ill. *Journal of Health and Social Behavior,* 33: 299-315.

Ryan, C. P. (1995). Work isn't what it used to be: implications, recommendations, and strategies for vocational rehabilitation. *Journal of Rehabilitation,* 8-15.

Sackman, B. S. and Ingham, M. (1992). Methods for calculating hedonic loss. *NARRPS Journal and News,* 7(1): 7-14.

Sands, D. J. and Kozleski, E. B. (1994). Quality of life differences between adults with and without disabilities. *Education and Training in Mental Retardation and Developmental Disabilities,* 90-101.

Sartorius, N. (1995). Rehabilitation and Quality of Life. *International Journal of Mental Health,* 24(1): 7-13.

Satcher, J. (1993). Improving the quality of work life for persons with learning disabilities: ADA rights and responsibilities. *Journal of Applied Rehabilitation Counseling,* 24(1): 16-18.

Schalock, R. L. (1990a). Attempts to conceptualize and measure quality of life. In R. L. Schalock, (Ed.), *Quality of Life: Perspectives and Issues,* pp. 141-148 . Washington, D.C.: American Association of Mental Retardation.

Schalock, R. L. (1990b). Where do we go from here? In R. L. Schalock, (Ed.), *Quality of Life: Perspectives and Issues,* pp. 235-240. Washington, D.C.: American Association of Mental Retardation.

Schalock, R. L. (1996). Quality of life and quality assurance. In Renwick, I. Brown, and M. Nagler (Eds.), *Quality of Life in Health Promotion and Rehabilitation,* pp. 104-118. Thousand Oaks, CA: Sage Publications.

Schalock, R. L. and Lilley, M. A. (1986). Placement from community-based mental retardation programs: how well do clients do after 8 to 10 years? *American Journal of Mental Deficiency,* 90(6): 669-676.

Scherer, M. J. (1990). Assistive device utilization and quality of life in adults with spinal cord injuries or cerebral palsy two years later. *Journal of Applied Rehabilitation Counseling,* 21(4): 36-44.

Scott, B. (1996). Testimony presented by Bruce Scott, Consumer Representative, on the behalf of the American Therapeutic Recreation Association to the House Appropriations Subcommittee on Labor, Health and Human Services, and Education.
http://cwis.unomaha.edu/%7Ebrasile/testimny.htm

Scuccimarra, D. J. and Speece, D. L. (1990). Employment outcomes and social integration of students with mild handicaps: the quality of life two years after high school. *Journal of Learning Disabilities,* 23(4): 213-219.

Shain, M. (1996). Work, employment, and mental health: implications for quality of life. In R. Renwick, I. Brown, and M. Nagler (Eds.), *Quality of Life in Health Promotion and Rehabilitation,* pp. 327-341. Thousand Oaks, CA: Sage Publications.

Shank, J. W., Coyle, C. P., Boyd, R., and Kinney, W. B. (1996). A classification scheme for therapeutic recreation research grounded in the rehabilitative sciences. *Therapeutic Research Journal,* 178-196.

Sinnott-Oswald, M., Gliner, J. A., and Spencer, K. C. (1991). Supported and sheltered employment: quality of life issues among workers with disabilities. *Education and Training in Mental Retardation,* 388-397.

Stark, J. A. and Goldsbury, R. (1990). Quality of life from childhood to adulthood. In R. L. Schalock, (Ed.), *Quality of Life: Perspectives and Issues,* pp. 71-92 . Washington, D.C.: American Association of Mental Retardation.

Taylor, S. J. and Bogdan, R. (1990). Quality of life and the individual's perspective. In R. L. Schalock, (Ed.), *Quality of Life: Perspectives and Issues,* pp. 27-40. Washington, D.C.: American Association of Mental Retardation.

Turk, M. A. (1996). The impact of disability on fitness in women: musculoskeletal issues. In D. M. Krotoski, M. A. Nosek, and M. A. Turk (Eds.), *Women with Physical Disabilities: Achieving and Maintaining Health and Well-Being,* pp. 391-401. Baltimore: Paul H. Brookes.

Vandergriff, D. V. and Chubon, R. A. (1994). Quality of life experienced by persons with mental retardation in various residential settings. *Journal of Rehabilitation,* 30-37.

Vaughan, C. E. and Hobson, S. (1990). Reducing late-life dependence resulting from declining visual acuity. *Journal of Visual Impairment and Blindness,* 370-372.

Verbrugge, L. M., Reoma, J. M., and Gruber-Baldini, A. L. (1994). Short-term dynamics of disability and well-being. *Journal of Health and Social Behavior,* 35: 97-117.

Walker, D. E., Blankenship, V., Ditty, J. A., and Lynch, K. P. (1987). Prediction of recovery for closed-head-injured adults: an evaluation of the MMPI, the Adaptive Behavior Scale, and a Quality of Life Rating Scale. *Journal of Clinical Psychology,* 43(6): 699-707.

Ward, N. (1990). Reflections on my quality of life: then and now. In R. L. Schalock (Ed.), *Quality of Life: Perspectives and Issues,* pp. 9-16. Washington, D.C.: American Association of Mental Retardation.

Warren, L., Wrigley, M., Yoels, W. C., and Fine, P. R. (1996). Factors associated with life satisfaction among a sample of persons with neurotrauma. *Journal of Rehabilitation Research and Development,* 33(4): 404-408.

West, M., Kregel, J., and Banks, P. D. (1990). Fringe benefits available to supported employment participants. *Rehabilitation Counseling Bulletin,* 34(2): 126-138.

Whelton, C., Pawlick, J., and Cardamone, J. (1997). Involving families in psychosocial rehabilitation. *Psychiatric Rehabilitation Journal,* 20(3): 57-60.

Whitaker, S. (1989). Quality of life and people with a very profound handicap. *British Journal of Mental Subnormality,* 35(68): 3-7.

APPENDIX 35
Seizures and Quality of Life (QOL) Literature

Source	Population	Measures/Method	Domains
Hays, Vickrey, Hermann, Perrine, Cramer, Meador, Spritzer, and Devinsky (1995)	292 Patients with epilepsy and their designated proxies	Used 89-item QOL Inventory	Physical functioning, pain, health perception, role disability (due to, physical or emotional health) support, emotional well-being, overall QOL, social isolation, energy/fatigue, language/memory/attention cognitive function, seizure distress, work and driving
Helmstaedter and Elger (1994)	Presurgical epileptic patients	Evaluated subjective reports of psychosocial impairments with a questionnaire	Physical status, emotional status, capability, work, social life, independence and self-determination
Hermann (1995)	Epilepsy patients	Reviews phases of QOL research for epilepsy patients	Cognitive, behavioral, psychosocial function; fear of seizures, social effects, perceived stigma, limitations and discrimination, behavior ratings, personality, psychosocial
Langfitt (1995)	71 Epilepsy patients	Epilepsy Surgery Inventory, Sickness Profile, Washington Psychosocial Seizure Inventory	Symptoms, functional status, self-care, impact mobility, physical activity, energy and vitality, sleep and rest, social functioning, emotional status, cognition, health perceptions, general life satisfaction, work and household management
National Institutes of Health (1990)	A consensus development conference on surgery for epilepsy with neurologists, neurosurgeons, psychologists, and other health care providers	Addressed issues of epilepsy surgery including patient selection and management	Seizure elimination or reduction, short-term surgical outcome, physical health, mental health, cognitive function and memory, social health, general health
Vickrey, Hays, Graber et al. (1992)	239 Adults with epilepsy	Epilepsy Surgery Inventory, Mood Profile, Seizure Classification	Energy/fatigue, overall QOL, social function, emotional well-being, cognitive function, physical function, pain, role limitations

References

Hays, R. D., Vickrey, B. G., Hermann, B. P., Perrine, K., Cramer, J., Meador, K., Spritzer, K., and Devinsky, O. (1995). Agreement between self reports and proxy reports of quality of life in epilepsy patients. *Quality of Life Research,* 4: 159-168.

Helmstaedter, C. and Elger, C. E. (1994). Cognitive-behavioral aspects of quality of life in presurgical patients with epilepsy. *Journal of Epilepsy,* 7: 220-231.

Hermann, B. P. (1995). The evolution of health-related quality of life assessment in epilepsy. *Quality of Life Research,* 4: 87-100.

Langfitt, J. T. (1995). Comparison of the psychometric characteristics of three quality of life measures in intractable epilepsy. *Quality of Life Research,* 4: 101-114.

National Institutes of Health. (1990). Surgery for epilepsy. *NIH Consensus Statement Online,* 8(2): 1-20.
Vickrey, B. G., Hays, R. D., Graber, J., Rausch, R., Engel, J., and Brook, R. H. (1992). A health-related quality of life instrument for patients evaluated for epilepsy surgery. *Medical Care*, 30(4): 299-319.

APPENDIX 36
Sexual Abuse and Quality of Life Literature

Source	Population	Measures/Method	Domains
Nagler (1996)	39 Persons with disabilities who have experienced sexual abuse	Interviews and essay on QOL issues and sexual abuse	Social, emotional, sexuality, work, friends, self-esteem, marriage, education, emotional and physical well-being
Zweig, Barber, and Eccles (1997)	Young adults: 872 women and 527 men	Data from MI Study of Adolescent Life used to examine sexual coercion and well-being	Psychological and social adjustment, depressed mood, self-esteem, coping

References

Nagler, M. (1996). Quality of life of people with disabilities who have experienced sexual abuse. In R. Renwick, I. Brown, and M. Nagler (Eds.), *Quality of Life in Health Promotion and Rehabilitation,* pp. 190-203. Thousand Oaks, CA: Sage Publications.
Zweig, J. M., Barber, B. L., and Eccles, J. S. (1997). Sexual coercion and well-being in young adulthood: comparisons by gender and college status. *Journal of Interpersonal Violence,* 12(2): 291-308.

APPENDIX 37
Spinal Cord Injury and Quality of Life (QOL) Research Literature

Source	Population	Measures/Method	Domains
Boschen (1996)	222 Young adults with spinal cord injuries living in Toronto	Living with a Spinal Cord Injury Questionnaire, Latitude of Choice Scale, Self-Concept Semantic Differential Scale, Locus of Control Scale	Autonomy, control, and daily life choices with postinjury accommodations
Clayton and Chubon (1994)	100 SCI patients (89% male, 20% female)	Life Situation Survey Social Health Battery	Educational level, employment status, income, social activities, and severity of disability
Krause (1996)	449 Persons with spinal cord injuries	Life Situation Questionnaire and collection of prospective data on life adjustment in 1974, 1985, 1989	Subjective well-being, social and vocational functioning, and life satisfaction

APPENDIX 37 (continued)
Spinal Cord Injury and Quality of Life (QOL) Research Literature

Source	Population	Measures/Method	Domains
Rintala, Hart, and Fuhrer (1996)	661 Persons with spinal cord injuries	Questionnaires and Perceived Stress Scale Center for Epidemiological Studies Depression Scale, Life Satisfaction Index, Craig Handicap Assessment and Reporting Technique, ASIA Total Motor Index, Functional Independence Measure, Hassles Scale, Life Events Scale, Personal Independence Profile, Satisfaction with Personal Assistance, Interpersonal Support Evaluation List	Depression, life satisfaction, morbidity, mobility, occupation, social integration and support, independence, pressure sores
Scherer (1990)	Persons with spinal cord injury (SCI) and cerebral palsy (CP)	Compared persons with SCI and CP using assistive devices (AD), interviews and observations, Personal Capacities Questionnaire, Functional Assessment Inventory, Taylor-Johnson Temperament Analysis	Personal capacities, adaptive behavior, vocational qualifications, motor functioning
Turk (1996)	Women with disabilities: neuromuscular diseases, late effects of polio, spinal cord pathology, multiple sclerosis, osteoporosis in disability	Essay on fitness as an optimal state of physical well-being. Call for research on fitness issues for women with physical disabilities	Flexibility, muscular strength and endurance, cardiopulmonary conditioning
Warren, Wrigley, Yoels, and Fine (1996)	137 Persons with traumatic brain injury, 38 spinal cord injury persons	Life Satisfaction Index-A, Functional Independence Measure, Family Satisfaction Scale	Family satisfaction, employment status, memory independence, bowel independence, marital status, self blame

References

Boschen, K. A. (1996). Correlates of life satisfaction, residential satisfaction, and locus of control among adults with spinal cord injuries. *Rehabilitation Counseling Bulletin,* 39(4): 230-243.

Clayton, K.S. and Chubon, R. A. (1994). Factors associated with the quality of life of long-term spinal cord injured persons. *Archives of Physical Medicine and Rehabilitation*, 75, 633-638.

Krause, J. S. (1996). Prediction of mortality after spinal cord injury: a 20-year prospective study. *Rehabilitation R & D Progress Reports*, 34: 298-299.

Rintala, D. H., Hart, K. A., and Fuhrer, M. J. (1996). Perceived stress in individuals with spinal cord injuries. In D. M. Krotoski, M. A. Nosek, and M. A. Turk (Eds.), *Women with Physical Disabilities: Achieving and Maintaining Health and Well-Being,* pp. 223-242. Baltimore: Paul H. Brookes Publishing.

Scherer, M. J. (1990). Assistive device utilization and quality of life in adults with spinal cord injuries or cerebral palsy two years later. *Journal of Applied Rehabilitation Counseling*, 21(4): 36-44.

Warren, L., Wrigley, M., Yoels, W. C., and Fine, P. R. (1996). Factors associated with life satisfaction among a sample of persons with neurotrauma. *Journal of Rehabilitation Research and Development,* 33(4): 404-408.

APPENDIX 38
Substance Abuse and Quality of Life (QOL) Literature

Source	Population	Measures/Method	Domains
Harper (1990)	Couples in couple therapy dealing with the recovery of a chemically dependent partner	Treatment model with three phases of recovery for the relationship in which their QOL is questioned	Trust, communication, intimacy, sex, and partnership
Lennox (1994)	Chronic substance abusers	Center for Epidemiological Studies Depression Scale	Somatic complaints, depressed affect, positive affect, and interpersonal relations
Mehrabian and Ross (1979)	293 Undergraduate students	Checklists, questionnaires, and measures of personality	Life changes, physical illness and symptoms, psychosomatic symptoms, accidents, psychological symptoms
Nation, Benshoff and Malkin (1996)	Adolescents in substance abuse treatment facilities	Random survey of substance abuse treatment programs using therapeutic recreation	Social skills, self-esteem, self-efficacy and improve cooperation and trust; QOL not a specific goal
Stillson, White, and Harris (1986)	Alcoholism treatment personnel	Review of aspects of stress management techniques to improve QOL	Psychotherapy, meditation/visualization and time management

References

Harper, J. (1990). Recovery for the relationship: a treatment model for couples with a recovering chemically dependent partner. *Alcoholism Treatment Quarterly,* 7(2): 1-21.

Lennox, R. D. (1994). Measurement error issues in substance abuse services research: lessons from structural equation modeling and psychometric theory. *Evaluation and Program Planning,* 17(4): 399-407.

Mehrabian, A. and Ross, M. (1979). Illness, accidents, and alcohol use as functions of the arousing quality and pleasantness of life changes. *Psychological Reports,* 45: 31-43.

Nation, J. M., Benshoff, J. J., and Malkin, M. M. (1996). Therapeutic recreation programs for adolescents in substance abuse treatment facilities. *Journal of Rehabilitation,* 10-16.

Stillson, K., White, J., and Harris, E. F. (1986). Helping the helper: stress management for alcoholism treatment personnel. *Alcoholism Treatment Quarterly,* 3(3): 107-123.

APPENDIX 39
Traumatic Brain Injuries and Quality of Life (QOL) Research Literature

Source	Population	Measures/Method	Domains
Burton and Volpe (1993)	33 Persons with traumatic brain injury	Social Adjustment Scale to evaluate functioning in various categories	Work, social and leisure, extended family, marital, parental, family

APPENDIX 39 (continued)
Traumatic Brain Injuries and Quality of Life (QOL) Research Literature

Source	Population	Measures/Method	Domains
Condeluci, Ferris, and Bogdan (1992)	Persons in head injury rehabilitation	Review of three surveys from the survivors' perspective	Independence in activities of daily living, living situation, communication skills, health status, mobility, problem behaviors, need for rehabilitation and supervision, employment status, family, income, and educational status
Kaplan (1993)	25 Individuals with traumatic brain injury	Portland Adaptability Inventory	Temperament and emotionality, activities and social behavior, physical capabilities
Turk (1996)	Women with disabilities: neuromuscular diseases, late effects of polio, spinal cord pathology, multiple sclerosis, osteoporosis in disability	Essay on fitness as an optimal state of physical well-being; call for research on fitness issues for women with physical disabilities	Flexibility, muscular strength and endurance, cardiopulmonary conditioning
Walker, Blankenship, Ditty, and Lynch (1987)	25 Closed-head-injured adults (1 female and 24 males)	MMPI, Adaptive Behavior Scale, Quality of Life Rating Scale	Vocational, educational, family participation, community service, avocational, artistic, and scholarly pursuits
Warren, Wrigley, Yoels, and Fine (1996)	137 Persons with traumatic brain injury, 38 spinal cord injury persons	Life Satisfaction Index–A, Functional Independence Measure, Family Satisfaction Scale	Family satisfaction, employment status, memory independence, bowel independence, marital status, self blame
West, Kregel, and Banks (1990)	1,550 Individuals placed in supported employment (65% with mental retardation, 9% with long-term mental illness, and 10% with head injuries and cerebral palsy)	*Data Management System Operations Manual* for form completion by 96 provider agencies	Evaluation of QOL in worklife by looking availability of fringe benefits

References

Burton, L. A. and Volpe, B. (1993). Social adjustment scale assessments in traumatic brain injury. *Journal of Rehabilitation,* 34-37.

Condeluci, A., Ferris, L. L., and Bogdan, A. (1992). Outcome and value: the survivor perspective. *Journal of Head Trauma Rehabilitation,* 7(4): 37-45.

Kaplan, S. P. (1993). Five-year tracking of psychosocial changes in people with severe traumatic brain injury. *Rehabilitation Counseling Bulletin,* 36(3): 151-159.

Turk, M. A. (1996). The impact of disability on fitness in women: musculoskeletal issues. In D. M. Krotoski, M. A. Nosek, and M. A. Turk (Eds.), *Women with Physical Disabilities: Achieving and Maintaining Health and Well-Being,* pp. 391-401. Baltimore: Paul H. Brookes.

Walker, D. E., Blankenship, V., Ditty, J. A., and Lynch, K. P. (1987). Prediction of recovery for closed-head-injured adults: an evaluation of the MMPI, the Adaptive Behavior Scale, and a Quality of Life Rating Scale. *Journal of Clinical Psychology,* 43(6): 699-707.

Warren, L., Wrigley, M., Yoels, W. C., and Fine, P. R. (1996). Factors associated with life satisfaction among a sample of persons with neurotrauma. *Journal of Rehabilitation Research and Development,* 33(4): 404-408.

West, M., Kregel, J., and Banks, P. D. (1990). Fringe benefits available to supported employment participants. *Rehabilitation Counseling Bulletin,* 34(2): 126-138.

Index

I

J

N

O

P